MyMISLab™: Improves Student Engagement Before, During, and After Class

Prep and Engagement

- **NEW! VIDEO LIBRARY –** Robust video library with over 100 new book-specific videos that include easy-to-assign assessments, the ability for instructors to add YouTube or other sources, the ability for students to upload video submissions, and the ability for polling and teamwork.

- **Decision-making simulations – NEW and improved feedback for students.** Place your students in the role of a key decision-maker! Simulations branch based on the decisions students make, providing a variation of scenario paths. Upon completion students receive a grade, as well as a detailed report of the choices and the associated consequences of those decisions.

- **Video exercises – UPDATED with new exercises.** Engaging videos that bring business concepts to life and explore business topics related to the theory students are learning in class. Quizzes then assess students' comprehension of the concepts covered in each video.

- **Learning Catalytics –** A "bring your own device" student engagement, assessment, and classroom intelligence system helps instructors analyze students' critical-thinking skills during lecture.

- **Dynamic Study Modules (DSMs) – UPDATED with additional questions.** Through adaptive learning, students get personalized guidance where and when they need it most, creating greater engagement, improving knowledge retention, and supporting subject-matter mastery. Also available on mobile devices.

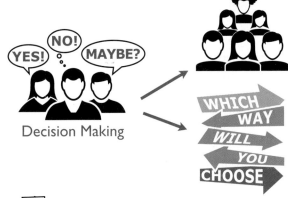

Decision Making

Critical Thinking

- **Writing Space – UPDATED with new commenting tabs, new prompts, and a new tool for students called Pearson Writer.** A single location to develop and assess concept mastery and critical thinking, the Writing Space offers automatic graded, assisted graded, and create your own writing assignments, allowing you to exchange personalized feedback with students quickly and easily.

  Writing Space can also check students' work for improper citation or plagiarism by comparing it against the world's most accurate text comparison database available from **Turnitin**.

- **Additional Features –** Included with the MyLab are a powerful homework and test manager, robust gradebook tracking, Reporting Dashboard, comprehensive online course content, and easily scalable and shareable content.

http://www.pearsonmylabandmastering.com

PEARSON

Dear Student,

College is a fun time in your life. You've experienced the freedom of living on your own, made new friends, and enjoyed once-in-a-lifetime experiences. However, at this point in your college career you've begun to realize that a life transition is on your horizon. You will graduate and you will need to find a career—not just another job. Now is the time for you to start thinking about that career and how to prepare for it.

Most students say they want a successful career. But defining *successful* is different for each person. Most students want an exciting, stable, well-paying job. You owe it to yourself to think about what that job is and how you're going to get it. Which jobs pay the salary you want? Are some jobs more stable than others? What type of work do you want to do for the next 40 years?

This MIS course is important for answering those questions. Over time, technology creates new jobs...examples today are mobile application developers, social media analysts, information security specialists, business intelligence analysts, and data architects, to consider just a few jobs that didn't exist 20, even 10, years ago. Similarly, the best jobs 20 years from now probably don't currently exist.

The trick to turning information systems to your advantage is getting ahead of their effect. During your career, you will find many opportunities for the innovative application of information systems in business and government—but only if you know how to look for them.

Once found, those opportunities become your opportunities when you—as a skilled, creative, non-routine problem solver—apply emerging technology to facilitate your organization's strategy. This is true whether your job is in marketing, operations, sales, accounting, finance, entrepreneurship, or another discipline.

Using technology in innovative ways enabled superstars like Steve Jobs, Bill Gates, Larry Ellison, Mark Zuckerberg, Larry Page, Sergey Brin, and Jeff Bezos to earn billions and revolutionize commerce. You may not be such a superstar, but you can exceed beyond your expectations by applying the knowledge you learn in this class.

Congratulations on deciding to study business. Use this course to help you obtain and then thrive in an interesting and rewarding career. Learn more than just the MIS terminology—understand the ways information systems are transforming business and the many, many ways you can participate in that transformation.

In this endeavor, we wish you, a future business professional, the very best success!

David Kroenke & Randy Boyle

The Guides

Each chapter includes three unique **guides** that focus on current issues in information systems. In each chapter, one of the guides focuses on an ethical issue in business, and the second focuses on security. The third guide addresses the application of the chapter's contents to some other dimension of business. The content of each guide is designed to stimulate thought, discussion, and active participation in order to help *you* develop your problem-solving skills and become a better business professional.

Learning Aids for Students

We have structured this book so you can maximize the benefit from the time you spend reading it. As shown in the following table, each chapter includes various learning aids to help you succeed in this course.

Resource	Description	Benefit	Example
Guides	Each chapter includes three guides that focus on current issues in information systems. One addresses ethics, one addresses security, and the third addresses other business topics.	Stimulate thought and discussion. Address ethics and security once per chapter. Help develop your problem-solving skills.	Chapter 5, Ethics Guide: Querying Inequality? Chapter 8, Security Guide: Digital Is Forever Chapter 9, Guide: Data Mining in the Real World
Chapter Introduction Business Example	Each chapter begins with a description of a business situation that motivates the need for the chapter's contents. We focus on two different businesses over the course of the text: Falcon Security, a provider of aerial surveillance and inspection services, and PRIDE, a cloud-based, healthcare startup opportunity.	Understand the relevance of the chapter's content by applying it to a business situation.	Chapter 9, opening vignette: Business Intelligence Systems and PRIDE
Query-Based Chapter Format	Each chapter starts with a list of questions, and each major heading is a question. The Active Review contains tasks for you to perform in order to demonstrate your ability to answer the questions.	Use the questions to manage your time, guide your study, and review for exams.	Chapter 1, Q1-4: How Can You Use the Five Component Model? Chapter 6, Q6-4: How Do Organizations Use the Cloud?
So What?	Each chapter of this text includes an exercise called "So What?" This feature challenges the students to apply the knowledge they've gained from the chapter to themselves, often in a personal way. The goal is to drive home the relevancy of the chapter's contents to their future professional lives. It presents a current issue in IS that is relevant to the chapter content and asks you to consider why that issue matters to you as a future business professional.	Understand how the material in the chapter applies to everyday situations.	Chapter 2, So What? Augmented Collaboration

Resource	Description	Benefit	Example
2026?	Each chapter concludes with a discussion of how the concepts, technology, and systems described in that chapter might change by 2026.	Learn to anticipate changes in technology and recognize how those changes may affect the future business environment.	Chapter 7, 2026? discusses the future of ERP applications
Active Review	This review provides a set of activities for you to perform in order to demonstrate your ability to answer the primary questions addressed by the chapter.	After reading the chapter, use the Active Review to check your comprehension. Use for class and exam preparation.	Chapter 9, Active Review
Using Your Knowledge	These exercises ask you to take your new knowledge one step further by applying it to a practice problem.	Test your critical-thinking skills.	Chapter 4, Using Your Knowledge
Collaboration Exercises	These exercises and cases ask you to collaborate with a group of fellow students, using collaboration tools introduced in Chapter 2.	Practice working with colleagues toward a stated goal.	Collaboration Exercise 3 discusses how to tailor a high-end resort's information system to fit its competitive strategy
Case Studies	Each chapter includes a case study at the end.	Apply newly acquired knowledge to real-world situations.	Case Study 6, Cloud Solutions that Test for Consumer Risk and Financial Stability
Application Exercises	These exercises ask you to solve situations using spreadsheet (Excel) or database (Access) applications.	Develop your computer skills.	AE10-1 builds on your knowledge from Chapter 10 by asking you to score the websites you visit using WOT
International Dimension	This module at the end of the text discusses international aspects of MIS. It includes the importance of international IS, the localization of system components, the roles of functional and cross-functional systems, international applications, supply chain management, and challenges of international systems development.	Understand the international implications and applications of the chapters' content.	International Dimension QID-3, How Do Inter-enterprise IS Facilitate Global Supply Chain Management?

Using MIS

David M. Kroenke

Randall J. Boyle

NINTH EDITION

GLOBAL EDITION

PEARSON

Boston   Columbus   Indianapolis   New York   San Francisco   Amsterdam
Cape Town   Dubai   London   Madrid   Milan   Munich   Paris   Montréal   Toronto
Delhi   Mexico City   São Paulo   Sydney   Hong Kong   Seoul   Singapore   Taipei   Tokyo

Vice President, Business Publishing: Donna Battista
Editor-in-Chief: Stephanie Wall
Acquisitions Editor: Nicole Sam
Development Editor: Laura Town
Editorial Assistant: Olivia Vignone
Editorial Assistant, Global Edition: Alice Dazeley
Assistant Project Editor, Global Edition: Saptarshi Deb
Vice President, Product Marketing: Maggie Moylan
Director of Marketing, Digital Services and Products: Jeanette Koskinas
Executive Field Marketing Manager: Adam Goldstein
Field Marketing Manager: Lenny Ann Raper
Product Marketing Assistant: Jessica Quazza
Team Lead, Program Management: Ashley Santora
Program Manager: Denise Weiss
Team Lead, Project Management: Jeff Holcomb
Project Manager: Karalyn Holland
Project Manager, Global Edition: Sudipto Roy
Senior Manufacturing Controller, Global Edition: Kay Holman

Operations Specialist: Carol Melville
Creative Director: Blair Brown
Senior Art Director: Janet Slowik
Vice President, Director of Digital Strategy and Assessment: Paul Gentile
Manager of Learning Applications: Paul DeLuca
Digital Editor: Brian Surette
Director, Digital Studio: Sacha Laustsen
Digital Studio Manager: Diane Lombardo
Digital Studio Project Manager: Regina DaSilva
Digital Studio Project Manager: Alana Coles
Digital Studio Project Manager: Robin Lazrus
Full-Service Project Management and Composition: Integra Software Services, Pvt. Ltd.
Media Production Manager, Global Edition: Jayaprakash K.
Assistant Media Producer, Global Edition: Naina Singh
Interior Designer: Karen Quigley
Interior Illustrations: Simon Alicea
Cover Image: © Marina Strizhak/ 123RF

Pearson Education Limited
Edinburgh Gate
Harlow
Essex CM20 2JE
England

and Associated Companies throughout the world

Visit us on the World Wide Web at: www.pearsonglobaleditions.com

© Pearson Education Limited 2017

ISBN 10: 1-292-16522-7
ISBN 13: 978-1-292-16522-6

British Library Cataloguing-in-Publication Data
A catalogue record for this book is available from the British Library.

Typeset in Photina MT Pro by Integra India
Printed in Malaysia (CTP-VVP)

To C.J., Carter, and Charlotte
—David Kroenke

To Courtney, Noah, Fiona, and Layla
—Randy Boyle

Brief Contents

Describes how this course teaches four key skills for business professionals. Defines *MIS, information systems,* and *information.*

Describes characteristics, criteria for success, and the primary purposes of collaboration.

Discusses components of collaboration IS and describes collaboration for communication and content sharing. Illustrates use of Google Drive, SharePoint, and other collaboration tools.

Describes reasons why organizations create and use information systems: to gain competitive advantage, to solve problems, and to support decisions.

Describes the manager's essentials of hardware and software technology. Discusses open source, Web applications, mobile systems, and BYOD policies.

Explores database fundamentals, applications, modeling, and design. Discusses the entity-relationship model. Explains the role of Access and enterprise DBMS products. Defines *BigData* and describes nonrelational and NoSQL databases.

Explains why the cloud is the future. Describes basic network technology that underlies the cloud, how the cloud works, and how organizations, including Falcon Security, can use the cloud. Explains SOA and summarizes fundamental Web services standards.

Discusses workgroup, enterprise, and interenterprise IS. Describes problems of information silos and cross-organizational solutions. Presents CRM, ERP, and EAI. Discusses ERP vendors and implementation challenges.

Describes components of social media IS (SMIS) and explains how SMIS can contribute to organizational strategy. Discusses the theory of social capital and how revenue can be generated using social media. Explains the ways organizations can use ESN and manage the risks of SMIS.

Describes business intelligence and knowledge management, including reporting systems, data mining, and social media-based knowledge management systems.

Describes organizational response to information security: security threats, policy, and safeguards.

Describes the role, structure, and function of the IS department; the role of the CIO and CTO; outsourcing; and related topics.

Discusses the need for BPM and the BPM process. Introduces BPMN. Differentiates between processes and information systems. Presents SDLC stages. Describes agile technologies and scrum and discusses their advantages over the SDLC.

CONTENTS

Part 1 : Why MIS?

1: THE IMPORTANCE OF MIS 37

2: COLLABORATION INFORMATION SYSTEMS 71

3: STRATEGY AND INFORMATION SYSTEMS   117

Part 2: Information Technology

4: HARDWARE, SOFTWARE, AND MOBILE SYSTEMS 149

5: DATABASE PROCESSING   195

6: THE CLOUD   237

Part 3: Using IS for Competitive Advantage

7: PROCESSES, ORGANIZATIONS, AND INFORMATION SYSTEMS   283

8: SOCIAL MEDIA INFORMATION SYSTEMS 325

9: BUSINESS INTELLIGENCE SYSTEMS   369

Part 4: Information Systems Management

10: INFORMATION SYSTEMS SECURITY   419

11: INFORMATION SYSTEMS MANAGEMENT 461

12: INFORMATION SYSTEMS DEVELOPMENT 489

PREFACE

In Chapter 1, we claim that MIS is the most important class in the business curriculum. That's a bold statement, and every year we ask whether it remains true. Is there any discipline having a greater impact on contemporary business and government than IS? We continue to doubt there is. Every year brings important new technology to organizations, and many of these organizations respond by creating innovative applications that increase productivity and otherwise help them accomplish their strategies.

Over the past year, we've seen the largest IPO in history ($25 billion) come from e-commerce giant Alibaba. Amazon revealed that it's using an army of Kiva robots to increase productivity in its fulfillment centers by 50 percent. And we've seen an unprecedented flurry of IoT smart devices aimed at personal, home, and automobile automation services hit the market. It seems like every industry is running full tilt toward the smart door. Technology is fundamentally changing the way organizations operate. It's forcing them to be more productive, innovative, and adaptable.

Even innovations that we've known about for several years took big leaps forward this year. MakerBot made huge strides in 3D printing by introducing new composite filaments that can print materials that look just like wood, metal, and stone—not just plastics. Mercedes-Benz was the hit of CES 2015 when it debuted its new driverless F 015 car with saloon-style doors, complete touch-screen interface, and front-room seating. And Google announced it was deploying 25 of its driverless cars around Mountain View, California, starting in summer 2015.

Large-scale data breaches were a major problem again this year. eBay, Home Depot, JP Morgan Chase, and Anthem all suffered enormous data losses. Sony Pictures lost more than 100 TB of confidential corporate data, and Apple lost hundreds of explicit celebrity photos to hackers. And these are just a fraction of the total number of organizations affected this year.

In addition, normal revisions were needed to address emergent technologies such as cloud-based services, mobile devices, innovative IS-based business models like that at zulily, changes in organizations' use of social media, and so on.

More sophisticated and demanding users push organizations into a rapidly changing future—one that requires continual adjustments in business planning. To participate, our graduates need to know how to apply emerging technologies to better achieve their organizations' strategies. Knowledge of MIS is critical. And this pace continues to remind us of Carrie Fisher's statement "The problem with instantaneous gratification is that it's just not fast enough."

Why This Ninth Edition?

The changes in this ninth edition, Global Edition, are listed in Table 1. Substantial changes were made in Chapter 1 to strengthen the argument that MIS is the most important course in the business curriculum. The chapter now looks at the Digital Revolution and the exponential change happening to technology. It discusses how digital devices are changing due to increased processing power (Moore's Law), connectivity (Metcalfe's Law), network speed (Nielsen's Law), and storage capacity (Kryder's Law). It then gives examples of how new technology creates entirely new types of businesses and forces existing businesses to change the way they operate.

Chapter 1 also includes new salary data projections from the Bureau of Labor Statistics through 2022. These salary projections cover pay ranges for typical information systems jobs, general business occupations, and managerial-level positions.

TABLE 1 : CHANGES IN THE NINTH EDITION

Chapter	Change
1	New Falcon Security Part 1 introduction
1	New Falcon Security chapter introduction
1	New So What? Feature: Biggest IPO Ever: Alibaba
1	Updated industry statistics throughout the chapter
1	New Q1-1 covering the Information Age, Digital Revolution, and power of exponential change
1	New discussion about the forces pushing digital change: Bell's Law, Moore's Law, Metcalfe's Law, Nielsen's Law, and Kryder's Law
1	New Q1-2 looking at the way changes in technology will affect student's future job security
1	New statistics about projected technology job growth from BLS
1	Combined discussion about MIS, IS, and IT
1	Updated 2026? discussion in Q1-7
2	New Falcon Security chapter introduction
2	New So What? Feature: Augmented Collaboration
2	New Security Guide: Evolving Security
2	Updated terms *Microsoft Lync* to *Skype for Business*, *Google Grid* to *Google Drive*, *Microsoft Web Apps* to *Microsoft Office Online*, *SkyDrive* to *OneDrive*, *Hotmail* to *Outlook.com*
2	Updated instructions and images for Google Drive
3	New Falcon Security chapter introduction
3	New So What? Feature: Driving Strategy
3	New Security Guide: Hacking Smart Things
3	New five forces, value chain, and business process examples using Falcon Security
3	Updated statistics in the chapter and Amazon case study
4	New Falcon Security chapter introduction
4	New So What? Feature: New from CES 2015
4	New Ethics Guide: Free Apps for Data
4	Updated industry statistics throughout
4	New discussion about augmented reality hardware
4	Updated developments in 3D printing, self-driving cars, and IoT
4	Updated terms *Internet Explorer* to *Edge*, *Windows 8* to *Windows 10*
5	New Falcon Security chapter introduction
5	New justification for learning database technology
5	Updated E-R notation for minimum cardinality to conform to contemporary usage
5	New Q5-7 about the possibility of Falcon Security maintaining video metadata in a database
5	New discussion of NewSQL and in-memory DBMS
5	New Collaboration Exercise
6	New Falcon Security chapter introduction
6	New So What? Feature: Net Neutrality Enabled
6	New Security Guide: From Anthem to Anathema

Chapter	Change
6	Added discussion of new net neutrality regulations
6	Added discussion about personal area networks (PANs) and Bluetooth
6	Updated statistics and AWS offerings
7	Updated ERP vendor rankings and comments
7	Added new technology as a fifth implementation challenge
7	Added discussion of the effect of mobility, security threats, and the Internet of Things on enterprise applications in a new 2026? discussion
8	New Ethics Guide: Synthetic Friends
8	New Security Guide: Digital Is Forever
8	New discussion about the use of social media in recruiting
8	Expanded discussion of social capital using a YouTube channels example
8	Expanded discussion of mobile ad spending
8	Updated social media statistics throughout the chapter
9	Included latest CEO surveys on the importance of BI
9	Replaced predictive policing example with reporting application in medicine
9	Updated parts analysis example to remove AllRoad Parts and keep the example anonymous
9	New So What? exercise about BI for securities trading
9	Updated Web trends, HD Insight description, and 2026? discussion
10	New So What? Feature: New from Black Hat 2014
10	New Security Guide: EMV to the Rescue
10	New discussion of notable APTs
10	Updated security statistics and figures throughout the chapter
10	New discussion of ransomware
10	New discussion of recent large-scale data breaches
11	New Security Guide: Selling Privacy
11	New Ethics Guide: Privacy Versus Productivity: The BYOD Dilemma
11	Updated IS jobs, descriptions, and salary data
12	New So What? Feature: Using This Knowledge for Your Number-One Priority
12	Revised 2026? discussion
Appl Ex	New exercise using open source software (LibreOffice)
Appl Ex	New exercise using software to compress and encrypt files (7-Zip)
International Dimension	New discussion of localization using IBM's Watson
International Dimension	Expanded discussion of EU's "right to be forgotten" law

Chapters 1 through 6 begin with a new discussion of Falcon Security, a privately owned company that provides surveillance and inspection services for companies using flying drones. Chapters 7–12 continue to be introduced by PRIDE Systems, a cloud-based virtual exercise competition and healthcare startup. In addition to motivating the chapter material, both case scenarios provide numerous opportunities for students to practice one of Chapter 1's key skills: "Assess, evaluate, and apply emerging technology to business."

This edition continues to have a focus on teaching ethics. Every Ethics Guide asks students to apply Immanuel Kant's categorical imperative, Bentham and Mill's utilitarianism, or both to the business situation described in the guide. We hope you find the ethical considerations richer and deeper with these exercises. The categorical imperative is introduced in the Ethics Guide in Chapter 1 (pages 56–57), and utilitarianism is introduced in the Ethics Guide in Chapter 2 (pages 92–93).

As shown in Table 1, additional changes were made to every chapter, including six new Security Guides, six new So What? Features, three new Ethics Guides, and updates to chapter cases. Additional figures, like the one showing mobile ad spending in Chapter 8, were added to make the text more accessible. Numerous changes were made throughout the chapters in an attempt to keep them up to date. MIS moves fast, and to keep the text current, we checked every fact, data point, sentence, and industry reference for obsolescence and replaced them as necessary.

To reiterate the preface of earlier editions, we believe it is exceedingly important to make these frequent adaptations because of the delays associated with a 2-year revision cycle. Text materials we develop in April of one year are published in January of the next year and are first used by students in September—a minimum 17-month delay.

For some areas of study, a year and a half may not seem long because little changes in that amount of time. But in MIS, entire companies can be founded and then sold for billions of dollars in just a few years. YouTube, for example, was founded in February 2005 and then sold in November 2006 to Google for $1.65B (21 months). Facebook started in 2004 and currently (2015) has a market capitalization exceeding $212B. MIS changes fast—very fast. We hope this new edition is the most up-to-date MIS textbook available.

Importance of MIS

As stated, we continue to believe we are teaching the single most important course in the business school. The rationale for this bold statement is presented in Chapter 1, starting on page 1. In brief, the argument relies on two observations.

First, processing power, interconnectivity of devices, storage capacity, and bandwidth are all increasing so rapidly that it's fundamentally changing how we use digital devices. Businesses are increasingly finding—and, more importantly, increasingly *required* to find—innovative applications for information systems. The incorporation of Facebook and Twitter into marketing systems is an obvious example, but this example is only the tip of the iceberg. For at least the next 10 years, every business professional will, at the minimum, need to be able to assess the efficacy of proposed IS applications. To excel, business professionals will also need to define innovative IS applications.

Further, professionals who want to emerge from the middle ranks of management will, at some point, need to demonstrate the ability to manage projects that develop these innovative information systems. Such skills will not be optional. Businesses that fail to create systems that take advantage of changes in technology will fall prey to competition that can create such systems. So, too, will business professionals.

The second premise for the singular importance of the MIS class relies on the work of Robert Reich, former Secretary of Labor for the Clinton administration. In *The Work of Nations*,[1] Reich identifies four essential skills for knowledge workers in the 21st century:

- Abstract thinking
- Systems thinking

- Collaboration
- Experimentation

For reasons set out in Chapter 1, we believe the MIS course is the single best course in the business curriculum for learning these four key skills.

Today's Role for Professors

What is our role as MIS professors? Students don't need us for definitions; they have the Web for that. They don't need us for detailed notes; they have the PowerPoints. Consequently, when we attempt to give long and detailed lectures, student attendance falls. And this situation is even more dramatic for online courses.

We need to construct useful and interesting experiences for students to apply MIS knowledge to their goals and objectives. In this mode, we are more like track coaches than the chemistry professor of the past. And our classrooms are more like practice fields than lecture halls.[2]

Of course, the degree to which each of us moves to this new mode depends on our goals, our students, and our individual teaching styles. Nothing in the structure or content of this edition assumes that a particular topic will be presented in a nontraditional manner. But every chapter contains materials suitable for use with a coaching approach, if desired.

In addition to the chapter feature titled So What?, all chapters include a collaboration exercise that students can use for team projects inside and outside of class. As with earlier editions, each chapter contains three guides that describe practical implications of the chapter contents that can be used for small in-class exercises. Additionally, every chapter concludes with a case study that can be the basis for student activities. Finally, this edition contains 39 application exercises (see page 520).

Falcon Security and PRIDE Cases

Each part and each chapter opens with a scenario intended to get students involved emotionally, if possible. We want students to mentally place themselves in the situation and to realize that this situation—or something like it—could happen to them. Each scenario sets up the chapter's content and provides an obvious example of why the chapter is relevant to them. These scenarios help support the goals of student motivation and learning transfer.

Furthermore, both of these introductory cases involve the application of new technology to existing businesses. Our goal is to provide opportunities for students to see and understand how businesses are affected by new technology and how they need to adapt while, we hope, providing numerous avenues for you to explore such adaptation with your students.

In developing these scenarios, we endeavor to create business situations rich enough to realistically carry the discussions of information systems while at the same time simple enough that students with little business knowledge and even less business experience can understand. We also attempt to create scenarios that will be interesting to teach. This edition introduces the new Falcon Security case and continues the PRIDE Systems case from the eighth edition.

Falcon Security

The chapters in Parts 1 and 2 are introduced with dialogue from key players at Falcon Security, a privately owned company that provides surveillance and inspection services for companies using flying drones. We wanted to develop the case around an interesting business model that students would want to learn more about. Drones get a lot of attention in the press, but students may not know a lot about how they're used in business. Drones are getting cheaper and easier to fly and have a lot more functionality than they did just a few years ago. It's likely that students will see drones deployed widely during their careers.

Falcon Security is considering strengthening its competitive advantage by 3D printing its own drones. Buying fleets of drones is expensive, and the drones become outdated quickly. However, were the company to do so, it would be changing its fundamental business model, or at least adding to it. Making drones would require Falcon Security to hire new employees, develop new business processes, and potentially develop a new IS to support the custom-built drones. All of this is good fodder for Chapter 3 and for underlining the importance of the ways that IS needs to support evolving business strategy.

Ultimately, Falcon Security determines that it does not want to become a drone manufacturer. It could print some drone parts, but not enough to make it cost effective. The company would still have to buy a lot of expensive component parts to assemble an airworthy drone, something it's not sure it can do consistently. Falcon decides to focus on its core strength of providing integrated security services.

Students may object that, in studying Falcon Security, they devoted considerable time to an opportunity that ultimately didn't make business sense and was rejected. But this outcome is at least as informative as a successful outcome. The example uses knowledge of processes as well as application of business intelligence to avoid making a serious blunder and wasting substantial money. Falcon Security didn't have to open a factory and 3D-print a fleet of custom-built drones just to find out it would be a mistake. It could make a prototype, *analyze* the costs and benefits, and then avoid making the mistake in the first place. The very best way to solve a problem is not to have it!

PRIDE Systems

The Performance Recording, Integration, Delivery, and Evaluation (PRIDE) system was first developed for the sixth edition. In that version, it was an embryonic, entrepreneurial opportunity that used mobile devices, data-gathering exercise equipment, and the cloud to share integrated data among healthcare providers, heart surgery patients, health clubs, health insurance companies, and employers.

PRIDE is a real-world prototype developed for the owner of a health club who wanted to connect the workout data of his club members to their workout data at home and to their employers, insurance companies, and healthcare professionals. PRIDE is written in C#, and the code runs against an Azure database in the cloud. The PRIDE system uses the Windows Phone emulator that is part of Visual Studio. PRIDE was going to be ported to iOS and Android devices after demonstrating feasibility and after the club owner obtained financing.

As reflected in the PRIDE case, the developers realized it was unlikely to succeed because, as Zev says in Chapter 7, "Doctors don't care about exercise." Dr. Flores was too busy as a cardiac surgeon to make his startup a success. Therefore, he sold it to a successful businessman who changed the staff and the strategy and repurposed the software. All of this is described at the start of Chapter 7.

Use of the Categorical Imperative and Utilitarianism in Ethics Guides

Since the introduction of the Ethics Guides into the first edition of this text, we believe there has been a shift in students' attitudes about ethics. Students seem, at least many of them, to be more cynical and callous about ethical issues. As a result, in the seventh edition, we began to use Kant's categorical imperative and Bentham and Mill's utilitarianism to ask students, whose ethical standards are often immature, to adopt the categorical imperative and utilitarian perspectives rather than their own perspectives and, in some cases, in addition to their own perspectives. By doing so, the students are asked to "try on" those criteria, and we hope in the process they think more deeply about ethical principles than they do when we allow them simply to apply their personal biases.

The Ethics Guide in Chapter 1 introduces the categorical imperative, and the guide in Chapter 2 introduces utilitarianism. If you choose to use these perspectives, you will need to assign both of those guides.

2026?

Every chapter concludes with a question labeled "2026?" This section presents our guesses about how the subject of that chapter is likely to change between now and 2026. Clearly, if we had a crystal ball that would give good answers to that question, we wouldn't be writing textbooks.

However, we make what we believe is a reasonable stab at an answer. You will probably have different ideas, and we hope students will have different ideas as well. The goal of these sections is to prompt students to think, wonder, assess, and project about future technology. These sections usually produce some of the most lively in-class discussions.

Why Might You Want Your Students to Use SharePoint?

The difficult part of teaching collaboration is knowing how to assess it. Collaboration assessment is not simply finding out which students did the bulk of the work. It also involves assessing feedback and iteration; that is, identifying who provided feedback, who benefited from the feedback, and how well the work product evolved over time.

Microsoft SharePoint is a tool that can help assess collaboration. It automatically maintains detailed records of all changes that have been made to a SharePoint site. It tracks document versions, along with the date, time, and version author. It also maintains records of user activity—who visited the site, how often, what site features they visited, what work they did, what contributions they made, and so forth. SharePoint makes it easy to determine which students were making sincere efforts to collaborate by giving and receiving critical feedback throughout the project assignment and which students were making a single contribution 5 minutes before midnight the day before the project was due.

Additionally, SharePoint has built-in facilities for team surveys, team wikis, and member blogs as well as document and list libraries. All of this capability is backed up by a rich and flexible security system. To be clear, we do not use SharePoint to run our classes; we use either Blackboard or Canvas for that purpose. However, we do require students to use SharePoint for their collaborative projects. A side benefit is that they can claim, rightfully, experience and knowledge of using SharePoint in their job interviews.

You might also want to use Office 365 because it includes Skype, hosted Exchange, 1TB online storage, and SharePoint Online as an add-on. Microsoft offers Office 365 to academic institutions as a whole or to students directly at reduced educational rates.

Why Are the Chapters Organized by Questions?

The chapters of *Using MIS* are organized by questions. According to Marilla Svinicki,[3] a leading researcher on student learning at the University of Texas, we should not give reading assignments such as "Read pages 50 through 70." The reason is that today's students need help organizing their time. With such a reading assignment, they will fiddle with pages 50 through 70 while texting their friends, surfing the Internet, and listening to their iPods. After 30 or 45 minutes, they will conclude they have fiddled enough and will believe they have completed the assignment.

Instead, Svinicki states we should give students a list of questions and tell them their job is to answer those questions, treating pages 50 through 70 as a resource for that purpose. When students can answer the questions, they have finished the assignment.

Using that philosophy, every chapter in this text begins with a list of questions. Each major heading in the chapter is one of those questions, and the Active Review at the end of each chapter provides students a set of actions to take in order to demonstrate that they are able to answer the questions. Since learning this approach from Professor Svinicki, we have used it in our classes and have found that it works exceedingly well.

How Does This Book Differ from *Experiencing MIS* and from *Processes, Systems, and Information*?

In addition to *Using MIS*, we've written an MIS text titled *Experiencing MIS*. These two texts provide different perspectives for teaching this class. The principal difference between *Using MIS* and *Experiencing MIS* is that the latter is modular in design and has a more "in your face" attitude about MIS. Modularity definitely has a role and place, but not every class needs or appreciates the flexibility and brevity a modular text offers. A shorter, more custom version of *Experiencing MIS* is also available as *MIS Essentials*.

There is also a fourth MIS text titled *Processes, Systems, and Information: An Introduction to MIS* coauthored with Earl McKinney of Bowling Green State University. It represents a third approach to this class and is structured around business processes. It has a strong ERP emphasis and includes two chapters on SAP as well as two chapter tutorials for using the SAP Alliance Global Bikes simulation. Earl has taught SAP for many years and has extensive experience in teaching others how to use the Global Bikes simulation.

In *Using MIS*, we have endeavored to take advantage of continuity and to build the discussion and knowledge gradually through the chapter sequence, in many places taking advantage of knowledge from prior chapters.

The goal in writing these books is to offer professors a choice of approach. We are committed to each of these books and plan to revise them for some time. We sincerely hope that one of them will fit your style and objectives for teaching this increasingly important class.

Instructor Resources

At the Instructor Resource Center, *www.pearsonglobaleditions.com/Kroenke*, instructors can easily register to gain access to a variety of instructor resources available with this text in downloadable format. If assistance is needed, a dedicated technical support team is ready to help with the media supplements that accompany this text. Visit *https://support.pearson.com/getsupport/s/* for answers to frequently asked questions and toll-free user support phone numbers.

The following supplements are available with this text:

- Test Bank
- TestGen® Computerized Test Bank
- PowerPoint Presentation

AACSB Learning Standards Tags

What Is the AACSB?

The Association to Advance Collegiate Schools of Business (AACSB) is a nonprofit corporation of educational institutions, corporations, and other organizations devoted to the promotion and improvement of higher education in business administration and accounting. A collegiate institution offering degrees in business administration or accounting may volunteer for AACSB accreditation review. The AACSB makes initial accreditation decisions and conducts periodic reviews to promote continuous quality improvement in management education. Pearson Education is a proud member of the AACSB and is pleased to provide advice to help you apply AACSB Learning Standards.

What Are AACSB Learning Standards?

One of the criteria for AACSB accreditation is the quality of the curricula. Although no specific courses are required, the AACSB expects a curriculum to include learning experiences in such areas as:

- Communication Abilities
- Ethical Understanding and Reasoning Abilities
- Analytic Skills
- Use of Information Technology
- Dynamics of the Global Economy
- Multicultural and Diversity Understanding
- Reflective Thinking Skills

These seven categories are AACSB Learning Standards. Questions that test skills relevant to these standards are tagged with the appropriate standard. For example, a question testing the moral questions associated with externalities would receive the Ethical Understanding tag.

How Can I Use These Tags?

Tagged questions help you measure whether students are grasping the course content that aligns with AACSB guidelines. In addition, the tagged questions may help to identify potential applications of these skills. This, in turn, may suggest enrichment activities or other educational experiences to help students achieve these goals.

Acknowledgments

First, we wish to thank Earl McKinney, professor of information systems at Bowling Green University and author of *Processes, Systems, and Information*, for many hours of insightful conversation about the role of processes in this MIS course as well as for his deep insights into the theory of information. We also thank David Auer of Western Washington University for help with data communications technology and Jeffrey Proudfoot of Bentley University for his insights on information security.

Many thanks as well to Jeff Gains of San Jose State University for helpful feedback about prior editions of this text; Jeff's comments have strongly influenced revisions for years. Also, a special thanks to Harry Reif at James Madison University for most insightful observations about ways to improve this text.

At Microsoft, we are grateful for the help of Randy Guthrie, who supports MIS professors in many ways, including facilitating use of DreamSpark as well as giving many presentations to students. Also, we thank Rob Howard for conversations and consulting about SharePoint and SharePoint Designer and Steve Fox for helpful conversations about both SharePoint and Microsoft

Azure. Regarding our SharePoint program, a very special thanks to David Auer of Western Washington University and Laura Atkins of James Madison University, who serve as the community proctors for our SharePoint MIS community site, which enables dozens of professors and hundreds of students to learn how to use SharePoint. Our SharePoint solution is hosted by NSPI in Atlanta, Georgia.

Thanks to Neil Miyamoto, co-owner of The Firm (*http://thefirmmpls.com/*), for the ideas behind the PRIDE case. Additionally, we thank Don Nilson, a certified scrum master, for essential ideas and guidance on the new material on agile development and scrum.

Laura Town is the development editor on all of our MIS books, and we continue to be grateful for her support, knowledge, expertise, and great attitude through thick and thin! The textbook industry is undergoing dramatic changes at this time, and Laura's knowledge, guidance, and wisdom on the textbook production process are most appreciated.

We would like to thank those who contributed to the development of our excellent Instructor Resources: Instructor's Manual, Roberta M. Roth; PowerPoints, Steve Loy; and Test Bank, Katie Trotta/ANSR Source. We would also like to express our thanks to the following authors for creating a superb set of resources for our MyLab: Roberta M. Roth, University of Northern Iowa; J. K. Sinclaire, Arkansas State University; Melody White, University of North Texas; and John Hupp, Columbus State University.

Pearson Education is a great publishing company, chock-full of dedicated, talented, and creative people. We thank Karalyn Holland for taking over production management of a complex set of texts and doing it so efficiently and willingly. We also thank Janet Slowik, art director, and her team for redesigning this book so beautifully. Finally, we thank Sue Nodine of Integra-Chicago for managing the production of the book.

No textbook makes its way into the hands of students without the active involvement of a dedicated and professional sales force. We thank the Pearson sales team and especially Anne Fahlgren, the marketing manager for this text. Thanks also goes to our former, and now happily retired, editor Bob Horan for his years of friendship, support, and wise counsel. Finally, like so many authors in college publishing, we owe tremendous thanks to our current editor, Nicole Sam. Nicole continues to provide us with the skilled guidance necessary to make these texts a great success.

David Kroenke
Randy Boyle

Thanks to Our Reviewers

The following people deserve special recognition for their review work on this and previous editions of the book—for their careful reading, thoughtful and insightful comments, sensitive criticism, and willingness to follow up with email conversations, many of which were lengthy when necessary. Their collaboration on this project is truly appreciated.

Dennis Adams, *University of Houston, Main*
Heather Adams, *University of Colorado*
Hans-Joachim Adler, *University of Texas, Dallas*
Mark Alexander, *Indiana Wesleyan University*
Paul Ambrose, *University of Wisconsin, Whitewater*
Craig Anderson, *Augustana College*
Michelle Ashton, *University of Utah*
Laura Atkins, *James Madison University*
Cynthia Barnes, *Lamar University*
Reneta Barneva, *SUNY Fredonia*
Michael Bartolacci, *Penn State Lehigh Valley*

Ozden Bayazit, *Central Washington University*
Jack Becker, *University of North Texas*
Paula Bell, *Lock Haven University*
Kristi Berg, *Minot State University*
Doug Bickerstaff, *Eastern Washington University*
Hossein Bidgoli, *California State University, Bakersfield*
James Borden, *Villanova University*
Mari Buche, *Michigan Technological University*
Sheryl Bulloch, *Columbia Southern University*
Thomas Case, *Georgia Southern University*
Thomas Cavaiani, *Boise State University*

Vera Cervantez, *Collin County Community College*
Siew Chan, *University of Massachusetts, Boston*
Andrea Chandler, *independent consultant*
Joey Cho, *Utah State University*
Jimmy Clark, *Austin Community College*
Tricia Clark, *Penn State University, Capital Campus*
Carlos Colon, *Indiana University Bloomington*
Daniel Connolly, *University of Denver*
Jeff Corcoran, *Lasell College*
Jami Cotler, *Siena University*
Stephen Crandell, *Myers University*
Michael Cummins, *Georgia Institute of Technology*
Mel Damodaran, *University of Houston, Victoria*
Charles Davis, *University of St. Thomas*
Roy Dejoie, *Purdue University*
Charles DeSassure, *Tarrant County College*
Carol DesJardins, *St. Claire Community College*
Dawna Dewire, *Babson College*
Michael Doherty, *Marian College of Fond du Lac*
Mike Doherty, *University of Wyoming*
Richard Dowell, *The Citadel*
Chuck Downing, *University of Northern Illinois*
Dave Dulany, *Aurora University*
Charlene Dykman, *University of St. Thomas*
William Eddins, *York College*
Lauren Eder, *Rider University*
Kevin Elder, *Georgia Southern Statesboro*
Kevin Lee Elder, *Georgia Southern University*
Sean Eom, *Southeast Missouri State University*
Patrick Fan, *Virginia Polytechnic Institute and State University*
Badie Farah, *Eastern Michigan University*
M. Farkas, *Fairfield University*
Lawrence Feidelman, *Florida Atlantic University*
Daniel Fischmar, *Westminster College*
Robert W. Folden, *Texas A&M University*
Charles Bryan Foltz, *University of Tennessee at Martin*
Jonathan Frank, *Suffolk University*
Jonathan Frankel, *University of Massachusetts, Boston Harbor*
Linda Fried, *University of Colorado, Denver*
William H. Friedman, *University of Central Arkansas*
Sharyn Gallagher, *University of Massachusetts, Lowell*
Gary Garrison, *Belmont University*
Beena George, *University of St. Thomas*
Biswadip Ghosh, *Metropolitan State College of Denver*
Dawn Giannoni, *Nova Southeastern University*
Ernest Gines, *Tarrant County College*
Steven Gordon, *Babson College*
Donald Gray, *independent consultant*
George Griffin, *Regis University*
Randy Guthrie, *California Polytechnic State University, Pomona*
Tom Hankins, *Marshall University*
Bassam Hasan, *University of Toledo*

Richard Herschel, *St. Joseph's University*
Vicki Hightower, *Elon University*
Bogdan Hoanca, *University of Alaska Anchorage*
Richard Holowczak, *Baruch College*
Walter Horn, *Webster University*
Dennis Howard, *University of Alaska Anchorage*
James Hu, *Santa Clara University*
Adam Huarng, *California State University, Los Angeles*
John Hupp, *Columbus State University*
Brent Hussin, *University of Wisconsin*
Mark Hwang, *Central Michigan University*
James Isaak, *Southern New Hampshire University*
Wade Jackson, *University of Memphis*
Thaddeus Janicki, *Mount Olive College*
Chuck Johnston, *Midwestern State University*
Susan Jones, *Utah State University*
Iris Junglas, *University of Houston, Main*
George Kelley, *Erie Community College-City Campus*
Richard Kesner, *Northeastern University*
Jadon Klopson, *United States Coast Guard Academy*
Brian Kovar, *Kansas State University*
Andreas Knoefels, *Santa Clara University*
Chetan Kumar, *California State University, San Marcos*
Subodha Kumar, *University of Washington*
Stephen Kwan, *San Jose State University*
Jackie Lamoureux, *Central New Mexico Community College*
Yvonne Lederer-Antonucci, *Widener University*
Joo Eng Lee-Partridge, *Central Connecticut State University*
Diane Lending, *James Madison University*
David Lewis, *University of Massachusetts, Lowell*
Keith Lindsey, *Trinity University*
Stephen Loy, *Eastern Kentucky University*
Steven Lunce, *Midwestern State University*
Efrem Mallach, *University of Massachusetts*
Purnendu Mandal, *Marshall University*
Ronald Mashburn, *West Texas A&M University*
Richard Mathieu, *James Madison University*
Sathasivam Mathiyalakan, *University of Massachusetts, Boston*
Dan Matthews, *Trine University*
Ron McFarland, *Western New Mexico University*
Patricia McQuaid, *California Polytechnic State University, San Luis Obispo*
Stephanie Miserlis, *Hellenic College*
Wai Mok, *University of Alabama in Huntsville*
Janette Moody, *The Citadel*
Ata Nahouraii, *Indiana University of Pennsylvania*
Adriene Nawrocki, *John F. Kennedy University*
Anne Nelson, *Nova Southeastern University*
Irina Neuman, *McKendree College*
Donald Norris, *Southern New Hampshire University*
Margaret O'Hara, *East Carolina University*

Ravi Patnayakuni, *University of Alabama, Huntsville*
Ravi Paul, *East Carolina University*
Lowell Peck, *Central Connecticut State University*
Richard Peschke, *Minnesota State University, Mankato*
Doncho Petkov, *Eastern Connecticut State University*
Olga Petkova, *Central Connecticut State University*
Leonard Presby, *William Paterson University of New Jersey*
Terry Province, *North Central Texas College*
Uzma Raja, *University of Alabama*
Adriane Randolph, *Kennesaw State University*
Harry Reif, *James Madison University*
Karl Reimers, *Mount Olive College*
Wes Rhea, *Kennesaw State University*
Frances Roebuck, *Wilson Technical Community College*
Richard Roncone, *United States Coast Guard Academy*
Roberta Roth, *University of Northern Iowa*
Cynthia Ruppel, *Nova Southeastern University*
Bruce Russell, *Northeastern University*
Ramesh Sankaranarayanan, *University of Connecticut*
Eric Santanen, *Bucknell University*
Atul Saxena, *Mercer University*
Charles Saxon, *Eastern Michigan University*
David Scanlan, *California State University, Sacramento*
Herb Schuette, *Elon University*
Ken Sears, *University of Texas, Arlington*
Robert Seidman, *Southern New Hampshire University*
Tom Seymour, *Minot State University*
Sherri Shade, *Kennesaw State University*
Ganesan Shankar, *Boston University*
Emily Shepard, *Central Carolina Community College*
Lakisha Simmons, *Indiana State University*
David Smith, *Cameron University*

Glenn Smith, *James Madison University*
Stephen Solosky, *Nassau Community College*
Howard Sparks, *University of Alaska Fairbanks*
George Strouse, *York College*
Gladys Swindler, *Fort Hays State University*
Arta Szathmary, *Bucks County Community College*
Robert Szymanski, *Georgia Southern University*
Albert Tay, *Idaho State University*
Winston Tellis, *Fairfield University*
Asela Thomason, *California State University, Long Beach*
Lou Thompson, *University of Texas, Dallas*
Anthony Townsend, *Iowa State University*
Goran Trajkovski, *Towson University*
Kim Troboy, *Arkansas Technical University*
Jonathan Trower, *Baylor University*
Ronald Trugman, *Cañada College*
Nancy Tsai, *California State University, Sacramento*
Betty Tucker, *Weber State University*
William Tucker, *Austin Community College*
David VanOver, *Sam Houston State University*
Therese Viscelli, *Georgia State University*
Linda Volonino, *Canisius University*
William Wagner, *Villanova University*
Rick Weible, *Marshall University*
Melody White, *University of North Texas*
Robert Wilson, *California State University, San Bernardino*
Elaine Winston, *Hofstra University*
Joe Wood, *Webster University*
Michael Workman, *Florida Institute of Technology*
Kathie Wright, *Salisbury University*
James Yao, *Montclair State University*
Don Yates, *Louisiana State University*

Thanks to our Global Edition Contributors

The following people deserve special recognition for their contributions to this Global Edition.
Robert Manderson, *University of Roehampton*
Sahil Raj, *Punjabi University*
Neerja Sethi, *Nayang Technological University*

Thanks to our Global Edition Reviewers

We would also like to thank the following people for reviewing the global content and sharing their feedback to help improve the content.

Nurul Nuhu Binti Abdul Molok, *Kulliyyah Of Information And Communication Technology*
Yannis Pollalis, *University of Piraeus*

Shamikh Siddiqui, *Jumeira University*
Mathy Paesen, Technical Consultant at *Belfius Insurance*

ENDNOTES

1. Robert B. Reich, *The Work of Nations* (New York: Alfred A. Knopf, 1991), p. 229.
2. Some instructors take the next step and replace their lectures with their own recorded PowerPoints, in what is coming to be known as *flipping the classroom.* The So What? features, guides, collaboration exercises, and case studies in this text support that approach if you choose it. See the article titled "How the Flipped Classroom Is Radically Transforming Learning" on www.thedailyriff.com for more about this technique.
3. Marilla Svinicki, *Learning and Motivation in the Postsecondary Classroom* (Bolton, MA: Anker Publishing, 2004).

ABOUT THE AUTHORS

David Kroenke has many years of teaching experience at Colorado State University, Seattle University, and the University of Washington. He has led dozens of seminars for college professors on the teaching of information systems and technology; in 1991, the International Association of Information Systems named him Computer Educator of the Year. In 2009, David was named Educator of the Year by the Association of Information Technology Professionals-Education Special Interest Group (AITP-EDSIG).

David worked for the U.S. Air Force and Boeing Computer Services. He was a principal in the startup of three companies, serving as the vice president of product marketing and development for the Microrim Corporation and as chief of database technologies for Wall Data, Inc. He is the father of the semantic object data model. David's consulting clients have included IBM, Microsoft, and Computer Sciences Corporations, as well as numerous smaller companies. Recently, David has focused on using information systems for teaching collaboration and teamwork.

His text *Database Processing* was first published in 1977 and is now in its 14th edition. He has authored and coauthored many other textbooks, including *Database Concepts*, 7th ed. (2015), *Experiencing MIS*, 7th ed. (2017), *SharePoint for Students* (2012), *Office 365 in Business* (2012), and *Processes, Systems, and Information: An Introduction to MIS*, 2nd ed. (2015).

Randall J. Boyle received his Ph.D. in Management Information Systems from Florida State University in 2003. He also has a master's degree in Public Administration and a B.S. in Finance. He has received university teaching awards at Longwood University, the University of Utah, and the University of Alabama in Huntsville. He has taught a wide variety of classes, including Introduction to MIS, Cyber Security, Networking & Servers, System Analysis and Design, Telecommunications, Advanced Cyber Security, Decision Support Systems, and Web Servers.

His research areas include deception detection in computer-mediated environments, secure information systems, the effects of IT on cognitive biases, the effects of IT on knowledge workers, and e-commerce. He has published in several academic journals and has authored several textbooks, including *Experiencing MIS*, 7th ed., *Corporate Computer and Network Security*, 4th ed., *Applied Information Security*, 2nd ed., and *Applied Networking Labs*, 2nd ed.

PART 1

Why MIS?

FALCON Security is a 5-year-old, privately owned company that uses aerial drones to provide surveillance and inspection services for customers. Its customers are large industrial companies that want to reduce their physical security labor costs or need periodic inspection services for industrial sites. Falcon has contracts with several large oil refineries in Texas to provide real-time video surveillance of their sizable industrial facilities. It also does occasional safety inspections on critical infrastructure components (e.g., flare stacks), which would be difficult and dangerous to do in person.

Falcon Security's CEO and cofounder is Mateo Thomas. In the early part of his career Mateo was a major in the United States Army in charge of physical security at a large military base in the Middle East. After retiring from the Army, Mateo went to work as the director of security at a large Texas-based industrial manufacturer. While serving on a security policy steering committee with business unit managers, he met the young and ambitious Joni Campbell. He told Joni the company was paying way too much for physical security. He thought the company could buy a few drones to do the work of several physical security guards at a fraction of the cost. From his time in the military he'd seen how drones could be used successfully to improve security with much less time and effort. The problem was that he didn't know much about actually operating the drones. Neither did Joni.

FALCON Security

A week later, Joni was at a friend's wedding and saw a wedding video that included amazing aerial shots of the bride and groom on the beach, driving, and walking in the park. Curious, she approached the photographer, Camillia (Cam) Forset, and asked her how she produced those stunning videos. Turns out that Cam did weddings part-time during the summer months. Her day job, which she didn't especially like, was as a regional sales representative for a drone manufacturer. She experimented with drones at a few photo shoots and the results were spectacular. Everyone who saw the aerial footage wanted it. She was the only photographer in the metro area who could produce aerial video, and her business thrived. But weddings were mostly seasonal, and she still needed her day job to pay the bills. Joni knew she'd found the drone expert she needed and asked Cam if she'd like to have lunch with her and Mateo the following Saturday.

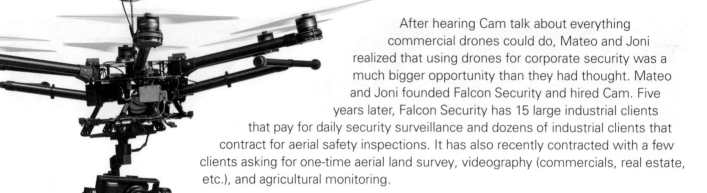

Source: Alexander Kolomietz/Fotolia

After hearing Cam talk about everything commercial drones could do, Mateo and Joni realized that using drones for corporate security was a much bigger opportunity than they had thought. Mateo and Joni founded Falcon Security and hired Cam. Five years later, Falcon Security has 15 large industrial clients that pay for daily security surveillance and dozens of industrial clients that contract for aerial safety inspections. It has also recently contracted with a few clients asking for one-time aerial land survey, videography (commercials, real estate, etc.), and agricultural monitoring.

Falcon Security has revenues of about $14 million per year, most of which comes from providing physical security to its large industrial clients. Mateo wants to grow Falcon Security nationally. He knows there are plenty of industrial clients outside of Texas that would pay for its services, possibly even a lucrative contract with the federal government. Joni is worried that Falcon is not ready. It's been a bumpy ride. Buying fleets of drones (planes and helicopters) has been expensive and, at times, frustrating. People have to be trained to operate the drones, the drones seem to break frequently, and newer models are always coming out. Then there's the hugely expensive systems development project that's currently under way to automate the collection, storage, and analysis of the data from the drones.

Mateo has also been exploring 3D printing as a way to reduce the costs of the drones. Cam's team was able to rapidly create an innovative prototype of a new passive recharging platform using a 3D printer. Now Falcon's drones can land, charge, and take off again without any human intervention. This has saved countless hours managing the drones and has increased the overall effective range of the drones. Fleets of autonomous drones can now be deployed across long distances by stopping every 10 to 15 miles at a recharging station.

Mateo hopes the company can have the same success in making its own drones. But he's not sure he wants to manufacture drones. How many new employees will he need to hire and train? How much will it cost to buy additional equipment and information systems to support the manufacturing process? Will these new drones be compatible with the existing data collection and processing system? Mateo asks Joni and Cam to figure out if manufacturing drones is the right move for Falcon Security.

The Importance of MIS

"Fired? You're firing me?"

"Well, *fired* is a harsh word, but ... well, Falcon Security has no further need for your services."

"But, Joni, I don't get it. I really don't. I worked hard, and I did everything you told me to do."

"Jennifer, that's just it. You did everything *I* told you to do."

"I put in so many hours. How could you fire me?"

"Your job was to find ways to reduce our fleet costs using 3D printing."

"Right! And I did that."

"No, you didn't. You followed up on ideas *that I gave you*. But we don't need someone who can follow up on my plans. We need someone who can figure out what we need to do, create her own plans, and bring them back to me.... and others."

"How could you expect me to do that? I've only been here 6 months!"

"It's called teamwork. Sure, you're just learning our business, but I made sure all of our senior staff would be available to you ..."

"I didn't want to bother them."

"Well, you succeeded. I asked Cam what she thought of the plans you're working on. 'Who's Jennifer?' she asked."

"But doesn't she work down at the hangar?"

"Right. She's the operations manager ... and it would seem to be worth talking to her."

"I'll go do that!"

"Jennifer, do you see what just happened? I gave you an idea and you said you'd do it. That's not what I need. I need you to find solutions on your own."

"I worked really hard. I put in a lot of hours. I've got all these reports written."

"Has anyone seen them?"

"I talked to you about some of them. But I was waiting until I was satisfied with them."

"Right. That's not how we do things here. We develop ideas and then kick them around with each other. Nobody has all the smarts. Our plans get better when we comment and rework them… I think I told you that."

"Maybe you did. But I'm just not comfortable with that."

"Well, it's a key skill here."

"I know I can do this job."

"Jennifer, you've been here almost 6 months; you have a degree in business. Several weeks ago, I asked you for your first idea for a process that would identify potential drones, or drone parts, that could be 3D-printed. Do you remember what you said?"

"Yes, I wasn't sure how to proceed. I didn't want to just throw something out that might not work."

"But how would you find out if it would work?"

"I don't want to waste money …"

"No, you don't. So, when you didn't get very far with that task, I backed up and asked you to send me a list of parts that could be printed based on our existing drones, a list of replacement repair parts we buy on a regular basis, the specifications for future drones that we might buy, and a description of how existing 3D-printed drones are made. Not details, just an overview."

"Yes, I sent you those part lists and specifications."

"Jennifer, they made no sense. Your lists included parts that can't be 3D-printed, and your list of potential future drones included models that can't even carry cameras."

"I know which parts can be printed, I just wasn't sure which ones to include. But I'll try again!"

"Well, I appreciate that attitude, but we're a small company, really still a startup in many ways. Everyone needs to pull more than their own weight here. Maybe if we were a bigger company, I'd be able to find a spot for you, see if we could bring you along. But we can't afford to do that now."

"What about my references?"

"I'll be happy to tell anyone that you're reliable, that you work 40 to 45 hours a week, and that you're honest and have integrity."

"Those are important!"

"Yes, they are. But today, they're not enough."

"But today, they're not enough."

Image source: rommma/Fotolia

STUDY QUESTIONS

Q1-1 Why is Introduction to MIS the most important class in the business school?

Q1-2 How will MIS affect me?

Q1-3 What is MIS?

Q1-4 How can you use the five-component model?

Q1-5 What is information?

Q1-6 What are necessary data characteristics?

Q1-7 2026?

CHAPTER PREVIEW

"But today, they're not enough."

Do you find that statement sobering? And if hard work isn't enough, what is? We'll begin this book by discussing the key skills that Jennifer (and you) need and explaining why this course is the single best course in the business school for teaching you those key skills.

You may find that last statement surprising. If you are like most students, you have no clear idea of what your MIS class will be about. If someone were to ask you, "What do you study in that class?" you might respond that the class has something to do with computers and maybe computer programming. Beyond that, you might be hard-pressed to say more. You might add, "Well, it has something to do with computers in business," or maybe, "We are going to learn to solve business problems with computers using spreadsheets and other programs." So, how could this course be the most important one in the business school?

We begin with that question. After you understand how important this class will be to your career, we will discuss fundamental concepts. We'll wrap up with some practice on one of the key skills you need to learn.

Q 1-1 Why Is Introduction to MIS the Most Important Class in the Business School?

Introduction to MIS is the most important class in the business school. This wasn't always the case. A couple decades ago, majoring in "computers" was considered a nerdy thing do to. But things have changed—a lot. Now the hottest jobs are found in tech companies. People brag about working for tech startups. Apple Inc. is the largest corporation in the world with a market cap of $740B. The largest IPO offering in history ($25B) came from the online e-commerce giant Alibaba (Alibaba Holdings Group) in 2014.

But why? Why has information technology changed from a minor corporate support function to a primary driver of corporate profitability? Why are tech jobs some of the highest paid? Why is working for a tech company considered über cool?

The answer has to do with the way technology is fundamentally changing business.

The Digital Revolution

You've probably heard that we live in the **Information Age**, or a period in history where the production, distribution, and control of information is the primary driver of the economy. The Information Age started in the 1970s with the **Digital Revolution**, or the conversion from mechanical and analog devices to digital devices. This shift to digital devices meant monumental changes for companies, individuals, and our society as a whole.

The problem was, people couldn't really understand how, or even why, this shift was going to affect them. Much like people today, they based their future projections on past events. They knew factories, bureaucracies, mass production, and operational efficiency. But this knowledge didn't prepare them for the changes that were coming.

The Digital Revolution didn't just mean that new "digital" equipment was replacing old mechanical, or analog, equipment. These new digital devices could now be connected to other digital devices and share data among themselves. They could also work faster as processor speed increased. This was groundbreaking. In 1972, computer scientist Gordon Bell recognized that these digital devices would change the world as they evolved and became widely used. He formulated **Bell's Law**, which states that "a new computer class forms roughly each decade establishing a new industry."[1] In other words, digital devices will evolve so quickly that they will enable new platforms, programming environments, industries, networks, and information systems every 10 years.

And it has happened just as Bell predicted. About every 10 years since 1970, entirely new classes of digital devices have emerged. They have created entirely new industries, companies, and platforms. In the 1980s, we saw the rise of the personal computer (PC) and small local networks. In the 1990s, we saw the rise of the Internet and widespread adoption of cellular phones. In the 2000s, we saw a push toward making all "things" network-enabled. Social networking and cloud-based services really took off, creating a flurry of new companies.

The evolution of digital technology has fundamentally altered businesses and become a primary driver of corporate profitability. And it will probably continue to do so for at least the next few decades. The key to understanding how businesses will be affected by this digital evolution is understanding the forces pushing the evolution of these new digital devices.

Evolving Capabilities

To understand the fundamental forces pushing the evolution of digital devices, let's imagine your body is evolving at the same rate as digital devices. Suppose you can run 8 miles per hour today. That's about average. Now suppose, hypothetically, that your body is changing so quickly that you can run twice as fast every 18 months. In 18 months, you'd be able to run 16 mph. In another 18 months, you'd be at 32 mph. Then 64, 128, 256, and 512. Then, after 10 1/2 years of growth, you'd be running 1,024 mph—on foot! How would this change your life?

Well, you'd certainly give up your car. It would be much too slow. Air travel would also probably be a thing of the past. You could start a very profitable package delivery business and quickly corner the market. You could live outside of the city because your commute would be shorter. You'd also need new clothes and some really tough shoes! And this is the key point—not only would *you* change, but *what* you do and *how* you do it would also change. This is Bell's Law. This same thing is happening to digital devices.

This example may seem silly at first, but it helps you understand how exponential change is affecting digital devices. Processing power, interconnectivity of devices, storage capacity, and bandwidth are all increasing extremely rapidly—so rapidly that it's changing how these devices are used. Let's explore some of these forces by looking at the laws that describe them.

Moore's Law

In 1965, Gordon Moore, cofounder of Intel Corporation, stated that because of technology improvements in electronic chip design and manufacturing, "The number of transistors per square inch on an integrated chip doubles every 18 months." This became known as **Moore's Law**. His statement has been commonly misunderstood to be "The speed of a computer doubles every 18 months," which is incorrect but captures the sense of his principle.

Because of Moore's Law, the ratio of price to performance of computers has fallen from something like $4,000 for a standard computing device to a fraction of a penny for that same computing device.[2] See Figure 1-1. Increasing processing power has had a greater impact on the global economy in the past 30 years than any other single factor. It has enabled new devices, applications, companies, and platforms. In fact, most tech companies would not exist today if processing power hadn't increased exponentially.

As a future business professional, however, you needn't care how fast of a computer your company can buy for $1,000. That's not the point. The point is, because of Moore's Law, the cost of data processing is approaching zero. Current applications like new drug development, artificial intelligence, and molecular modeling require massive amounts of processing power. Innovations

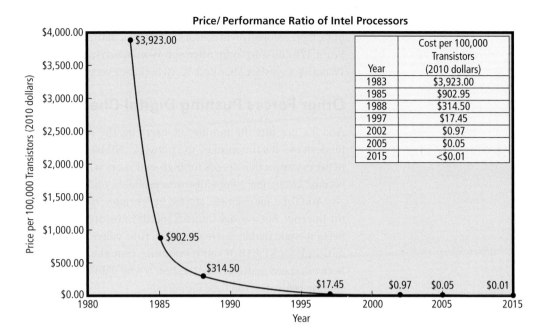

Figure 1-1
Computer Price/Performance
Ratio Decreases

in these areas are being held back because the cost of buying sufficient processing power is so high. But the good news is that the cost of processing is dropping—rapidly.

Metcalfe's Law

Another fundamental force that is changing digital devices is Metcalfe's Law, named after Robert Metcalfe, the inventor of Ethernet. **Metcalfe's Law** states that the value of a network is equal to the square of the number of users connected to it. In other words, as more digital devices are connected together, the value of that network will increase.[3] See Figure 1-2. Metcalfe's Law can be clearly seen in the dramatic rise of the Internet in the 1990s. As more users gained access to the Internet, it became more valuable. The dot-com boom ushered in tech giants like Google, Amazon, and eBay. None of these companies would have existed without large numbers of users connected to the Internet.

Metcalfe's Law isn't lost on tech companies, either. Google's Project Loon is a major effort to bring Internet access to everyone on the planet using a network of inflated balloons floating around the world. One of the primary metrics for social media companies is the number of monthly

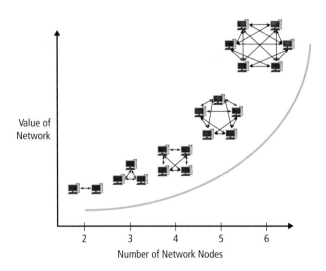

Figure 1-2
Increasing Value of Networks

active users (MAU) using their social network. The more people they can get in their network, the more their company will be worth. And look at the network effects of using products like Microsoft Word. Why do you pay for Microsoft Word when you could use a free word processor like LibreOffice Writer? You pay for Microsoft Word because everyone else uses it.

Other Forces Pushing Digital Change

And it's not just the number of users on the network that's changing the way we use digital devices—it's the *speed* of the network. **Nielsen's Law**, named after Jakob Nielsen, says that network connection speeds for high-end users will increase by 50 percent per year. As networks become faster, new companies, new products, and new platforms will emerge.

YouTube, for example, started in February 2005 when there wasn't a lot of video shared over the Internet. But average Internet speeds were increasing to the point where a typical Internet connection could handle a stream of YouTube videos. By November 2006, the company was bought by Google for $1.65B. If you're counting, that's less than 2 years to create a billion-dollar company. Network speed matters. The question is why didn't Google, Microsoft, IBM, or Apple think of video sharing before the YouTube founders?

There are other forces changing digital devices beyond Nielsen's Law, Metcalfe's Law, and Moore's Law (See Figure 1-3). **Kryder's Law**, named after Mark Kryder, the former chief technology officer of Seagate Corp., says that the storage density on magnetic disks is increasing at an exponential rate. Digital storage is so important that it's typically the first question you ask when you buy a new computer, smartphone, or tablet. There's also power consumption, image resolution, and interconnectivity between devices, all of which are changing, too. And this isn't a complete list.

This Is the Most Important Class in the School of Business

This takes us back to our original statement that Introduction to MIS is the most important class you will take in the school of business. Why? Because this class will show you how technology is fundamentally changing businesses. You'll learn why executives are constantly trying to find ways to use new technology to create a sustainable competitive advantage. This leads us to the first reason Introduction to MIS is the most important course in the business school today:

> **Future business professionals need to be able to assess, evaluate, and apply emerging information technology to business.**

You need the knowledge of this course to attain that skill.

Law	Meaning	Implications
Moore's Law	The number of transistors per square inch on an integrated chip doubles every 18 months.	Computers are getting exponentially faster. The cost of data processing is approaching zero.
Metcalfe's Law	The value of a network is equal to the square of the number of users connected to it.	More digital devices are connected together. The value of digital and social networks is increasing exponentially.
Nielsen's Law	Network connection speeds for high-end users will increase by 50 percent per year.	Network speed is increasing. Higher speeds enable new products, platforms, and companies.
Kryder's Law	The storage density on magnetic disks is increasing at an exponential rate.	Storage capacity is increasing exponentially. The cost of storing data is approaching zero.

Figure 1-3
Fundamental Forces Changing Technology

Q1-2 How Will MIS Affect Me?

Technological change is accelerating. So what? How is this going to affect you? You may think that the evolution of technology is just great. You can hardly wait for the next iGadget to come out.

But pause for a second and imagine you graduated from college in 2004 and went to work for one of the largest and most successful home entertainment companies in the United States—Blockbuster LLC. In 2004, Blockbuster had 60,000 employees and 9,000-plus stores with $5.9B in annual revenues. Everything looked peachy. Fast-forward 6 years to 2010 and Blockbuster was bankrupt! Why? Because streaming a video over the Internet is easier than driving to a store. High-speed Internet connections made it all possible.

The point is that after graduation you too may choose to go to work for a large, successful, well-branded company. And 6 years down the road, it could be bankrupt because technology changed and it didn't.

How Can I Attain Job Security?

Many years ago, I had a wise and experienced mentor. One day I asked him about job security, and he told me that the only job security that exists is "a marketable skill and the courage to use it." He continued, "There is no security in our company, there is no security in any government program, there is no security in your investments, and there is no security in Social Security." Alas, how right he turned out to be.

So, what is a marketable skill? It used to be that one could name particular skills, such as computer programming, tax accounting, or marketing. But today, because of Moore's Law, Metcalfe's Law, and Kryder's Law, the cost of data processing, storage, and communications is essentially zero. Any routine skill can and will be outsourced to the lowest bidder. And if you live in the United States, Canada, Australia, Europe, or another advanced economy, the lowest bidder is unlikely to be you.

Numerous organizations and experts have studied the question of what skills will be marketable during your career. Consider two of them. First, the RAND Corporation, a think tank located in Santa Monica, California, has published innovative and groundbreaking ideas for more than 60 years, including the initial design for the Internet. In 2004, RAND published a description of the skills that workers in the 21st century will need:

> Rapid technological change and increased international competition place the spotlight on the skills and preparation of the workforce, particularly the ability to adapt to changing technology and shifting demand. Shifts in the nature of organizations...favor strong nonroutine cognitive skills.[4]

Whether you're majoring in accounting, marketing, finance, or information systems, you need to develop strong nonroutine cognitive skills.

What are such skills? Robert Reich, former Secretary of Labor, enumerates four:[5]

- Abstract reasoning
- Systems thinking
- Collaboration
- Ability to experiment

Figure 1-4 shows an example of each. Reread the Falcon Security case that started this chapter, and you'll see that Jennifer lost her job because of her inability to practice these key skills. Even though Reich's book was written in the early 1990s, the cognitive skills he mentions are still relevant today because humans, unlike technology, aren't changing that rapidly.[6]

How Can Intro to MIS Help You Learn Nonroutine Skills?

Introduction to MIS is the best course in the business school for learning Reich's four key skills because every topic requires you to apply and practice them. Here's how.

Skill	Example	Jennifer's Problem at Falcon Security
Abstract Reasoning	Construct a model or representation.	Hesitancy and uncertainty when conceptualizing a method for identifying 3D-printable drone parts.
Systems Thinking	Model system components and show how components' inputs and outputs relate to one another.	Inability to model Falcon Security's operational needs.
Collaboration	Develop ideas and plans with others. Provide and receive critical feedback.	Unwilling to work with others on work-in-progress.
Ability to Experiment	Create and test promising new alternatives, consistent with available resources.	Fear of failure prohibited discussion of new ideas.

Figure 1-4

Examples of Critical Skills for Nonroutine Cognition

Abstract Reasoning

Abstract reasoning is the ability to make and manipulate models. You will work with one or more models in every course topic and book chapter. For example, later in this chapter you will learn about a *model* of the five components of an information system. This chapter will describe how to use this model to assess the scope of any new information system project; other chapters will build upon this model.

In this course, you will not just manipulate models that we have developed, you will also be asked to construct models of your own. In Chapter 5, for example, you'll learn how to create data models, and in Chapter 12 you'll learn to make process models.

Systems Thinking

Can you go to a grocery store, look at a can of green beans, and connect that can to U.S. immigration policy? Can you watch tractors dig up a forest of pulpwood trees and connect that woody trash to Moore's Law? Do you know why Cisco Systems is one of the major beneficiaries of YouTube? Answers to all of these questions require systems thinking. **Systems thinking** is the ability to model the components of the system to connect the inputs and outputs among those components into a sensible whole that reflects the structure and dynamics of the phenomenon observed.

As you are about to learn, this class is about information *systems.* We will discuss and illustrate systems; you will be asked to critique systems; you will be asked to compare alternative systems; you will be asked to apply different systems to different situations. All of those tasks will prepare you for systems thinking as a professional.

Collaboration

Collaboration is the activity of two or more people working together to achieve a common goal, result, or work product. Chapter 2 will teach you collaboration skills and illustrate several sample collaboration information systems. Every chapter of this book includes collaboration exercises that you may be assigned in class or as homework.

Here's a fact that surprises many students: Effective collaboration isn't about being nice. In fact, surveys indicate the single most important skill for effective collaboration is to give and receive critical feedback. Advance a proposal in business that challenges the cherished program of the VP of marketing, and you'll quickly learn that effective collaboration skills differ from party manners at the neighborhood barbeque. So, how do you advance your idea in the face of the VP's resistance? And without losing your job? In this course, you can learn both skills and information systems for such collaboration. Even better, you will have many opportunities to practice them.

Ability to Experiment

"I've never done this before."

"I don't know how to do it."

"But will it work?"

"Is it too weird for the market?"

Fear of failure: the fear that paralyzes so many good people and so many good ideas. In the days when business was stable, when new ideas were just different verses of the same song, professionals could allow themselves to be limited by fear of failure.

Let's look at an example of the application of social networking to the oil change business. Is there a legitimate application of social networking there? If so, has anyone ever done it? Is there anyone in the world who can tell you what to do? How to proceed? No. As Reich says, professionals in the 21st century need to be able to experiment.

Successful experimentation is not throwing buckets of money at every crazy idea that enters your head. Instead, **experimentation** is making a reasoned analysis of an opportunity, envisioning potential solutions, evaluating those possibilities, and developing the most promising ones, consistent with the resources you have.

In this course, you will be asked to use products with which you have no familiarity. Those products might be Microsoft Excel or Access, or they might be features and functions of Blackboard that you have not used. Or you may be asked to collaborate using OneDrive or SharePoint or Google Drive. Will your instructor explain and show every feature of those products that you'll need? You should hope not. You should hope your instructor will leave it up to you to experiment, to envision new possibilities on your own, and to experiment with those possibilities, consistent with the time you have available.

Jobs

Employment is another factor that makes the Introduction to MIS course vitally important to you. Accenture, a technology consulting and outsourcing company, conducted a survey of college graduates in 2014. It found that 69 percent of 2014 college graduates say they will need additional training or education before they get their desired job. Further, 46 percent of recent graduates were working in jobs that did not require their degree or were otherwise underemployed.[7] But this is not the case in job categories related to information systems.

Spence and Hlatshwayo studied employment in the United States from 1990 to 2008.[8] They defined a *tradable job* as one that was not dependent on a particular location; this distinction is important because such jobs can be outsourced overseas. As shown in Figure 1-5, computer systems design and related services had the strongest growth of any job type in that category. The number of jobs dipped substantially after the dot-com bust in 2000; since 2003, however, job growth has not only recovered but accelerated dramatically. While this category includes technical positions such as computer programmer and database administrator, it includes nontechnical sales, support, and business management jobs as well. By the way, because Figure 1-5 shows tradable jobs, it puts an end to the myth that all the good computer jobs have gone overseas. According to their data analysis, sourced from the U.S. Bureau of Labor Statistics, that simply has not happened.

The data in Figure 1-5 stops at 2009 and, unfortunately, Spence and Hlatshwayo have not updated their study. However, Figure 1-6 shows the U.S. Bureau of Labor Statistics recent job projections for business managers, computer and information technology, and other business occupations for the years 2012 to 2022.[9] Growth rates of all information systems–related jobs are above the 11 percent average for all occupations.

Information systems and computer technology provide job and wage benefits beyond just IS professionals. Acemoglu and Autor published an impressive empirical study of jobs and wages

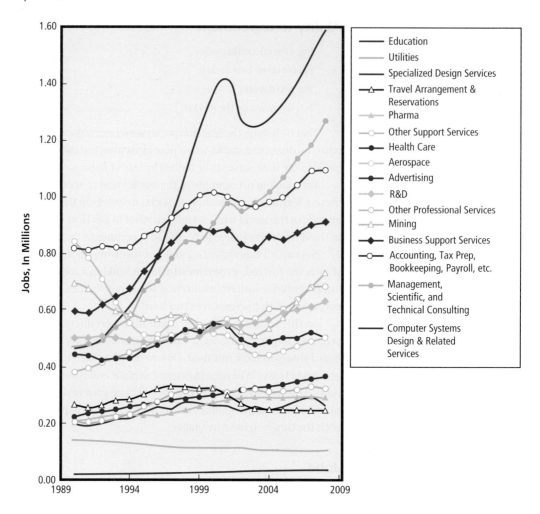

Figure 1-5

Growth of Jobs by Sector from 1989 to 2009

Source: From *The Evolving Structure of the American Economy* and the *Employment Challenge* by Michael Spence and Sandile Hlatshwayo. Copyright © 2011 by The Council on Foreign Relations Press. Reprinted with permission.

in the United States and parts of Europe from the 1960s to 2010. They found that early in this period, education and industry were the strongest determinants of employment and salary. However, since 1990, the most significant determinant of employment and salary is the nature of work performed. In short, as the price of computer technology plummets, the value of jobs that benefit from it increases dramatically.[10] For example, plentiful, high-paying jobs are available to business professionals who know how to use information systems to improve business process quality, or those who know how to interpret data mining results for improved marketing, or those who know how to use emerging technology like 3D printing to create new products and address new markets. See the Guide on pages 62–63 for more thoughts on why you might consider an IS-related job.

What Is the Bottom Line?

The bottom line? This course is the most important course in the business school because:

1. **It will give you the background you need to assess, evaluate, and apply emerging information systems technology to business.**
2. **It can give you the ultimate in job security—marketable skills—by helping you learn abstraction, systems thinking, collaboration, and experimentation.**
3. **Many well-paid MIS-related jobs are in high demand.**

	2012 Median Pay	Job Growth (%) 2012–22	Job Growth (N) 2012–22
Business Managers			
Marketing Managers	$115,750	12%	25,400
Information Systems Managers	$120,950	15%	50,900
Financial Managers	$109,740	9%	47,100
Human Resources Managers	$ 99,720	13%	13,600
Sales Managers	$105,260	8%	29,800
Computer and Information Technology			
Computer Network Architects	$ 91,000	15%	20,900
Computer Systems Analysts	$ 79,680	25%	127,700
Database Administrators	$118,700	15%	17,900
Information Security Analysts	$ 87,170	37%	27,400
Network and Systems Admin.	$ 72,560	12%	42,900
Software Developers	$ 93,350	22%	222,600
Web Developers	$ 62,500	20%	28,500
Business Occupations			
Accountants and Auditors	$ 63,550	13%	166,700
Financial Analysts	$ 76,950	16%	39,300
Management Analysts	$ 78,600	19%	133,800
Market Research Analysts	$ 60,300	32%	131,500
Logisticians	$ 72,780	22%	27,600
Human Resources Specialists	$ 55,640	7%	32,500

Figure 1-6
Bureau of Labor Statistics Occupational Outlook 2012–2022
Source: Based on Bureau of Labor Statistics, "Computer Systems Analysts," Occupational Outlook Handbook, accessed April 16, 2015, *www.bls.gov/ooh.*

Q1-3   What Is MIS?

We've used the term *MIS* several times, and you may be wondering exactly what it is. **MIS** stands for **management information systems**, which we define as *the management and use of information systems that help organizations achieve their strategies.* MIS is often confused with the closely related terms *information technology* and *information systems.* An **information system (IS)** is an assembly of hardware, software, data, procedures, and people that produces information. In contrast, **information technology (IT)** refers to the products, methods, inventions, and standards used for the purpose of producing information.

How are MIS, IS, and IT different? You cannot buy an IS. But you can buy IT; you can buy or lease hardware, you can license programs and databases, and you can even obtain predesigned procedures. Ultimately, however, it is *your* people who will assemble the IT you purchase and execute those procedures to employ that new IT. Information technology drives the development of new information systems.

For any new system, you will always have training tasks (and costs), you will always have the need to overcome employees' resistance to change, and you will always need to manage the employees as they use the new system. Hence, you can buy IT, but you cannot buy IS. Once your new information system is up and running, it must be managed and used effectively in order to achieve the organization's overall strategy. This is MIS.

Consider a simple example. Suppose your organization decides to develop a Facebook page. Facebook provides the IT. It provides the hardware and programs, the database structures, and standard procedures. You, however, must create the IS. You have to provide the data to fill your portion of its database, and you must extend its standard procedures with your own procedures for keeping that data current. Those procedures need to provide, for example, a means to review your page's content regularly and a means to remove content that is judged inappropriate. Furthermore, you need to train employees on how to follow those procedures and manage those employees to ensure that they do. MIS is the management of your Facebook page to achieve your overall organization's strategy. Managing your own Facebook page is as simple an IS as exists. Larger, more comprehensive IS that involve many, even dozens, of departments and thousands of employees require considerable work.

The definition of MIS has three key elements: *management and use, information systems*, and *strategies*. Let's consider each, starting first with information systems and their components.

Components of an Information System

A **system** is a group of components that interact to achieve some purpose. As you might guess, an *information system (IS)* is a group of components that interacts to produce information. That sentence, although true, raises another question: What are these components that interact to produce information?

Figure 1-7 shows the **five-component framework**—a model of the components of an information system: **computer hardware**, **software**, **data**, **procedures**, and **people**. These five components are present in every information system, from the simplest to the most complex. For example, when you use a computer to write a class report, you are using hardware (the computer, storage disk, keyboard, and monitor), software (Word, WordPerfect, or some other word-processing program), data (the words, sentences, and paragraphs in your report), procedures (the methods you use to start the program, enter your report, print it, and save and back up your file), and people (you).

Consider a more complex example, say, an airline reservation system. It, too, consists of these five components, even though each one is far more complicated. The hardware consists of thousands of computers linked together by data communications hardware. Hundreds of different programs coordinate communications among the computers, and still other programs perform the reservations and related services. Additionally, the system must store millions upon millions of characters of data about flights, customers, reservations, and other facts. Hundreds of different procedures are followed by airline personnel, travel agents, and customers. Finally, the information system includes people, not only the users of the system but also those who operate and service the computers, those who maintain the data, and those who support the networks of computers.

The important point here is that the five components in Figure 1-7 are common to all information systems, from the smallest to the largest. As you think about any information system, including a new one like social networking, learn to look for these five components. Realize, too, that an information system is not just a computer and a program, but rather an assembly of computers, programs, data, procedures, and people.

As we will discuss later in this chapter, these five components also mean that many different skills are required besides those of hardware technicians or computer programmers when building or using an information system. See the Guide starting on page 62 for more.

Before we move forward, note that we have defined an information system to include a computer. Some people would say that such a system is a **computer-based information system**. They would note that there are information systems that do not include computers, such as a calendar hanging on the wall outside of a conference room that is used to schedule the room's use. Such systems have been used by businesses for centuries. Although this point is true, in this book we focus on computer-based information systems. To simplify and shorten the book, we will use the term *information system* as a synonym for *computer-based information system*.

Management and Use of Information Systems

The next element in our definition of MIS is the *management and use* of information systems. Here we define management to mean develop, maintain, and adapt. Information systems do not pop

Figure 1-7

Five Components of an Information System

Five-Component Framework

Hardware	Software	Data	Procedures	People

up like mushrooms after a hard rain; they must be developed. They must also be maintained, and, because business is dynamic, they must be adapted to new requirements.

You may be saying, "Wait a minute, I'm a finance (or accounting or management) major, not an information systems major. I don't need to know how to manage information systems." If you are saying that, you are like a lamb headed for shearing. Throughout your career, in whatever field you choose, information systems will be built for your use and sometimes under your direction. To create an information system that meets your needs, you need to take an *active role* in that system's development. Even if you are not a programmer or a database designer or some other IS professional, you must take an active role in specifying the system's requirements and in managing the system's development project. You will also have an important role in testing the new system. Without active involvement on your part, it will only be good luck that causes the new system to meet your needs.

As a business professional, you are the person who understands business needs and requirements. If you want to apply social networking to your products, you are the one who knows how best to obtain customer responses. The technical people who build networks, the database designers who create the database, the IT people who configure the computers—none of these people know what is needed and whether the system you have is sufficient or whether it needs to be adapted to new requirements. You do!

Security is critically important when using information systems today. You'll learn much more about it in Chapter 10. But you need to know about strong passwords and their use now, before you get to that chapter. Read and follow the Security Guide on pages 60–61.

In addition to management tasks, you will also have important roles to play in the *use* of information systems. Of course, you will need to learn how to employ the system to accomplish your job tasks. But you will also have important ancillary functions as well. For example, when using an information system, you will have responsibilities for protecting the security of the system and its data. You may also have tasks for backing up data. When the system fails (all do, at some point), you will have tasks to perform while the system is down as well as tasks to accomplish to help recover the system correctly and quickly.

Achieving Strategies

The last part of the definition of MIS is that information systems exist to help organizations *achieve their strategies*. First, realize that this statement hides an important fact: Organizations themselves do not "do" anything. An organization is not alive, and it cannot act. It is the people within a business who sell, buy, design, produce, finance, market, account, and manage. So, information systems exist to help people who work in an organization to achieve the strategies of that business.

Information systems are not created for the sheer joy of exploring technology. They are not created so the company can be "modern" or so the company can show it has a social networking presence on the Web. They are not created because the information systems department thinks it needs to be created or because the company is "falling behind the technology curve."

This point may seem so obvious that you might wonder why we mention it. Every day, however, some business somewhere is developing an information system for the wrong reasons. Right now, somewhere in the world, a company is deciding to create a Facebook presence for the sole reason that "every other business has one." This company is not asking questions such as:

- "What is the purpose of our Facebook page?"
- "What is it going to do for us?"
- "What is our policy for employees' contributions?"
- "What should we do about critical customer reviews?"
- "Are the costs of maintaining the page sufficiently offset by the benefits?"

For more information on how an understanding of MIS can broaden your career options, see the Guide on pages 62–63.

But that company should ask those questions! Chapter 3 addresses the relationship between information systems and strategy in more depth. Chapter 8 addresses social media and strategy specifically.

Again, MIS is the development and use of information systems that help businesses achieve their strategies. You should already be realizing that there is much more to this class than buying a computer, working with a spreadsheet, or creating a Web page.

Q1-4   How Can You Use the Five-Component Model?

The five-component model in Figure 1-7 can help guide your learning and thinking about IS, both now and in the future. To understand this framework better, first note in Figure 1-8 that these five components are symmetric. The outermost components, hardware and people, are both actors; they can take actions. The software and procedure components are both sets of instructions: Software is instructions for hardware, and procedures are instructions for people. Finally, data is the bridge between the computer side on the left and the human side on the right.

Now, when we automate a business task, we take work that people are doing by following procedures and move it so that computers will do that work, following instructions in software. Thus, the process of automation is a process of moving work from the right side of Figure 1-8 to the left.

The Most Important Component—You

You are part of every information system that you use. When you consider the five components of an information system, the last component, people, includes you. Your mind and your thinking are not merely a component of the information systems you use; they are the most important component.

As you will learn later in this chapter, computer hardware and programs manipulate data, but no matter how much data they manipulate, it is still just data. It is only humans that produce information. When you take a set of data, say, a list of customer responses to a marketing campaign, that list, no matter if it was produced using 10,000 servers and Hadoop (Chapter 9), is still just data. It does not become information until you or some other human take it into your mind and are informed by it.

Even if you have the largest computer farm in the world and even if you are processing that data with the most sophisticated programs, if you do not know what to do with the data those programs produce, you are wasting your time and money. The quality of your thinking is what determines the quality of the information that is produced.

Substantial cognitive research has shown that although you cannot increase your basic IQ, you can dramatically increase the quality of your thinking. That is one reason we have emphasized the need for you to use and develop your abstract reasoning. The effectiveness of an IS depends on the abstract reasoning of the people who use it.

All Components Must Work

Information systems often encounter problems—despite our best efforts, they don't work right. And in these situations, blame is frequently placed on the wrong component. You will often hear people complain that the computer doesn't work, and certainly hardware or software is sometimes at fault. But with the five-component model, you can be more specific, and you have more suspects to consider. Sometimes the data is not in the right format or, worse, is incorrect. Sometimes, the procedures are not clear and the people using the system are not properly trained. By using the five-component model, you can better locate the cause of a problem and create effective solutions.

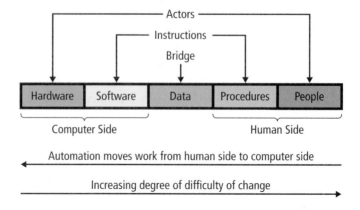

Figure 1-8

Characteristics of the Five Components

Biggest IPO Ever: Alibaba

Have you ever thought about starting your own business? It's not easy to turn a new idea into a profitable company. But the Information Age has created an environment in which anyone can grow a small business with minimal investment and marginal risk. Sometimes even technical requirements can be outsourced.

For example, companies like Squarespace.com allow entrepreneurs lacking Web development skills to create dynamic, visually appealing platforms to sell their goods or services. And if you don't want to sit around packing and shipping your products to customers, let Fulfillment by Amazon (FBA) do it for you!

But fledgling entrepreneurs aren't the only ones benefiting from the resources provided by a growing digital economy; companies of all sizes dealing in business-to-business (B2B), business-to-consumer (B2C), and consumer-to-consumer (C2C) commerce are also profiting from new opportunities to find cheaper raw materials, higher-quality trading goods, and, most importantly, customers.

What Is Alibaba.com?

Founded by Jack Ma in 1999, Alibaba.com started out as an e-commerce portal for buying and selling goods and has since grown to include a variety of financial, auction, and commerce services. Alibaba's mission is to connect suppliers and buyers around the globe.[11]

Alibaba boasts millions of products, dozens of product categories, and thousands of messages exchanged daily between buyers and sellers. While this may be the first time you have heard of Alibaba.com, it has become a major product and information interchange for buying and selling wholesale goods.

The influence Alibaba.com has on global commerce is even more evident when you consider the size of its IPO in the fall of 2014 (NYSE: BABA). BABA broke the record for biggest-ever IPO by roughly $3B with an IPO of $25B.[12] By comparison, Facebook raised $16B in its 2012 IPO, and General Motors' IPO raised $15.7B after emerging from bankruptcy in 2010. Interestingly, Ma started Alibaba.com with less than $70,000 in 1999 and is now the richest man in China.

Growing Pains

Alibaba rapidly evolved from a "new idea" to a leading global retailer and supplier with the biggest IPO of all time. Given the company's meteoric rise, it might be tempting to assume that Alibaba.com is going to be the dominant worldwide retailer and

Source: Yeong-Ung Yang/Corbis

supplier. But this may not be the case. The site has been mired with suppliers selling counterfeit products despite roughly $16M invested annually to combat the sale of fraudulent goods.[13]

Alibaba.com has sought to combat counterfeit goods by allowing suppliers to obtain "Gold Supplier" status, a vetting process including site visits by verification services. However, you can imagine the logistical complexities associated with vetting global suppliers and responding to fraud claims by global buyers.

What Can Alibaba.com Do for You?

If you are thinking of importing wholesale goods and selling them on your own e-commerce site or in your flagship brick-and-mortar location, then Alibaba.com might end up being a great supplier for you. Even if you don't end up buying products from Alibaba, lessons can be learned from Alibaba's success.

First, Alibaba.com is a perfect example of how managing information can be as profitable as selling a high-quality product. Consider the fact that Alibaba may be the largest retailer in the world, but it has little or no inventory at all.

Second, Alibaba.com demonstrates the complexities associated with operating in a global economy. Managing customer relationships can be more difficult when buyers and sellers are located around the world.

Finally, the story of Alibaba.com illustrates what can be accomplished in a relatively short period of time with a laptop, a good idea, and a lot of hard work. So stop checking your friends' status updates and get to work on your idea for the next great tech company!

Questions

1. Take a few minutes to browse Alibaba.com and look at some examples of products for sale on the site. What are some of the logistical differences between buying something on Alibaba.com and buying something on Amazon.com?

2. How has reading this article changed your perception of the difficulty associated with starting a new business?

3. Think about companies that currently have high stock prices. Do these companies sell a product or service, or do they offer something else? How is Alibaba.com similar to or different from these companies?

4. What are some of the challenges associated with operating an international business not discussed in this feature?

5. Think about your own purchasing habits and the buying habits of your friends/coworkers. Can you identify a product people need that is available on Alibaba.com? Is there a different Web site on which you could purchase this product for wholesale prices and sell it to customers for a profit?

High-Tech Versus Low-Tech Information Systems

Information systems differ in the amount of work moved from the human side (people and procedures) to the computer side (hardware and programs). For example, consider two different versions of a customer support information system: A system that consists only of a file of email addresses and an email program is a very low-tech system. Only a small amount of work has been moved from the human side to the computer side. Considerable human work is required to determine when to send which emails to which customers.

In contrast, a customer support system that keeps track of the equipment that customers have and the maintenance schedules for that equipment and then automatically generates email reminders to customers is a higher-tech system. This simply means that more work has been moved from the human side to the computer side. The computer is providing more services on behalf of the humans.

Often, when considering different information systems alternatives, it will be helpful to consider the low-tech versus high-tech alternatives in light of the amount of work being moved from people to computers.

The Ethics Guide in each chapter of this book considers the ethics of information systems use. These guides challenge you to think deeply about ethical standards, and they provide for some interesting discussions with classmates. The Ethics Guide on pages 56–57 considers the ethics of presenting data that deceives the viewer.

Understanding the Scope of New Information Systems

The five-component framework can also be used when assessing the scope of new systems. When in the future some vendor pitches the need for a new technology to you, use the five components to assess how big of an investment that new technology represents. What new hardware will you need? What programs will you need to license? What databases and other data must you create? What procedures will need to be developed for both use and administration of the information system? And, finally, what will be the impact of the new technology on people? Which jobs will change? Who will need training? How will the new technology affect morale? Will you need to hire new people? Will you need to reorganize?

Components Ordered by Difficulty and Disruption

Finally, as you consider the five components, keep in mind that Figure 1-8 shows them in order of ease of change and the amount of organizational disruption. It is a simple matter to order additional hardware. Obtaining or developing new programs is more difficult. Creating new databases or changing the structure of existing databases is still more difficult. Changing procedures, requiring people to work in new ways, is even more difficult. Finally, changing personnel responsibilities and reporting relationships and hiring and terminating employees are all very difficult and very disruptive to the organization.

Q1-5 What Is Information?

Based on our earlier discussions, we can now define an information system as an assembly of hardware, software, data, procedures, and people that interact to produce information. The only term left undefined in that definition is *information*, and we turn to it next.

Definitions Vary

Information is one of those fundamental terms that we use every day but that turns out to be surprisingly difficult to define. Defining information is like defining words such as *alive* and *truth*. We know what those words mean, we use them with each other without confusion, but nonetheless, they are difficult to define.

In this text, we will avoid the technical issues of defining information and will use common, intuitive definitions instead. Probably the most common definition is that **information** is knowledge derived from data, whereas *data* is defined as recorded facts or figures. Thus, the facts that employee James Smith earns $70.00 per hour and that Mary Jones earns $50.00 per hour are *data*. The statement that the average hourly wage of all the graphic designers is $60.00 per hour is *information*. Average wage is knowledge derived from the data of individual wages.

Another common definition is that *information is data presented in a meaningful context*. The fact that Jeff Parks earns $30.00 per hour is data.[14] The statement that Jeff Parks earns less than half the average hourly wage of the company's Web designers, however, is information. It is data presented in a meaningful context.

Another definition of information that you will hear is that *information is processed data* or, sometimes, *information is data processed by summing, ordering, averaging, grouping, comparing, or other similar operations*. The fundamental idea of this definition is that we do something to data to produce information.

There is yet a fourth definition of information, which was set out by the great research psychologist Gregory Bateson. He defined information as *a difference that makes a difference.*

For the purposes of this text, any of these definitions of information will do. Choose the definition of information that makes sense to you. The important point is that you discriminate between data and information. You also may find that different definitions work better in different situations.

Where Is Information?

Suppose you create a graph of Amazon.com's stock price and net income over its history, like that shown in Figure 1-9. Does that graph contain information? Well, if it shows a difference that

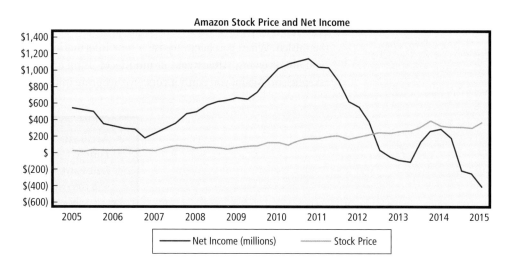

Figure 1-9

Amazon.com Stock Price and Net Income

makes a difference or if it presents data in a meaningful context, then it fits two of the definitions of information, and it's tempting to say that the graph contains information.

However, show that graph to your family dog. Does your dog find information in that graph? Well, nothing about Amazon.com, anyway. The dog might learn what you had for lunch, but it won't obtain any information about Amazon.com's stock price over time.

Reflect on this experiment and you will realize that the graph is not, itself, information. The graph is data that you and other humans *perceive*, and from that perception you *conceive* information. In short, if it's on a piece of paper or on a digital screen, it's data. If it's in the mind of a human, it's information.

Why, you're asking yourself, do I care? Well, for one, it further explains why you, as a human, are the most important part of any information system you use. The quality of your thinking, of your ability to conceive information from data, is determined by your cognitive skills. *The data is just the data; the information you conceive from it is the value that you add to the information system.*

Furthermore, people have different perceptions and points of view. Not surprisingly, then, they will conceive different information from the same data. You cannot say to someone, "Look, it's right there in front of you, in the data" because it's not right there in the data. Rather, it's in your head and in their heads, and your job is to explain what you have conceived so that others can understand it.

Finally, once you understand this, you'll understand that all kinds of common sentences make no sense. "I sent you that information" cannot be true. "I sent you the data, from which you conceived the information" is the most we can say. During your business career, this observation will save you untold frustration if you remember to apply it.

Q1-6 What Are Necessary Data Characteristics?

You have just learned that humans conceive information from data. As stated, the quality of the information that you can create depends, in part, on your thinking skills. It also depends, however, on the quality of the data you are given. Figure 1-10 summarizes critical data characteristics.

Accurate

First, good information is conceived from accurate, correct, and complete data that has been processed correctly as expected. Accuracy is crucial; business professionals must be able to rely on the results of their information systems. The IS function can develop a bad reputation in the organization if a system is known to produce inaccurate data. In such a case, the information system becomes a waste of time and money as users develop work-arounds to avoid the inaccurate data.

A corollary to this discussion is that you, a future user of information systems, ought not to rely on data just because it appears in the context of a Web page, a well-formatted report, or a fancy query. It is sometimes hard to be skeptical of data delivered with beautiful, active graphics. Do not be misled. When you begin to use a new information system, be skeptical. Cross-check the data you are receiving. After weeks or months of using a system, you may relax. Begin, however, with skepticism. Again, you cannot conceive accurate information from inaccurate data.

> - **Accurate**
> - **Timely**
> - **Relevant**
>   - To context
>   - To subject
> - **Just sufficient**
> - **Worth its cost**

Figure 1-10

Data Characteristics Required for Good Information

Timely

Good information requires that data be timely—available in time for its intended use. A monthly report that arrives 6 weeks late is most likely useless. The data arrives long after the decisions have been made that needed your information. An information system that sends you a poor customer credit report after you have shipped the goods is unhelpful and frustrating. Notice that timeliness can be measured against a calendar (6 weeks late) or against events (before we ship).

When you participate in the development of an IS, timeliness will be part of the requirements you specify. You need to give appropriate and realistic timeliness needs. In some cases, developing systems that provide data in near real time is much more difficult and expensive than producing data a few hours later. If you can get by with data that is a few hours old, say so during the requirements specification phase.

Consider an example. Suppose you work in marketing and you need to be able to assess the effectiveness of new online ad programs. You want an information system that not only will deliver ads over the Web but that also will enable you to determine how frequently customers click on those ads. Determining click ratios in near real time will be very expensive; saving the data in a batch and processing it some hours later will be much easier and cheaper. If you can live with data that is a day or two old, the system will be easier and cheaper to implement.

Relevant

Data should be relevant both to the context and to the subject. Considering context, you, the CEO, need data that is summarized to an appropriate level for your job. A list of the hourly wage of every employee in the company is unlikely to be useful. More likely, you need average wage information by department or division. A list of all employee wages is irrelevant in your context.

Data should also be relevant to the subject at hand. If you want data about short-term interest rates for a possible line of credit, then a report that shows 15-year mortgage interest rates is irrelevant. Similarly, a report that buries the data you need in pages and pages of results is also irrelevant to your purposes.

Just Barely Sufficient

Data needs to be sufficient for the purpose for which it is generated, but just barely so. We are inundated with data; one of the critical decisions that each of us has to make each day is what data to ignore. The higher you rise into management, the more data you will be given, and because there is only so much time, the more data you will need to ignore. So, data should be sufficient, but just barely.

Worth Its Cost

Data is not free. There are costs for developing an information system, costs of operating and maintaining that system, and costs of your time and salary for reading and processing the data the system produces. For data to be worth its cost, an appropriate relationship must exist between the cost of data and its value.

Consider an example. What is the value of a daily report of the names of the occupants of a full graveyard? Zero, unless grave robbery is a problem for the cemetery. The report is not worth the time required to read it. It is easy to see the importance of economics for this silly example. It will be more difficult, however, when someone proposes new technology to you. You need to be ready to ask, "What's the value of the information I can conceive from this data?" "What is the cost?" "Is there an appropriate relationship between value and cost?" Information systems should be subject to the same financial analyses to which other assets are subjected.

Ethics Guide

Suppose you're a young marketing professional who has just taken a new promotional campaign to market. The executive committee asks you to present a summary of the sales effect of the campaign, and you produce the graph shown in Figure 1. As shown, your campaign was just in the nick of time; sales were starting to fall the moment your campaign kicked in. After that, sales boomed.

But note the vertical axis has no quantitative labels. If you add quantities, as shown in Figure 2, the performance is less impressive. It appears that the substantial growth amounts to less than 20 units. Still the curve of the graph is impressive, and if no one does the arithmetic, your campaign will appear successful.

This impressive shape is only possible, however, because Figure 2 is not drawn to scale. If you draw it to scale, as shown in Figure 3, your campaign's success is, well, problematic, at least for you.

Which of these graphs do you present to the committee? Each chapter of this text includes an Ethics Guide that explores ethical and responsible behavior in a variety of MIS-related contexts. In this chapter, we'll examine the ethics of data and information.

Centuries of philosophical thought have addressed the question "What is right behavior?" and we can't begin to discuss all of it here. You will learn much of it, however, in your business ethics class. For our purposes, we'll use two of the major pillars in the philosophy of ethics. We introduce the first one here and the second in Chapter 2.

The German philosopher Immanuel Kant defined the *categorical imperative* as the principle that *one should behave only in a way that one would want the behavior to be a universal law.* Stealing is not such behavior because if everyone steals, nothing can be owned. Stealing cannot be a universal law. Similarly, lying cannot be consistent with the categorical imperative because if everyone lies, words are useless.

When you ask whether a behavior is consistent with this principle, a good litmus test is "Are you willing to publish your behavior to the world? Are you willing to put it on your Facebook page? Are you willing to say what you've done to all the players involved?" If not, your behavior is not ethical, at least not in the sense of Kant's categorical imperative.

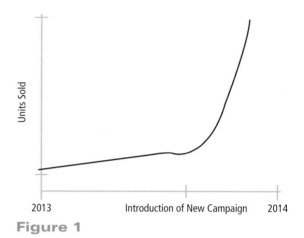

Figure 1

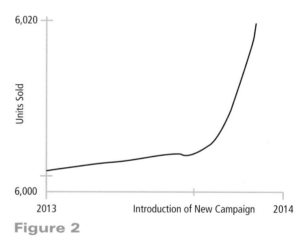

Figure 2

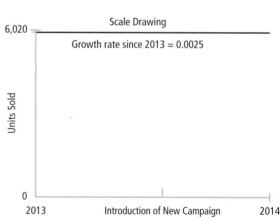

Figure 3

Kant defined *duty* as the necessity to act in accordance with the categorical imperative. *Perfect duty* is behavior that must always be met. Not lying is a perfect duty. *Imperfect duty* is action that is praiseworthy but not required according to the categorical imperative. Giving to charity is an example of an imperfect duty.

Kant used the example of cultivating one's own talent as an imperfect duty, and we can use that example as a way of defining professional responsibility. Business professionals have an imperfect duty to obtain the skills necessary to accomplish their jobs. We also have an imperfect duty to continue to develop our business skills and abilities throughout our careers.

We will apply these principles in the chapters that follow. For now, use them to assess your beliefs about Figures 1 through 3 by answering the following questions.

Source: Pressmaster/Fotolia

? DISCUSSION QUESTIONS

1. Restate Kant's categorical imperative using your own words. Explain why cheating on exams is not consistent with the categorical imperative.

2. While there is some difference of opinion, most scholars believe that the Golden Rule ("Do unto others as you would have them do unto you.") is not equivalent to Kant's categorical imperative. Justify this belief.

3. Using the Bateson definition (discussed in Q5) that information is a difference that makes a difference:
   a. Explain how the features of the graph in Figure 1 influence the viewer to create information.
   b. Explain how the features of the graph in Figure 3 influence the viewer to create information.
   c. Which of these graphs is consistent with Kant's categorical imperative?

4. Suppose you created Figure 1 using Microsoft Excel. To do so, you keyed the data into Excel and clicked the Make Graph button (there is one, though it's not called that). Voilà, Excel created Figure 1 without any labels and drawn out of scale as shown. Without further consideration, you put the result into your presentation.
   a. Is your behavior consistent with Kant's categorical imperative? Why or why not?
   b. If Excel automatically produces graphs like Figure 1, is Microsoft's behavior consistent with Kant's categorical imperative? Why or why not?

5. Change roles. Assume now you are a member of the executive committee. A junior marketing professional presents Figure 1 to the committee, and you object to the lack of labels and the scale. In response, the junior marketing professional says, "Sorry, I didn't know. I just put the data into Excel and copied the resulting graph." What conclusions do you, as an executive, make about the junior marketing professional in response to this statement?

6. Is the junior marketing person's response in question 5 a violation of a perfect duty? Of an imperfect duty? Of any duty? Explain your response.

7. If you were the junior marketing professional, which graph would you present to the committee?

8. According to Kant, lying is not consistent with the categorical imperative. Suppose you are invited to a seasonal barbeque at the department chair's house. You are served a steak that is tough, overcooked, and so barely edible that you secretly feed it to the department chair's dog (who appears to enjoy it). The chairperson asks you, "How is your steak?" and you respond, "Excellent, thank you."
   a. Is your behavior consistent with Kant's categorical imperative?
   b. The steak seemed to be excellent to the dog. Does that fact change your answer to part a?
   c. What conclusions do you draw from this example?

Q1-7 2026?

In Q1-1, we said that future businesspeople need to be able to assess, evaluate, and apply emerging technology. What technology might that be? And how might it pertain to future business?

Let's take a guess at technology in the year 2026. Of course, we won't have perfect insight, and, in fact, these guesses will probably seem ludicrous to the person who finds this book for sale for a dollar at a Goodwill store in 2026. But let's exercise our minds in that direction.

One near certainty is that most computers won't look like computers. Apple's iPad, for example, does not look like a traditional desktop or laptop, but you can use it to watch videos, listen to music, read books, store photos, surf the Internet, and network online. You can also buy apps for the iPad that are educational, such as ones designed to aid toddlers in learning their ABCs and others focused on helping high school students learn the periodic table.

Consider how your smartphone will change by 2026. Imagine it has a 1Gbps network connection, 1 Exabyte of storage, and over a teraflop in processing power and can connect to any electrical device that consumes energy. You can store or stream every song and movie ever made to any device including your tablet, TV, car, refrigerator, windows, mirrors, and walls. Oh… and its battery life is now over a month on a single charge. Nice. Think about how differently you'll use this device.

By 2026, it's possible that desktop and portable computers as we know them today will have disappeared. They'll be replaced by mobile devices of many different types. Your employer might not even provide you a computer; you may be expected to bring your own computing device to work, or maybe all workplaces will have computing devices that you make personal by signing in. We explore these possibilities further in Chapter 4.

Beyond the changes to traditional "computers" and mobile devices, it's likely that more everyday things will have similar functionality. Tanita offers a scale that sends an electrical pulse through your body and then provides not only your weight but also your body fat, bone mass, metabolism, and level of hydration. You can wear a watch that counts the calories you have burned, the number of miles you have walked or run, and how well you've slept and reports this data back to a Web site. You could link this data with your doctor's office so that your physician could actually prescribe exercise, just like drugs.

Imagine some middle-aged, overweight man sitting at a Pizza Hut when the 911 staff arrives to carry him away.

"Why are you here?" he'll say. "I'm fine."

"Oh, no you're not. Your pacemaker called us because you're having a heart attack."

But let's apply systems thinking to the social implications of these changes. If everyone in 2026 is wearing Google Glass or Microsoft's HoloLens, would shoplifters, bank robbers, or mass-murdering bombers be caught in minutes? Bad behavior by anyone could be instantly streamed to the whole world. Doing so would require not just the image data but also huge networks of computers to process the image data in real time. And, if so, what does that mean for privacy? And where are the business opportunities in all of that?[15]

Will people still go to work? Why? Yahoo! CEO Marissa Mayer required her employees to come to work and earned the disdain of many. Is she on the wrong side of that trend? She says important work gets done in informal meetings around the coffee pot, but will this matter when meeting at the coffee pot is a virtual experience? And what about organizations? What will we need organizations for? Will talented employees need organizations? Or will they band together in temporary teams, work together, and then band together in another way?

Bring this closer to home. What about classrooms?

Why go to class if you have a classroom in a box? Let's phrase this differently because the traditional classroom does have value, especially to those students who learn from comments and questions asked by more able students.[16] Put it this way: Suppose you can go to a traditional classroom for $25,000 a year or go to the classroom in a box for $3,500 per year. Either way, you earn a degree; maybe the box's degree is not as prestigious, but it is an accredited degree. Which would you choose?

We'll take a 2026 look at the end of each chapter. For now, just realize one certainty: Knowledge of information systems and their use in business will be more important, not less.

Security Guide

PASSWORDS AND PASSWORD ETIQUETTE

Many forms of computer security use passwords to control access to systems and data. Most likely, you have a university account that you access with a username and password. When you set up that account, you were probably advised to use a "**strong password**." That's good advice, but what is a strong password? Probably not "sesame," but what then?

Microsoft, a company that has many reasons to promote effective security, provides the following guidelines for creating a strong password. A strong password should:

- Have at least 10 characters; 12 is even better
- Not contain your username, real name, or company name
- Not contain a complete dictionary word in any language
- Be different from previous passwords you have used
- Contain both upper- and lowercase letters, numbers, and special characters (such as ~ ! @; # $ % ^ &; * () _+; =; { } | [] \: "; ' <; >;?,./)

Examples of good passwords are:

- Qw37^T1bb?at
- 3B47qq<3>5!7b

The problem with such passwords is that they are nearly impossible to remember. And the last thing you want to do is write your password on a piece of paper and keep it near the device where you use it. Never do that!

One technique for creating memorable, strong passwords is to base them on the first letter of the words in a phrase. The phrase could be the title of a song or the first line of a poem or one based on some fact about your life. For example, you might take the phrase "I was born in Rome, New York, before 2000." Using the first letters from that phrase and substituting the character < for the word *before*, you create the password IwbiR,NY<2000. That's an acceptable password, but it would be better if all of the numbers were not placed on the end. So, you might try the phrase, "I was born at 3:00 AM in Rome, New York." That phrase yields the password Iwba 3:00AMiR,NY which is a strong password that is easily remembered.

Once you have a strong password you want to avoid *reusing* the same password at every site you visit. Not all sites provide the same level of protection for your data. In fact, sometimes they lose your password to hackers. Then hackers can use those passwords to access other sites that you regularly use. Password variety is your friend. Never use the same password for less important sites (e.g., social networking) that you'd use to access more important sites (e.g., online banking).

You also need to protect your password with proper behavior. Never write down your password, do not share it with others, and never ask others for their passwords.

Source: iQoncept/Fotolia

Occasionally, an attacker will pretend to be an administrator and ask users for their passwords. You'll never have to give your password to a real administrator. He or she doesn't need it and won't ask for it. He or she already has full access to all corporate computers and systems.

But what if you need someone else's password? Suppose, for example, you ask someone to help you with a problem on your computer. You sign on to an information system, and for some reason, you need to enter that other person's password. In this case, say to the other person, "We need your password," and then get out of your chair, offer your keyboard to the other person, and look away while she enters the password. Among professionals working in organizations that take security seriously, this little "do-si-do" move—one person getting out of the way so another person can enter her password—is common and accepted.

If someone asks for your password, do not give it out. Instead, get up, go over to that person's machine, and enter your own password yourself. Stay present while your password is in use, and ensure that your account is logged out at the end of the activity. No one should mind or be offended in any way when you do this. It is the mark of a professional.

 DISCUSSION QUESTIONS

1. Here is a line from Shakespeare's *Macbeth:* "Tomorrow and tomorrow and tomorrow, creeps in its petty pace." Explain how to use these lines to create a password. How could you add numbers and special characters to the password in a way that you will be able to remember?

2. List two different phrases that you can use to create a strong password. Show the password created by each.

3. One of the problems of life in the cyberworld is that we all are required to have multiple passwords—one for work or school, one for bank accounts, another for eBay or other auction sites, and so forth. Of course, it is better to use different passwords for each. But in that case you have to remember three or four different passwords. Think of different phrases you can use to create a memorable, strong password for each of these different accounts. Relate the phrase to the purpose of the account. Show the passwords for each.

4. Explain proper behavior when you are using your computer and you need to enter, for some valid reason, another person's password.

5. Explain proper behavior when someone else is using her computer and that person needs to enter, for some valid reason, your password.

Guide

FIVE-COMPONENT CAREERS

Some years, even some decades, students can wait until their last semester to think seriously about jobs. They can pick a major, take the required classes, and prepare to graduate, all the while assuming that job recruiters will be on campus, loaded with good jobs, sometime during their senior year. *Alas, today is not one of those periods.*

In the current employment situation, you need to be proactive and aggressive in your job search. Think about it: You will be spending one-third of your waking life in your job. One of the best things you can do for yourself is to begin to think seriously about your career prospects now. You don't want to find yourself working as a barista after 4 years of business school, unless, of course, you're planning on starting the next Starbucks.

So, start here. Are you interested in a career in MIS? At this point, you don't know enough to know, but Figure 1-5 and Figure 1-6 should catch your attention. With job growth like that, in a category of jobs that is net of outsourcing, you should at least ponder whether there is a career for you in IS and related services.

But what does that mean? If you go to the U.S. Bureau of Labor Statistics, you can find that there are more than a million computer programmers in the United States today and more than 600,000 systems analysts. You probably have some notion of what a programmer does, but you don't yet know what a systems analyst is. Examine the five components in Figure 1-7, however, and you can glean some idea. Programmers work primarily with the software component, while systems analysts work with

the entire system, with all five components. So, as a systems analyst, you work with system users to determine what the organizational requirements are and then with technical people (and others) to help develop that system. You work as a cultural broker: translating the culture of technology into the culture of business, and the reverse.

Fortunately for you, many interesting jobs are not captured by the bureau's data. Why fortunate? Because you can use what you're learning in this course to identify and obtain jobs that other students may not think about or even know about. If so, you've gained a competitive advantage.

The chart on the next page provides a framework for thinking about careers in an unconventional way. As you can see, there are technical jobs in MIS but fascinating, challenging, high-paying, nontechnical ones as well. Consider, for example, professional sales. Suppose you have the job of selling

Source: Tyler Olson/Fotolia

enterprise-class software to the Mayo Clinic. You will sell to intelligent, highly motivated professionals with tens of millions of dollars to spend. Or suppose you work for the Mayo Clinic on the receiving end of that sales pitch. How will you spend your tens of millions? You will need knowledge of your business, and you will need to understand enough technology to ask intelligent questions and interpret the responses.

Give this some thought by answering the questions that follow, even if they aren't assigned for a grade!

	Hardware	Software	Data	Procedures	People
Sales & Marketing	Vendors (IBM, Cisco, etc.)	Vendors (Microsoft, Oracle, etc.)	Vendors (Acxiom, Google, etc.)	Vendors (SAP, Infor, Oracle)	Recruiters (Robert Half, Lucas Group)
Support	Vendors Internal MIS	Vendors Internal MIS	Database administration Security	Vendors and internal customer support	Customer support Training
Development	Computer engineering Internal MIS	Application programmer Quality test Engineer	Data modeler Database design	Business process management Process reengineering	Training Internal MIS recruiting
Management	Internal MIS	Internal MIS	Data administration	Project management	Technical management
Consulting	Project management, development, pre- and postsale support				

DISCUSSION QUESTIONS

1. What does the phrase *in a category of jobs that is net of outsourcing* mean? Reread the discussion of Figure 1-5 if you're not certain. Why is this important to you?

2. Examine the five-component careers chart and choose the row that seems most relevant to your interests and abilities. Describe a job in each component column of that row. If you are uncertain, Google the terms in the cells of that row.

3. For each job in your answer to question 2, describe what you think are the three most important skills and abilities for that job.

4. For each job in your answer to question 2, describe one innovative action that you can take this year to increase your employment prospects.

ACTIVE REVIEW

Use this Active Review to verify that you understand the ideas and concepts that answer the chapter's study questions.

Q1-1 Why is Introduction to MIS the most important class in the business school?

Define *Bell's Law* and explain why its consequences are important to business professionals today. Describe how *Moore's Law*, *Metcalfe's Law*, *Nielsen's Law*, and *Kryder's Law* are changing how digital devices are used. State how business professionals should relate to emerging information technology.

Q1-2 How will MIS affect me?

Give the text's definition of *job security* and use Reich's list to explain how this course will help you attain that security. Summarize IS-related job opportunities. According to the Bureau of Labor Statistics, how does the growth rate of IS-related jobs compare with the average growth rate of all jobs nationally?

Q1-3 What is MIS?

Explain why you can buy IT, but you can never buy IS. What does that mean to you as a potential future business manager? Identify the three important phrases in the definition of *MIS*. Name the five components of an information system. Using the five-component model, explain the difference between IT and IS. Explain why end users need to be involved in the management of information systems. Explain why it is a misconception to say that organizations do something.

Q1-4 How can you use the five-component model?

Name and define each of the five components. Explain the symmetry in the five-component model. Show how automation moves work from one side of the five-component structure to the other. Name the most important component and state why it is the most important. Use the five-component model to describe the differences between high-tech and low-tech information systems. Explain how the components are ordered according to difficulty of change and disruption.

Q1-5 What is information?

State four different definitions of information. Identify the one that is your favorite and explain why. State the difference between data and information. Explain why information can never be written on a piece of paper or shown on a display device.

Q1-6 What are necessary data characteristics?

Create a mnemonic device for remembering the characteristics of good data. Explain how these data characteristics relate to information quality.

Q1-7 2026?

What trends do you expect to see in 2026? How might you use your smartphone differently in 2026? What everyday devices might be able to connect to the Internet in 2026? Explain the term *classroom in a box*. Why is your college or university challenged by classrooms in a box? Is it seriously challenged, or is this just a passing fad? Summarize how answering these questions contributes to your skill as a nonroutine thinker.

Using Your Knowledge with Falcon Security

Reread the Falcon Security vignette at the start of this chapter. Using the knowledge you've gained from this chapter, especially that in Q2, identify five mistakes that Jennifer made. For each, explain what you would do differently. Be specific.

KEY TERMS AND CONCEPTS

MyMISLab™

To complete the problems with the ⭐, go to EOC Discussion Questions in the MyLab.

USING YOUR KNOWLEDGE

⭐ **1-1. a.** What importance do you give to non-routine skills? Provide an example from your own life where you found that non-routine skills played an important role in your success. Divide your own non-routine skills into abstract reasoning skills, system thinking skills, collaboration skills, and ability-to-experiment skills. Analyze and rate yourself on these parameters. Find out which skill you excel at and which you lack in. Try to find the reasons for your lacking in that specific non-routine skill.

b. How do you think that non-routine skills are going to contribute in your major or area of specialization. List which the non-routine skills i.e. abstract reasoning skills, system thinking skills, collaboration skills, and ability-to-experiment skills is most important in your future job endeavors.

c. Your college/university wants to start a new MBA specialization programme. The administration, however, is in a dilemma as to whether to start a specialization in MBA (IT) or MBA (IS). In your opinion, is there any difference between these two? If yes, what advice would you give the administration regarding which specialization it should start and why? Give reasons for your answer.

⭐ **1-2. a.** According to Metcalf's law, "the value of a network is equal to the square of the number of users connected to it." See its implementation of law in your college/university computer lab. Find out the number of systems that are connected and sharing the information through a shared network. Evaluate the value of network vis a-vis the number of users connected to it.

b. According to Bell's law, "a new computer class forms roughly each decade, establishing a new industry." Going by this law, we may say that a new industry has evolved due to the advent of social networking that is changing the conventional rules of business. Find out how social networking has changed the way organizations do business. For answering this question, select a particular organization which has evolved due the emergence of social networking.

c. According to Moore's law, "the number of transistors per square inch on an integrated chip doubles every 18 months." Do you think comparable advances have been made in business processes that support the advancement of computer processing.

d. According to Nielsen's law, "network computer connection speeds for high-end users will increase by 50% per year." Thus, based on this, we have seen a lot of advancement in network speed and recently YouTube has launched YouTube Music. Do you think YouTube Music can give stiff competition to Spotify and Apple Music?

⭐ **1-3.** There are various definitions of information given in this chapter. Out of varying definitions, one thing that is quite similar is that the quality of information depends on the quality of data. Accordingly, various important characteristics of data have also been listed in this chapter (Figure 1-10).

　a. State whether the necessary characteristics of data are same as that of information

　b. If yes, which characteristic of information do you weigh more. Why?

　c. If no, suggest the possible characteristics of information.

　d. "MIS is the most important subject in your business school". "Would you categorize this statement as an information or data. Give reasons to support your answer.

　e. If it is data for you, state the facts that should be added to this statement to make it information.

COLLABORATION EXERCISE 1

Collaborate with a group of fellow students to answer the following questions. For this exercise, do not meet face to face. Coordinate all of your work using email and email attachments only. Your answers should reflect the thinking of the entire group, not just one or two individuals.

1-4. Abstract reasoning.

　a. Define *abstract reasoning*, and explain why it is an important skill for business professionals.

　b. Explain how a list of items in inventory and their quantity on hand is an abstraction of a physical inventory.

　c. Give three other examples of abstractions commonly used in business.

　d. Explain how Jennifer failed to demonstrate effective abstract-reasoning skills.

　e. Can people increase their abstract-reasoning skills? If so, how? If not, why not?

1-5. Systems thinking.

　a. Define *systems thinking*, and explain why it is an important skill for business professionals.

　b. Explain how you would use systems thinking to explain why Moore's Law caused a farmer to dig up a field of pulpwood trees. Name each of the elements in the system, and explain their relationships to each other.

　c. Give three other examples of the use of systems thinking with regard to consequences of Bell's Law, Moore's Law, or Metcalfe's Law.

　d. Explain how Jennifer failed to demonstrate effective systems-thinking skills.

　e. Can people improve their systems-thinking skills? If so, how? If not, why not?

1-6. Collaboration.

　a. Define *collaboration*, and explain why it is an important skill for business professionals.

　b. Explain how you are using collaboration to answer these questions. Describe what is working with regard to your group's process and what is not working.

　c. Is the work product of your team better than any one of you could have done separately? If not, your collaboration is ineffective. If that is the case, explain why.

　d. Does the fact that you cannot meet face to face hamper your ability to collaborate? If so, how?

　e. Explain how Jennifer failed to demonstrate effective collaboration skills.

　f. Can people increase their collaboration skills? If so, how? If not, why not?

1-7. Experimentation.

　a. Define *experimentation*, and explain why it is an important skill for business professionals.

　b. Explain several creative ways you could use experimentation to answer this question.

　c. How does the fear of failure influence your willingness to engage in any of the ideas you identified in part b?

　d. Explain how Jennifer failed to demonstrate effective experimentation skills.

　e. Can people increase their willingness to take risks? If so, how? If not, why not?

1-8. Job security.

　a. State the text's definition of *job security*.

b. Evaluate the text's definition of job security. Is it effective? If you think not, offer a better definition of job security.

c. As a team, do you agree that improving your skills on the four dimensions in the Collaboration Exercise Questions will increase your job security?

d. Do you think technical skills (accounting proficiency, financial analysis proficiency, etc.) provide job security? Why or why not? Do you think you would have answered this question differently in 1990? Why or why not?

CASE STUDY 1

zulily

On November 15, 2013, zulily, a Seattle corporation, issued its initial stock (i.e., went public) at $22 a share. By the end of the day, the stock was trading at $38, and 4 months later it reached $62, nearly tripling its initial price. At $62, the holdings of the company's chairman, Mark Vadon, totaled more than $2B.

Before dismissing this as just another successful public offering, consider the company. What is its business model? A high-tech company offering the latest gee-whiz technology? A new tablet? A new Facebook competitor? Another way of sharing pictures? No, no, no, and no. zulily sells to mothers: primarily children's clothes and toys, but also women's clothes, accessories, and décor items. The oldest and most traditional forms of retail. So what is the excitement? Cofounders Mark Vadon and Darrell Cavens found a way to harness information technology to provide an entertaining shopping experience to mothers, one that offers name-brand goods as well as unique and difficult-to-find off-brands and often sells them at substantial discounts. According to the zulily prospectus, 45 percent of its sales occur over mobile devices, as mothers churn through the day's specials while they sit in playgrounds, in cars waiting for kids at soccer practice, or anywhere else young mothers have a break long enough to shop on their mobile devices.

One of your goals for this class should be to learn *to assess, evaluate, and apply emerging information technology to business.* Seem like an empty platitude? Not to Mr. Vadon, who turned that exact principle into $2B... so far.

The zulily Business Model

zulily conducts flash sales of children's and women's clothing and other items of interest to women. Sales open at 6 AM Pacific time each day and last 72 hours. Customers find brand-name merchandise intermingled with hard-to-find boutique products. zulily uses the term *curated sale* to mean the sale of items specifically selected and grouped by its shopping experts to be exciting to women. Because these curated sales provide interesting variety, women enjoy the thrill of discovery while shopping. zulily thus provides entertainment as well as a

Figure 1-11
zulily Merchandise Variety
Courtesy of Zuilly Inc. Used by permission

	2010	2011	2012	2013	2014
Number of active customers (thousands)	157	791	1,580	3,200	4,900
Revenue (millions)	$18	$143	$331	$696	$1,200
Sales per active customer	$117	$180	$210	$218	$245

Figure 1-12
zulily Performance

rewarding shopping experience. And those low prices, some as low as 70 percent off retail, are available for only 72 hours. So, shop and buy now, ladies!

Does it work? Apparently so. As shown in Figure 1-12, in 4 years zulily increased the number of its active customers by 3,121 percent while increasing revenue per active customer by 209 percent. That combination resulted in revenue growth from $18M to $1.2B; that's a 185 percent annual growth rate!

How zulily Did It

The sales process begins when zulily buyers identify goods to be sold. Buyers negotiate with vendors to establish both wholesale and retail prices, terms, and maximum quantities by size. zulily then obtains sample merchandise and, if necessary, photographs it in-house. It also writes ad copy to be displayed along with the photos during the sale. By taking photos when needed and writing its own ad copy, zulily ensures a consistent quality of presentation on its site. zulily also adds considerable value to smaller vendors who do not otherwise have access to such high-quality expertise.

Items are then grouped together into 3-day sales events. zulily accepts orders for items up to the maximum quantity negotiated with the vendor. At that point, the item (or a particular size of an item) is marked as no longer available, thus increasing pressure to buy remaining items *now*. After the event closes, zulily orders the items from the vendor, receives them, packages them, and then ships the items to customers. zulily thus maintains almost no inventory. Customers receive their items in zulily packaging, thus reinforcing the zulily brand.

zulily is subject to errors and mistakes from vendors. If, for example, the vendor promises to ship 1,000 pairs of shoes of a particular size and zulily sells all 1,000 pairs, but later the vendor delivers only, say, 900 pairs in that size, some customers will be disappointed. And those customers will hold zulily, not the vendor, responsible for their disappointment.

Use of Technology

zulily's business model would be infeasible without information systems. For one, it needs the Internet to reach customers, and it needs mobile technology to do so on phones and other mobile devices. Further, zulily buyers use the Internet to find vendors and items to sell. But what else?

In the prospectus for its initial public offering, zulily stated, "Continual innovation through investment in technology is core to our business."[17] It states that it developed a proprietary technology platform to manage the enormous spikes in Web processing demand that occur due to the nature of flash sales. Reflect on the challenges of such development: In 2010, zulily's platform supported $18M in sales; 4 years later, it supported $1.2B in sales, a 66-fold increase in demand. You will learn some of the ways that such enormous growth can be accommodated in Chapter 6. For now, understand that such growth would be impossible in a world without information systems.

But there's more. In that same prospectus, zulily stated that it has developed "extensive data collection and analytics capabilities" that enable it to anticipate its customers' shopping preferences and to tailor the customers' shopping experiences accordingly. So, as with any good salesperson, what you see and how it is shown to you depend on what you've purchased in the past. That same data can also be analyzed to help buyers determine the items customers are most likely to purchase. You will learn about data analytics in Chapter 9.

Growth-Management Problems

Such spectacular growth does not come without problems. According to its 2014 annual report (SEC Form 10-K), zulily increased its headcount from 329 at the end of 2011 to 2,907 at the end of 2014. That's an 884 percent increase in zulily's workforce in 3 years. That rate of growth is exceedingly difficult to manage, a fact the company recognized:

> To support continued growth, we must effectively integrate, develop and motivate a large number of new employees, while maintaining our corporate culture. In particular, we intend to continue to make substantial investments to expand our merchandising and technology personnel.[18]

Unfortunately, zulily is located just down the street from Amazon and Nordstrom and just across a lake from Microsoft. Finding (and retaining) those merchandising and technology personnel in Seattle will be difficult. In its annual report, zulily mentioned particularly the need to hire mid-level managers.

Learning from zulily

zulily is remarkable for its spectacular growth, but it's even more remarkable because that growth occurred in a very traditional market. What's more basic than selling clothes to women? Who would think that the founder of a company in that market could turn his holdings into $1.7B in 5 years? Or that the company could increase its workforce by 884 percent in 3 years?

In the final analysis, zulily succeeded because its founders developed an innovative application of information systems technology. As you will learn, the technology zulily uses is not groundbreaking. All that technology was described in the fourth edition of this textbook in 2009 when zulily was founded. The creative genius was finding a way to apply that technology to a business opportunity and then to have the managerial skill to develop that idea into a thriving business. Without doubt, dozens of such opportunities lie in front of you. You just need to recognize and build on them.

QUESTIONS

1-9. Go to zulily.com and register. Identify features of the site that make shopping entertaining to mothers and explain why those features entertain. Explain why this is important to the zulily business model.

1-10. Go to Nordstrom.com and shop for children's clothes. How does the zulily shopping experience differ from that at Nordstrom? Briefly describe the advantages and disadvantages of each type of experience.

1-11. If you were a buyer for zulily, what data would you like to have about customer purchase habits?

1-12. If you were a buyer for zulily, what data would you like to have about past vendor performance?

1-13. In the general course of life, 2-year-old boys become 3-year-old boys, 4-year-old girls become 5-year-old girls, and so on. How can zulily use this not-so-remarkable phenomenon to customize a customer's shopping experience? What data would you need to do this?

1-14. As a business professional, it is likely information systems professionals will ask you data questions like those in questions 1-11 to 1-13 above. What is the best way for you to respond? Verbally in a meeting? With a written document? With a sketch or diagram? How will you know if you have been understood?

1-15. At the April 2015 stock price of $14.59, the market values zulily at $1.86B. This is a big drop from the February 2014 high of $68.39 a share price. Describe zulily's principle assets. Does a $1.86B valuation seem appropriate, given your description of the company's assets? Justify your answer.

b. Click the Similar Occupations link at the bottom of the page. Find another job that you might want. Describe that job, median salary, and educational requirements.

c. The BLS data is comprehensive, but it is not up to date for fast-changing disciplines such as IS. For example, one very promising career today is social media marketing, a job that does not appear in the BLS data. Describe one way that you might learn about employment prospects for such emerging job categories.

d. Considering your answer to part c, describe an IS-related job that would be the best match for your skills and interests. Describe how you can learn if that job exists.

ENDNOTES

1. *http://research.microsoft.com/pubs/64155/tr-27-146.pdf*

2. These figures represent the cost of 100,000 transistors, which can roughly be translated into a unit of a computing device. If you doubt any of this, just look at your $139 Kindle Fire and realize that you pay nothing for its wireless access. Geoff Colvin claims the cost of 125,000 transistors is less than the cost of a grain of rice. See *http://chowtimes.com/2010/09/11/food-for-though/food-for-thought.*

3. Zipf's Law is a more accurate, though less easily understood, way of explaining how the value of a network increases as additional network nodes are added. See Briscoe, Odlyzko, and Tilly's 2006 article "Metcalfe's Law Is Wrong" for a better explanation: *http://spectrum.ieee.org/computing/networks/metcalfes-law-is-wrong.*

4. Lynn A. Kaoly and Constantijn W. A. Panis, *The 21st Century at Work* (Santa Monica, CA: RAND Corporation, 24), p. xiv.

5. Robert B. Reich, *The Work of Nations* (New York: Alfred A. Knopf, 1991), p. 229.

6. In the 2011 book "Literacy Is NOT Enough: 21st Century Fluencies for the Digital Age," Lee Crockett, Ian Jukes, and Andrew Churches list problem solving, creativity, analytical thinking, collaboration, communication, and ethics, action, and accountability as key skills workers need for the 21st century.

7. Accenture, "Accenture 2014 College Graduate Employment Survey," last modified April 16, 2014, *www.accenture.com/sitecollectiondocuments/pdf/accenture-2014-college-graduates-survey.pdf.*

8. Michael Spence and Sandile Hlatshwayo, *The Evolving Structure of the American Economy and the Employment Challenge* (New York: Council on Foreign Relations, 2011).

9. Bureau of Labor Statistics, "Computer Systems Analysts," *Occupational Outlook Handbook*, accessed April 16, 2015, *www.bls.gov/ooh.*

10. Daron Acemoglu and David Autor, "Skills, Tasks, and Technologies: Implications for Employment and Earnings" (working paper, National Bureau of Economic Research, June 2010), *www.nber.org/papers/w16082.*

11. Alibaba.com, "About Alibaba.com," accessed April 6, 2015, *http://activities.alibaba.com/alibaba/following-about-alibaba.php.*

12. Leslie Picker and Lulu Yilun Chen, "Alibaba's Banks Boost IPO Size to Record of $25 Billion," September 22, 2014, accessed April 4, 2015, *www.bloomberg.com/news/articles/2014-09-22/alibaba-s-banks-said-to-increase-ipo-size-to-record-25-billion.*

13. Carlos Tejada, "China Raps Alibaba for Fakes," January 28, 2015, accessed April 6, 2015, *www.wsj.com/articles/chinas-saic-criticizes-alibaba-over-fake-goods-1422425378.*

14. Actually, the word *data* is plural; to be correct, we should use the singular form *datum* and say, "The fact that Jeff Parks earns $30.00 per hour is a datum." The word *datum*, however, sounds pedantic and fussy, and we will avoid it in this text.

15. Anton Wahlman, "Could Google Glass Catch the Boston Bomber?" *TheStreet*, last updated April 18, 2013, *http://money.msn.com/technology-investment/post.aspx?post=f0d8f47e-1d83-4c0b-a9f1-c6bbf250fc3c.*

16. Louise Nemanich, Michael Banks, and Dusya Vera, "Enhancing Knowledge Transfer in Classroom Versus OnLine Settings: The Interplay Among Instructor, Student, and Context," *Decision Sciences Journal of Innovative Education* 7, no. 1 (29): 140.

17. zulily Prospectus, *www.sec.gov/Archives/edgar/data/1478484/0119312513443794/d552850d424b4.htm.*

18. zulily, Inc. (2014). Form 10-K 2014. Retrieved from zulily.com, *http://investor.zulily.com/secfiling.cfm?filingid=1478484-15-18.*

Collaboration
Information
Systems

"No, Felix! Not again! Over, and over, and over! We decide something one meeting and then go over it again the next meeting and again the next. What a waste!"

"What do you mean, Cam?" asks Felix, Falcon Security's customer service manager. "I think it's important we get this right."

"Well, Felix, if that's the case, why don't you come to the meetings?"

"I just missed a couple."

"Right. Last week we met here for, oh, 2, maybe 3 hours, and we decided to print and assemble a new prototype quadcopter using as many 3D-printed parts as possible."

"But Cam, 3D printing a stationary recharging platform is a lot different than 3D printing a complex machine like a drone. What difference does it make if we print a drone that can't fly?"

"Felix! We discussed that last week. We found some existing drone plans that we can use for free. They've already been tested, and they do work. We're going to see if we can use existing internal components from an existing quadcopter in the new 3D-printed quadcopter. It might even be possible to use generic parts to reduce costs even more."

"Look, Cam, Joni just wants something reasonable to tell Mateo. If we tell her these new 3D-printed quadcopters can't fly, which they probably won't, Mateo will cancel this project and we can get back to work … flying high-quality drones manufactured by those who know what they're doing!"

"Felix, you're driving me nuts. We discussed this *ad nauseam* last week. Let's make some progress. Why don't some of you other guys help me? Alexis, what do you think?"

"Felix, Cam is right," Alexis, Falcon Security's head of sales, chimes in. "We did have a long discussion on how to go about this—and we did agree to focus first on building a functional drone that might reduce our costs. This could save us a lot of money and give us a more customizable drone platform."

"Well, Alexis, I think it's a mistake. Why didn't anyone tell me? I put a lot of time looking into flight performance of these 3D-printed drones."

"Did you read the email?" Alexis asks tentatively.

"What email?"

"The meeting summary email that I send out each week," Alexis says with a sigh.

"I got the email, but I couldn't download the attachment. Something weird about a virus checker couldn't access a gizmo or something like that …" Felix trails off.

Cam can't stand that excuse. "Here, Felix, take a look at mine. I'll underline the part where we concluded that we'd focus on building the prototype first so you can be sure to see it."

"Cam, there's no reason to get snippy about this. I thought I had a good idea," Felix says, sounding hurt.

"OK, so we're agreed—*again this week*—that we're going to make the prototype drone using 3D-printed parts based off the free plans. Now, we've wasted enough time covering old ground. Let's get some new thinking on how we're going to do that."

Felix slumps back into his chair and looks down at his cell phone.

"Oh, no, I missed a call from Mapplethorpe. Ahhhh."

"Felix, what are you talking about?" asks Cam.

"I got the email, but I couldn't download the attachment."

Image source: rommma/Fotolia

STUDY QUESTIONS

Q2-1 What are the two key characteristics of collaboration?

Q2-2 What are three criteria for successful collaboration?

Q2-3 What are the four primary purposes of collaboration?

Q2-4 What are the requirements for a collaboration information system?

Q2-5 How can you use collaboration tools to improve team communication?

Q2-6 How can you use collaboration tools to manage shared content?

Q2-7 How can you use collaboration tools to manage tasks?

Q2-8 Which collaboration IS is right for your team?

Q2-9 2026?

"Mapplethorpe, my contact at Gulf Oil. He wants to know how to read the new multispectral images of his flare stacks. I'm sorry, but I've got to call him. I'll be back in a few minutes."

Felix leaves the room.

Cam looks at the two team members who are left.

"Now what?" she asks. "If we go forward, we'll have to rediscuss everything when Felix comes back. Maybe we should just take a break?"

Alexis shakes her head. "Cam, let's not. It's tough for me to get to these meetings. I don't have to work until tonight, so I drove down here just for this. I've got to pick up Simone from day care. We haven't done anything yet. Let's just ignore Felix."

"OK, Alexis, but it isn't easy to ignore Felix."

The door opens and Joni walks in.

"Hi everyone! How's it going?" she asks brightly. "Is it OK if I sit in on your meeting?"

CHAPTER PREVIEW

Business is a social activity. While we often say that organizations accomplish their strategy, they don't. *People* in organizations accomplish strategy by working with other people, almost always working in groups. People do business with people.

Over the years, technology has increasingly supported group work. In your grandfather's day, communication was done using letter, phone, and office visits. Those technologies were augmented in the 1980s and 1990s with fax and email and more recently by texting, conference calls, and videoconferencing. Today, products such as Office 365 provide a wide array of tools to support collaborative work.

This chapter investigates ways that information systems can support collaboration. We begin by defining collaboration, discussing collaborative activities, and setting criteria for successful collaboration. Next, we'll address the kinds of work that collaborative teams do. Then we'll discuss requirements for collaborative information systems and illustrate important collaborative tools for improving communication and sharing content. After that, we'll bring this closer to your needs today and investigate the use of three different collaboration IS that can improve your student collaborations. Finally, we'll wrap up with a discussion of collaboration in 2026!

Q2-1 What Are the Two Key Characteristics of Collaboration?

To answer this question, we must first distinguish between the terms *cooperation* and *collaboration*. **Cooperation** is a group of people working together, all doing essentially the same type of work, to accomplish a job. A group of four painters, each painting a different wall in the same room, are working cooperatively. Similarly, a group of checkers at the grocery store or clerks at the post office are working cooperatively to serve customers. A cooperative group can accomplish a given task faster than an individual working alone, but the cooperative result is usually not better in quality than the result of someone working alone.

In this text, we define **collaboration** as a group of people working together to achieve a common goal *via a process of feedback and iteration*. Using feedback and iteration, one person will produce something, say, the draft of a document, and a second person will review that draft and provide critical feedback. Given the feedback, the original author or someone else will then revise the first draft to produce a second. The work proceeds in a series of stages, or *iterations*, in which something is produced, members criticize it, and then another version is produced. Using iteration and feedback, the group's result can be better than what any single individual can produce alone. This is possible because different group members provide different perspectives. "Oh, I never thought of it that way" is a typical signal of collaboration success.

Many, perhaps most, student groups incorrectly use cooperation rather than collaboration. Given an assignment, a group of five students will break it up into five pieces, work to accomplish their piece independently, and then merge their independent work for grading by the professor. Such a process will enable the project to be completed more quickly, with less work by any single individual, but it will not be better than the result obtained if the students were to work alone.

In contrast, when students work collaboratively, they set forth an initial idea or work product, provide feedback to one another on those ideas or products, and then revise in accordance with feedback. Such a process can produce a result far superior to that produced by any student working alone.

Importance of Effective Critical Feedback

Given this definition, for collaboration to be successful members must provide and receive *critical* feedback. A group in which everyone is too polite to say anything critical cannot collaborate. As Darwin John, the world's first chief information officer (CIO) (see Chapter 11), once said, "If two of you have the exact same idea, then we have no need for one of you." On the other hand, a group that is so critical and negative that members come to distrust, even hate, one another cannot effectively collaborate either. For most groups, success is achieved between these extremes.

To underline this point, consider the research of Ditkoff, Allen, Moore, and Pollard. They surveyed 108 business professionals to determine the qualities, attitudes, and skills that make a good collaborator.[1] Figure 2-1 lists the most and least important characteristics reported in the survey. Most students are surprised to learn that 5 of the top 12 characteristics involve disagreement (highlighted in blue in Figure 2-1). Most students believe that "we should all get along" and more or less have the same idea and opinions about team matters. Although it is important for the team to be sociable enough to work together, this research indicates that it is also important for team members to have different ideas and opinions and to express them to each other.

When we think about collaboration as an iterative process in which team members give and receive feedback, these results are not surprising. During collaboration, team members learn from each other, and it will be difficult to learn if no one is willing to express different, or even unpopular, ideas. The respondents also seem to be saying, "You can be negative, as long as you care about what we're doing." These collaboration skills do not come naturally to people who have been taught to "play well with others," but that may be why they were so highly ranked in the survey.

The characteristics rated *not relevant* are also revealing. Experience as a collaborator or in business does not seem to matter. Being popular also is not important. A big surprise, however, is that being well organized was rated 31st out of 39 characteristics. Perhaps collaboration itself is not a very well-organized process.

Guidelines for Giving and Receiving Critical Feedback

Giving and receiving critical feedback is the single most important collaboration skill. So, before we discuss the role that information systems can play for improving collaboration, study the guidelines for giving and receiving critical feedback shown in Figure 2-2.

The Most Important Characteristics for an Effective Collaborator

1. Is enthusiastic about the subject of our collaboration.

2. Is open-minded and curious.

3. Speaks his or her mind even if it's an unpopular viewpoint.

4. Gets back to me and others in a timely way.

5. Is willing to enter into difficult conversations.

6. Is a perceptive listener.

7. Is skillful at giving/receiving negative feedback.

8. Is willing to put forward unpopular ideas.

9. Is self-managing and requires "low maintenance."

10. Is known for following through on commitments.

11. Is willing to dig into the topic with zeal.

12. Thinks differently than I do/brings different perspectives.

…

31. Is well organized.

32. Is someone I immediately liked. The chemistry is good.

33. Has already earned my trust.

34. Has experience as a collaborator.

35. Is a skilled and persuasive presenter.

36. Is gregarious and dynamic.

37. Is someone I knew beforehand.

38. Has an established reputation in field of our collaboration.

39. Is an experienced businessperson.

Figure 2-1
Important Characteristics of
a Collaborator

Many students have found that when they first form a collaborative group, it's useful to begin with a discussion of critical feedback guidelines like those in Figure 2-2. Begin with this list, and then, using feedback and iteration, develop your own list. Of course, if a group member does not follow the agreed-upon guidelines, someone will have to provide critical feedback to that effect as well.

Warning!

If you are like most undergraduate business students, especially freshmen or sophomores, your life experience is keeping you from understanding the need for collaboration. So far, almost everyone you know has the same experiences as you and, more or less, thinks like you. Your friends and associates have the same educational background, scored more or less the same on standardized tests, and have the same orientation toward success. So, why collaborate? Most of you think the same way, anyway: "What does the professor want, and what's the easiest, fastest way to get it to her?"

So, consider this thought experiment. Your company is planning to build a new facility that is critical for the success of a new product line and will create 300 new jobs. The county government won't issue a building permit because the site is prone to landslides. Your engineers believe your

Guideline	Example
Be specific.	"I was confused until I got to Section 2" rather than "The whole thing is a disorganized mess."
Offer suggestions.	"Consider moving Section 2 to the beginning of the document."
Avoid personal comments.	Never: "Only an idiot would miss that point … or write that document."
Strive for balance.	"I thought Section 2 was particularly good. What do you think about moving it to the start of the document?"
Question your emotions.	"Why do I feel so angry about the comment he just made? What's going on? Is my anger helping me?"
Do not dominate.	If there are five members of the group, unless you have special expertise, you are entitled to just 20 percent of the words/time.
Demonstrate a commitment to the group.	"I know this is painful, but if we can make these changes our result will be so much better." or "Ouch. I really didn't want to have to redo that section, but if you all think it's important, I'll do it."

Figure 2-2
Guidelines for Providing and Receiving Critical Feedback

design overcomes that hazard, but your chief financial officer (CFO) is concerned about possible litigation in the event there is a problem. Your corporate counsel is investigating the best way to overcome the county's objections while limiting liability. Meanwhile, a local environmental group is protesting your site because it believes the site is too close to an eagle's nest. Your public relations director is meeting with these local groups every week.

Do you proceed with the project?

To decide, you create a working team of the chief engineer, the CFO, your legal counsel, and the PR director. Each of those people has different education and expertise, different life experience, and different values. In fact, the only thing they have in common is that they are paid by your company. That team will participate collaboratively in ways that are far different from your experience so far. Keep this example in mind as you read this chapter.

Bottom line: The two key characteristics of collaboration are iteration and feedback.

Q2-2 What Are Three Criteria for Successful Collaboration?

J. Richard Hackman studied teamwork for many years, and his book *Leading Teams* contains many useful concepts and tips for future managers.[2] According to Hackman, there are three primary criteria for judging team success:

- Successful outcome
- Growth in team capability
- Meaningful and satisfying experience

Successful Outcome

Most students are primarily concerned with the first criterion. They want to achieve a good outcome, measured by their grade, or they want to get the project done with an acceptable grade while minimizing the effort required. For business professionals, teams need to accomplish their goals: make a decision, solve a problem, or create a work product. Whatever the objective is, the first success criterion is "Did we do it?"

Although not as apparent in student teams, most business teams also need to ask, "Did we do it within the time and budget allowed?" Teams that produce a work product too late or far over budget are not successful, even if they did achieve their goal.

Growth in Team Capability

The other two criteria are surprising to most students, probably because most student teams are short-lived. But, in business, where teams often last months or years, it makes sense to ask, "Did the team get better?" If you're a football fan, you've undoubtedly heard your college's coach say, "We really improved as the season progressed." (Of course, for the team with 2 wins and 12 losses, you didn't hear that.) Football teams last only a season. If the team is permanent, say, a team of customer support personnel, the benefits of team growth are even greater. Over time, as the team gets better, it becomes more efficient; thus, over time the team provides more service for a given cost or the same service for less cost.

How does a team get better? For one, it develops better work processes. Activities are combined or eliminated. Linkages are established so that "the left hand knows what the right hand is doing," or needs, or can provide. Teams also get better as individuals improve at their tasks. Part of that improvement is the learning curve; as someone does something over and over, he or she gets better at it. But team members also teach task skills and give knowledge to one another. Team members also provide perspectives that other team members need.

Meaningful and Satisfying Experience

The third element of Hackman's definition of team success is that team members have a meaningful and satisfying experience. Of course, the nature of team goals is a major factor in making work meaningful. But few of us have the opportunity to develop a life-saving cancer vaccine or safely land a stricken airliner in the middle of the Hudson River in winter. For most of us, it's a matter of making the product, or creating the shipment, or accounting for the payment, or finding the prospects, and so on.

So, in the more mundane world of most business professionals, what makes work meaningful? Hackman cites numerous studies in his book, and one common thread is that the work is perceived as meaningful by the team. Keeping prices up to date in the product database may not be the most exciting work, but if that task is perceived by the team as important, it will become meaningful.

Furthermore, if an individual's work is not only perceived as important, but the person doing that work is also given credit for it, then the experience will be perceived as meaningful. So, recognition for work well done is vitally important for a meaningful work experience.

Another aspect of team satisfaction is camaraderie. Business professionals, just like students, are energized when they have the feeling that they are part of a group, each person doing his or her own job and combining efforts to achieve something worthwhile that is better than any could have done alone.

Q2-3 What Are the Four Primary Purposes of Collaboration?

Collaborative teams accomplish four primary purposes:

- Become informed
- Make decisions
- Solve problems
- Manage projects

These four purposes build on each other. For example, making a decision requires that team members be informed. In turn, to solve a problem, the team must have the ability to make decisions (and become informed). Finally, to conduct a project, the team must be able to solve problems (and make decisions and become informed).

Before we continue, understand you can use the hierarchy of these four purposes to build your professional skills. You cannot make good decisions if you do not have the skills to inform yourself. You cannot solve problems if you are unable to make good decisions. And you cannot manage projects if you don't know how to solve problems!

In this question, we will consider the collaborative nature of these four purposes and describe requirements for information systems that support them, starting with the most basic: becoming informed.

Becoming Informed

Informing is the first and most fundamental collaboration purpose. Recall from Chapter 1 that two individuals can receive the same data but construct different interpretations or, as stated in the terms of Chapter 1, conceive different information. The goal of the informing is to ensure, as much as possible, that team members are conceiving information in the same way.

For example, as you read in the opening scenario, the team at Falcon Security has been assigned the task of investigating the 3D printing opportunity. One of the team's first tasks is to ensure that everyone understands that goal and, further, understands the basics of 3D printing technology and what is required to implement it.

Informing, and hence all of the purposes of collaboration, presents several requirements for collaborative information systems. As you would expect, team members need to be able to share data and to communicate with one another to share interpretations. Furthermore, because memories are faulty and team membership can change, it is also necessary to document the team's understanding of the information conceived. To avoid having to go "over and over and over" a topic, a repository of information, such as a wiki, is needed. We will say more about this in Q5.

Making Decisions

Collaboration is used for some types of decision making, but not all. Consequently, to understand the role for collaboration, we must begin with an analysis of decision making. Decisions are made at three levels: *operational, managerial,* and *strategic.*

Operational Decisions

Operational decisions are those that support operational, day-to-day activities. Typical operational decisions are: How many widgets should we order from vendor A? Should we extend credit to vendor B? Which invoices should we pay today?

Managerial Decisions

Managerial decisions are decisions about the allocation and utilization of resources. Typical decisions are: How much should we budget for computer hardware and programs for department A next year? How many engineers should we assign to project B? How many square feet of warehouse space do we need for the coming year?

In general, if a managerial decision requires consideration of different perspectives, then it will benefit from collaboration. For example, consider the decision of whether to increase employee pay in the coming year. No single individual has the answer. The decision depends on an analysis of inflation, industry trends, the organization's profitability, the influence of unions, and other factors. Senior managers, accountants, human resources personnel, labor relationships managers, and others will each bring a different perspective to the decision. They will produce a work product for the decision, evaluate that product, and make revisions in an iterative fashion—the essence of collaboration.

Strategic Decisions

Strategic decisions are those that support broad-scope, organizational issues. Typical decisions at the strategic level are: Should we start a new product line? Should we open a centralized warehouse in Tennessee? Should we acquire company A?

Strategic decisions are almost always collaborative. Consider a decision about whether to move manufacturing operations to China. This decision affects every employee in the organization, the organization's suppliers, its customers, and its shareholders. Many factors and many perspectives on each of those factors must be considered.

The Decision Process

Information systems can be classified based on whether their decision processes are *structured* or *unstructured.* These terms refer to the method or process by which the decision is to be made, not to the nature of the underlying problem. A **structured decision** process is one for which there is an understood and accepted method for making the decision. A formula for computing the reorder quantity of an item in inventory is an example of a structured decision process. A standard method for allocating furniture and equipment to employees is another structured decision process. Structured decisions seldom require collaboration.

An **unstructured decision** process is one for which there is no agreed-on decision-making method. Predicting the future direction of the economy or the stock market is a classic example. The prediction method varies from person to person; it is neither standardized nor broadly accepted. Another example of an unstructured decision process is assessing how well suited an employee is for performing a particular job. Managers vary in the manner in which they make such assessments. Unstructured decisions are often collaborative.

The Relationship Between Decision Type and Decision Process

The decision type and decision process are loosely related. Decisions at the operational level tend to be structured, and decisions at the strategic level tend to be unstructured. Managerial decisions tend to be both structured and unstructured.

We use the words *tend to be* because there are exceptions to the relationship. Some operational decisions are unstructured (e.g., "How many taxicab drivers do we need on the night before the homecoming game?"), and some strategic decisions can be structured (e.g., "How should we assign sales quotas for a new product?"). In general, however, the relationship holds.

Decision Making and Collaboration Systems

As stated, few structured decisions involve collaboration. Deciding, for example, how much of product A to order from vendor B does not require the feedback and iteration among members that typify collaboration. Although the process of generating the order might require the coordinated work of people in purchasing, accounting, and manufacturing, there is seldom a need for one person to comment on someone else's work. In fact, involving collaboration in routine, structured decisions is expensive, wasteful, and frustrating. "Do we have to have a meeting about everything?" is a common lament.

The situation is different for unstructured decisions because feedback and iteration are crucial. Members bring different ideas and perspectives about what is to be decided, how the decision will be reached, what criteria are important, and how decision alternatives score against those criteria. The group may make tentative conclusions and discuss potential outcomes of those conclusions, and members will often revise their positions. Figure 2-3 illustrates the change in the need for collaboration as decision processes become less structured.

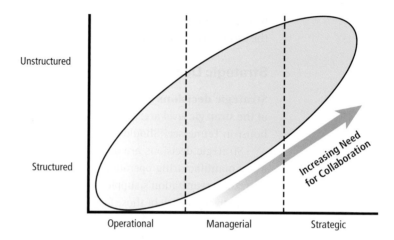

Figure 2-3
Collaboration Needs
for Decision Making

Solving Problems

Solving problems is the third primary reason for collaborating. A **problem** is a perceived difference between what is and what ought to be. Because it is a perception, different people can have different problem definitions.

Therefore, the first and arguably the most important task for a problem-solving collaborative group is defining the problem. For example, the Falcon Security team has been assigned the problem of determining whether 3D printing drones is a viable option. As stated as part of the informing purpose, the group needs first to ensure that the team members understand this goal and have a common understanding of what 3D printing entails.

See the Guide on pages 106–107 to learn one technique that business professionals use to obtain a common definition of a problem. That technique requires effective communication.

However, because a problem is a difference between what is and what ought to be, the statement "reduce operational expenses" does not go far enough. Is saving one dollar enough of a reduction? Is saving $100,000 enough? Does it take $1,000,000 for the reduction to be enough? A better problem definition would be to reduce operational expenses by 10 percent or by $100,000 or some other more specific statement of what is desired.

Figure 2-4 lists the principal problem-solving tasks. Because this text is about information systems and not about problem solving per se, we will not delve into those tasks here. Just note the work that needs to be done, and consider the role of feedback and iteration for each of these tasks.

Managing Projects

Managing projects is a rich and complicated subject, with many theories and methods and techniques. Here we will just touch on the collaborative aspects of four primary project phases.

Projects are formed to create or produce something. The end goal might be a marketing plan, the design of a new factory, or a new product, or it could be performing the annual audit. Because projects vary so much in nature and size, we will summarize generic project phases here. Figure 2-5 shows project management with four phases, the major tasks of each, and the kinds of data that collaborative teams need to share.

> - Define the problem.
> - Identify alternative solutions.
> - Specify evaluation criteria.
> - Evaluate alternatives.
> - Select an alternative.
> - Implement solution.

Figure 2-4
Problem-Solving Tasks

Phase	Tasks	Shared Data
Starting	Set team authority. Set project scope and initial budget. Form team. Establish team roles, responsibilities, and authorities. Establish team rules.	Team member personal data Start-up documents
Planning	Determine tasks and dependencies. Assign tasks. Determine schedule. Revise budget.	Project plan, budget, and other documents
Doing	Perform project tasks. Manage tasks and budget. Solve problems. Reschedule tasks, as necessary. Document and report progress.	Work in process Updated tasks Updated project schedule Updated project budget Project status documents
Finalizing	Determine completion. Prepare archival documents. Disband team.	Archival documents

Figure 2-5
Project Management Tasks
and Data

Starting Phase

The fundamental purpose of the starting phase is to set the ground rules for the project and the team. In industry, teams need to determine or understand what authority they have. Is the project given to the team? Or is part of the team's task to identify what the project is? Is the team free to determine team membership, or is membership given? Can the team devise its own methods for accomplishing the project, or is a particular method required? Student teams differ from those in industry because the team's authority and membership are set by the instructor. However, although student teams do not have the authority to define the project, they do have the authority to determine how that project will be accomplished.

Other tasks during the starting phase are to set the scope of the project and to establish an initial budget. Often this budget is preliminary and is revised after the project has been planned. An initial team is formed during this phase with the understanding that team membership may change as the project progresses. It is important to set team member expectations at the outset. What role will each team member play, and what responsibilities and authority will he or she have? Team rules are also established as discussed under decision making.

Planning Phase

The purpose of the planning phase is to determine "who will do what and by when." Work activities are defined, and resources such as personnel, budget, and equipment are assigned to them. As you'll learn when we discuss project management in Chapter 12, tasks can depend on one another. For example, you cannot evaluate alternatives until you have created a list of alternatives to evaluate. In this case, we say that there is a *task dependency* between the task *Evaluate alternatives* and the task *Create a list of alternatives*. The *Evaluate alternatives* task cannot begin until the completion of the *Create a list of alternatives* task.

Once tasks and resources have been assigned, it is possible to determine the project schedule. If the schedule is unacceptable, more resources can be added to the project or the project scope can be reduced. Risks and complications arise here, however, as will be discussed in Chapter 12. The project budget is usually revised at this point as well.

Doing Phase

Project tasks are accomplished during the doing phase. The key management challenge here is to ensure that tasks are accomplished on time and, if not, to identify schedule problems as early as possible. As work progresses, it is often necessary to add or delete tasks, change task assignments, add or remove task labor or other resources, and so forth. Another important task is to document and report project progress.

Finalizing Phase

Are we done? This question is an important and sometimes difficult one to answer. If work is not finished, the team needs to define more tasks and continue the doing phase. If the answer is yes, then the team needs to document its results, document information for future teams, close down the project, and disband the team.

Review the third column of Figure 2-5. All of this project data needs to be stored in a location accessible to the team. Furthermore, all of this data is subject to feedback and iteration. That means there will be hundreds, perhaps thousands, of versions of data items to be managed. We will consider ways that collaborative information systems can facilitate the management of such data in Q2-6.

Q2-4 What Are the Requirements for a Collaboration Information System?

As you would expect, a **collaboration information system**, or, more simply, a **collaboration system**, is an information system that supports collaboration. In this section, we'll discuss the components of such a system and use the discussions in Q2-1 and Q2-2 to summarize the requirements for a collaboration IS.

A collaboration information system is a practical example of IS, one that you and your teammates can, and should, build. Because you are new to thinking about IS, we begin first with a summary of the five components of such a system, and then we will survey the requirements that teams, including yours, should consider when constructing a collaboration IS.

The Five Components of an IS for Collaboration

As information systems, collaboration systems have the five components of every information system: hardware, software, data, procedures, and people. Concerning hardware, every team member needs a device for participating in the group's work, either a personal computer or a mobile device like an iPad. In addition, because teams need to share data, most collaboration systems store documents and other files on a server somewhere. Google Drive and Microsoft OneDrive provide servers that are accessed via the Internet, in what is called *the cloud*, which you will learn about in Chapter 6. For now, think of it as one or more computers that store and retrieve your files, somewhere out on the Internet.

Collaboration programs are applications like email or text messaging, Google Docs, Microsoft Office Online, and other tools that support collaborative work. We will survey those tools in Q2-5 through Q2-7.

Regarding the data component, collaboration involves two types. **Project data** is data that is part of the collaboration's work product. For example, for a team designing a new product, design documents are examples of project data. A document that describes a recommended solution is project data for a problem-solving project. **Project metadata** is data used to manage the project. Schedules, tasks, budgets, and other managerial data are examples of project metadata. Both types of data, by the way, are subject to iteration and feedback.

Criterion for Team Success	Requirement
Complete the work, on time, on budget	Communicate (feedback) Manage many versions of content (iteration) Manage tasks (on time, on budget)
Growth in team capability	Record lessons learned Document definitions, concepts, and other knowledge Support intra–team training
Meaningful and satisfying experience	Build team esprit Reward accomplishment Create sense of importance

Figure 2-6
Requirements for
a Collaboration IS

Collaboration information systems procedures specify standards, policies, and techniques for conducting the team's work. An example is procedures for reviewing documents or other work products. To reduce confusion and increase control, the team might establish a procedure that specifies who will review documents and in what sequence. Rules about who can do what to which data are also codified in procedures. Procedures are usually designed by the team; sometimes they need to be adjusted because of limitations in the collaboration tools being used.

The final component of a collaboration system is, of course, people. We discussed the importance of the ability to give and receive critical feedback in Q1. In addition, team members know how and when to use collaboration applications.

Primary Functions: Communication and Content Sharing

Figure 2-6 shows requirements categorized according to Hackman's three criteria for team success (discussed in Q2-2). For doing the work on time and on budget, teams need support from their collaboration system to communicate, to manage many versions of content, and to manage tasks. We will discuss tools that support each of those requirements in Q2-5 through Q2-7. Notice that these requirements support iteration and feedback, as you would expect for an IS that supports collaboration. Figure 2-6 also shows requirements for growth in team capability and for creating a meaningful and satisfying experience.

As you will learn, there are numerous alternatives for constructing an IS to meet those requirements. We will investigate three in Q2-8. You will then have the opportunity of creating an IS for your team in Collaboration Exercise 2 on page 110. Doing so will be greatly beneficial because it will teach you firsthand the role of each of the five components and it will also give you a result that you can use with other teams, in other courses, and, of course, during your career.

Figure 2-7 lists the four purposes of collaboration activities discussed in Q2-3 and summarizes IS requirements for collaboration systems for each purpose. When you construct your own collaboration IS, first determine the type of effort you are engaged in and then use Figure 2-7 to help you determine your requirements.

Q2-5 How Can You Use Collaboration Tools to Improve Team Communication?

Because of the need to provide feedback, team communication is essential to every collaborative project. In addition to feedback, however, communication is important to manage content, project tasks, and the other requirements shown in Figures 2-6 and 2-7. Developing an effective communication facility is the first thing your team should do, and it is arguably the most important feature of a collaboration IS.

Team Purpose	Requirements
Become informed	Share data Support group communication Manage project tasks Store history
Make decisions	Share decision criteria, alternative descriptions, evaluation tools, evaluation results, and implementation plan Support group communication Manage project tasks Publish decision, as needed Store analysis and results
Solve problems	Share problem definitions, solution alternatives, costs and benefits, alternative evaluations, and solution implementation plan Support group communication Manage project tasks Publish problem and solution, as needed Store problem definition, alternatives, analysis, and plan
Manage projects	Support starting, planning, doing, and finalizing project phases (Figure 2–5) Support group communication Manage project tasks

Figure 2-7
Requirements for Different
Collaboration Purposes

The particular tools used depend on the ways that the team communicates, as summarized in Figure 2-8. **Synchronous communication** occurs when all team members meet at the same time, such as with conference calls or face-to-face meetings. **Asynchronous communication** occurs when team members do not meet at the same time. Employees who work different shifts at the same location or team members who work in different time zones around the world must meet asynchronously.

The Ethics Guide on pages 92–93 addresses some of the ethical challenges that arise when team members have opposing viewpoints.

Most student teams attempt to meet face to face, at least at first. Arranging such meetings is always difficult, however, because student schedules and responsibilities differ. If you are going to arrange such meetings, consider creating an online group calendar in which team members post their availability, week by week. Also, use the meeting facilities in Microsoft Outlook to issue invitations and gather RSVPs. If you don't have Outlook, use an Internet site such as Evite (*www.evite.com*) for this purpose.

For most face-to-face meetings, you need little; the standard Office applications or their freeware lookalikes, such as LibreOffice, will suffice. However, research indicates that face-to-face

Synchronous		Asynchronous
Shared calendars Invitation and attendance		
Single location	Multiple locations	Single or multiple locations
Office applications such as Word and PowerPoint Shared whiteboards	Conference calls Multiparty text chat Screen sharing Webinars Videoconferencing	Email Discussion forums Team surveys

Virtual meetings

Figure 2-8
Collaboration Tools for
Communication

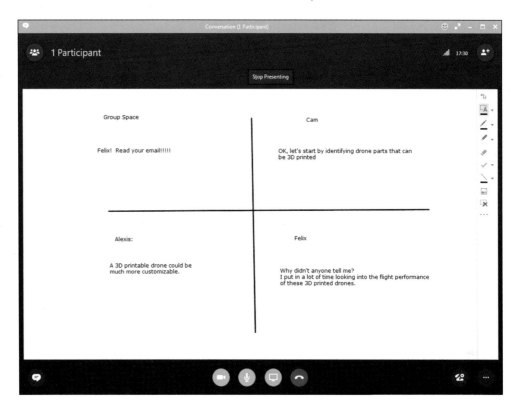

Figure 2-9

Skype for Business Whiteboard Showing Simultaneous Contributions

Source: Used by permission from Skype Corporation.

meetings can benefit from shared, online workspaces, such as that shown in Figure 2-9.[3] With such a whiteboard, team members can type, write, and draw simultaneously, which enables more ideas to be proposed in a given period of time than when team members must wait in sequence to express ideas verbally. If you have access to such a whiteboard, try it in your face-to-face meetings to see if it works for your team.

However, *given today's communication technology, most students should forgo face-to-face meetings.* They are too difficult to arrange and seldom worth the trouble. Instead, learn to use **virtual meetings** in which participants do not meet in the same place and possibly not at the same time.

If your virtual meeting is synchronous (all meet at the same time), you can use conference calls, multiparty text chat, screen sharing, webinars, or videoconferencing. Some students find it weird to use text chat for school projects, but why not? You can attend meetings wherever you are, without using your voice. Google Hangouts support multiparty text chat, as does Skype for Business. Google or Bing "multiparty text chat" to find other, similar products.

Screen-sharing applications enable users to view the same whiteboard, application, or other display. Figure 2-9 shows an example whiteboard for a Falcon Security meeting. This whiteboard, which is part of Skype for Business, allows multiple people to contribute simultaneously. To organize the simultaneous conversation, the whiteboard real estate is divided among the members of the group, as shown. Some groups save their whiteboards as minutes of the meeting.

A **webinar** is a virtual meeting in which attendees view one of the attendees' computer screens for a more formal and organized presentation. WebEx (*www.webex.com*) is a popular commercial webinar application used in virtual sales presentations.

If everyone on your team has a camera on his or her computer, you can also do **videoconferencing**, like that shown in Figure 2-10. You can use Google Hangouts, WebEx, or Skype for Business, which we will discuss in Q8. Videoconferencing is more intrusive than text chat (you have to comb your hair), but it does have a more personal touch.

In some classes and situations, synchronous meetings, even virtual ones, are impossible to arrange. You just cannot get everyone together at the same time. In this circumstance, when

Figure 2-10
Videoconferencing Example
Source: Tom Merton/Getty Images

the team must meet asynchronously, most students try to communicate via **email**. The problem with email is that there is too much freedom. Not everyone will participate because it is easy to hide from email. (Was Felix, in the opening scenario, really unable to open the attachment?) Email threads become disorganized and disconnected. After the fact, it is difficult to find particular emails, comments, or attachments.

Discussion forums are an alternative. Here, one group member posts an entry, perhaps an idea, a comment, or a question, and other group members respond. Figure 2-11 shows an example. Such forums are better than email because it is harder for the discussion to get off track. Still, however, it remains easy for some team members not to participate.

Figure 2-11
Example Discussion Forum
Source: © Access 2013, Microsoft Corporation

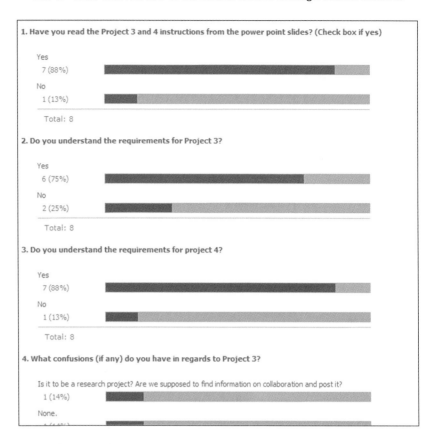

Figure 2-12
Example Survey Report

Team surveys are another form of communication technology. With these, one team member creates a list of questions and other team members respond. Surveys are an effective way to obtain team opinions; they are generally easy to complete, so most team members will participate. Also, it is easy to determine who has not yet responded. Figure 2-12 shows the results of one team survey. SurveyMonkey (*www.surveymonkey.com*) is one common survey application program. You can find others on the Internet. Microsoft SharePoint has a built-in survey capability, as we discuss in Q8.

Video and audio recordings are also useful for asynchronous communication. Key presentations or discussions can be recorded and played back for team members at their convenience. Such recordings are also useful for training new employees.

Q2-6 How Can You Use Collaboration Tools to Manage Shared Content?

Content sharing is the second major function of collaboration systems. To enable iteration and feedback, team members need to share both project data (such as documents, spreadsheets, and presentations) and work-product data as well as project metadata (such as tasks, schedules, calendars, and budgets). The applications teams use and the means by which they share data depend on the type of content. Figure 2-13 provides an overview.[4]

For teams that are sharing Office documents such as Word, Excel, and PowerPoint, the gold standard of desktop applications is Microsoft Office. However, it is also the most expensive. To minimize costs, some teams use either LibreOffice (*www.libreoffice.org*) or Apache OpenOffice (*www.openoffice.org*). Both are license-free, open-source products. (You'll learn more about these terms in Chapter 4; for now, think free.) These products have a small subset of the features and functions of Microsoft Office, but they are robust for what they do and are adequate for many businesses and students.

Content Type	Desktop Application	Web Application	Cloud Drive
Office documents (Word, Excel, PowerPoint)	Microsoft Office LibreOffice OpenOffice	Google Docs (Import/ Export non–Google Docs) Microsoft Office Online (Microsoft Office only)	Google Drive Microsoft OneDrive Microsoft SharePoint Drop Box
PDFs	Adobe Acrobat	Viewers in Google Drive and Microsoft Web OneDrive and SharePoint	Google Drive Microsoft OneDrive Microsoft SharePoint Dropbox
Photos, videos	Adobe Photoshop, Camtasia, and numerous others	Google Picasa	Google Drive Microsoft OneDrive Microsoft SharePoint Apple iCloud Dropbox
Other (engineering drawings)	Specific application (Google SketchUp)	Rare	Google Drive Microsoft OneDrive Microsoft SharePoint Dropbox

Figure 2-13
Content Applications and
Storage Alternatives

Teams that share documents of other types need to install applications for processing those particular types. For examples, Adobe Acrobat processes PDF files, Photoshop and Google Picasa process photos, and Camtasia produces computer screen videos that are useful for teaching team members how to use computer applications.

In addition to desktop applications, teams can also process some types of content using Web applications inside their browsers (Firefox, Chrome, and so on). Both Google Docs and Microsoft Office Online can process Word, Excel, and PowerPoint files. However, Google has its own versions of these files. Consequently, if the user uploads a Word document that was created using a desktop application and then wishes to edit that document, he or she must convert it into Google Docs format by opening it with Google Docs. After editing the document, if the user wants to place the document back into Word format, he or she will need to specifically save it in Word format. This is not difficult once the user is aware of the need to do so. Of course, if the team never uses a desktop application and instead uses Google Docs to create and process documents via the Web, then no conversion between the desktop and Google Docs formats is needed. Microsoft Office Online can be used in a similar way, but Office Online will edit only documents that were created using Microsoft Office. Documents created using LibreOffice and OpenOffice cannot be edited using Microsoft Office Online.

Browser applications require that documents be stored on a cloud server. Google Docs documents must be stored on Google Drive; Microsoft Office Online must be stored on either Microsoft OneDrive or Microsoft SharePoint. We will illustrate the use of Google Docs and Google Drive when we discuss version management later in this chapter.

Documents other than Office documents can be stored (but not processed via the browser) on any cloud server. Team members store the documents on the server for other team members to access. Dropbox is one common alternative, but you can use Google Drive, Microsoft OneDrive, and SharePoint as well. You can also store photos and videos on Apple's iCloud.

Figure 2-14 lists collaboration tools for three categories of content: no control, version management, and version control.

Shared Content with No Control

The most primitive way to share content is via email attachments. However, email attachments have numerous problems. For one, there is always the danger that someone does not receive an email, does not notice it in his or her inbox, or does not bother to save the attachments. Then,

Alternatives for Sharing Content		
No Control	Version Management	Version Control
Email with attachments Shared files on a server	Google Docs Microsoft Office Online Microsoft Office	Microsoft SharePoint

Figure 2-14
Collaboration Tools for Sharing Content

Increasing degree of content control

too, if three users obtain the same document as an email attachment, each changes it, and each sends back the changed document via email, then different, incompatible versions of that document will be floating around. So, although email is simple, easy, and readily available, it will not suffice for collaborations in which there are many document versions or for which there is a desire for content control.

Another way to share content is to place it on a shared **file server**, which is simply a computer that stores files…just like the disk in your local computer. If your team has access to a file server at your university, you can put documents on the server and others can download them, make changes, and upload them back onto the server. You can also store files on the cloud servers listed in Figure 2-13.

Storing documents on servers is better than using email attachments because documents have a single storage location. They are not scattered in different team members' email boxes, and team members have a known location for finding documents.

However, without any additional control, it is possible for team members to interfere with one another's work. For example, suppose team members A and B download a document and edit it, but without knowing about the other's edits. Person A stores his version back on the server and then person B stores her version back on the server. In this scenario, person A's changes will be lost.

Furthermore, without any version management, it will be impossible to know who changed the document and when. Neither person A nor person B will know whose version of the document is on the server. To avoid such problems, some form of version management is recommended.

Shared Content with Version Management on Google Drive

Systems that provide **version management** track changes to documents and provide features and functions to accommodate concurrent work. For office documents, you can obtain version management services from Google Drive, Microsoft OneDrive, and Microsoft SharePoint. Here we will discuss the use of Google Drive.

Google Drive is a free service that provides a virtual drive in the cloud into which you can create folders and store files. You can upload files of any type, but only files that are processed by Google Docs receive version management. We'll restrict the rest of this discussion to files of those types.

To use Google Drive, you need a Google Account, which you obtain by creating a gmail address. (If you already have a gmail address, you already have a Google Account with the same name as your gmail address.) To create a Google account, go to *http://accounts.google.com* and fill out the form shown in Figure 2-15.

In this form, you need not provide a value for your current email address, though it's a good idea to provide one if you can. That address is used by Google in the event you forget your password and for other security backup purposes.

To create a Google document, go to *http://drive.google.com* (note that there is no *www* in this address). Sign in with your Google Account (your gmail address). From that point on, you can

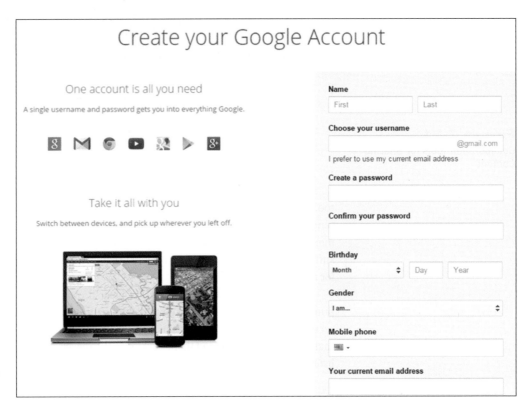

Figure 2-15

Form for Creating a Google Drive Account

Source: Google and the Google logo are registered trademarks of Google Inc., Used with permission.

create, upload, process, save, and download documents. Figure 2-16 shows a folder named MIS 2016 with the same document in both Word and Google Docs format. After editing the user can save the Google Docs version back to Word if necessary. Types of documents that can be created on Google Drive are shown under the NEW button.

With Google Drive, you can make documents available to others by entering their email addresses or Google accounts. Those users are notified that the document exists and are given a link by which they can access it. If they have a Google account, they can edit the document; otherwise, they can just view the document. To see who can share one of the documents in Figure 2-16, right-click on any document the screen, click Share, and click Advanced. A screen showing those who share the document will appear like that in Figure 2-17.

Because folders and documents are stored on Google Drive, server users can simultaneously see and edit documents. In the background, Google Docs merges the users' activities into a single

Figure 2-16

Available Types of Documents on Google Drive

Source: Google and the Google logo are registered trademarks of Google Inc., Used with permission.

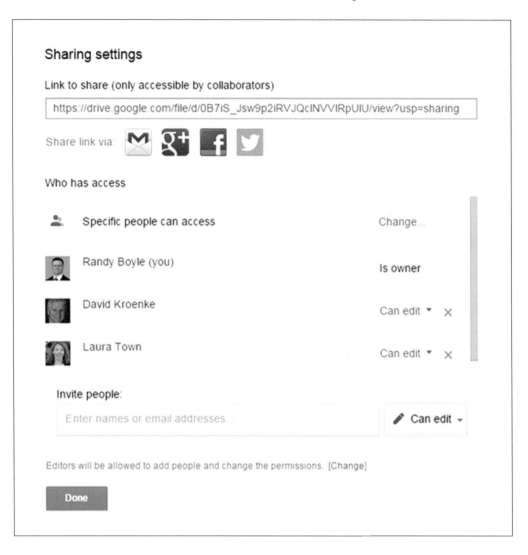

Figure 2-17

Document Sharing on Google Drive

Source: Google and the Google logo are registered trademarks of Google Inc., Used with permission.

document. You are notified that another user is editing a document at the same time as you are, and you can refresh the document to see his or her latest changes. Google tracks document revisions, with brief summaries of changes made. Figure 2-18 shows a sample revision document that has been edited by two users.

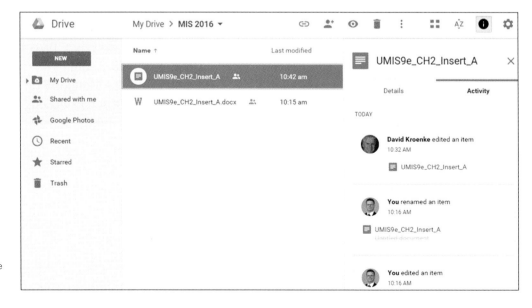

Figure 2-18

Example of Editing a Shared Document on Google Drive

Source: Google and the Google logo are registered trademarks of Google Inc., Used with permission.

Ethics Guide

I KNOW WHAT'S BETTER, REALLY

Suppose you work for a small startup company involved in the innovative application of 3D printing technology, like Falcon Security. Your company is 2 years old, employs 50 people, and, like many startup companies, is short of money. Even though you're relatively junior, you've impressed the company's founders, and they have asked you to take a leadership role on a number of special projects. Recently, the company has been investigating developing an information system to store 3D engineering designs and make them available to customers for purchase. You've been assigned to a committee that is developing alternative IS designs for consideration by senior management.

You and a coworker, Leslie Johnson, have developed two different alternatives for consideration by the committee. You believe that Alternative Two is vastly preferable to Alternative One, but Leslie believes just the opposite. You think if Leslie's alternative is chosen, the result will be a major financial loss, one that your young startup company is unlikely to survive. Even if that does not occur, so much time will be lost pursuing Leslie's alternative that your company will fall behind the competition in your dynamic, developing market and will lose substantial market share to the competition as a result.

Unfortunately, Leslie is called away due to a family emergency on the day the two of you are to present your alternatives. You so strongly believe that Leslie's plan is likely to cause irreparable harm to the company that you decide to present only your plan. While you never lie outright, you lead the committee to believe that both of you strongly support your plan. The committee adopts your plan, and Leslie never learns that the committee saw only one alternative. Is your behavior ethical?

The Ethics Guide in Chapter 1 introduced Kant's categorical imperative as one way of assessing ethical conduct. This guide introduces a second way, one known as *utilitarianism*. The basis of this theory goes back to early Greek philosophers, but the founders of the modern theory are considered to be Jeremy Bentham and John Stuart Mill, as you will learn in your business ethics class.

According to utilitarianism, the morality of an act is determined by its outcome. Acts are judged to be moral if they result in the greatest good to the greatest number or if they maximize happiness and reduce suffering. The prior sentence contains a great deal of subtlety that has led to numerous flavors of utilitarianism—flavors that are beyond the scope of this text. Here we will work with the gist of those statements.

Using utilitarianism as a guide, killing can be moral if it results in the greatest good to the greatest number. Killing Adolf Hitler would have been moral if it stopped the Holocaust. Similarly, utilitarianism can assess lying or other forms of deception as moral if the act results in the greatest good to the greatest number. Lying to someone with a fatal illness that you're certain he or she will recover is moral if it increases that person's happiness and decreases his or her suffering.

Our Recommended Alternatives

~~Alternative One~~
- ~~In-house stores 3D diagrams~~
- ~~Direct connect to e-commerce server~~

~~Alternative Two~~ **Use the Cloud**
- 3D diagrams stored on elastic cloud servers
- Use MongoDB on AWS
- SOA connections to e-commerce server

DISCUSSION QUESTIONS

1. According to Kant's categorical imperative, is your action not to present Leslie's alternative ethical?
2. According to utilitarianism, is your action not to present Leslie's alternative ethical?
3. Assume:
   a. You were right. Had the company embarked on Leslie's alternative, it would have driven the company into bankruptcy. Does this fact make your actions more ethical? Explain your answer.
   b. You were wrong. Leslie's alternative would have been far superior to yours for the company's future. Does this fact make your actions less ethical? Explain your answer.
4. In your opinion, do the intended consequences or the actual consequences have more bearing when assessing ethics from a utilitarian perspective?
5. You could postpone the meeting until Leslie is able to attend and thus allow Leslie to present the alternative to yours. Doing so, however, increases the likelihood that the committee selects Leslie's alternative, and you firmly believe that decision will be fatal to the company.
   a. According to Kant's categorical imperative, is a decision not to postpone ethical?
   b. According to utilitarianism, is a decision not to postpone ethical?
6. Suppose Leslie learns you presented only your alternative, and you two become archenemies. To the company's disadvantage, the two of you are never able to work together again. According to utilitarianism, does this outcome change the ethics of your behavior?
7. Suppose that instead of not presenting Leslie's alternative at all, you present it, but in a very negative light. You are honest when you focus the bulk of your description of it on disadvantages because that's what you believe. However, you also know that Leslie does not agree with the way you see the situation. Given your biased presentation, the committee selects your alternative.
   a. According to Kant's categorical imperative, is your behavior ethical?
   b. According to utilitarianism, is your behavior ethical?
8. What would you do in this circumstance? Justify the ethics of your decision.

You can improve your collaboration activity even more by combining Google Drive with Google+.

Google Drive is free and very easy to use. Google Drive, Dropbox, and Microsoft OneDrive are all far superior to exchanging documents via email or via a file server. If you are not using one of these three products, you should. Go to *http://drive.google.com*, *www.dropbox.com*, or *www.onedrive.com* to check them out. You'll find easy-to-understand demos if you need additional instruction.

Shared Content with Version Control

Version management systems improve the tracking of shared content and potentially eliminate problems caused by concurrent document access. They do not, however, provide **version control**, the process that occurs when the collaboration tool limits, and sometimes even directs, user activity. Version control involves one or more of the following capabilities:

- User activity limited by permissions
- Document checkout
- Version histories
- Workflow control

Microsoft SharePoint is a large, complex, and very robust application for all types of collaboration. It has many features and functions, including all of those just listed. It also contains features for managing tasks, sharing non-Office documents, keeping calendars, publishing blogs, and many more capabilities. Some organizations install SharePoint on their own Windows servers; others access it over the Internet using SharePoint Online. Office 365 Professional and other versions of Office 365 include SharePoint.

SharePoint is an industrial-strength product, and if you have an opportunity to use it, by all means learn to do so. SharePoint is used by thousands of businesses, and SharePoint skills are in high demand. The latest version is SharePoint 2013; we will illustrate its use here. Consider the SharePoint implementation of the four functions listed.

Permission-Limited Activity

Monitoring and vetting collaborators can help stop malicious insiders. The Security Guide on pages 104–105 discusses why monitoring user behavior has become necessary.

With SharePoint (and other version control products), each team member is given an account with a set of permissions. Then shared documents are placed into shared directories, sometimes called **libraries**. For example, on a shared site with four libraries, a particular user might be given read-only permission for library 1; read and edit permission for library 2; read, edit, and delete permission for library 3; and no permission even to see library 4.

Document Checkout

With version control applications, document directories can be set up so that users are required to check out documents before they can modify them. When a document is checked out, no other user can obtain it for the purpose of editing it. Once the document has been checked in, other users can obtain it for editing.

Figure 2-19 shows a screen for a user of Microsoft SharePoint 2013. The user is checking out the document UMIS 8e Chapter 2. Once it has been checked out, the user can edit it and return it to this library. While it is checked out, no other user will be able to edit it, and the user's changes will not be visible to others.

With SharePoint, Microsoft manages concurrent updates on office documents (Word, Excel, etc.) and documents need not normally be checked out. In Figure 2-19, the user has checked out an Acrobat PDF (indicated by a green arrow next to the PDF icon), which is not an Office document.

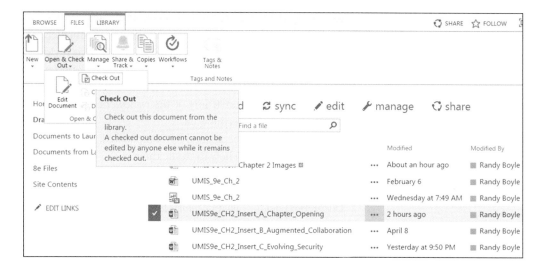

Figure 2-19

Checking Out a Document

Source: © Access 2013, Microsoft
Corporation

Version History

Because collaboration involves feedback and iteration, it is inevitable that dozens, or even hundreds, of documents will be created. Imagine, for example, the number of versions of a design document for the Boeing 787. In some cases, collaboration team members attempt to keep track of versions by appending suffixes to file names. The result for a student project is a file name like *Project1_lt_kl_092911_most_ recent_draft.docx* or something similar. Not only are such names ugly and awkward, no team member can tell whether this is the most current version.

Collaboration tools that provide version control have the data to readily provide histories on behalf of the users. When a document is changed (or checked in), the collaboration tool records the name of the author and the date and time the document is stored. Users also have the option of recording notes about their version. You can see an example of a version history report produced by SharePoint 2013 later in the chapter in Figure 2-33 (page 114).

Workflow Control

Collaboration tools that provide **workflow control** manage activities in a predefined process. If, for example, a group wants documents to be reviewed and approved by team members in a particular sequence, the group would define that workflow to the tool. Then the workflow is started, and the emails to manage the process are sent as defined. For example, Figure 2-20 shows a SharePoint workflow in which the group defined a document review process that involves a sequence of

Figure 2-20

Example Workflow

Source: © Access 2013, Microsoft
Corporation

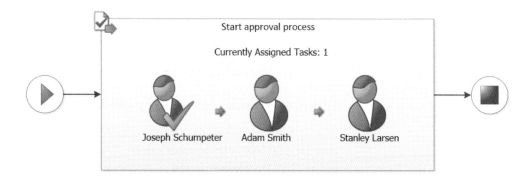

reviews by three people. Given this definition, when a document is submitted to a library, SharePoint assigns a task to the first person, Joseph Schumpeter, to approve the document and sends an email to him to that effect. Once he has completed his review (the green checkmark means that he has already done so), SharePoint assigns a task for and sends an email to Adam Smith to approve the document. When all three reviewers have completed their review, SharePoint marks the document as approved. If any of the reviewers disapprove, the document is marked accordingly and the workflow is terminated.

Workflows can be defined for complicated, multistage business processes. See *SharePoint for Students*[5] for more on how to create them.

Numerous version control applications exist. For general business use, SharePoint is the most popular. Other document control systems include MasterControl (*www.mastercontrol.com*) and Document Locator (*www.documentlocator.com*). Software development teams use applications such as CVS (*www.nongnu.org/cvs*) or Subversion (*http://subversion.apache.org*) to control versions of software code, test plans, and product documentation.

Q2-7 How Can You Use Collaboration Tools to Manage Tasks?

As you will learn in project management classes, one of the keys for making team progress is keeping a current task list. Good project managers make sure that every team meeting ends with an updated list of tasks, including who is responsible for getting each task done and the date by which he or she will get it done. We've all been to meetings in which many good ideas were discussed, even agreed upon, but nothing happened after the meeting. When teams create and manage task lists, the risks of such nonaction diminish. Managing with a task list is critical for making progress.

Task descriptions need to be specific and worded so it is possible to decide whether the task was accomplished. "Create a good requirements document" is not an effective, testable task description, unless all team members already know what is supposed to be in a good requirements document. A better task would be "Define the contents of the requirements document for the XYZ project."

In general, one person should be made responsible for accomplishing a task. That does not mean that the assigned person does the task; it means that he or she is responsible for ensuring that it gets done. Finally, no benefit will come from this list unless every task has a date by which it is to be completed. Further, team leaders need to follow up on tasks to ensure they are done by that date. Without accountability and follow-up, there is no task management.

As you'll learn in your project management classes, you can add other data to the task list. You might want to add critical resources that are required, and you might want to specify tasks that need to be finished before a given task can be started. We will discuss such task dependencies further in Chapter 12, when we discuss the management of systems development projects.

For team members to utilize the task list effectively, they need to share it. In this question, we will consider two options: sharing a task spreadsheet on Google Drive and using the task list feature in Microsoft SharePoint. Google gmail and Calendar also have a task list feature, but as of this writing, it is impossible to share it with others, so it is not useful for collaboration.

Sharing a Task List on Google Drive

Sharing a task list on Google Drive is simple. To do so, every team member needs to obtain a Google account. Then one team member can create a team folder and share it with the rest of the team, giving everyone edit permission on documents that it contains. One of the team members then creates a task spreadsheet on that folder.

Augmented Collaboration

When was the last time you turned to the Internet for help solving a problem? Only a decade or two ago, the world was a very different place. If you wanted to learn something new, you had to make a considerable effort—like checking out a book from the library or using a landline phone to call a friend.

Today, there are limitless resources for you to draw from that are only a mouse click away. These include high-definition videos, message boards, interactive Web sites, collaboration tools, and more! Every day people are turning to sites like YouTube to learn how to do things like change a car tire, write a new programming script, or better manage a supply chain.

But you may be wondering, what's next? Will there ever be a *better* approach to learning besides simply reading a message board or watching a video? If you look at new innovations currently under development by Facebook, Google, and Microsoft, the answer to that question is a resounding "yes!"

What Is Microsoft HoloLens (aka "Project Baraboo")?

You may have heard about Oculus Rift or Google Glass, but do you know the difference? Oculus Rift, with its development now under Facebook's control, is a virtual reality headset geared to 3D gaming and new forms of social media. Google Glass was designed to provide augmented reality, meaning that the real world is still visible but with the Glass interface superimposed on top of it. As a new entrant to this market, Microsoft recently announced the HoloLens, which is also an augmented reality headset.[6] Recent reviews of the HoloLens indicate that this innovation may be a game changer for business, productivity, and collaboration.

A recent demonstration of the HoloLens pointed to its usability as a collaboration platform. In a demo conducted at Microsoft corporate headquarters, reporters were allowed to test the HoloLens for use in a number of applications, including the installation of a light switch.[7] However, the evaluator would not receive help from the HoloLens by simply searching the Web or watching a video.

Using HoloLens, the evaluator would receive live instruction from an expert electrician using its custom Skype application. When the task began, a video conferencing window was superimposed in the field of view of the HoloLens user showing a live feed from the expert. The expert was able to remotely see a live feed of the field of view of the user. The expert could draw directions on his or her own device, which would then appear superimposed in the field of view of the user wearing the HoloLens.

Source: Corbis News/Corbis

Within 5 minutes, a number of complicated steps were completed and the switch was properly installed and tested. The expert was then free to move on to the "next call."

How Can HoloLens Change Collaboration and Business?

Installing a light switch may be a relatively simple task for some people. But what does this basic demonstration mean for the future of collaboration? HoloLens, and other types of headsets, can create new interaction and collaboration opportunities for countless businesses and industries. Think about the impact of this type of technology on health care. Suppose complications arise during a surgery and the medical team on hand is struggling to resolve them. A specialist across the country can be patched in using an augmented reality headset to provide both direction and detailed instructions that can be superimposed in the field of view of the surgeon.

Similarly, imagine how complex sequences of operations in a manufacturing facility or nuclear power plant could be carried out by a novice operator who is working under the supervision of a seasoned expert communicating through a HoloLens. These two examples are only the tip of the iceberg, but like the HoloLens, they may help you see the future of collaboration in an entirely new way!

Questions

1. This feature provides two examples of possible business uses for the HoloLens. Think about the future impact of this innovation by identifying other industries that may benefit from the development of augmented reality technology.

2. What is the difference between the Oculus Rift and the Microsoft HoloLens?

3. How could this type of technology benefit your collaborations as a student? Think about how you interact with tutors and fellow students on group projects and how you seek and receive help from your instructor.

4. Privacy concerns are one of the factors that prompted Google to delay a full release of the Google Glass. What are the security and privacy implications of releasing a product like the HoloLens?

5. Virtual reality and augmented reality headsets are currently a novelty, but that will change over the coming years. How might these new innovations affect collaboration and business 10 or 20 years from now?

Figure 2-21 shows a sample task list containing the name of each task, the name of the person to whom it is assigned, the date it is due, the task's status, and remarks. Because every member of the team has edit permission, everyone can contribute to this task list. Google Drive will allow simultaneous edits. Because Google Drive tracks version history, it will be possible, if necessary, to learn who made which changes to the task list.

Setting up such a list is easy, and having such a list greatly facilitates project management. The key for success is to keep it current and to use it to hold team members accountable.

Sharing a Task List Using Microsoft SharePoint

SharePoint includes a built-in content type for managing task lists that provides robust and powerful features. The standard task list can be readily modified to include user-customized columns, and many different views can be constructed to show the list in different ways for different users. Like the rest of SharePoint, its task lists are industrial-strength.

Figure 2-22 shows a task list that we used for the production of this text. The first three columns are built-in columns that SharePoint provides. The last column, named Book Title, is the book for which the task was assigned. For example, UMIS stands for the book titled *Using MIS*. When one of our team members opens this site, the view of the task list shown in Figure 2-23 is displayed. The tasks in this view are sorted by Due Date value and are filtered on the value of Task Status so any task that has been completed is not shown. Hence, this is a to-do list. Another view of

Figure 2-21

Sample Task List Using Google Drive

Source: Google and the Google logo are registered trademarks of Google Inc., Used with permission.

	Sample Task List				
	A	B	C	D	E
1	Task	Assigned To	Due Date	Status	Remarks
2	Get Set Up:				
3	Determine how we will meet	Kroenke	4/10/2017	Complete	Kroenke will set up the meeting and drive the discussion to conclusion
4	Decide communication method	Boyle	4/15/2017	Complete	Boyle will identify alternatives to show the team... and get team decision
5	Identify cloud server alternatives	Boyle	4/10/2017	Complete	Boyle will do this via email... until we can get our cloud server up
6	Select a cloud server	Kroenke	4/20/2017	Late	Kroenke will drive us to a decision and document it
7	Set up a cloud server	Kroenke	4/24/2017	In process	Set up the server for use by the team; communicate to all how to use it.
8	Determine office document alternatives	Town	4/26/2017	In process	Use cloud server from here on out!
9	Select office document applications	Town	4/28/2017	In process	Laura will drive the team to a decision and document.
10	Specify task list contents	Kroenke	4/28/2017	Complete	Done, but can't place on cloud server until Kroenke finishes.
11	Determine how to store task list	Town	5/2/2017	Not started	Laura will drive the team to a decision here.
12	Document requirements	Boyle	5/3/2017	Not started	Document all the requirements document on our cloud server

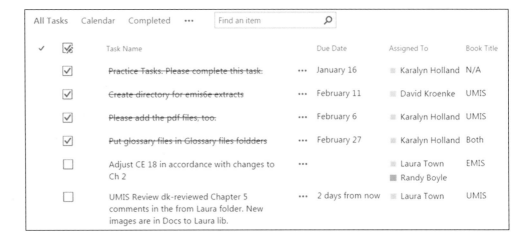

Figure 2-22

UMIS Production Task List in SharePoint

Source: © Access 2013, Microsoft Corporation

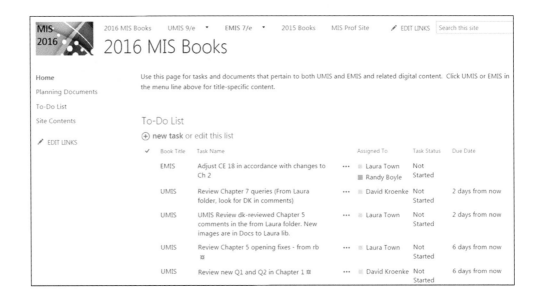

Figure 2-23

UMIS To-Do List in SharePoint

Source: © Access 2013, Microsoft Corporation

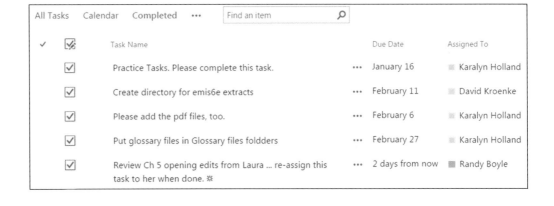

Figure 2-24

UMIS Completed Tasks in SharePoint

Source: © Access 2013, Microsoft Corporation

this list, shown in Figure 2-24, includes only those tasks in which Status equals Completed. That view is a "what we've done so far" list.

Alerts are one of the most useful features in SharePoint task lists. Using alerts, team members can request SharePoint to send emails when certain events occur. Our team sets alerts so Share-Point sends a team member an email whenever a task is created that is assigned to him or her. We also have SharePoint send alerts to a task's creator whenever a task is modified. Figure 2-31 (on page 113) shows such an email.

SharePoint task lists provide features and functions that are far superior to the spreadsheet shown in Figure 2-21. Again, if you can obtain access to SharePoint, you should strongly consider using it, a possibility we address in the next question.

Q2-8 Which Collaboration IS Is Right for Your Team?

Your MIS class will help you gain knowledge and skills that you'll use throughout your business career. But why wait? You can benefit from this knowledge right now and put it to use tonight. Most business courses involve a team project; why not use what you've learned to construct a collaboration IS that will make teamwork easier and can help your team achieve a better product? In this question, we will define and set up your evaluation of three sets of collaboration tools.

Three Sets of Collaboration Tools

Figure 2-25 summarizes three different sets of collaboration tools that you might use.

The *Minimal* Collaboration Tool Set

The first, the Minimal set, has the minimum possible set of tools and is shown in the second column of Figure 2-25. With this set, you should be able to collaborate with your team, though you will get little support from the software. In particular, you will need to manage concurrent access by setting up procedures and agreements to ensure that one user's work doesn't conflict with another's. Your collaboration will be with text only; you will not have access to audio or video so you cannot hear or see your collaborators. You also will not be able to view documents or whiteboards during your meeting. This set is probably close to what you're already doing.

	Three Collaboration Tool Sets		
	Minimal	Good	Comprehensive
Communication	Email; multiparty text chat	Google Hangouts	Microsoft Skype for Business
Content Sharing	Email or file server	Google Drive	SharePoint
Task Management	Word or Excel files	Google Calendar	SharePoint lists integrated with email
Nice-to-Have Features		Discussion boards, surveys, wikis, blogs, share pictures/videos from third-party tools	Built-in discussion boards, surveys, wikis, blogs, picture/video sharing
Cost	Free	Free	$10/month per user or Free
Ease of Use (time to learn)	None	1 hour	3 hours
Value to Future Business Professional	None	Limited	Great
Limitations	All text, no voice or video; no tool integration	Tools not integrated, must learn to use several products	Cost, learning curve required

Figure 2-25
Three Collaboration Tool Sets

Component	Features
Skype for Business	Multiparty text chat Audio- and videoconferencing Online content sharing Webinars with PowerPoint
SharePoint Online	Content management and control using libraries and lists Discussion forums Surveys Wikis Blogs
Exchange	Email integrated with Skype for Business and SharePoint Online
Office 2013	Concurrent editing for Word, Excel, PowerPoint, and OneNote
Hosted integration	Infrastructure built, managed, and operated by Microsoft

Figure 2-26

Office 365 Features You Need for the Comprehensive Tool Set

The *Good* Collaboration Tool Set

The second set, the Good set, shown in the third column of Figure 2-25, shows a more sophisticated set of collaboration tools. With it, you will have the ability to conduct multiparty audio and video virtual meetings, and you will also have support for concurrent access to document, spreadsheet, and presentation files. You will not be able to support surveys, wikis, and blogs and share pictures and videos with this set. If you want any of them, you will need to search the Internet to find suitable tools.

The *Comprehensive* Collaboration Tool Set

The third set of collaboration tools, the Comprehensive set, is shown in the last column of Figure 2-25. You can obtain this tool set with certain versions of Office 365. However, Microsoft continually revises the versions and what's included in them, so you'll need to investigate which version provides the features of the comprehensive tool set. Look for a version (perhaps a free trial) that includes all the products shown in Figure 2-26. If your school has adopted Office 365 for Education, then you should be able to obtain these features for free.

This set is the best of these three because it includes content management and control, workflow control, and online meetings with sharing as just described. Furthermore, this set is integrated; SharePoint alerts can send emails via the Microsoft email server Exchange when tasks or other lists and libraries change. You can click on users' names in emails or in SharePoint, and Office 365 will automatically start a Skype for Business text, audio, or video conversation with that user if he or she is currently available. All text messages you send via Skype for Business are automatically recorded and stored in your email folder.

Choosing the Set for Your Team

Which set should you choose for your team? Unless your university has already standardized on the Office 365 version you need, you will have to pay for it. You can obtain a 30-day free trial, and if your team can finish its work in that amount of time, you might choose to do so. Otherwise, your team will need to pay a minimum of $10 per month per user. So, if cost is the only factor, you can rule out the comprehensive tool set.

And even if you can afford the most comprehensive set, you may not want to use it. As noted in Figure 2-25, team members need to be willing to invest something on the order of 3 hours to begin to use the basic features. Less time, on the order of an hour, will be required to learn to use the Good tool set, and you most likely already know how to use the Minimal set.

When evaluating learning time, consider Figure 2-27. This diagram is a product **power curve**, which is a graph that shows the relationship of the power (the utility that one gains from a

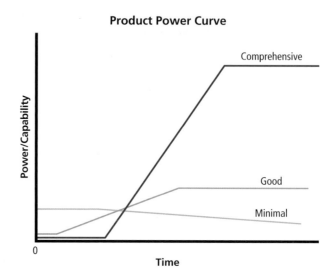

Figure 2-27
Product Power Curve

software product) as a function of the time using that product. A flat line means you are investing time without any increase in power. The ideal power curve starts at a positive value at time zero and has no flat spots.

The Minimal product set gives you some power at time zero because you already know how to use it. However, as you use it over time, your project will gain complexity and the problems of controlling concurrent access will actually cause power to decrease. The Good set has a short flat spot as you get to know it. However, your power then increases over time until you reach the most capability your team can do with it. The Comprehensive set has a longer flat spot in the beginning because it will take longer to learn. However, because it has such a rich collaboration feature set, you will be able to gain considerable collaborative power, much more so than the Good set, and the maximum capability is much greater than the Good set.

Finally, consider the next-to-last row in Figure 2-25. The Minimal set has no value to you as a future professional and contributes nothing to your professional competitive advantage. The Good set has some limited value; as you know, there are organizations that use Google Drive and Hangouts. The Comprehensive set has the potential to give you a considerable competitive advantage, particularly because SharePoint skills are highly valued in industry. You can use knowledge of it to demonstrate the currency of your knowledge in job interviews.

So, which is the right set for your team? It's up to you. See Collaboration Exercise 2 on page 110.

Don't Forget Procedures and People!

One last and very important point: Most of this chapter focuses on collaboration tools, the software component of an information system. Regarding the other four components, you need not worry about hardware, at least not for the Good or Comprehensive sets, because those tools are hosted on hardware in the cloud. The data component is up to you; it will be your content as well as your metadata for project management and for demonstrating that your team practiced iteration and feedback.

As you evaluate alternatives, however, you need to think seriously about the procedure and people components. How are team members going to use these tools? Your team needs to have agreement on tools usage, even if you do not formally document procedures. As noted, such procedures are especially necessary for controlling concurrent access in the minimal system. You need to have agreement not only on how to use these tools but also on what happens when teammates don't use these tools. What will you do, for example, if teammates persist in emailing documents instead of using Google Drive or SharePoint?

Additionally, how will your team train its members in the use of these tools? Will you divvy up responsibility for learning features and then teach the skills to one another? You will find a plethora of training materials on the Web.[8] But who will find them, learn them, and then teach the others?

Finally, does your team need to create any special jobs or roles? Do you want to identify, for example, someone to monitor your shared documents to ensure that deliverables are stored appropriately? Do you want someone identified to store minutes of meetings? Or to remove completed tasks from a task list? Or to keep the task list in agreement with current planning? Consider these and similar needs and, if needed, appoint such a person before problems develop.

Remember this example as a future business professional: In commerce, we are never selecting just software; to put that software to use as a system, we need to create all five of the IS components!

Q2-9 2026?

So, how will we collaborate in 2026? Where will the current trends take us? Clearly, free data communications and data storage will make collaboration systems cheaper and easier to use. One consequence is that by 2026 face-to-face (F2F) meetings will be rare.

F2F meetings require everyone to be in the same place at the same time, and both of those *sames* can be problematic. When employees work in different locations, bringing them together is expensive in travel cost and time. Employees standing in line in airport security or waiting in their cars in traffic are hardly productive. And bringing everyone together is unfriendly to the environment.

Even when employees work at the same location, they may have schedule conflicts or they may not work at that location at the same time. And, unless employees are providing an in-person service, such as physical training, or surgery, or construction, why do they need to work in the same location?

Furthermore, what happens when you finally do get employees together? Say you bring the top managers into the home office for training. They no sooner sit down than their cell phones ring, and off they go to the lobby to handle some raging problem back home. Twenty minutes later, they're back for another 5 minutes before their phones ring again. Meanwhile, a good portion of the managers who stayed in the meeting are texting their offices throughout the training.

In 2026, employees whose services need not be provided in person will work at home, if not full time, then at least several days a week. Nearly all corporate training will be online. Most will be asynchronous.

A mining company (that chooses to remain anonymous) in Washington State provided an international example back in 2011. The company is located in the United States, close to the Canadian border, but owns several mines in Canada. For its annual audit, the company needed the services of a Canadian-chartered accounting firm from Vancouver, British Columbia. During the audit period, the border crossing was crowded, and the auditors were billing dozens of hours of expensive time while sitting unproductively in their cars at the crossing. To reduce the audit expense, the company eliminated most of this travel by storing audit data in SharePoint libraries.

But, by 2026, why be unproductive in your car? By then, you should be able to use the full capabilities of whatever collaboration tools you choose on any mobile device. So, as long as you're not driving, you'll use your device in your car, or your golf cart, or your boat to get work done.

Further, as the example provided shows, by 2026 collaboration systems will greatly ease international business. If teams meet virtually most of the time and if it doesn't matter where team members are located, then projects can involve the best, or perhaps the most affordable, workers worldwide. Further, work can follow the sun. Workers in the United States can submit documents for feedback from team members in Asia. The Asian workers can contribute their feedback during their normal workday and pass the documents along to European team members for review during *their* normal workday. All the reviewed work will be available to the U.S. workers when their next day begins.

Business travel will be a shadow of its former self. The travel industry will reorganize for mostly recreational travel. Even conventions will become, well, virtual.

Because of these trends, now is a great time for you to learn online, asynchronous collaboration skills. It's also a good time for you, as a future knowledge worker, to prepare yourself for global opportunities . . . and global competition. And, finally, when you're buying commercial real estate, buy that hotel in Hawaii, not the one in Paramus, New Jersey (unless, of course, it has a water slide for kids, a spa, a nearby golf course, and a casino)!

Security Guide

EVOLVING SECURITY

In the past, protecting an organization's information systems and data was often equated to protecting a castle. Castles used defenses like moats, large walls, and towers to protect inhabitants from enemies lurking outside their walls. Information security professionals used the *castle model* as a metaphor to describe how security measures such as firewalls and intrusion detection systems (IDS) could be used to create a barrier between internal information systems and hackers working to compromise them. However, the castle model is no longer feasible for most organizations.

The rapid spread of smartphones, laptops, and other network-enabled devices has completely transformed organizations' network architecture. Physical boundaries are nearly gone. Organizations now have hundreds, and in some cases thousands, of devices (e.g., laptops, tablets, and phones) that are used by employees both inside and outside the company. Employees can use these devices to access corporate servers remotely and store corporate data locally.

Information security professionals now use a *city model* to describe their efforts to secure corporate information systems. In the city model, authorized users, as well as visitors, are free to roam the digital city with any device they'd like. But access to individual buildings, servers, and data is restricted. Users can access resources only if they're authorized.

But the city model isn't perfect. If users' devices are compromised, hackers could use them to access remote corporate networks or steal data directly from the device's local hard drive. Trying to secure this type of digital environment is even more challenging when you consider the diversity of devices, operating systems, and applications being used. It's a daunting task.

The loss of physical boundaries and the proliferation of devices mean that information security professionals need to be more careful about controlling access to resources. They also have to monitor user behavior much more closely than before. Not everyone in the city can be trusted.

Vetting Insiders

Employees acting maliciously *within* an organization are often viewed as one of the biggest concerns of information security professionals[9] (remember Edward Snowden and the NSA). Employers try to reduce the risk of rogue employees by conducting thorough background checks before hiring. They conduct interviews, run credit reports, and administer personality surveys. But what happens when a company

Source: Tim Robberts/The Image Bank/Getty Images

engages in a collaborative project with another firm? How can team leaders be sure their corporate partners have been evaluated with the same level of scrutiny?

The hard truth is that these types of assurances cannot be made in most cases. Granting network access to outside collaborators can pose a considerable threat. A temporary collaborator granted access to an internal network could steal corporate data more easily than a cybercriminal attacking it from the outside. In a way, it's similar to trusting your siblings. You may trust your brother or sister, but do you trust their friends?

Employee Monitoring

You may be wondering if there is anything employers can do to mitigate the risks of an insider threat or a sketchy corporate partner. Employers are increasingly monitoring Internet usage, tracking GPS information on vehicles and mobile devices, recording keystrokes, monitoring social media activity, and reviewing emails.[10] While some of these activities are illegal for employers to conduct in some states, many or all of these activities are permitted in most states. Monitoring activities can be used to provide a fairly robust picture of employee behavior. They can also be used to identify risk levels for each employee within the organization.

For example, in a recent study by Paul Taylor at Lancaster University,[11] researchers found that employees who were planning to act maliciously changed the way they interacted with their coworkers. They started to use singular pronouns (like *I, me,* or *my*) rather than plural pronouns (like *us, we,* or *our*). They became more negative, and their language became more nuanced and error-prone.

Researchers are also developing new technologies that can be used to monitor and interpret not only what users are typing or clicking on but also *how* they are typing and *how* they are moving their mouse. These measurements can then be used for any number of applications, like making sure you are not reusing corporate passwords[12] or identifying stress or anxiety while you are writing an email. By the time you enter the workforce, almost everything you do for your company has the potential to be monitored and analyzed!

QUESTIONS

1. This guide emphasizes how information security strategy has changed over the past two decades due to advancements in technology. What do these changes mean for you personally in managing and securing your own personal systems and data?

2. Take a few minutes to conduct an Internet search on insider threats. Besides some of the high-profile cases of employees stealing and selling or distributing corporate data, what other examples can you find?

3. What kinds of collaboration tools have you used to complete class assignments and projects? Could these collaboration tools pose a risk to you? How?

4. How do you feel about the trend of companies using new technologies to monitor their employees? Would you want to work for a company that uses monitoring technologies? Why or why not?

5. Monitoring digital activity is not exclusive to the workplace. Internet service providers monitor your Web traffic, and many Web sites monitor everything that you do while interacting with their site. What does this mean for users working from home? How might an ISP's monitoring activities be a threat to corporations?

Guide

EGOCENTRIC VERSUS EMPATHETIC THINKING

As stated earlier, a problem is a perceived difference between what is and what ought to be. When developing information systems, it is critical for the development team to have a common definition and understanding of the problem. This common understanding can be difficult to achieve, however.

Cognitive scientists distinguish between egocentric and empathetic thinking. Egocentric thinking centers on the self; someone who engages in egocentric thinking considers his or her view as "the real view" or "what really is." In contrast, those who engage in empathetic thinking consider their view as one possible interpretation of the situation and actively work to learn what other people are thinking.

Different experts recommend empathetic thinking for different reasons. Religious leaders say that such thinking is morally superior; psychologists say that empathetic thinking leads to richer, more fulfilling relationships. In business, empathetic thinking is recommended because it is smart. Business is a social endeavor, and those who can understand others' points of view are always more effective. Even if you do not agree with others' perspectives, you will be much better able to work with them if you understand their views.

Consider an example. Suppose you say to your MIS professor, "Professor Jones, I couldn't come to class last Monday. Did we do anything important?" Such a statement is a prime example of egocentric thinking. It takes no account of your professor's point of view and implies that your professor talked about nothing important. As a professor, it is tempting to say, "No, when I noticed you weren't there, I took out all the important material."

To engage in empathetic thinking, consider this situation from the professor's point of view. Students who do not come to class cause extra work for their professors. It does not matter how valid your reason for not attending class; you may actually have been contagious with a fever of 102. But, no matter what, your not coming to class is more work for your professor. He or she must do something extra to help you recover from the lost class time.

Using empathetic thinking, you would do all you can to minimize the impact of your absence on your professor. For example, you could say, "I couldn't come to class, but I got the class notes from Mary. I read through them, and I have a question about establishing alliances as competitive advantage....Oh, by the way, I'm sorry to trouble you with my problem."

Before we go on, let's consider a corollary to this scenario: Never, ever, send an email to your boss that says, "I couldn't come to the staff meeting on Wednesday. Did we do anything important?" Avoid this for the same reasons as those for missing class. Instead, find a way to minimize the impact of your absence on your boss.

Now, what does all of this have to do with MIS? Consider the Falcon Security team at the start of this chapter. What is the problem? Cam thinks a big problem is that Felix doesn't come to meetings. Felix thinks the team is focused on the

Source: BlueSkyImages/Fotolia

flight performance of the drones. Alexis thinks the team should determine which drone parts could be 3D-printed. Joni, once she understands what is going on, is likely to be focused on wasted employee time and the lack of consensus among team members.

Now imagine yourself in that meeting. If everyone engages in egocentric thinking, what will happen? The meeting will be argumentative and acrimonious and likely will end with nothing accomplished.

Suppose, instead, that the attendees think empathetically. In this case, Cam may make an effort to find out why Felix is missing meetings. Felix would make an effort to understand why his behavior is a problem to the team.

The team would make a concerted effort to address the different points of view, and the outcome will be much more positive—possibly a recognition that the team should be meeting virtually and asynchronously. Either way, the attendees have the same information; the difference in outcomes results from the thinking style of the attendees.

Empathetic thinking is an important skill in all business activities. Skilled negotiators always know what the other side wants; effective salespeople understand their customers' needs. Buyers who understand the problems of their vendors get better service. And students who understand the perspective of their professors get better...

 # DISCUSSION QUESTIONS

1. In your own words, explain how egocentric and empathetic thinking differ.
2. Suppose you miss a staff meeting. Using empathetic thinking, explain how you can get needed information about what took place in the meeting.
3. How does empathetic thinking relate to problem definition?
4. Suppose you and another person differ substantially on a problem definition. Suppose she says to you, "No, the real problem is that..." followed by her definition of the problem. How do you respond?
5. Again, suppose you and another person differ substantially on a problem definition. Assume you understand his definition. How can you make that fact clear?
6. Explain the following statement: "In business, empathetic thinking is smart." Do you agree?

ACTIVE REVIEW

Use this Active Review to verify that you understand the ideas and concepts that answer the chapter's study questions.

Q2-1 What are the two key characteristics of collaboration?

In your own words, explain the difference between cooperation and collaboration. Name the two key characteristics of collaboration and explain how they improve group work. Name the key component of a collaboration IS and explain why the text claims this is so. Summarize important skills for collaborators and list what you believe are the best ways to give and receive critical feedback.

Q2-2 What are three criteria for successful collaboration?

Name and describe three criteria for collaboration success. Summarize how these criteria differ between student and professional teams.

Q2-3 What are the four primary purposes of collaboration?

Name and describe four primary purposes of collaboration. Explain their relationship. Describe ways that collaboration systems can contribute to each purpose.

Q2-4 What are the requirements for a collaboration information system?

Name and describe the five components of a collaboration information system. Summarize the primary requirements for collaboration information systems and relate those requirements to the need for iteration and feedback as well as the three criteria for successful collaboration.

Q2-5 How can you use collaboration tools to improve team communication?

Explain why communication is important to collaboration. Define *synchronous* and *asynchronous communication* and explain when each is used. Name two collaboration tools that can be used to help set up synchronous meetings. Describe collaboration tools that can be used for face-to-face meetings. Describe tools that can be used for virtual, synchronous meetings. Describe tools that can be used for virtual, asynchronous meetings.

Q2-6 How can you use collaboration tools to manage shared content?

Summarize alternatives for processing Office documents on the desktop as well as over the Internet. Describe two ways that content is shared with no control and explain the problems that can occur. Explain the difference between version management and version control. Describe how user accounts, passwords, and libraries are used to control user activity. Explain how check-in/checkout works. Describe workflows and give an example.

Q2-7 How can you use collaboration tools to manage tasks?

Explain why managing tasks is important to team progress. Demonstrate how a task should be described. List the minimal content of a task list. Summarize the advantages and disadvantages of using a spreadsheet and Microsoft SharePoint for managing tasks.

Q2-8 Which collaboration IS is right for your team?

Describe the three collaboration tool sets described and indicate how each meets the minimum requirements for collaboration. Explain the differences among them. Summarize the criteria for choosing the right set for your team. Explain the meaning of the power curve and discuss the power curve for each of the three alternatives described.

Q2-9 2026?

Describe the impact that free data storage and data communications have on collaboration systems. Explain why F2F meetings are expensive in both cost and time. Explain why meetings such as F2F training sessions can be ineffective. Summarize the ways collaboration systems reduce the costs and difficulties of international business. Explain how collaboration systems are changing the scope of workers with whom you will compete. Describe consequences of all this to the travel industry. If you disagree with any of the conclusions in this 2026, explain how and why.

Using Your Knowledge with Falcon Security

Reread the Falcon Security scenario at the start of this chapter. Using the knowledge you've gained from this chapter, explain how this team could use collaboration tools to be more effective. Describe how such tools can solve Felix's problems as well as result in better communication and higher-quality results for the team.

KEY TERMS AND CONCEPTS

MyMISLab™

To complete the problems with the ⭐, go to EOC Discussion Questions in the MyLab.

USING YOUR KNOWLEDGE

⭐ **2-1.** Using your past experience of working in teams, do you think, your team understood the difference between cooperation and collaboration? If it was collaborative, then what was the extent of its success? To what extent did the team grow in its efficiency and for how long have they worked in collaboration? Was the team's experience satisfactory?

⭐ **2-2.** Using the past experience of decision making in teams, give an example illustrating the levels of decisions made by the team? Was the decision making process in the team structured or unstructured? What extent of collaboration was required for that particular decision making?

⭐ **2-3.** The success of a business school is dependent on the constant evaluation of its teaching approach, which also helps to upgrade its syllabus. Although these decisions are taken by senior management, there is always active involvement of teachers and students in the form of their feedback. Take the opinion of your teachers and fellow students on the extent of collaboration in changing course curriculum or teaching pedagogy in your business school. Try to find out the extent of collaboration (between senior management and teachers) and the kind of decisions (operational, managerial, and strategic decisions) taken by the senior management. Is more preference given to collaboration in one type of decision making? If so, give reasons for the same. Find out from your teachers on whether there is any application of collaborative information system. Based on knowledge gained from this chapter, suggest how you could improve the collaborative decision making process.

2-4. Having the read the difference between cooperation and collaboration in this chapter, choose your favorite team sport, like rugby, cricket or football, and comment on whether the players of the selected sporting team are cooperating with each other or collaborating with each other. Justify your answer by taking into the account the roles and responsibility of each player in the team.

COLLABORATION EXERCISE 2

In this exercise, you will first build a collaboration IS and then use that IS to answer four questions in a collaborative fashion. You might want to read the four questions (in item 2-8 below) before you build your IS.

Until you answer question 2-5, you'll have to make do with email or face-to-face meeting. Once you've answered that question, use your communication method to answer question 2-6. Once you've answered question 2-6, use your communication and your content-sharing method to answer question 2-7. Then use the full IS to answer question 2-8.

2-5. Build a communication method:
   a. Meet with your team and decide how you want to meet in the future. Use Figure 2-8 as a guide.
   b. From the discussion in a, list the requirements for your communication system.
   c. Select and implement a communication tool. It could be Skype, Google Hangouts, or Skype for Business.
   d. Write procedures for the team to use when utilizing your new communication tool.

2-6. For this collaborative exercise, make a group of 5 students. The group is a given a task to make an assignment on "Knowledge of MIS enhances the job prospects of MBA students".
   a. Complete this assignment by using the cooperation method.
   b. Applying collaboration, complete the same assignment.
   c. Find out the difference between the two approaches and the results of the assignments.
   d. If the team decides to choose a collaboration tool to share the content among the group members, which tool will you select and why?

2-7. Make a group of 10 members and divide the group into two subgroups of 5 members each.
   a. Fix on a topic on which the team members want to communicate. Members of both subgroups should decide on one topic.
   b. The first subgroup should choose single location synchronous communication tool to share information among themselves. Give reasons for selecting a particular single location synchronous communication tool.

   c. The second subgroup should choose multi locations synchronous communication tool to share information among themselves. Give reasons for selecting a particular multi- locations synchronous communication tool.
   d. In the end, compile the contents of two subgroups using the asynchronous communication tool. Write down the procedure on how these two subgroups will communicate by selecting the appropriate asynchronous communication tool.

2-8. Using your new collaboration information system, answer the following questions:
   a. What is collaboration? Reread Q2-1 in this chapter, but do not confine yourselves to that discussion. Consider your own experience working in collaborative teams, and search the Web to identify other ideas about collaboration. Dave Pollard, one of the authors of the survey on which Figure 2-1 is based, is a font of ideas on collaboration.
   b. What characteristics make for an effective team member? Review the survey of effective collaboration skills in Figure 2-1 and the guidelines for giving and receiving critical feedback, and discuss them as a group. Do you agree with them? What skills or feedback techniques would you add to this list? What conclusions can you, as a team, take from this survey? Would you change the rankings in Figure 2-1?
   c. What would you do with an ineffective team member? First, define an ineffective team member. Specify five or so characteristics of an ineffective team member. If your group has such a member, what action do you, as a group, believe should be taken?
   d. How do you know if you are collaborating well? When working with a group, how do you know whether you are working well or poorly? Specify five or so characteristics that indicate collaborative success. How can you measure those characteristics?
   e. Briefly describe the components of your new collaboration IS.
   f. Describe what your team likes and doesn't like about using your new collaboration system.

CASE STUDY 2

Eating Our Own Dog Food

Dogfooding is the process of using a product or idea that you develop or promote. The term arose in the 1980s in the software industry when someone observed that the company wasn't using the product it developed. Or "they weren't eating their own dog food." Wikipedia attributes the term to Brian Val-

entine, test manager for Microsoft LAN Manager in 1988, but I recall using the term before that date. Whatever its origin, if, of their own accord, employees choose to dogfood their own product or idea, many believe that product or idea is likely to succeed.

You may be asking, "So what?" Well, this text was developed by a collaborative team, using Office 365 Professional and many of the techniques described in this chapter. We dogfooded the ideas and products in this chapter.

Figure 2-28 shows a diagram of the process that transforms a draft chapter in Word, PowerPoint, and PNG image format into PDF pages. You will learn more about process diagrams like this in Chapter 10. For now, just realize that each column represents the activities taken by a role, which in this case is a particular person. The process starts with the thin-lined circle in the top left and ends with the thick-lined circle near the bottom right. The dashed lines represent the flow of data from one activity to another.

As shown in Figure 2-28, the authors work closely with the developmental editor, who ensures that the text is complete and complies with the market requirements, as specified by the acquisitions editor. We need not delve into this process in detail here; just observe that many different versions of chapter text and chapter art are created as people playing the various roles edit and approve and adjust edits.

Face-to-face meetings are impossible because the people fulfilling the roles in Figure 2-28 live in different geographic locations. In the past, the developmental process was conducted using the phone, email, and a file server. As you can imagine, considerable confusion can ensue with the hundreds of documents, art exhibits, and multiple reviewed copies of each.

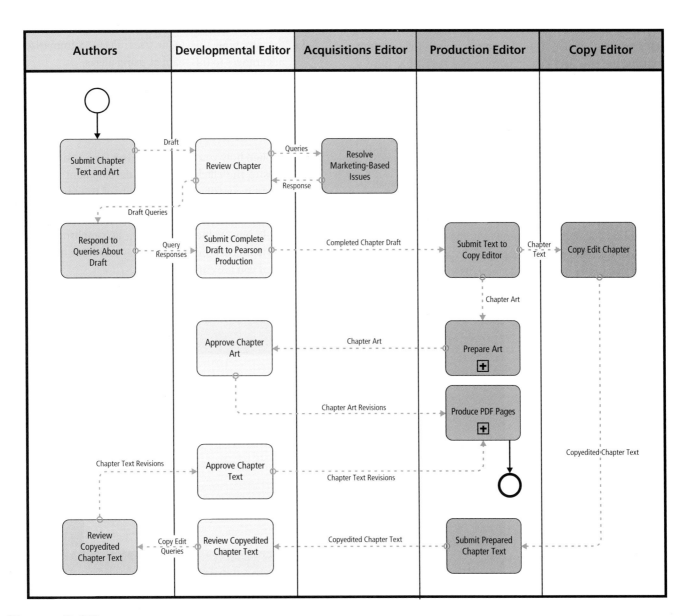

Figure 2-28
Chapter Development Process

Furthermore, task requests delivered via email are easily lost. Dropped tasks and incorrect versions of documents and art are not common, but they do occur.

When we decided to begin publishing a new edition every year, we knew we needed to find some way of increasing our productivity. Consequently, our development team decided to eat its own dog food and use Office 365 Professional. During this process, the author, the developmental editor Laura Town, and the production editors met frequently using Google Hangouts (we couldn't use Skype for Business because Pearson would not allow its employees to install it). Figure 2-29 shows a typical hangout. Notice that the three actors in this process are sharing a common whiteboard. Each can write or draw on that whiteboard. At the end of the meeting, the whiteboards were saved and placed on the team's SharePoint site to be used as minutes of the meeting.

Figure 2-30 shows the team's top-level SharePoint site. The **Quick Launch** (left-side vertical menu) has links to important content on the site. The center portion has tasks that have a value other than "Completed" for Status.

The team set up alerts so that when new tasks were created in the Tasks list, SharePoint would send an email to the person who had been assigned that task. As shown in Figure 2-31, emails were also sent to a task's creator when that task status was changed by others.

All documents and figures were stored and managed in SharePoint libraries. Figure 2-32 shows the contents of the Draft Documents Chapter 2 library at the time this chapter was written. By storing documents in SharePoint, the team took advantage of library version tracking. Figure 2-33 shows a portion of the version history of one of the documents in this library.

When it is completed, Laura will need to review the final chapter version, so a task should be created asking her to do so. That new task will spawn an email to her like the email in Figure 2-31. I will create that task just as soon as I finish this sentence! That's dogfooding!

QUESTIONS

2-9. In your own words, define *dogfooding*. Do you think dogfooding is likely to predict product success? Why or why not? When would dogfooding not predict product success?

2-10. Explain how this team uses the shared whiteboard to generate minutes. What are the advantages of this technique?

2-11. Explain how this team uses alerts. Summarize the advantages to this team of using alerts.

2-12. Explain why this team does not use Skype for Business.

2-13. Summarize the advantages to this team of using Share-Point.

2-14. Explain how you think Office 365 Professional contributes to the efficiency of the development team. How might it contribute to the quality of this text?

2-15. Which aspects of Office 365 Professional described here could have value to you when accomplishing student team projects? Explain why they add value compared to what you are currently doing.

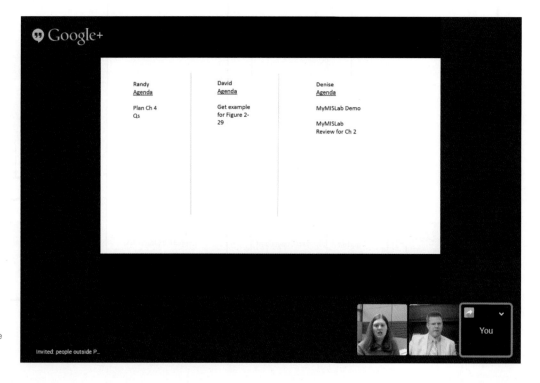

Figure 2-29
Google Hangout Group Conversation
Source: Google and the Google logo are registered trademarks of Google Inc., Used with permission.

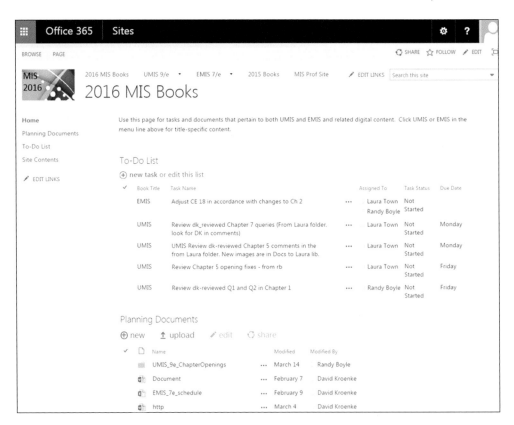

Figure 2-30
Using MIS 9th Edition SharePoint Development Site
Source: © Access 2013, Microsoft Corporation

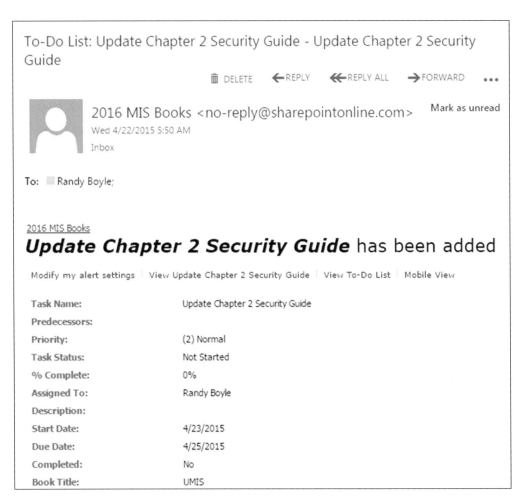

Figure 2-31
Example Email from SharePoint
Source: © Access 2013, Microsoft Corporation

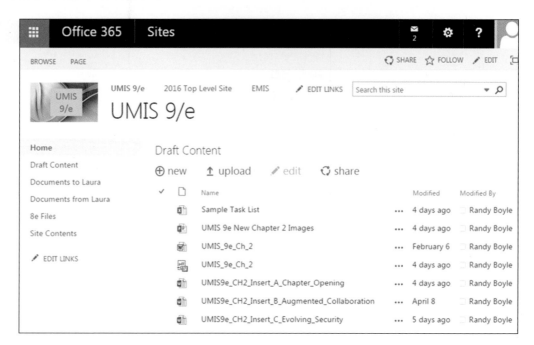

Figure 2-32
First Draft Document Library Contents
Source: © Access 2013, Microsoft Corporation

Version History

Delete All Versions

No. ↓	Modified	Modified By	Size	Comments
7.0	4/18/2015 7:49 AM	Randy Boyle	1.7 MB	
6.0	4/18/2015 7:00 AM	Randy Boyle	1.5 MB	
5.0	4/18/2015 6:25 AM	Randy Boyle	1008.7 KB	
4.0	4/18/2015 5:57 AM	Randy Boyle	824.8 KB	
3.0	4/18/2015 4:53 AM	Randy Boyle	199.7 KB	
2.0	4/18/2015 3:52 AM	Randy Boyle	85 KB	
1.0	4/18/2015 1:32 AM	Randy Boyle	97.4 KB	
	Title	Figure 4-???		

Figure 2-33
Version History
Source: © Access 2013, Microsoft Corporation

MyMISLab™

Go to the Assignments section of your MyLab to complete these writing exercises.

2-16. Reread about 2026 in Q2-9. Do you agree with the conclusions? Why or why not? If F2F meetings become rare, what additional impacts do you see on the travel industry? In light of this change, describe travel industry investments that make sense and those that do not. What are promising investments in training? What are promising investments in other industries?

2-17. Groupware is a software used to support multiple users in remote locations working on the same set of tasks. It is also known as collaborative software. The major benefit is that the groupware has a mechanism by which the tasks can be coordinated.

The major component of groupware is email. This is used to update members of the team, elicit responses and send out alerts. Find out more about groupware and then answer the following questions:

a. What do the emails have live links to and what is the other main form of communication between team members?

b. Groupware can be described as either process or information centered, what does this mean?

c. What are the drawbacks of collaborative software that relies on email?

ENDNOTES

1. Mitch Ditkoff, Tim Moore, Carolyn Allen, and Dave Pollard, "The Ideal Collaborative Team," *Idea Champions*, accessed April 26, 2014, *www.ideachampions.com/downloads/collaborationresults.pdf.*

2. J. Richard Hackman, *Leading Teams: Setting the Stage for Great Performances* (Boston: Harvard Business Press, 2002).

3. Wouter van Diggelen, *Changing Face-to-Face Communication: Collaborative Tools to Support Small-Group Discussions in the Classroom* (Groningen: University of Groningen, 2011).

4. Warning: The data in this figure is changing rapidly. The features and functions of both Web applications and cloud drives may have been extended from what is described here. Check the vendor's documentation for new capabilities.

5. Carey Cole, Steve Fox, and David Kroenke, *SharePoint for Students* (Upper Saddle River, NJ: Pearson Education, 2012), pp. 116–129.

6. Jessi Hempel, "Project HoloLens: Our Exclusive Hands-On with Microsoft's Holographic Goggles," *Wired.com*, January 21, 2015, accessed April 5, 2015, *www.wired.com/2015/01/microsoft-hands-on.*

7. Matt Rosoff, "I Just Tried Microsoft's Remarkable Holographic Headset—Here's What It's Like," *BusinessInsider.com*, January 21, 2015, accessed April 5, 2015, *www.businessinsider.com/microsoft-hololens-hands-on-2015-1.*

8. See also David Kroenke and Donald Nilson, *Office 365 in Business* (Indianapolis, IN: John Wiley & Sons, 2011).

9. Grant Hatchimonji, "Report Indicates Insider Threats Leading Cause of Data Breaches in Last 12 Months," *CSO Online*, October 8, 2013, accessed April 13, 2015, *www.csoonline.com/article/2134056/network-security/report-indicates-insider-threats-leading-cause-of-data-breaches-in-last-12-months.html.*

10. Donna Ballman, "10 New (and Legal) Ways Your Employer is Spying on You," *AOL Jobs*, September 29, 2013, accessed April 13, 2015, *http://jobs.aol.com/articles/2013/09/29/new-ways-employer-spy.*

11. Paul Taylor, "Employers Can Predict Rogue Behavior Using Your Emails," *The Conversation*, February 18, 2014, accessed April 14, 2015, *https://theconversation.com/employers-can-predict-rogue-behaviour-using-your-emails-23338.*

12. J. L. Jenkins, M. Grimes, J. G. Proudfoot, and P. B. Lowry, "Improving Password Cyber-security Through Inexpensive and Minimally Invasive Means: Detecting and Deterring Password Reuse Through Keystroke-Dynamics Monitoring and Just-in-Time Fear Appeals. *Information Technology for Development* 20, no. 2 (2014), 196–213.

Strategy and
Information Systems

"Hey Cam, let's get some lunch. I need to hear more about the new LiDAR imaging we're going to start offering," says a well-dressed Alexis as she pops into the development lab where Cam is closely watching an employee testing a large quadcopter.

"Yeah, sure, I could use the break."

"What's that? Are you testing a new quad?"

"Um, well…yes. Mateo wanted to see if we could 3D-print our own drones. We're testing a new prototype we just finished building. It might be a lot cheaper than buying them. But I've never *built* a drone before."

"Wow. So, we've decided to get into the drone-making business?"

Cam motions to Alexis to move out into the hall so they can talk privately.

"Honestly, I hope not. But we'll see how this turns out. We're still trying to figure out if it will save us enough money to make it worth our while."

"Well, better you than me. They've got the right woman for the job!" Alexis smiles and tries to keep the conversation light.

"Yeah, well, this project is the least of my worries." Cam rolls her eyes and looks sincerely frustrated.

"What do you mean?"

"Who are we?"

"What do you mean?" Alexis is a little taken aback.

"Well, as a company, who are we? We've always been known as a company that provides security monitoring, and we've got some big contracts. I get that. But...there's a lot of money we could be making in agricultural survey, industrial inspection, real estate videos, and wedding videos. I think we're really missing out."

"Have you talked with Mateo about this?"

"Yes, he agreed that these are all good ideas, but he wants to stay focused on big security contracts. He's even talking about contracting with law enforcement agencies, search and rescue, and the federal government."

"And...what's the downside?" Alexis asks. "It sounds like if I could close a few big sales, we'd be sittin' pretty. From the sales side, I'd be doing less work for more money."

"Yeah, but that's a big 'if.' What if we can't sign them? What if the funding dries up? What if the public doesn't like the idea of the U.S. federal government using drones to video its citizens?"

"I don't know. If the money's as good as Mateo thinks it is, it might be worth a shot."

"Yes, but we could be spending our time and money developing accounts that we already know are profitable and will be for a long time. People are always getting married. It just seems like a no-brainer to think of Falcon Security as more than just a 'security' company. There's so much money on the table." Cam is clearly frustrated and shakes her head.

"Cam, I completely agree. The side projects we've done have been profitable. There's no arguing that."

"Well?"

"Well, it comes down to focus. We can't be everything to everybody. Providing long-term security monitoring for a chemical company is very different from doing a weekend wedding photo shoot."

"But what about all the money we could be making right now? If we don't earn it, somebody else will."

Alexis starts to smile and says, "Hey, let's grab Joni on the way out to lunch. She's the one who really needs to hear this. You two can talk strategy while I get some of those tasty fish tacos!"

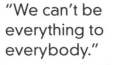

"We can't be everything to everybody."

Image source: rommma/Fotolia

STUDY QUESTIONS

Q3-1 How does organizational strategy determine information systems structure?

Q3-2 What five forces determine industry structure?

Q3-3 How does analysis of industry structure determine competitive strategy?

Q3-4 How does competitive strategy determine value chain structure?

Q3-5 How do business processes generate value?

Q3-6 How does competitive strategy determine business processes and the structure of information systems?

Q3-7 How do information systems provide competitive advantages?

Q3-8 2026?

CHAPTER PREVIEW

Recall from Chapter 1 that MIS is the development and use of information systems that enables organizations to achieve their strategies. In Chapter 2, you learned how information systems can help people collaborate. This chapter focuses on how information systems support competitive strategy and how IS can create competitive advantages. As you will learn in your organizational behavior classes, a body of knowledge exists to help organizations analyze their industry, select a competitive strategy, and develop business processes. In the first part of this chapter, we will survey that knowledge and show how to use it, via several steps, to structure information systems. Then, toward the end of the chapter, we will discuss how companies use information systems to gain a competitive advantage.

Falcon Security provides a good example. Its strategy has been to differentiate itself by providing security surveillance services using drones. It has systems and processes to do that. But, as Cam states, what if the company can't secure additional security contracts? How will the company grow if it doesn't get them? Even if it did get those new contracts, does it have the systems and process to handle them?

Q3-1 How Does Organizational Strategy Determine Information Systems Structure?

According to the definition of MIS, information systems exist to help organizations achieve their strategies. As you will learn in your business strategy class, an organization's goals and objectives are determined by its *competitive strategy*. Thus, ultimately, competitive strategy determines the structure, features, and functions of every information system.

Figure 3-1 summarizes this situation. In short, organizations examine the structure of their industry and determine a competitive strategy. That strategy determines value chains, which, in turn, determine business processes. The structure of business processes determines the design of supporting information systems.

Michael Porter, one of the key researchers and thinkers in competitive analysis, developed three different models that can help you understand the elements of Figure 3-1. We begin with his five forces model.

Figure 3-1
Organizational Strategy
Determines Information Systems

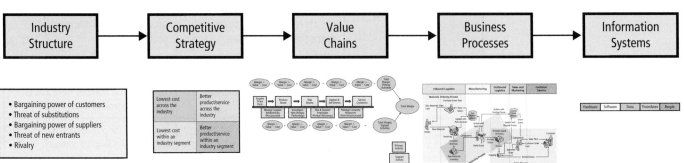

Q3-2 What Five Forces Determine Industry Structure?

Organizational strategy begins with an assessment of the fundamental characteristics and structure of an industry. One model used to assess an industry structure is Porter's **five forces model**,[1] summarized in Figure 3-2. According to this model, five competitive forces determine industry profitability: bargaining power of customers, threat of substitutions, bargaining power of suppliers, threat of new entrants, and rivalry among existing firms. The intensity of each of the five forces determines the characteristics of the industry, how profitable it is, and how sustainable that profitability will be.

To understand this model, consider the strong and weak examples for each of the forces in Figure 3-3. A good check on your understanding is to see if you can think of different forces of each category in Figure 3-3. Also, take a particular industry—say, auto repair—and consider how these five forces determine the competitive landscape of that industry.

In the opening vignette of this chapter, Cam is concerned that focusing only on physical security may place Falcon Security at a competitive disadvantage. She thinks the company could expand into agricultural survey, industrial inspection, real estate videos, and wedding videos. She's also worried about being financially dependent on a few large industrial accounts. Figure 3-4 shows an analysis of the competitive landscape Falcon Security faces.

The large industrial accounts that Falcon Security serves could demand more services or lower prices because they account for a large percentage of Falcon Security's revenue. The threat of substitutions, like customers choosing to install wireless digital Web cameras, is somewhat strong. But these substitutions may not be viable options for some of the industrial clients due to the lack of internal technical expertise or physical distance limitations. A new entrant, like Amazon starting to offer surveillance service using its delivery drones, could be a substantial threat. But Falcon Security could respond to this by offering additional services, like real-time 3D mapping. Or it could enter new markets like agricultural survey and industrial inspection.

Figure 3-2

Porter's Five Forces Model of Industry Structure

Source: Based on Michael E. Porter, *Competitive Advantage: Creating and Sustaining Superior Performance* (The Free Press, a Division of Simon & Schuster Adult Publishing Group). Copyright © 1985, 1998 by Michael E. Porter.

- Bargaining power of customers
- Threat of substitutions
- Bargaining power of suppliers
- Threat of new entrants
- Rivalry

Force	Example of Strong Force	Example of Weak Force
Bargaining power of customers	Toyota's purchase of auto paint (because Toyota is a huge customer that will purchase paint in large volume)	Your power over the procedures and policies of your university
Threat of substitutions	Frequent traveler's choice of auto rental	Patients using the only drug effective for their type of cancer
Bargaining power of suppliers	New car dealers (because they control what the "true price" of a vehicle is and the customer cannot reliably verify the accuracy of that price)	Grain farmers in a surplus year (an oversupply makes the product less valuable and less profitable)
Threat of new entrants	Corner latte stand (because it is an easy business to replicate)	Professional football team (because the number of teams is tightly controlled by the NFL)
Rivalry	Used car dealers (because there are many to choose from)	Google or Bing (expensive to develop and market a search engine)

Figure 3-3

Examples of Five Forces

Force	Falcon Security Example	Force Strength	Falcon Security's Response
Bargaining power of customers	A large account wants more services at a lower price	Strong	Lower prices or diversify into other markets
Threat of substitutions	Replace drones with wireless IP Web cameras	Medium	Offer differentiating services, like LiDAR, that cameras can't provide
Bargaining power of suppliers	We're increasing the cost of the drones we sell	Weak	We'll make our own drones
Threat of new entrants	Amazon begins offering package delivery and surveillance via drones	Medium	Offer differentiating services and enter other markets
Rivalry	A new drone company expands its operations into the state	Weak	Offer additional features like direct streaming video to the customer

Figure 3-4
Five Forces at Falcon Security

The other forces are not as worrisome to Falcon Security. The bargaining power of drone suppliers is weak because there are lots of drone manufacturers to choose from. And it always has the option of 3D printing its own drones. The threat from rivals isn't strong because Falcon Security has developed a self-charging drone platform and an integrated video processing system that wouldn't be easy for rivals to replicate.

Like Falcon Security, organizations examine these five forces and determine how they intend to respond to them. That examination leads to competitive strategy.

Q3-3 How Does Analysis of Industry Structure Determine Competitive Strategy?

See the Ethics Guide on pages 122–123 to learn how a change in strategy can greatly affect a company's culture.

An organization responds to the structure of its industry by choosing a **competitive strategy**. Porter followed his five forces model with the model of four competitive strategies, shown in Figure 3-5.[2] According to Porter, firms engage in one of these four strategies. An organization can focus on being the cost leader, or it can focus on differentiating its products or services from those of the competition. Further, the organization can employ the cost or differentiation strategy across an industry, or it can focus its strategy on a particular industry segment.

Consider the car rental industry, for example. According to the first column of Figure 3-5, a car rental company can strive to provide the lowest-cost car rentals across the industry, or it can seek to provide the lowest-cost car rentals to an industry segment—say, U.S. domestic business travelers.

As shown in the second column, a car rental company can seek to differentiate its products from the competition. It can do so in various ways—for example, by providing a wide range of high-quality cars, by providing the best reservation system, by having the cleanest cars or the fastest check-in, or by some other means. The company can strive to provide product differentiation across the industry or within particular segments of the industry, such as U.S. domestic business travelers.

	Cost	**Differentiation**
Industry-wide	Lowest cost across the industry	Better product/service across the industry
Focus	Lowest cost within an industry segment	Better product/service within an industry segment

Figure 3-5
Porter's Four Competitive Strategies

Ethics Guide

YIKES! BIKES

Suppose you are an operations manager for Yikes! Bikes, a manufacturer of high-end mountain bicycles. Yikes! has been in business more than 25 years and has an annual revenue of $35M. The founder and sole owner recently sold the business to an investment group, Major Capital. You know nothing about the sale until your boss introduces you to Andrea Parks, a partner at Major Capital, who is in charge of the acquisition. Parks explains to you that Yikes! has been sold to Major Capital and that she will be the temporary general manager. She explains that the new owners see great potential in you, and they want to enlist your cooperation during the transition. She hints that if your potential is what she thinks it is, you will be made general manager of Yikes!

Parks explains that the new owners decided there are too many players in the high-end mountain bike business, and they plan to change the competitive strategy of Yikes! from high-end differentiation to lowest-cost vendor. Accordingly, they will eliminate local manufacturing, fire most of the manufacturing department, and import bikes from China. Further, Major Capital sees a need to reduce expenses and plans a 10 percent across-the-board staff reduction and a cut of two-thirds of the customer support department. The new bikes will be of lesser quality than current Yikes! bikes, but the price will be substantially less. The new ownership group believes it will take a few years for the market to realize that Yikes! bikes are not the same quality as they were. Finally, Parks asks you to attend an all-employee meeting with the founder and her.

At the meeting, the founder explains that, due to his age and personal situation, he decided to sell Yikes! to Major Capital and that starting today Andrea Parks is the general manager. He thanks the employees for their many years of service, wishes them well, and leaves the building. Parks introduces herself to the employees and states that Major Capital is very excited to own such a great company

with a strong, quality brand. She says she will take a few weeks to orient herself to the business and its environment and plans no major changes to the company.

You are reeling from all this news when Parks calls you into her office and explains that she needs you to prepare two reports. In one, she wants a list of all the employees in the manufacturing department, sorted by their salary (or wage for hourly employees). She explains that she intends to cut the most costly employees first. "I don't want to be inflexible about this, though," she says. "If there is someone whom you think we should keep, let me know, and we can talk about it."

She also wants a list of the employees in the customer support department, sorted by the average amount of time each support rep spends with customers. She explains, "I'm not so concerned with payroll expense in customer support. It's not how much we're paying someone, it's how much time they're wasting with customers. We're going to have a bare-bones support department, and we want to get rid of the gabby chatters first."

You are, understandably, shocked and surprised...not only at the speed with which the transition has occurred, but also because you don't think the founder would do this to the employees. You call him at home and tell him what is going on.

"Look," he explains, "when I sold the company, I asked them to be sure to take care of the employees. They said they would. I'll call Andrea, but there's really nothing I can do at this point; they own the show."

In a black mood of depression, you realize you don't want to work for Yikes! anymore, but your wife is 6 months pregnant with your first child. You need medical insurance for her at least until the baby is born. But what miserable tasks are you going to be asked to do before then? And you suspect that if you balk at any task, Parks won't hesitate to fire you, too.

As you leave that night, you run into Lori, the most popular customer support representative and one of your favorite employees. "Hey," Lori asks you, "what did you think of that meeting? Do you believe Andrea? Do you think they'll let us continue to make great bikes?"

 DISCUSSION QUESTIONS

1. In your opinion, did the new owners take any illegal action? Is there evidence of a crime in this scenario?

2. Consider the ethics of the statement that Parks made to all of the employees. Using both the categorical imperative (pages 56–57) and utilitarianism (pages 92–93), assess the ethics of that statement. Were you to question her about the ethics of her statement, how do you think she would justify herself?

3. What do you think Parks will tell the founder if he calls as a result of your conversation with him? Does he have any legal recourse? Is Major Capital's behavior toward him unethical? Why or why not?

4. Parks is going to use data to perform staff cuts. What do you think about her criteria? Ethically, should she consider other factors, such as number of years of service, past employee reviews, or other criteria?

5. How do you respond to Lori? What are the consequences if you tell her what you know? What are the consequences of lying to her? What are the consequences of saying something noncommittal? Consider both the categorical imperative and utilitarianism perspectives in your response.

6. If you actually were in this situation, would you leave the company? Why or why not?

7. In business school, we talk of principles like competitive strategy as interesting academic topics. But, as you can see from the Yikes! case, competitive strategy decisions have human consequences. How do you plan to resolve conflicts between human needs and tough business decisions?

8. How do you define *job security*?

According to Porter, to be effective, the organization's goals, objectives, culture, and activities must be consistent with the organization's strategy. To those in the MIS field, this means that all information systems in the organization must reflect and facilitate the organization's competitive strategy.

Q3-4 How Does Competitive Strategy Determine Value Chain Structure?

Organizations analyze the structure of their industry, and, using that analysis, they formulate a competitive strategy. They then need to organize and structure the organization to implement that strategy. If, for example, the competitive strategy is to be *cost leader*, then business activities need to be developed to provide essential functions at the lowest possible cost.

A business that selects a *differentiation* strategy would not necessarily structure itself around least-cost activities. Instead, such a business might choose to develop more costly processes, but it would do so only if those processes provided benefits that outweighed their costs. Joni at Falcon Security knows that buying the best commercial drones is expensive, and she judges the costs worthwhile. She may find that 3D printing Falcon's own custom drones to be worthwhile, too.

Porter defined **value** as the amount of money that a customer is willing to pay for a resource, product, or service. The difference between the value that an activity generates and the cost of the activity is called the **margin**. A business with a differentiation strategy will add cost to an activity only as long as the activity has a positive margin.

A **value chain** is a network of value-creating activities. That generic chain consists of five **primary activities** and four **support activities**.

Primary Activities in the Value Chain

To understand the essence of the value chain, consider one of Falcon Security's suppliers, a medium-sized drone manufacturer (see Figure 3-6). First, the manufacturer acquires raw materials using the inbound logistics activity. This activity concerns the receiving and handling of raw materials and other inputs. The accumulation of those materials adds value in the sense that even a pile of unassembled parts is worth something to some customer. A collection of the parts needed to build a

Figure 3-6
Drone Manufacturer's Value Chain

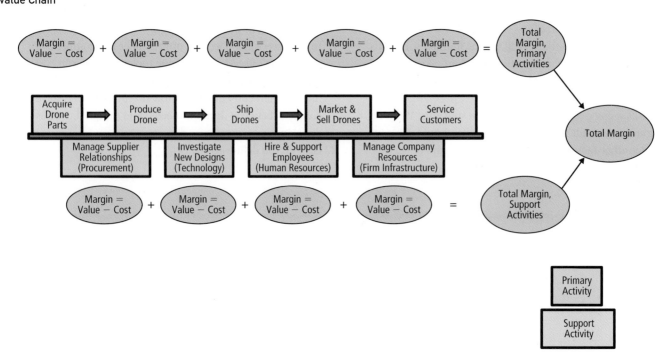

Primary Activity	Description
Inbound Logistics	Receiving, storing, and disseminating inputs to the products
Operations/Manufacturing	Transforming inputs into the final products
Outbound Logistics	Collecting, storing, and physically distributing the products to buyers
Sales and Marketing	Inducing buyers to purchase the products and providing a means for them to do so
Customer Service	Assisting customers' use of the products and thus maintaining and enhancing the products' value

Figure 3-7

Task Descriptions for Primary Activities of the Value Chain

Source: Based on Michael E. Porter, *Competitive Advantage: Creating and Sustaining Superior Performance* (The Free Press, a Division of Simon & Schuster Adult Publishing Group). Copyright © 1985, 1998 by Michael E. Porter.

drone is worth more than an empty space on a shelf. The value is not only the parts themselves, but also the time required to contact vendors for those parts, to maintain business relationships with those vendors, to order the parts, to receive the shipment, and so forth.

In the operations activity, the drone maker transforms raw materials into a finished drone, a process that adds more value. Next, the company uses the outbound logistics activity to deliver the finished drone to a customer. Of course, there is no customer to send the drone to without the marketing and sales value activity. Finally, the service activity provides customer support to the drone users.

Each stage of this generic chain accumulates costs and adds value to the product. The net result is the total margin of the chain, which is the difference between the total value added and the total costs incurred. Figure 3-7 summarizes the primary activities of the value chain.

Support Activities in the Value Chain

The support activities in the generic value chain contribute indirectly to the production, sale, and service of the product. They include procurement, which consists of the processes of finding vendors, setting up contractual arrangements, and negotiating prices. (This differs from inbound logistics, which is concerned with ordering and receiving in accordance with agreements set up by procurement.)

Porter defined technology broadly. It includes research and development, but it also includes other activities within the firm for developing new techniques, methods, and procedures. He defined human resources as recruiting, compensation, evaluation, and training of full-time and part-time employees. Finally, firm infrastructure includes general management, finance, accounting, legal, and government affairs.

Supporting functions add value, albeit indirectly, and they also have costs. Hence, as shown in Figure 3-6, supporting activities contribute to a margin. In the case of supporting activities, it would be difficult to calculate the margin because the specific value added of, say, the manufacturer's lobbyists in Washington, D.C., is difficult to know. But there is a value added, there are costs, and there is a margin—even if it is only in concept.

Value Chain Linkages

Porter's model of business activities includes **linkages**, which are interactions across value activities. For example, manufacturing systems use linkages to reduce inventory costs. Such a system uses sales forecasts to plan production; it then uses the production plan to determine raw material needs and then uses the material needs to schedule purchases. The end result is just-in-time inventory, which reduces inventory sizes and costs.

By describing value chains and their linkages, Porter recognized a movement to create integrated, cross-departmental business systems. Over time, Porter's work led to the creation of a new discipline called business process design. The central idea is that organizations should not automate or improve existing functional systems. Rather, they should create new, more efficient business processes that integrate the activities of all departments involved in a value chain. You will see an example of a linkage in the next section.

Value chain analysis has a direct application to manufacturing businesses like the drone manufacturer. However, value chains also exist in service-oriented companies such as medical clinics. The difference is that most of the value in a service company is generated by the operations, marketing and sales, and service activities. Inbound and outbound logistics are not typically as important.

Q3-5 How Do Business Processes Generate Value?

A **business process** is a network of activities that generate value by transforming inputs into outputs. The **cost** of the business process is the cost of the inputs plus the cost of the activities. The margin of the business process is the value of the outputs minus the cost.

A business process is a network of activities. Each **activity** is a business function that receives inputs and produces outputs. An activity can be performed by a human, by a computer system, or by both. The inputs and outputs can be physical, like drone parts, or they can be data, such as a purchase order. A **repository** is a collection of something; a database is a repository of data, and a raw material repository is an inventory of raw materials. We will refine and extend these definitions in Chapter 7 and again in Chapter 12, but these basic terms will get us started.

Consider the three business processes for a drone manufacturer shown in Figure 3-8. The materials ordering process transforms cash[3] into a raw materials inventory. The manufacturing process transforms raw materials into finished goods. The sales process transforms finished goods into cash. Notice that the business processes span the value chain activities. The sales process involves sales and marketing as well as outbound logistics activities, as you would expect.

Figure 3-8
Three Examples of Business Processes

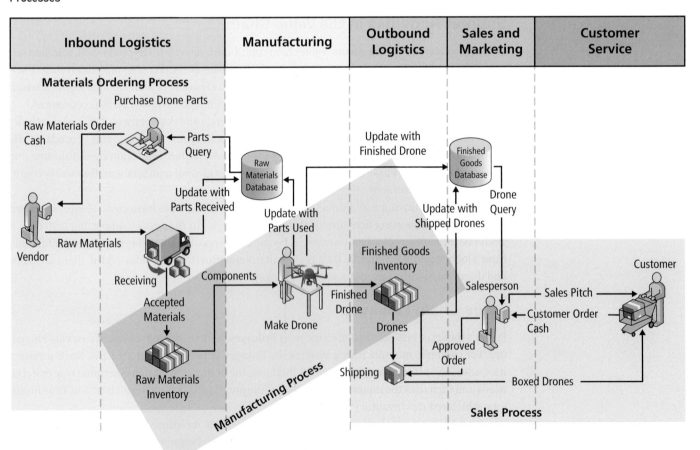

Note, too, that while none of these three processes involve a customer-service activity, customer service plays a role in other business processes

Also notice that activities get and put data resources from and to databases. For example, the purchase-drone parts activity queries the raw materials database to determine the materials to order. The receiving activity updates the raw materials database to indicate the arrival of materials. The make-drone activity updates the raw materials database to indicate the consumption of materials. Similar actions are taken in the sales process against the finished goods database.

Business processes vary in cost and effectiveness. In fact, the streamlining of business processes to increase margin (add value, reduce costs, or both) is key to competitive advantage. You will learn about process design when we discuss **business process management** in Chapter 12. To get a flavor of process design, however, consider Figure 3-9, which shows an alternate process for the drone manufacturer. Here the purchase-drone-parts activity not only queries the raw materials inventory database, it also queries the finished goods inventory database. Querying both databases allows the purchasing department to make decisions not just on raw materials quantities but also on customer demand. By using this data, purchasing can reduce the size of raw materials inventory, reducing production costs and thus adding margin to the value chain. This is an example of using a linkage across business processes to improve process margin.

As you will learn, however, changing business processes is not easy to do. Most process design requires people to work in new ways and to follow different procedures, and employees often resist such change. In Figure 3-9, the employees who perform the purchase-drone-parts activity need to learn to adjust their ordering processes to use customer purchase patterns. Another complication is that data stored in the finished goods database likely will need to be redesigned to keep track of customer demand data. As you will learn in Chapter 12, that redesign effort will require that some application programs be changed as well.

Figure 3-9

Improved Material Ordering Process

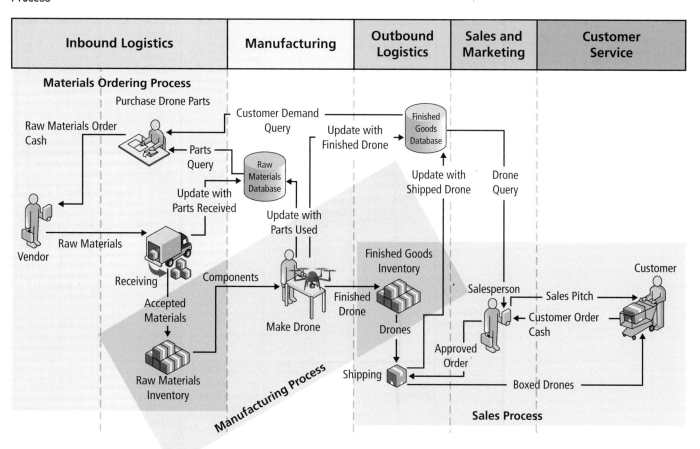

Q3-6 How Does Competitive Strategy Determine Business Processes and the Structure of Information Systems?

Figure 3-10 shows a business process for renting bicycles. The value-generating activities are shown in the top of the table, and the implementation of those activities for two companies with different competitive strategies is shown in the rows below.

The first company has chosen a competitive strategy of low-cost rentals to students. Accordingly, this business implements business processes to minimize costs. The second company has chosen a differentiation strategy. It provides "best-of-breed" rentals to executives at a high-end conference resort. Notice that this business has designed its business processes to ensure superb service. To achieve a positive margin, it must ensure that the value added will exceed the costs of providing the service.

Now, consider the information systems required for these business processes. The student rental business uses a shoebox for its data facility. The only computer/software/data component in its business is the machine provided by its bank for processing credit card transactions.

The high-service business, however, makes extensive use of information systems, as shown in Figure 3-11. It has a sales tracking database that tracks past customer rental activity and an inventory database that is used to select and up-sell bicycle rentals as well as to control bicycle inventory with a minimum of fuss to its high-end customers.

	Value-Generating Activity	Greet Customer →	Determine Needs →	Rent Bike →	Return Bike & Pay
Low-cost rental to students	Message that implements competitive strategy	"You wanna bike?"	"Bikes are over there. Help yourself."	"Fill out this form, and bring it to me over here when you're done."	"Show me the bike." "OK, you owe $23.50. Pay up."
	Supporting business process	None.	Physical controls and procedures to prevent bike theft.	Printed forms and a shoebox to store them in.	Shoebox with rental form. Minimal credit card and cash receipt system.
High-service rental to business executives at conference resort	Message that implements competitive strategy	"Hello, Ms. Henry. Wonderful to see you again. Would you like to rent the WonderBike 4.5 that you rented last time?"	"You know, I think the WonderBike Supreme would be a better choice for you. It has ... "	"Let me just scan the bike's number into our system, and then I'll adjust the seat for you."	"How was your ride?" "Here, let me help you. I'll just scan the bike's tag again and have your paperwork in just a second." "Would you like a beverage?" "Would you like me to put this on your hotel bill, or would you prefer to pay now?"
	Supporting business process	Customer tracking and past sales activity system.	Employee training and information system to match customer and bikes, biased to "up-sell" customer.	Automated inventory system to check bike out of inventory.	Automated inventory system to place bike back in inventory. Prepare payment documents. Integrate with resort's billing system.

Figure 3-10

Operations Value Chains for Bicycle Rental Companies

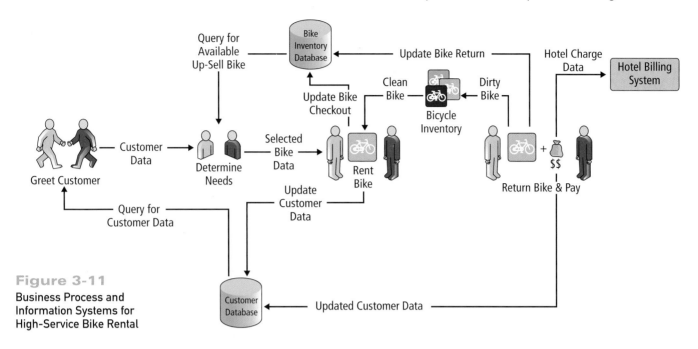

Figure 3-11

Business Process and
Information Systems for
High-Service Bike Rental

Q3-7 How Do Information Systems Provide Competitive Advantages?

In your business strategy class, you will study the Porter models in greater detail than we have discussed here. When you do so, you will learn numerous ways that organizations respond to the five competitive forces. For our purposes, we can distill those ways into the list of principles shown in Figure 3-12. Keep in mind that we are applying these principles in the context of the organization's competitive strategy.

You can also apply these principles to your personal competitive advantage, as discussed in the Guide on pages 138–139.

Some of these competitive techniques are created via products and services, and some are created via the development of business processes. Consider each.

Competitive Advantage via Products

The first three principles in Figure 3-12 concern products or services. Organizations gain a competitive advantage by creating *new* products or services, by *enhancing* existing products or services, and by *differentiating* their products and services from those of their competitors.

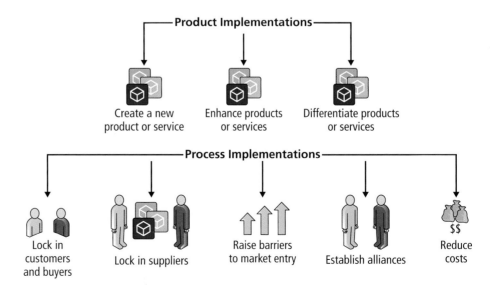

Figure 3-12

Principles of Competitive
Advantage

Driving Strategy

How many hours do you spend per week driving a car? Think about the productivity boost you could get if you spent that time studying for exams, applying for a job, or responding to orders placed on your new Web site. Also, think about how much time your car just sits there—unused and unproductive. Could your car be used more productively if it was shared with a friend, sibling, or spouse? Maybe a driverless car, like those mentioned in Chapter 4, could drop you off at school and then return home to be used by someone else?

Businesses can also recognize gains in efficiency, productivity, and sales that will come from using driverless vehicles. For example, Mercedes is developing a driverless truck that can operate autonomously once it is on the highway (a driver is required to get the truck on and off of the interstate).[4] Not only can this vehicle transport a shipment to its destination faster, it can also make roads safer by eliminating fatigued drivers and distracted driving.

To identify another potential business application of driverless vehicles, take a look at one of Amazon's new projects. Amazon recently filed a patent application for delivery trucks outfitted with 3D printers.[5] The purpose of these vehicles is to rapidly respond to orders by manufacturing goods while the vehicle is en route to the delivery location. You may be wondering what this has to do with a driverless car, but if you combine Amazon's innovation *with* a driverless vehicle, you now have an autonomous factory on wheels! Think about the strategic value of being able to instantly deploy manufacturing capabilities to any geographic location on demand.

Driving Existing Markets to Change

Businesses are constantly fine-tuning and adapting their business strategies to create and maintain competitive advantages. Markets are sometimes disrupted by new entrants, substitute products, or new innovations. It is clear that Über is revolutionizing transportation services around the world. In a few short years, it has become a major player in the transportation industry with a $40B valuation.[6] But is Über invincible to new forms of competition?

Could a new entrant start a transportation company using only driverless vehicles? One of the biggest concerns consumers have with Über is the lack of background checks and other vetting processes required of its drivers. What if you removed drivers from the business model entirely?

Source: chombosan/Fotolia

This driverless taxi company would have other benefits as well. Passengers wouldn't have to worry about safety. Profit margins for the company would probably increase due to reduced labor costs, healthcare costs, and accidents. Vehicles would never have to stop for rest, food, bathroom breaks, and so on, so the company could continuously make money (except for vehicle maintenance and filling gas tanks, but both of these activities occur even with human operators).

The implications of driverless vehicles are not just limited to the transportation sector. They could also influence industries like shipping, aviation, and law enforcement. If you still think new innovations cannot take down juggernaut companies, just ask Polaroid!

Questions

1. One mechanism that could help (1) inform the navigation of driverless cars and (2) update the vehicle with current road conditions is Internet connectivity to other autonomous vehicles operating in the area. What vulnerabilities could be exploited by equipping one of these vehicles with Internet access?

2. The feature describes a scenario in which Amazon's mobile manufacturing vehicles could be operated autonomously. What are some logistical issues that could arise from a delivery vehicle functioning without a human operator?

3. Creating driverless vehicles that can operate safely is clearly a complex problem. Based on the promising results found in this domain, what other complex tasks exist that may prove feasible for automation?

4. New innovations often disrupt existing markets and force them to adapt or be eliminated (e.g., look at how iTunes and Apple devices have reshaped the music industry). How might the proliferation of driverless cars influence the automotive insurance industry?

5. How would you feel riding in a car that is changing lanes and swerving to avoid debris or poor road conditions all without your control? Do you think a driverless vehicle is something that everyone would want to own, even if it is sold at an affordable price?

Information systems create competitive advantages either as part of a product or by providing support to a product. Consider, for example, a car rental agency like Hertz or Avis. An information system that produces information about the car's location and provides driving instructions to destinations is part of the car rental, and thus is part of the product itself (see Figure 3-13a). In contrast, an information system that schedules car maintenance is not part of the product but instead supports the product (see Figure 3-13b). Either way, information systems can help achieve the first three principles in Figure 3-12.

The remaining five principles in Figure 3-12 concern competitive advantage created by the implementation of business processes.

Competitive Advantage via Business Processes

Organizations can *lock in customers* by making it difficult or expensive for customers to switch to another product. This strategy is sometimes called establishing high **switching costs**. Organizations can *lock in suppliers* by making it difficult to switch to another organization or, stated

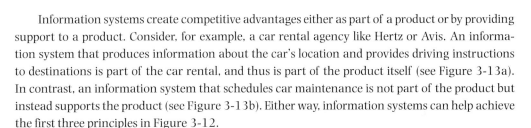

a. Information System as Part of a Car Rental Product

b. Information System That Supports a Car Rental Product

Daily Service Schedule – June 15, 2017

StationID   22

StationName   Lubrication

ServiceDate	ServiceTime	VehicleID	Make	Model	Mileage	ServiceDescription
06/15/2017	12:00 AM	155890	Ford	Explorer	2244	Std. Lube
06/15/2017	11:00 AM	12448	Toyota	Tacoma	7558	Std. Lube

StationID   26

StationName   Alignment

ServiceDate	ServiceTime	VehicleID	Make	Model	Mileage	ServiceDescription
06/15/2017	9:00 AM	12448	Toyota	Tacoma	7558	Front end alignment inspect

StationID   28

StationName   Transmission

ServiceDate	ServiceTime	VehicleID	Make	Model	Mileage	ServiceDescription
06/15/2017	11:00 AM	155890	Ford	Explorer	2244	Transmission oil change

Figure 3-13

Two Roles for Information Systems Regarding Products

positively, by making it easy to connect to and work with the organization. Finally, competitive advantage can be gained by *creating entry barriers* that make it difficult and expensive for new competition to enter the market.

One advantage a company can create is ensuring that it produces secure products. For more information, see the Security Guide on pages 136–137.

Another means to gain competitive advantage is to *establish alliances* with other organizations. Such alliances establish standards, promote product awareness and needs, develop market size, reduce purchasing costs, and provide other benefits. Finally, organizations can gain competitive advantage by *reducing costs*. Such reductions enable the organization to reduce prices and/or to increase profitability. Increased profitability means not just greater shareholder value but also more cash, which can fund further infrastructure development for even greater competitive advantage.

All of these principles of competitive advantage make sense, but the question you may be asking is "How do information systems help to create competitive advantage?" To answer that question, consider a sample information system.

How Does an Actual Company Use IS to Create Competitive Advantages?

ABC, Inc.,[7] is a worldwide shipper with sales well in excess of $1B. From its inception, ABC invested heavily in information technology and led the shipping industry in the application of information systems for competitive advantage. Here we consider one example of an information system that illustrates how ABC successfully uses information technology to gain competitive advantage.

ABC maintains customer account data that include not only the customer's name, address, and billing information, but also data about the people, organizations, and locations to which the customer ships. Figure 3-14 shows a Web form that an ABC customer is using to schedule a shipment. When the ABC system creates the form, it fills the Company name drop-down list with the names of companies that the customer has shipped to in the past. Here the user is selecting Pearson Education.

When the user clicks the Company name, the underlying ABC information system reads the customer's contact data from a database. The data consist of names, addresses, and phone numbers of recipients from past shipments. The user then selects a Contact name, and the system inserts that contact's address and other data into the form using data from the database, as shown in Figure 3-15. Thus, the system saves customers from having to reenter data for recipients to whom they have shipped in the past. Providing the data in this way also reduces data-entry errors.

Figure 3-14

ABC, Inc., Web Page to Select a Recipient from the Customer's Records

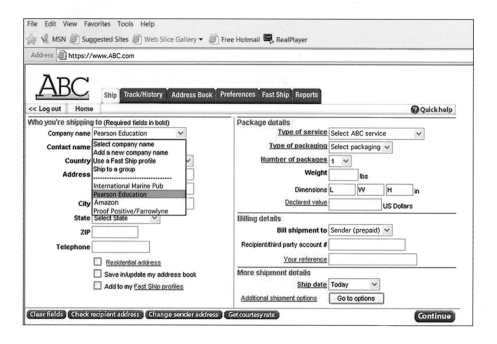

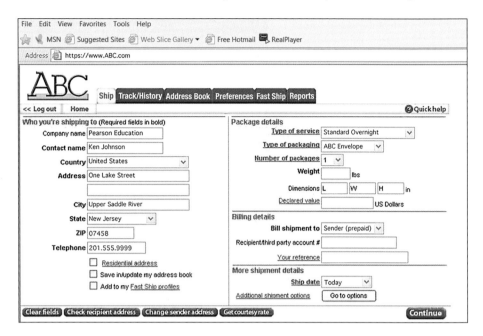

Figure 3-15

ABC, Inc., Web Page to Select a Contact from the Customer's Records

Figure 3-16 shows another feature of this system. On the right-hand side of this form, the customer can request that ABC send email messages to the sender (the customer), the recipient, and others as well. The customer can opt for ABC to send an email when the shipment is created and when it has been delivered. In Figure 3-16, the user has provided three email addresses. The customer wants all three addresses to receive delivery notification, but only the sender will receive shipment notification. The customer can add a personal message as well. By adding this capability to the shipment scheduling system, ABC has extended its product from a package-delivery service to a package- *and* information-delivery service.

Figure 3-17 shows one other capability of this information system. It has generated a shipping label, complete with bar code, for the user to print. By doing this, the company not only reduces

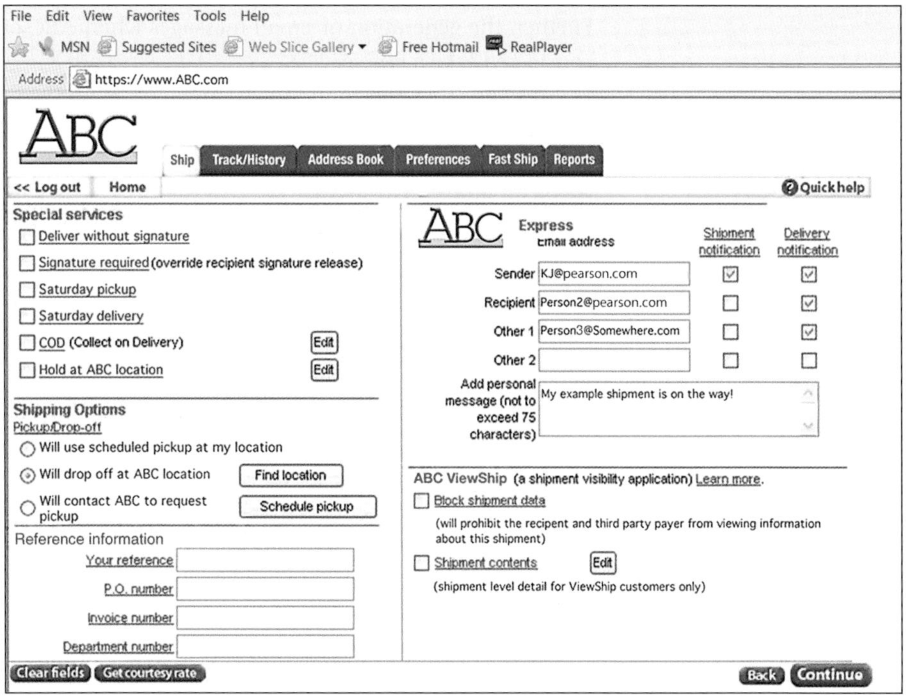

Figure 3-16

ABC, Inc., Web Page to Specify Email Notification

Figure 3-17
ABC, Inc., Web Page to Print a Shipping Label

errors in the preparation of shipping labels, but it also causes the customer to provide the paper and ink for document printing! Millions of such documents are printed every day, resulting in a considerable savings to the company.

How Does This System Create a Competitive Advantage?

Now consider the ABC shipping information system in light of the competitive advantage factors in Figure 3-12. This information system *enhances* an existing service because it eases the effort of creating a shipment to the customer while reducing errors. The information system also helps to *differentiate* the ABC package delivery service from competitors that do not have a similar system. Further, the generation of email messages when ABC picks up and delivers a package could be considered to be a *new* service.

Because this information system captures and stores data about recipients, it reduces the amount of customer work when scheduling a shipment. Customers will be *locked in* by this system: If a customer wants to change to a different shipper, he or she will need to rekey recipient data for that new shipper. The disadvantage of rekeying data may well outweigh any advantage of switching to another shipper.

This system achieves a competitive advantage in two other ways as well. First, it raises the barriers to market entry. If another company wants to develop a shipping service, it will not only have to be able to ship packages, but it will also need to have a similar information system. In addition, the system reduces costs. It reduces errors in shipping documents, and it saves ABC paper, ink, and printing costs.

Of course, to determine if this system delivers a *net savings* in costs, the cost of developing and operating the information system will need to be offset against the gains in reduced errors and paper, ink, and printing costs. It may be that the system costs more than the savings. Even still, it may be a sound investment if the value of intangible benefits, such as locking in customers and raising entry barriers, exceeds the net cost.

Before continuing, review Figure 3-12. Make sure you understand each of the principles of competitive advantage and how information systems can help achieve them. In fact, the list in Figure 3-12 probably is important enough to memorize because you can also use it for non-IS applications. You can consider any business project or initiative in light of competitive advantage.

Q3-8   2026?

Models of business strategy, competitive advantages, and their relationship to processes and IS are unlikely to change in the next 10 years. They may evolve, there may be some new models that rise to the surface, but those new models are likely to be extensions of existing models, within the existing paradigms.

What is likely to change, however, is pace. Because of the Internet and related technology, the speed of business is accelerating. The Web, Twitter, Facebook, and other social sites enable the rapid spread of new ideas and innovations and require businesses to be constantly on the alert for changes that may affect their strategy in short periods of time.

Falcon Security is an excellent example. It has had a successful, growing business providing security services for some time. But, as discussed in Figure 3-4, it is very dependent on a few large industrial clients. These clients could force Falcon Security to lower its fees or install their own wireless Web cameras. Both of these possibilities threaten Falcon Security's differentiation strategy of providing premium aerial security surveillance services.

One technology that is likely to have a major affect on competitive strategies is self-driving vehicles. For many products, transportation is a major cost. Self-driving cars, possibly even drones, will dramatically reduce these costs, with major consequences. Augmented reality devices, like Google Glass and Microsoft's HoloLens, will also change the competitive landscape in the next 10 years.

So, we can reasonably assume that the pace of change and the pace of integration of new technology will be fast and increasing, possibly accelerating, in the next 10 years. We can lament this fact; we can ignore it, but doing so is like standing on the shore of the Mississippi River, telling it to flow elsewhere.

Instead, we, and especially *you*, need to view this increased pace as rapidly creating opportunities in which you can excel. You know it's coming; you know that, if not self-driving vehicles on the ground or in the air, then some other product that is today being constructed in someone's garage, maybe with 3D printing, some new technology-based products will change the competitive landscape for the company for which you will work. Knowing that, how can you take advantage of it?

When gold was discovered along the Colorado River in Arizona in the 1850s, thousands of pioneers ran to the mine fields. The odds were slim on success, and only a few struck it rich. A much surer bet was made by those who started the clothing and supply stores, or the railroads that moved the raw ore to the smelter, or the steamships that carried goods up the Colorado from the Sea of Cortez.

Maybe you want to be a modern-day prospector and use technology to create new products like 3D printing. If so, do it. But, maybe, like Falcon Security, you want to attend to the innovative products that others are making and create new strategies or build new businesses that take advantage of the opportunities that new products create. You can be certain that, 10 years from now, you will have even more opportunity to do so.

Security Guide

HACKING SMART THINGS

You may have noticed a recent trend in TV commercials for cars. Many car manufacturers are focusing on technology-centric special features. One of the most popular add-ons right now is adding the capability to turn your car into an Internet hot spot. Sure, allowing your friends to check their social media updates using your car's Wi-Fi sounds pretty cool. But there may be some unintended risks associated with incorporating this capability into your car—or any device, for that matter. What if one of your passengers used that Wi-Fi connection to access your car's brakes?

Internet of Things (IoT)

You may have already heard of the *Internet of Things* (IoT), or the idea that objects are becoming connected to the Internet so they can interact with other devices, applications, or services. Countless companies are working to capitalize on the possibilities of new "smart" products designed to automatically communicate with other devices and exchange data with little or no intervention by the user. The trend of developing new Internet-enabled devices is so widespread that some estimates place the number of IoT devices at roughly 26 billion by 2020.[8]

But what can all of these new smart devices be used for? Take home automation, for example. The home automation market is growing rapidly with new Internet-enabled devices like thermostats, smoke detectors, light bulbs, surveillance cameras, and door locks gaining in popularity.[9] These devices allow a homeowner to remotely monitor the temperature of the home, turn lights on or off, or remotely keep an eye on the family dog by tapping into a webcam feed. While all of these capabilities seem like a great idea and add convenience to daily life, the trend of outfitting every object with Internet access may prove to be a hazardous, even dangerous, proposition.

Internet of Threats

You might already be aware of some of the types of security threats on the Internet. If you tune in to the evening news on any given night, you will see stories about data stolen

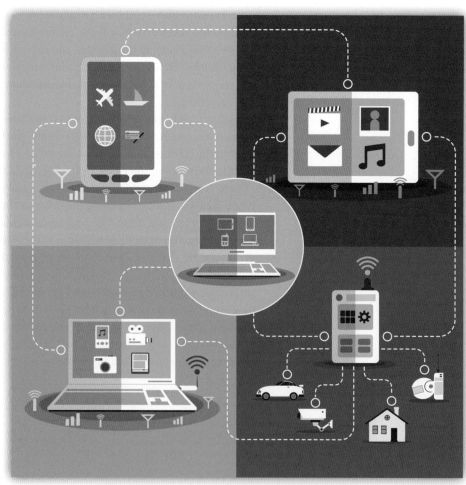

Source: macrovector/Fotolia

from large corporations, government insiders leaking sensitive information, or cyberattacks launched from around the globe.

What does this have to do with you? Well, you have sensitive information, too. How would you feel if your bank statements, medical records, and email history for the past 5 years were stolen and posted online? You probably are taking steps to avoid these threats like running antivirus software, enabling automatic updates, using your operating system's default firewall, avoiding suspicious emails, and staying away from shady Web sites.

But what about securing your data stored on these new Internet-enabled smart devices? Think about the security implications of having to protect 10, 20, or 30 different Internet-enabled devices in your home. Will you have to buy antivirus software for your refrigerator or configure a firewall on your thermostat? Could a hacker hijack the webcam in your living room or, worse, actually hijack your car?

Taking Back-Seat Driver to a Whole New Level

Yes, a hacker could potentially compromise your car if it is connected to the Internet. If a hacker takes control of your vehicle, he or she could then remotely control various functions of the vehicle (e.g., the brakes), keep tabs on your GPS coordinates, activate the Bluetooth microphone and listen to anything taking place inside of the car, or access data about the vehicle's operations and performance.[10] The thought of someone eavesdropping on your conversations in the car is bad enough. But what would happen if the hacker activates the brakes, or disables them, while you are driving? What happens when driverless cars become widely adopted and hackers could have complete control over the vehicle?

As more and more devices are accessible over some form of network, users will have to weigh the pros and the cons of using them. But securing these new smart devices will take additional work. The same thing that makes these devices great will also make them vulnerable to attack. Yes, of course, a smart thermostat will save you money. But what happens when it gets a virus? Will you be the one running a temperature?

 # DISCUSSION QUESTIONS

1. How many devices in your home are connected to the Internet? How much time do you spend daily, weekly, or monthly trying to ensure that these devices have the latest updates and are secure? What are the implications of maintaining dozens of smart devices?

2. The guide discusses the potential threat of a hacker accessing a vehicle and downloading data about the car's performance and operations. Aside from a malicious hacker acting alone, are there any businesses or government agencies that could benefit from accessing these data? How?

3. Has this guide changed your perception of the Internet of Things? Do the benefits of smart devices outweigh the risk of data loss or your personal privacy? Why or why not?

4. The Internet of Things is not solely focused on home automation or private consumer products. Businesses are using the Internet of Things to manage supply chains and streamline various business processes. What benefits or risks are associated with businesses adopting new Internet-enabled devices?

Guide

YOUR PERSONAL COMPETITIVE ADVANTAGE

Consider the following possibility: You work hard, earning your degree in business, and you graduate, only to discover that you cannot find a job in your area of study. You look for 6 weeks or so, but then you run out of money. In desperation, you take a job waiting tables at a local restaurant. Two years go by, the economy picks up, and the jobs you had been looking for become available. Unfortunately, your degree is now 2 years old; you are competing with students who have just graduated with fresh degrees (and fresh knowledge). Two years of waiting tables, good as you are at it, does not appear to be good experience for the job you want. You're stuck in a nightmare—one that will be hard to get out of, and *one that you cannot allow to happen.*

Examine Figure 3-12 again, but this time consider those elements of competitive advantage as they apply to you personally. As an employee, the skills and abilities you offer are your personal product. Examine the first three items in the list and ask yourself, "How can I use my time in school—and in this MIS class, in particular—to create new skills, to enhance those I already have, and to differentiate my skills from the competition?" (By the way, you will enter a national/international market. Your competition is not just the students in your class; it's also students in classes in Ohio, California, British Columbia, Florida, New York, and every place else they're teaching MIS today.)

Suppose you are interested in professional sales. Perhaps you want to sell in the pharmaceutical industry. What skills can you learn from your MIS class that will make you more competitive as a future salesperson? Ask yourself, "How does the pharmaceutical industry use MIS to gain competitive advantage?" Get on the Internet and find examples of the use of information systems in the pharmaceutical

industry. How does Pfizer, for example, use a customer information system to sell to doctors? How can your knowledge of such systems differentiate you from your competition for a job there? How does Pfizer use a knowledge management system? How does the firm keep track of drugs that have an adverse effect on each other?

The fourth and fifth items in Figure 3-12 concern locking in customers, buyers, and suppliers. How can you interpret those elements in terms of your personal competitive advantage? Well, to lock in a relationship, you first have to have one. So do you have an internship? If not, can you get one? And once you have an internship, how can you use your knowledge of MIS to lock in your job so that you get a job offer? Does the company you are interning for have a sales tracking system (or any other information system that is important to the company)? If users are happy with the system, what characteristics make it worthwhile? Can you lock in a job by becoming an expert user of this system? Becoming an expert user not only locks you into your job, but it also raises barriers to entry for others who might be competing for the job. Also, can you suggest ways to improve the system, thus

using your knowledge of the company and the system to lock in an extension of your job?

Human resources personnel say that networking is one of the most effective ways of finding a job. How can you use this class to establish alliances with other students? Is there an email list server for the students in your class? What about Facebook? LinkedIn? Twitter? How can you use those facilities to develop job-seeking alliances with other students? Who in your class already has a job or an internship? Can any of those people provide hints or opportunities for finding a job?

Don't restrict your job search to your local area. Are there regions of your country where jobs are more plentiful? How can you find out about student organizations in those regions? Search the Web for MIS classes in other cities, and make contact with students there. Find out what the hot opportunities are in other cities.

Finally, as you study MIS, think about how the knowledge you gain can help you save costs for your employers. Even more, see if you can build a case that an employer would actually save money by hiring you. The line of reasoning might be that because of your knowledge of IS, you will be able to facilitate cost savings that more than compensate for your salary.

In truth, few of the ideas that you generate for a potential employer will be feasible or pragmatically useful. The fact that you are thinking creatively, however, will indicate to a potential employer that you have initiative and are grappling with the problems that real businesses have. As this course progresses, keep thinking about competitive advantage, and strive to understand how the topics you study can help you to accomplish, personally, one or more of the principles in Figure 3-12.

? DISCUSSION QUESTIONS

1. Summarize the efforts you have taken thus far to build an employment record that will lead to job offers after graduation.

2. Considering the first three principles in Figure 3-12, describe one way in which you have a competitive advantage over your classmates. If you do not have such a competitive advantage, describe actions you can take to obtain one.

3. In order to build your network, you can use your status as a student to approach business professionals. Namely, you can contact them for help with an assignment or for career guidance. For example, suppose you want to work in banking and you know that your local bank has a customer information system. You could call the manager of that bank and ask him or her how that system creates a competitive advantage for the bank. You also could ask to interview other employees and go armed with the list in Figure 3-12. Describe two specific ways in which you can use your status as a student and the list in Figure 3-12 to build your network in this way.

4. Describe two ways that you can use student alliances to obtain a job. How can you use information systems to build, maintain, and operate such alliances?

ACTIVE REVIEW

Use this Active Review to verify that you understand the ideas and concepts that answer the chapter's study questions.

Q3-1 How does organizational strategy determine information systems structure?

Diagram and explain the relationship of industry structure, competitive strategy, value chains, business processes, and information systems. Working from industry structure to IS, explain how the knowledge you've gained in these first three chapters pertains to that diagram.

Q3-2 What five forces determine industry structure?

Name and briefly describe the five forces. Give your own examples of both strong and weak forces of each type, similar to those in Figure 3-3.

Q3-3 How does analysis of industry structure determine competitive strategy?

Describe four different strategies as defined by Porter. Give an example of four different companies that have implemented each of the strategies.

Q3-4 How does competitive strategy determine value chain structure?

Define the terms *value, margin,* and *value chain.* Explain why organizations that choose a differentiation strategy can use value to determine a limit on the amount of extra cost to pay for differentiation. Name the primary and support activities in the value chain and explain the purpose of each. Explain the concept of linkages.

Q3-5 How do business processes generate value?

Define *business process, cost,* and *margin* as they pertain to business processes. Explain the purpose of an activity and describe types of repository. Explain the importance of business process redesign and describe the difference between the business processes in Figure 3-8 and those in Figure 3-9.

Q3-6 How does competitive strategy determine business processes and the structure of information systems?

In your own words, explain how competitive strategy determines the structure of business processes. Use the examples of a clothing store that caters to struggling students and a clothing store that caters to professional businesspeople in a high-end neighborhood. List the activities in the business process for the two companies and create a chart like that in Figure 3-9. Explain how the information systems' requirements differ between the two stores.

Q3-7 How do information systems provide competitive advantages?

List and briefly describe eight principles of competitive advantage. Consider your college bookstore. List one application of each of the eight principles. Strive to include examples that involve information systems.

Q3-8 2026?

Describe the ways that business strategies are likely to change in the next 10 years. Using Google Glass as an example, describe companies whose strategy is likely to be challenged. Summarize the lesson that gold mining on the Colorado River in the 1850s can teach us.

Using Your Knowledge with Falcon Security

Explain in your own words how Falcon Security's competitive strategy is threatened by relying on a few large industrial accounts. Describe Falcon Security's planned response and summarize the problems that Cam perceives with that response. Recommend a course of action for Falcon Security. Use Cam's idea of diversifying the type of work the company does to illustrate your answer.

KEY TERMS AND CONCEPTS

Activity   126
Business process   126
Business process management   127
Competitive strategy   121
Cost   126

Five forces model   120
Linkages   124
Margin   124
Primary activities   124
Repository   126

Support activities   124
Switching costs   131
Value   124
Value chain   124

MyMISLab™

To complete the problems with the ✪, go to EOC Discussion Questions in the MyLab.

USING YOUR KNOWLEDGE

✪ **3-1.** Choose four organizations in a particular industry. The first organization should be following the competitive strategy of lower cost across the industry, the second should be following the competitive strategy of lower cost within an industry segment, the third should be following the competitive strategy of better service/ products across the industry, and the last should be following the competitive strategy of better products/ services within an industry segment. Compare their strategies and analyze how the information system could be used for each shortlisted organization to gain competitive advantage.

✪ **3-2.** Suppose that your college wants to open another branch in some other city. You are being hired as a consultant by your college. To guide the administration in deciding whether to open a new branch or not. You need to know the financial viability of the new project, which is dependent on the future intake of students and also the competitors. For this you decide to implement Porter's competitive forces model into practice.

   a. Analyze the present scenario of this industry according to the Porter's competitive forces model.

   b. Based on the analysis conducted in part a, recommend a competitive strategy.

   c. Consult your teachers to find out new courses that should be included in the new college.

   d. Suppose that you suggest a differentiation strategy to start a new mode of teaching, i.e. online distance education courses to target the working executives. In this new mode of teaching (online teaching), list the primary value chain activities as they apply to this business.

   e. After identification of the primary activities for on-line teaching, identify the support chain activities as they apply to this new code of teaching.

   f. Describe how information system could be used to support traditional classroom teaching.

✪ **3-3.** John owns and operates two hotels, Budget 99 and Luxury 100. John never attended a professional course in any university. He has worked for years in his uncle's hotel and eventually gained experience and confidence to start his own business. Budget 99 is a budget hotel that focuses on college tours, middle or lower income groups, whereas Luxury 100 targets high income groups, like business executives. John has never heard of Michael Porter or any his theories. He operates his business by his 'gut feeling.'

   a. Explain how the knowledge of the Porter's competitive model can help John to run his hotels in a better way.

   b. Refer to Figure 3.5 to enlist possible competitive strategies that John can formulate.

   c. Refer to Figure 3.7 and list the task descriptions of the primary activities of the value chain of the hotels.

   d. Refer to Figure 3.10 and make a detailed chart of operations value chains at the reception counter for both Budget 99 and Luxury 100 hotels.

   e. Considering the above answers, how can John use information system for his Luxury 100 hotel. While answering this question, take both perspectives into account, i.e. operational as well as customer perspective, and then give reasons on how the implementation of an information system will yield positive results for John.

COLLABORATION EXERCISE 3

Using the collaboration IS you built in Chapter 2 (page 110), collaborate with a group of students to answer the following questions.

Singing Valley Resort is a top-end 50-unit resort located high in the Colorado mountains. Rooms rent for $400 to $4,500 per night, depending on the season and the type of accommodations. Singing Valley's clientele are well-to-do; many are famous entertainers, sports figures, and business executives. They are accustomed to, and demand, superior service.

Singing Valley resides in a gorgeous mountain valley and is situated a few hundred yards from a serene mountain lake. It prides itself on superior accommodations; tip-top service; delicious, healthful, organic meals; and exceptional wines. Because it has been so successful, Singing Valley is 90 percent occupied except during the "shoulder seasons" (November, after the leaves change and before the snow arrives, and late April, when winter sports are finished but the snow is still on the ground).

Singing Valley's owners want to increase revenue, but because the resort is nearly always full and because its rates are already at the top of the scale, it cannot do so via occupancy revenue. Thus, over the past several years it has focused on upselling to its clientele activities such as fly-fishing, river rafting, cross-country skiing, snowshoeing, art lessons, yoga and other exercise classes, spa services, and the like.

To increase the sales of these optional activities, Singing Valley prepared in-room marketing materials to advertise their availability. Additionally, it trained all registration personnel on techniques of casually and appropriately suggesting such activities to guests on arrival.

The response to these promotions was only mediocre, so Singing Valley's management stepped up its promotions. The first step was to send email to its clientele advising them of the activities available during their stay. An automated system produced emails personalized with names and personal data.

Unfortunately, the automated email system backfired. Immediately upon its execution, Singing Valley management received numerous complaints. One long-term customer objected that she had been coming to Singing Valley for 7 years and asked if they had yet noticed that she was confined to a wheelchair. If they had noticed, she said, why did they send her a personalized invitation for a hiking trip? The agent of another famous client complained that the personalized email was sent to her client and her husband, when anyone who had turned on a TV in the past 6 months knew the two of them were involved in an exceedingly acrimonious divorce. Yet an-

other customer complained that, indeed, he and his wife had vacationed at Singing Valley 3 years ago, but he had not been there since. To his knowledge, his wife had not been there, either, so he was puzzled as to why the email referred to their visit last winter. He wanted to know if, indeed, his wife had recently been to the resort, without him. Of course, Singing Valley had no way of knowing about customers it had insulted who never complained.

During the time the automated email system was operational, sales of extra activities were up 15 percent. However, the strong customer complaints conflicted with its competitive strategy so, in spite of the extra revenue, Singing Valley stopped the automated email system, sacked the vendor who had developed it, and demoted the Singing Valley employee who had brokered the system. Singing Valley was left with the problem of how to increase its revenue.

Your team's task is to develop two innovative ideas for solving Singing Valley's problem. At the minimum, include the following in your response:

a. An analysis of the five forces of the Singing Valley market. Make and justify any necessary assumptions about their market.

b. A statement of Singing Valley's competitive strategy.

c. A statement of the problem. Recall from Chapter 2 that a problem is a perceived difference between what is and what ought to be. If the members of your group have different perceptions of the problem, all the better. Use a collaborative process to obtain the best possible problem description to which all can agree.

d. Document in a general way (like the top row of Figure 3-10) the process of up-selling an activity.

e. Develop two innovative ideas for solving the Singing Valley problem. For each idea, provide:
   - A brief description of the idea.
   - A process diagram (like Figure 3-11) of the idea. Figure 3-11 was produced using Microsoft Visio; if you have access to that product, you'll save time and have a better result if you also use it.
   - A description of the information system needed to implement the idea.

f. Compare the advantages and disadvantages of your alternatives in part e and recommend one of them for implementation.

CASE STUDY 3

The Amazon of Innovation

On Cyber Monday, December 1, 2014, Amazon.com customers ordered more than 18 toys per *second*. And almost 60 percent of Amazon's holiday shoppers bought gifts using a mobile device. This contributed to a 20 percent increase in Amazon's total annual sales of $89B. Amazon's last order for the holiday season was placed on December 24 at 10:24 PM and was delivered at 11:06 PM just in time for Christmas. (Some of Amazon's major innovations are listed in Figure 3-18.)

You may think of Amazon as simply an online retailer, and that is indeed where the company achieved most of its success. To do this, Amazon had to build enormous supporting infrastructure—just imagine the information systems and fulfillment facilities needed to ship toys ordered at a rate of 18 per second. That infrastructure, however, is needed only during the busy holiday season. Most of the year, Amazon is left with excess infrastructure capacity. Starting in 2000, Ama-

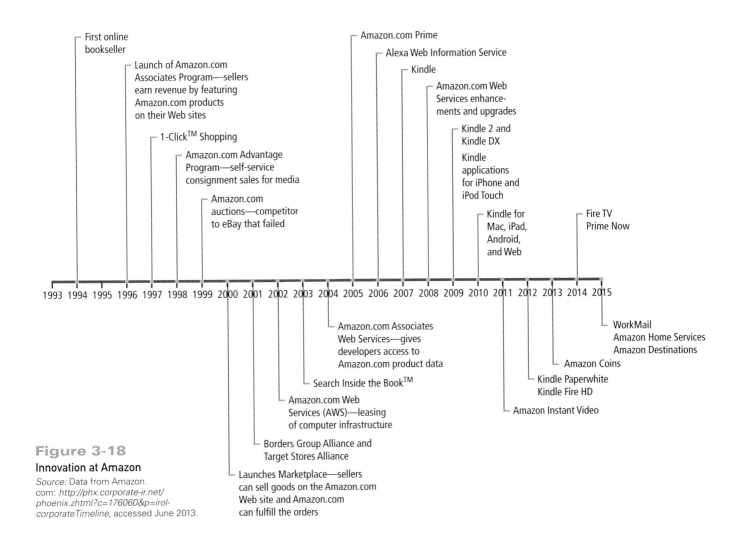

Figure 3-18

Innovation at Amazon

Source: Data from Amazon. com: *http://phx.corporate-ir.net/ phoenix.zhtml?c=176060&p=irol-corporateTimeline*, accessed June 2013.

zon began to lease some of that capacity to other companies. In the process, it played a key role in the creation of what are termed *cloud services*, which you will learn about in Chapter 6. For now, just think of cloud services as computer resources somewhere out in the Internet that are leased on flexible terms.

Today, Amazon's business lines can be grouped into three major categories:

- Online retailing
- Order fulfillment
- Cloud services

Consider each.

Amazon created the business model for online retailing. It began as an online bookstore, but every year since 1998 it has added new product categories. The company is involved in all aspects of online retailing. It sells its own inventory. It incentivizes you, via the Associates program, to sell its inventory as well. Or it will help you sell your inventory within its product pages or via one of its consignment venues. Online auctions are the major aspect of online sales in which Amazon does not participate. It tried auctions in 1999, but it could never make inroads against eBay.[11]

Today, it's hard to remember how much of what we take for granted was pioneered by Amazon. "Customers who bought this, also bought that;" online customer reviews; customer ranking of customer reviews; books lists; Look Inside the Book; automatic free shipping for certain orders or frequent customers; and Kindle books and devices were all novel concepts when Amazon introduced them.

Amazon's retailing business operates on very thin margins. Products are usually sold at a discount from the stated retail price, and 2-day shipping is free for Amazon Prime members (who pay an annual fee of $99). How does it do it? For one, Amazon drives its employees incredibly hard. Former employees claim the hours are long, the pressure is severe, and the workload is heavy. But what else? It comes down to Moore's Law and the innovative use of nearly free data processing, storage, and communication.

In addition to online retailing, Amazon also sells order fulfillment services. You can ship your inventory to an Amazon warehouse and access Amazon's information systems just as if they were yours. Using technology known as Web services (discussed in Chapter 6), your order processing information systems can directly integrate, over the Web, with Amazon's inventory, fulfillment, and shipping applications. Your customers need not know that Amazon played any role at all. You can also sell that same inventory using Amazon's retail sales applications.

Amazon Web Services (AWS) allow organizations to lease time on computer equipment in very flexible ways. Amazon's Elastic Cloud 2 (EC2) enables organizations to expand and contract the computer resources they need within minutes. Amazon has a variety of payment plans, and it is possible to buy computer time for less than a penny an hour. Key to this capability is the ability for the leasing organization's computer programs to interface with Amazon's to automatically scale up and scale down the resources leased. For example, if a news site publishes a story that causes a rapid ramp-up of traffic, that news site can, programmatically, request, configure, and use more computing resources for an hour, a day, a month, whatever.

With its Kindle devices, Amazon has become both a vendor of tablets and, even more importantly in the long term, a vendor of online music and video. And to induce customers to buy Kindle apps, in 2013 Amazon introduced its own currency, Amazon Coins. In 2014, Amazon opened a 3D printing store from which customers can customize their own toys, jewelry, dog bones, and dozens of other products. It also made a push to provide video services by introducing Fire TV.[12]

In 2015 Amazon introduced WorkMail, a potential cloud-based replacement for Microsoft Exchange. It also introduced Amazon Home Services (local professional services), Amazon Destinations (travel site), and Amazon Dash (a one-button reordering device).[13]

Finally, Jeff Bezos announced in 2014 that Amazon was experimenting with package delivery using drones, a service called Prime Air.[14] In March 2015, the U.S. Federal Aviation Administration gave Amazon permission to start testing its drones in the United States.[15] But drone delivery is something that will happen in the future; consider a business service that Amazon.com is offering right now.

Fulfillment by Amazon (FBA)

Fulfillment by Amazon (FBA) is an Amazon service by which other sellers can ship goods to Amazon warehouses for stocking, order packaging, and shipment. FBA customers pay a fee for the service as well as for inventory space. Amazon uses its own inventory management and order fulfillment business processes and information systems to fulfill the FBA customers' orders.

FBA customers can sell their goods on Amazon.com, sell them via their own sales channels, or both. If the FBA customer sells on Amazon.com, Amazon will provide customer service for order processing (handling returns, fixing erroneously packed orders, answering customer order queries, and the like).

The costs for Fulfillment by Amazon depend on the type and size of the goods to be processed. The FBA fees for standard-size products as of February 2015 are shown in the table.

	FBA Costs[16]
Order handling (per order)	$1.00
Pick & pack (per item)	$1.04
Weight handling (per pound)	Between $0.50 for less than 1 pound, to $1.59 plus $0.39 per pound for items over 2 pounds
Storage (cubic foot per month)	$0.51 between January and September and $0.68 from October to December

If goods are sold via Amazon.com, Amazon uses its own information systems to drive the order fulfillment process. However, if the goods are sold via an FBA customer's sales channel, then the FBA customer must connect its own information systems with those at Amazon. Amazon provides a standardized interface by which this is done called Amazon Marketplace Web Service (MWS). Using Web-standard technology (see Chapter 6), FBA customers' order and payment data are directly linked to Amazon's information systems.

FBA enables companies to outsource order fulfillment to Amazon, thus avoiding the cost of developing their own processes, facilities, and information systems for this purpose.

QUESTIONS

3-4. Based on the facts presented in this case, what do you think is Amazon.com's competitive strategy? Justify your answer.

3-5. Jeff Bezos, CEO of Amazon.com, has stated that the best customer support is none. What does that mean?

3-6. Suppose you work for Amazon or a company that takes innovation as seriously as Amazon does. What do you suppose is the likely reaction to an employee who says to his or her boss, "But, I don't know how to do that!"?

3-7. Using your own words and your own experience, what skills and abilities do you think you need to have to thrive at an organization like Amazon?

3-8. What should UPS and FedEx be doing in response to Amazon.com's interest in drone delivery?

3-9. Summarize the advantages and disadvantages for brick-and-mortar retailers to sell items via Amazon.com. Would you recommend that they do so?

3-10. If a brick-and-mortar retailer were to use FBA, what business processes would it not need to develop? What costs would it save?

3-11. If a brick-and-mortar retailer were to use FBA, what information systems would it not need to develop? What costs would it save?

3-12. If a brick-and-mortar retailer were to use FBA, how would it integrate its information systems with Amazon's? (To add depth to your answer, Google the term *Amazon MWS.*)

MyMISLab™

Go to the Assignments section of your MyLab to complete these writing exercises.

3-13. Saeed has come up with what he hopes is a great idea. He has developed a smart phone app that can be used use to find all the ingredients in a food store that you need for your chosen recipe. It uses a clever combination of bar codes and GPS tracking. Saeed intends to create bespoke versions of the app for each of the major grocery chains.

Very soon Saeed realizes that not only will the chains not return his calls, but that many of them have their own cut-down versions aimed at increasing sales and flow around their stores.

a. Explain how an understanding of the basics of the grocery industry would have alerted Saeed to the difficulties he is now facing.

b. Where do you think that Saeed's app might fit into the value chain, if it has a place?

c. How would Saeed's app fit into the business process system and at what stage?

d. Explain Saeed's competitive strategy and how an analysis of Porter's five forces model would benefit him.

3-14. YourFire, Inc., is a small business owned by Curt and Julie Robards. Based in Brisbane, Australia, YourFire manufactures and sells a lightweight camping stove called the YourFire. Curt, who previously worked as an aerospace engineer, invented and patented a burning nozzle that enables the stove to stay lit in very high winds—up to 90 miles per hour. Julie, an industrial designer by training, developed an elegant folding design that is small, lightweight, easy to set up, and very stable. Curt and Julie manufacture the stove in their garage, and they sell it directly to their customers over the Internet and via phone.

   a. Explain how an analysis of the five competitive forces could help YourFire.

   b. What does the YourFire competitive strategy seem to be?

   c. Briefly summarize how the primary value chain activities pertain to YourFire. How should the company design these value chains to conform to its competitive strategy?

   d. Describe business processes that YourFire needs in order to implement its marketing and sales and its service value chain activities.

   e. Describe, in general terms, information systems to support your answer to part d.

3-15. A friend of yours from college, who you haven't talked to in 3 years, sends you an email asking you to meet him for lunch. He says he's got a great idea for a business and wants to run it by you. At first you're hesitant because your friend, while obviously intelligent, doesn't always think things though. You agree to meet for lunch and talk about the idea. At lunch, he explains that he's been developing new flexible screens for his employer that are incredibly tough, waterproof, and use very little energy. His idea is to use these new flexible screens to create wearable computing clothing that can connect directly to smartphones and push ads, promotions, and video. His only problem is that he knows nothing about business. He's not sure where to start.

   a. Explain how you could use the five forces model to help your friend understand the potential success of his wearable flex screens.

   b. How might understanding the unique forces affecting this industry determine the competitive advantage for your friend's new company?

ENDNOTES

1. Michael Porter, *Competitive Strategy: Techniques for Analyzing Industries and Competitors* (New York: Free Press, 1980).
2. Based on Michael Porter, *Competitive Strategy* (New York: Free Press, 1985).
3. For simplicity, the flow of cash is abbreviated in Figure 3-8. Business processes for authorizing, controlling, making payments, and receiving revenue are, of course, vital.
4. Chris Welch, "Mercedes Built a Self-Driving Truck That Could Save Thousands of Lives Every Year," *The Verge*, October 7, 2014, accessed April 10, 2015, *www.theverge.com/2014/10/7/6939809/mercedes-self-driving-truck-could-save-thousands-lives-each-year.*
5. Lee Matthews, "Amazon Files Patent for 3D Printing Delivery Trucks," *Geek.com*, February 25, 2015, accessed April 10, 2015, *www.geek.com/news/amazon-files-patent-for-3d-printing-delivery-trucks-1616525.*
6. Maxwell Wessel, "Making Sense of Über's $40 Billion Valuation," *HBR.org*, December 10, 2014, accessed April 10, 2015, *https://hbr.org/2014/12/making-sense-of-ubers-40-billion-valuation.*
7. The information system described here is used by a major transportation company that did not want its name published in this textbook.
8. P. Middleton, P. Kjeldsen, and J. Tully, "Forecast: The Internet of Things, Worldwide, 2013," November 18, 2013, accessed April 18, 2015, *www.gartner.com/doc/2625419/forecast-internet-things-worldwide.*
9. *https://nest.com/works-with-nest/*
10. J. Markoff, "Researchers Show How a Car's Electronics Can Be Taken Over Remotely," *The New York Times*, March 9, 2011, p. B3.
11. For a fascinating glimpse of this story from someone inside the company, see "Early Amazon: Auctions" at *http://glinden.blogspot.com/2006/04/early-amazon-auctions.html*, accessed August 2012.
12. *http://www.amazon.com/b?ie=UTF8&node=8323871011.*
13. Andy Meek, "Amazon's Roadmap for 2015: Move Fast, Launch as Much as Possible," *BGR Media*, April 24, 2015, accessed May 16, 2015, *https://bgr.com/2015/04/24/amazon-earnings-q1-2015-analysis-roadmap.*
14. George Anders, "Amazon's Drone Team Is Hiring: Look at These Nifty Job Ads," *Forbes*, accessed May 22, 2014, *www.forbes.com/sites/georgeanders/2014/05/19/amazons-drone-team-is-hiring-look-at-these-nifty-job-ads/.*
15. Bart Jansen, "FAA Approves Amazon Drone Research Again," *USA Today*, accessed April 30, 2015, *www.usatoday.com/story/money/2015/04/09/faa-amazon-drone-approval-prime-air/25534485.*
16. "Fulfillment by Amazon Fee Changes 2015," *Amazon.com*, accessed April 30, 2015, *www.amazon.com/gp/help/customer/display.html/?nodeId=201119410.*

PART 2

Information Technology

The next three chapters address the technology that underlies information systems. You may think that such technology is unimportant to you as a business professional. However, as you will see, today's managers and business professionals work with information technology all the time as consumers, if not in a more involved way.

Chapter 4 discusses hardware, software, and open source alternatives and defines basic terms and fundamental computing concepts. It briefly touches on new developments in self-driving cars, 3D printing, and the Internet of Things. It also looks at the importance of Web applications and mobile systems.

Chapter 5 addresses the data component of information systems by describing database processing. You will learn essential database terminology and will be introduced to techniques for processing databases. We will also introduce data modeling because you may be required to evaluate data models for databases that others develop for you.

Chapter 6 continues the discussion of computing devices begun in Chapter 4 and describes data communications, Internet technologies, and cloud-based services. It looks at how organizations can use the cloud effectively and addresses potential security problems that may come from using the cloud.

The purpose of these three chapters is to teach technology sufficient for you to be an effective IT consumer, like Mateo, Joni, Cam, and Alexis at Falcon Security. You will learn basic terms, fundamental concepts, and useful frameworks so that you will have the knowledge to ask good questions and make appropriate requests of the information systems professionals who will serve you.

FALCON Security

It's difficult to stay up to date on the latest technology changes because things are changing so quickly. Every year, a slew of new innovations come out. Some of them may represent real threats to your organization's strategy. Others may represent potential new opportunities for growth. It's important to be able to understand the strategic implications these new technologies represent. You need to be able to ask the right questions.

The concepts and frameworks presented in these chapters will be far more useful to you than learning latest technology trends. Trends come and go. The technology you're using now will be outdated in 10 years. Understanding how to assess the business implications behind any new innovation will be a benefit to you through your entire career.

Hardware, Software, and Mobile Systems

Cam Forset, the operations manager of Falcon Security, asked Mateo Thomas, CEO, Joni Campbell, CFO, and Alexis Moore, head of sales, to come down to the small hangar bay to see how the testing of the new 3D-printed drone is coming along. Mateo asked Cam to investigate the possibility of using 3D-printed parts to make drones in-house rather than buy them from vendors. This could be a tremendous cost-savings opportunity and give the company greater flexibility in updating its current fleet of drones.

Cam waves to Mateo and Joni to come over and look at the screen that she and Alexis are looking at. The screen is showing a live video feed from the new drone as it flies around the perimeter of the building.

"Well, it works—sort of," Cam says to Mateo and Joni with a forced smile. "It's *pretty* stable, and we can get streaming video. I just wish it hadn't taken 2 weeks to get it running." Cam's voice has an undeniably displeased tone.

"That's OK. What was the total cost to make it?" Mateo asks.

"Well, this specific quad cost nearly nothing. We harvested all of the internals from a couple broken quads we had lying around. Everything else we printed." Cam points to a rack of dismantled quadcopters. "We found

some free designs on the Web, but we had to make some changes so they would work with our internals."

"Well, that's good news, isn't it?" Mateo asks.

"Well, not really," Cam says with a skeptical tone. "If we wanted to build more drones, we'd need to harvest more parts from existing drones or buy generic parts and try to see if they'll work together."

Joni and Mateo both look confused. Mateo shakes his head and asks, "Well, why didn't you build it with generic parts in the first place?"

"Honestly, we weren't sure we could make it work even if we used existing internal components. I've never *made* a quadcopter before," Cam says flatly. "We ended up printing about 20 parts, but we still needed motors, a speed controller, a flight control board, a radio transmitter and receiver, propellers, batteries, and a charger."

"We also needed to make sure it could integrate with our internal systems. We didn't want to start experimenting with generic components until we knew we could actually make a quad that could fly," she adds.

"So your next step is to take out the existing internal components and replace them with generic parts to see if they will work, right?" Mateo asks.

"Well..." Cam starts to say.

Joni interrupts, "It probably won't matter if the generic components work or not. Essentially we've just replaced the frame, skids, and a few other parts to hold the camera. We still have to buy the other nonprintable component parts. Those won't be cheap. Add in the additional labor costs to assemble and test each quad..." she trails off.

"Plus the time and labor to integrate them with our internal systems," Alexis picks up her train of thought. "It won't be easy or cheap."

"Exactly," Cam says. "3D printing our own drones isn't going to save us enough money. There aren't enough parts that can be replaced. Yes, the passive recharging platform we developed using 3D-printed parts was a huge success. It has allowed us to automate the recharging process and extend the reach of our drones. But I just

"3D printing our own drones isn't going to save us enough money."

Image source: rommma/Fotolia

STUDY QUESTIONS

Q4-1 What do business professionals need to know about computer hardware?

Q4-2 How can new hardware affect competitive strategies?

Q4-3 What do business professionals need to know about software?

Q4-4 Is open source software a viable alternative?

Q4-5 What are the differences between native and Web applications?

Q4-6 Why are mobile systems increasingly important?

Q4-7 What are the challenges of personal mobile devices at work?

Q4-8 2026?

don't think 3D printing our own drones is going reduce our hardware costs enough to justify us becoming a drone manufacturer."

Mateo looks disappointed. "Well, maybe you're right. I really wish there was some way to make it work. It just seems like we keep burning through cash buying dozens of drones that become obsolete in a few years. It's really frustrating being on the cutting edge."

"You mean the bleeding edge...right?" Joni says with a smirk.

CHAPTER PREVIEW

What would you do if you were Mateo? Or Joni? Would you go ahead and build your own customized drones? It might give you a unique competitive advantage down the road. You might be able to hire someone who is an expert at building drones and save a lot of money. Is Cam being too conservative? If you're wondering why, as a future business professional, you need to know about hardware and software, think about those questions. Those and others of greater complexity—most likely ones involving technology that will be invented between now and the time you start working—will come your way.

You don't need to be an expert. You don't need to be a hardware engineer or a computer programmer. You do need to know enough, however, to be an effective consumer. You need the knowledge and skills to ask important, relevant questions and understand the answers.

We begin with basic hardware concepts and how innovations in hardware could affect businesses. Next, we will discuss software concepts, open source software development, and the differences between native and Web applications. Following that, we'll discuss the importance of mobile systems and the challenges created when employees bring their computers to work. Finally, we'll wrap up by forecasting trends in hardware and software in 2026.

Q4-1 What Do Business Professionals Need to Know About Computer Hardware?

Most people think of computer hardware as a laptop, a desktop, a server, or maybe even a tablet. As time passes, the way we think of computer hardware is changing. Take phones as an example. Twenty-five years ago, they were strictly used for voice communication. No one would have considered a phone a piece of computer hardware.

Fast-forward to today. Smartphones have substantial processing power, the ability to connect to networks, internal memory, and virtual keyboards and can interconnect with other devices. Now a "phone" is essentially a powerful piece of computing hardware. Computing hardware is also being integrated into other devices such as watches, glasses, TVs, cars, and even toothbrushes.

Computer hardware consists of electronic components and related gadgetry that input, process, output, and store data according to instructions encoded in computer programs or software. All hardware today has more or less the same components, at least to the level that is important to us. We'll begin with those components, and then we'll quickly survey basic types of computers.

Hardware Components

Over the course of your career, application software, hardware, and firmware will change, sometimes rapidly. The Guide on pages 186–187 challenges you to choose a strategy for addressing this change.

Every computer has a **central processing unit (CPU)**, which is sometimes called "the brain" of the computer. Although the design of the CPU has nothing in common with the anatomy of animal brains, this description is helpful because the CPU does have the "smarts" of the machine. The CPU selects instructions, processes them, performs arithmetic and logical comparisons, and stores results of operations in memory. Some computers have two or more CPUs. A computer with two CPUs is called a **dual-processor** computer. **Quad-processor** computers have four CPUs. Some high-end computers have 16 or more CPUs.

CPUs vary in speed, function, and cost. Hardware vendors such as Intel, Advanced Micro Devices, and National Semiconductor continually improve CPU speed and capabilities while reducing CPU costs (as discussed under Moore's Law in Chapter 1). Whether you or your department needs the latest, greatest CPU depends on the nature of your work.

The CPU works in conjunction with **main memory**. The CPU reads data and instructions from memory and then stores the results of computations in main memory. Main memory is sometimes called **RAM**, for random access memory.

All computers include **storage hardware**, which is used to save data and programs. Magnetic disks (also called hard disks) are the most common storage device. Solid-state storage (aka an SSD drive) is much faster than a hard drive and gaining in popularity, but it is several times more expensive. USB flash drives are small, portable solid-state storage devices that can be used to back up data and transfer it from one computer to another. Optical disks such as CDs and DVDs also are popular portable storage media.

Types of Hardware

Figure 4-1 lists the basic types of hardware. **Personal computers** (PCs) are classic computing devices that are used by individuals. In the past, PCs were the primary computer used in business. Today, they are gradually being supplanted by tablets and other mobile devices. The Mac Pro is an example of a modern PC. Apple brought **tablets** to prominence with the iPad. In 2012, Microsoft announced Surface and Google announced the Nexus series, all tablets. Smartphones are cell phones with processing capability; the Samsung Galaxy S6 is a good example. Today, because it's hard to find a cell phone that isn't "smart," people often just call them phones.

A **server** is a computer that is designed to support processing requests from many remote computers and users. A server is essentially a PC on steroids. A server differs from a PC principally because of what it does. The relationship between PCs and servers is similar to the relationship between clients and servers at a typical restaurant. Servers take requests from clients and then bring them things. In restaurants this is food and silverware. In computing environments servers can send Web pages, email, files, or data to PCs. PCs, tablets, and smartphones that access servers are called **clients**. As of 2016, a good example of a server is the Dell PowerEdge server.

Hardware Type	Example (s)
Personal Computer (PC) *Including desktops and laptops*	Apple Mac Pro
Tablet *Including e-book readers*	iPad, Microsoft Surface, Google Nexus, Kindle Fire
Smartphone	Samsung Galaxy, iPhone
Server	Dell PowerEdge 12G Server
Server Farm	Racks of servers (Figure 4-2)

Figure 4-1
Basic Types of Hardware

Figure 4-2
Server Farm
Source: © Andrew Twort/Alamy

Finally, a **server farm** is a collection of, typically, thousands of servers. (See Figure 4-2.) Server farms are often placed in large truck trailers that hold 5,000 servers or more. Typically a trailer has two large cables coming out of it; one is for power, and the other is for data communications. The operator of the farm backs a trailer into a pre-prepared slab (in a warehouse or sometimes out in the open air), plugs in the power and communications cables, and, voilà, thousands of servers are up and running!

Increasingly, server infrastructure is delivered as a service via the Internet that is often referred to as *the cloud*. We will discuss cloud computing in Chapter 6, after you have some knowledge of data communications.

The capacities of computer hardware are specified according to data units, which we discuss next.

Computer Data

Computers represent data using **binary digits**, called **bits**. A bit is either a zero or a one. Bits are used for computer data because they are easy to represent physically, as illustrated in Figure 4-3. A switch can be either closed or open. A computer can be designed so that an open switch represents

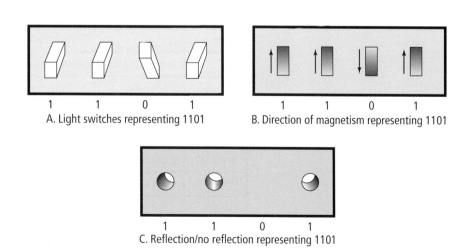

Figure 4-3
Bits Are Easy to Represent Physically

zero and a closed switch represents one. Or the orientation of a magnetic field can represent a bit: magnetism in one direction represents a zero; magnetism in the opposite direction represents a one. Or, for optical media, small pits are burned onto the surface of the disk so that they will reflect light. In a given spot, a reflection means a one; no reflection means a zero.

Computer Data Sizes

All forms of computer data are represented by bits. The data can be numbers, characters, currency amounts, photos, recordings, or whatever. All are simply a string of bits. For reasons that interest many but are irrelevant for future managers, bits are grouped into 8-bit chunks called **bytes**. For character data, such as the letters in a person's name, one character will fit into one byte. Thus, when you read a specification that a computing device has 100 million bytes of memory, you know that the device can hold up to 100 million characters.

Bytes are used to measure sizes of noncharacter data as well. Someone might say, for example, that a given picture is 100,000 bytes in size. This statement means the length of the bit string that represents the picture is 100,000 bytes or 800,000 bits (because there are 8 bits per byte).

The specifications for the size of main memory, disk, and other computer devices are expressed in bytes. Figure 4-4 shows the set of abbreviations that are used to represent data storage capacity. A **kilobyte**, abbreviated **KB**, is a collection of 1,024 bytes. A **megabyte**, or **MB**, is 1,024 kilobytes. A **gigabyte**, or **GB**, is 1,024 megabytes; a **terabyte**, or **TB**, is 1,024 gigabytes; a **petabyte**, or **PB**, is 1,024 terabytes; an **exabyte**, or **EB**, is 1,024 petabytes; and a **zettabyte**, or **ZB**, is 1,024 exabytes. Sometimes you will see these definitions simplified as 1KB equals 1,000 bytes and 1MB equals 1,000K, and so on. Such simplifications are incorrect, but they do ease the math.

To put these sizes in perspective consider that, as of 2014, Walmart stores about 2.5 PB worth of customer data.[1] Facebook processes about 600 TB each day, in a 300PB data warehouse.[2] The super-secret NSA data center in Utah is estimated to hold about 12 EB of data.[3] And Cisco estimates that annual global Internet traffic volume will exceed 1.6 ZB by the end of 2018.[4]

Specifying Hardware with Computer Data Sizes

Computer disk capacities are specified according to the amount of data they can contain. Thus, a 500GB disk can contain up to 500GB of data and programs. There is some overhead, so it is not quite 500GB, but it's close enough.

You can purchase computers with CPUs of different speeds. CPU speed is expressed in cycles called *hertz*. In 2015, a slow personal computer had a speed of 3.0 Gigahertz. A fast personal computer had a speed of 3.5+ Gigahertz, with dual processors. As predicted by Moore's Law, CPU speeds continually increase.

An employee who does only simple tasks such as word processing does not need a fast CPU; a 2.0 Gigahertz CPU will be fine. However, an employee who processes large, complicated spreadsheets or

Term	Definition	Abbreviation
Byte	Number of bits to represent one character	
Kilobyte	1,024 bytes	KB
Megabyte	1,024 K = 1,048,576 bytes	MB
Gigabyte	1,024 MB = 1,073,741,824 bytes	GB
Terabyte	1,024 GB = 1,099,511,627,776 bytes	TB
Petabyte	1,024 TB = 1,125,899,906,842,624 bytes	PB
Exabyte	1,024 PB = 1,152,921,504,606,846,976 bytes	EB
Zettabyte	1,024 EB = 1,180,591,620,717,411,303,424 bytes	ZB

Figure 4-4

Important Storage-Capacity Terminology

who manipulates large database files or edits large picture, sound, or video files needs a fast computer like a dual processor with 3.5 Gigahertz or more. Employees whose work requires them to use many large applications at the same time need 12 GB or more of RAM. Others can do with less.

One last comment: The cache and main memory are **volatile**, meaning their contents are lost when power is off. Magnetic and optical disks are **nonvolatile**, meaning their contents survive when power is off. If you suddenly lose power, the contents of unsaved memory—say, documents that have been altered—will be lost. Therefore, get into the habit of frequently (every few minutes or so) saving documents or files that you are changing. Save your documents before your roommate trips over the power cord.

Q4-2 How Can New Hardware Affect Competitive Strategies?

Organizations are interested in new hardware because they represent potential opportunities, or threats, to their ability to generate revenue. It's important to keep an eye on new tech hardware for the same reason you watch the weather forecast. You care about how the future will affect you.

Below we will look at three new hardware developments that have the potential to disrupt existing organizations.

Internet of Things

The first disruptive force that has the power to change business is the **Internet of Things (IoT)**. This is the idea that objects are becoming connected to the Internet so they can interact with other devices, applications, or services. Everyday objects are being embedded with hardware capable of sensing, processing, and transmitting data. Objects can then connect to a network and share data with any other application, service, or device.

Take your mobile phone, for example; it's probably a smartphone. But it wasn't always "smart." It started out as a simple device that just handled voice calls. Over time it became a **smart device** by adding more processing power, more memory, Internet access, Wi-Fi connectivity, and the ability to interconnect with other devices and applications (Figure 4-5). People began to use their mobile phones much differently than before. It also changed the way businesses operate. In 2014, Amazon.com reported that more than 60 percent of its customers shopped using a mobile device.[5]

Another class of smart devices that is showing a lot of potential is augmented reality (AR). **Augmented reality** is the combination of the real world with virtual images or objects, whereas **virtual reality** is a completely computer-generated virtual world. Industry leaders in the AR market, like Google (Glass), Microsoft (HoloLens), and Meta (Meta Pro), are fighting for a projected $120 billion market by 2020.[6] These smart glasses are developing in much the same way cellular phones developed over the past 20 years. In fact, it's entirely possible that the AR market could disrupt the smartphone market. Imagine taking calls, browsing the Web, messaging friends, and watching a movie without ever taking your smartphone out of your pocket.

What happens when other devices become smart? How would your life change if you had access to a smart car, smart home appliances, or an entire smart building? Within a few short decades it's possible that you could interact with nearly every object around you from your smartphone. In fact, your devices will be able to talk to other devices, anticipate your actions, make changes, and configure themselves.

This shift away from "dumb" devices to interconnected smart devices is not lost on businesses. Consumers like smart devices and are willing to pay more for them. Businesses want to improve the existing devices they manufacture into a smart devices and then sell them for twice as much. If they don't, someone else will.

Figure 4-5
Smartphone Development
Source: Grgroup/Fotolia

The iPhone, for example, was introduced by Apple Inc., a computing hardware and software company. The mobile phone market was already mature. Industry leaders could have created a smartphone, but they didn't. Apple's success with portable audio players (iPod) and mobile phones (iPhone) was a shot across the bow of other hardware manufacturers. A wave of smart devices is coming.

Impact of the Internet of Things

The impact of IoT will be felt by many different high-tech industries. Smart devices need microprocessors, memory, wireless network connections, a power source, and new software. These devices will also need new protocols, more bandwidth, and tighter security, and they will consume more energy.

A good example of this push toward smart devices is General Electric's (GE) Industrial Internet.[7] GE's Industrial Internet is a broad program focused on creating smart devices, analyzing the data from these devices, and then making changes that increase efficiencies, reduce waste, and improve decision making. GE sees the greatest potential for smart devices in hospitals, power grids, railroads, and manufacturing plants.

GE estimates that an average airline using smart devices in its jet aircraft could save an average of 2 percent in fuel consumption. The resulting fuel and carbon dioxide savings would be the equivalent of removing 10,000 cars from the road.[8]

Microsoft has also made tremendous gains using smart devices. Microsoft has created a network of 125 smart buildings spread over 500 acres in Redmond, Washington (Figure 4-6).[9] Its operations center processes 500 million data transactions every day from 30,000 devices, including heaters, air conditioners, lights, fans, and doors.

Microsoft engineers were able to reduce energy costs by 6 percent to 10 percent a year by identifying problems like wasteful lighting, competing heating and cooling systems, and rogue fans. For Microsoft, that's millions of dollars. What if every corporate building were a smart

Figure 4-6
Microsoft's Redmond, WA,
Campus
Source: Ian Dagnall/Alamy

building? When you consider that 40 percent of the world's energy is consumed in corporate buildings, you can start to get an idea of the immense cost savings.

Self-driving Cars

The second disruptive force that could change the way businesses operate is self-driving cars. A **self-driving car** (also known as a driverless car) uses a variety of sensors to navigate like a traditional car but without human intervention. It will be full of advanced hardware and integrated software and is the epitome of a mobile system. In fact, it will be so mobile that it will be able to move without anyone being in the car (Figure 4-7). Yes, self-driving cars are in your very near future.

A recent report by KPMG and the Center for Automotive Research indicates that self-driving cars will be a reality as soon as 2019.[10] Google is shooting for 2018, and most auto manufacturers (Mercedes-Benz, Nissan, Audi, and BMW) say they will have self-driving cars by 2020.[11] As of 2015, Google's latest self-driving car is a two-seater with no steering wheel, brake pedals, or accelerator.[12] Google's cars have logged more than 700,000 miles without a single accident. The Mercedes-Benz F 015 was the hit of the CES 2015 show when it drove itself on stage and opened its saloon-style doors revealing passenger seats facing each other. It looks like the race to develop self-driving cars is heating up. The competition will be fierce.

Self-driving cars will make things easier, cheaper, and safer. They'll also disrupt well-established industries.

Self-driving Cars Make Things Easier

Imagine how a self-driving car will change the lives of a typical family. A self-driving car could allow Dad to review sales reports while "driving" to work. He's much less stressed out—and more productive—during his commute than he was with his old car. The self-driving car could then drop off the kids at school—without Dad in the car—and return home to take Mom to work.

After work the family goes shopping and is dropped off curbside at the store. No need to park anymore. It's safer too. While shopping, Dad gets a message from his college-aged daughter that she needs the car sent to pick her up from the airport. Dad's glad he won't have to drive all the way out there.

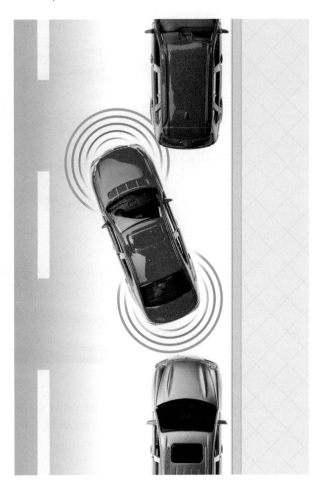

Figure 4-7
Future Cars Will Drive Themselves
Source: Dan Race/Fotolia

Dad remembers when he had to drive himself. It was a long and painful process. Now the car plans the route for him, fills itself up with gas, communicates with intersections so he never gets a red light, and reroutes itself if there's an accident or traffic. Most importantly, he doesn't get mad at other drivers. Traveling is just easier now.

Later the family plans a vacation to a distant locale. Taking the self-driving car is the way to go. No airport security lines, family members don't have to get frisked by overzealous TSA agents, they get comfortable seats that face each other, they don't have to pay for their bags, and they don't have to rent a car when they get there. Plus, they can leave anytime they like.

Sometimes it's nice to leave for vacation at night and sleep while you're "driving." Driving isn't bad when you don't actually drive.

Self-driving Cars Make Things Cheaper

You've seen how a self-driving car can make your life easier. But what about cost? Will it be more expensive or less expensive than the car you have now?

Self-driving cars will probably be much less expensive over time than your current car. Early adopters will pay a premium when self-driving cars first hit the market, but that's true of most new products.

Cost savings will show up in several ways. In the above scenario, you may have noticed that the family had only one car. Self-driving cars will be used more effectively than cars are used now. Most cars sit dormant for 22 hours a day. Sharing a self-driving car could eliminate the need to have multiple cars. That's a big cost savings.

You'll see more cost savings because a self-driving car will drive better than you. You'll save on fuel because it will drive more efficiently (less braking, revving the engine, and street racing!). You will avoid costly traffic tickets, parking tickets, and DUI citations.

Your car insurance will drop dramatically. It may be so low that you won't even need it anymore. One of the largest insurers in the United States, Travelers, said, "Driverless cars or technologies that facilitate ride or home sharing, could disrupt the demand for our products from current customers, create coverage issues or impact the frequency or severity of losses, and we may not be able to respond effectively."[13]

They're probably right. Self-driving cars will probably take a big chunk out of the $100B, paid each year in car insurance premiums. And they should. Your future self-driving car will be safer because its crash avoidance systems will apply the brakes before you're even aware of a problem. It will be able to know the exact locations, velocities, and routes of all cars within the vicinity. Automobile accidents may become a thing of the past.

Self-driving Cars Will Make Things Safer

Yes, you read that right—safer. Currently, 90 percent of motor vehicle crashes are caused by human error.[14] Motor vehicle crashes are the leading cause of death for people ages 3 to 33. Spending time driving may be the most dangerous thing you do all day.

Your car will be able to see better than you, react more quickly than you, and have better information about your driving environment. It will be able to communicate with other cars around it, dynamically analyze traffic patterns, avoid construction sites, and contact emergency services if needed.

Self-driving cars will mean safer driving, fewer accidents, fewer drunk drivers, fewer road-rage incidents, and fewer auto–pedestrian accidents. Cars will be able to go faster with fewer accidents. In the future, manual driving may be a risky and expensive hobby.

Self-driving Cars Will Disrupt Businesses

Self-driving cars have the potential to disrupt well-established industries. Self-driving cars may mean fewer cars on the road. Fewer cars on the road may mean fewer cars sold (transportation), fewer auto loans written (finance), fewer automobile insurance policies underwritten (insurance), fewer auto parts sold due to fewer accidents (manufacturing), and fewer parking lots (real estate). If they didn't have to drive, consumers might take more trips by car than by plane or train (transportation).

The production of self-driving cars will mean more jobs for engineers, programmers, and systems designers. There will be more computer hardware, sensors, and cameras in the vehicle. Corporations may not completely see the far-reaching effects of self-driving cars on existing industries.

How will self-driving cars disrupt your personal life? Suppose you get married in a few years and have a child. Will your child ever drive a car? Will driving a "manual" car be too costly? Your potential offspring may never learn how to drive a car. But that may not be too strange. Do you know how to ride a horse? Your ancestors did.

3D Printing

The third disruptive force that has the power to change businesses is 3D printing. As you learned in Chapter 3, 3D printing will not only change the competitive landscape, but it may change the nature of businesses themselves. Think back to the Falcon Security case at the start of this chapter. The Falcon Security team chose not to make its own drones because doing so wasn't going to save the company enough money. It didn't want to use 3D printing to become a drone manufacturer.

While manufacturing wasn't right for Falcon, it is a viable option for some companies. Consider how Nike has used 3D printing to improve the way it designs and creates shoes. It recently used a 3D printer to create the world's first 3D-printed cleat plate for a shoe called the Nike Vapor Laser

Figure 4-8
3D Printer
Source: Seraficus/iStock/Getty Images

Talon.[15] Nike chose to use a 3D printer to produce the cleat because it could create the optimal geometric shapes for optimal traction. Using a 3D printer, it could design and produce a lighter and stronger cleat much more quickly than before. Even more interesting, in late 2014 Nike filed a patent for a new type of 3D printer that can print objects on fabric that won't distort when stretched.

3D printers have the potential to affect a broad array of industries beyond sporting equipment. You can get an idea of the scope of change when you realize that 3D printers can print in more than just plastics (Figure 4-8). They can print in metals, ceramics, foods, and biological material too.

At CES 2015, industry leader MakerBot announced that it will begin selling composite filaments that can be used in its 3D printers. These new composite filaments combine traditional PLA (polylactic acid) thermoplastic with materials like wood, bronze, iron, and limestone. While each type of composite filament will require a new 3D print head, the printed objects will look and behave like their real-world counterparts.

Take the ability to 3D-print in a variety of materials and look for opportunities across the aerospace, defense, automotive, entertainment, and healthcare industries. What happens when it becomes feasible to 3D-print extra-large objects like cars,[16] planes, boats, houses, and drones?

Below are three examples of nontraditional 3D printing. Consider how disruptive each one would be to its respective industry:

- 3D Systems new ChefJet™ Pro can print complex sugary structures in flavors like chocolate, vanilla, mint, cherry, sour apple, and watermelon.[17] With a ChefJet, even a culinary novice could produce intricate, beautiful, and fully customized deserts.
- Researchers at the Harvard School of Engineering and Applied Sciences were able to print a 3D biological structure with blood vessels that could deliver nutrients and remove waste.[18] This development means doctors will be able to print fully functional replacements for damaged tissues by simply pressing print. Not only could this save lives, but it could also lower insurance premiums and the overall cost of health care.
- Professor Behrokh Khoshnevis of the University of Southern California has built a large-scale 3D printer that can print an entire house in 24 hours.[19] This 3D home printer would create more stable and better insulated structures, use less materials, reduce workplace injuries, automatically install heating and plumbing, and produce the home at a fraction of the cost.

Q4-3 What Do Business Professionals Need to Know About Software?

Operating systems can become infected with malware. Read the Security Guide on pages 184–185 to learn more.

As a future manager or business professional, you need to know the essential terminology and software concepts that will enable you to be an intelligent software consumer. To begin, consider the basic categories of software shown in Figure 4-9.

Every computer has an **operating system (OS)**, which is a program that controls that computer's resources. Some of the functions of an operating system are to read and write data, allocate main memory, perform memory swapping, start and stop programs, respond to error conditions, and facilitate backup and recovery. In addition, the operating system creates and manages the user interface, including the display, keyboard, mouse, and other devices.

Although the operating system makes the computer usable, it does little application-specific work. If you want to check the weather or access a database, you need application programs such as an iPad weather application or Oracle's customer relationship management (CRM) software.

Both client and server computers need an operating system, though they need not be the same. Further, both clients and servers can process application programs. The application's design determines whether the client, the server, or both process it.

You need to understand two important software constraints. First, a particular version of an operating system is written for a particular type of hardware. For example, Microsoft Windows works only on processors from Intel and companies that make processors that conform to the Intel instruction set (the commands that a CPU can process). With other operating systems, such as Linux, many versions exist for many different instruction sets.

Second, two types of application programs exist. **Native applications** are programs that are written to use a particular operating system. Microsoft Access, for example, will run only on the Windows operating system. Some applications come in multiple versions. For example, there are Windows and Macintosh versions of Microsoft Word. But unless you are informed otherwise, assume that a native application runs on just one operating system. Native applications are sometimes called **thick-client applications**.

A **Web application** (also known as a thin-client application) is designed to run within a computer browser such as Firefox, Chrome, Opera, or Edge (formerly Internet Explorer). Web applications run within the browser and can run on any type of computer. Ideally, a Web application can also run within any browser, though this is not always true as you will learn.

Consider next the operating system and application program categories of software.

What Are the Major Operating Systems?

The major operating systems are listed in Figure 4-10. Consider each.

Nonmobile Client Operating Systems

Nonmobile client operating systems are used on personal computers. The most popular is **Microsoft Windows**. Some version of Windows resides on more than 85 percent of the world's desktops, and, if we consider just business users, the figure is more than 95 percent. The most

	Operating System	**Application Programs**
Client	Programs that control the client computer's resources	Applications that are processed on client computers
Server	Programs that control the server computer's resources	Applications that are processed on server computers

Figure 4-9
Categories of Computer Software

Category	Operating System	Used for	Remarks
Nonmobile Clients	Windows	Personal Computer Clients	Most widely used operating system in business. Current version is Windows 10. Includes a touch interface.
	Mac OS	Macintosh Clients	First used by graphic artists and others in arts community; now used more widely. First desktop OS to provide a touch interface. Current version is the Mac OS X El Capitan.
	Unix	Workstation Clients	Popular on powerful client computers used in engineering, computer-assisted design, architecture. Difficult for the nontechnical user. Almost never used by business clients.
	Linux	Just about anything	Open-source variant of Unix. Adapted to almost every type of computing device. On a PC, used with Libre Office application software. Rarely used by business clients.
Mobile Clients	Symbian	Nokia, Samsung, and other phones	Popular worldwide, but less so in North America.
	Blackberry OS	Research in Motion Blackberries	Device and OS developed for use by business. Very popular in beginning, but losing market share to iOS and Android.
	iOS	iPhone, iPod Touch, iPad	Rapidly increasing installed base with success of the iPhone and iPad. Based on Mac OS X.
	Android	Samsung, Google, HTC, and Sony smartphones; tablets	Linux-based phone/tablet operating system from Google. Rapidly increasing market share.
	Windows 10 (mobile)	Nokia and Microsoft Surface	Windows 10 tailored specifically for mobile devices. Full Windows 10 on Surface Pro.
Servers	Windows Server	Servers	Businesses with a strong commitment to Microsoft.
	Unix	Servers	Fading from use. Replaced by Linux.
	Linux	Servers	Very popular. Aggressively pushed by IBM.

Figure 4-10
Major Operating Systems

recent version of Windows is Windows 10. Net Applications estimates that overall market share of Windows as of 2015 is Windows 10 at 0.1 percent, Windows 8.1 at 11.2 percent, Windows 8 at 3.5 percent, Windows 7 at 58.4 percent, Windows Vista at 2.0 percent, and Windows XP at 16.0 percent.[20] It's interesting to note that Microsoft dropped support for Windows XP in 2014 despite the fact that it is still more popular than Windows Vista, Windows 8, Windows 8.1, and Windows 10.

Windows 8 was a major rewrite of prior versions. Windows 8 was distinguished by what Microsoft calls **modern-style applications**.[21] These applications, now carried over into Windows 10, are touch-screen oriented and provide context-sensitive, pop-up menus. They can also be used with a mouse and keyboard. Microsoft claims that modern-style applications work just as well on portable, mobile devices, such as tablet computers, as they do on desktop computers. One key feature of modern-style applications is the minimization of menu bars, status lines, and other visual overhead. Figure 4-11 shows an example of a modern-style version of searching for images in Windows Explorer.

Apple Computer, Inc., developed its own operating system for the Macintosh, **Mac OS**. The current version is Mac OS X El Capitan. Apple touts it as the world's most advanced desktop operating system, and, until Windows 8, it was without doubt. Windows 10 now gives it a run for the money in terms of that title.

Figure 4-11

Example of the Modern-Style Interface

Source: © Access 2013, Microsoft Corporation

Until recently, Mac OS was used primarily by graphic artists and workers in the arts community. But for many reasons, Mac OS has made headway into the traditional Windows market. According to Net Applications, as of 2015, desktop operating system market share was divided between versions of Windows (91.0 percent), OS X (5.8 percent), and Linux (1.5 percent).[22]

Mac OS was designed originally to run the line of CPU processors from Motorola, but today a Macintosh with an Intel processor is able to run both Windows and the Mac OS.

Unix is an operating system that was developed at Bell Labs in the 1970s. It has been the workhorse of the scientific and engineering communities since then. Unix is seldom used in business.

Linux is a version of Unix that was developed by the open source community. This community is a loosely coupled group of programmers who mostly volunteer their time to contribute code to develop and maintain Linux. The open source community owns Linux, and there is no fee to use it. Linux can run on client computers, but usually only when budget is of paramount concern. By far, Linux is most popular as a server OS. According to *DistroWatch.com*, the top five most popular versions of Linux as of 2015 were Linux Mint, Ubuntu, Debian GNU/Linux, openSUSE, and Fedora.[23]

Mobile Client Operating Systems

Figure 4-10 also lists the five principal mobile operating systems. **Symbian** is popular on phones in Europe and the Far East, but less so in North America. **BlackBerry OS** was one of the most successful early mobile operating systems and was used primarily by business users on BlackBerry devices. It has lost market share to iOS, Android, and Windows 10.

iOS is the operating system used on the iPhone, iPod Touch, and iPad. When first released, it broke new ground with its ease of use and compelling display, features that are now being copied by the BlackBerry OS and Android. With the popularity of the iPhone and iPad, Apple has been increasing its market share of iOS, and, according to Net Applications, it is used on 39 percent of mobile devices.[24] The current version of iOS is iOS 8.

Android is a mobile operating system licensed by Google. Android devices have a very loyal following, especially among technical users. Net Applications estimates Android's market share to be nearly 52 percent.

Most industry observers would agree that Apple has led the way, both with the Mac OS and the iOS, in creating easy-to-use interfaces. Certainly, many innovative ideas have first appeared in a Macintosh or iSomething and then later were added, in one form or another, to Android and Windows.

Users who want Windows 10 on mobile devices will get either **Windows 10 (mobile)** on smartphones or a full version of Windows 10 on Surface Pro devices. Windows garners about 2 percent of the mobile OS market share.

The smartphone market has always been huge, but recently, e-book readers and tablets have substantially increased the market for mobile client operating systems. As of April 2015, 64 percent of Americans owned a smartphone, and 53 percent owned a tablet in addition to their smartphone.[25]

Server Operating Systems

The last three rows of Figure 4-10 show the three most popular server operating systems. **Windows Server** is a version of Windows that has been specially designed and configured for server use. It has much more stringent and restrictive security features than other versions of Windows and is popular on servers in organizations that have made a strong commitment to Microsoft.

Unix can also be used on servers, but it is gradually being replaced by Linux.

Linux is frequently used on servers by organizations that want, for whatever reason, to avoid a server commitment to Microsoft. IBM is the primary proponent of Linux and in the past has used it as a means to better compete against Microsoft. Although IBM does not own Linux, IBM has developed many business systems solutions that use Linux. By using Linux, neither IBM nor its customers have to pay a license fee to Microsoft.

Virtualization

Virtualization is the process by which one physical computer hosts many different virtual (not literal) computers within it. One operating system, called the **host operating system**, runs one or more operating systems as applications. Those hosted operating systems are called **virtual machines (vm)**. Each virtual machine has disk space and other resources allocated to it. The host operating system controls the activities of the virtual machines it hosts to prevent them from interfering with one another. With virtualization, each vm is able to operate exactly the same as it would if it were operating in a stand-alone, nonvirtual environment.

Three types of virtualization exist:

- PC virtualization
- Server virtualization
- Desktop virtualization

With **PC virtualization**, a personal computer, such as a desktop or laptop, hosts several different operating systems. Say a user needs to have both Linux and Windows running on a computer for a training or development project. In that circumstance, the user can load software like Oracle VirtualBox or VMWare Workstation on the host operating system in order to create Linux and Windows virtual machines. The user can run both systems on the same hardware at the same time if the host operating system has sufficient resources (i.e., memory and CPU power) as shown in Figure 4-12.

With **server virtualization**, a server computer hosts one or more other server computers. In Figure 4-13, a Windows Server computer is hosting two virtual machines. Users can log on to either of those virtual machines, and they will appear as normal servers. Figure 4-14 shows how virtual machine VM3 appears to a user of that server. Notice that a user of VM3 is running a browser that is accessing SharePoint. In fact, this virtual machine was used to generate many of the SharePoint figures in Chapter 2. Server virtualization plays a key role for cloud vendors, as you'll learn in Chapter 6.

Figure 4-12

Linux Mint Virtual Machine Running in Microsoft Windows 7 Professional

Source: © Access 2013, Microsoft Corporation

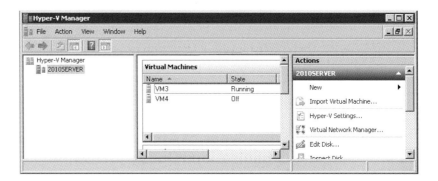

Figure 4-13

Windows Server Computer Hosting Two Virtual Machines

Source: © Access 2013, Microsoft Corporation

Figure 4-14

Virtual Machine Example

Source: © Access 2013, Microsoft Corporation

PC virtualization is interesting as well as quite useful, as you will learn in Chapter 6. Desktop virtualization, on the other hand, has the potential to be revolutionary. With **desktop virtualization**, a server hosts many versions of desktop operating systems. Each of those desktops has a complete user environment and appears to the user to be just another PC. However, the desktop can be accessed from any computer to which the user has access. Thus, you could be at an airport and go to a terminal computer and access your virtualized desktop. To you, it appears as if that airport computer is your own personal computer. Using a virtual desktop also means that you wouldn't have to worry about losing a corporate laptop or confidential internal data. Meanwhile, many other users could have accessed the computer in the airport, and each thought he or she had his or her personal computer. IBM offers PC virtualization for as low as $12 a month per PC.

Desktop virtualization is in its infancy, but it might have major impact during the early years of your career.

Own Versus License

When you buy a computer program, you are not actually buying that program. Instead, you are buying a **license** to use that program. For example, when you buy a Mac OS license, Apple is selling you the right to use Mac OS. Apple continues to own the Mac OS program. Large organizations do not buy a license for each computer user. Instead, they negotiate a **site license**, which is a flat fee that authorizes the company to install the product (operating system or application) on all of that company's computers or on all of the computers at a specific site.

In the case of Linux, no company can sell you a license to use it. It is owned by the open source community, which states that Linux has no license fee (with certain reasonable restrictions). Large companies such as IBM and smaller companies such as RedHat can make money by *supporting* Linux, but no company makes money selling Linux licenses.

What Types of Applications Exist, and How Do Organizations Obtain Them?

Some applications are designed to be free but gather data about the people who use them. Read the Ethics Guide on pages 176–177 about how this is done.

Application software performs a service or function. Some application programs are general purpose, such as Microsoft Excel or Word. Other application programs provide specific functions. QuickBooks, for example, is an application program that provides general ledger and other accounting functions. We begin by describing categories of application programs and then describe sources for them.

Horizontal-market application software provides capabilities common across all organizations and industries. Word processors, graphics programs, spreadsheets, and presentation programs are all horizontal-market application software.

Examples of such software are Microsoft Word, Excel, and PowerPoint. Examples from other vendors are Adobe's Acrobat, Photoshop, and PageMaker and Jasc Corporation's Paint Shop Pro. These applications are used in a wide variety of businesses across all industries. They are purchased off the shelf, and little customization of features is necessary (or possible). They are the automobile equivalent of a sedan. Everybody buys them and then uses them for different purposes.

Vertical-market application software serves the needs of a specific industry. Examples of such programs are those used by dental offices to schedule appointments and bill patients, those used by auto mechanics to keep track of customer data and customers' automobile repairs, and those used by parts warehouses to track inventory, purchases, and sales. If horizontal-market applications are sedans, then vertical-market applications would be construction vehicles, like an excavator. They meet the needs of a specific industry.

Vertical applications usually can be altered or customized. Typically, the company that sold the application software will provide such services or offer referrals to qualified consultants who can provide this service.

Software Source

	Off-the-shelf	Off-the-shelf and then customized	Custom-developed
Software Type Horizontal applications			
Vertical applications			
One-of-a-kind applications			

Figure 4-15
Software Sources and Types

One-of-a-kind application software is developed for a specific, unique need. The U.S. Department of Defense develops such software, for example, because it has needs that no other organization has.

You can think of one-of-a-kind application software as the automotive equivalent of a military tank. Tanks are developed for a very specific and unique need. Tanks cost more to manufacture than sedans, and cost overruns are common. They take longer to make and require unique hardware components. However, tanks are highly customizable and fit the requirements of a heavy-duty battle vehicle very well.

If you're headed into battle, you wouldn't want to be driving a four-door sedan. Sometimes paying for a custom vehicle, while expensive, is warranted. It all depends on what you're doing. Militaries, for example, purchase sedans, construction vehicles, and tanks. Each vehicle fills its own need. You can buy computer software in exactly the same ways: **off-the-shelf software**, **off-the-shelf with alterations software**, or **custom-developed software**.

Organizations develop custom application software themselves or hire a development vendor. Like buying a tank, such development is done in situations where the needs of the organization are so unique that no horizontal or vertical applications are available. By developing custom software, the organization can tailor its application to fit its requirements.

Custom development is difficult and risky. Staffing and managing teams of software developers is challenging. Managing software projects can be daunting. Many organizations have embarked on application development projects only to find that the projects take twice as long—or longer—to finish than planned. Cost overruns of 200 percent and 300 percent are not uncommon. We will discuss such risks further in Chapter 12.

In addition, every application program needs to be adapted to changing needs and changing technologies. The adaptation costs of horizontal and vertical software are amortized over all the users of that software, perhaps thousands or millions of customers. For custom-developed software, however, the using organization must pay all of the adaptation costs itself. Over time, this cost burden is heavy.

Because of the risk and expense, custom development is the last-choice alternative, used only when there is no other option. Figure 4-15 summarizes software sources and types.

What Is Firmware?

Firmware is computer software that is installed into devices such as printers, print servers, and various types of communication devices. The software is coded just like other software, but it is installed into special, read-only memory of the printer or other device. In this way, the program becomes part of the device's memory; it is as if the program's logic is designed into the device's circuitry. Therefore, users do not need to load firmware into the device's memory. Firmware can be changed or upgraded, but this is normally a task for IS professionals.

Q4-4   Is Open Source Software a Viable Alternative?

To answer this question, you first need to know something about the open source movement and process. Most computer historians would agree that Richard Matthew Stallman is the father of the movement. In 1983, he developed a set of tools called **GNU** (a self-referential acronym meaning *GNU Not Unix*) for creating a free Unix-like operating system. Stallman made many other contributions to open source, including the **GNU general public license (GPL) agreement,** one of the standard license agreements for open source software. Stallman was unable to attract enough developers to finish the free Unix system but continued making other contributions to the open source movement.

In 1991 Linus Torvalds, working in Helsinki, began work on another version of Unix, using some of Stallman's tools. That version eventually became Linux, the high-quality and very popular operating system discussed previously.

The Internet proved to be a great asset for open source, and many open source projects became successful, including:

- LibreOffice (default office suite in Linux distributions)
- Firefox (a browser)
- MySQL (a DBMS, see Chapter 5)
- Apache (a Web server, see Chapter 6)
- Ubuntu (a Windows-like desktop operating system)
- Android (a mobile device operating system)
- Cassandra (a NoSQL DBMS, see Chapter 5)
- Hadoop (a BigData processing system, see Chapter 9)

Why Do Programmers Volunteer Their Services?

To a person who has never enjoyed writing computer programs, it is difficult to understand why anyone would donate his or her time and skills to contribute to open source projects. Programming is, however, an intense combination of art and logic, and designing and writing a complicated computer program can be exceedingly pleasurable (and addictive). Many programmers joyfully write computer programs—day after day. If you have an artistic and logical mind, you ought to try it.

The first reason that people contribute to open source is that it is great fun! Additionally, some people contribute to open source because it gives them the freedom to choose the projects they work on. They may have a programming day job that is not terribly interesting—say, writing a program to manage a computer printer. Their job pays the bills, but it's not fulfilling.

In the 1950s, Hollywood studio musicians suffered as they recorded the same style of music over and over for a long string of uninteresting movies. To keep their sanity, those musicians would gather on Sundays to play jazz, and a number of high-quality jazz clubs resulted. That's what open source is to programmers: a place where they can exercise their creativity while working on projects they find interesting and fulfilling.

Another reason for contributing to open source is to exhibit one's skill, both for pride and to find a job or consulting employment. A final reason is to start a business selling services to support an open source product.

How Does Open Source Work?

The term **open source** means that the source code of the program is available to the public. **Source code** is computer code as written by humans and understandable by humans. Figure 4-16 shows a portion of the computer code written for the PRIDE project (see Chapter 7 opener).

SO WHAT?

New from CES 2015

Source: VECTORWORKS_ENTERPRISE/Shutterstock

What's new in hardware? It's the Consumer Electronics Show (CES) held in Las Vegas every January: 3,600 exhibitors and 170,000-plus hardware-gawking attendees whipped to frenzy by loud music, screaming video, and hyperventilating media. It's a show that only Las Vegas can do!

What's hot this year? How about:

1. **Mercedes-Benz F015:** At the top of everyone's list of must-see innovations at CES 2015 was the new driverless Mercedes-Benz F015. This isn't just a driverless car. It's one of the first cars designed specifically as a driverless vehicle, not just an adaptation of a traditional driver-centric vehicle. It's more like a futuristic silver carriage with saloon-style doors. Inside the F015, passengers sit facing each other, chatting while the car does the driving. They are surrounded by interactive touch screens that can control the entire vehicle. Passengers can even control the car using hand gestures and eye movements.

    The F015 is a fuel-cell plug-in hybrid with a range of about 680 miles. Those aren't stressful driving miles either. Passengers can chat, work, or even sleep the whole way. The Mercedes-Benz F015 will likely change the way people think about travel.

    Oh, and the F015 can talk too. Pedestrians walking in front of the F015's hear its voice telling them that it's safe to cross in front of it. The F015 then projects a crosswalk in front of the car to guide pedestrians across the street. If you want to see what cars will look like 10 to 15 years from now, check out the F015.

2. **Works with Nest:** Nest Labs made big strides over the past year after being acquired by Google in 2014 for $3.2B. Nest Labs is best known for its smart thermostat and smart smoke detector. But Nest Labs is quickly becoming known more broadly as a home automation company. Network-enabled smart devices using Nest standards can be controlled remotely and interact with other devices and applications.

    At the CES 2015 show, the list of "Works with Nest" partners grew beyond Whirlpool, LG, Mercedes-Benz, Logitech, and August Smart Lock. New companies included Pebble (smartwatch), Rachio (sprinklers), Interactive Voice (voice-activated alarm clock), and Life360 (smartphone tracking app). Nest Labs is positioning itself to be the leader in home automation services.

    As more IoT devices come online, expect to see them get the Works with Nest label. This will allow devices to dynamically communicate with each other to create new synergies that didn't exist before. Imagine your car telling your thermostat that you're 20 minutes away and that it should start warming the house up. Your bread maker is nearly done with a fresh loaf of bread, your lights are ready to turn on the instant you pull in the drive, and you're getting live streaming video of your dog playing in the backyard.

    The convergence between home automation and IoT is going to produce some really interesting products over the next couple of years. Watch for new announcements from Nest Labs at CES 2016.

3. **Composite Filaments:** MakerBot really pushed 3D printing ahead this year when it introduced several new *composite* filaments. These composite filaments combine traditional PLA (polylactic acid) thermoplastic with materials like wood, bronze, iron, and limestone. They can be used to 3D-print objects that look and behave like their real-world counterparts.

    Wood furniture can be printed, sanded, and stained just like real wood. And it feels like wood too. Metal objects like jewelry, tools, and parts can be printed and polished and look just like their pure-metal cousins. Even the limestone composite filament produces objects that look and feel like real limestone.

    MakerBot's new composite filaments are important because they make it economical to now print in metal, wood, and stone. In the past it was possible to 3D-print in metal, but metal laser sintering was expensive. These new composite filaments make it possible to print objects like a hammer that have both metal and wood parts. The downside is that printing with these new composite filaments requires a unique print head for each type of filament. For most consumers, the cost of an additional print head to print in each additional material will probably be a minor issue.

MakerBot's introduction of new composite filaments has the potential to push 3D printing beyond the use of hobbyists, inventors, and manufacturers. A reasonably priced 3D printer that can print more than 50 percent of the objects in a typical household could be a valuable home appliance.

Questions

1. What would be the benefits of Mercedes-Benz's new "carriage"-type driverless car over a traditional car that has been converted to be driverless?

2. Why would Mercedes-Benz want its new driverless cars to talk to pedestrians?

3. How could a Nest thermostat save you money?

4. What advantages would a Nest-compliant washing machine have over a traditional one?

5. Why are 3D printers a potentially disruptive technology to manufacturing?

6. How could new composite filaments affect innovation, prototyping, and new product development?

Source code is compiled into **machine code** that is processed by a computer. Machine code is, in general, not understandable by humans and cannot be modified. When a user accesses a Web site, the machine code version of the program runs on the user's computer. We do not show machine code in a figure because it would look like this:

11010010100101111110011101111001000111000001111110111011101111100111...

In a **closed source** project, say, Microsoft Office, the source code is highly protected and only available to trusted employees and carefully vetted contractors. The source code is protected like gold in a vault. Only those trusted programmers can make changes to a closed source project.

Figure 4-16
Source Code Sample

```
/// <summary>
/// Allows the page to draw itself.
/// </summary>
private void OnDraw(object sender, GameTimerEventArgs e)
{
    SharedGraphicsDeviceManager.Current.GraphicsDevice.Clear(Color.CornflowerBlue);

    SharedGraphicsDeviceManager.Current.GraphicsDevice.Clear(Color.Black);

    // Render the Silverlight controls using the UIElementRenderer.
    elementRenderer.Render();

    // Draw the sprite
    spriteBatch.Begin();

    // Draw the rectangle in its new position
    for (int i = 0; i < 3; i++)
    {
        spriteBatch.Draw(texture[i], bikeSpritePosition[i], Color.White);
    }

    // Using the texture from the UIElementRenderer,

    // draw the Silverlight controls to the screen.
    spriteBatch.Draw(elementRenderer.Texture, Vector2.Zero, Color.White);

    spriteBatch.End();
}
```

With open source, anyone can obtain the source code from the open source project's Web site. Programmers alter or add to this code depending on their interests and goals. In most cases, programmers can incorporate code they find into their own projects. They may be able to resell those projects depending on the type of license agreement the project uses.

Open source succeeds because of collaboration. A programmer examines the source code and identifies a need or project that seems interesting. He or she then creates a new feature, redesigns or reprograms an existing feature, or fixes a known problem. That code is then sent to others in the open source project who evaluate the quality and merits of the work and add it to the product, if appropriate.

Typically, there is a lot of give and take. Or, as described in Chapter 2, there are many cycles of iteration and feedback. Because of this iteration, a well-managed project with strong peer reviews can result in very high quality code, like that in Linux.

So, Is Open Source Viable?

The answer depends on to whom and for what. Open source has certainly become legitimate. According to *The Economist*, "It is now generally accepted that the future will involve a blend of both proprietary and open-source software."[26] During your career, open source will likely take a greater and greater role in software. However, whether open source works for a particular situation depends on the requirements and constraints of that situation. You will learn more about matching requirements and programs in Chapter 12.

In some cases, companies choose open source software because it is "free." It turns out that this advantage may be less important than you'd think because in many cases support and operational costs swamp the initial licensing fee.

Q4-5 What Are the Differences Between Native and Web Applications?

Applications can be categorized as native applications that run on just one operating system or Web applications that run in browsers. In the latter case, the browser provides a more or less consistent environment for the application; the peculiarities of operating systems and hardware are handled by the browser's code and hidden from the Web application.

Figure 4-17 contrasts native and Web applications on their important characteristics. Consider the Native Applications column first.

Developing Native Applications

Native applications are developed using serious, heavy-duty, professional programming languages. Mac OS and iOS applications are constructed using Objective-C or the **Swift** programming language. Linux (Android) applications are constructed using Java, and Windows applications are constructed using C#, VB.NET, C++, and others. All of these languages are **object-oriented**, which means they can be used to create difficult, complex applications and, if used properly, will result in high-performance code that is easy to alter when requirements change. The particular characteristics of object-oriented languages are beyond the scope of this text.

Object-oriented languages can be used only by professional programmers who have devoted years to learning object-oriented design and coding skills. Typically, such developers were computer science majors in college.

The benefit of such languages is that they give programmers close control over the assets of the computing device and enable the creation of sophisticated and complex user interfaces. If the programs are well written, they perform fast and use memory efficiently. The limits on native

	Native Applications	**Web Applications**
Development Languages	Objective-C Java C#, C++, VB.NET, Swift (object-oriented languages)	html5 css3 JavaScript (scripting language)
Developed by	Professional programmers, only	Professional programmers and technically oriented Web developers and business professionals
Skill level required	High	Low to high
Difficulty	High	Easy to hard, depending on application requirements
Developer's Degree	Computer science	Computer science Information systems Graphics design
User Experience	Can be superb, depending on programming quality	Simple to sophisticated, depending on program quality
Possible applications	Whatever you can pay for…	Some limits prohibit very sophisticated applications
Dependency	iOS, Android, Windows	Browser differences, only
Cost	High. Difficult work by highly paid employees, multiple versions required.	Low to high … easier work by lesser-paid employees, only multiple browser files necessary. Sophisticated applications may require high skill and pay.
Application distribution	Via application stores (e.g., Apple Store)	Via Web sites
Example	Vanguard iPad application (free in Apple's iTunes store)	Seafood Web site: www.wildrhodyseafood.com Picozu editor: www.picozu.com/editor

Figure 4-17
Characteristics of Native and Web Applications

applications are usually budgetary, not technological. As a businessperson, you can get just about any application you can afford.

The downside of native applications is that they are, well, native. They only run on the operating system for which they are programmed. An iOS application must be completely recoded in order to run on Android and recoded again to run on Windows.[27] Thus, to reach all users, an organization will need to support and maintain three separate versions of the same application. It will also have to staff and manage three different development teams, with three different skill sets.

As a general rule, the cost of native applications is high. Many organizations reduce that cost by outsourcing development to India and other countries (see the introduction to Chapter 11), but native applications are still expensive relative to Web applications. The standard way to distribute native applications is via a company store, such as iTunes, owned by Apple. An excellent example of a native application is Vanguard's iPad application. It is easy to use, has complex functionality, and is highly secure, as you would expect. Companies such as Vanguard must and can afford to pay for exceedingly high-quality applications.

Developing Web Applications

The third column in Figure 4-17 summarizes Web application characteristics. Such applications run inside a browser such as Firefox, Chrome, Opera, or Edge. The browser handles the idiosyncrasies of the operating system and underlying hardware. In theory, an organization should be able to develop a single application and have it run flawlessly on all browsers on all devices. Unfortunately, there are some differences in the way that browsers implement the Web code. This means that some applications won't run correctly in some browsers.

As shown in the first row of Figure 4-17, Web development languages are html5, css3, and Javascript. html5 is the latest version of html, which you will learn about in Chapter 6. The advantages of this version are support for graphics, animation, 2D animations, and other sophisticated user experiences. css3 is used with html5 to specify the appearance of content coded in html. JavaScript is a scripting programming language that is much easier to learn than native-client languages. It is used to provide the underlying logic of the application.

Web applications can be written by professional programmers, and, indeed, most are. However, it is possible for technically oriented Web developers and business professionals to develop them as well. The entry-level technical skill required is low, and simple applications are relatively easy to develop. But sophisticated user experiences are difficult. Web application developers may have degrees in computer science, information systems, or graphics design.

The user experience provided by a Web application varies considerably. Some are simply fancy Web-based brochures (*www.wildrhodyseafood.com*); others are quite sophisticated, such as SpiroCanvas in Figure 4-18 (*www.gethugames.in/*) or, even more impressive, *www.biodigital.com* in Figure 4-19.

Web applications are limited by the capabilities of the browser. While browsers are becoming increasingly sophisticated, they cannot offer the full capabilities of the underlying operating system and hardware. Thus, Web applications are unable to support very specialized and complex applications, though this becomes less true each year.

As stated, the major advantage of Web over native applications is that they will run on any operating system and device. There are some browser differences, but these differences are very minor when compared with the differences among iOS, Android, and Windows. In general, unlike native applications, you can assume that a Web application has one code base and one development team.

Because Web applications can be developed by less skilled, lesser-paid employees and because only one code base and one development team are necessary, they are considerably cheaper to develop than native applications. However, this statement assumes applications of equivalent complexity. A simple native application can be cheaper to develop than a complex Web application.

Users obtain Web applications via the Internet. For example, when you go to *www.picozu.com/editor* the required html5, css3, and JavaScript files are downloaded automatically over the Web.

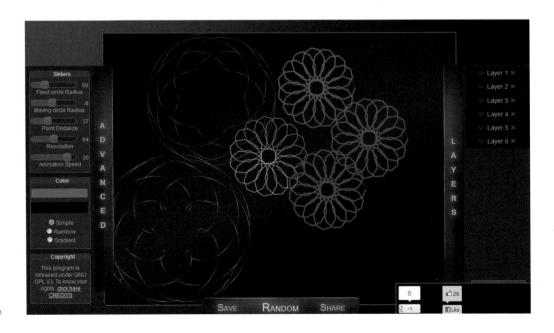

Figure 4-18

GethuGames' SpiroCanvas

Source: www.gethugames.in/ spirocanvas/ Reprinted by permission

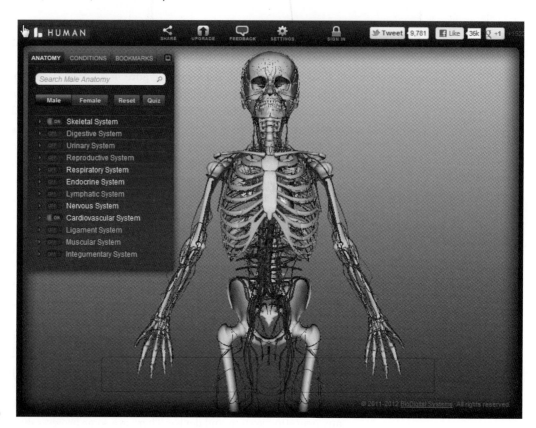

Figure 4-19
Sophisticated html5 Application
Source: Image created using the
BioDigital Human (*www.biodigital.com*)

Updates to the application are automatic and seamless. You need not install (or reinstall) anything. This difference is an advantage to the user; it makes it more difficult, however, to earn money from your application. Amazon, for example, will sell your native application and pay you a royalty. However, unless you require users to buy your Web application (which is possible, but rare), you'll have to give it away.

Which Is Better?

You know the answer to that question. If it were clear-cut, we'd only be discussing one alternative. It's not. The choice depends on your strategy, your particular goals, the requirements for your application, your budget, your schedule, your tolerance for managing technical projects, your need for application revenue, and other factors. In general, Web applications are cheaper to develop and maintain, but they may lack the wow factor. You and your organization have to decide for yourselves!

Q4-6 Why Are Mobile Systems Increasingly Important?

Mobile systems are information systems that support users in motion. Mobile systems users access the system from *any place*—at home, at work, in the car, on the bus, or at the beach—using any smart device, such as a smartphone, tablet, or PC. The possibilities are endless.

Mobile systems users move not only geographically but also from device to device. The user who starts reading a book on an iPad on a bus, continues reading that book on a PC at work, and finishes it on a Kindle Fire at home is mobile both geographically and across devices.

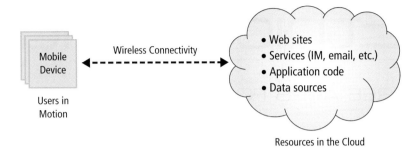

Figure 4-20

Elements of a Mobile Information System

As shown in Figure 4-20, the major elements in a mobile system are *users in motion, mobile devices, wireless connectivity,* and a *cloud-based resource.* A **mobile device** is a small, lightweight, power-conserving, computing device that is capable of wireless connectivity. Almost all mobile devices have a display and some means for data entry. Mobile devices include smartphones, tablets, smartwatches, and small, light laptops. Desktop computers, Xboxes, and large, heavy, power-hungry laptops are not mobile devices.

You will learn about wireless connectivity and the cloud in Chapter 6. For now, just assume that the cloud is a group of servers on the other end of a connection with a mobile device. When downloading a book for a Kindle, for example, the cloud is one or more servers on the other end that store that book and download a copy of it to your device.

The major reason for the importance of mobile systems is the size of their market. According to Cisco, at the end of 2014 there were 7.4 billion mobile devices generating 2.5 exabytes of traffic per month.[28] By 2019, this will jump to 11.5 billion mobile devices generating more than 24.3 exabytes per month. That's 1.5 devices for every person on the planet. Smartphones will account for nearly 75 percent of global mobile traffic.[29]

It took seven years after the launch of the first iPhone (2007–2014) for smartphones to achieve mainstream use by 70 percent of the U.S. market.[30] That's faster than any other technology except television in the early 1950s, which tied the smartphone adoption rate. The February 2015 comScore Report shows 182 million people in the United States owned smartphones, which accounted for 74.9 percent of the mobile phone market.[31] The size of the mobile e-commerce, or **m-commerce**, market is expected to exceed $113B by 2017.[32]

Additionally, mobile use is favored by the young. According to Nielsen's measures of mobile device use, the younger the age group, the greater the percentage of people with mobile devices. Further, younger people have more devices per capita than older groups.[33] These young cohorts will further increase mobile systems use in the years to come.

Because of this vast and growing market, mobile systems are having a major impact on business and society today—impact that is forcing industry change while creating new career opportunities for mobile-IS-savvy professionals, as well as large numbers of new, interesting mobile-IS-related jobs.

Ethics Guide

FREE APPS FOR DATA

You're sitting in your Introduction to MIS class, and the professor starts talking about how profitable software development can be. He points out that billionaires like Bill Gates (Microsoft), Larry Ellison (Oracle), Larry Page (Google), and Mark Zuckerberg (Facebook) all made their fortunes by developing useful software. But a vocal classmate jumps in and points out that he's never paid any of those people a penny. He uses Google Search, Gmail, and Facebook all for free. Yes, he uses Microsoft Office, but it's the free online version through OneDrive. Even the apps on his smartphone are free.

Then comes the perennial question, which also happens to be a major point of frustration for the tech industry: How do you make money from free apps? The professor says something about capturing market share, potential income, and future innovation. You're not buying it. You're interested in *real* income, not *potential* income.

Nick the Data Broker

The person sitting next to you, Nick, starts smiling broadly and nods his head. He's in your group for your big class project. He leans over and whispers, "If you're not paying for it, *you* are the product. Data is where you make money, not software. Give them the software, take the data, and make the money. It's simple."

You're a little confused at first. But then you think back to last Wednesday when you first met Nick. He said he was coming back to school to get a degree in MIS because he needed the technical knowledge for his new job with his brother's company. He explained that his brother was a data broker (sometimes called an information broker). He buys data about individuals from companies and then sells it to other companies for a profit. It sounded like they were doing really well. Before you could even ask if it was legal or ethical, Nick quipped, "Yes, of course it's legal. Everyone does it." He had obviously gotten this question before.

But was Nick right? He isn't a billionaire like Bill Gates. Nick was only concerned with buying and selling data. He wasn't interested in application development. But he did make a good point, and it got you thinking. What if you started a business that made applications that were designed to collect individual data? You could make dozens of useful apps, collect individual data, and then sell it to Nick.

But what data would Nick pay for? How much of it could you get? He wouldn't care about gaming data. But he would pay for data about user behavior like which Web sites they visit, where they're located, who their friends are, and what they purchase.

Flashlight Apps

At lunch, you do a few searches about how mobile applications can access data on smartphones. It turns out that users just have to grant the application permission(s), and it can access *any* data on the phone. Could that be right? *Any* data? This could be a gold mine. You get excited at the prospect of harvesting thousands of terabytes of data and selling them to Nick. You could retire in a month.

But then a sinking feeling comes over you. What if you're not the first person to think of this idea? What if someone else is already giving away apps and harvesting users' data. You decide to check the permissions for one of the most useful free applications you have on your phone—your flashlight app. You search for "flashlight app permissions" and you see dozens of news articles referencing a threat report by SnoopWall.[34]

The SnoopWall report looked at the permissions required by the top 10 flashlight apps for Android smartphones. The results were shocking. All of these apps did more than just turn a light on and off. They required permission to access data about your location, network connectivity, and USB storage. They also required permissions to install shortcuts, receive data to/from the Internet, modify your system settings, and disable your screen lock.

The app you use was third on the list. Not good. You decide to check to see whether the report was accurate. Were these apps harvesting all this data? You look at the first five flashlight apps that show up in Google Play. The results are shown in the table below. The bottom two rows show the changes in the number of permissions from 2013 to 2014.

Seeing all of the permissions required by these simple flashlight apps is distressing. Why would your flashlight need your GPS coordinates? Who was getting this data? What were they using it for? It looks like someone had already thought of your data-harvesting idea. It may be too late to make any money off the free-app-for-individual-data scheme. All of a sudden, these free apps don't look as attractive to you—as a consumer.

Permissions	1 Super-Bright LED Flashlight	2 Tiny Flashlight + LED	3 Brightest LED Flashlight	4 Flashlight	5 Brightest Flashlight Free	6 Color Flashlight	7 High-Powered Flashlight	8 Super Bright Flashlight
Take pictures and videos	X	X	X	X	X	X	X	X
Receive data from Internet	X		X				X	
Control flashlight	X	X	X		X	X	X	
Change system display settings	X		X			.	X	
Modify system settings	X		X				X	
Prevent device from sleeping	X	X	X	X	X		X	
View network connections	X	X	X	X	X	X	X	X
Full network access	X	X	X	X	X	X	X	X
Run at startup		X						
Control vibration		X						
Retrieve running apps			X				X	
Modify or delete the contents of your USB storage			X		X		X	
Read the contents of your USB storage			X		X		X	
View Wi-Fi connections			X		X		X	
Read phone status and identity			X		X		X	
Read Home settings and shortcuts				X	X			
Write Home settings and shortcuts				X				
Disable your screen lock				X				
Install shortcuts				X	X			
Uninstall shortcuts				X	X			
Approximate location					X		X	
Precise location					X		X	
Disable or modify status bar					X			
Count Now	8	7	13	9	15	4	15	3
Count Then	20	6	13	9	15	4	15	NA

DISCUSSION QUESTIONS

1. Consider the decision to create a free application designed to harvest individual data.
   a. Is this decision ethical according to the categorical imperative (pages 56–57)?
   b. Is this decision ethical according to the utilitarian perspective (pages 92–93)?
   c. How would users react if they knew their data was being harvested in exchange for a free app?
2. Suppose Google becomes aware that apps in the Google Play store are harvesting user data unrelated to the function of the application.
   a. Does it have a *legal* obligation to find out which apps are harvesting data inappropriately?
   b. Does it have an *ethical* obligation to find out which apps are harvesting data inappropriately?
   c. Does Google provide free apps in exchange for individual data? Why?
3. How hard should Google work at curating apps in Google Play to ensure that appropriate permissions are set?
4. In 2014, Symantec found that 17 percent of all Android apps were malware in disguise.[35] But a report by Google found that less than 1 percent of all Android devices had a potentially harmful application installed.[36]
   a. Is it ethical for Google to remove applications it considers inappropriate? Consider both the categorical imperative and utilitarian perspectives.
   b. Is it ethical for Google to limit permissions for certain applications? Consider both the categorical imperative and utilitarian perspectives.

	Hardware	Software	Data	Procedures	People
Impact of mobile systems growth	Many, many more mobile devices will be sold.	Compact interfaces; new technology for active users; application scaling.	More data, but more information? Less device real estate means fewer ads possible.	Always on, always at work. Employee lifestyle becomes hybrid of personal and professional.	Ability to thrive in a dynamic environment more important.
Industry changes	PCs less important; high demand (and requirement) for innovative devices as well as cheap copycats.	html5, css3, and JavaScript increase capability of thin-clients.	Loss of control. Ad model in danger?	Personal mobile devices at work.	More part-time employees and independent contractors.
Career opportunities	Jobs for mobile device sales, marketing, support.	New technology levels the playing field for html5. Business expertise needed for mobile requirements. New companies!	Reporting and data mining even more important. Design of effective mobile reports.	Innovative use of just-in-time data. Need for adjusting business processes gives another premium to non-routine problem solvers.	Independent contractors (and some employees) work where and when they want. What is this new social organism?

Figure 4-21
Five Components of Mobile Change and Opportunity

Figure 4-21 summarizes the mobile-system impact for each of the five components of an information system. We will discuss each of the components in this figure, starting with hardware.

Hardware

Clearly, increasing demand for mobile systems means the sales of many more mobile devices, often at the expense of PC sales. Hewlett-Packard, a large PC manufacturer, learned this fact when it didn't respond quickly enough to the onslaught of mobile devices and was forced to eliminate 27,000 jobs in 2012. In the future, there will be high demand for innovative mobile devices as well as cheap copycats.

If you're reading this book, you're unlikely to be a hardware engineer, and if you're not living in Asia, you're also unlikely to be involved in hardware manufacturing. However, any market having 3.9 billion prospects is ripe with opportunities in marketing, sales, logistics, customer support, and related activities.

Software

The reduced size of mobile devices requires the invention of new, innovative interfaces. The mobile user is an active user and expects an active screen experience. The premium will be for moving graphics, changing Web pages, and animation. Applications will need to scale from the very smallest to the very largest, while providing a user experience appropriate to the device's size.

Rapid technology change in mobile software continually levels the playing field. Today, for example, expert programmers in Objective-C better not relax. html5 and css3 are gaining popularity, and they will reduce the need for Objective-C expertise. Further, as you learned in Q5, while languages like Objective-C are difficult and time-consuming to learn, html5, css3, and JavaScript are less so. With the reduced barrier to entry, hordes of less experienced and less educated new entrants will appear as competitors. You might be one of them.

Additionally, continually evolving software means new and exciting entrepreneurial opportunities. Are you sorry that you missed the early days working at Facebook? Right now, somewhere, there is another Mark Zuckerberg starting…well, what? Because of the continually changing software environment, new opportunities abound and will continue to do so for decades.

Data

Many more mobile systems mean an incredible amount of new data, data that professionals can use to create much more information. But, as you learned in Chapter 1, more data doesn't necessarily mean more information. In fact, many business professionals believe they're drowning in data while starving for information. What can be done with all of this mobile-systems data to enable humans to conceive information of greater value to them? Data mining and better reporting are possibilities for you that are discussed in Chapter 9.

On the other hand, not all the news is good, at least not for many organizations. For one, smaller screens means less room for advertising, a factor that limited the success of the Facebook public offering in May 2012. Also, mobile systems increase the risk of organizations losing control over their data. In the past, employees used only computer equipment provided by the employer and connected only via employer-managed networks. In that situation, it is possible for the organization to control who does what with which data and where. No longer. Employees come to work with their own mobile devices. Data leakage is inevitable.

With more people switching to mobile devices and with less room for ads, online advertising revenue may be sharply reduced, possibly endangering the revenue model that supports most of the Web's free content. If this happens, dramatic change is just around the corner!

Procedures

Mobile systems are always on. They have no business hours. And people who use mobile systems are equally always on. In the mobile world, we're always open for business. It is impossible to be out of the office. One consequence of always-on is the blending of our personal and professional lives. Such blending means, in part, that business will intrude on your personal life, and your personal life will intrude on your business. This intrusion can be distracting and stressful; on the other hand, it can lead to richer, more complex relationships.

Employees will expect to use their mobile devices at work, but should they? In truth, who can keep them from it? If the organization blocks them from connecting to the work-related networks, they can connect over the wireless networks that they pay for themselves. In this case, the organization is entirely out of the loop. Could employees send confidential corporate information through their personal mobile devices? We will discuss these issues in more detail in Q4-7.

Mobile systems offer the potential of **just-in-time data**, which is data delivered to the user at the precise time it is needed. A pharmaceutical salesperson uses just-in-time data when she accesses a mobile system to obtain the latest literature on a new drug while waiting for the doctor to whom she will pitch it. She needn't remember the drug's characteristics any longer than it takes her to walk down the hallway and make the sale.

Furthermore, some organizations will passively wait for change to happen, while others will proactively reengineer their processes to incorporate mobile systems for higher process quality. Either way, the need for business process change creates opportunity for creative, nonroutine business problem solvers.

People

Mobile systems change the value of our thinking. For example, just-in-time data removes the premium on the ability to memorize vast quantities of product data, but creates a premium for the ability to access, query, and present that data. Mobile systems increase the speed of business, giving an advantage to those who can nimbly respond to changing conditions and succeed with the unexpected.

With the ability to be connected and always on, organizations may find they can be just as effective with part-time employees and independent contractors. The increasing regulatory complexity and cost of full-time employees will create an incentive for organizations to do just that.

As that occurs, professionals who can thrive in a dynamic environment with little need for direct supervision will find that they can work both where and when they want, at least a good part of the time. Once you're always on and remote, it doesn't matter if you're always on in New Jersey or at a ski area in Vermont. New lifestyle choices become possible for such workers.

These mobile workers can work where they want and for whom they want. There won't be a boss looking over their shoulder. They can work multiple jobs with different companies at the same time! Companies may have to change the way they pay workers. Instead of paying employees by the hour, they would need to focus more on paying for productivity. This shift toward focusing on performance will empower great employees and make it harder for slackers to hide out in an organization. Companies will benefit from mobile workers too. They won't need as much expensive commercial office space. What an incredible time to be starting a business career!

Q4-7 What Are the Challenges of Personal Mobile Devices at Work?

Protecting company computers and software from malware is essential to corporate success. Read the Security Guide on pages 184–185 to learn about one of the most virulent technological threats.

So far, we've focused on mobile applications that organizations create for their customers and others to use. In this question we will address the use of mobile systems *within* organizations.

In truth, organizations today have a love/hate relationship with their employees' use of their own mobile devices at work. They love the cost-saving possibility of having employees buy their own hardware, but they hate the increased vulnerability and loss of control. The result, at least today, is a wide array of organizational attitudes.

Consider a recent Gartner report that estimates by 2016, nearly 38 percent of companies will stop providing devices to their workers altogether.[37] You'll have to bring your own device. David Willis, a senior analyst at Gartner, notes, "BYOD strategies are the most radical change to the economics and the culture of client computing in business in decades."[38] Yet only 43 percent of all organizations have created an official mobile-use policy.[39]

Advantages and Disadvantages of Employee Use of Mobile Systems at Work

Figure 4-22 summarizes the advantages and disadvantages of employee use of mobile systems at work. Advantages include the cost savings just mentioned as well as greater employee satisfaction of using devices that they chose according to their own preferences rather than organization-supplied PCs. Because employees are already using these devices for their own purposes, they need less training and can be more productive. All of this means reduced support costs.

On the other hand, employee use of mobile devices has significant disadvantages. First, there is the real danger of lost or damaged data. When data is brought into employee-owned computing devices, the organization loses control over where it goes or what happens to it. In May 2012, IBM disallowed the use of Apple's voice searching application, Siri, on employees' mobile devices for just that reason.[40] Also, if an employee loses his or her device, the data goes with it, and when employees leave the organization, the data on their personal devices needs to be deleted somehow.

Advantages	Disadvantages
Cost savings	Data loss or damage
Greater employee satisfaction	Loss of control
Reduced need for training	Compatibility problems
Higher productivity	Risk of infection
Reduced support costs	Greater support costs

Figure 4-22
Advantages and Disadvantages of Employee Use of Mobile Systems at Work

Organizations also lose control over the updating of software and the applications that users employ. This control loss leads to compatibility problems; users can process data, for example edit documents, with software that is incompatible with the organization's standard software. The result to the organization is a mess of inconsistent documents.

Possibly the greatest disadvantage of employee use of their own devices is the risk of infection. The organization cannot know where the users have been with their devices or what they've done when they've been there. The possibility of severe viruses infecting the organization's networks is real. Finally, all of these disadvantages can also lead, ironically, to greater support costs.

Given all that, organizations cannot avoid the issue. Whatever the costs and risks, employees are bringing their own devices to work. Ignoring the issue will simply make matters worse.

Survey of Organizational BYOD Policy

A **bring your own device (BYOD) policy** is a statement concerning employees' permissions and responsibilities when they use their own device for organizational business. Figure 4-23 arranges BYOD policies according to functionality and control. Starting in the lower left-hand corner, the most primitive policy is to ignore mobile use. That posture, which provides neither functionality to the employee nor control to the organization, has no advantages and, as just stated, cannot last.

The next step up in functionality is for the organization to offer its wireless network to mobile devices, as if it were a coffee shop. The advantage to the organization of this policy is that the organization can sniff employees' mobile traffic, thus learning how employees are using their devices (and time) during work.

The next policy provides more functionality and somewhat more control. Here the organization creates secure application services using https (explained in Chapter 10) that require employee sign-on and can be accessed from any device, mobile or not. Such applications can be used when employees are at work or elsewhere. These services provide controlled access to some organizations' assets.

A fourth policy is more of a strategic maneuver than a policy. The organization tells employees that they can sign on to the organization's network with their mobile devices, but the employee is financially responsible for any damage he or she does. The hope is that few employees know what their exposure is and hence decide not to do so.

A more enlightened policy is to manage the users' devices as if they were owned by the organization. With this policy, employees turn over their mobile devices to the IS department, which cleanses and reloads software and installs programs that enable the IS department to manage the device remotely. Numerous vendors license products called **mobile device management**

	Control					
		Low ←				→ High
High	Full VPN Access to Organizational Systems			You're responsible for damage	We'll check it out, reload software and data, and manage it remotely	If you connect it, we own it
Functionality	Organizational Services on Public Internet		We'll offer limited systems you can access from any device			
	Access to Internet	We'll be a coffee shop				
Low	None	They don't exist				

Figure 4-23
Six Common BYOD Policies

BYOD Policy	Description	Advantage to Organization
They don't exist	Organization looks the other way when employees bring mobile devices to work.	None
We'll be a coffee shop	You'll be able to sign in to our wireless network using your mobile device.	Packet sniffing of employee mobile device use at work.
We'll offer limited systems you can access from any device	Organization creates https applications with sign-in and offers access to noncritical business systems.	Employees gain public access from any device, not just mobile devices, without having to use VPN accounts.
You're responsible for damage	Threatening posture to discourage employee use of mobile devices at work.	Appear to be permissive without actually being so.
We'll check it out, reload software, then manage remotely	Employees can use their mobile devices just as if they were computers provided by the corporate IS department.	Employee buys the hardware (perhaps with an employer's contribution).
If you connect it, we own it	Employees are not to use mobile devices at work. If they do, they lose them. Part of employment agreement.	Ultimate in control for highly secure work situations (intelligence, military).

Figure 4-24
Advantages of Example BYOD Policies

(MDM) software that assist this process. These products install and update software, back up and restore mobile devices, wipe employer software and data from devices in the event the device is lost or the employee leaves the company, report usage, and provide other mobile device management data.

This policy benefits the organization, but some employees resist turning over the management of their own hardware to the organization. This resistance can be softened if the organization pays at least a portion of the hardware expense.

The most controlling policy is for the organization to declare that it owns any mobile device that employees connect to its network. To be enforceable, this policy must be part of the employee's contract. It is taken by organizations that manage very secure operations and environments. In some military/intelligence organizations, the policy is that any smart device that ever enters the workplace may never leave it. The advantages of these six policies are summarized in Figure 4-24.

BYOD policies are rapidly evolving, and many organizations have not yet determined what is best for them. If your employer has a committee to develop such policies, join it if you can. Doing so will provide a great way to gain exposure to the leading technology thinkers at your organization.

Q4-8   2026?

There's a really old movie called *You've Got Mail* (1998) starring Tom Hanks and Meg Ryan. In it, the characters get really excited when they get "mail." The term *email* was so new at the time that it hadn't even caught on yet. You can see people in the movie reading newspapers and paper books. Oh, how times have changed.

Fast-forward to today. Email now comes in seconds after it's sent. You check your email during commercial breaks while you're watching TV, while you're driving in traffic, and while you're sitting on the toilet. Instead of checking your email with bated breath, you're dreading seeing more work pile up in your inbox. Or worse—bills, spam, and viruses.

New hardware and software have changed everyday life. People are always on, always connected, always communicating, always working and playing. This trend will continue. The Internet of Things will allow us to be continually connected to more and more devices. You'll be able to control your home, and everything in it, from your smartphone. Your home will be so smart that it will analyze you. It will see what, how, and when you do things and then anticipate your needs.

Imagine your TV turning on every morning at just the right time so you can watch the markets open (see Figure 4-25). You smell fresh-baked bread, your shower turns on by itself, and your car knows exactly when to self-start so it's warm when you get in. Your self-driving car will let you work on your way to work. You'll see these anticipatory systems at your job too.

How will advances in hardware and software affect the types of jobs you'll go to? Ten years from now, the best-paying jobs will be ones that don't currently exist. The following are hot jobs today: IoT architect, marketing technologist, BigData architect, and DevOps manager. These job titles didn't exist 10 years ago. Ten years from now, there will be an entirely new set of jobs that you haven't heard of before.

How do you prepare for future jobs? What types of jobs will pay well? Regardless of your current college major, your future job will probably require a high level of tech skill. The best way to prepare for these types of jobs is to cultivate creativity, novel problem solving, and good judgment and have a sincere desire to learn new things.

Figure 4-25
Smart Home
Source: Si-Gal/iStock Vectors/Getty Images

Security Guide

ANATOMY OF A HEARTBLEED

Every once in a while there is a problem so big that it affects nearly everyone. In the past, World Wars I and II were so far reaching that they affected nearly everyone on the planet. Fast-forward to today. Most people use some form of technology like a cell phone, tablet, or computer on a daily basis. What if there was a technology problem so serious that it affected nearly every piece of hardware, software, and system on the earth? That problem was named Heartbleed, and it became known to the public on April 7, 2014.

Bruce Schneier, a world-renowned computer security expert, called the Heartbleed vulnerability "catastrophic" and "on the scale of 1 to 10, this is an 11."[41] At the time it was estimated that at least 17 percent to 25 percent of all Web sites were vulnerable to attack. Add in vulnerable software, hardware, operating systems, embedded systems, cell phones, and networking appliances. Heartbleed quickly became one of the most widespread and potentially dangerous computing vulnerabilities ever.

What Is Heartbleed?

Heartbleed is a vulnerability that comes from a flaw in the code for the open source OpenSSL cryptographic library. The OpenSSL library is widely used to secure Internet traffic. When you access a secure Internet site, you'll see a padlock symbol and "https" in your Web browser's address bar. An attacker can use the Heartbleed vulnerability to extract information being held in a computer's memory that is hosting a secure Web site. This could include usernames, passwords, session cookies, cryptographic keys, and so on. Anything that's in memory can be extracted.

How Does It Work?

Suppose you're a "client" accessing a secure "server." A client sends a certain amount of random data (say, 65Kb) to a server. The server makes a copy of that random data and sends it back to the client. This is called a "heartbeat" (not Heartbleed). A heartbeat is used to make sure both the client and server are OK.

The "bleed" part comes when the client sends the server *too little* data. The client says it's sending 65Kb of data, but it's really only sending 1 byte of data. This is the flaw. It never checks to see that there really was 65Kb of data sent. The server takes the 1 byte of data received from the client and adds 65Kb of data from its own memory containing confidential data. Then it sends it back to the client. This process can be done many times and leaves no record that it ever occurred.

Who's at Risk?

The short answer is nearly everyone. Mashable posted a short list of some of the more well-known Web sites that were vulnerable to the Heartbleed vulnerability.[42] This list included

Instagram, Pinterest, Tumblr, Google, Yahoo!, Flickr, Etsy, YouTube, Dropbox, and Wikipedia. This is not a comprehensive list. If you haven't changed your passwords after April 7, 2014, you should.

If that sounds bad, hold on, it gets worse. Those are just vulnerable Web servers. What about other servers (i.e., email, Web, IM, etc.), software, hardware, and embedded systems? Gmail and Yahoo! Mail made the list. Siemens issued updates for some of its hardware that controls factory systems. Some cell phones running Android needed to be updated as well as Apple's AirPort Time Capsule and AirPort Extreme appliances.[43] The list goes on and on.

Why Didn't I Know About This?

Surprisingly, the reaction to the Heartbleed vulnerability outside the tech industry was tepid. The Pew Research Center found that during the peak of the Heartbleed scare about 60 percent of American adults had heard of Heartbleed. However, only 40 percent had taken steps to secure their accounts by changing their passwords.[44] Even more worrisome, 74 percent of the world's largest 2,000 companies were still vulnerable a year after Heartbleed became widely known.[45]

Suppose you didn't change your passwords. What would happen if just one company lost your login information? Do you reuse your passwords at multiple sites or systems? Is it possible that hackers know about password reuse? The combination of a widespread vulnerability like Heartbleed and users reusing their password at multiple sites is concerning.

The Heartbleed vulnerability reminds us just how pervasive, important, and potentially vulnerable computing has become. We are constantly interacting with hardware and software. Information systems are also becoming interconnected at a dizzying rate. Could a future vulnerability similar to Heartbleed cause widespread data loss…across the globe? Time will tell.

DISCUSSION QUESTIONS

1. Do you use the same password for multiple Web sites? How could data loss at one Web site affect the security of other Web sites?
2. Is checking a Web site for the Heartbleed vulnerability illegal? Why?
3. Do you use any of the Web sites listed by Mashable? Did you change your passwords on those systems? Why or why not?
4. The person who wrote the portion of OpenSSL code containing the Heartbleed vulnerability said the error slipped through because there weren't enough eyes looking at the code for possible errors. Because OpenSSL is open source, could a shortage of paid code checkers mean there might be more errors like Heartbleed? Why?
5. If a hardware or software maker finds a vulnerability in one of its products, how should it respond? Does it have a legal responsibility to warn its users? Does it have an ethical responsibility to do so? Why or why not?
6. Could state-sponsored organizations exploit vulnerabilities as part of a cyber-war campaign or an information-gathering operation? Would this be ethical?

Guide

KEEPING UP TO SPEED

Have you ever been to a cafeteria where you put your lunch tray on a conveyor belt that carries the dirty dishes into the kitchen? That conveyor belt reminds me of technology. Like the conveyor, technology just moves along, and all of us run on top of the technology conveyor, trying to keep up. We hope to keep up with the relentless change of technology for an entire career without ending up in the techno-trash.

Technology change is a fact, and the only appropriate question is, "What am I going to do about it?" One strategy you can take is to bury your head in the sand: "Look, I'm not a technology person. I'll leave it to the pros. As long as I can send email and use the Internet, I'm happy. If I have a problem, I'll call someone to fix it."

That strategy is fine, as far as it goes, and many businesspeople have used it. Following that strategy won't give you a competitive advantage over anyone, and it will give someone else a competitive advantage over you, but as long as you develop your advantage elsewhere, you'll be OK—at least for yourself.

What about your department, though? If an expert says, "You should be buying your employees Windows 10 tablet devices," are you going to nod your head and say, "Great. Sell 'em to me!"? Or are you going to know enough to realize that it may be too early to know what the success of Windows 10 will be? Or to know that maybe you'll have problems getting homegrown, in-house applications down from whatever stores Microsoft sets up?

At the other end of the spectrum are those who love technology. You'll find them everywhere—they may be accountants, marketing professionals, or production-line supervisors who not only know their field but also enjoy information technology. Maybe they were IS majors or had double majors that combined IS with another area of expertise (e.g., IS with accounting). These people read *CNET News* and *ZDNet* most days, and they can tell you the latest on desktop virtualization or html5 or Windows 10. Those people are sprinting along the technology conveyor belt; they will never end up in the techno-trash, and they will use their knowledge of IT to gain competitive advantage throughout their careers.

Many business professionals fall in between these extremes. They don't want to bury their heads, but they don't have the desire or interest to become technophiles (lovers of technology), either. What to do? There are a couple of strategies. For one, don't allow yourself to ignore technology. When you see a technology article in *The Wall Street Journal*, read it. Don't just skip it because it's about technology. Read

Source: Rawpixel/Fotolia

the technology ads too. Many vendors invest heavily in ads that instruct without seeming to. Another option is to take a seminar or pay attention to professional events that combine your specialty with technology. For example, when you go to the bankers' convention, attend a panel or two on "Mobile Device Use at Banks." There are always sessions like that, and you might make a contact with similar problems and concerns in another company.

Probably the best option, if you have the time for it, is to get involved as a user representative on technology committees in your organization. Or, if your company is doing a review of its BYOD policy, see if you can get on the review committee. Alternatively, when there's a need for a representative from your department to discuss needs

for the next-generation helpline system, sign up. Or, later in your career, become a member of the business practice technology committee or whatever it is called at your organization.

Just working with such groups will add to your knowledge of technology. Presentations made to such groups, discussions about uses of technology, and ideas about using IT for competitive advantage will all add to your IT knowledge. You'll gain important contacts and exposure to leaders in your organization as well.

It's up to you. You get to choose how you relate to technology. But be sure you choose; don't let your head get stuck in the sand without thinking about it.

 DISCUSSION QUESTIONS

1. Do you agree that the change of technology is relentless? What do you think that means to most business professionals? To most organizations?
2. Think about the three postures toward technology presented here. Which camp will you join? Why?
3. Write a two-paragraph memo to yourself justifying your choice in question 2. If you chose to ignore technology, explain how you will compensate for the loss of competitive advantage. If you're going to join one of the other two groups, explain why, and describe how you're going to accomplish your goal.
4. Given your answer to question 2, assume that you're in a job interview and the interviewer asks about your interest in and knowledge of technology. Write a three-sentence response to the interviewer's question.

ACTIVE REVIEW

Use this Active Review to verify that you understand the ideas and concepts that answer the chapter's study questions.

Q4-1   What do business professionals need to know about computer hardware?

List types of hardware and give an example of each. Define *bit* and *byte*. Explain why bits are used to represent computer data. Define the units of bytes used to size memory.

Q4-2   How can new hardware affect competitive strategies?

Define *IoT* and describe a smart device. Explain why smart devices are desirable. Give two examples of how businesses could benefit from smart devices. Describe how self-driving cars could be safer and cheaper and make life easier. Explain how 3D printing works and how it could affect new product design, manufacturing, distribution, and consumer purchasing.

Q4-3   What do business professionals need to know about software?

Review Figure 4-10 and explain the meaning of each cell in this table. Describe three kinds of virtualization and explain the use of each. Explain the difference between software ownership and software licenses. Explain the differences among horizontal-market, vertical-market, and one-of-a-kind applications. Describe the three ways that organizations can acquire software.

Q4-4   Is open source software a viable alternative?

Define *GNU* and *GPL*. Name three successful open source projects. Describe four reasons programmers contribute to open source projects. Define *open source, closed source, source code*, and *machine code*. In your own words, explain why open source is a legitimate alternative but may or may not be appropriate for a given application.

Q4-5   What are the differences between native and Web applications?

In your own words, summarize the differences between native applications and Web applications. In high-level terms, explain the difference between object-oriented languages and scripting languages. Explain each cell of Figure 4-17. State which is better: native or Web applications. Justify your answer.

Q4-6   Why are mobile systems increasingly important?

Define *mobile systems*. Name and describe the four elements of a mobile system. Describe the size of the mobile market and explain why there are 3.9 billion mobile prospects. Explain why the mobile market will become stronger in the future. Explain why a problem for one organization is an opportunity for another. Using the five-component model, describe particular opportunities for each component. Define *just-in-time data* and explain how it changes the value of human thinking.

Q4-7   What are the challenges of personal mobile devices at work?

Summarize the advantages and disadvantages of employees' using mobile systems at work. Define *BYOD* and *BYOD policy*. Name six possible policies and compare them in terms of functionality and organizational control. Summarize the advantage of each to employers.

Q4-8   2026?

Explain how email usage has changed over the past 15 years. Describe how an anticipatory system might work. Explain how advances in hardware and software might change the types of jobs you take in the future.

Using Your Knowledge with Falcon Security

Suppose you are part of this Falcon Security team. Briefly summarize how the knowledge in this chapter would help you contribute. Explain why Falcon Security decided not make its own drones using 3D printing. Summarize the challenges it would face if it did decide to make its own drones.

KEY TERMS AND CONCEPTS

Android   163
Application software   166
Augmented reality (AR)   155
Binary digits   153
Bits   153
BlackBerry OS   163
Bring your own device (BYOD)
   policy   181
Bytes   154
Central processing unit (CPU)   152
Client   152
Closed source   170
Computer hardware   151
Custom-developed software   167
Desktop virtualization   166
Dual processor   152
Exabyte (EB)   154
Firmware   167
Gigabyte (GB)   154
GNU   168
GNU general public license (GPL)
   agreement   168
Horizontal-market application   166
Host operating system   164
Internet of Things (IoT)   155
iOS   163
Just-in-time data   179

Kilobyte (KB)   154
License   166
Linux   163
Mac OS   162
Machine code   170
Main memory   152
M-commerce   175
Megabyte (MB)   154
Microsoft Windows   161
Mobile device   175
Mobile device management (MDM)
   software   181
Mobile systems   174
Modern-style application   162
Native application   161
Nonvolatile   155
Object-oriented   171
Off-the-shelf software   167
Off-the-shelf with alterations
   software   167
One-of-a-kind application   167
Open source   168
Operating system (OS)   161
PC virtualization   164
Personal computers   152
Petabyte (PB)   154

PixelSense   190
Quad processor   152
RAM   152
Self-driving car   157
Server   152
Server farm   153
Server virtualization   164
Site license   166
Smart device   155
Source code   168
Storage hardware   152
Swift   171
Symbian   163
Tablets   152
Terabyte (TB)   154
Thick-client application   161
Unix   163
Vertical-market application   166
Virtualization   164
Virtual machines (vm)   164
Virtual reality   155
Volatile   155
Web application   161
Windows 10 (mobile)   164
Windows Server   164
Zettabyte (ZB)   154

MyMISLab™

To complete the problems with the ⭐, go to EOC Discussion Questions in the MyLab.

USING YOUR KNOWLEDGE

 **4-1. a.** Make a list of types of hardware devices you are using after referring to Figure 4.1. Try to fill the figure with hardware types and give examples of each type that you are using.

   b. After listing the types of hardware that you are using, refer to Figure 4-4 and make a list of storage capacity of each hardware device.

   c. Since CPU speed matters a lot in the processing of data, find out the speed of the CPU of devices that you are using. Try to figure out whether the present speed of the CPU is enough to support the kind of operations that you perform.

   d. Either (1) download and install the programs in your answer to part d or (2) explain why you would choose not to do so.

e. Does DreamSpark provide an unfair advantage to Microsoft? Why or why not?

⭐ 4-2. Visit the Open Source Initiative's Web site at *www.opensource.org*. Summarize the mission of this foundation. Find the definition of open source on this site, and summarize that definition in your own words. Explain this foundation's role with regard to open source licenses. Summarize the process for having a license approved by the foundation. Describe the advantage of having the foundation's approval.

⭐ 4-3. Suppose that you are Cam at Falcon Security. List five criteria you would use in helping Falcon Security decide whether it should make its own drones. Justify your criteria.

4-4. Refer to Figure 4-10 and list the non-mobile and mobile client operating systems that you are using. Make a list of unique features that you like the most, compare the non-mobile operating system with its latest edition (if you are using the latest edition, compare with the old version) and find out additional features provided by non-mobile client operating system used by you.

4-5. Mark says that "Open service softwares cannot replace licensed software. Peter disagrees with this statement. Now, as a friend of Peter, download Libre Office and compare the features of MS Word and LibreOffice. On the basis of the comparison, give your verdict on the statement made by Mark.

4-6. In case of server operating system, there are three options which are discussed in this chapter, i.e. Windows Server, UNIX and Linux. Find out which type of server operating system is being installed in your college/university computer lab after interviewing the IT admin. Find the reasons for selecting a particular server operating system.

COLLABORATION EXERCISE 4

Using the collaboration IS you built in Chapter 2 (page 110), collaborate with a group of students to answer the following questions.

In the past few years, Microsoft has been promoting **PixelSense,** a hardware–software product that enables people to interact with data on the top of a table. PixelSense initiates a new product category, and the best way to understand it is to view one of Microsoft's promotional videos at *www.microsoft.com/en-us/pixelsense/default.aspx.*

PixelSense paints the top of the 30-inch table with invisible, near-infrared light to detect the presence of objects. It can respond to as many as 52 different touches at the same time. According to Microsoft, this means that four people sitting around the PixelSense table could use all 10 of their fingers to manipulate up to 12 objects, simultaneously.

PixelSense uses wireless and other communications technologies to connect to devices that are placed on it, such as cameras or cell phones. When a camera is placed on PixelSense, pictures "spill" out of it, and users can manipulate those pictures with their hands. Products can be placed on PixelSense, and their product specifications are displayed. Credit cards can be placed on PixelSense, and items to be purchased can be dragged or dropped onto the credit card.

Currently, Microsoft PixelSense is marketed and sold to large-scale commercial organizations in the financial services, healthcare, hospitality, retail, and public service business sectors. Also, smaller organizations and individuals can purchase a PixelSense unit from Samsung (*www.samsunglfd.com/solution/sur40.do*).

One of the first implementers of PixelSense was the iBar lounge at Harrah's Rio All-Suite Hotel and Casino in Las Vegas, Nevada. The subtitle for the press release announcing iBar's system read, "Harrah's Reinvents Flirting and Offers New Uninhibited Fun and Play to iBar Patrons."[46]

The potential uses for PixelSense are staggering. Maps can display local events, and consumers can purchase tickets to those events by just using their fingers. PixelSense can also be used for new computer games and gambling devices. Children can paint on PixelSense with virtual paintbrushes. Numerous other applications are possible. Microsoft envisions PixelSense as a ubiquitous billion dollar technology that will find its way to tabletops, countertops, and mirrors.[47]

As you can see at the PixelSense Web site, this product can be used for many different purposes in many different places, such as restaurants, retail kiosks, and eventually at home. Probably most of the eventual applications for PixelSense have not yet been envisioned. One clear application, however, is in the gambling and gaming industry. Imagine placing your credit card on a PixelSense gambling device and playing the night away. Every time you lose, a charge is made against your credit card. Soon, before you know it, you've run up $15,000 in debt, which you learn when PixelSense tells you you've reached the maximum credit limit on your card.

Recall the RAND study cited in Chapter 1 that stated there will be increased worldwide demand for workers who can apply new technology and products to solve business problems in innovative ways. PixelSense is an excellent example of a new technology that will be applied innovatively.

4-7. Consider uses for PixelSense at your university. How might PixelSense be used in architecture, chemistry, law, medicine, business, geography, political science, art, music, or any other discipline in which your team has interest? Describe one potential application for PixelSense for five different disciplines.

4-8. List specific features and benefits for each of the five applications you selected in question 4-7.

4-9. Describe, in general terms, the work that needs to be accomplished to create the applications you identified in question 4-7.

4-10. It is clear from the above case that many new applications are coming up in the market, as a result of which, new career opportunities have risen. Do you think that knowledge of information systems will enhance prospects of better job opportunities in the context of rapid growth of mobile systems? Perform a SWOT analysis to provide your answer.

4-11. Visit the website https://www.microsoft.com/surface/en-us/business/smb and go through the business applications of Microsoft Surface. Make a comprehensive report of these applications and then comment on the future potential of Microsoft Surface.

CASE STUDY 4

PSA Cruising with Information System

Singapore is a small island with abundant natural resources, a large protected harbor, and skilled manpower in addition to being strategically located on major trade routes. Singapore has put these resources to good use and is considered to be one of the best port cities in the world. Singapore's port is the world's second busiest port in terms of total shipping tonnage; the port transships one-fifth of the world's shipping containers and half of the world's annual supply of crude oil. This makes it the world's busiest transshipment port (transshipment is the transfer of containers from one vessel to another vessel bound for the cargo's final destination). Until 1964, the Singapore Harbour Board managed all port facilities, but since the expansion of port facilities that year, the Port of Singapore Authority (PSA) has taken over. At present, the Port of Singapore Authority offers five terminals and various facilities to those who conduct maritime trade operations in Singapore's harbors. The Port of Singapore Authority also provides specialized cargo handling services for hazardous chemicals and refrigerated cargo at each container terminal. These include 24-hour technical support to ensure smooth operation of refrigerated containers (Reefer-Care), professional care and consultation on the safe handling of dangerous goods (DG), as mandated by local and international authorities (ChemCare), and on-dock facilities with a full range of container depot services (BoxCare).

The success of the Port of Singapore Authority cannot be solely attributed to the strategic location of Singapore since there are other ports on the same east-west sea lanes. Ports like Port Klang and Port of Tanjung Pelepas (both in Malaysia), located at the southwest tip of the state of Johor, which is a stone's throw from Singapore, collect nowhere near as much revenue as the Port of Singapore Authority. The main reason behind the success of the Port of Singapore Authority is the unmatched value proposition provided by information systems. PSA has very rightfully identified that the success of a port depends on the effective management of containers that arrive at the port and hence one of the most important application of information system at PSA is Computer Integrated Terminal Operation System (CITOS), which addresses this issue. When a ship arrives, CITOS allocates an appropriate berth to the ship for a specified time and decides upon the number of cranes that will be required to unload the containers into the stacking yard. Considering the kind of traffic of ships and volume of containers at Singapore port, it is impossible for the Port of Singapore Authority to manually manage the unloading of containers onto another ship or schedule pickup for domestic delivery by freight forwarders. But through CITOS, work instructions regarding these critical activities are transmitted to all the machine operators using real-time wireless data transmission, which helps to effectively manage reloading or domestic forwarding of containers. CITOS is divided into various subsystems to accomplish the multitude of tasks at the port. The Container Recognition Subsystem helps to electronically recognize each character of a container's ID, and automatically cross checks this against the existing record of expected containers. During transit, container numbers written on them in paint tend to erode, but by applying neural network technology, the Container Recognition Subsystem is able to read and recognize the container number with precision. This is accomplished through a set of video cameras, with each camera being focused on the part of the container where the numbers should be. The picture from the cameras is transferred to a personal computer which digitizes the pictures. This allows the neural network software based on artificial intelligence, which mimics the learning process of the human brain so as to extract patterns from collected data, to attempt recognizing each character with precision against previously declared numbers. In this way, comprehensive records on incoming and outgoing container trucks are maintained. Another subsystem of CITOS is the Gate Automation Subsystem which records the arrival of a container at the gate, lists its weight, and either assigns a location or directs delivery of containers, all within 45 seconds. The third subsystem of CITOS is the Ship Planning Subsystem which manages the loading and unloading of containers. It positions the containers inside each vessel and allocates and sequences cranes for unloading and loading.

Another major concern in a port is the turnaround time of ships, which must be as quick as possible so as to manage the huge volume of incoming ships. Here again PSA has implemented information system to manage the turnaround time. The Yard Planning Expert Subsystem of CITOS sorts containers for the optimum utilization of yard space, which eventually helps to save time when containers are being unloaded or loaded. The Resource Allocation Subsystem of CITOS manages the huge operational staff of the Port of Singapore Authority. It allocates duties to operational staff and forecasts the exact requirements of staff for managing operations. It also produces a deployment plan for operations to be executed. Changes in the resource requirements for crane equipment are detected instantaneously and adjusted accordingly in the deployment plan during the deployment process.

Not resting on its laurels, PSA is constantly finding avenues where it can implement information systems and yet another application of information system at PSA is PORTNET. PORTNET is an EDI facility specifically designed for effective coordination between the Port of Singapore Authority and shipping companies. Shipping companies send a message through the system to the Port of Singapore Authority before the arrival of a ship in Singapore. The company clearly indicates the time/date of arrival and number of containers on board, and electronically applies for required berth spaces. This is a 24 × 7 electronic data interchange system which works in tandem with CITOS. The application received from PORTNET is transferred to CITOS and the whole network handles the scheduling of the unloading and loading of containers.

Realizing the urgent need of managing the ever increasing movement of ships, PSA has implemented CIMOS i.e. Computer Integrated Marine Operation System. CIMOS tracks the movement of ships in the Singapore Straits and port waters, and one of its most important functions is to notify ships that are on collision paths with each other, so that the port operator can contact the ships by radio to warn them to change their course. CIMOS has a Vessel Traffic Information Subsystem, which monitors the Singapore Straits and port waters using five remote radars. All of this information is stored in a database linked to PORTNET through which shippers can locate information about specific ships.

DISCUSSION QUESTIONS

4-12. How is PSA taking the help of information system in order to manage the containers at the Port of Singapore?

4-13. Discuss the application of the information system in reducing the turnaround time of ships at the Port of Singapore.

4-14. How is information system being applied to maintain coordination between PSA and shipping companies at the Port of Sinagpore?

4-15. How is CIMOS helping PSA to manage the movement of ships at port of Singapore?

4-16. Visit the website (https://www.singaporepsa.com/) and make a note of other services provided by of Port of Singapore.

4-17. As one of the main job at PSA is the management of ships in the proper manner, visit your nearby parking facility and try to find out about the hardware being put in practice to manage the vehicles.

4-18. Since the concept of Augmented Reality (AR) has been discussed in this chapter, do you think that AR can help PSA in managing its activities at the port.

MyMISLab™

Go to the Assignments section of your MyLab to complete these writing exercises.

4-19. Suppose your first job after graduating from college is working at a large insurance company. Your boss asks you to analyze the impact self-driving cars will have on revenues from car insurance policies. List four ways self-driving cars could impact the insurance industry. Justify your answers.

4-20. Visit www.distrowatch.com. Click on one of the top five listed Linux distributions (like Mint, Ubuntu, Debian, Fedora, or OpenSUSE). Click on the Screenshots link for that distribution. List some similarities between this operating system and your current operating system. Summarize the advantages and disadvantages of switching from your current operating system to a Linux distribution.

ENDNOTES

1. SAS Institute Inc., "Big Data Meets Big Data Analytics," SAS.com, accessed May 14, 2014, www.sas.com/resources/whitepaper/wp_46345.pdf.
2. Pamela Vagata and Kevin Wilfong, "Scaling the Facebook Data Warehouse to 300 PB," Facebook.com, accessed May 14, 2014, https://code.facebook.com/posts/229861827208629/scaling-the-facebook-data-warehouse-to-300-pb.
3. Kashmir Hill, "Blueprints of NSA's Ridiculously Expensive Data Center in Utah Suggest It Holds Less Info than Thought," Forbes.com, accessed May 14, 2014, www.forbes.com/sites/kashmirhill/2013/07/24/blueprints-of-nsa-data-center-in-utah-suggest-its-storage-capacity-is-less-impressive-than-thought.
4. Cisco Systems, Inc., "VNI Forecast Highlights," Cisco.com, accessed April 30, 2015, www.cisco.com/web/solutions/sp/vni/vni_forecast_highlights/index.html.
5. Jillian D'Onfro, "Amazon: Here's the Final Tally for All the Insane Shopping Everyone Did This Holiday Season," Business Insider, December 26, 2014, accessed May 1, 2015, www.businessinsider.com/amazon-christmas-shopping-release-2014-12.
6. John Gaudiosi, "How Augmented Reality and Virtual Reality Will Generate $150 Billion in Revenue by 2020," Fortune, April 25, 2015, accessed May 1, 2015, http://fortune.com/2015/04/25/augmented-reality-virtual-reality.
7. Peter C. Evans and Marco Annunziata, "Industrial Internet: Pushing the Boundaries of Minds and Machines," General Electric, November 26, 2012, accessed May 21, 2014, www.ge.com/docs/chapters/Industrial_Internet.pdf.
8. Ibid.
9. Jennifer Warnick, "88 Acres: How Microsoft Quietly Built the City of the Future," Microsoft Corp., accessed May 21, 2014, www.microsoft.com/en-us/news/stories/88acres/88-acres-how-microsoft-quietly-built-the-city-of-the-future-chapter-1.aspx.
10. KPMG and the Center for Automotive Research, "Self-Driving Cars: Are We Ready," 2013, accessed May 1, 2015, www.kpmg.com/US/en/IssuesAndInsights/ArticlesPublications/Documents/self-driving-cars-are-we-ready.pdf.
11. Glenn Garvin, "Automakers Say Self-Driving Cars Are on the Horizon," Miami Herald, March 21, 2014, accessed May 22, 2014, www.tampabay.com/news/business/autos/automakers-say-self-driving-cars-are-on-the-horizon/2171386.
12. Steven Musil, "Google Unveils Self-Driving Car, Sans Steering Wheel," CNET, May 27, 2014, accessed May 28, 2014, www.cnet.com/news/google-unveils-self-driving-car-sans-steering-wheel.
13. The Travelers Indemnity Company, "2014 Annual Report," Travelers.com, December 31, 2014, accessed May 1, 2015, http://investor.travelers.com/corporateprofile.aspx.
14. Network of Employers for Traffic Safety, "10 Facts Employers Must Know," accessed May 1, 2015, http://trafficsafety.org/safety/fleet-safety/10-facts-employers-must-know.
15. Liz Stinson, "For Super Bowl, Nike Uses 3-D Printing to Create a Faster Football Cleat," Wired, January 10, 2014, accessed May 23, 2014, www.wired.com/2014/01/nike-designed-fastest-cleat-history.
16. See EDAG's GENESIS prototype car at www.EDAG.de.
17. Venessa Wong, "A Guide to All the Food That's Fit to 3D Print (So Far)," BusinessWeek, January 28, 2014, accessed May 23, 2014, www.businessweek.com/articles/2014-01-28/all-the-food-thats-fit-to-3d-print-from-chocolates-to-pizza.
18. Dan Ferber, "An Essential Step Toward Printing Living Tissues," Harvard School of Engineering and Applied Sciences, February 19,

2014, accessed May 23, 2014, *www.seas.harvard.edu/news/2014/02/essential-step-toward-printing-living-tissues*.

19. Ryan Bushey, "Researchers Are Making a 3D Printer That Can Build a House in 24 Hours," *Business Insider*, January 9, 2014, accessed May 23, 2014, *www.businessinsider.com/3d-printer-builds-house-in-24-hours-2014-1*.

20. "Net Applications," accessed May 15, 2015, *www.netapplications.com*.

21. Previously called metro-style. Name change by Microsoft, reputedly because of a trademark lawsuit from Europe.

22. "Net Applications," accessed May 15, 2015, *www.netapplications.com*.

23. DistroWatch.com, accessed May 15, 2015, *www.distrowatch.com*.

24. "Net Applications," accessed July 15, 2013, *www.netapplications.com*.

25. Pew Research Center, "U.S. Smartphone Use in 2015," *PewInternet.org*, accessed May 2015, *www.pewinternet.org/files/2015/03/PI_Smartphones_0401151.pdf*.

26. "Unlocking the Cloud," *The Economist*, May 28, 2009.

27. Not quite true. Much of the design and possibly some of the code can be reused between native applications. But, for your planning, assume that it all must be redone. Not enough will carry over to make it worth considering.

28. Cisco Systems Inc., "Cisco Visual Networking Index: Global Mobile Data Traffic Forecast Update, 2014–2019," *Cisco.com*, February 3, 2015, accessed May 22, 2015, *www.cisco.com/c/en/us/solutions/collateral/service-provider/visual-networking-index-vni/white_paper_c11-520862.html*.

29. Ibid.

30. Horace Dediu, "Late Late Majority," *Asymco.com*, July 8, 2014, accessed July 7, 2015, *www.asymco.com/2014/07/08/late-late-majority*.

31. comScore, "comScore Reports March 2015 U.S. Smartphone Subscriber Market Share," February 9 2015, accessed May 16, 2015, *www.comscore.com/Insights/Market-Rankings/comScore-Reports-December-2014-US-Smartphone-Subscriber-Market-Share*.

32. eMarketer, "Mobile Commerce Roundup," *eMarketer.com*, October 2013, accessed June 10, 2014, *www.emarketer.com/public_media/docs/eMarketer_Mobile_Commerce_Roundup.pdf*.

33. The Nielsen Company, "Survey New U.S. Smartphone Growth By Age and Income," accessed May 2012, *www.nielsen.com/us/en/insights/news/2012/survey-new-u-s-smartphone-growth-by-age-and-income.html*.

34. SnoopWall, "SnoopWall Flashlight Apps Threat Assessment Report," October 1, 2014, *SnoopWall.com*, accessed April 27, 2015, *www.snoopwall.com/threat-reports-10-01-2014*.

35. Symantec Corporation, "Internet Security Report," *Symantec.com*, Volume 20, April 2015, accessed April 27, 2015, *www4.symantec.com/mktginfo/whitepaper/ISTR/21347932_GA-internet-security-threat-report-volume-20-2015-social_v2.pdf*.

36. Google, "Android Security 2014 Year in Review," *GoogleUserContent.com*, accessed April 27, 2015, *http://static.googleusercontent.com/media/source.android.com/en/us/devices/tech/security/reports/Google_Android_Security_2014_Report_Final.pdf*.

37. David Willis, "Bring Your Own Device: The Facts and the Future," Gartner Inc., April 11, 2013.

38. Ibid.

39. "CDH," accessed July 15, 2013, *www.cdh.com*.

40. Robert McMillan, "IBM Worries iPhone's Siri Has Loose Lips," last modified May 24, 2012, *www.cnn.com/2012/05/23/tech/mobile/ibm-siri-ban/index.html?iphoneemail*.

41. Bruce Schneier, "Heartbleed," *Schneier on Security*, April 9, 2014, accessed May 9, 2014, *www.schneier.com/blog/archives/2014/04/heartbleed.html*.

42. Mashable Team, "The Heartbleed Hit List: The Passwords You Need to Change Right Now," April 9, 2014, accessed May 9, 2014, *http://mashable.com/2014/04/09/heartbleed-bug-websites-affected*.

43. Shaun Nichols, "Apple Stabs Heartbleed Bug in AirPort Extreme, Time Capsule Gear," *The Register*, April 24, 2014, accessed May 9, 2014, *www.theregister.co.uk/2014/04/24/apple_posts_updates_for_heartbleed_flaw_in_airport*.

44. Pew Research Center, "Heartbleed's Impact," April 30, 2014, accessed May 9, 2014, *http://www.pewinternet.org/files/2014/04/PIP_Heartbleed-impact_043014.pdf*.

45. Robert Hackett, "On Heartbleed's Anniversary, 3 of 4 Big Companies Are Still Vulnerable," *Fortune.com*, April 7, 2015, accessed May 2, 2015, *http://fortune.com/2015/04/07/heartbleed-anniversary-vulnerable*.

46. Microsoft press release, "Harrah's Entertainment Launches Microsoft Surface at Rio iBar, Providing Guests with Innovative and Immersive New Entertainment Experiences," last modified June 11, 2008, *www.microsoft.com/presspass/press/2008/jun08/06-11HETSurfacePR.mspx*.

47. Microsoft press release, May 29, 2007.

48. http://bschool.nus.edu/staff/bizteosh/LeePartridgeTeoLimJSIS2000P

49. http://www.sba.oakland.edu/faculty/lauer/downloads/MIS625/Readings/singapore%20case.pdf

50. https://www.singaporepsa.com/about-us/mission-and-values

51. https://www.singaporepsa.com/

Database Processing

It's Friday night, and Camillia (Cam) Forset is on her way to an art show opening. She gets an urgent call from Jess Denkar, the head of security at PetroTex. PetroTex is a large oil refinery based in Texas and one of Falcon Security's biggest industrial clients. Jess is looking for information that could help him find out who stole almost $75,000 worth of custom piping and copper wiring.

Cam made sure Jess had her personal cell phone number and told him to call her anytime—day or night. She knows it's important to show Jess that the money PetroTex spends on Falcon's services is worth it. She immediately calls Toshio Sato, director of IT Services, and tells him to come back into the office. She also sends a text message to CEO Mateo Thomas and CFO Joni Campbell.

"Have you found anything yet?" Joni asks. She quickly sets down her purse at a nearby workstation and begins hovering behind Toshio.

"Not yet—we're working as fast as we can," Cam replies tersely. Cam wants to focus on helping Toshio find the correct security footage, not discuss the importance of the PetroTex account to Falcon Security.

"Is there anything I can do to help?" Joni wonders.

"No, we're just trying to find the right footage. There's a lot of it to review," Cam sighs.

"What's the problem? Why do we have to look through so much footage?"

Toshio is tempted to tell Joni that "we" aren't looking through anything. He's the one doing the searching. But he holds his tongue. "Well, the problem is we have footage of dozens of different buildings at PetroTex, from several different drones, over about a 2-week period. Tracking down the footage of exactly when the equipment was stolen means we have to search through hundreds of different video files. This could take all night," he answers matter-of-factly.

"There's got to be a faster way to do this. Can't we just search for the footage somehow?" Joni says.

"No," Toshio says calmly. "We don't have a way to track the data about the videos. The video files are sequentially numbered and stored in directories for a specific company. We can also see the date and time the video file was created, but there are several different drones. It's just…"

Cam interrupts Toshio to try to keep him from getting distracted. "Toshio and I have talked about creating a database to track all of our video files. We've just been busy trying to automate the data collection and storage process."

"Well, how long would it take to make it? How much would it cost?" Joni asks.

"We're not sure. We don't even know which database management system we'd use. Toshio and I have both used Microsoft Access, but Toshio mentioned something called MongoDB that might be better for tracking video files."

Toshio pauses the video he's reviewing and starts pointing at a listing of video files in a directory. "Instead of searching through all of these manually, I could just specify characteristics about each video like company name, building name, date, time, and elevation. It would return the URLs for videos matching those characteristics. We'd know right where they are on our file server."

"Sounds good to me. Anything to keep us from spending our Friday nights looking through video footage. Let's do it," Joni quips.

Cam tries to get things back on track. "OK, great, we'll put it on our list. There's no doubt that a database will keep us from having to search through all this footage. For now, though, we should probably focus on finding the footage for Jess. We've got a lot to go through tonight."

"We don't have a way to track the data about the videos."

Image source: rommma/Fotolia

STUDY QUESTIONS

Q5-1   What is the purpose of a database?

Q5-2   What is a database?

Q5-3   What is a database management system (DBMS)?

Q5-4   How do database applications make databases more useful?

Q5-5   How are data models used for database development?

Q5-6   How is a data model transformed into a database design?

Q5-7   How can Falcon Security benefit from a database system?

Q5-8   2026?

CHAPTER PREVIEW

Although you may not realize it, you access dozens, if not hundreds, of databases every day. Every time you make a cell phone call, log on to the Internet, or buy something online using a credit card, applications behind the scenes are processing numerous databases. Use Snapchat, Facebook, Twitter, or LinkedIn, and again applications are processing databases on your behalf. Google something, and yet again dozens of databases are processed to obtain the search results.

As a user, you need know nothing about the underlying technology. From your perspective, "it just works," to quote the late Steve Jobs. However, as a business professional in the 21st century, it's a different story. You need the knowledge of this chapter for four principal reasons:

1. When you participate in the development of any new business initiative, you need to know if database technology can facilitate your project goals. If so, you need sufficient knowledge to assess whether building that database is akin to building a small shed or is closer to building a skyscraper. Joni, in the opening vignette of this chapter, needs to have some knowledge to assess how hard (and thus how expensive) building that new database will be.
2. Because databases are ubiquitous in commerce, billions upon billions of bytes of data are stored every day. You need to know how to turn that data into a format from which you can construct useful information. To that end, you might use one of many different graphical tools to query that data. Or, to become truly proficient, you might learn SQL, an international standard language for querying database. Many business professionals have done just that. See the So What? feature of this chapter on page 205.
3. Business is dynamic, and information systems must adapt. Often such adaptation means that the structure of the database needs to be changed. Sometimes it means that entirely new databases must be created. As you will learn in this chapter, only the users, such as yourself, know what and how detail should be stored. You may be asked to evaluate a data model like those described in Q5-4 to facilitate database change and creation.
4. Finally, you might someday find yourself or your department in a material mess. Maybe you don't know who has which equipment, or where certain tools are located, or what's really in your supply closet. In that case, you might choose to build your own database. Unless you're an IS professional, that database will be small and relatively simple, but it can still be very useful to you and your colleagues. Case Study 5 on page 230 illustrates one such example.

This chapter addresses the why, what, and how of database processing. We begin by describing the purpose of a database and then explain the important components of database systems. Next, we discuss data modeling and show how IS professionals use data models to design database structure. We then discuss how a database system could be used to solve the tracking problem at Falcon Security. We'll wrap up with pondering where database technology might be in 2026.

Q5-1 What Is the Purpose of a Database?

The purpose of a database is to keep track of things. When most students learn that, they wonder why we need a special technology for such a simple task. Why not just use a list? If the list is long, put it into a spreadsheet.

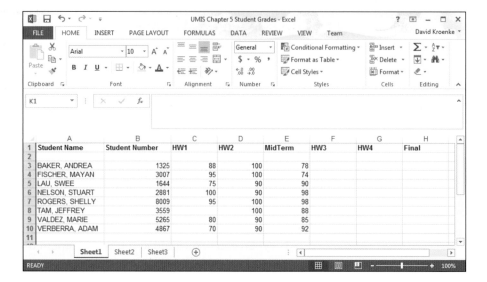

Figure 5-1

A List of Student Grades Presented in a Spreadsheet

Source: © Access 2013, Microsoft Corporation

In fact, many professionals do keep track of things using spreadsheets. If the structure of the list is simple enough, there is no need to use database technology. The list of student grades in Figure 5-1, for example, works perfectly well in a spreadsheet.

Suppose, however, that the professor wants to track more than just grades. Say that the professor wants to record email messages as well. Or perhaps the professor wants to record both email messages and office visits. There is no place in Figure 5-1 to record that additional data. Of course, the professor could set up a separate spreadsheet for email messages and another one for office visits, but that awkward solution would be difficult to use because it does not provide all of the data in one place.

Instead, the professor wants a form like that in Figure 5-2. With it, the professor can record student grades, emails, and office visits all in one place. A form like the one in Figure 5-2 is difficult, if not impossible, to produce from a spreadsheet. Such a form is easily produced, however, from a database.

The key distinction between Figures 5-1 and 5-2 is that the data in Figure 5-1 is about a single theme or concept. It is about student grades only. The data in Figure 5-2 has multiple themes; it shows student grades, student emails, and student office visits. We can make a general rule from these examples: Lists of data involving a single theme can be stored in a spreadsheet; lists that involve data with multiple themes require a database. We will say more about this general rule as this chapter proceeds.

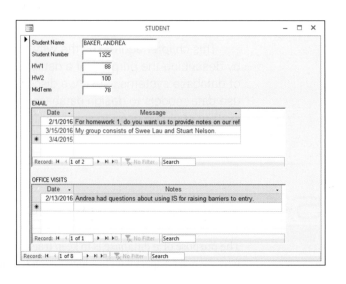

Figure 5-2

Student Data Shown in a Form from a Database

Source: © Access 2013, Microsoft Corporation

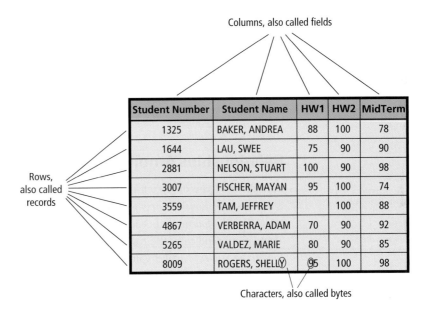

Figure 5-3
Student Table (also called a file)

Q5-2 What Is a Database?

A **database** is a self-describing collection of integrated records. To understand the terms in this definition, you first need to understand the terms illustrated in Figure 5-3. As you learned in Chapter 4, a **byte** is a character of data. In databases, bytes are grouped into **columns**, such as *Student Number* and *Student Name*. Columns are also called **fields**. Columns or fields, in turn, are grouped into **rows**, which are also called **records**. In Figure 5-3, the collection of data for all columns (*Student Number, Student Name, HW1, HW2,* and *MidTerm*) is called a *row* or a *record*. Finally, a group of similar rows or records is called a **table** or a **file**. From these definitions, you can see a hierarchy of data elements, as shown in Figure 5-4.

It is tempting to continue this grouping process by saying that a database is a group of tables or files. This statement, although true, does not go far enough. As shown in Figure 5-5, a database is a collection of tables *plus* relationships among the rows in those tables, *plus* special data, called *metadata*, that describes the structure of the database. By the way, the cylindrical symbol 🛢 labeled "database" in Figure 5-5 represents a computer disk drive. It is used like this because databases are most frequently stored on disks.

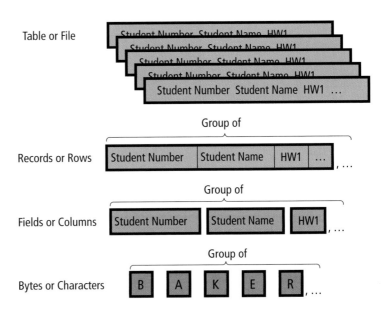

Figure 5-4
Hierarchy of Data Elements

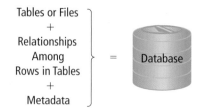

Figure 5-5
Components of a Database

Relationships Among Rows

Consider the terms on the left-hand side of Figure 5-5. You know what tables are. To understand what is meant by *relationships among rows in tables*, examine Figure 5-6. It shows sample data from the three tables *Email*, *Student*, and *Office_Visit*. Notice the column named *Student Number* in the *Email* table. That column indicates the row in *Student* to which a row of *Email* is connected. In the first row of *Email*, the *Student Number* value is 1325. This indicates that this particular email was received from the student whose *Student Number* is 1325. If you examine the *Student* table, you will see that the row for Andrea Baker has this value. Thus, the first row of the *Email* table is related to Andrea Baker.

Now consider the last row of the *Office_Visit* table at the bottom of the figure. The value of *Student Number* in that row is 4867. This value indicates that the last row in *Office_Visit* belongs to Adam Verberra.

From these examples, you can see that values in one table relate rows of that table to rows in a second table. Several special terms are used to express these ideas. A **key** (also called a **primary key**) is a column or group of columns that identifies a unique row in a table. *Student Number* is the key of the *Student* table. Given a value of *Student Number*, you can determine one and only one row in *Student*. Only one student has the number 1325, for example.

Figure 5-6
Example of Relationships
Among Rows

Email Table

EmailNum	Date	Message	Student Number
1	2/1/2016	For homework 1, do you want us to provide notes on our references?	1325
2	3/15/2016	My group consists of Swee Lau and Stuart Nelson.	1325
3	3/15/2016	Could you please assign me to a group?	1644

Student Table

Student Number	Student Name	HW1	HW2	MidTerm
1325	BAKER, ANDREA	88	100	78
1644	LAU, SWEE	75	90	90
2881	NELSON, STUART	100	90	98
3007	FISCHER, MAYAN	95	100	74
3559	TAM, JEFFREY		100	88
4867	VERBERRA, ADAM	70	90	92
5265	VALDEZ, MARIE	80	90	85
8009	ROGERS, SHELLY	95	100	98

Office_Visit Table

VisitID	Date	Notes	Student Number
2	2/13/2016	Andrea had questions about using IS for raising barriers to entry.	1325
3	2/17/2016	Jeffrey is considering an IS major. Wanted to talk about career opportunities.	3559
4	2/17/2016	Will miss class Friday due to job conflict.	4867

Every table must have a key. The key of the *Email* table is *EmailNum*, and the key of the *Office_ Visit* table is *VisitID*. Sometimes more than one column is needed to form a unique identifier. In a table called *City*, for example, the key would consist of the combination of columns (*City*, *State*) because a given city name can appear in more than one state.

Student Number is not the key of the *Email* or the *Office_Visit* tables. We know that about *Email* because there are two rows in *Email* that have the *Student Number* value 1325. The value 1325 does not identify a unique row; therefore, *Student Number* cannot be the key of *Email*.

Nor is *Student Number* a key of *Office_Visit*, although you cannot tell that from the data in Figure 5-6. If you think about it, however, there is nothing to prevent a student from visiting a professor more than once. If that were to happen, there would be two rows in *Office_Visit* with the same value of *Student Number*. It just happens that no student has visited twice in the limited data in Figure 5-6.

In both *Email* and *Office_Visit*, *Student Number* is a key, but it is a key of a different table, namely *Student*. Hence, the columns that fulfill a role like that of *Student Number* in the *Email* and *Office_ Visit* tables are called **foreign keys**. This term is used because such columns are keys, but they are keys of a different (foreign) table than the one in which they reside.

Before we go on, databases that carry their data in the form of tables and that represent relationships using foreign keys are called **relational databases**. (The term *relational* is used because another, more formal name for a table like those we're discussing is **relation**.) You'll learn about another kind of database, or data store, in Q5-8 and in Case Study 5.

Metadata

Recall the definition of database: A database is a self-describing collection of integrated records. The records are integrated because, as you just learned, rows can be linked together by their key/ foreign key relationship. Relationships among rows are represented in the database. But what does *self-describing* mean?

Database technology puts unprecedented ability to conceive information into the hands of users. But what do you do with that information when you find something objectionable? See the Ethics Guide on pages 202–203 for an example case.

It means that a database contains, within itself, a description of its contents. Think of a library. A library is a self-describing collection of books and other materials. It is self-describing because the library contains a catalog that describes the library's contents. The same idea also pertains to a database. Databases are self-describing because they contain not only data, but also data about the data in the database.

Metadata is data that describes data. Figure 5-7 shows metadata for the *Email* table. The format of metadata depends on the software product that is processing the database. Figure 5-7 shows the

Figure 5-7

Sample Metadata (in Access)

Source: © Access 2013, Microsoft Corporation

Ethics Guide

QUERYING INEQUALITY?

MaryAnn Baker works as a data analyst in human relations at a large, multinational corporation. As part of its compensation program, her company defines job categories and assigns salary ranges to each category. For example, the category M1 is used for first-line managers and is assigned the salary range of $75,000 to $95,000. Every job description is assigned to one of these categories, depending on the knowledge and skills required to do that job. Thus, the job titles Manager of Customer Support, Manager of Technical Writing, and Manager of Product Quality Assurance are all judged to involve about the same level of management expertise and are all assigned to category M1.

One of MaryAnn's tasks is to analyze company salary data and determine how well actual salaries conform to established ranges. When discrepancies are noted, human relations managers meet to determine whether the discrepancy indicates a need to:

- Adjust the category's salary range;
- Move the job title to a different category;
- Define a new category; or
- Train the manager of the employee with the discrepancy on the use of salary ranges in setting employee compensation.

MaryAnn is an expert in creating database queries. Initially, she used Microsoft Access to produce reports, but much of the salary data she needs resides in the organization's Oracle database. At first she would ask the IS Department to extract certain data and move it into Access, but over time she learned that it was faster to ask IS to move all employee data from the operational Oracle database into another Oracle database created just for HR data analysis. Although Oracle provides a graphical query interface like that in Access, she found it easier to compose complex queries directly in SQL, so she learned it and, within a few months, became a SQL expert.

"I never thought I'd be doing this," she said. "But it turns out to be quite fun, like solving a puzzle, and apparently I'm good at it."

One day, after a break, MaryAnn signed into her computer and happened to glance at the results of a query that she'd left running while she was gone. "That's odd," she thought, "all the people with Hispanic surnames have lower salaries than the others." She wasn't looking for that

202

pattern; it just happened to jump out at her as she glanced at the screen.

As she examined the data, she began to wonder if she was seeing a coincidence or if there was a discriminatory pattern within the organization. Unfortunately for Mary-Ann's purposes, the organization did not track employee race in its database, so she had no easy way of identifying employees of Hispanic heritage other than reading through the list of surnames. But, as a skilled problem solver, that didn't stop MaryAnn. She realized that many employees having Hispanic origins were born in certain cities in Texas, New Mexico, Arizona, and California. Of course, this wasn't true for all employees; many non-Hispanic employees were born in those cities, too, and many Hispanic employees were born in other cities. This data was still useful, however, because MaryAnn's sample queries revealed that the proportion of employees with Hispanic surnames who were also born in those cities

was very high. "OK," she thought, "I'll use those cities as a rough surrogate."

Using birth city as a query criterion, MaryAnn created queries that determined employees who were born in the selected cities earned, on average, 23 percent less than those who were not. "Well, that could be because they work in lower-pay-grade jobs." After giving it a bit of thought, MaryAnn realized that she needed to examine wages and salaries within job categories. "Where," she wondered, "do people born in those cities fall in the ranges of their job categories?" So, she constructed SQL to determine where within a job category the compensation for people born in the selected cities fell. "Wow!" she said to herself, "almost 80 percent of the employees born in those cities fall into the bottom half of their salary range."

MaryAnn scheduled an appointment with her manager for the next day.

DISCUSSION QUESTIONS

When answering the following questions, suppose that you are MaryAnn:

1. Given these query results, do you have an ethical responsibility to do something? Consider both the categorical imperative (pages 56–57) and the utilitarian (pages 92–93) perspectives.

2. Given these query results, do you have a personal or social responsibility to do something?

3. What is your response if your manager says, "You don't know anything; it could be that starting salaries are lower in those cities. Forget about it."

4. What is your response if your manager says, "Don't be a troublemaker; pushing this issue will hurt your career."

5. What is your response if your manager says, "Right. We already know that. Get back to the tasks that I've assigned you."

6. Suppose your manager gives you funding to follow up with a more accurate analysis, and, indeed, there is a pattern of underpayment to people with Hispanic surnames. What should the organization do? For each choice below, indicate likely outcomes:

a. Correct the imbalances immediately.

b. Gradually correct the imbalances at future pay raises.

c. Do nothing about the imbalances, but train managers not to discriminate in the future.

d. Do nothing.

7. Suppose you hire a part-time person to help with the more accurate analysis, and that person is so outraged at the outcome that he quits and notifies newspapers in all the affected cities of the organization's discrimination.

a. How should the organization respond?

b. How should you respond?

8. Consider the adage "Never ask a question for which you do not want the answer."

a. Is following that adage ethical? Consider both the categorical imperative and utilitarian perspectives.

b. Is following that adage socially responsible?

c. How does that adage relate to you, as MaryAnn?

d. How does that adage relate to you, as a future business professional?

e. With regard to employee compensation, how does that adage relate to organizations?

metadata as it appears in Microsoft Access. Each row of the top part of this form describes a column of the *Email* table. The columns of these descriptions are *Field Name, Data Type,* and *Description. Field Name* contains the name of the column, *Data Type* shows the type of data the column may hold, and *Description* contains notes that explain the source or use of the column. As you can see, there is one row of metadata for each of the four columns of the *Email* table: *EmailNum, Date, Message,* and *Student Number.*

The bottom part of this form provides more metadata, which Access calls *Field Properties,* for each column. In Figure 5-7, the focus is on the *Date* column (note the light rectangle drawn around the *Date* row). Because the focus is on *Date* in the top pane, the details in the bottom pane pertain to the *Date* column. The Field Properties describe formats, a default value for Access to supply when a new row is created, and the constraint that a value is required for this column. It is not important for you to remember these details. Instead, just understand that metadata is data about data and that such metadata is always a part of a database.

The presence of metadata makes databases much more useful. Because of metadata, no one needs to guess, remember, or even record what is in the database. To find out what a database contains, we just look at the metadata inside the database.

Q5-3 What Is a Database Management System (DBMS)?

A **database management system (DBMS)** is a program used to create, process, and administer a database. As with operating systems, almost no organization develops its own DBMS. Instead, companies license DBMS products from vendors such as IBM, Microsoft, Oracle, and others. Popular DBMS products are **DB2** from IBM, **Access** and **SQL Server** from Microsoft, and **Oracle Database** from the Oracle Corporation. Another popular DBMS is **MySQL**, an open source DBMS product that is license-free for most applications.[1] Other DBMS products are available, but these five process the great bulk of databases today.

Note that a DBMS and a database are two different things. For some reason, the trade press and even some books confuse the two. A DBMS is a software program; a database is a collection of tables, relationships, and metadata. The two are very different concepts.

Creating the Database and Its Structures

Database developers use the DBMS to create tables, relationships, and other structures in the database. The form in Figure 5-7 can be used to define a new table or to modify an existing one. To create a new table, the developer just fills the new table's metadata into the form.

To modify an existing table—say, to add a new column—the developer opens the metadata form for that table and adds a new row of metadata. For example, in Figure 5-8 the developer has added a new column called *Response?.* This new column has the data type *Yes/No,* which means that the column can contain only one value—*Yes* or *No.* The professor will use this column to indicate whether he has responded to the student's email. A column can be removed by deleting its row in this table, though doing so will lose any existing data.

Processing the Database

SQL is essential for processing a database, but it can be misused by criminals to steal data. This kind of SQL injection attack is described in the Security Guide on pages 224–225.

The second function of the DBMS is to process the database. Such processing can be quite complex, but, fundamentally, the DBMS provides applications for four processing operations: to read, insert, modify, or delete data. These operations are requested in application calls upon the DBMS. From a form, when the user enters new or changed data, a computer program behind the form calls the DBMS to make the necessary database changes. From a Web application, a program on the client or on the server calls the DBMS to make the change.

Not What the Data Says ...

Two product managers, Jeremey Will and Neil Town, are arguing about the effectiveness of a September product sales promotion in front of their boss, Sarah Murphy.

SARAH: "So, should we repeat that promotion in October?"

JEREMEY: "No way. It was expensive, and there was no increase in sales."

NEIL: "I disagree. Well, wait, I agree there was no increase in sales from August, but if you look at sales history, we have a substantial increase over past Septembers."

JEREMEY: "Where'd you get that data?"

NEIL: "Extracted it from the sales database. Anyway, on average, our sales are up 11 percent from past years. And, even better, most of that increase is from new customers."

JEREMEY: "I don't think so. I called four different sales reps, and they said they can't get any prospects to bite."

NEIL: "Not what the data says. I put it into Access and then did a series of queries. Nineteen percent of sales in September were from new customers."

SARAH: "Amazing. But can you relate that to the campaign?"

NEIL: "Yes, strongly. Turns out of the new customers' sales, almost two-thirds used a coupon."

SARAH: "Neil, put this into a report for me. I want to take it to the executive meeting tomorrow."

1. Do you want to be Jeremey or Neil? Justify your answer.
2. What skills and abilities will you need to be Neil?

Source: StockLite/Shutterstock

3. List specific sales data you need to provide answers as Neil does.
4. In words, describe how that data needs to be processed in order to produce Neil's responses.
5. All of the results that Neil provides are readily produced by Access or by any SQL-processing DBMS. With a basic understanding of SQL, you could write the queries in 5 minutes or less. However, this chapter will give you necessary background, but it won't teach you SQL queries. Consult your university's course catalog and find a course that would teach you the necessary skills. Name that course and explain why you will (or won't) take it.

Structured Query Language (SQL) is an international standard language for processing a database. All five of the DBMS products mentioned earlier accept and process SQL (pronounced "see-quell") statements. As an example, the following SQL statement inserts a new row into the *Student* table:

```
INSERT INTO Student
([Student Number], [Student Name], HW1, HW2, MidTerm)
VALUES
(1000, 'Franklin, Benjamin', 90, 95, 100);
```

As stated, statements like this one are issued "behind the scenes" by programs that process forms and reports. Alternatively, they can be issued directly to the DBMS by an application program.

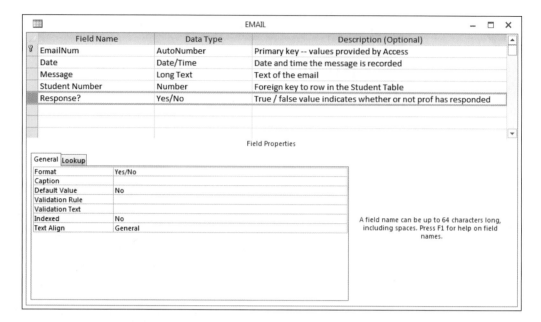

Figure 5-8
Adding a New Column
to a Table (in Access)

Source: © Access 2013, Microsoft
Corporation

You do not need to understand or remember SQL language syntax. Instead, just realize that SQL is an international standard for processing a database. SQL can also be used to create databases and database structures. You will learn more about SQL if you take a database management class.

Administering the Database

A third DBMS function is to provide tools to assist in the administration of the database. **Database administration** involves a wide variety of activities. For example, the DBMS can be used to set up a security system involving user accounts, passwords, permissions, and limits for processing the database. To provide database security, a user must sign on using a valid user account before she can process the database.

Permissions can be limited in very specific ways. In the Student database example, it is possible to limit a particular user to reading only *Student Name* from the *Student* table. A different user could be given permission to read the entire *Student* table, but limited to update only the *HW1*, *HW2*, and *MidTerm* columns. Other users can be given still other permissions.

In addition to security, DBMS administrative functions include backing up database data, adding structures to improve the performance of database applications, removing data that are no longer wanted or needed, and similar tasks.

For important databases, most organizations dedicate one or more employees to the role of database administration. Figure 5-9 summarizes the major responsibilities for this function. You will learn more about this topic if you take a database management course.

Q5-4   How Do Database Applications Make Databases More Useful?

A set of database tables, by itself, is not very useful; the tables in Figure 5-6 contain the data the professor wants, but the format is awkward at best. The data in database tables can be made more useful, or more available for the conception of information, when it is placed into forms like that in Figure 5-2 or other formats.

A **database application** is a collection of forms, reports, queries, and application programs[2] that serves as an intermediary between users and database data. Database applications reformat

Category	Database Administration Task	Description
Development	Create and staff DBA function	Size of DBA group depends on size and complexity of database. Groups range from one part-time person to small group.
	Form steering committee	Consists of representatives of all user groups. Forum for community-wide discussions and decisions.
	Specify requirements	Ensure that all appropriate user input is considered.
	Validate data model	Check data model for accuracy and completeness.
	Evaluate application design	Verify that all necessary forms, reports, queries, and applications are developed. Validate design and usability of application components.
Operation	Manage processing rights and responsibilities	Determine processing rights/restrictions on each table and column.
	Manage security	Add and delete users and user groups as necessary; ensure that security system works.
	Track problems and manage resolution	Develop system to record and manage resolution of problems.
	Monitor database performance	Provide expertise/solutions for performance improvements.
	Manage DBMS	Evaluate new features and functions.
Backup and Recovery	Monitor backup procedures	Verify that database backup procedures are followed.
	Conduct training	Ensure that users and operations personnel know and understand recovery procedures.
	Manage recovery	Manage recovery process.
Adaptation	Set up request tracking system	Develop system to record and prioritize requests for change.
	Manage configuration change	Manage impact of database structure changes on applications and users.

Figure 5-9
Summary of Database Administration (DBA) Tasks

database table data to make it more informative and more easily updated. Application programs also have features that provide security, maintain data consistency, and handle special cases.

The specific purposes of the four elements of a database application are:

Forms	View data; insert new, update existing, and delete existing data
Reports	Structured presentation of data using sorting, grouping, Filtering, and other operations
Queries	Search based on data values provided by the user
Application programs	Provide security, data consistency, and special purpose processing, e.g., handle out-of-stock situations

Database applications came into prominence in the 1990s and were based on the technology available at that time. Many existing systems today are long-lived extensions to those applications; the ERP system SAP (discussed in Chapter 7) is a good example of this concept. You should expect to see these kinds of applications during the early years of your career.

Today, however, many database applications are based on newer technology that employs browsers, the Web, and related standards. These browser-based applications can do everything the older ones do, but they are more dynamic and better suited to today's world. To see why, consider each type.

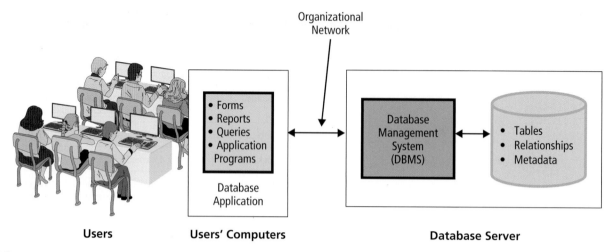

Figure 5-10

Components of a Database Application System

Traditional Forms, Queries, Reports, and Applications

In most cases, a traditional database is shared among many users. In that case, the application shown in Figure 5-10 resides on the users' computers and the DBMS and database reside on a server computer. A network, in most cases *not* the Internet, is used to transmit traffic back and forth between the users' computers and the DBMS server computer.

Single-user databases like those in Microsoft Access are an exception. With such databases, the application, the DBMS, and the database all reside on the user's computer.

Traditional forms appeared in window-like displays like that in Figure 5-2. They serve their purpose; users can view, insert, modify, and delete data with them, but by today's standards, they look clunky.

Figure 5-11 shows a traditional report, which is a static display of data, placed into a format that is meaningful to the user. In this report, each of the emails for a particular student is shown after the student's name and grade data. Figure 5-12 shows a traditional query. The user specifies query criteria in a window-like box (Figure 5-12a), and the application responds with data that fit those criteria (Figure 5-12b).

Traditional database application programs are written in object-oriented languages such as C++ and VisualBasic (and even in earlier languages like COBOL). They are thick applications that need to be installed on users' computers. In some cases, all of the application logic is contained in a program on users' computers and the server does nothing except run the DBMS and serve up data. In other cases, some application code is placed on both the users' computers and the database server computer.

Student Homework Progress with Emails

Student Name		Student Number	HW1	HW2
BAKER, ANDREA		1325	88	100

	Email Date	Message		
	3/15/2016	My group consists of Swee Lau and Stuart Nelson.		
	2/1/2016	For homework 1, do you want us to provide notes on our references?		
LAU, SWEE		1644	75	90

	Email Date	Message		
	3/15/2016	Could you please assign me to a group?		

Figure 5-11

Example of a Student Report

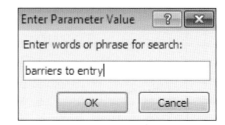

Figure 5-12a

Sample Query Form Used to Enter Phrase for Search

Figure 5-12b

Sample Query Results of Query Operation

Source: © Access 2013, Microsoft Corporation

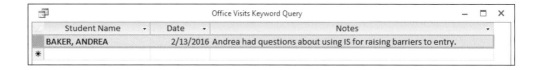

As stated, in the early years of your career, you will still see traditional applications, especially for enterprise-wide applications like ERP and CRM. Most likely, you will also be concerned, as a user if not in a more involved way, with the transition from such traditional applications into browser-based applications.

Browser Forms, Reports, Queries, and Applications

The databases in browser-based applications are nearly always shared among many users. As shown in Figure 5-13, the users' browsers connect over the Internet to a Web server computer, which in turn connects to a database server computer (often many computers are involved on the server side of the Internet).

Browser applications are thin-client applications that need not be preinstalled on the users' computers. In most cases, all of the code for generating and processing the application elements is shared between the users' computers and the servers. JavaScript is the standard language for user-side processing. Languages like C# and Java are used for server-side code, though JavaScript is starting to be used on the server with an open source product named Node.js.

Browser database application forms, reports, and queries are displayed and processed using html and, most recently, using html5, css3, and JavaScript as you learned in Chapter 4.

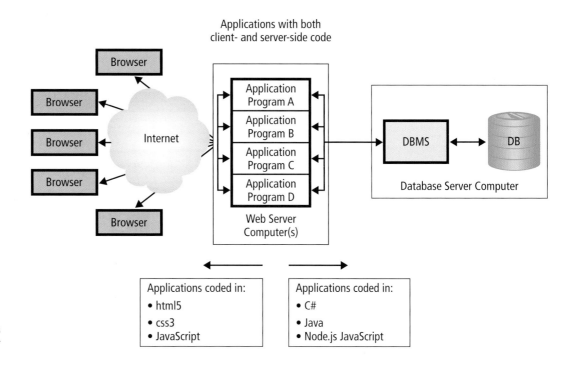

Figure 5-13

Four Application Programs on a Web Server Computer

Microsoft
Online Services

New user

1. **Details**
2. Settings
3. Licenses
4. Email
5. Results

Details
Name

* Required

First name: Drew
Last name: Mills
* Display name: Drew
* User name: Drew   @ Office365inBusiness.com ▼

Additional details ▾

Next   Cancel

Figure 5-14
Account Creation Browser Form
Source: © Access 2013, Microsoft
Corporation

Figure 5-14 shows a browser form that is used to create a new user account in Office 365. The form's content is dynamic; the user can click on the blue arrow next to *Additional Details* to see more data. Also, notice the steps in the left-hand side that outline the process that administrator will follow when creating the new account. The current step is shown in color. Compare and contrast this form with that in Figure 5-2; it is cleaner, with much less chrome.

Figure 5-15 illustrates a browser report that shows the content of a SharePoint site. The content is dynamic; almost all of the items can be clicked to produce other reports or take other actions. The user can search the report in the box in the upper-right-hand corner to find specific items.

Browser-based applications can support traditional queries, but more exciting are **graphical queries**, in which query criteria are created when the user clicks on a graphic. Figure 5-16 shows a map of one of the facilities protected by Falcon Security. The user can click on any one of the video icons on the map, and the click will initiate a query to return a list of all the videos available from that location.

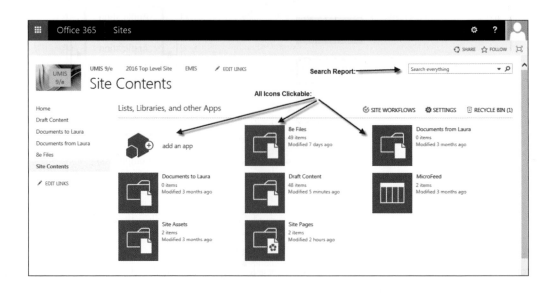

Figure 5-15
Browser Report
Source: © Access 2013, Microsoft
Corporation

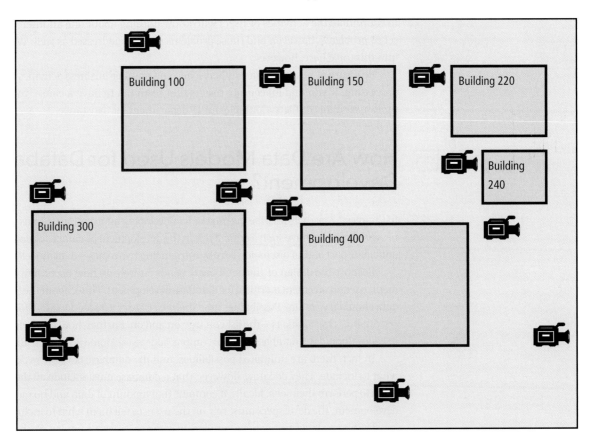

Figure 5-16

Graphical Query: User Clicks on
Video Icon to Find All Videos from
That Location

Security requirements are more stringent for browser-based Internet applications than for traditional ones. Most traditional applications run within a corporate network protected from threats common on the Internet. Browser-based applications that are open to the public, over the Internet, are far more vulnerable. Thus, protecting security is a major function for browser-based Internet application programs. Like traditional database application programs, they need to provide for data consistency and to handle special conditions as well. As an example of the need for data consistency, consider the problems introduced by multi-user processing.

Multi-user Processing

Most traditional and browser-based applications involve multiple users processing the same database. While such **multi-user processing** is common, it does pose unique problems that you, as a future manager, should know about. To understand the nature of those problems, consider the following scenario, which could occur on either a traditional or browser-based application.

At a ticket vendor's Web site, two customers, Andrea and Jeffrey, are both attempting to buy tickets to a popular event. Andrea uses her browser to access the site and finds that two tickets are available. She places both of them in her shopping cart. She doesn't know it, but when she opened the order form, she invoked an application program on the vendor's servers that read a database to find that two tickets are available. Before she checks out, she takes a moment to verify with her friend that they still want to go.

Meanwhile, Jeffrey uses his browser and also finds that two tickets are available because his browser activates that same application that reads the database and finds (because Andrea has not yet checked out) that two are available. He places both in his cart and checks out.

Meanwhile, Andrea and her friend decide to go, so she checks out. Clearly, we have a problem. Both Andrea and Jeffrey have purchased the same two tickets. One of them is going to be disappointed.

This problem, known as the **lost-update problem**, exemplifies one of the special characteristics of multi-user database processing. To prevent this problem, some type of locking must be used to coordinate the activities of users who know nothing about one another. Locking brings its own set of problems, however, and those problems must be addressed as well. We will not delve further into this topic here, however.

Be aware of possible data conflicts when you manage business activities that involve multi-user processing. If you find inaccurate results that seem not to have a cause, you may be experiencing multi-user data conflicts. Contact your IS department for assistance.

Q5-5   How Are Data Models Used for Database Development?

In Chapter 12, we will describe the process for developing information systems in detail. However, business professionals have such a critical role in the development of database applications that we need to anticipate part of that discussion here by introducing two topics—data modeling and database design.

Because the design of the database depends entirely on how users view their business environment, user involvement is critical for database development. Think about the Student database. What data should it contain? Possibilities are: *Students, Classes, Grades, Emails, Office_Visits, Majors, Advisers, Student_Organizations*—the list could go on and on. Further, how much detail should be included in each? Should the database include campus addresses? Home addresses? Billing addresses?

In fact, there are unlimited possibilities, and the database developers do not and cannot know what to include. They do know, however, that a database must include all the data necessary for the users to perform their jobs. Ideally, it contains that amount of data and no more. So, during database development, the developers must rely on the users to tell them what to include in the database.

Database structures can be complex, in some cases very complex. So, before building the database the developers construct a logical representation of database data called a **data model**. It describes the data and relationships that will be stored in the database. It is akin to a blueprint. Just as building architects create a blueprint before they start building, so, too, database developers create a data model before they start designing the database.

For a philosophical perspective on data models, see the Guide on pages 226–227.

Figure 5-17 summarizes the database development process. Interviews with users lead to database requirements, which are summarized in a data model. Once the users have approved (validated) the data model, it is transformed into a database design. That design is then implemented into database structures. We will consider data modeling and database design briefly in the next two sections. Again, your goal should be to learn the process so that you can be an effective user representative for a development effort.

What Is the Entity-Relationship Data Model?

The **entity-relationship (E-R) data model** is a tool for constructing data models. Developers use it to describe the content of a data model by defining the things (*entities*) that will be stored in the database and the *relationships* among those entities. A second, less popular tool for data modeling is

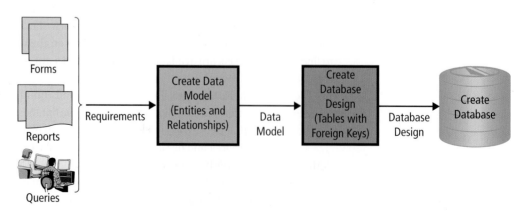

Figure 5-17
Database Development Process

the **Unified Modeling Language (UML)**. We will not describe that tool here. However, if you learn how to interpret E-R models, with a bit of study you will be able to understand UML models as well.

Entities

An **entity** is some thing that the users want to track. Examples of entities are *Order, Customer, Salesperson,* and *Item.* Some entities represent a physical object, such as *Item* or *Salesperson;* others represent a logical construct or transaction, such as *Order* or *Contract.* For reasons beyond this discussion, entity names are always singular. We use *Order,* not *Orders; Salesperson,* not *Salespersons.*

Entities have **attributes** that describe characteristics of the entity. Example attributes of *Order* are *OrderNumber, OrderDate, SubTotal, Tax, Total,* and so forth. Example attributes of *Salesperson* are *SalespersonName, Email, Phone,* and so forth.

Entities have an **identifier**, which is an attribute (or group of attributes) whose value is associated with one and only one entity instance. For example, *OrderNumber* is an identifier of *Order* because only one *Order* instance has a given value of *OrderNumber.* For the same reason, *CustomerNumber* is an identifier of *Customer.* If each member of the sales staff has a unique name, then *SalespersonName* is an identifier of *Salesperson.*

Before we continue, consider that last sentence. Is the salesperson's name unique among the sales staff? Both now and in the future? Who decides the answer to such a question? Only the users know whether this is true; the database developers cannot know. This example underlines why it is important for you to be able to interpret data models because only users like you will know for sure.

Figure 5-18 shows examples of entities for the Student database. Each entity is shown in a rectangle. The name of the entity is just above the rectangle, and the identifier is shown in a section at the top of the entity. Entity attributes are shown in the remainder of the rectangle. In Figure 5-18, the *Adviser* entity has an identifier called *AdviserName* and the attributes *Phone, CampusAddress,* and *EmailAddress.*

Observe that the entities *Email* and *Office_Visit* do not have an identifier. Unlike *Student* or *Adviser,* the users do not have an attribute that identifies a particular email. We *could* make one up. For example, we could say that the identifier of *Email* is *EmailNumber,* but if we do so we are not modeling how the users view their world. Instead, we are forcing something onto the users. Be aware of this possibility when you review data models about your business. Do not allow the database developers to create something in the data model that is not part of your business world.

Relationships

Entities have **relationships** to each other. An *Order,* for example, has a relationship to a *Customer* entity and also to a *Salesperson* entity. In the Student database, a *Student* has a relationship to an *Adviser,* and an *Adviser* has a relationship to a *Department.*

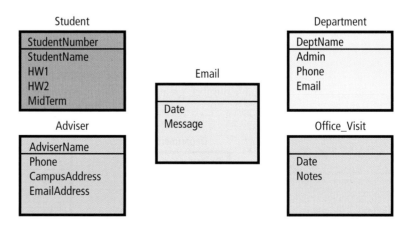

Figure 5-18
Student Data Model Entities

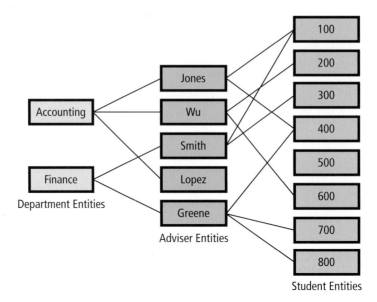

Figure 5-19

Example of Department, Adviser, and Student Entities and Relationships

Figure 5-19 shows sample *Department, Adviser*, and *Student* entities and their relationships. For simplicity, this figure shows just the identifier of the entities and not the other attributes. For this sample data, *Accounting* has three professors—Jones, Wu, and Lopez—and *Finance* has two professors—Smith and Greene.

The relationship between *Advisers* and *Students* is a bit more complicated because in this example, an adviser is allowed to advise many students and a student is allowed to have many advisers. Perhaps this happens because students can have multiple majors. In any case, note that Professor Jones advises students 100 and 400 and that student 100 is advised by both Professors Jones and Smith.

Diagrams like the one in Figure 5-19 are too cumbersome for use in database design discussions. Instead, database designers use diagrams called **entity-relationship (E-R) diagrams**. Figure 5-20 shows an E-R diagram for the data in Figure 5-19. In this figure, all of the entities of one type are represented by a single rectangle. Thus, there are rectangles for the *Department, Adviser*, and *Student* entities. Attributes are shown as before in Figure 5-18.

Additionally, a line is used to represent a relationship between two entities. Notice the line between *Department* and *Adviser*, for example. The vertical bar on the left side of the relationship means that an adviser works in just one department. The forked lines on the right side of that line signify that a department may have more than one adviser. The angled lines, which are referred to as **crow's feet**, are shorthand for the multiple lines between *Department* and *Adviser* in Figure 5-19. Relationships like this one are called **1:N**, or **one-to-many relationships**, because one department can have many advisers, but an adviser has at most one department.

Now examine the line between *Adviser* and *Student*. Notice the crow's feet that appear at each end of the line. This notation signifies that an adviser can be related to many students and that a student can be related to many advisers, which is the situation in Figure 5-19. Relationships like this one are called **N:M**, or **many-to-many relationships**, because one adviser can have many students and one student can have many advisers.

Students sometimes find the notation N:M confusing. Interpret the N and M to mean that a variable number, greater than one, is allowed on each side of the relationship. Such a relationship

Figure 5-20

Sample Relationships Version 1

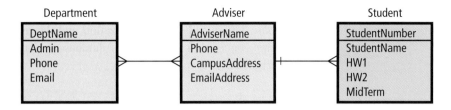

Figure 5-21
Sample Relationships Version 2

is not written *N:N* because that notation would imply that there are the same number of entities on each side of the relationship, which is not necessarily true. *N:M* means that more than one entity is allowed on each side of the relationship and that the number of entities on each side can be different.

Figure 5-21 shows the same entities with different assumptions. Here, advisers may advise in more than one department, but a student may have only one adviser, representing a policy that students may not have multiple majors.

Which, if either, of these versions is correct? Only the users know. These alternatives illustrate the kinds of questions you will need to answer when a database designer asks you to check a data model for correctness.

Figures 5-20 and 5-21 are typical examples of an entity-relationship diagram. Unfortunately, there are several different styles of entity-relationship diagrams. This one is called, not surprisingly, a **crow's-foot diagram** version. You may learn other versions if you take a database management class.

The crow's-foot notation shows the maximum number of entities that can be involved in a relationship. Accordingly, they are called the relationship's **maximum cardinality**. Common examples of maximum cardinality are 1:N, N:M, and 1:1 (not shown).

Another important question is "What is the minimum number of entities required in the relationship?" Must an adviser have a student to advise, and must a student have an adviser? Constraints on minimum requirements are called **minimum cardinalities**.

Figure 5-22 presents a third version of this E-R diagram that shows both maximum and minimum cardinalities. The second vertical bar on the lines means that at least one entity of that type is required. The small oval means that the entity is optional; the relationship *need not* have an entity of that type. Using this notation, if there are two vertical bars, both the minimum and maximum cardinality are one. If there is a vertical bar with a crow's foot, then the minimum cardinality is one and the maximum is many.

Thus, in Figure 5-22 a department is not required to have a relationship to any adviser, but an adviser is required to belong to a department. Similarly, an adviser is not required to have a relationship to a student, but a student is required to have a relationship to an adviser. Note, also, that the maximum cardinalities in Figure 5-22 have been changed so that both are 1:N.

Is the model in Figure 5-22 a good one? It depends on the policy of the university. Again, only the users know for sure.

Q5-6 How Is a Data Model Transformed into a Database Design?

Database design is the process of converting a data model into tables, relationships, and data constraints. The database design team transforms entities into tables and expresses relationships by defining foreign keys. Database design is a complicated subject; as with data modeling, it occupies

Figure 5-22
Sample Relationships Showing Both Maximum and Minimum Cardinalities

weeks in a database management class. In this section, however, we will introduce two important database design concepts: normalization and the representation of two kinds of relationships. The first concept is a foundation of database design, and the second will help you understand important design considerations.

Normalization

Normalization is the process of converting a poorly structured table into two or more well-structured tables. A table is such a simple construct that you may wonder how one could possibly be poorly structured. In truth, there are many ways that tables can be malformed—so many, in fact, that researchers have published hundreds of papers on this topic alone.

Consider the *Employee* table in Figure 5-23a. It lists employee names, hire dates, email addresses, and the name and number of the department in which the employee works. This table seems innocent enough. But consider what happens when the Accounting department changes its name to Accounting and Finance. Because department names are duplicated in this table, every row that has a value of "Accounting" must be changed to "Accounting and Finance."

Data Integrity Problems

Suppose the Accounting name change is correctly made in two rows, but not in the third. The result is shown in Figure 5-23b. This table has what is called a **data integrity problem:** Some rows indicate that the name of Department 100 is "Accounting and Finance," and another row indicates that the name of Department 100 is "Accounting."

This problem is easy to spot in this small table. But consider a table like the *Customer* table in the Amazon.com database or the eBay database. Those databases have millions of rows. Once a table that large develops serious data integrity problems, months of labor will be required to remove them.

Data integrity problems are serious. A table that has data integrity problems will produce incorrect and inconsistent results. Users will lose confidence in the data, and the system will develop a poor reputation. Information systems with poor reputations become serious burdens to the organizations that use them.

Employee

Name	HireDate	Email	DeptNo	DeptName
Jones	Feb 1, 2010	Jones@ourcompany.com	100	Accounting
Smith	Dec 3, 2012	Smith@ourcompany.com	200	Marketing
Chau	March 7, 2012	Chau@ourcompany.com	100	Accounting
Greene	July 17, 2011	Greene@ourcompany.com	100	Accounting

(a) Table Before Update

Employee

Name	HireDate	Email	DeptNo	DeptName
Jones	Feb 1, 2010	Jones@ourcompany.com	100	Accounting and Finance
Smith	Dec 3, 2012	Smith@ourcompany.com	200	Marketing
Chau	March 7, 2012	Chau@ourcompany.com	100	Accounting and Finance
Greene	July 17, 2011	Greene@ourcompany.com	100	Accounting

Figure 5-23
A Poorly Designed
Employee Table

(b) Table with Incomplete Update

Employee

Name	HireDate	Email	DeptNo
Jones	Feb 1, 2010	Jones@ourcompany.com	100
Smith	Dec 3, 2012	Smith@ourcompany.com	200
Chau	March 7, 2012	Chau@ourcompany.com	100
Greene	July 17, 2011	Greene@ourcompany.com	100

Department

DeptNo	DeptName
100	Accounting
200	Marketing
300	Information Systems

Figure 5-24
Two Normalized Tables

Normalizing for Data Integrity

The data integrity problem can occur only if data are duplicated. Because of this, one easy way to eliminate the problem is to eliminate the duplicated data. We can do this by transforming the table design in Figure 5-23a into two tables, as shown in Figure 5-24. Here the name of the department is stored just once; therefore, no data inconsistencies can occur.

Of course, to produce an employee report that includes the department name, the two tables in Figure 5-24 will need to be joined back together. Because such joining of tables is common, DBMS products have been programmed to perform it efficiently, but it still requires work. From this example, you can see a trade-off in database design: Normalized tables eliminate data duplication, but they can be slower to process. Dealing with such trade-offs is an important consideration in database design.

The general goal of normalization is to construct tables such that every table has a *single* topic or theme. In good writing, every paragraph should have a single theme. This is true of databases as well; every table should have a single theme. The problem with the table design in Figure 5-23 is that it has two independent themes: employees and departments. The way to correct the problem is to split the table into two tables, each with its own theme. In this case, we create an *Employee* table and a *Department* table, as shown in Figure 5-24.

As mentioned, there are dozens of ways that tables can be poorly formed. Database practitioners classify tables into various **normal forms** according to the kinds of problems they have. Transforming a table into a normal form to remove duplicated data and other problems is called *normalizing* the table.[3] Thus, when you hear a database designer say, "Those tables are not normalized," she does not mean that the tables have irregular, not-normal data. Instead, she means that the tables have a format that could cause data integrity problems.

Summary of Normalization

As a future user of databases, you do not need to know the details of normalization. Instead, understand the general principle that every normalized (well-formed) table has one and only one theme. Further, tables that are not normalized are subject to data integrity problems.

Be aware, too, that normalization is just one criterion for evaluating database designs. Because normalized designs can be slower to process, database designers sometimes choose to accept non-normalized tables. The best design depends on the users' processing requirements.

Representing Relationships

Figure 5-25 shows the steps involved in transforming a data model into a relational database design. First, the database designer creates a table for each entity. The identifier of the entity becomes the key of the table. Each attribute of the entity becomes a column of the table. Next, the

Figure 5-25
Transforming a Data Model into a
Database Design

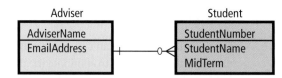

- Represent each entity with a table
  - Entity identifier becomes table key
  - Entity attributes become table columns
- Normalize tables as necessary
- Represent relationships
  - Use foreign keys
  - Add additional tables for N:M relationships

resulting tables are normalized so that each table has a single theme. Once that has been done, the next step is to represent relationship among those tables.

For example, consider the E-R diagram in Figure 5-26a. The *Adviser* entity has a 1:N relationship to the *Student* entity. To create the database design, we construct a table for *Adviser* and a second table for *Student*, as shown in Figure 5-26b. The key of the *Adviser* table is *AdviserName*, and the key of the *Student* table is *StudentNumber*.

Adviser

| AdviserName |
| EmailAddress |

Student

| StudentNumber |
| StudentName |
| MidTerm |

(a) 1:N Relationship Between Adviser and Student Entities

Adviser Table—Key Is AdviserName

AdviserName	EmailAddress
Jones	Jones@myuniv.edu
Choi	Choi@myuniv.edu
Jackson	Jackson@myuniv.edu

Student Table—Key Is StudentNumber

StudentNumber	StudentName	MidTerm
100	Lisa	90
200	Jennie	85
300	Jason	82
400	Terry	95

(b) Creating a Table for Each Entity

Adviser Table—Key Is AdviserName

AdviserName	EmailAddress
Jones	Jones@myuniv.edu
Choi	Choi@myuniv.edu
Jackson	Jackson@myuniv.edu

Foreign key column represents relationship

Student—Key Is StudentNumber

StudentNumber	StudentName	MidTerm	AdviserName
100	Lisa	90	Jackson
200	Jennie	85	Jackson
300	Jason	82	Choi
400	Terry	95	Jackson

Figure 5-26
Representing a 1:N Relationship

(c) Using the *AdviserName* Foreign Key to Represent the 1:N Relationship

Further, the *EmailAddress* attribute of the *Adviser* entity becomes the *EmailAddress* column of the *Adviser* table, and the *StudentName* and *MidTerm* attributes of the *Student* entity become the *StudentName* and *MidTerm* columns of the *Student* table.

The next task is to represent the relationship. Because we are using the relational model, we know that we must add a foreign key to one of the two tables. The possibilities are: (1) place the foreign key *StudentNumber* in the *Adviser* table or (2) place the foreign key *AdviserName* in the *Student* table.

The correct choice is to place *AdviserName* in the *Student* table, as shown in Figure 5-26c. To determine a student's adviser, we just look into the *AdviserName* column of that student's row. To determine the adviser's students, we search the *AdviserName* column in the *Student* table to determine which rows have that adviser's name. If a student changes advisers, we simply change the value in the *AdviserName* column. Changing *Jackson* to *Jones* in the first row, for example, will assign student 100 to Professor Jones.

For this data model, placing *StudentNumber* in *Adviser* would be incorrect. If we were to do that, we could assign only one student to an adviser. There is no place to assign a second adviser.

This strategy for placing foreign keys will not work for N:M relationships, however. Consider the data model in Figure 5-27a; here advisers and students have a many-to-many relationship. An adviser may have many students, and a student may have multiple advisers (for multiple majors).

To see why the foreign key strategy we used for 1:N relationships will not work for N:M relationships, examine Figure 5-27b. If student 100 has more than one adviser, there is no place to record second or subsequent advisers.

To represent an N:M relationship, we need to create a third table, as shown in Figure 5-27c. The third table has two columns, *AdviserName* and *StudentNumber*. Each row of the table means that the given adviser advises the student with the given number.

As you can imagine, there is a great deal more to database design than we have presented here. Still, this section should give you an idea of the tasks that need to be accomplished to create a database. You should also realize that the database design is a direct consequence of decisions made in the data model. If the data model is wrong, the database design will be wrong as well.

Users' Role in the Development of Databases

As stated, a database is a model of how the users view their business world. This means that the users are the final judges as to what data the database should contain and how the records in that database should be related to one another.

The easiest time to change the database structure is during the data modeling stage. Changing a relationship from one-to-many to many-to-many in a data model is simply a matter of changing the 1:N notation to N:M. However, once the database has been constructed and loaded with data and forms, reports, queries, and application programs have been created, changing a one-to-many relationship to many-to-many means weeks of work.

You can glean some idea of why this might be true by contrasting Figure 5-26c with Figure 5-27c. Suppose that instead of having just a few rows, each table has thousands of rows; in that case, transforming the database from one format to the other involves considerable work. Even worse, however, is that someone must change application components as well. For example, if students have at most one adviser, then a single text box can be used to enter *AdviserName*. If students can have multiple advisers, then a multiple-row table will need to be used to enter *AdviserName* and a program will need to be written to store the values of *AdviserName* into the *Adviser_Student_Intersection* table. There are dozens of other consequences, consequences that will translate into wasted labor and wasted expense.

Thus, *user review of the data model is crucial.* When a database is developed for your use, you must carefully review the data model. If you do not understand any aspect of it, you should ask for clarification until you do. *Entities must contain all of the data you and your employees need to do your*

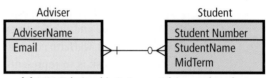

(a) N:M Relationship Between Adviser and Student

Adviser—Key Is AdviserName

AdviserName	Email
Jones	Jones@myuniv.edu
Choi	Choi@myuniv.edu
Jackson	Jackson@myuniv.edu

No room to place second or third AdviserName

Student—Key Is StudentNumber

StudentNumber	StudentName	MidTerm	AdviserName
100	Lisa	90	Jackson
200	Jennie	85	Jackson
300	Jason	82	Choi
400	Terry	95	Jackson

(b) Incorrect Representation of N:M Relationship

Adviser—Key Is AdviserName

AdviserName	Email
Jones	Jones@myuniv.edu
Choi	Choi@myuniv.edu
Jackson	Jackson@myuniv.edu

Student—Key Is StudentNumber

StudentNumber	StudentName	MidTerm
100	Lisa	90
200	Jennie	85
300	Jason	82
400	Terry	95

Adviser_Student_Intersection

AdviserName	StudentNumber
Jackson	100
Jackson	200
Choi	300
Jackson	400
Choi	100
Jones	100

Student 100 has three advisers

(c) Adviser_Student_Intersection Table Represents the N:M Relationship

Figure 5-27
Representing an N:M
Relationship

jobs, and relationships must accurately reflect your view of the business. If the data model is wrong, the database will be designed incorrectly, and the applications will be difficult to use, if not worthless. Do not proceed unless the data model is accurate.

As a corollary, when asked to review a data model, take that review seriously. Devote the time necessary to perform a thorough review. Any mistakes you miss will come back to haunt you, and by then the cost of correction may be very high with regard to both time and expense. This brief introduction to data modeling shows why databases can be more difficult to develop than spreadsheets.

How Can Falcon Security Benefit from a Database System?

Falcon Security wants to be able to find videos by querying their characteristics. For example, it wants responses to questions like "Which videos do we have of the Beresford Building in October 2015, shot from 3,000 feet or less?" And, from time to time, Falcon employees analyze some of the videos, and they want to record comments about their analyses for potential later use.

Falcon can choose one of two database architectures. For one, it can store the video footage on a file server and keep metadata about each video in a relational database that it can query. That metadata will include the address of the video footage on the file server. Alternatively, Falcon can utilize one of the new NoSQL DBMS products like **MongoDB**—an open source document-oriented DBMS—to store the video footage in the same database as the metadata. (See Q5-8).

Toshio Sato investigates these two alternatives and discusses his findings with Cam Forset. They are both intrigued by the possible use of MongoDB, but they know that their interest is, in part, a desire to learn something new. They don't really know how well that product works, nor do they know how robust the MongoDB query facility will be.

On the other hand, they can readily build a simple Access database to store the metadata. In the metadata, they can store the URL of the file server location that has the video (for example, *https://abc.Falcon.com/Video1*). In this way, they can use Access to store the data and then query it using the Access graphical query facility. Because Access can also process native SQL, they can use it for the most sophisticated query operations if needed.

Toshio and Cam discuss these alternatives and decide to use Access to store the metadata. They know this approach is less risky because it uses known technology. Also, both of them are skilled at using Access, and they can develop the database and application quickly with less risk. Toshio and Cam create a short presentation of this recommendation and present it to Mateo, who approves it.

After the approval, Toshio creates the E-R diagram shown in Figure 5-28 and discusses it with Cam. She thinks that they might want to add an Employee entity rather than just the employee's name in the Analysis entity. They decide, however, that they don't yet have that many employees and that adding the extra entity might make the application too hard to use, at least at present. So with that decision, they proceed to create the database and related applications. You'll have an opportunity to do the same with a team of your colleagues in Collaboration Exercise 5, page 230.

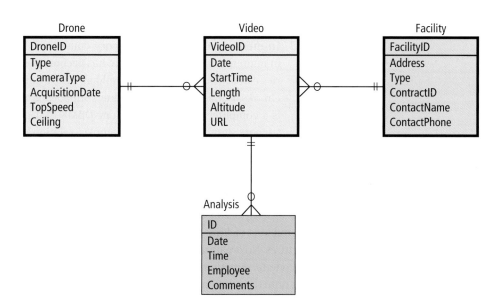

Figure 5-28

E-R Diagram for Falcon
Security's Database

Q5-8   2026?

With ever-cheaper data storage and data communications, we can be sure that the volume of database data will continue to grow, probably exponentially, through 2026. All that data contains patterns that can be used to conceive information to help businesses and organizations achieve their strategies. That will make business intelligence, discussed in Chapter 9, even more important. Furthermore, as databases become bigger and bigger, they're more attractive as targets for theft or mischief, as we recently saw at Sony Entertainment. Those risks will make database security even more important, as we discuss in Chapter 10.

Additionally, the DBMS landscape is changing. While for years relational DBMS products were the only game in town, the Internet changed that by posing new processing requirements. As compared to traditional database applications, some Internet applications process many, many more transactions against much simpler data. A tweet has a much simpler data structure than the configuration of a Kenworth truck, but there are so many more tweets than truck configurations!

Also, traditional relational DBMS products devote considerable code and processing power to support what are termed **ACID** (atomic, consistent, isolated, durable) transactions. In essence, this acronym means that either all of a transaction is processed or none of it is (atomic), that transactions are processed in the same manner (consistent) whether processed alone or in the presence of millions of other transactions (isolated), and that once a transaction is stored it never goes away—even in the presence of failure (durable).

ACID transactions are critical to traditional commercial applications. Even in the presence of machine failure, Vanguard must process both the sell and the buy sides of a transaction; it cannot process part of a transaction. Also, what it stores today must be stored tomorrow. But many new Internet applications don't need ACID. Who cares if, one time out of 1 million, only half of your tweet is stored? Or if it's stored today and disappears tomorrow?

These new requirements have led to three new categories of DBMS:

1. **NoSQL DBMS**. This acronym is misleading. It really should be NotRelational DBMS. It refers to new DBMS products that support very high transaction rates processing relatively simple data structures, replicated on many servers in the cloud, without ACID transaction support. MongoDB, Cassandra, Bigtable, and Dynamo are NoSQL products

2. **NewSQL DBMS**. These DBMS products process very high levels of transactions, like the NoSQL DBMS, but provide ACID support. They may or may not support the relational model. Such products are a hotbed of development with new vendors popping up nearly every day. Leading products are yet unknown.

3. **In-memory DBMS**. This category consists of DBMS products that process databases in main memory. This technique has become possible because today's computer memories can be enormous and can hold an entire database at one time, or at least very large chunks of it. Usually these products support or extend the relational model. SAP HANA is a computer with an in-memory DBMS that provides high volume ACID transaction support simultaneously with complex relational query processing. Tableau Software's reporting products are supported by a proprietary in-memory DBMS using an extension to SQL.

Does the emergence of these new products mean the death knell for relational databases? It seems unlikely because organizations have created thousands of traditional relational databases with millions of lines of application code that process SQL statements against relational data structures. No organization wants to endure the expense and effort of converting those databases and code to something else. There is also a strong social trend among older technologists to hang onto the relational model. However, these new products are loosening the stronghold that relational technology has enjoyed for decades, and it is likely that by 2026 many NoSQL, NewSQL, and in-memory databases will exist in commerce.

Furthermore, existing DBMS vendors like Oracle, Microsoft, and IBM will not sit still. With substantial cash and highly skilled developers, they will likely incorporate features of these new categories of DBMS into their existing or new products. Acquisitions of some of the NewSQL startups, in particular, are likely.

What does that mean to you as a business professional? First, such knowledge is useful; stay abreast of developments in this area. When you are given a problem, like the need to query videos at Falcon, you might choose to utilize one of these new types of database. Unless you are an IT professional, however, you won't work with them directly. It will be to your advantage to know about them, however, and to suggest their use to the IS personnel who support your requirements.

Also, watch these developments from an investor's perspective. Not all such products will be open source; even if they are, there will be companies that integrate them into their product or service offerings, and those companies may well be good investment opportunities.

If you're interested in IS as a discipline or as a second major, pay attention to these products. You still need to learn the relational model and the processing of relational databases; they will be the bread-and-butter of the industry, even in 2026. But exciting new opportunities and career paths will also develop around these new DBMS products. Learn about them as well, and use that knowledge to separate yourself from the competition when it comes to job interviews.

Security Guide

THEFT BY SQL INJECTION

Warning You are about to learn a technique for compromising an information system called *SQL injection.* Do not try it on existing systems. SQL injection attacks leave log entries with your IP address attached. Attempting SQL injection on a system without permission is illegal. You can be identified, tracked, and charged. Felony hacking convictions are not resume builders.

SQL injection is a popular way to steal data because it can be done from anywhere in the world. You don't even need to physically enter the target country. You need some smart people with time to invest and a couple modest computers. From a criminal's point of view it's a low-risk and high-reward proposition.

SQL injection is a criminal attack on an information system to illegally extract data from a database. It can add or delete data, drop tables and their data, and even shut down an information system. And, because it can be done from anywhere in the world, criminals can rob from countries that don't extradite criminals, such as Russia, China, North Korea, and others.

Criminals have caught on to theft-by-SQL-injection. Imperva®, an enterprise data security firm, listed the following key findings in its 2013 Imperva Web Application Attack Report:[4]

1. Retailers suffer two times as many SQL injection attacks as other industries.
2. Most Web applications receive four or more Web attack campaigns per month, and others are constantly under attack (176 out of 180 days).
3. One Web site received 94,057 SQL injection attack requests in one day.

Let those numbers sink in: Your corporate Web site is likely being attacked on a regular basis.

How Does SQL Injection Work?

SQL injection, as it sounds, is a way of inserting your own SQL code into someone else's information system. To understand this, consider what happens when you normally log in to a Web site. You enter your username (**JohnDoe001**) and a password (**password1234**) and then press the Enter key.

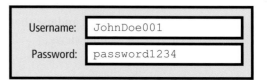

| Username: | JohnDoe001 |
| Password: | password1234 |

Source: Federico Caputo/iStock/Thinkstock

In a site that is vulnerable to SQL injection, the following SQL statement is sent to the Web site's DBMS.

```
SELECT * FROM Users WHERE username= 'JohnDoe001'
        AND password='password1234';
```

If the username and password are both correct, you'll be allowed in. The "injection" part of SQL injection happens when you enter in *unexpected* text into that Web form. You enter text into the login form that changes the way the SQL statement is processed.

Instead of entering a real username and password, put in a random username (in this case, we kept it **JohnDoe001**) and a malformed, but tricky, statement into the password field (**anything' or 1=1 --**).

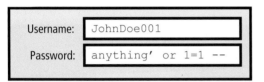

Note that the single quote (') in the password changes the SQL statement by enclosing the word "anything" and allowing 1=1 to be included. (The double hyphen indicates the rest of the SQL statement, which is not shown because it's not relevant to this guide.)

```
SELECT * FROM Users WHERE username='JohnDoe001'
            AND password='anything' or 1=1 --';
```

The word "anything" will *not* match the correct password in the database, but because "or 1=1" was included the resulting comparison will always be "true." This is because 1=1 is true, and only one side of the comparison needs to be true if "or" is included. This SQL statement will enable you to bypass the login screen and gain access to the system. Similar malformed SQL statements can be used to extract, add, or delete data. There is even software available that largely automates the SQL injection process.

SQL injection can be readily prevented. The particular techniques are beyond the scope of this text, but they come down to never writing computer programs to append user-entered data to a SQL statement. Instead, the users' data is passed to a program controlled by the DBMS that inspects that user-entered data and then uses it without changing any SQL code.[5]

Unfortunately, not all companies take the time to protect themselves from SQL injection. Sony Corp. lost more than 100 million accounts to SQL injection attacks in 2011. In 2014, two U.S. Navy systems administrators on a nuclear aircraft carrier used SQL injection to get the private data of 220,000 sailors. They said they did it out of "boredom."

 DISCUSSION QUESTIONS

1. Why is data theft attractive to criminals?
2. How common is SQL injection?
3. How does SQL injection work?
4. What can an attacker do to a database using SQL injection?
5. How can organizations prevent SQL injection attacks from being successful?
6. If you were a senior manager at an organization that had serious losses due to SQL injection, what would you do about it?
7. Suppose an organization not only prevents SQL injection from success but also tracks the identity of sites that attempt such attacks. What should the organization do with that attack data?

Guide

IMMANUEL KANT, DATA MODELER

Only the users can say whether a data model accurately reflects their business environment. What happens when the users disagree among themselves? What if one user says orders have a single salesperson, but another says that sales teams produce some orders? Who is correct?

It's tempting to say, "The correct model is the one that better represents the real world." The problem with this statement is that data models do not model "the real world." A data model is simply a model of what the data modeler perceives. This very important point can be difficult to understand, but if you do understand it, you will save many hours in data model validation meetings and be a much better data modeling team member.

The German philosopher Immanuel Kant reasoned that what we perceive as reality is based on our perceptive apparatus. That which we perceive he called phenomena. Our perceptions, such as of light and sound, are processed by our brains and made meaningful. But we do not and cannot know whether the images we create from the perceptions have anything to do with what might or might not really be.

Kant used the term *noumenal world* to refer to the essence of "things in themselves"—to whatever it is out there that gives rise to our perceptions and images. He used the term *phenomenal world* to refer to what we humans perceive and construct.

It is easy to confuse the noumenal world with the phenomenal world, because we share the phenomenal world with other humans. All of us have the same mental apparatus, and we all make the same constructions. If you ask your roommate to hand you the toothpaste, she hands you the toothpaste, not a hairbrush. But the fact that we share this mutual view does not mean that the mutual view describes in any way what is truly out there. Dogs construct a world based on smells, and orca whales construct a world based on sounds. What the "real world" is to a dog, a whale, and a human are completely different. All of this means that we cannot ever justify a data model as a "better representation of the real world." Nothing that humans can do represents the real, noumenal world. A data model, therefore, is a model of

a human's model of what appears to be "out there." For example, a model of a salesperson is a model of the model that humans make of salespeople.

To return to the question that we started with, what do we do when people disagree about what should be in a data model? First, realize that anyone attempting to justify her data model as a better representation of the real world is saying, quite arrogantly, "The way I think of the world is

Source: Lebrecht Music and Arts Photo Library/Alamy

the way that counts." Second, in times of disagreement we must ask the question, "How well does the data model fit the mental models of the people who are going to use the system?" The person who is constructing the data model may think the model under construction is a weird way of viewing the world, but that is not the point. The only valid point is whether it reflects how the users view their world. Will it enable the users to do their jobs?

DISCUSSION QUESTIONS

1. What does a data model represent?

2. Explain why it is easy for humans to confuse the phenomenal world with the noumenal world.

3. If someone were to say to you, "My model is a better model of the real world," how would you respond?

4. In your own words, how should you proceed when two people disagree on what is to be included in a data model?

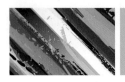

ACTIVE REVIEW

Use this Active Review to verify that you understand the ideas and concepts that answer the chapter's study questions.

Q5-1 What is the purpose of a database?

State the purpose of a database. Explain the circumstances in which a database is preferred to a spreadsheet. Describe the key difference between Figures 5-1 and 5-2.

Q5-2 What is a database?

Define the term *database*. Explain the hierarchy of data and name three elements of a database. Define *metadata*. Using the example of *Student* and *Office_Visit* tables, show how relationships among rows are represented in a database. Define the terms *primary key*, *foreign key*, and *relational database*.

Q5-3 What is a database management system (DBMS)?

Explain the acronym DBMS and name its functions. List five popular DBMS products. Explain the difference between a DBMS and a database. Summarize the functions of a DBMS. Define *SQL*. Describe the major functions of database administration.

Q5-4 How do database applications make databases more useful?

Explain why database tables, by themselves, are not very useful to business users. Name the four elements of a database application and describe the purpose of each. Explain the difference between a database application and a database application program. Describe the nature of traditional database applications. Explain why browser-based applications are better than traditional ones. Name the primary technologies used to support browser-based applications.

Q5-5 How are data models used for database development?

Explain why user involvement is critical during database development. Describe the function of a data model. Sketch the database development process. Define *E-R model, entity, relationship, attribute*, and *identifier*. Give an example, other than one in this text, of an E-R diagram. Define *maximum cardinality* and *minimum cardinality*. Give

an example of three maximum cardinalities and two minimum cardinalities. Explain the notation in Figures 5-21 and 5-22.

Q5-6 How is a data model transformed into a database design?

Name the three components of a database design. Define *normalization* and explain why it is important. Define *data integrity problem* and describe its consequences. Give an example of a table with data integrity problems and show how it can be normalized into two or more tables that do not have such problems. Describe two steps in transforming a data model into a database design. Using an example not in this chapter, show how 1:N and N:M relationships are represented in a relational database. Describe the users' role in the database development. Explain why it is easier and cheaper to change a data model than to change an existing database. Use the examples of Figures 5-26c and 5-27c in your answer.

Q5-7 How can Falcon Security benefit from a database system?

Summarize the two database architectures that Falcon could use for its video database. Describe the architecture it used and explain the rationale for that choice.

Q5-8 2026?

Explain how an increase in database data in the next decade will affect business intelligence and security. Summarize two major requirements that some Internet database applications created. Explain the characteristics of the ACID processing of a transaction. Briefly describe the characteristics of NoSQL, NewSQL, and in-memory DBMS products. Summarize how you should respond to these developments.

Using Your Knowledge with Falcon Security

You can readily understand why the knowledge of this chapter would be useful to you if you have a job like Toshio or Cam. But what if you are Mateo (the CEO) or Joni (the CFO)? The knowledge in this chapter will prepare you to make better decisions like the one that Mateo made in Q5-7. It will also help Joni understand the level of budget required to fund this project. Even if you never create a single query during your career, you will make many decisions that involve the use, creation, and maintenance of databases.

KEY TERMS AND CONCEPTS

MyMISLab™

To complete the problems with the ★, go to EOC Discussion Questions in the MyLab.

USING YOUR KNOWLEDGE

★ 5-1. What are the steps involved in creating a database? Which step is the most crucial and why?

★ 5-2. A professor teaches many courses in a university. However, some professors who are the administrative heads (such as Department heads) may not teach a course. Some courses are taught jointly by more than one professor. Identify the entities and their relationship in the above scenario. What is the maximum cardinality of this relationship? Can this relationship be implemented in a database? Why or Why not?

★ 5-3. Identify two entities in the data entry form in Figure 5-29. What attributes are shown for each? What do you think are the identifiers?

5-4. Visit *www.acxiom.com*. Navigate the site to answer the following questions.
   a. According to the Web site, what is Acxiom's privacy policy? Are you reassured by its policy? Why or why not?

   b. Make a list of 10 different products that Acxiom provides.
   c. Describe Acxiom's top customers.
   d. Examine your answers in parts b and c and describe, in general terms, the kinds of data that Acxiom must be collecting to be able to provide those products to those customers.
   e. What is the function of InfoBase?
   f. What is the function of PersonicX?
   g. In what ways might companies like Acxiom need to limit their marketing so as to avoid a privacy outcry from the public?
   h. Should there be laws that govern companies like Acxiom? Why or why not?
   i. Should there be laws that govern the types of data services that governmental agencies can buy from companies like Acxiom? Why or why not?

Employee Class Attendance

EmployeeNumber: 1299393

FirstName: Mary

LastName: Lopez

Email: Mlopez@somewhere.com

Class:

	CourseName	CourseDate	Instructor	Remarks
	Presentation Skills I	3/17/2016	Johnson	Excellent presenter!
	CRM Administrator	5/19/2016	Wu	Needs work on security administration
*				

Record: 1 of 2   No Filter   Search

Figure 5-29
Sample Data Entry Form

COLLABORATION EXERCISE 5

Using the collaboration IS you built in Chapter 2 (page 110), collaborate with a group of students to answer the following questions.

The Falcon Security problem is an excellent example of the use of small databases in business. It is also within reach for you to develop as a practice exercise. To do so, work with your team to answer the following questions:

5-5. Study Figure 5-28 to understand the entities and their relationships. Justify each of the cardinalities in this model.

5-6. Working with your team, develop a list of seven queries that together use all of the entities in Figure 5-28.

5-7. Modify the E-R model in Figure 5-28 to include a *Contact* entity that is related to the Facility entity. Create the relationship, and specify and justify the relationship's cardinalities.

5-8. Discuss the advantages and disadvantages of the model you created in your answer to question 5-7 and the model in Figure 5-28.

5-9. Transform the data model in Figure 5-28 into a relational database design. *Hint:* Create a table for each entity and relate those tables as shown in Q6.

5-10. Create an Access database for your design in question 5-9.

5-11. Fill your database with sample data. Because you do not have files on a server, leave the URL column blank.

5-12. A Big Data Analytics organization has launched a connecting program around the UK to train faculty members across 500 campuses. Each year at least 20 faculty members from each campus need to register for this program. The faculty members will be trained on the big data analytics and other emerging technologies. As a coordinator of this program, you need to track faculty members, their campuses and the technology they have registered for in the current term. You have decided to represent this situation with an ER diagram. Hence,
a. Identify various entities in this given scenario.
b. After identification of entities, find out the attributes of the identified entities .
c. The next task is to list down the identifiers to be used in the final ER diagram.
d. Before going for the depiction of the given scenario using ER Diagram, figure out the relationship among identified the entities.
e. After performing above steps, make an ER Diagram to depict the above findings.

CASE STUDY 5

Searching for Classic and Vintage Car Parts...

Shane Ashley-Carter is a highly qualified and experienced car mechanic, having served apprenticeships with both British luxury car marquees Jaguar and Bentley in the early part of his career, which now spans more than 20 years. He is a typical luxury car mechanic, whose expertise and experience is sought after in the United Kingdom and world-wide, including the Middle-East, Africa, Asia, Australia, and the United States. Shane specializes in classic and vintage models as well those in the current ranges. In his spare time, he also renovates and repairs interior fixtures and fittings, and exterior body panels at his workshop in Oxfordshire, England. (See *http://www.a-cl.co.uk*). During the months of June, July, and August, he works on repairs and restorations of car exteriors and interiors when the weather is reliably warm and dry, and during the remainder of the year he repairs and replaces mechanical components.

Before the global financial crisis of 2008, he did a brisk trade in acquiring, restoring, renovating, reselling, and retrofitting car parts to classic and vintage Jaguars and Bentleys, especially of the former because of the global brand recognition that resulted from the famous Oxford-based detective television series, *Inspector Morse*. During this time, he rarely needed to maintain significant stocks of the various car components as there was a balance between supply and demand. However, during the period leading up to 2010, he found that his stock of car parts increased due to a severe down-turn in the world economy, which significantly affected his trade in fitting and reselling classic and vintage car parts. At one point he had a stock of 200 car components.

Clearly, 200 car components can range in size and complexity depending on their location in the classic and vintage cars, from small temperature sensor units to large engine components and their assemblies and sub-assemblies of ancillary systems as are found in fuel, exhaust, and electrical systems. Initially, Shane stored them in his workshop in the rack system that he had been extending as the number of parts grew. Although his business had slowed significantly, he found that he was spending an increasing amount of time managing access to his stock of parts and determining their availability for customers' classic and vintage car repairs and restorations. The manual labeling and

inventory system that he had successfully used previously was becoming cumbersome, unwieldy, and increasingly inaccurate.

Once the economic recovery began in 2013, demand for his classic and vintage car parts increased again as his car repairs and restoration business expanded. At this point, he decided that he would minimize his stock of parts as quickly as possible by capitalizing on the available demand for his services. However, Shane had two problems. First, he did not reliably know which classic and vintage car parts he had in stock and where they were located in his workshop. Second, he wasn't willing to exhaust himself climbing the storage racks in order to locate components that are sometimes small in size.

To address the problems, Shane created a Microsoft Access database with only one table: Part. To populate the database with data, Shane had to initially take stock of all the classic and vintage car parts and record the data as shown in the columns of Figure 5-33.

Obviously, a single-table database could have been stored in Excel, but Shane needs to query his data in a number of different ways. For example, he wants to know the location of the engine temperature sensors in his workshop racking system that have a temperature range suitable for the cooler conditions of the Scotland region. He also wants to know which fuel system component parts are available for different grades of fuel. Further, customers have special needs. For example, one might want an exhaust system component that generates a particular sound note during acceleration, which is in accord with the original manufacturer's specification of the classic and vintage car. In the absence of a database, he doesn't know whether he has the part or not. Alternatively, he might want to know of all of the electrical parts concerned when he decides that he needs to refurbish an electrical part with a new component, and so on. Because of his changing needs, particularly concerning his questions regarding the data stored in his database and his vast reserve of motor parts, Shane uses the Access query facility. Figure 5-34 shows an example query that returns the location of temperature sensors in the workshop racking system that is suitable for the Scotland region, and Figure 5-35 shows the result of that query.

Figure 5-30
Steering wheel of a vintage car
Source: Claire Plumridge/ Shutterstock

Figure 5-31
Engine Parts
Source: © MR. TEERASAK
KHEMNGERN/Shutterstock

Figure 5-32
Car Parts
Source: © sima/Shuttetstock

QUESTIONS

5-13. Explain why a simple, one-table only, Access database can be defined as a database with all of its benefits even though the data could be straightforwardly stored as an Excel spreadsheet.

5-14. Justify the decision to use Access to store the classic and vintage car parts data.

5-15. Examine the columns in Figure 5-33.
   a. Name three features of classic and vintage car parts that are not represented in this table.
   b. If you were a business analyst advising Shane, what criteria should you use in deciding whether to include the additional data?

5-16 Suppose that, in addition to the data about car parts, Shane wants to store data about the manufacturer such as its address, its years of manufacture, and general comments about the manufacturer.
   a. Design a Manufacturer table.

b. Alter the design of the Part table (Figure 5-33) to represent the relationship between Part and Manufacturer. State and justify any assumptions.

5-17. Using the data in Figure 5-34, draw conclusions about the location and characteristics of the temperature sensor parts, their brand, and their location in the racking system.

5-18. Explain the statement "A database is an abstraction of some aspects of a business." Using this example, explain the ways that processing an abstraction is more effective than examining car parts. Generalize your observation to databases for business in general.

5-19. This database will soon become useless if it is not kept up-to-date. List procedures that Shane needs to create and follow to keep his database current.

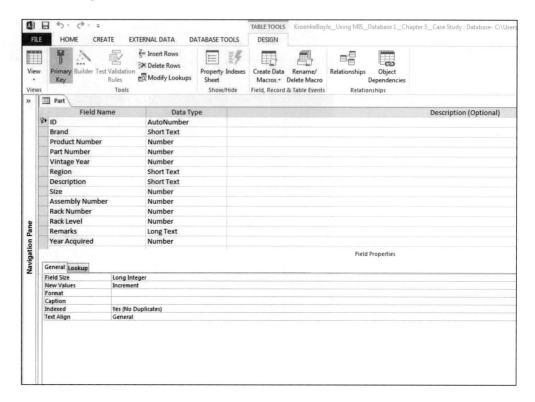

Figure 5-33

Columns in the Part Table

Source: © Access 2013, Microsoft Corporation

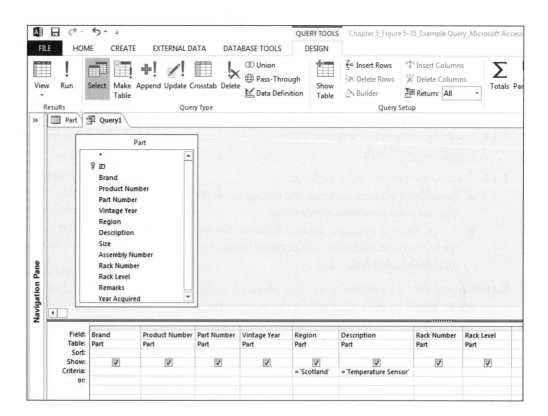

Figure 5-34

Example of Access Query

Source: © Access 2013, Microsoft Corporation

Figure 5-35

Results of Query from Figure 5-34

Source: © Access 2013, Microsoft Corporation

Brand	Product Number	Part Number	Vintage Year	Region	Description	Size	Assembly Number	Rack Number	Rack Level
Jaguar	1234	5678	1972	Scotland	Temperature Sensor	23	18	1	3
Jaguar	1234	3432	1983	Scotland	Temperature Sensor	18	23	3	1
Bentley	1234	7654	1965	Scotland	Temperature Sensor	22	12	2	0

MyMISLab™

Go to the Assignments section of your MyLab to complete these writing exercises.

5-20. Go to *http://aws.amazon.com* and search for AWS database offerings. Explain the differences among Amazon's RDS, DynamoDB, ElastiCache, and Redshift services. Which of these three would you recommend for storing Falcon Security's data? (By the way, whenever you query the Internet for any AWS product, be sure to include the keyword AWS in your search. Otherwise, your search will result in Amazon's lists of books about the item you're searching for.)

5-21. Suppose you are the accounts manager at a wholesale auto parts distributor. You use spreadsheets to keep track of just about everything. So do your employees. You have hundreds of different spreadsheets to update, back up, and share. Some of them are getting extremely large and unwieldy. You're worried about losing track of them, or worse, having a malicious employee permanently destroy them. A new hire fresh out of college says building a database would solve most of your problems. How would you determine if a database would really solve your problems? If you chose to develop a centralized database, how would you choose the employees to create the database? What criteria would you use to select those employees? How would you justify allocating people and money to developing this database?

ENDNOTES

1. MySQL was supported by the MySQL company. In 2008, that company was acquired by Sun Microsystems, which was, in turn, acquired by Oracle later that year. However, because MySQL is open source, Oracle does not own the source code.
2. Watch out for confusion between a *database application* and a *database application program*. A database application includes forms, reports, queries, and database application programs.
3. See David Kroenke and David Auer, *Database Concepts*, 7th ed., pp. 81–86 (Upper Saddle River, NJ: Pearson Education, 2015) for more information.
4. Imperva, "Imperva Web Application Attack Report," July 2013, accessed May 19, 2014, *www.imperva.com/docs/HII_Web_Application_Attack_Report_Ed4.pdf*.
5. To learn more about how to prevent SQL injection you can visit OWASP.org. It has a helpful SQL Injection Prevention Cheat Sheet that explains how to parameterize queries and use stored procedures to stop SQL injection. See *www.owasp.org/index.php/SQL_Injection_Prevention_Cheat_Sheet*.
6. Performance and Prestige Cars Limited, The Premier Car Company for Specialist Car Servicing and Repairs, www.a-cl.co.uk, accessed on January 2016.

The Cloud

"What's your plan, Toshio?" Mateo Thomas, CEO of Falcon Security, is meeting with Toshio Sato, IT director, and Joni Campbell, CFO, to discuss Falcon Security's data storage costs.

"Right now, Mateo, we're fine. We just got our new NAS online, and we've increased our storage capacity by almost 30 percent, but ..." Toshio trails off.

Joni can't stand this. "Well, we're fine until you look at the bills we're running up. The money we've spent on storage has increased 350 percent *in 1 year.*"

"Yes, Joni, it has, but our volume's gone up 400 percent," Toshio replies.

"True enough, but ..."

Mateo has had enough and interrupts. "We've been over this before. No need to rehash it. We all agree that our storage costs are too high. Toshio, I'd asked you to look into alternatives. What have you got?"

"The cloud."

"The *what?*" Joni hopes he's not losing it.

"The cloud," Toshio repeats. "We move all of our video to the cloud."

Mateo is curious. "OK, Toshio, I'll bite. What's the cloud?"

"It's a movement—I'd call it a fad, except I think it's here to stay."

"So how does it help us?" Mateo asks.

"We lease storage capacity from a third party."

Joni's confused. "You mean we'd lease hard drives rather than buy them?"

"Well, not exactly," Mateo explains. "We wouldn't be installing any more hard drives in our data center. We can lease online storage on very, very flexible, pay-as-you-go terms. If we get a large new client, we can acquire more storage and scale it to meet our needs."

"You mean each day? We can change the terms of our lease on a daily basis?" Joni thinks that's not possible. "OK, so how much does it cost? This can't be cheap."

"How about $10 per terabyte?"

Mateo's puzzled at that. "What do you mean, $10 per terabyte?"

"I mean we can get 1 terabye of online storage for about $10 per month." Toshio grins as he says this.

"*What?*" Joni's dumbfounded.

"Yeah, that's it. We can get as much storage as we want, and our systems automatically upload all incoming data from our drones. The net difference would be that our average monthly storage costs would be at least 50 percent less than they are now. And that's not counting the power savings, the time saved doing backups, or the fact that we wouldn't have to configure any more new hardware." Toshio isn't quite sure, but he thinks the actual storage costs could be less.

"Toshio, you've got to be kidding. We can save tens of thousands of dollars in storage costs. This is *huge*." As Joni says this, in the back of her mind she's thinking, "If it's true."

"Well, it's good; I don't know about huge. We'd have additional development costs to set up our systems, and that will take some time."

"Toshio, give me a plan. I want a plan." Mateo's thinking what these savings could mean to their next two quarters … and beyond.

"I'll give you something next week," Toshio says.

"I want it by Friday, Toshio."

"How about $10 per terabyte?"

Image source: rommma/Fotolia

STUDY QUESTIONS

CHAPTER PREVIEW

If you go into business for yourself, there's an excellent chance you'll have a problem just like Falcon Security's. What is the best way to support your Web site or other information systems? Should you use the cloud? Most likely, the answer will be yes. So, then, which of your applications should use it and how? You need the knowledge of this chapter to participate in the conversations you'll have. Of course, you could just rely on outside experts, but that doesn't work in the 21st century. Many of your competitors will be able to ask and understand those questions—and use the money their knowledge saves them for other purposes.

Or what if you work for a large company that has embraced the Internet of Things (IoT)? Will you make products that send and receive data across the Internet? How will your products connect to the cloud? Will a cloud offering make sense for you and your customers? How will you know without some knowledge of the cloud?

We begin this chapter with an overview of why the cloud is the future for most organizations. Then, in Q6-2 and Q6-3, we will discuss background technology you need to know to better understand how the cloud works and what organizations can do with it. We'll discuss local area networks, the fundamentals of the Internet, how Web servers function, and the purpose of basic cloud technologies. Then we'll return to discussing how organizations can use the cloud, basic steps for setting up a cloud presence, and cloud security. We'll wrap up with the cloud in 2026.

Q6-1 Why Is the Cloud the Future for Most Organizations?

Until 2010 or so, most organizations constructed and maintained their own computing infrastructure. Organizations purchased or leased hardware, installed it on their premises, and used it to support organizational email, Web sites, e-commerce sites, and in-house applications such as accounting and operations systems (you'll learn about those in the next chapter). After about 2010, however, organizations began to move their computing infrastructure to the cloud, and it is likely that in the future all, or nearly all, computing infrastructure will be leased from the cloud. So, just what is the cloud, and why is it the future?

What Is the Cloud?

We define the **cloud** as the *elastic* leasing of *pooled* computer resources *over the Internet*. The term *cloud* is used because most early diagrams of three-tier and other Internet-based systems used a cloud symbol to represent the Internet (see Figure 5-13 for an example), and organizations came to view their infrastructure as being "somewhere in the cloud."

Elastic

Consider each of the italicized terms in the definition. The term **elastic**, which was first used this way by Amazon.com, means that the computing resources leased can be increased or decreased dynamically, programmatically, in a short span of time and that organizations pay for just the resources they use.

Suppose a car manufacturer creates an ad to run during the Academy Awards. It believes it has a fantastic ad that will result in millions of hits on its Web site. However, it doesn't know ahead of time if there will be a thousand, or a million, or ten million, or even more site visits. Further, the

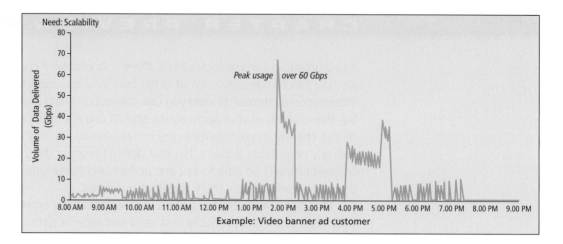

Figure 6-1

Example Video Banner
Ad Customer

ad may appeal more to one nationality than to another. Will 70 percent of those visits arise in the United States and the rest in Europe? Or will there be millions from Japan? Or Australia? Given this uncertainty, how does the car manufacturer prepare its computing infrastructure? The car manufacturer knows that if it cannot provide very short response time (say, a fraction of a second), it will lose the benefit of an incredibly expensive ad. On the other hand, if the ad is a flop, preprovisioning of thousands of servers will add to the accumulation of wasted money.

Figure 6-1 shows an example of this situation, based on a real case supported by Amazon.com's CloudFront. Suppose Figure 6-1 shows the processing on the car manufacturer's Web site during the Academy Awards. Throughout the day, the car manufacturer is delivering less than 10 Gbps of its content to users. However, as soon as its ad runs (2 PM in the Hawaii-Aleutian time zone where the data was collected), demand increases seven-fold and stays high for half an hour. After the announcement of Best Picture, when its ad runs again, demand again increases to 30 and 40 Gpbs for an hour and then returns to its base level.

Without an increase in servers, response time will be 3 or 5 seconds or more, which is far too long to maintain the attention of a charged-up Academy Awards viewer. However, the car manufacturer has contracted with its cloud vendor to add servers, wherever needed worldwide, to keep response time to less than 0.5 seconds. Using cloud technology, the cloud vendor will programmatically increase its servers to keep response time below the 0.5-second threshold. As demand falls after the ad runs a second time, it will release the excess servers and reallocate them at the end of the awards.

In this way, the car manufacturer need not build or contract for infrastructure that supports maximum demand. Had it done so, the vast majority of its servers would have been idle for most of the evening. And, as you'll learn, the cloud vendor can provision servers worldwide using the cloud; if a good portion of the excess demand is in Singapore, for example, it can provision extra servers in Asia and reduce wait time due to global transmission delays.

Pooled

The second key in the definition of cloud is *pooled*. Cloud resources are **pooled** because many different organizations use the same physical hardware; they share that hardware through virtualization. Cloud vendors dynamically allocate virtual machines to physical hardware as customer needs increase or decrease. Thus, servers that advertisers need for the Academy Awards can be reallocated to CPA firms that need them later that same day, to textbook publishers who need them for online student activity on Monday, or to the hotel industry that needs them later the next week.

An easy way to understand the essence of this development is to consider electrical power. In the very earliest days of electric power generation, organizations operated their own generators to create power for their company's needs. Over time, as the power grid expanded, it became

Figure 6-2
Apple Data Center in Maiden, NC
Source: Google Earth

possible to centralize power generation so that organizations could purchase just the electricity they needed from an electric utility.

Both cloud vendors and electrical utilities benefit from *economies of scale*. According to this principle, the average cost of production decreases as the size of the operation increases. Major cloud vendors operate enormous Web farms. Figure 6-2 shows the building that contains the computers in the Web farm that Apple constructed in 2011 to support its iCloud offering. This billion-dollar facility contains more than 500,000 square feet.[1] Amazon.com, IBM, Google, Microsoft, Oracle, and other large companies each operate several similar farms worldwide.

Over the Internet

Finally, with the cloud, the resources are accessed **over the Internet**. "Big deal," you're saying. "I use the Internet all the time." Well, think about that for a minute. The car manufacturer in the previous example has contracted with the cloud vendor for a maximum response time; the cloud vendor adds servers as needed to meet that requirement. As stated, the cloud vendor may be provisioning, nearly instantaneously, servers all over the world. How does it do that? And not for just one customer, like the car manufacturer, but for thousands?

In the old days, for such interorganizational processing to occur, developers from the car manufacturer had to meet with developers from the cloud vendor and design an interface. "Our programs will do this, providing this data, and we want your programs to do that, in response, sending us this other data back." Such meetings took days and were expensive and error-prone. Given the design, the developers then returned home to write code to meet the agreed-on interface design, which may not have been understood in the same way by all parties.

It was a long, slow, expensive, and prone-to-failure process. If organizations had to do that today, cloud provisioning would be unaffordable and infeasible.

Instead, the computer industry settled on a set of standard ways of requesting and receiving services over the Internet. You will learn about some of these standards in Q6-3. For now, just realize those standards enable computers that have never "met" before to organize a dizzying, worldwide dance to deliver and process content to users on PCs, iPads, Google phones, Xboxes, and even exercise equipment in a tenth of second or less. It is absolutely fascinating and gorgeous technology! Unfortunately, you will have the opportunity to learn only a few basic terms in Q6-2 and Q6-3. Before we define and explain those terms, however, let's consider factors that make the cloud the future.

Why Is the Cloud Preferred to In-House Hosting?

Figure 6-3 compares and contrasts cloud-based and in-house hosting. As you can see, the positives are heavily tilted toward cloud-based computing. The cloud vendor Rackspace will lease you one medium server for less than a penny per hour. You can obtain and access that server today, actually within a few minutes. Tomorrow, if you need thousands of servers, you can readily scale up to obtain them. Furthermore, you know the cost structure; although you might have a surprise in regard to how many customers want to access your Web site, you won't have any surprises as to how much it will cost.

Another positive is that as long as you're dealing with large, reputable organizations, you'll be receiving best-of-breed security and disaster recovery (discussed in Chapter 10). In addition, you need not worry that you're investing in technology that will soon be obsolete; the cloud vendor is taking that risk. All of this is possible because the cloud vendor is gaining economies of scale by selling to an entire industry, not just to you.

The negatives of cloud computing involve loss of control. You're dependent on a vendor; changes in the vendor's management, policy, and prices are beyond your control. Further, you don't know where your data—which may be a large part of your organization's value—is located. Nor do you know how many copies of your data there are or even if they're located in the same

Figure 6-3

Comparison of Cloud and In-House Alternatives

Cloud	In-House
Positive:	
Small capital requirements	Control of data location
Speedy development	In-depth visibility of security and disaster preparedness
Superior flexibility and adaptability to growing or fluctuating demand	
Known cost structure	
Possibly best-of-breed security/disaster preparedness	
No obsolescence	
Industry-wide economies of scale, hence cheaper	
Negative:	
Dependency on vendor	Significant capital required
Loss of control over data location	Significant development effort
Little visibility into true security and disaster preparedness capabilities	Annual maintenance costs
	Ongoing support costs
	Staff and train personnel
	Increased management requirements
	Difficult (impossible?) to accommodate fluctuating demand
	Cost uncertainties
	Obsolescence

country as you are. Finally, you have no visibility into the security and disaster preparedness that is actually in place. Your competition could be stealing your data and you won't know it.

The positives and negatives of in-house hosting are shown in the second column of Figure 6-3. For the most part, they are the opposite of those for cloud-based computing; note, however, the need for personnel and management. With in-house hosting, not only will you have to construct your own data center, you'll also need to acquire and train the personnel to run it and then manage those personnel and your facility.

Storing valuable information online can be risky. The Security Guide on pages 270–271 looks at why your information may not be as safe as you think.

Why Now?

A skeptic might respond to Figure 6-3 by saying, "If it's so great, why hasn't cloud hosting been used for years? Why now?"

In fact, cloud-based hosting (or a version of it under a different name) has been around since the 1960s. Long before the creation of the personal computer and networks, time-sharing vendors provided slices of computer time on a use-fee basis. However, the technology of that time, continuing up until the first decade of this century, did not favor the construction and use of enormous data centers, nor did the necessary Internet standards exist.

Three factors have made cloud-based hosting advantageous today. First, processors, data communication, and data storage are so cheap that they are nearly free. At the scale of a Web farm of hundreds of thousands of processors, providing a virtual machine for an hour costs essentially nothing, as suggested by the 1.5 cent-per-hour price. Because data communication is so cheap, getting the data to and from that processor is also nearly free.

Companies can save a lot of money by using the cloud, and these savings translate into profit. This profit does not come without ethical concerns, however. The Ethics Guide on pages 244–245 examines these concerns.

Second, virtualization technology enables the near instantaneous creation of a new virtual machine. The customer provides (or creates in the cloud) a disk image of the data and programs of the machine it wants to provision. Virtualization software takes it from there. Finally, as stated, Internet-based standards enable cloud-hosting vendors to provide processing capabilities in flexible yet standardized ways.

When Does the Cloud Not Make Sense?

Cloud-based hosting makes sense for most organizations. The only organizations for which it may not make sense are those required by law or by industry standard practice to have physical control over their data. Such organizations might be forced to create and maintain their own hosting infrastructure. A financial institution, for example, might be legally required to maintain physical control over its data. Even in this circumstance, however, it is possible to gain many of the benefits of cloud computing using private clouds and virtual private clouds, possibilities we consider in Q6.

Q6-2 What Network Technology Supports the Cloud?

A computer **network** is a collection of computers that communicate with one another over transmission lines or wirelessly. As shown in Figure 6-4, the four basic types of networks are personal area networks, local area networks, wide area networks, and internets.

Type	Characteristic
Personal area network (PAN)	Devices connected around a single person
Local area network (LAN)	Computers connected at a single physical site
Wide area network (WAN)	Computers connected between two or more separated sites
The Internet and internets	Networks of networks

Figure 6-4
Basic Network Types

Ethics Guide

CLOUDY PROFIT?

Alliance Partners (a fictitious name) is a data broker. You'll learn about data brokers in Chapter 9, but for now, just know that such companies acquire and buy consumer and other data from retailers, other data brokers, governmental agencies, and public sources and aggregate it into data profiles of individuals. Alliance specializes in acquiring and analyzing market, buyer, and seller data for real estate agents. Alliance sells an individual profile to qualified real estate agents for $100 to $1,500, depending on the amount of data and type of analysis requested.

Alliance is owned by three partners who started the business in 1999. They endured tough times during the dot-com collapse at the turn of the century, but crawled out of that hole and were doing well until they encountered severe revenue shortfalls in the 2008 real estate collapse. In late 2008, in order to reduce operational costs to survive the downturn, Alliance transitioned its data storage and processing from its own Web farm to the cloud. The elastic flexibility of the cloud enables Alliance to improve the speed and quality of its data services at a fraction of prior costs. Furthermore, using the cloud enabled it to reduce the in-house hardware support staff by 65 percent.

The partners meet twice a year to review their financial performance, evaluate strategy, and plan for both the next six months and the longer term. In 2008, in the midst of their revenue shortfalls, they met in a small suite in the local Hamilton Inn, ate stale doughnuts, and drank watery orange juice. This year, they've rented a facility in the British Virgin Islands in the Caribbean. The following conversation occurred between two of the partners at the onset of this year's meeting:

"Bart, what are we doing here?" Shelly, the partner in charge of sales and marketing, is challenging Bart Johnson, Alliance's managing partner.

"What do you mean, Shelly? Don't you like it here?"

"I *love* it here. So does my husband. But I also know we're paying $15,000 a night to rent this island!" Shelly rubs sunscreen on her hands as she talks.

"Well, we don't have the entire island." Bart sounds defensive.

"No, I guess not," she says. "They have to let some of the staff stay here. We're the only paying customers...the only nonlocals.

"But," Shelly continues, "that's not my point. My point is, how can we afford this level of expense? We'll pay nearly $200,000 for this meeting alone. Where are we meeting next? Some five-star resort on the moon?"

"Look, Shelly, as you're about to hear, our gross margin last year was 74 percent. We're a money machine! We're swimming in profit! We can't spend money fast enough.

Source: Eunikas/Fotolia

One of the items on our agenda is whether we want to issue a $1 million, a $3 million, or a $5 million partners' distribution."

"No!" Shelly sounds stunned.

"Yup. Using the cloud, we've reduced our operational expense from 62 percent of our revenue to 9 percent. I'm plowing money back into R&D as fast as I can, but there's only so much that Jacob and his crew can absorb. Meanwhile, order the lobster and wait until you taste tonight's wines."

"That's disgusting."

"OK," Bart says. "Don't drink the wine. You want your distribution?"

"No; I mean yes, but this is crazy. It can't last."

"Probably not. But it's what we've got right now."

 # DISCUSSION QUESTIONS

When answering the following questions, assume that Alliance has done nothing illegal, including paying all federal, state, and local taxes on a timely basis.

1. From the perspective of Kant's categorical imperative (pages 56–57), are Alliance's partners' meeting expenses and intended partner distribution unethical?

2. From the utilitarian perspective (pages 92–93), are Alliance's partners' meeting expenses and intended partner distribution unethical?

3. Milton Friedman, world-renowned economist at the University of Chicago, stated that corporate executives have a responsibility to make as much money as possible as long as they don't violate rules embodied in law and in ethical custom.[2]

   a. Do you agree with his statement? Why or why not?

   b. Friedman defined *ethical custom* narrowly to mean no *fraud* or *deception*. Using his definition, has Alliance acted ethically?

   c. Define, using your own words, *ethical custom*.

   d. Using your definition of *ethical custom*, has Alliance acted ethically?

4. Do you find any of the following excessive? Explain your answers:

   a. Spending nearly $200,000 on a five-day partners' meeting for three partners and their spouses?

   b. Earning a 74 percent gross profit?

   c. Paying a semiannual distribution of $1M, $3M, or $5M? If so, which level is excessive to you?

5. Describe the primary driver in Alliance's current profitability.

6. From the data presented, what else might Alliance have done with its excess profits?

7. Do you think profitable companies, especially very profitable companies, have an ethical obligation to:

   a. Contribute to charity?

   b. Lower prices when it is possible to do so and continue to earn a reasonable profit?

   c. Contribute to environmental causes?

   d. When possible, pay large bonuses to all employees, not just senior management?

8. To most students, someone who earns $500,000 a year in income is rich. To someone who makes $500,000 a year, partners who pay themselves $1M to $5M every 6 months are rich. To someone making $2M to $10M a year, billionaires are rich. What do you think classifies someone as rich?

9. Do you think rich people have an ethical obligation to:

   a. Contribute to charity?

   b. Contribute to environmental causes?

   c. Forego governmental benefits to which they are entitled, for example, not take Social Security that they don't need?

A **personal area network (PAN)** connects devices located around a *single person.* Most PAN devices connect wirelessly to other devices located within 10 meters. A **local area network (LAN)** connects computers that reside in a single geographic location on the premises of the company that operates the LAN. The number of connected computers can range from two to several hundred. The distinguishing characteristic of a LAN is *a single location.* A **wide area network (WAN)** connects computers at different geographic locations. The computers in two separated company sites must be connected using a WAN. To illustrate, a smartwatch or fitness tracker will create a PAN by connecting to a student's smartphone. The computers for a college of business located on a single campus can be connected via a LAN. The computers for a college of business located on multiple campuses must be connected via a WAN.

The single-versus multiple-site distinction between LANs and WANs is important. With a LAN, an organization can place communications lines wherever it wants because all lines reside on its premises. The same is not true for a WAN. A company with offices in Chicago and Atlanta cannot run a wire down the freeway to connect computers in the two cities. Instead, the company contracts with a communications vendor licensed by the government and that already has lines or has the authority to run new lines between the two cities.

An **internet** is a network of networks. Internets connect LANs, WANs, and other internets. The most famous internet is "**the Internet**" (with an uppercase letter *I*), the collection of networks you use when you send email or access a Web site. In addition to the Internet, private networks of networks, called *internets,* also exist. A private internet used exclusively within an organization is sometimes called an **intranet**.

The networks that make up an internet use a large variety of communication methods and conventions, and data must flow seamlessly across them. To provide seamless flow, an elaborate scheme called a *layered protocol* is used. The details of protocols are beyond the scope of this text. Just understand that a **protocol** is a set of rules and data structures for organizing communication. Computers need to use protocols so they can exchange data. People use similar protocols to communicate. People, for example, follow a conversational protocol that says when one person talks, the other person listens. They switch back and forth until they are done communicating. Without a protocol for conversations, people would continually talk over each other and nothing would be communicated.

There are many different protocols; some are used for PANs, some are used for LANs, some are used for WANs, some are used for internets and the Internet, and some are used for all of these. We will identify several common protocols in this chapter.

What Are the Components of a LAN?

Employers can and do monitor employees' online activities. What is the purpose of this monitoring, and how is it done? Is there anything employees can do about it? The Guide on pages 272–273 considers these questions.

As stated, a LAN is a group of computers connected together on a single site. Usually the computers are located within a half-mile or so of each other. The key distinction, however, is that all of the computers are located on property controlled by the organization that operates the LAN. This means that the organization can run cables wherever needed to connect the computers.

Figure 6-5 shows a LAN typical of those in a **small office or home office (SOHO)**. Typically, such LANs have fewer than a dozen or so computers and printers. Many businesses, of course, operate LANs much larger than this one. The principles are the same for a larger LAN, but the additional complexity is beyond the scope of this text.

The computers and printers in Figure 6-5 communicate via a mixture of wired and wireless connections. Some devices use wired connections, and others use wireless connections. The devices and protocols used differ for wired and wireless connectivity.

The Institute for Electrical and Electronics Engineers (IEEE, pronounced "I triple E") sponsors committees that create and publish protocol and other standards. The committee that addresses LAN standards is called the *IEEE 802 Committee.* Thus, IEEE LAN protocols always start with the numbers 802.

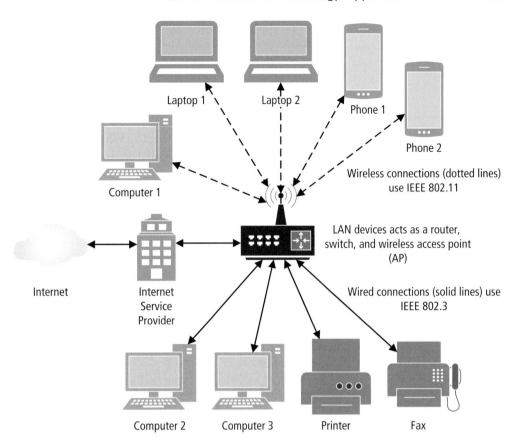

Figure 6-5

Typical Small Office/Home Office (SOHO) LAN

The **IEEE 802.3 protocol** is used for wired LAN connections. This protocol standard, also called **Ethernet**, specifies hardware characteristics, such as which wire carries which signals. It also describes how messages are to be packaged and processed for wired transmission over the LAN.

Most personal computers today support what is called **10/100/1000 Ethernet**. These products conform to the 802.3 specification and allow for transmission at a rate of 10, 100, or 1,000 Mbps (megabits per second). Switches detect the speed a given device can handle and communicate with it at that speed. If you check computer listings at Dell, Lenovo, and other manufacturers, you will see PCs advertised as having 10/100/1000 Ethernet. Today, speeds of up to 1 Gbps are possible on wired LANs.

By the way, the abbreviations used for communications speeds differ from those used for computer memory. For communications equipment, K stands for 1,000, not 1,024 as it does for memory. Similarly, M stands for 1,000,000, not $1,024 \times 1,024$; G stands for 1,000,000,000, not $1,024 \times 1,024 \times 1,024$. Thus, 100 Mbps is 100,000,000 bits per second. Also, communications speeds are expressed in *bits*, whereas memory sizes are expressed in *bytes*. These are different units of measurement. One byte consists of eight bits. This means a 1 MB file would consist of 8,388,608 bits. If you sent a 1 MB file over a 1 Mbps connection, it would take more than 8 seconds to send because your connection speed is measured in bits per second, not bytes per second.

Wireless LAN connections use the **IEEE 802.11 protocol**. Several versions of 802.11 exist, and as of 2015, the most current one is IEEE 802.11ac. The differences among these versions are beyond the scope of this discussion. Just note that the current standard, 802.11ac, allows speeds of up to 1.3 Gbps, though few users have an Internet connection fast enough to take full advantage of that speed.

Bluetooth is another common wireless protocol used to make PAN connections. It is designed for transmitting data over short distances, replacing cables. Devices, such as wireless mice, keyboards, printers, and headphones, use Bluetooth to connect to desktop computers. Other devices like smartwatches and fitness trackers can use Bluetooth to connect to smartphones and send data over the Internet. More and more devices like clothing, automobiles, and sports equipment are becoming Bluetooth enabled.

Connecting Your LAN to the Internet

Although you may not have realized it, when you connect your SOHO LAN, phone, iPad, or Kindle to the Internet, you are connecting to a WAN. You must do so because you are connecting to computers that are not physically located on your premises. You cannot start running wires down the street to plug in somewhere.

When you connect to the Internet, you are actually connecting to an **Internet service provider (ISP)**. An ISP has three important functions. First, it provides you with a legitimate Internet address. Second, it serves as your gateway to the Internet. The ISP receives the communications from your computer and passes them on to the Internet, and it receives communications from the Internet and passes them on to you. Finally, ISPs pay for the Internet. They collect money from their customers and pay access fees and other charges on your behalf.

Figure 6-6 shows the three common alternatives for connecting to the Internet. Notice that we are discussing how your computer connects to the Internet via a WAN; we are not discussing the structure of the WAN itself. WAN architectures and their protocols are beyond the scope of this text. Search the Web for "leased lines" or "PSDN" if you want to learn more about WAN architectures.

SOHO LANs (such as that in Figure 6-5) and individual home and office computers are commonly connected to an ISP in one of three ways: a special telephone line called a DSL line, a cable TV line, or a wireless-phone-like connection.

Digital Subscriber Line (DSL)

A **digital subscriber line (DSL)** operates on the same lines as voice telephones, but it operates so it does not interfere with voice telephone service. Because DSL signals do not interfere with telephone signals, DSL data transmission and telephone conversations can occur simultaneously.

Figure 6-6
Summary of LAN Networks

Type	Topology	Transmission Line	Transmission Speed	Equipment Used	Protocol Commonly Used	Remarks
Local area network	Local area network	UTP or optical fiber	Common: 10/100/1000 Mbps Possible: 1 Gbps	Switch NIC UTP or optical	IEEE 802.3 (Ethernet)	Switches connect devices, multiple switches on all but small LANs.
	Local area network with wireless	UTP or optical for nonwireless connections	Up to 600 Mbps	Wireless access point Wireless NIC	IEEE 802.11n, (802.11ac not yet common)	Access point transforms wired LAN (802.3) to wireless LAN (802.11).
Connections to the Internet	DSL modem to ISP	DSL telephone	Personal: Upstream to 1 Mbps, downstream to 40 Mbps (max 10 likely in most areas)	DSL modem DSL-capable telephone line	DSL	Can have computer and phone use simultaneously. Always connected.
	Cable modem to ISP	Cable TV lines to optical cable	Upstream to 1 Mbps Downstream 300 Kbps to 10 Mbps	Cable modem Cable TV cable	Cable	Capacity is shared with other sites; performance varies depending on others' use.
	WAN wireless	Wireless connection to WAN	500 Kbps to 1.7 Mbps	Wireless WAN modem	One of several wireless standards	Sophisticated protocols enables several devices to use the same wireless frequency.

A device at the telephone company separates the phone signals from the computer signals and sends the latter signal to the ISP. Digital subscriber lines use their own protocols for data transmission.

Cable Line

A cable line is the second type of WAN connection. **Cable lines** provide high-speed data transmission using cable television lines. The cable company installs a fast, high-capacity optical fiber cable to a distribution center in each neighborhood it serves. At the distribution center, the optical fiber cable connects to regular cable-television cables that run to subscribers' homes or businesses. Cable signals do not interfere with TV signals.

Because as many as 500 user sites can share these facilities, performance varies depending on how many other users are sending and receiving data. At the maximum, users can download data up to 50 Mbps and can upload data at 512 Kbps. Typically, performance is much lower than this. In most cases, the download speed of cable lines and DSL lines is about the same. Cable lines use their own protocols.

WAN Wireless Connection

A third way you can connect your computer, mobile device, or other communicating device is via a **WAN wireless** connection. Amazon.com's Kindle, for example, uses a Sprint wireless network to provide wireless data connections. The iPhone uses a LAN-based wireless network if one is available and a WAN wireless network if not. The LAN-based network is preferred because performance is considerably higher. As of 2015, WAN wireless provides average performance of 1.0 Mbps with peaks of up to 3.0 Mbps, as opposed to the typical 50 Mbps for LAN wireless.

Q6-3 How Does the Cloud Work?

Mateo and Joni are flabbergasted at the low cost of the cloud. They doubt that it's real. They would be less cautious if they understood how the cloud operates. This section will give you the basic understanding they lack and enable you to be an effective consumer of cloud services.

The cloud resides in the Internet. So, in order to learn how the cloud works, you need a basic understanding of how the Internet works. With that background, you will learn how it is possible for a cloud vendor to provide dramatic elasticity to support the workload shown in Figure 6-1.

The technology that underlies the Internet and the additional technology that enables the cloud to work are complicated. Here, we will stay at a high level and help you learn overarching concepts and basic definitions. We begin with a simple example.

An Internet Example

Figure 6-7 illustrates one use of the Internet. Suppose you are sitting in snowbound Minneapolis, and you want to communicate with a hotel in sunny, tropical northern New Zealand. Maybe you are making a reservation using the hotel's Web site, or maybe you are sending an email to a reservations clerk inquiring about facilities or services.

To begin, note that this example is an internet because it is a network of networks. It consists of two LANs (yours and the hotel's) and four networks. (In truth, the real Internet consists of tens of thousands of networks, but to conserve paper, we don't show all of them.) A **hop** is the movement from one network to another. As drawn, in Figure 6-7, the shortest path from you to the hotel's LAN consists of four hops. This term is frequently used by cloud vendors when they discuss provisioning servers to minimize the number of hops.

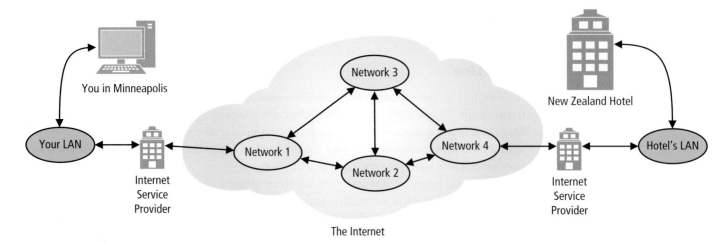

Figure 6-7
Using the Internet for a Hotel
Reservation

Carriers and Net Neutrality

As your message, or **packet**, moves across the Internet, it passes through networks owned by large telecommunication providers known as **carriers**. Some of these large carriers include Sprint, AT&T, Verizon Business, and XO Communications. These large carriers exchange traffic freely without charging each other access fees via **peering** agreements. Carriers make revenue by collecting subscription fees from end users, but not from peers.

The problem with peering is that some people use more bandwidth than others. Netflix, for example, accounts for about 33 percent of all Internet traffic in North America between 9:00 PM and 12:00 AM.[3] Carriers argue that they should be able to charge varying rates based on content, application, or the user requesting the data.

Netflix, eBay, Yahoo!, and Amazon.com say this could hurt consumers and innovation. They believe in the **net neutrality** principle, where all data is treated equally. They argue that carriers should not be allowed to decide which sites load quickly, which apps are allowed on a network, and which content is acceptable.

In 2015, the Federal Communications Commission (FCC) approved new net neutrality regulations that ensure ISPs cannot discriminate between different types of Internet traffic. This means all consumers would have access to content on an equal basis. This ruling in many ways renders the Internet a utility like water or electricity that would be governed by comparable regulations. Several large carriers have already begun fighting these new regulations in court.

Internet Addressing

Just like regular surface mail, every location on the Internet needs an address. For reasons beyond this discussion, an Internet address is called an **IP address**, which is a number that identifies a particular device. **Public IP addresses** identify a particular device on the public Internet. In order to get on the Internet, every device must have access to a public IP address. Because public IP addresses must be unique, worldwide, their assignment is controlled by a public agency known as **ICANN (Internet Corporation for Assigned Names and Numbers)**.

Private IP addresses identify a particular device on a private network, usually on a LAN. Their assignment is controlled within the LAN, usually by a LAN device like the one shown in Figure 6-5. When you sign on to a LAN at a coffee shop, for example, the LAN device lends you a private IP address to use while you are connected to the LAN. When you leave the LAN, it reuses that address.

Use of Private IP Addresses

When your computer accesses a public site, say, *www.pearsonhighered.com*, from within a LAN at, say, a coffee shop, your traffic uses your private IP address until it gets to the LAN device. At that point, the LAN device substitutes your private IP address with its public IP address and sends your traffic out onto the public Internet.

This private/public IP address scheme has two major benefits. First, public IP addresses are conserved. All of the computers on the LAN use only one public IP address. Second, by using private IP addresses, you are protected from attackers directly attacking you because they cannot send attack packets to private IP addresses. They can only send packets to devices with public IP addresses.

Public IP Addresses and Domain Names

IP addresses have two formats. The most common form, called **IPv4**, has a four-decimal dotted notation such as 165.193.123.253; the second, called **IPv6**, has a longer format and will not concern us here. In your browser, if you enter *http://165.193.140.14*, your browser will connect with the device on the public Internet that has been assigned to this address.

Nobody wants to type IP addresses such as *http://165.193.140.14* to find a particular site. Instead, we want to enter names such as *www.pandora.com* or *www.woot.com* or *www.pearsonhighered.com*. To facilitate that desire, ICANN administers a system for assigning names to IP addresses. First, a **domain name** is a worldwide-unique name that is affiliated with a public IP address. When an organization or individual wants to register a domain name, it goes to a company that applies to an ICANN-approved agency to do so. GoDaddy (*www.godaddy.com*) is an example of such a company (Figure 6-8).

GoDaddy or a similar agency, will first determine if the desired name is unique worldwide. If so, then it will apply to register that name to the applicant. Once the registration is completed, the applicant can affiliate a public IP address with the domain name. From that point onward, traffic for the new domain name will be routed to the affiliated IP address.

Note two important points: First, several (or many) domain names can point to the same IP address. Second, the affiliation of domain names with IP addresses is dynamic. The owner of the domain name can change the affiliated IP addresses at its discretion.

In 2014, the U.S. Department of Commerce announced it was giving up oversight over ICANN. Critics worry that less-free countries will now try to force ICANN to disallow domain names for dissident groups, thereby kicking them off the Internet. At this point, it's still unclear how ICANN will be governed.

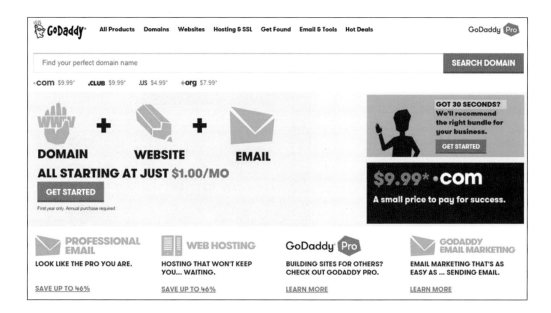

Figure 6-8
GoDaddy Screenshot
Source: © 2015 GoDaddy Operating Company, LLC. All rights reserved.

Before we leave addressing, you need to know one more term. A **URL (Uniform Resource Locator)** is an address on the Internet. Commonly, it consists of a protocol (such as http:// or ftp://) followed by a domain name or public IP address. A URL is actually quite a bit more complicated than this description, but that detailed knowledge is beyond the scope of this text, so we'll hurry along. The preferred pronunciation of URL is to say the letters U, R, L.

Processing on a Web Server

At this point, you know basic networking terms and have a high-level view of how the Internet works. To understand the value of the cloud, and how it works and how your organization can use it, you need to know a bit about the processing that occurs on a Web server. For this discussion, we will use the example of a Web storefront, which is a server on the Web from which you can buy products.

Suppose you want to buy an item from zulily, a private buyer's site that sells clothing. To do so, you go to *www.zulily.com* and navigate to the product(s) you want to buy (see Figure 6-9). When you find something you want, you add it to your shopping cart and keep shopping. At some point, you check out by supplying credit card data. But what happens when your order data arrives at the server?

Three-Tier Architecture

Almost all Web applications use the **three-tier architecture**, which is a design of user computers and servers that consists of three categories, or tiers, as shown in Figure 6-10. The **user tier** consists of computers, phones, and other mobile devices that have browsers that request and process Web pages. The **server tier** consists of computers that run Web servers and process application programs. The **database tier** consists of computers that run a DBMS that processes requests to retrieve and store data. Figure 6-10 shows only one computer at the database tier. Some sites have multicomputer database tiers as well.

Figure 6-9

Sample of Commerce Server Pages; Product Offer Pages

Source: Courtesy of Zuilly Inc. Used by permission.

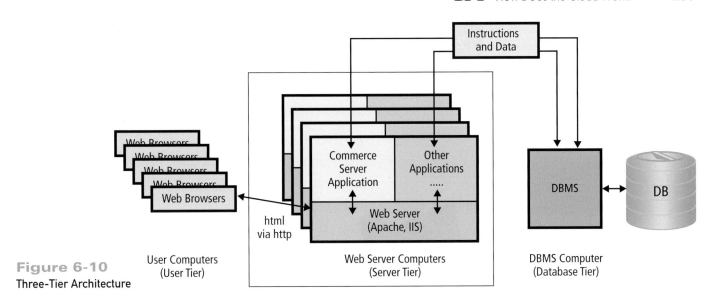

Figure 6-10
Three-Tier Architecture

When you enter *www.zulily.com* in your browser, the browser sends a request that travels over the Internet to a computer in the server tier at the zulily site. In response to your request, a server-tier computer sends back a **Web page**, which is a document coded in, usually, html (and, as discussed in Chapter 4, probably includes CSS, JavaScript, and other data).

Web servers are programs that run on a server-tier computer and manage traffic by sending and receiving Web pages to and from clients. A **commerce server** is an application program that runs on a server-tier computer. Typical commerce server functions are to obtain product data from a database, manage the items in a shopping cart, and coordinate the checkout process. When a request comes to the server, the Web server examines it and sends it to the proper program for processing. Thus, the Web server passes e-commerce traffic to the commerce server. It passes requests for other applications to those applications. In Figure 6-10, the server-tier computers are running a Web server program, a commerce server application, and other applications having an unspecified purpose.

Watch the Three Tiers in Action!

Suppose the user of the Web page in Figure 6-9 clicks on shoes and then selects a particular shoe, say, the Darkish Gray Dorine Mary Jane shoe. When the user clicks on that shoe, the commerce server requests that shoe's data from the DBMS, which reads it from the database and then returns the data (including pictures) to the commerce server. That server then formats the Web page with the data and sends the html version of that page to the user's computer. The result is the page shown in Figure 6-11.

Service-Oriented Architecture (SOA)

The cloud would be impossible without a design philosophy called the **service-oriented architecture (SOA)**. According to this philosophy, all interactions among computing devices are defined as services in a formal, standardized way. This philosophy enables all the pieces of the cloud to fit together, as you will see. However, understanding SOA (pronounced SO-ah) in depth requires you to learn more computer science than you need as a business professional. So, the best way for you to understand SOA is via a business analogy.

A SOA Analogy

Figure 6-12 shows an arrangement of departments at a hypothetical online bicycle part retailer named Best Bikes. The Sales Department receives order requests and follows a process to have them approved for shipping. On request, the Credit Department verifies customer credit

Figure 6-11
Product Page
Source: Courtesy of Zuilly Inc.
Used by permission

as needed to approve orders, and the Inventory Department verifies the availability of the inventory needed to fulfill an order.

In an informal, non-SOA-type organization, one salesperson would contact someone he or she knows in Credit and ask something like, "Can you approve an allocation of $10,000 of credit to the ABC Bicycle Company?" In response, the credit person might say, "Sure," and the salesperson might note the name of the person who approved the amount. Some days, he or she might remember to record the date; other days, not so. Another salesperson might do something else, say, contact a different person in Credit and ask something like, "I need $5,000 in credit for Order 12345," and that other person in Credit might say, "I don't know, send the order over, and if I can, I'll write 'Approved' on it." Other irregular, but similar, interactions could occur between the Sales and the Inventory departments.

Such operations are definitely *not* service-oriented. People are asking for credit verification in different ways and receiving responses in different ways. The process for approving an order varies

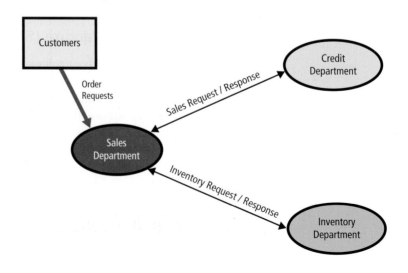

Figure 6-12

Approval Request Interactions
Among Three Departments

from salesperson to salesperson, and possibly from day to day with the same salesperson. The records of approvals are inconsistent. Such an organization will have varying levels of process quality and inconsistent results, and should the company decide to open a facility in another city, these operations cannot be readily duplicated, nor should they be.

Using SOA principles, each department would formally define the services it provides. Examples are:

For the Credit Department:

- CheckCustomerCredit
- ApproveCustomerCredit

For the Inventory Department

- VerifyInventoryAmount
- AllocateInventory
- ReleaseAllocatedInventory

Further, for each service, each department would formally state the data it expects to receive with the request and the data it promises to return in response. Every interaction is done exactly the same way. There is no personal contact between certain people in the departments; no salesperson need know who works in Credit or Inventory. Instead, requests are emailed to a generic email address in Credit or Inventory, and those departments decide who will process the request and how it will be processed. No department has or need have any knowledge of who works in another department nor how the department accomplishes its work. Each department is free to change personnel task assignments and to change the way it performs its services, and no other department needs to know that a change occurred. In SOA terms, we would say the work of the department is **encapsulated** in the department.

With this organization, if Best Bikes wants to add another Inventory Department in another city, it can do so and no salesperson need change the way he or she sets up, submits, or receives responses to requests. Sales continues to send a VerifyInventoryAmount service request, formatted in the standard way, to the same email address.

With multiple sites, the Inventory function would change the way it implements service requests to first identify which of the several Inventory Departments should process the request. Sales would not know, nor need to know, this happened. Best Bikes could dynamically create 1,000 Inventory Departments and the Sales Department need not change anything it does. Later, it could reduce those 1,000 Inventory Departments to three, and, again, sales need not make any change.

SOA for Three-Tier Architecture

From this discussion, you can see how SOA is used to enable cloud processing. The description and advantages and disadvantages of this analogy for SOA are the same for the cloud. Consider Figure 6-13, which shows the three-tier architecture with SOA drawn in. In this case, the commerce server application formally defines services that browsers can request, the data they must provide with the request, and the data that each will receive in response to the request. Sample services are:

- ObtainPartData
- ObtainPartImages
- ObtainPartQuantityOnHand
- OrderPart

And so forth. Again, each service also documents the data it expects and the data it will return.

Now, JavaScript (or another code language) is written to invoke these services correctly. That JavaScript is included as part of the Web pages the server sends to the browsers, and when users employ the browsers to purchase, the JavaScript behind the Web page invokes the services in the correct way.

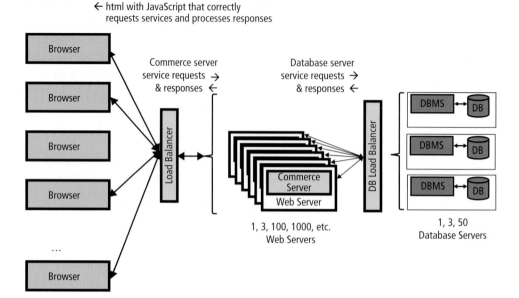

Figure 6-13
SOA Principles Applied
to Three-Tier Architecture

The server tier can consist of three servers at 3 AM, 3,000 servers at 11 AM, 6,000 servers at 6 PM, and 100 servers at 10 PM. Furthermore, those servers can move around the world; at one time of day, they can be all located in the United States, and at another time of day, they can all be located in Europe, and so on. Nothing, absolutely nothing, in the browsers need change as these servers are adjusted.

To take advantage of the multiple Web servers, a load-balancing program receives requests and sends them to an available server. The load-balancing program keeps data about the speed and health of all its assigned Web servers and allocates work to maximize throughput.

In addition, on the back end, SOA services are defined between the Web server and the database server. Accordingly, the database server need do nothing as the number and location of Web servers is adjusted. And that's a two-way street. Nothing in the Web servers need be changed if the number and location of database servers is adjusted. However, load balancing for database servers is considerably more complicated.

Do not infer from this discussion that SOA services and the cloud are only used for three-tier processing. Such services and the cloud are used for multitudes of applications across the Internet. This three-tier application is just an example.

From this discussion, you can understand how cloud elasticity is possible. However, for many organizations to use the cloud and to be able to mix and match Web services, they need to agree on standard ways of formatting and processing service requests and data. That leads us to cloud standards and protocols. Again, we discuss these at a very high level.

Protocols Supporting Web Services

A protocol is a set of rules and data structures for organizing communication. Because the cloud's Web services use the Internet, the protocols that run the Internet also support cloud processing. We will start with them.

TCP/IP Protocol Architecture

The basic plumbing of the Internet is governed by protocols that are defined according to an arrangement called the **TCP/IP protocol architecture**. This architecture has five layers; one or more protocols are defined at each layer. Data communications and software vendors write computer programs that implement the rules of a particular protocol. (For protocols at the bottom layer, the physical layer, they build hardware devices that implement the protocol.)

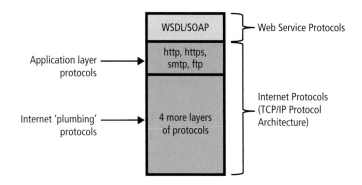

Figure 6-14
Protocols That Support Web Services

Internet Protocols: http, https, smtp, and ftp

The only Internet protocols that you as a business professional are likely to encounter are those at the top, or the application layer of the TCP/IP architecture, shown in Figure 6-14. **Hypertext Transfer Protocol (http)** is the protocol used between browsers and Web servers. When you use a browser such as Microsoft Edge, Safari, or Chrome, you are using a program that implements the http protocol. At the other end, at the New Zealand hotel mentioned earlier, for example, there is a server that also processes http. Even though your browser and the server at the hotel have never "met" before, they can communicate with one another because they both follow the rules of http. Similarly, in Figure 6-13, the browsers send and receive service requests to and from the commerce server using http.

As you will learn in Chapter 10, there is a secure version of http called **https**. Whenever you see *https* in your browser's address bar, you have a secure transmission and you can safely send sensitive data like credit card numbers. When you are on the Internet, if you do not see *https*, then you should assume that all of your communication is open and could be published on the front page of your campus newspaper tomorrow morning. Hence, when you are using http, email, text messaging, chat, videoconferencing, or anything other than https, know that whatever you are typing or saying could be known by anyone else.

Two additional TCP/IP application-layer protocols are common. **smtp**, or **Simple Mail Transfer Protocol**, is used for email transmissions (along with other protocols). **ftp**, or **File Transfer Protocol**, is used to move files over the Internet. Google Drive and Microsoft OneDrive use ftp behind the scenes to transmit files to and from their cloud servers to your computer.

WSDL, SOAP, XML, and JSON

To wrap up the discussion, we will briefly consider four standards used extensively for Web services and the cloud. Those standards and their purpose are as follows:

WSDL (Web Services Description Language)	A standard for describing the services, inputs and outputs, and other data supported by a Web service. Documents coded according to this standard are machine readable and can be used by developer tools for creating programs to access the service.
SOAP (no longer an acronym)	A protocol for requesting Web services and for sending responses to Web service requests.
XML (eXtensible Markup Language)	A markup language used for transmitting documents. Contains much metadata that can be used to validate the format and completeness of the document, but includes considerable overhead (see Figure 6-15a).
JSON (JavaScript Object Notation)	A markup language used for transmitting documents. Contains little metadata and is preferred for transmitting volumes of data between servers and browsers. While the notation is the format of JavaScript objects, JSON documents can be processed by any language (see Figure 6-15b).

```
<person>
    <firstName>Kelly</firstName>
    <lastName>Summers</lastName>
    <dob>12/28/1985</dob>
    <address>
        <streetAddress>309 Elm Avenue</streetAddress>
        <city>San Diego</city>
        <state>CA</state>
        <postalCode>98225</postalCode>
    </address>
    <phoneNumbers>
        <phoneNumber type="home">685 555-1234</phoneNumber>
        <phoneNumber type="cell">685 555-5678</phoneNumber>
    </phoneNumbers>
</person>
```

Figure 6-15a
Example XML Document

```
{
    "firstName": "Kelly",
    "lastName": "Summers",
    "dob": "12/28/1985",
    "address": {
        "streetAddress": "309 Elm Avenue",
        "city": "San Diego",
        "state": "CA",
        "postalCode": "98225"
    },
    "phoneNumber": [
        {
            "type": "home",
            "number": "685 555-1234"
        },
        {
            "type": "cell",
            "number": "685 555-5678"
        }
    ]
}
```

Figure 6-15b
Example JSON Document

Service authors (computer programmers) create WSDL documents to describe the services they provide and the inputs and outputs required. These WSDL documents are seldom read by humans. Instead, developer tools like Microsoft Visual Studio read the WSDL to configure the programming environment for programmers who write code to access that service.

As shown in Figure 6-14, SOAP, which is not an acronym though it looks like one, is a protocol that sits on top of http and the lower-level Internet protocols. *Sits on top of* means that it uses http to send and receive SOAP messages. (SOAP can also use smtp.) Programs that use Web services issue SOAP messages to request services; the Web service uses SOAP messages to return responses to service requests.

Finally, XML and JSON are ways of marking up documents so that both the service requestor and the service provider know what data they're processing. Figure 6-15 shows a simple example of both. As you can see, XML documents contain as much metadata as they do application data. These metadata are used to ensure that the document is complete and properly formatted. XML is used when relatively few messages are being transmitted and when ensuring a complete and correct document is crucial. Both WSDLs and SOAP messages are coded in XML.

As its name indicates, JSON uses the notation for JavaScript objects to format data. It has much less metadata and is preferred for the transmission of voluminous application data. Web servers use JSON as their primary way of sending application data to browsers.

With this technical background, you should no longer be skeptical that the benefits of the cloud are real. They are. However, this fact does not mean that every organization uses the cloud well. In the remainder of this chapter, we will describe generic ways that organizations can use the cloud, discuss how Falcon Security in particular can use the cloud, and, finally, discuss an exceedingly important topic: cloud security.

Q6-4 How Do Organizations Use the Cloud?

Organizations can use the cloud in several different ways. The first, and by far most popular, is to obtain cloud services from cloud service vendors.

Cloud Services from Cloud Vendors

In general, cloud-based service offerings can be organized into the three categories shown in Figure 6-16. An organization that provides **software as a service (SaaS)** provides not only hardware infrastructure, but an operating system and application programs as well. For example, Salesforce.com provides hardware and programs for customer and sales tracking as a service. Similarly, Google provides Google Drive and Microsoft provides OneDrive as a service. With Office 365, Exchange, Skype for Business, and SharePoint applications are provided as a service "in the cloud."

You've probably heard of, or used, Apple's iCloud. It's a cloud service that Apple uses to sync all of its customers' iOS devices. As of 2015, Apple provides 10 free applications in the iCloud. Calendar is a good example. When a customer enters an appointment in her iPhone, Apple automatically pushes that appointment into the calendars on all of that customer's iOS devices. Further, customers can share calendars with others that will be synchronized as well. Mail, pictures, applications, and other resources are also synched via iCloud.

An organization can move to SaaS simply by signing up and learning how to use it. In Apple's case, there's nothing to learn. To quote the late Steve Jobs, "It just works."

The second category of cloud hosting is **platform as a service (PaaS)**, whereby vendors provide hosted computers, an operating system, and possibly a DBMS. Microsoft Windows Azure, for example, provides servers installed with Windows Server. Customers of Windows Azure then add their own applications on top of the hosted platform. Microsoft SQL Azure provides a host with Windows Server and SQL Server. Oracle On Demand provides a hosted server with Oracle Database. Again, for PaaS, organizations add their own applications to the host. Amazon EC2 provides servers with Windows Server or Linux installed.

The most basic cloud offering is **infrastructure as a service (IaaS)**, which is the cloud hosting of a bare server computer or data storage. Rackspace provides hardware for customers to load whatever operating system they want, and Amazon.com licenses S3 (Simple Storage Service), which provides unlimited, reliable data storage in the cloud.

Cloud Category	Examples
SaaS (software as a service)	Salesforce.com iCloud Office 365
PaaS (platform as a service)	Microsoft Azure Oracle On Demand
IaaS (infrastructure as a service)	Amazon EC2 (Elastic Cloud 2) Amazon S3 (Simple Storage Service)

Figure 6-16
Three Fundamental Cloud Types

Benefits of Content Delivery Networks

- Decreased, even guaranteed, loadtime
- Reduced load on origin server
- Increased reliability
- Protection form DOS attacks
- Reduced delivery costs for mobile users
- Pay-as-you-go

Figure 6-17
Benefits of Content Delivery
Networks

Content Delivery Networks

A second major use of the cloud is to deliver content from servers placed around the world. A **content delivery network (CDN)** is a system of hardware and software that stores user data in many different geographical locations and makes those data available on demand. A CDN provides a specialized type of PaaS but is usually considered in its own category, as it is here.

Consider CDN applications: A news organization could use a CDN to store copies of its news articles. The CDN vendor replicates articles on servers, possibly worldwide, so as to speed response time. When a news reader accesses an article, the request is transmitted to a routing server that determines which CDN server is likely to deliver the article to the user the fastest. Because traffic changes rapidly, especially for popular sites, such calculations are made in real time. A request for content at one moment in time could be served by a computer in, say, San Diego, and a few moments later, that same request from that same user might be served by a computer in Salt Lake City.

In addition to news articles, CDNs are often used to store and deliver content that seldom changes. For example, the company banner on an organization's Web page might be stored on many CDN servers. Various pieces of the Web page could be obtained from different servers on the CDN; all such decisions are made in real time to provide the fastest content delivery possible.

Figure 6-17 summarizes CDN benefits. The first two are self-explanatory. Reliability is increased because data are stored on many servers. If one server fails, any of a potentially large number of other servers can deliver the content. You will learn about denial-of-service (DOS) attacks in Chapter 10. For now, just understand that such security threats send so much data to a given server that the server's performance for legitimate traffic becomes unacceptable. By having multiple servers, CDNs help to protect against such attacks.

In some cases, CDNs reduce access costs for mobile users (those who do have a limited data account). By delivering the data faster, site connection charges can be reduced. Finally, many (but not all) CDN services are offered on a flexible, pay-as-you-go basis. Customers need not contract for fixed services and payments; they pay only for what they use, when they use it. Figure 6-18 shows an example of how CDN servers might be distributed. A number of vendors offer CDN.

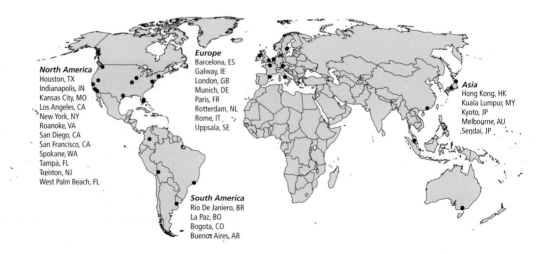

North America
Houston, TX
Indianapolis, IN
Kansas City, MO
Los Angeles, CA
New York, NY
Roanoke, VA
San Diego, CA
San Francisco, CA
Spokane, WA
Tampa, FL
Trenton, NJ
West Palm Beach, FL

Europe
Barcelona, ES
Galway, IE
London, GB
Munich, DE
Paris, FR
Rotterdam, NL
Rome, IT
Uppsala, SE

Asia
Hong Kong, HK
Kuala Lumpur, MY
Kyoto, JP
Melbourne, AU
Sendai, JP

South America
Rio De Janiero, BR
La Paz, BO
Bogota, CO
Buenos Aires, AR

Figure 6-18
Servers Used in a Typical CDN
Service

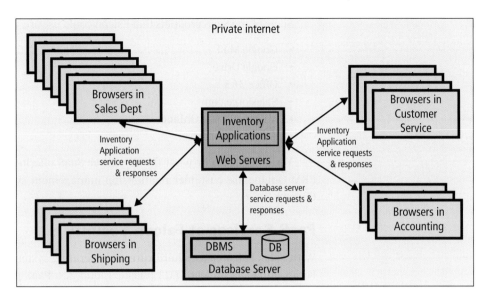

Figure 6-19
Web Services Principles Applied
to Inventory Applications

Using Web Services Internally

The third way that organizations can use cloud technology is to build internal information systems using Web services. Strictly speaking, this is not using the cloud because it does not provide elasticity nor the advantages of pooled resources. It does advantageously use cloud standards, however, so we include it here.

Figure 6-19 shows a Web services inventory application at a hypothetical online bicycle part retailer named Best Bikes. In this example, Best Bikes is running its own servers on its own infrastructure. To do so, Best Bikes sets up a private internet within the company, an internet that is generally not reachable from outside the company. Best Bikes writes the applications for processing inventory using Web services standards; applications publish a WSDL; the Web services are accessed by other applications within the company using SOAP; and data are delivered using JSON. Application users access the inventory Web services using JavaScript that is sent down to the users' browsers.

Users of the inventory Web services include Sales, Shipping, Customer Service, Accounting, and other departments. Internal applications can use the inventory Web services like building blocks. They can use the services that they need—and no more. Because the Web services are encapsulated, the inventory system can be altered without affecting other applications. In this way, systems development is more flexible, and it will be faster and hence less costly.

As stated, however, this is not a cloud. In this example, Best Bikes has a fixed number of servers; no attempt is made to make them elastic. Also, the servers are dedicated to inventory. During idle periods, they are not dynamically reused for other purposes. Some organizations remove this limit by creating a private cloud, as discussed in Q6-6.

Q6-5 How Can Falcon Security Use the Cloud?

Falcon Security is an innovative startup company with a small IT department. As such, it is unlikely to have the resources necessary to develop a large server infrastructure. Instead, it is far more likely to take advantage of cloud services provided by cloud vendors.

SaaS Services at Falcon Security

Software as a service requires little investment in the hardware and software system components. The SaaS vendor administers and manages the cloud servers and makes the software available, usually as a thin-client. Falcon will, however, need to transfer existing data, create new data, develop procedures, and train users.

Some of the SaaS products that Falcon could use are:

- Google Mail
- Google Drive
- Office 365
- Salesforce.com
- Microsoft CRM OnLine
- And many others ...

You already know what the first three SaaS offerings are. Salesforce.com and Microsoft's CRM OnLine are customer relationship management systems, which you will learn about in Chapter 7.

PaaS Services at Falcon Security

With PaaS, Falcon leases hardware and operating systems in the cloud from the cloud vendor. For example, it can lease EC2 (Elastic Cloud 2, a PaaS product offered by Amazon.com), and Amazon.com will preinstall either Linux or Windows Server on the cloud hardware. Given that basic capability, Falcon would then install its own software. For example, it could install its own, in-house developed applications, or it could install other applications licensed from a software vendor. It could also license a DBMS, say, SQL Server from Microsoft, and place it on an EC2 Windows Server instance. In the case of software licensed from others, Falcon must purchase licenses that permit replication because Amazon.com will replicate it when it increases servers.

Some cloud vendors include DBMS products in their PaaS services. Thus, Falcon could obtain Windows Servers with SQL Server already installed from the Microsoft Azure cloud offerings. That option is likely what Toshio was considering when he mentioned the $10 per TB per month.

DBMS are also included in other vendors' cloud offerings. As of May 2015 Amazon.com offers the following DBMS products with EC2:

Amazon Relational Database Service (RDS)	A relational database service supporting MySQL, Oracle, SQL Server, or PostgreSQL
Amazon DynamoDB	A fast and scalable NoSQL database service
MongoDB	A NoSQL DBMS product that stores objects in JSON format
Amazon ElastiCache	An very fast in-memory cache database service
Amazon Redshift	A petabyte-scale data warehouse

Finally, Falcon might use a CDN to distribute its content worldwide and to respond to leads generated from advertising as described in Q6-1.

IaaS Services at Falcon Security

As stated, IaaS provides basic hardware in the cloud. Some companies acquire servers this way and then load operating systems onto them. Doing so requires considerable technical expertise and management, and hence a company like Falcon is unlikely to do so.

Falcon might, however, obtain data storage services in the cloud. Amazon.com, for example, offers data storage with its S3 product. Using it, organizations can place data in the cloud and even have that data be made elastically available. Again, however, an organization like Falcon would more likely use SaaS and PaaS because of the added value they provide.

Q6-6 How Can Organizations Use Cloud Services Securely?

The Internet and cloud services based on Internet infrastructure provide powerful processing and storage services at a fraction of the cost of private data centers. However, the Internet is a jungle of threats to data and computing infrastructure, as discussed in Chapter 10. How can organizations realize the benefits of cloud technology without succumbing to those threats?

The answer involves a combination of technologies that we will address, at a very high level, in this question. As you read, realize that no security story is ever over; attackers constantly strive to find ways around security safeguards, and occasionally they succeed. Thus, you can expect that cloud security will evolve beyond that described here throughout your career. We begin with a discussion of VPNs, a technology used to provide secure communication over the Internet.

Virtual Private Networks (VPNs)

A **virtual private network (VPN)** uses the Internet to create the appearance of private, secure connections. In the IT world, the term *virtual* means something that appears to exist but in fact does not. Here, a VPN uses the public Internet to create the appearance of a private connection on a secure network.

A Typical VPN

Figure 6-20 shows one way to create a VPN to connect a remote computer, perhaps an employee working at a hotel in Miami, to a LAN at a Chicago site. The remote user is the VPN client. That client first establishes a public connection to the Internet. The connection can be obtained by accessing a local ISP, as shown in Figure 6-20, or, in some cases, the hotel itself provides a direct Internet connection.

In either case, once the Internet connection is made, VPN software on the remote user's computer establishes a connection with the VPN server in Chicago. The VPN client and VPN server then have a secure connection. That connection, called a **tunnel**, is a virtual, private pathway over a public or shared network from the VPN client to the VPN server. Figure 6-21 illustrates the connection as it appears to the remote user.

To secure VPN communications over the public Internet, the VPN client software *encrypts*, or codes (see Chapter 10, page 417), messages so their contents are protected from snooping. Then the VPN client appends the Internet address of the VPN server to the message and sends that package over the Internet to the VPN server. When the VPN server receives the message, it strips its address off the front of the message, *decrypts* the coded message, and

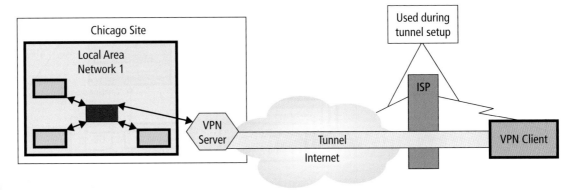

Figure 6-20
Remote Access Using VPN: Actual Connections

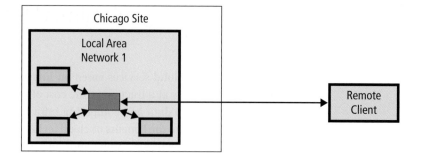

Figure 6-21
Remote Access Using VPN:
Apparent Connection

sends the plain text message to the original address inside the LAN. In this way, secure private messages are delivered over the public Internet.

Using a Private Cloud

A **private cloud** is a cloud owned and operated by an organization for its own benefit. To create a *private* cloud, the organization creates a private internet and designs applications using Web services standards just as shown in Figure 6-19 (page 261). The organization then creates a farm of servers and manages those servers with elastic load balancing just as the cloud service vendors do. Because of the complexity of managing multiple database servers, most organizations choose not to replicate database servers. Figure 6-22 illustrates this possibility.

Private clouds provide security *within* the organizational infrastructure but do not provide secure access from outside that infrastructure. To provide such access, organizations set up a VPN and users employ it to securely access the private cloud as shown in Figure 6-23.

Private clouds provide the advantages of elasticity, but to questionable benefit. What can organizations do with their idle servers? They could realize some cost savings by shutting down the idle servers. But unlike the cloud vendors, they cannot repurpose them for use by other companies. Possibly a large conglomerate or major international company could balance processing loads across subsidiary business units and across different geographical regions. 3M, for example,

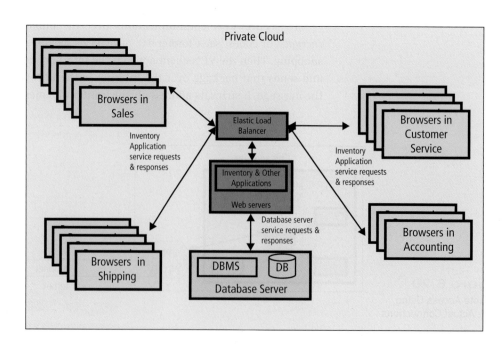

Figure 6-22
Private Cloud for Inventory
and Other Applications

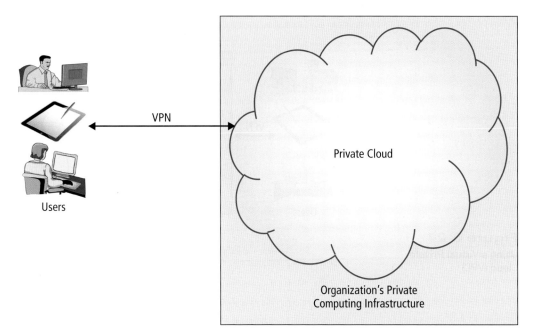

Figure 6-23

Accessing Private Cloud over a Virtual Private Network

might balance processing for its different product groups and on different continents, but it is difficult to imagine that, in doing so, it would save money or time. A company like Falcon Security is very unlikely to develop a private cloud.

Microsoft, Amazon.com, Oracle, IBM, and other major cloud service vendors employ thousands of highly trained, very highly skilled personnel to create, manage, administer, and improve their cloud services. It is unimaginable that any noncloud company, even large ones like 3M, could build and operate a cloud service facility that competes. The only situation in which this might make sense is if the organization is required by law or business custom to maintain physical control over its stored data. Even in that case, however, the organization is unlikely to be required to maintain physical control over all data, so it might keep critically sensitive data on-premises and place the rest of the data and related applications into the facilities of a public cloud vendor. It might also use a virtual private cloud, which we consider next.

Using a Virtual Private Cloud

A **virtual private cloud (VPC)** is a subset of a public cloud that has highly restricted, secure access. An organization can build its own VPC on top of public cloud infrastructure like AWS or that provided by other cloud vendors. The means by which this is done are beyond the scope of this text, but think of it as VPN tunneling on steroids.

Using a VPC, an organization can store its most sensitive data on its own infrastructure and store the less sensitive data on the VPC. In this way, organizations that are required to have physical control over some of their data can place that data on their own servers and locate the rest of their data on the VPC as shown in Figure 6-24. By doing so, the organization gains the advantages of cloud storage and possibly cloud processing for that portion of its data that it need not physically control.

In some cases, organizations have obtained permission from regulating bodies to store even their very sensitive data on a VPC. For example, Case Study 6 (pages 277–278) discusses FinQloud, a VPC set up and managed by NASDAQ OMX, the owner of the NASDAQ and other financial exchanges.

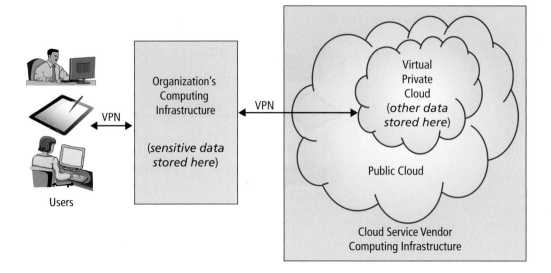

Figure 6-24
Using a Virtual Private Cloud (VPC)

 Q6-7 2026?

So where does the cloud go in the next 10 years? Absent some unknown factor such as a federal tax on Internet traffic, cloud services will become faster, more secure, easier to use, and cheaper. Fewer and fewer organizations will set up their own computing infrastructure; instead, they will benefit from the pooling of servers across organizations and from the economies of scale produced by cloud vendors.

But, looking a bit deeper, the cloud brings both good and bad news. The good news is that organizations can readily obtain elastic resources at very low cost. This trend will benefit everyone from individuals on the iCloud or Google Drive, to small groups using Office 365, to companies like Falcon Security using PaaS, to huge organizations like NASDAQ OMX (Case Study 6) using IaaS.

The overall size of the cloud is getting bigger too. For example, Google's Project Loon looks to seed the atmosphere with high-altitude balloons capable of providing Internet access to previously unreachable parts of the planet. And Google isn't stopping there. It's also making the cloud faster. Google Fiber aims to offer users 1 Gbps connections to the Internet. That's 100 times faster than the average broadband connection. Comcast responded to Google's plans by announcing its own gigabit-per-second service.

So what's the bad news? Remember that 500,000-square-foot Apple Web farm in Figure 6-2? Note the size of the parking lot. That tiny lot accommodates the entire operations staff. According to *Computerworld,* that building employs an operations staff of 50 people, which, spread over three shifts, 24/7, means that not many more than eight people will be running that center at any one time. Seems impossible, but is it? Again, look at the size of the parking lot.

And it's not just large companies like Apple. In 2015, every city of almost any size still supports small companies that install and maintain in-house email Exchange and other servers. If SaaS products like Google Drive or Office 365 replace those servers, what happens to those local jobs? They're gone! See Collaboration Exercise 6, page 276, for more on this topic.

But, with computing infrastructure so much cheaper, there have to be new jobs somewhere. By 2026, where will they be? For one, there will be more startups. Cheap and elastic cloud services enable small startups like the football player evaluation company Hudl (*www.hudl.com*) to access CDN and other cloud services for next to nothing, a capability that would have taken years and thousands of dollars in the past. Go to its site to check its response time; it's fast!

An organization like Falcon Security can reduce its storage costs by 50 percent if it moves its data to the cloud. If the move is successful, Falcon Security can increase profitability, have a

SO WHAT?

Net Neutrality Enabled

Have you ever wondered what it would have been like to live during the time of the Wild West? Outlaws were abundant, and early settlers were free to stake claim to land with minimal response or oversight from the government. If you stop and think about it, the spread of Internet-connected devices has, in many ways, created a similar environment—a digital Wild West.

The digital Wild West has many parallels to the old American frontier. Modern-day cyberspace bandits can commit deviant or criminal acts (e.g., cyberbullying, stealing data, denial-of-service attacks, cybervandalism, cyberwarfare) and are rarely caught or prosecuted. This lack of legal response to criminal acts is often due to an absence of existing laws needed to convict such offenders. Cybercriminals are also difficult to physically track down.

In the old American frontier, land was "up for grabs," and people rushed to stake claim to valuable land. Similarly, today's digital resources are up for grabs. Companies are trying to stake claim to intellectual property, data streams, and bandwidth. Internet service providers (ISPs), for example, have little control over the amount, type, or origin of the content they deliver. Why is this a problem? Consider the fact that in roughly the past 5 years, Netflix's streaming services have grown so rapidly that 30 percent of all Internet traffic in the United States during peak hours is associated with people watching movies and TV shows using Netflix.[4]

As an ISP, you may feel that Netflix should pay you a fee for clogging up your fiber lines with the release of a new season of a popular TV show. On the other hand, consumers and content providers want net neutrality. This would mean that all users and content providers would be treated equally. There wouldn't be "fast" and "slow" lanes on the Internet. ISPs wouldn't be allowed to block, or even slow, content associated with competing ISPs. They also couldn't charge heavy Internet users additional fees or taxes.

To address these issues, the Federal Communications Commission (FCC) recently made an important ruling on net neutrality and became the new sheriff in town!

Neutralizing Innovation?

In early 2015, the FCC approved new regulations to ensure that ISPs cannot discriminate between different types of Internet traffic. In short, all consumers will have access to content on an equal basis.[5] This ruling in many ways renders the Internet a utility. It

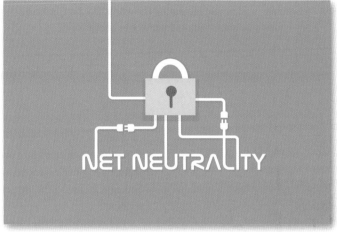

Source: bakhtiarzein/Fotolia

would be governed much like standard utilities (e.g., water and electricity) are by comparable regulations. Many people applauded this ruling. They pointed to the benefits of an Internet free of "fast" lanes and "slow" lanes. However, while on its surface it seems that this ruling can only be a good thing, there may be downsides to net neutrality.

People against net neutrality argue that it is yet another instance of the government interfering with free markets. This argument is based on laissez-faire economics, which advocates for a marketplace in which government intervention is not allowed. According to this principle, if a company is going to fail, it should fail and the marketplace will correct itself.

In the case of net neutrality, ISPs want to have the freedom to oversee Internet traffic flowing through their infrastructure. They want to be able to throttle it up or down based on whether content providers are paying them for better access. Because this capability has been ruled out by the FCC, ISPs are arguing that the loss of this potential revenue stream will inhibit infrastructure development, limit growth, and stifle new innovation.

Will we ever know if this claim by the ISPs is true? Maybe or maybe not. ISPs are working on finding ways to overturn this ruling. So while this battle is over, the larger war on net neutrality may have only just begun!

Questions

1. The feature states that access to the Internet can be compared to other utilities due to the regulations that government agencies are beginning to enforce. Do you agree or

disagree with the notion that the Internet is a utility? Explain your reasoning.

2. Imagine if the Internet was not protected by net neutrality. If you were an entrepreneur starting a new e-commerce company, how could your business be hurt by ISPs creating "fast" and "slow" lanes on the Internet?

3. The Internet is a resource used by governments, universities, businesses, and people all around the world. Do you think any one country or organization should be in charge of it?

4. Some economists may frown on the FCC getting involved in the operations of telecommunications companies and ISPs. Think of some examples of other potential harmful effects of net neutrality (besides the potential of lost revenue and stifled innovation).

5. Netflix was used as an example of a company that is instigating large volumes of Internet traffic. In what ways will the enforcement of net neutrality benefit Netflix?

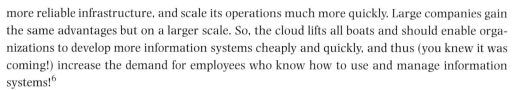

more reliable infrastructure, and scale its operations much more quickly. Large companies gain the same advantages but on a larger scale. So, the cloud lifts all boats and should enable organizations to develop more information systems cheaply and quickly, and thus (you knew it was coming!) increase the demand for employees who know how to use and manage information systems![6]

But what else? The cloud will foster new categories of work. By 2026, everything will be connected to everything else, with most data stored in the cloud. Mobile systems will be the standard; desktops will be relegated to content creators. So what new opportunities might arise?

Consider **remote action systems**, IS that provide computer-based activity or action at a distance. By enabling action at a distance, remote action systems save time and travel expense and make the skills and abilities of an expert available in places where he or she is not physically located. They also enable experts to scale their expertise. Let's look at a few examples.

Telediagnosis is a remote action system that healthcare professionals use to diagnose illness for patients in rural or remote areas. **Telesurgery** uses telecommunications to link surgeons to robotic equipment at distant locations. In 2001, Dr. Jacques Marescaux, located in New York City, performed the first trans-Atlantic surgery when he successfully operated on a patient in Strasbourg, France. Such examples, which are still rare, have problems that must be overcome, but they will become more common by 2026. In fact, the largest healthcare provider in the U.S., UnitedHealthcare, recently announced that all video-based doctor visits will be covered just like regular doctor visits.[7]

Other uses for remote systems include **telelaw enforcement**, such as the RedFlex system that uses cameras and motion-sensing equipment to issue tickets for red-light and speeding violations. The RedFlex Group, headquartered in South Melbourne, Victoria, Australia, earns 87 percent of its revenue from traffic violations in the United States. It offers a turn-key traffic citation information system that includes all five components.[8]

Many remote systems are designed to provide services in dangerous locations, such as robots that clean nuclear reactors or biologically contaminated sites. Drones and other unoccupied military equipment are examples of remote systems used in war zones. Private security and law enforcement will increasingly take advantage of remotely controlled flying drones and robots. You may see an upgraded form of Knightscope's 300-pound robot, named K5, patrolling your neighborhood in 2026.

But, even with these new opportunities, the news isn't all good. New York's Metropolitan Opera is arguably the finest opera company in the world. To see a live performance, you can drive to Manhattan, park your car, taxi to Lincoln Center, and pay $300 per seat. Or you can watch the same opera, remotely broadcast via Met Live, at a local movie theater, park your car for free, pay $12, and take a seat in the fourth row, where via the magic of digital broadcasting you can see details like the stitching on the singers' costumes. Details you just can't see from the $300 seats at the Met. And the sound quality is better. Wonderful, but now, who will go to a local opera performance?

Teleaction reduces the value of local mediocrity. The claim "Well, I'm not the best, but at least I'm here" loses value in a teleaction world. In 1990, when former Secretary of Labor Robert Reich wrote *The Work of Nations*,[9] he could sensibly claim that those who provide routine face-to-face services are exempt from the dangers of offshoring. That claim loses validity in the teleaction world.

By 2026, the value of the top-notch performers increases, possibly exponentially. Four million people watch the average Met Live broadcast; agents for the artists who perform at that venue will negotiate a sizable part of that $120 million gate. A famous surgeon or skating coach can reach a bigger market, faster and better, and be much better paid. So, if you can be the world's best at something, do it!

But what about the rest of us? If you're not the world's expert at something, then find a way to be indispensable to someone who is. Own the theaters that broadcast Met Live. Own the skating rink for the remote figure skating coach. Be the vendor of the food at some teleaction event.

Or become essential to the development, use, and management of information systems that support these new opportunities. A business background with IS expertise will serve you very well between now and 2026. The next six chapters discuss many existing and new IS applications. Keep reading!

Security Guide

FROM ANTHEM TO ANATHEMA

Have you ever lost your smartphone, even just for an hour or two? If so, you probably recall the wave of panic that set in when you thought it might be gone forever. Losing any digital device can be extremely troubling for a number of reasons. First, mobile devices and laptops are not cheap. The thought of spending hundreds of dollars, or even a couple thousand dollars in the case of a laptop, to replace the lost device is distressing. However, what often creates the most panic is the thought of the person now possessing your device finding a way to access all of your data.

If you were to lose a digital device, what data would you be most concerned about—banking data, email archives, social media accounts, your collection of photos, or something else? There is no right or wrong answer to this question, and responses vary from person to person. However, what is certain is the likelihood that in the future someone will access your personal data. The frustrating part is that in most cases, the culprits will not even need physical access to your smartphone or laptop. Your data can be stolen just as easily from a company storing it in the cloud. Don't believe it? Just ask anyone covered by Anthem health care in February 2015.

Cloudy with a Chance of Theft

More and more data are being stored in the cloud. Why? Because data storage costs have plummeted and Internet access has become faster and cheaper. In 1990, 1 million transistors cost $527, a gigabyte of storage cost $569, and a gigabit per second of bandwidth cost $1,245.[10] But today 1 million transistors cost $0.05, a gigabyte of storage costs $0.02, and a gigabit per second of bandwidth costs $15.

Internet users want easy access to more and more data. Unfortunately, the downside to greater accessibility is that it becomes more accessible to hackers too.

In early 2015, Anthem Insurance Companies, Inc. reported a security breach resulting in the loss of roughly 80 million customer accounts.[11] Hackers stole sensitive account data like names, addresses, Social Security numbers, and salaries. While any nationally publicized security breach will cause concern, especially in light of the recent trend in breaches with the Target and Home Depot incidents, Anthem customers became more and more irate as details about the nature of the breach were reported. Anthem eventually disclosed that the account data stolen had been stored in plain text—not encrypted. This meant that hackers could immediately begin selling the data on the black market or using it for other nefarious purposes.

Security experts criticized Anthem for not encrypting sensitive customer account data. Numerous clients considered

Anthem's failure to encrypt account records negligent, and they subsequently filed lawsuits.

Bad for Business or Business as Usual?

How would you feel if your account data had been part of the Anthem breach? Would this incident make you want to switch to a different healthcare provider, or would you recognize that large corporate data breaches are just a fact of life in a digital world and that your new healthcare provider could be equally vulnerable? The reality is that data breaches are so pervasive that it is not a matter of if, but when, a company holding data about you will be hacked. In fact, about a month after the Anthem data breach,

Premera Blue Cross announced the loss of 11 million customer records. The lost customer records were even more sensitive because they included bank-account and medical data.[12]

Despite these threats, it is highly unlikely that companies will begin pulling data from the cloud. Consumers clearly want the ease of use that Web-based services provide. However, it is possible that corporations' security practices could evolve from being a necessary evil to becoming a competitive advantage. In fact, there could come a time when a company's reputation for information security could be more valuable than the very products or services it sells!

 DISCUSSION QUESTIONS

1. Think about all of the cloud services you use. How vulnerable are you right now to having your data stolen?

2. What are some of the ways you can lower the chances of your personal data being stolen?

3. The article explains how Anthem failed to encrypt sensitive account data. Why would encrypting account data make it more secure?

4. Have prior data breaches, like those at Home Depot or Target, affected your behavior as a consumer? How?

5. How can a greater awareness of security best practices help you in your current job?

Guide

IS IT SPYING OR JUST GOOD MANAGEMENT?

According to a 2007 survey by American Management Association, 66 percent of employers monitor employees' Internet connections.[13] They also monitor email (43 percent), keystrokes (45 percent), stored files (43 percent), blogs (12 percent), and social networking sites (10 percent). That survey is 8 years old, and it is likely that, if anything, employer monitoring of employee activities has increased. A number of different techniques are used:

- **Key loggers.** A key logger is a program that records all of your keystrokes. Employers can install key loggers without a problem on any corporate computer. If you allow your employer to configure your personal mobile device as part of its BYOD policy, it can install a key logger on it as well.

  Key loggers do just what their name implies; they record *everything* you key: user IDs, passwords, text messages, emails, documents, and so forth. They are agnostic about what they record. If you check your personal banking account on an employer-owned computer, your employer (and its IT personnel) has everything it needs to manage your banking account. If you write a love letter to your spouse, the key logger will record it.

- **Log files.** Computer systems are indefatigable diarists. Your employer-provided computer or mobile device and any employer server that you connect to with a personal device keep extensive logs of your activity. Those logs show, in part, when you start work, when you end work, how long your computer is idle at work, and possibly, if the device has GPS, where your device has been. Logs also show what files you process and much information about your activities over the employer-managed networks.

- **Packet sniffers.** A **packet sniffer** is a program that captures network traffic.

Most operate on wireless networks, but they are readily installed to work on wired networks as well. Packet sniffers obtain the text of unsecured email (most email), text messages, and Internet sites visited. They also can obtain voice traffic processed over the Internet. Any traffic that passes through an organization's networks, whether from your employer-provided device, your personal device, or your personal computer at home (if you're using the corporate network), can be sniffed.

Your employer could also have video surveillance cameras, audio recorders, office spies, and numerous other ways of watching you, but let's leave those aside.

As you think about the amount of data that key logging files, log files, and packet sniffing files contain, you may feel secure that out of the millions of messages sent and received, your employer is unlikely to find your problematic ones. **Text mining** is the application of statistical techniques on text streams for locating particular words or patterns of particular words and even correlating word counts and patterns with personality profiles. The results can be used to find undesirable employees such as thieves, sexual predators,

Source: Image Source/Getty Images

those engaged in an illicit romance, and any other profiles the employer creates (disgruntled employee?). So hiding in the company data pile is little protection.

Aha, you're thinking. What about the First Amendment? It protects me, no? Alas, no. The First Amendment preserves your free speech regarding laws Congress may enact, and while in some limited sense it does protect federal employees, it doesn't protect anyone else at work.

Well, you think, they can't fire me for just anything, can they? Alas, again, unless you have negotiated an employment contract, you are what the attorneys call *an employee at will.* That means the employer can fire you for any reason whatsoever.[14] The only exceptions are that you cannot be fired because of your race, gender, religion, or disability. You also cannot be fired for performing a public service such as jury duty. But, if you write an email on a computer at work that says your boss's spouse is a jerk, he or she can fire you (the boss, not the spouse).

 DISCUSSION QUESTIONS

1. List the types of data you think are appropriate for your employer to gather about you:
   a. On employer-provided devices.
   b. On personal devices used at work or at home on employer-provided networks.
2. As a manager, list the types of data you would like to obtain on your employees.
3. If there are differences between your answers to questions 1 and 2, explain and justify the differences.
4. Under what circumstances do you think it is appropriate for your employer to install a key logger on your personal mobile device?
5. Suppose someone from your IT department informs you that the company has evidence that one of your married subordinates is conducting an affair with someone not his or her spouse:
   a. What would you do if the affair involves two people who work at your employer?
   b. What would you do if the affair involves someone not employed by your company?
   c. Do you think obtaining such knowledge is appropriate?
6. Given what you have learned regarding electronic surveillance at work, state your own personal guidelines for computer use.
7. Reread the definition of job security in Chapter 1. Using that definition as a foundation, state what you can do, as an employee at will, to avoid being fired for a frivolous reason.

ACTIVE REVIEW

Use this Active Review to verify that you understand the ideas and concepts that answer the chapter's study questions.

Q6-1   Why is the cloud the future for most organizations?

Define *cloud* and explain the three key terms in your definition. Using Figure 6-3 as a guide, compare and contrast cloud-based and in-house hosting. Explain three factors that make cloud computing possible today. When does it not make sense to use a cloud-based infrastructure?

Q6-2   What network technology supports the cloud?

Define *computer network*. Explain the differences among PANs, LANs, WANs, intranets, internets, and the Internet. Describe protocol and explain the purpose of protocols. Explain the key distinction of a LAN. Describe the purpose of each component in Figure 6-5. Define *IEEE 802.3* and *802.11* and explain how they differ. List three ways of connecting a LAN or computer to the Internet. Explain the nature of each.

Q6-3   How does the cloud work?

Explain the statement, "The Internet is an internet." Define *IP address* and explain the different ways that public and private IP addresses are used. Describe the purpose of a domain name and explain how such names are associated with public IP addresses. Explain the role for agencies like GoDaddy. Define *URL*.

Define *three-tier architecture* and name and describe the role of each tier. Explain the role of each tier in Figure 6-10 as well as how the pages in Figures 6-9 and 6-11 are processed. Using the department analogy, define *SOA* and explain why departments are encapsulated. Summarize the advantages of using SOA in the three-tier architecture.

Define *TCP/IP protocol architecture* and explain, in general terms, the purpose of http, https, smtp, and ftp. Define the purpose and role of WSDL, SOAP, XML, and JSON. State a key difference between XML and JSON.

Q6-4   How do organizations use the cloud?

Define *SaaS, PaaS,* and *IaaS*. Provide an example of each. For each, describe the business situation in which it would be the most appropriate option. Define *CDN* and explain the purpose and advantages of a CDN. Explain how Web services can be used internally.

Q6-5   How can Falcon Security use the cloud?

First, state why Falcon is likely to use the cloud. Name and describe SaaS products that Falcon could use. Explain several ways that Falcon could use PaaS offerings. Summarize why it is unlikely that Falcon would use IaaS.

Q6-6   How can organizations use cloud services securely?

Explain the purpose of a VPN and describe, in broad terms, how a VPN works. Define the term *virtual* and explain how it relates to VPN. Define *private cloud*. Summarize why the benefits of a private cloud are questionable. What kind of organization might benefit from such a cloud? Explain why it is unlikely that even very large organizations can create private clouds that compete with public cloud utilities. Under what circumstance might a private cloud make sense for an organization? Define *VPC* and explain how and why an organization might use one.

Q6-7   2026?

What is the likely future for the cloud? Summarize the good and bad news the cloud brings. Explain why the photo in Figure 6-2 is disturbing. Explain the statement, "The cloud lifts all boats." Describe three categories of remote action systems. Explain how remote systems will increase the value of super-experts but diminish local mediocrity. What can other-than-super-experts do? Summarize how this 2026 discussion pertains to your career hopes.

Using Your Knowledge with Falcon Security

Name the principal advantage of the cloud to Falcon Security. For hosting its data, which cloud offering—SaaS, PaaS, or IaaS—makes the most sense, given the size and nature of Falcon's business? Explain how Falcon could use that offering. If Falcon were larger and employed a more sophisticated IT staff, name another alternative that would make sense. Explain why.

KEY TERMS AND CONCEPTS

MyMISLab™

To complete the problems with the ⭐, go to EOC Discussion Questions in the MyLab.

USING YOUR KNOWLEDGE

⭐ **6-1.** Search the web for TCO (Total Cost of Ownership). Explain the TCO model. How can TCO model help organizations decide whether to buy the software or obtain it from the cloud vendor?

⭐ **6-2.** Apple invested more than $1B in the North Carolina data center mentioned in Q6-1. For Apple to spend such a sum, it must perceive the iCloud as being a key component of its future. Using the principles discussed in Q3-7 of Chapter 3, explain all the ways you believe the iCloud will give Apple a competitive advantage over other mobile device vendors.

⭐ **6-3.** Suppose you manage a group of seven employees in a small business. Each of your employees wants to be connected to the Internet. Consider two alternatives:

Alternative A: Each employee has his or her own device and connects individually to the Internet.

Alternative B: The employees' computers are connected using a LAN, and the network uses a single device to connect to the Internet.

a. Sketch the equipment and lines required for eachalternative.

b. Explain the actions you need to take to create each alternative.

c. Which of these two alternatives would you recommend?

6-4. a. Is cloud- based hosting suitable for all organizations? Explain.

   b. Suppose that the cloud- based hosting is not suitable for an organization, but the organization still wants to use cloud computing to reap its benefits. Describe two different ways in which the company can still use cloud computing.

6-5. A company that sells news online, wants to deliver content to its customers more quickly and efficiently based on their geographic location. How can it achieve this? Explain.

6-6. Describe the three trends that have led to the growth of cloud computing.

COLLABORATION EXERCISE 6

Using the collaboration IS you built in Chapter 2 (page 110), collaborate with a group of students to answer the following questions.

The cloud is causing monumental changes in the information systems services industry. In every city, you will still see the trucks of local independent software vendors (ISVs) driving to their clients to set up and maintain local area networks, servers, and software. You'll know the trucks by the Microsoft, Oracle, and Cisco logos on their sides. For years, those small, local companies have survived, some very profitably, on their ability to set up and maintain LANs, connect user computers to the Internet, set up servers, sell Microsoft Exchange licenses, and install other software on both servers and user computers.

Once everything is installed, these companies continued to earn revenue by providing maintenance for problems that inevitably developed and support for new versions of software, connecting new user computers, and so forth. Their customers vary, but generally are smaller companies of, say, 3 to 50 employees—companies that are large enough to need email, Internet connections, and possibly some entry-level software applications such as QuickBooks.

6-7. Using the knowledge of this chapter and the intuition of the members of your team, summarize threats that cloud services present to such ISVs.

6-8. Suppose your team owns and manages one of these ISVs. You learn that more and more of your clients are choosing SaaS cloud services like Google for email, rather than setting up local email servers.

   a. What, if anything, can you do to prevent the encroachment of SaaS on your business?

   b. Given your answer to question 6-8a, identify three alternative ways you can respond.

   c. Which of the three responses identified in your answer to question 6-8b would you choose? Justify your choice.

6-9. Even if SaaS eliminates the need for email and other local servers, there will still remain viable services that you can provide. Name and describe those services.

6-10. Suppose instead of attempting to adapt an existing ISV to the threat of cloud services, you and your teammates decide to set up an entirely new business, one that will succeed in the presence of SaaS and other cloud services. Looking at businesses in and around your campus, identify and describe the IS needs those businesses will have in the cloud services world.

6-11. Describe the IS services that your new business could provide for the business needs you identified in your answer to question 6-10.

6-12. Given your answers to questions 6-7 through 6-11, would you rather be an existing ISV attempting to adapt to this new world or an entirely new company? Compare and contrast the advantages and disadvantages of each alternative.

6-13. Refer to Figure 6-6 and find out how the computers in your college/university are connected. Fill the first part of the table using this information. The next task is to find out the major DSL, cable line, and WAN wireless connection service providers in your city. Also, find out the connection to the internet in your college/ university lab. Fill the bottom half of the table using this information.

CASE STUDY 6

Cloud Solutions that Test for Consumer Risk and Financial Stability

In 1986, Europe's pre-eminent financial centre in the city of London was de-regulated, giving its financial services industry, centered on the London Stock Exchange, a major boost that enabled it to expand beyond the relatively constrained confines of its physical borders. This was termed a 'Big Bang' at the time, and continues to be a useful metaphor and short-hand today. This enabled financial services companies and banks, in particular, to do business more freely between themselves, their customers, and their international counterparts in Africa, Asia, the Middle East, the United States, and other European countries. Parallel regulatory developments were also taking place in other regional financial centers, including Singapore and Japan, centered on their respective stock exchanges. Although regulation of the financial services industry continued to be of critical importance to the government and regulators alike for reasons of consumer protection and general financial stability, it was believed that a lighter touch approach was appropriate at a time when information technologies were emerging as major business tools and replacing an increasing number of manual processes.

In 1986, regulatory authorities continued to use traditional approaches to audit and regulate, which relied predominantly on the paper documents and records of transactions that were certified by accountancy and ratings agencies according to the prevailing legal requirements of the time. In 1997, the majority of the manual processes of conducting financial services industry business had moved to information systems involving computer screen-based trading. By the 2000s, huge advances in computing power coupled with highly sophisticated financial algorithms meant that new, innovative financial products were being developed and traded in the same way as the more traditional ones. However, it soon became apparent after the onset of the global financial crisis of 2007 that the increasingly light touch to financial regulation, which was also a feature of this time, was inappropriate in light of the highly technical nature of the computer-based transactions and the speed of innovation in the financial services industry.

With the advent of economic recovery in 2013, regulators sought to introduce a regulatory framework that is sensitive to the creation of innovative products and services emerging from the financial services industry while at the same time applying an appropriate level of regulation. The major regional financial centers and their respective regulators were looking closely at the role new technology trends could play in transforming the financial services industry. The Monetary Authority of Singapore (MAS) was evaluating 'FinTech', and the Financial Services Agency of Japan (FSA) and its 'FISC' were evaluating new technology infrastructures, including those based on cloud. In Europe, the Sandbox toolkit developed by the United Kingdom's Financial Conduct Authority (FCA) in 2015 is indicative of the financial regulation that is intended to minimize risk to consumers of new financial products and services while at the same time preserving general financial stability. The FCA describes the Sandbox as

> "…a regulatory sandbox that is a 'safe space' in which businesses can test innovative products, services, business models, and delivery mechanisms without immediately incurring all the normal regulatory consequences of engaging in the activity in question … a sandbox could allow a firm to make their advice platform available to a limited number of consumers. As a safeguard, once the advice is issued, but before transactions are executed, financial advisers would review the advice. This would allow firms to learn how consumers interact with their advice platform and how their algorithm performs compared to human assessment."

From this description of the sandbox, it is clear that the new product or service to be tested is conducted under real-world conditions involving real consumers who remain subject to legal rules. Other constraints, which could put them at risk and be detrimental to the result, also need to be carefully considered before testing.

The FCA has proposed a virtual sandbox based on a Cloud solution to address the real-world concerns that will simulate the real-world data and interactions between the consumers and the new financial product or service being tested. The FCA describes this as

> "…a cloud-based solution set up and equipped in collaboration between the industry, which businesses then could customize for their products or services, run tests with public data sets or data provided by other firms through the virtual sandbox, and then invite firms or even consumers to try their new solution. In this environment, there is no risk of consumer detriment, risk to market integrity or financial stability while testing."

On the back end, the 'sandbox' Cloud uses Microsoft's Azure product to provide a scalable, elastic storage. When financial services companies wish to simulate their new products and services, they submit their algorithm to the 'sandbox' Cloud for storage, and processing, to test aspects of this, including the business model, with respect to regulatory requirements and risks to the consumer. The results of the simulation determine whether the model or some other aspect of the new financial product or service need adjustment (as codified in the algorithm) to bring these within acceptable risk profiles for the consumer and the more general financial environment.

QUESTIONS

6-14. In your own words, summarize the approaches to regulation of the financial services industry in the run-up to the 'Big Bang' and the global financial crash, and explain why for most financial services organizations, the Cloud offers the best future IT infrastructure solution.

6-15. In your own words, explain how a Cloud-based solution will reduce risks to consumers who use products of financial services organizations post the global financial crash.

6-16. Clearly, in the view of the FCA, a virtual, Cloud-based sandbox holds the promise of minimizing the risks of financial services and products offered to consumers globally. Justify this view.

6-17. Do you agree with the view put forth in question 6-16? Explain why or why not and place your answer in the context of how financial services organizations can use the Cloud services securely.

6-18. If you were a consultant to global financial services industry organizations, how would advise them about the extent of their involvement in the FCA's Cloud-based virtual 'sandbox' project?

6-19. If you were a consultant to a global financial services company, what else might you do to build their confidence in the Cloud-based virtual sandbox?

6-20. Explain how the knowledge you have gained so far in this course helps you to understand the FCA's 'sandbox' Cloud system proposal.

MyMISLab™

Go to the Assignments section of your MyLab to complete these writing exercises.

6-21. Suppose that you work at Falcon Security and Joni tells you that she doesn't believe that cheap, elastic provisioning of data storage is possible. "There has to be a catch somewhere," she says. Write a one-page memo to her explaining how the cloud works. In your memo, include the role of standards for cloud processing.

6-22. Suppose you manage a sales department that uses the SaaS product Salesforce.com. One of your key salespeople refuses to put his data into that system. "I just don't believe that the competition can't steal my data, and I'm not taking that risk." How do you respond to him?

ENDNOTES

1. Patrick Thibodeau, "Apple, Google, Facebook Turn N.C. into Data Center Hub," *Computerworld*, June 3, 2011, *www.computerworld.com/ s/article/9217259/Apple_Google_Facebook_turn_N.C._into_data_ center_hub*.

2. Milton Friedman, "The Social Responsibility of Business Is to Increase Its Profits," *The New York Times Magazine*, September 13, 1970.

3. Don Reisinger, "Netflix Gobbles a Third of Peak Internet Traffic in North America," *CNET*, November 7, 2012, accessed June 6, 2014, *www.cnet.com/news/ netflix-gobbles-a-third-of-peak-internet-traffic-in-north-america*.

4. M. Prince, "Thoughts on Network Neutrality, the FCC, and the Future of Internet Governance." February 27, 2015, accessed April 10, 2015, *https://blog.cloudflare.com/net-neutrality*.

5. Mike Snider, Roger Yu, and Emily Brown, "What Is Net Neutrality and What Does It Mean for Me?" *USA Today*, February 27, 2015, accessed April 10, 2015, *www.usatoday.com/story/tech/2015/02/24/ net-neutrality-what-is-it-guide/23237737*.

6. See, for example, *http://online.wsj.com/article/SB100014241278873 23744604578470900844821388.html?mod=itp, accessed May 2013*.

7. Issie Lapowsky, "Video Is About to Become the Way We All Visit the Doctor," *Wired*, April 30, 2015, accessed May 4, 2015, *www.wired. com/2015/04/united-healthcare-telemedicine*.

8. Traffic citation information system is not a commonly accepted term, but providing all five components is essentially IS as a service, or ISaaS.

9. Robert Reich, *Work of Nations: Preparing Ourselves for Twenty-first Century Capitalism* (New York: Vintage Books, 1992), p. 176.

10. Gene Marks, "Why the Anthem Breach Just Doesn't Matter Anymore," *Forbes*, February 9, 2015, accessed April 22, 2015, *www.forbes.com/sites/quickerbettertech/2015/02/09/ why-the-anthem-breach-just-doesnt-matter-anymore*.

11. Tom Huddleston, "Anthem's Big Data Breach Is Already Sparking Lawsuits," *Fortune*, February 6, 2015, accessed April 22, 2015, *http://fortune.com/2015/02/06/ anthems-big-data-breach-is-already-sparking-lawsuits*.

12. Coral Garnick, "Premera Negligent in Data Breach, 5 Lawsuits Claim," *Seattle Times*, March 27, 2015, accessed April 22, 2015, *www.seattletimes.com/seattle-news/ premera-negligent-in-data-breach-5-lawsuits-claim*.

13. American Management Association, "2007 Electronic Monitoring & Surveillance Survey," amanet.org, February 28, 2008, accessed May 5, 2015, *www.amanet.org/training/articles/The-Latest-on-Workplace-Monitoring-and-Surveillance.aspx*.

14. Lewis Maltby, *Can They Do That?* (New York: Penguin Group, 2009), pp. 60–62.

15. UK Financial Conduct Authority, "FCA Regulatory sandbox", www.fca.org.uk., accessed on January 2016. Monetary Authority of Singapore, "MAS sets up new FinTech and Innovation Group", www.mas.gov.sg., accessed on January 2016. Financial Services Agency of Japan, "The FSA's Center for Financial Industry Information Systems Cloud Report", www.fisc.or.jp/english., accessed on January 2016.

Using IS for Competitive Advantage

In the previous six chapters, you gained a foundation of IS fundamentals. In Chapters 7–12, you will apply those fundamentals to learn how organizations use information systems to achieve their strategies. Part 3, Chapters 7–9, focuses on application of IS; Part 4, Chapters 10–12, focuses on management of IS.

Chapters 7–12 are introduced using a cloud-based, mobile application for the healthcare industry. To our knowledge, the system described here does not yet exist. However, it is entirely plausible, may be an excellent entrepreneurial opportunity, and features some of today's most exciting emerging technology in one of today's most important industries.

Source: Nongkran_ch/iStock/Thinkstock/Getty Images; Christopher Futcher/E+/ Getty Images

Collaboration

FBA

Office 365

Jobs!

Google+ vs. Facebook

The figure on the next page shows the major actors involved in this system, which we will call Performance Recording, Integration, Delivery, and Evaluation (PRIDE). Using PRIDE, exercise workout data is collected from devices that conform to the ANT[1] protocol, which is a personal network communications protocol implemented by exercise equipment such as treadmills, stationary bikes, heart monitors, footpads, and the like. Using this protocol, data is transmitted from exercise devices to the Internet, either via a local area network or via a cell phone. That exercise data is then stored in a cloud database.

Once the data is stored in the cloud, individuals, healthcare professionals, health clubs, insurance companies, and employers can query and obtain exercise reports. Doctors can ensure that their patients are exercising neither too little nor too much; health clubs can integrate exercise class data with personal exercise data; insurance companies can use that data to adjust policy rates for policy holders with

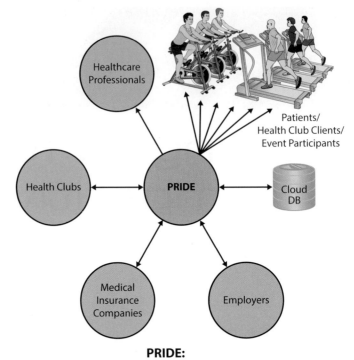

PRIDE:
Performance Recording, Integration, Display, and Evaluation

healthy lifestyles; and employers can assess the effectiveness of investments they make into improving employee health.

A prototype of this system was developed by a cardiac surgeon, Dr. Romero Flores, for use in his practice. The system was popular and helped patients recover from cardiac surgery, at least as long as Flores was pushing it in his own practice. Flores hoped to license this system to other doctors, but he had no success.

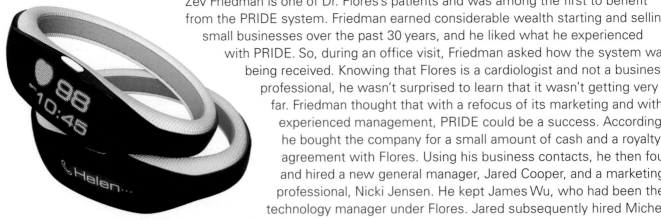

Source: Chesky_W/iStock/Thinkstock/Getty Images

Zev Friedman is one of Dr. Flores's patients and was among the first to benefit from the PRIDE system. Friedman earned considerable wealth starting and selling small businesses over the past 30 years, and he liked what he experienced with PRIDE. So, during an office visit, Friedman asked how the system was being received. Knowing that Flores is a cardiologist and not a business professional, he wasn't surprised to learn that it wasn't getting very far. Friedman thought that with a refocus of its marketing and with experienced management, PRIDE could be a success. Accordingly, he bought the company for a small amount of cash and a royalty agreement with Flores. Using his business contacts, he then found and hired a new general manager, Jared Cooper, and a marketing professional, Nicki Jensen. He kept James Wu, who had been the technology manager under Flores. Jared subsequently hired Michele Russell as sales director.

Processes, Organizations, and Information Systems

Zev Friedman, the owner of PRIDE Systems, Jared Cooper, general manager, Nicki Jensen, marketing professional, and James Wu, IS professional, are having an introductory meeting at Friedman's luxurious house on a Saturday morning.

After polite conversation, Zev gets down to business.

"Here's where Flores went wrong. Doctors don't care about exercise." Zev looks around the table as he speaks.

"They say they do." Nicki's not sure Zev will tolerate interruption, but it's not her style to sit back and listen.

"What people say and what they do are two different things. Doctors care about medicine and operations, and some care most about *expensive* operations. If they cared about exercise, they'd own health clubs." Zev's tone is matter of fact; Nicki's interruption didn't bother him at all.

"So we need to figure out who's got the pain and how much they'll pay." Jared, PRIDE Systems' new general manager, likes Zev's forthright manner.

"Right. Flores and his group demonstrated this thing works. You can use the cloud and all this exercise gear and mobile devices to collect, integrate, and report exercise data. So, who do we sell it to, and what do we tell 'em to induce them to buy?"

"I talked to a couple of insurance companies, and they're not promising." Jared looks at Zev.

"No? Why not?" Zev knows the answer, but he wants to see if Jared does.

"They don't like exercise. Exercise doesn't prevent disease. Well, maybe some cardiac diseases, and long term maybe some diabetes, but it doesn't do anything for cancer or Alzheimer's. The insurance companies think exercise just raises claims due to exercise-induced injury."

"You're kidding." Nicki can't believe what's she's hearing.

"Even worse, to them anyway, when you get in good shape, you last longer when you do get cancer or whatever. So, you live longer on your way out the door, and their care expenses increase."

"I can't believe I'm hearing this!" Nicki says what she's been thinking.

"How much money does a system own?"

Image source: jiris/Fotolia

"So, Zev, I'm wondering, do you think there's any government money in this? Obamacare funds we could tap?" Jared's looking right at Zev.

"Maybe. I'll ask some friends. That kind of money is slow to get, and the reporting requirements can be so painful it's not worth it. But I'll find out what I can. That won't help us immediately, though."

"Well, the real beneficiary of this is the whole system. All the players together." James speaks up for the first time.

"Young man, you may be right. But let me ask you, how much money does a system own?" Zev is gentle, but privately he's amazed at James's naiveté.

"Well, none, Mr. Friedman." James figures out where this is going.

"Then the system can't be a buyer, can it? Saying the system gets the benefits might make sense to you techies, but it won't make sense down at the bank." Zev is still gentle, but James is squirming.

"I see. OK." James is embarrassed but has the good sense to shut up.

"Well, besides the medical players, there are employers, health clubs, equipment manufacturers, and people who exercise." Jared is counting on his fingers as he speaks.

STUDY QUESTIONS

Q7-1 What are the basic types of processes?

Q7-2 How can information systems improve process quality?

Q7-3 How do information systems eliminate the problems of information silos?

Q7-4 How do CRM, ERP, and EAI support enterprise processes?

Q7-5 What are the elements of an ERP system?

Q7-6 What are the challenges of implementing and upgrading enterprise information systems?

Q7-7 How do inter-enterprise IS solve the problems of enterprise silos?

Q7-8 2026?

"Jared, take a look at those. I suspect employers will respond just as negatively as insurance companies, but maybe not, at least maybe not some. Find out."

"OK."

"You have to show the health clubs how PRIDE adds revenue to them, if it does. Same with the manufacturers." Zev looks at Nicki. "So, Nicki, what have you got to say?"

"Well, I think we should think about selling ads, you know, placing them on our competition sites and clicks. "

"Go on."

"Some sort of an ad revenue model based on use. But for that we need to get our numbers up. We have to get people using PRIDE in large groups. Maybe some events, social media–driven."

"I like that, but is it real? Let's find out. Jared, you look into the health clubs and employers. Nicki, you put some meat on your ad revenue idea, and James, you figure out if PRIDE can support, say, 10,000 people spinning at the same time, in the same contest. Questions?"

Everyone looks around the table; no one says a word.

"OK, see you next week."

CHAPTER PREVIEW

This chapter explores processes and their supporting information systems within levels of an organization. We will extend the business process discussion from Chapter 3 to investigate three types of processes and the scope of information systems they use. We will also investigate the concept of process quality and explain how information systems can be used to increase it. Then we will discuss how the use of information systems at one level of organization leads to information silos, explain the problems of such silos, and then show how those problems can be solved by information systems at the next level of organization. In particular, we'll discuss how enterprise systems such as CRM, ERP, and EAI (you'll learn the meaning of those terms) solve problems caused by workgroup information silos. ERP systems play a particularly important role, and we'll discuss their purpose and components and the major ERP vendors. Then we'll survey the major challenges that occur when implementing enterprise systems. We'll wrap up the chapter by showing how inter-enterprise IS can solve the problems of enterprise-level silos and finally, in 2026, discuss the implications of mobility and the cloud on future enterprise and inter-enterprise IS.

Q7-1 What Are the Basic Types of Processes?

As you learned in Chapter 3, a business process is a network of activities that generate value by transforming inputs into outputs. Activities are subparts of processes that receive inputs and produce outputs. Activities can be performed by humans only, by humans augmented by computer systems, and by computer systems only.

Figure 7-1 shows a simplified view of a three-activity process for approving customer orders. Each of these activities is, itself, a subprocess of this overall process. You can see that each step—check inventory, check customer credit, and approve special terms—receives inputs and transforms them into outputs. You will learn how to better diagram such processes in Chapter 12; for now, just view Figure 7-1 as showing the gist of a typical business process.

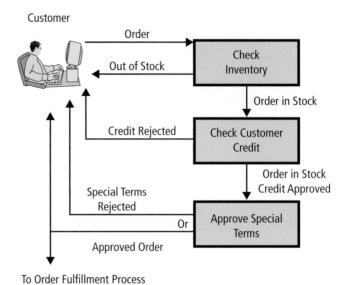

Figure 7-1

Business Process with
Three Activities

How Do Structured Processes Differ from Dynamic Processes?

Businesses have dozens, hundreds, even thousands of different processes. Some processes are stable, almost fixed sequences of activities and data flows. For example, the process of a sales-clerk accepting a return at Nordstrom, or other quality retail stores, is fixed. If the customer has a receipt, take these steps...if the customer has no receipt, take these other steps. That process needs to be standardized so that customers are treated consistently and correctly, so that returned goods are accounted for appropriately, and so that sales commissions are reduced in a way that is fair to the sales staff.

Other processes are less structured, less rigid, and often creative. For example, how does Nordstrom's management decide what women's clothes to carry next spring? Managers can look at past sales, consider current economic conditions, and make assessments about women's accep-tance of new styles at recent fashion shows, but the process for combining all those factors into orders of specific garments in specific quantities and colors is not nearly as structured as that for accepting returns.

In this text, we divide processes into two broad categories. **Structured processes** are for-mally defined, standardized processes that involve day-to-day operations: accepting a return, placing an order, purchasing raw materials, and so forth. They have the characteristics summa-rized in the left-hand column of Figure 7-2.

Dynamic processes are flexible, informal, and adaptive processes that normally involve stra-tegic and less structured managerial decisions and activities. Deciding whether to open a new store location and how best to solve the problem of excessive product returns are examples, as is using Twitter to generate buzz about next season's product line. Dynamic processes usually require human judgment. The right-hand column of Figure 7-2 shows characteristics of dynamic processes.

We will discuss structured processes and information systems that support them in this chapter. We have already discussed one dynamic process, collaboration, in Chapter 2, and we will discuss another, social media, in Chapter 8. Some aspects of business intelligence, in Chapter 9, are also dynamic processes.

For the balance of this chapter, we will use the term *process* to mean *structured process*.

How Do Processes Vary by Organizational Scope?

Processes are used at three levels of organizational scope: workgroup, enterprise, and inter-enterprise. In general, the wider the scope of the process, the more challenging the process is to manage. For example, processes that support a single workgroup function, say, accounts

Structured	Dynamic
Support operational and structured managerial decisions and activities	Support strategic and less structured managerial decision and activities
Standardized	Less specific, fluid
Usually formally defined and documented	Usually informal
Exceptions rare and not (well) tolerated	Exceptions frequent and expected
Process structure changes slowly and with organizational agony	Adaptive processes that change structure rapidly and readily
Example: Customer returns, order entry, purchasing, payroll, etc.	**Example:** Collaboration; social networking; ill-defined, ambiguous situations

Figure 7-2
Structured Versus Dynamic Processes

payable, are simpler and easier to manage than those that support a network of independent organizations, such as a supply chain. Consider processes at each of these three organizational scopes.

Workgroup Processes

A **workgroup process** exists to enable workgroups to fulfill the charter, purpose, and goals of a particular group or department. A physicians' partnership is a workgroup that follows processes to manage patient records, issue and update prescriptions, provide standardized postsurgery care, and so forth.

Figure 7-3 lists common workgroup processes. Notice that each of these processes is largely contained within a given department. These processes may receive inputs from other departments, and they may produce outputs used by other departments, but all, or at least the bulk of, the processes' activities lay within a single department.

A **workgroup information system** exists to support one or more processes within the workgroup. For example, an Operations department could implement an IS to support all three of the operations processes shown in Figure 7-3. Or an Accounting department might implement two or three different IS to support the accounting processes shown. Sometimes, workgroup information systems are called **functional information systems**. Thus, an operations management system is a functional information system, as are a general ledger system and a cost accounting system. The program component of a functional information system is called a **functional application**.

General characteristics of workgroup information systems are summarized in the top row of Figure 7-4. Typical workgroup information systems support 10 to 100 users. Because the procedures for using them must be understood by all members of the group, those procedures are often formalized in documentation. Users generally receive formal training in the use of those procedures as well.

When problems occur, they almost always can be solved within the group. If accounts payable duplicates the record for a particular supplier, the accounts payable group can make the fix. If the Web storefront has the wrong number of items in the inventory database, that count can be fixed within the storefront group.

(Notice, by the way, that the consequences of a problem are not isolated to the group. Because the workgroup information system exists to provide a service to the rest of the organization, its problems have consequences throughout the organization. The fix to the problem can usually be obtained within the group, however.)

Two or more departments within an organization can duplicate data, and such duplication can be very problematic to the organization, as we discuss in Q7-3. Finally, because workgroup

Workgroup	Workgroup Example Processes
Sales and marketing	• Lead generation • Lead tracking • Customer management • Sales forecasting • Product and brand management
Operations	• Order entry • Order management • Finished goods inventory management
Manufacturing	• Inventory (raw materials, goods-in-process) • Planning • Scheduling • Operations
Customer service	• Order tracking • Account tracking • Customer support
Human resources	• Recruiting • Compensation • Assessment • HR planning
Accounting	• General ledger • Financial reporting • Cost accounting • Accounts receivable • Accounts payable • Cash management • Budgeting • Treasury management

Figure 7-3
Common Workgroup Processes

information systems involve multiple users, changing them can be problematic. But, again, when problems do occur, they can be resolved within the workgroup.

Enterprise Processes

The Ethics Guide on pages 300–301 demonstrates how one person's actions can affect an entire company.

Enterprise processes span an organization and support activities in multiple departments. At a hospital, the process for discharging a patient supports activities in housekeeping, the pharmacy, the kitchen, nurses' stations, and other hospital departments.

Enterprise information systems support one or more enterprise processes. As shown in the second row of Figure 7-4, they typically have hundreds to thousands of users. Procedures are formalized and extensively documented; users always undergo formal procedure training. Sometimes enterprise systems include categories of procedures, and users are defined according to levels of expertise with the system as well as by level of authority.

The solutions to problems in an enterprise system involve more than one workgroup or department. As you will learn in this chapter, a major advantage of enterprise systems is that data duplication within the enterprise is either eliminated altogether or, if it is allowed to exist, changes to duplicated data are carefully managed to maintain consistency.

Because enterprise systems span many departments and involve potentially thousands of users, they are difficult to change. Changes must be carefully planned and cautiously implemented and users given considerable training. Sometimes users are given cash incentives and other inducements to motivate them to change.

CRM, ERP, and EAI are three enterprise information systems that we will define and discuss in Q7-4.

Scope	Example	Characteristics
Workgroup	Doctor's office/ medical practice	Support one or more workgroup processes. 10–100 users; procedures often formalized; problem solutions within group; workgroups can duplicate data; somewhat difficult to change
Enterprise	Hospital	Support one or more enterprise processes. 100–1,000+ users; procedures formalized; problem solutions affect enterprise; eliminate workgroup data duplication; difficult to change
Inter-enterprise	PRIDE system	Support one or more inter-enterprise processes. 1,000+ users; systems procedures formalized; problem solutions affect multiple organizations; can resolve problems of duplicated enterprise data; very difficult to change

Figure 7-4
Characteristics of Information Systems

Inter-enterprise Processes

Inter-enterprise processes span two or more independent organizations. For example, the process of buying a healthcare insurance policy via a healthcare exchange (see Case Study 7, pages 322–323) involves many insurance companies and governmental agencies. Each of these organizations has activities to fulfill, all of which are affected by laws, governmental policy, and competitive concerns of the insurance companies.

Inter-enterprise information systems support one or more inter-enterprise processes. Such systems typically involve thousands of users, and solutions to problems require cooperation among different, usually independently owned, organizations. Problems are resolved by meeting, by contract, and sometimes by litigation.

Data are often duplicated among organizations; such duplication is either eliminated (as will be done with PRIDE) or carefully managed. Because of their wide span, complexity, and use by multiple companies, such systems can be exceedingly difficult to change. Supply chain management (discussed in the International Dimension, pages 322–323) is the classic example of an inter-enterprise information system. We will study inter-enterprise PRIDE examples throughout the remaining chapters of this text.

Q7-2 How Can Information Systems Improve Process Quality?

Processes are the fabric of organizations; they are the means by which people organize their activities to achieve the organization's goals. As such, process quality is an important, possibly the most important, determinant of organizational success.[2]

The two dimensions of process quality are efficiency and effectiveness. **Process efficiency** is a measure of the ratio of process outputs to inputs. If an alternative to the process in Figure 7-1 can produce the same order approvals/rejections (output) for less cost or produce more approvals/ rejections for the same cost, it is more efficient.

Process effectiveness is a measure of how well a process achieves organizational strategy. If an organization differentiates itself on quality customer service and if the process in Figure 7-1 requires 5 days to respond to an order request, then that process is ineffective. Companies that provide customized manufacturing might make their processes more effective by using 3D printing.

How Can Processes Be Improved?

Organizations can improve the quality (efficiency and/or effectiveness) of a process in one of three ways:

- Change the process structure.
- Change the process resources.
- Change both process structure and resources.

Change the Process Structure

In some cases, process quality can be changed just by reorganizing the process. The order approval process in Figure 7-1 might be made more efficient if customer credit was done first and inventory was checked second. This change might be more efficient because it would save the cost of checking inventory for customers whose credit will be denied. However, that change would also mean that the organization would pay for a credit check on customers for which it did not have appropriate inventory. We will investigate such changes further in Chapter 12. For now, just note that process structure has a strong bearing on process efficiency.

Changing process structure can also increase process effectiveness. If an organization chooses a cost-leader strategy, then that strategy might mean that no special terms should ever be approved. If the process in Figure 7-1 results in the authorization of orders with special terms, then eliminating the third activity will make it more effective (most likely it will save on operational costs as well).

Change Process Resources

Business process activities are accomplished by humans and information systems. One way to improve process quality is to change the allocation of those resources. For example, if the process in Figure 7-1 is not effective because it takes too long, one way to make it more effective is to identify the source of delays and then to add more resources. If delays are caused by the check customer credit activity, one way to increase process effectiveness is to add more people to that activity. Adding people should decrease delays, but it will also add cost, so the organization needs to find the appropriate balance between effectiveness and efficiency.

Another way to shorten the credit check process would be to use an information system to perform the customer credit checks. Depending on the development and operational costs of the new system, that change might also be less costly and therefore more efficient.

Change Both Process Structure and Process Resources

Of course, it is possible to improve process quality by changing both the process's structure and resources. In fact, unless a structure change is only a simple reordering of tasks, changing the structure of a process almost always involves a change in resources as well.

How Can Information Systems Improve Process Quality?

Information systems can be used to improve process quality by:

- Performing an activity.
- Augmenting a human who is performing an activity.
- Controlling data quality and process flow.

Performing an Activity

Information systems can perform the entirety of a process activity. In Figure 7-1, for example, the check credit activity could be entirely automated. When you purchase from Amazon or another major online retailer, information systems check your credit while your transaction is being processed. Reserving a seat on an airline is done automatically; all of the reservation activity is done by an information system. (Except, of course, the passenger's activities: When making a reservation, you must choose the seat from available locations, but your time is free to the airline.)

Augmenting a Human Performing an Activity

A second way that information systems can improve process quality is by augmenting the actions of a human who is performing that activity. Consider the process of managing patient appointments. To schedule an appointment, patients call the doctor's office and talk with a receptionist who uses an appointment information system. That information system augments the appointment creation activity.

Controlling Data Quality Process Flow

A third way that information systems can improve process quality is by controlling data quality and process flow.

One of the major benefits of information systems is to control data quality. The IS can not only ensure that correct data values are being input, it can also ensure that data are complete before continuing process activities. The cheapest way to correct for data errors is at the source, and it avoids the problems that develop when process activities are begun with incomplete data.

Information systems also have a role in controlling process flow. Consider the order approval process in Figure 7-1. If this process is controlled manually, then someone, say, a salesperson, will obtain the order data from the customer and take whatever actions are needed to push that order through the three steps in the order process. If the salesperson gets busy or is distracted or away from work for a few days, or if there are unexpected delays in one of the activities, it is possible for an order to be lost or the approval unnecessarily delayed.

If, however, an information system is controlling the order approval process, then it can ensure that steps are performed in accordance with an established schedule. The information system can also be relied upon to make correct process-routing decisions for processes that are more complicated than that in Figure 7-1. SharePoint workflows, discussed in the context of collaboration in Chapter 2, can be used to automate structured processes.

Q7-3 How Do Information Systems Eliminate the Problems of Information Silos?

An **information silo** is the condition that exists when data are isolated in separated information systems. For example, consider the six workgroups and their information systems in Figure 7-3. Reflect on these information systems for a moment, and you'll realize that each one processes customer, sales, product, and other data, but each uses that data for its own purposes and will likely store slightly different data. Sales, for example, will store contact data for customers' purchasing agents, while Accounting will store contact data for customers' accounts payable personnel.

It's completely natural for workgroups to develop information systems solely for their own needs, but, over time, the existence of these separate systems will result in information silos that cause numerous problems.

What Are the Problems of Information Silos?

Figure 7-5 lists the major problems caused by information silos at the workgroup level, in this case, between the Sales and Marketing department and the Accounting department. First, data are duplicated. Sales and Marketing and Accounting applications maintain separate databases that store some of the same customer data. As you know, data storage is cheap, so the problem with duplication is not wasted disk storage. Rather, the problem is data inconsistency. Changes to customer data made in the Sales and Marketing application may take days or weeks to be made to the Accounting application's database. During that period, shipments will reach the customer without delay, but invoices will be sent to the wrong address. When an organization has inconsistent duplicated data, it is said to have a **data integrity** problem.

Additionally, when applications are isolated, business processes are disjointed. Suppose a business has a rule that credit orders over $15,000 must be preapproved by the Accounts Receivable department. If the supporting applications are separated, it will be difficult for the two activities to reconcile their data, and the approval will be slow to grant and possibly erroneous.

In the second row of Figure 7-5, Sales and Marketing wants to approve a $20,000 order with Ajax. According to the Sales and Marketing database, Ajax has a current balance of $17,800, so Sales and Marketing requests a total credit amount of $37,800. The Accounting database, however, shows Ajax with a balance of only $12,300 because the accounts receivable application has credited Ajax for a return of $5,500. According to Accounting's records, a total credit authorization of only $32,300 is needed in order to approve the $20,000 order, so that is all the department grants.

Sales and Marketing doesn't understand what to do with a credit approval of $32,300. According to its database, Ajax already owes $17,800, so if the total credit authorization is only $32,300, did Accounting approve only $14,500 of the new order? And why that amount? Both departments want to approve the order. It will take numerous emails and phone calls, however, to sort this out. These interacting business processes are disjointed.

A consequence of such disjointed activities is the lack of integrated enterprise information. For example, suppose Sales and Marketing wants to know if IndyMac is still a preferred customer. Assume that determining whether this is so requires a comparison of order history and payment history data. With information silos, that data will reside in two different databases and, in one of them, IndyMac is known by the name of the company that acquired it, OneWest Bank. Data

Figure 7-5
Problems Created
by Information Silos

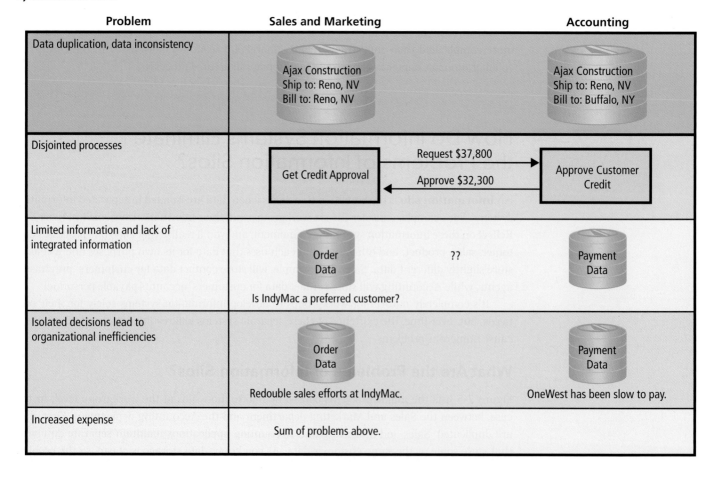

Problem	Sales and Marketing	Accounting
Data duplication, data inconsistency	Ajax Construction Ship to: Reno, NV Bill to: Reno, NV	Ajax Construction Ship to: Reno, NV Bill to: Buffalo, NY
Disjointed processes	Get Credit Approval — Request $37,800 → — ← Approve $32,300	Approve Customer Credit
Limited information and lack of integrated information	Order Data ?? Is IndyMac a preferred customer?	Payment Data
Isolated decisions lead to organizational inefficiencies	Order Data Redouble sales efforts at IndyMac.	Payment Data OneWest has been slow to pay.
Increased expense	Sum of problems above.	

Scope	Example	Example Information Silo	Enabling Technology
Workgroup	Doctor's office/ medical practice	Physicians and hospitals store separated data about patients. Unnecessarily duplicate tests and procedures.	Functional applications.
		⬇	Enterprise applications (CRM, ERP, EAI) on enterprise networks.
Enterprise	Hospital	Hospital and local drug store pharmacy have different prescription data for the same patient.	
		⬇	Distributed systems using Web service technologies in the cloud.
Inter-enterprise	Inter-agency prescription application	No silo: Doctors, hospitals, pharmacies share patients' prescription and other data.	

Figure 7-6
Information Silos as Drivers

integration will be difficult. Making the determination will require manual processes and days, when it should be readily answered in seconds.

This leads to the fourth consequence: inefficiency. When using isolated functional applications, decisions are made in isolation. As shown in the fourth row of Figure 7-5, Sales and Marketing decided to redouble its sales effort with IndyMac. However, Accounting knows that IndyMac was foreclosed by the FDIC and sold to OneWest and has been slow to pay. There are far better prospects for increased sales attention. Without integration, the left hand of the organization doesn't know what the right hand of the organization is doing.

Finally, information silos can result in increased cost for the organization. Duplicated data, disjointed systems, limited information, and inefficiencies all mean higher costs.

How Do Organizations Solve the Problems of Information Silos?

As defined, an information silo occurs when data is stored in isolated systems. The obvious way to fix such a silo is to integrate the data into a single database and revise applications (and business processes) to use that database. If that is not possible or practical, another remedy is to allow the isolation, but to manage it to avoid problems.

The arrows in Figure 7-6 show this resolution at two levels of organization. First, isolated data created by workgroup information systems are integrated using enterprise-wide applications.

Second, today, isolated data created by information systems at the enterprise level are being integrated into inter-enterprise systems using distributed applications (such as PRIDE). These applications process data in a single cloud database or connect disparate, independent databases so that those databases appear to be one database. We will discuss inter-enterprise systems further in Q7-7.

For now, to better understand how isolated data problems can be resolved, consider an enterprise system at a hospital.

An Enterprise System for Patient Discharge

Figure 7-7 shows some of the hospital departments and a portion of the patient discharge process. A doctor initiates the process by issuing a discharge patient order. That order is delivered to the appropriate nursing staff, who initiates activities at the pharmacy, the patient's family, and

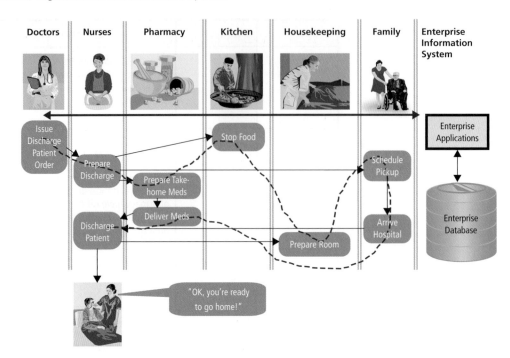

Figure 7-7
Example Enterprise Process
and Information System

kitchen. Some of those activities initiate activities back at the nursing staff. In Figure 7-7, the enterprise process (supported by the IS) is represented by a dotted blue line.

Prior to the enterprise system, the hospital had developed procedures for using a paper-based system and informal messaging via the telephone. Each department kept its own records. When the new enterprise information system was implemented, not only was the data integrated into a database, but new computer-based forms and reports were created. The staff needed to transition from the paper-based system to the computer-based system. They also needed to stop making phone calls and let the new information system make notifications across departments. These measures involved substantial change, and most organizations experience considerable anguish when undergoing such transitions.

Eliminating information silos is not without security risk; for more information, see the Security Guide on pages 314–315.

Q7-4 How Do CRM, ERP, and EAI Support Enterprise Processes?

Enterprise systems like the one in Figure 7-7 were not feasible until network, data communication, and database technologies reached a sufficient level of capability and maturity in the late 1980s and early 1990s. At that point, many organizations began to develop enterprise systems.

The Need for Business Process Engineering

As they did so, organizations realized that their existing business processes needed to change. In part, they needed to change to use the shared databases and to use new computer-based forms and reports. However, an even more important reason for changing business processes was that integrated data and enterprise systems offered the potential of substantial improvements in process quality. It became possible to do things that had been impossible before. Using Porter's language (Chapter 3, pages 119), enterprise systems enabled the creation of stronger, faster, more effective *linkages* among value chains.

For example, when the hospital used a paper-based system, the kitchen would prepare meals for everyone who was a patient at the hospital as of midnight the night before. It was not possible to obtain data about discharges until the next midnight. Consequently, considerable food was wasted at substantial cost.

With the enterprise system, the kitchen can be notified about patient discharges as they occur throughout the day, resulting in substantial reductions in wasted food. But when should the kitchen be notified? Immediately? And what if the discharge is cancelled before completion? Notify the kitchen of the cancelled discharge? Many possibilities and alternatives exist. So, to design its new enterprise system, the hospital needed to determine how best to change its processes to take advantage of the new capability. Such projects came to be known as **business process reengineering**, which is the activity of altering existing and designing new business processes to take advantage of new information systems.

Unfortunately, business process reengineering is difficult, slow, and exceedingly expensive. Business analysts need to interview key personnel throughout the organization to determine how best to use the new technology. Because of the complexity involved, such projects require high-level, expensive skills and considerable time. Many early projects stalled when the enormity of the project became apparent. This left some organizations with partially implemented systems, which had disastrous consequences. Personnel didn't know if they were using the new system, the old system, or some hacked-up version of both.

The stage was set for the emergence of enterprise application solutions, which we discuss next.

Emergence of Enterprise Application Solutions

When the process quality benefits of enterprise-wide systems became apparent, most organizations were still developing their applications in-house. At the time, organizations perceived their needs as being "too unique" to be satisfied by off-the-shelf or altered applications. However, as applications became more and more complex, in-house development costs became infeasible. As stated in Chapter 4, systems built in-house are expensive not only because of their high initial development costs, but also because of the continuing need to adapt those systems to changing requirements.

In the early 1990s, as the costs of business process reengineering were coupled to the costs of in-house development, organizations began to look more favorably on the idea of licensing preexisting applications. "Maybe we're not so unique, after all."

Some of the vendors who took advantage of this change in attitude were PeopleSoft, which licensed payroll and limited-capability human resources systems; Siebel, which licensed a sales lead tracking and management system; and SAP, which licensed something new, a system called *enterprise resource management*.

These three companies, and ultimately dozens of others like them, offered not just software and database designs. They also offered standardized business processes. These **inherent processes**, which are predesigned procedures for using the software products, saved organizations from the expense, delays, and risks of business process reengineering. Instead, organizations could license the software and obtain, as part of the deal, prebuilt processes that the vendors assured them were based on "industry best practices."

Despite the clear benefits of inherent processes and ERP, there can be an unintended consequence. See the Guide on pages 316–317 and consider that risk.

Some parts of that deal were too good to be true because, as you'll learn in Q7-5, inherent processes are almost never a perfect fit. But the offer was too much for many organizations to resist. Over time, three categories of enterprise applications emerged: customer relationship management, enterprise resource planning, and enterprise application integration. Consider each.

Customer Relationship Management (CRM)

A **customer relationship management (CRM) system** is a suite of applications, a database, and a set of inherent processes for managing all the interactions with the customer, from lead generation to customer service. Every contact and transaction with the customer is recorded in the CRM database. Vendors of CRM systems claim that using their products makes the organization *customer-centric*. Though that term reeks of sales hyperbole, it does indicate the nature and intent of CRM packages.

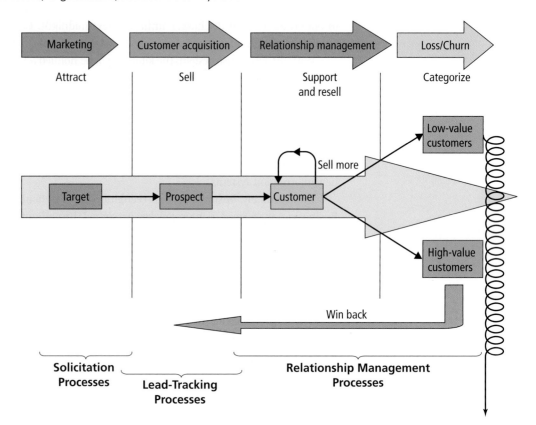

Figure 7-8

The Customer Life Cycle

Source: Used with permission from
Professor Douglas MacLachlan,
Foster School of Business,
University of Washington.

Figure 7-8 shows four phases of the **customer life cycle**: marketing, customer acquisition, relationship management, and loss/churn. Marketing sends messages to the target market to attract customer prospects. When prospects order, they become customers who need to be supported. Additionally, relationship management processes increase the value of existing customers by selling them more product. Inevitably, over time the organization loses customers. When this occurs, win-back processes categorize customers according to value and attempt to win back high-value customers.

Figure 7-9 illustrates the major components of a CRM application. Notice that components exist for each stage of the customer life cycle. As shown, all applications process a common customer database. This design eliminates duplicated customer data and removes the possibility of inconsistent data. It also means that each department knows what has been happening with the customer at other departments. Customer support, for example, will know not to provide $1,000 worth of support labor to a customer that has generated $300 worth of business over time.

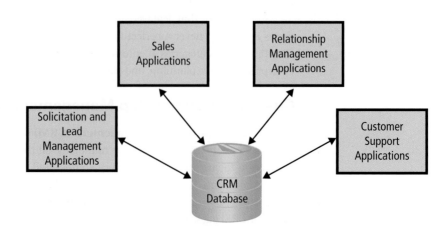

Figure 7-9

CRM Applications

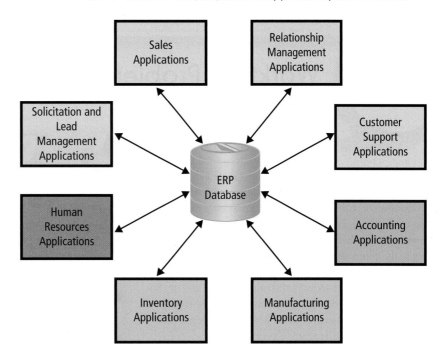

Figure 7-10
ERP Applications

However, it will know to bend over backward for customers that have generated hundreds of thousands of dollars of business. The result to the customers is that they feel like they are dealing with one entity, not many.

CRM systems vary in the degree of functionality they provide. One of the primary tasks when selecting a CRM package is to determine the features you need and to find a package that meets that set of needs. You might be involved in just such a project during your career.

Enterprise Resource Planning (ERP)

Enterprise resource planning (ERP) is a suite of applications called **modules**, a database, and a set of inherent processes for consolidating business operations into a single, consistent, computing platform. An **ERP system** is an information system based on ERP technology. As shown in Figure 7-10, ERP systems include the functions of CRM systems but also incorporate accounting, manufacturing, inventory, and human resources applications.

The primary purpose of an ERP system is integration; an ERP system allows the left hand of the organization to know what the right hand is doing. This integration allows real-time updates globally, whenever and wherever a transaction takes place. Critical business decisions can then be made on a timely basis using the latest data.

Workflow Problems

According to John Halamka, CIO of the Harvard Medical School and Group Health System, "Most IT problems are workflow problems, not software problems."[3] Using the knowledge of this chapter, you know that workflow problems concern either efficiency (ratio of costs to value delivered is too high) or effectiveness (not contributing to the competitive strategy). So what?

Who fixes a workflow problem? A computer programmer? A network engineer? A database administrator? No, no, and no. So who? Someone with knowledge of the business and, if the workflow involves an information system, someone who is knowledgeable and comfortable working with technical people.

Consider an example close to home. Suppose your university has a limited number of classrooms with sophisticated audiovisual display, and those classrooms are frequently assigned to professors who specialize in old-fashioned lecture and don't use audiovisual display. Meanwhile, professors who want to use, say, Learning Catalytics in their classrooms are making do with poor-quality, hard-to-view computer-based display.

How would you fix that problem? Change the software that allocates classrooms? But how? Who decides what changes need to be made? And does it need to be done in software? Could it be done by fixing a workflow? Is there a convenient point in the professor–class assignment process in which professors (or department chairs) can indicate which professors should teach in which classrooms? Or are classrooms allocated on a university-wide basis? Or maybe the audiovisual system is already generating metadata about its use, and without requiring anyone to provide any extra data, someone in the Assign-Classroom workflow could use this data to allocate the classrooms?

Who develops these alternatives? Who evaluates them? Who implements them with the workflow workers? You! Or it could be you. As you'll learn in Chapter 12, a *business analyst* is someone who knows business, who understands an organization's competitive strategy and ways to implement it, and who knows enough information systems technology to be able to model and design workflow changes and to work with technical personnel, when needed, to effectuate changes to information systems.

Source: Franz Pfluegl/Fotolia

To do this well, you need to know IS_and_something: IS_and_marketing, IS_and_ operations, IS_and_finance.

Questions

1. Using your own words, explain the meaning of the statement "Most IT problems are workflow problems, not software problems."

2. Consider the classroom assignment problem. Briefly describe three ways of solving that problem. Which of those three is the most promising? Why?

3. In your opinion, is the demand for professionals who know IS_and_something going to decrease? Increase? Stay about the same? Justify your response; search the Internet for data to support your claim.

4. If you were to become an expert in IS_and_something, what would the *something* be? Search the Internet for employment prospects for that career choice.

5. Examine your current plan of courses before you graduate. What courses do you need to add to your plan to learn IS_and_something? Will you add these courses? Why or why not?

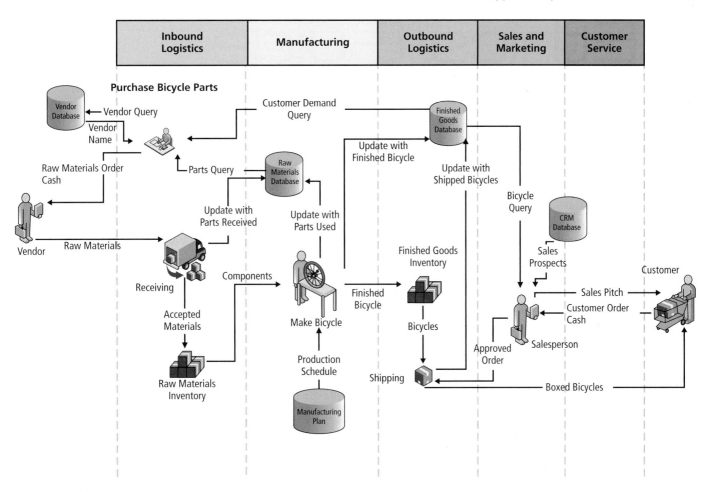

Figure 7-11
Pre-ERP Information Systems

To understand the utility of this integration, consider the pre-ERP systems shown in Figure 7-11. This diagram represents the same processes used by a bicycle manufacturer that we discussed in Chapter 3. It includes five different databases, one each for vendors, raw materials, finished goods, manufacturing plan, and CRM. Consider the problems that appear with such separated data when the Sales department closes a large order, say, for 1,000 bicycles.

First, should the company take the order? Can it meet the schedule requirements for such a large order? Suppose one of the primary parts vendors recently lost capacity due to an earthquake, and the manufacturer cannot obtain parts for the order in time. If so, the order schedule ought not to be approved. However, with such separated systems this situation is unknown.

Even if parts can be obtained, until the order is entered into the finished goods database, purchasing is unaware of the need to buy new parts. The same comment applies to manufacturing. Until the new order is entered into the manufacturing plan, the Production department doesn't know that it needs to increase manufacturing. And, as with parts, does the company have sufficient machine and floor capacity to fill the order on a timely basis? Does it have sufficient personnel with the correct skill sets? Should it be hiring? Can production meet the order schedule? No one knows before the order is approved.

Figure 7-11 does not show accounting. We can assume, however, that the company has a separate accounting system that is similarly isolated. Eventually, records of business activity find their way to the Accounting department and will be posted into the general ledger. With such a pre-ERP system, financial statements are always outdated, available several weeks after the close of the quarter or other accounting period.

Ethics Guide

DIALING FOR DOLLARS

Suppose you are a salesperson and your company's CRM forecasts that your quarterly sales will be substantially under quota. You call your best customers to increase sales, but no one is willing to buy more.

Your boss says that it has been a bad quarter for all the salespeople. It's so bad, in fact, that the vice president of sales has authorized a 20 percent discount on new orders. The only stipulation is that customers must take delivery prior to the end of the quarter so that accounting can book the order. "Start dialing for dollars," she says, "and get what you can. Be creative."

Using your CRM, you identify your top customers and present the discount offer to them. The first customer balks at increasing her inventory: "I just don't think we can sell that much."

"Well," you respond, "how about if we agree to take back any inventory you don't sell next quarter?" (By doing this, you increase your current sales and commission, and you also help your company make its quarterly sales projections. The additional product is likely to be returned next quarter, but you think, "Hey, that's then and this is now.")

"OK," she says, "but I want you to stipulate the return option on the purchase order."

You know that you cannot write that on the purchase order because accounting won't book all of the order if you do. So you tell her that you'll send her an email with that stipulation. She increases her order, and accounting books the full amount.

With another customer, you try a second strategy. Instead of offering the discount, you offer the product at full price but agree to pay a 20 percent credit in the next quarter. That way you can book the full price now. You pitch this offer as follows: "Our marketing department analyzed past sales using our fancy new computer system, and we know that increasing advertising will cause additional sales. So, if you order more product now, next quarter we'll give you 20 percent of the order back to pay for advertising."

Source: Roman Sigaev/Fotolia

In truth, you doubt the customer will spend the money on advertising. Instead, it will just take the credit and sit on a bigger inventory. That will kill your sales to the company next quarter, but you'll solve that problem then.

Even with these additional orders, you're still under quota. In desperation, you decide to sell product to a fictitious company that you say is owned by your brother-in-law. You set up a new account, and when accounting calls your brother-in-law for a credit check, he cooperates with your scheme. You then sell $40,000 of product to the fictitious company and ship the product to your brother-in-law's garage. Accounting books the revenue in the quarter, and you have finally made quota. A week into the next quarter, your brother-in-law returns the merchandise.

Meanwhile, unknown to you, your company's ERP system is scheduling production. The program that creates the production schedule reads the sales from your activities (and those of the other salespeople) and finds a sharp increase in product demand. Accordingly, it generates a schedule that calls for substantial production increases and schedules workers for the production runs. The production system, in turn, schedules the material requirements with the inventory application, which increases raw materials purchases to meet the increased production schedule.

 DISCUSSION QUESTIONS

1. Consider the email you write that agrees to take the product back.
   a. Is your action ethical according to the categorical imperative (pages 56–57) perspective?
   b. Is your action ethical according to the utilitarian perspective (pages 92–93)?
   c. If that email comes to light later, what do you think your boss will say?
2. Regarding your offer of the "advertising" discount:
   a. Is your action ethical according to the categorical imperative perspective?
   b. Is your action ethical according to the utilitarian perspective?
   c. What effect does that discount have on your company's balance sheet?
3. Regarding your shipping to the fictitious company:
   a. Is your action ethical according to the categorical imperative perspective?
   b. Is your action ethical according to the utilitarian perspective?
   c. Is your action legal?
4. Describe the effect of your activities on next quarter's inventories.
5. Setting aside ethical and legal issues, would you say the enterprise system is more of a help or a hindrance in this example?

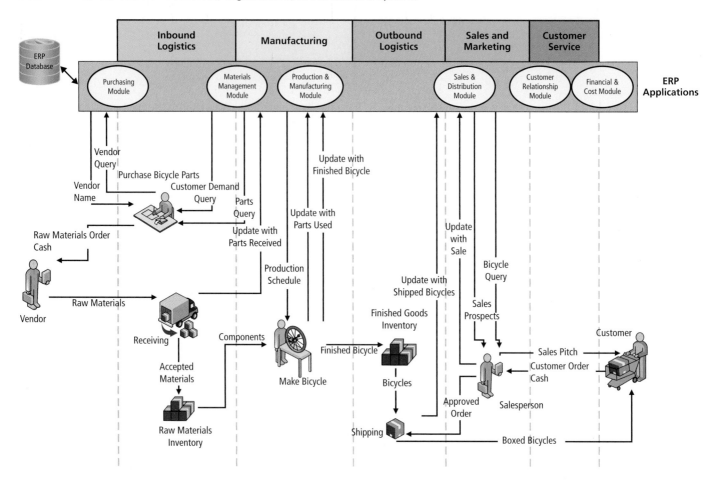

Figure 7-12
ERP Information Systems

Contrast this situation with the ERP system in Figure 7-12. Here, all activity is processed by ERP application programs (called *modules*), and consolidated data are stored in a centralized ERP database. When Sales is confronted with the opportunity to sell 1,000 bicycles, the information it needs to confirm that the order, schedule, and terms are possible can be obtained from the ERP system immediately. Once the order is accepted, all departments, including purchasing, manufacturing, human resources, and accounting, are notified. Further, transactions are posted to the ERP database as they occur; the result is that financial statements are available quickly. In most cases, correct financial statements can be produced in real time. With such integration, ERP systems can display the current status of critical business factors to managers and executives, as shown in the sales dashboard in Figure 7-13.

Of course, the devil is in the details. It's one thing to draw a rectangle on a chart, label it "ERP Applications," and assume that data integration takes all the problems away. It is far more difficult to write those application programs and to design the database to store that integrated data. Even more problematic, what procedures should employees and others use to process those application programs? Specifically, for example, what actions should salespeople take before they approve a large order? Here are some of the questions that need to be answered or resolved:

- How does the Sales department determine that an order is considered large? By dollars? By volume?
- Who approves customer credit (and how)?
- Who approves production capacity (and how)?
- Who approves schedule and terms (and how)?
- What actions need to be taken if the customer modifies the order?
- How does management obtain oversight on sales activity?

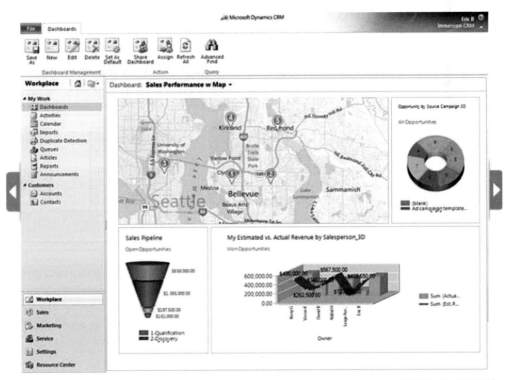

Figure 7-13
Sales Dashboard
Source: © Access 2013, Microsoft Corporation

SOURCE: Courtesy of Microsoft

As you can imagine, many other questions must be answered as well. Because of its importance to organizations today, we will discuss ERP in further detail in Q7-5. Before we do so, however, consider the third type of enterprise system: EAI.

Enterprise Application Integration (EAI)

ERP systems are not for every organization. For example, some nonmanufacturing companies find the manufacturing orientation of ERP inappropriate. Even for manufacturing companies, some find the process of converting from their current system to an ERP system too daunting. Others are quite satisfied with their manufacturing application systems and do not wish to change them.

Companies for which ERP is inappropriate still have the problems associated with information silos, however, and some choose to use **enterprise application integration (EAI)** to solve those problems. EAI is a suite of software applications that integrates existing systems by providing layers of software that connect applications together. EAI does the following:

- It connects system "islands" via a new layer of software/system.
- It enables existing applications to communicate and share data.
- It provides integrated information.
- It leverages existing systems—leaving functional applications as is but providing an integration layer over the top.
- It enables a gradual move to ERP.

The layers of EAI software shown in Figure 7-14 enable existing applications to communicate with each other and to share data. For example, EAI software can be configured to automatically carry out the data conversion required to make data compatible among different systems. When the CRM applications send data to the manufacturing application system, for example, the CRM system sends its data to an EAI software program. That EAI program makes the conversion and

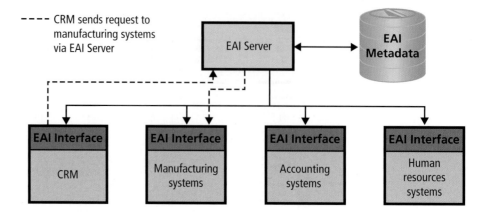

Figure 7-14
Design and Implementation for the Five Components

then sends the converted data to the ERP system. The reverse action is taken to send data back from the ERP to the CRM.

Although there is no centralized EAI database, the EAI software keeps files of metadata that describe data formats and locations. Users can access the EAI system to find the data they need. In some cases, the EAI system provides services that provide a "virtual integrated database" for the user to process.

The major benefit of EAI is that it enables organizations to use existing applications while eliminating many of the serious problems of isolated systems. Converting to an EAI system is not nearly as disruptive as converting to an ERP system, and it provides many of the benefits of ERP. Some organizations develop EAI applications as a stepping stone to complete ERP systems. Today, many EAI systems use Web services standards to define the interactions among EAI components. Some or all of the processing for those components can be moved to the cloud as well.

Q7-5 What Are the Elements of an ERP System?

Because of its importance to organizations today, we will consider ERP in more depth than CRM or EAI. To begin, the term *ERP* has been applied to a wide array of application solutions, in some cases erroneously. Some vendors attempted to catch the buzz for ERP by misapplying the term to applications that provided only one or two integrated functional applications.

The organization ERPsoftware360 publishes a wealth of information about ERP vendors, products, solutions, and applications. According to its Web site (*www.erpsoftware360.com/erp-101. htm*), for a product to be considered a true ERP product, it must include applications that integrate:

- Supply chain (procurement, sales order processing, inventory management, supplier management, and related activities)
- Manufacturing (scheduling, capacity planning, quality control, bill of materials, and related activities)
- CRM (sales prospecting, customer management, marketing, customer support, call center support)
- Human resources (payroll, time and attendance, HR management, commission calculations, benefits administration, and related activities)
- Accounting (general ledger, accounts receivable, accounts payable, cash management, fixed asset accounting)

An ERP solution is an information system and, as such, has all five components. We consider each in turn.

Hardware

Traditionally, organizations hosted ERP solutions on their own in-house, networked server computers. Such hosting is still the case for many large ERP applications, as well as for those ERP applications that were installed years ago and for which the hardware infrastructure is stable and well managed.

Increasingly, however, organizations are turning to cloud-based hosting in one of two modes:

- PaaS: Replace an organization's existing hardware infrastructure with hardware in the cloud. Install ERP software and databases on that cloud hardware. The using organization then manages the ERP software on the cloud hardware.
- SaaS: Acquire a cloud-based ERP solution. SAP, Oracle, Microsoft, and the other major ERP vendors offer their ERP software as a service. The vendor manages the ERP software and offers it to customers as a service.

During your career, existing in-house ERP solutions are likely to migrate to one of these two modes. Larger installations will likely move to PaaS; smaller and new ERP systems are likely to use SaaS.

ERP Application Programs

ERP vendors design application programs to be configurable so that development teams can alter them to meet an organization's requirements without changing program code. Accordingly, during the ERP development process, the development team sets configuration parameters that specify how ERP application programs will operate. For example, an hourly payroll application is configured to specify the number of hours in the standard workweek, hourly wages for different job categories, wage adjustments for overtime and holiday work, and so forth. Deciding on the initial configuration values and adapting them to new requirements is a challenging collaboration activity. It is also one that you might be involved in as a business professional.

Of course, there are limits to how much configuration can be done. If a new ERP customer has requirements that cannot be met via program configuration, then it needs to either adapt its business to what the software can do or write (or pay another vendor to write) application code to meet its requirements. As stated in Chapter 4, such custom programming is expensive, both initially and in long-term maintenance costs. Thus, choosing an ERP solution with applications that function close to the organization's requirements is critical to its successful implementation.

ERP Databases

An ERP solution includes a database design as well as initial configuration data. It does not, of course, contain the company's operational data. During development, the team must enter the initial values for that data as part of the development effort.

If your only experience with databases is creating a few tables in Microsoft Access, then you probably underestimate the value and importance of ERP database designs. SAP, the leading vendor of ERP solutions, provides ERP databases that contain more than 15,000 tables. The design includes the metadata for those tables, as well as their relationships to each other, and rules and constraints about how the data in some tables must relate to data in other tables. The ERP solution also contains tables filled with initial configuration data.

Reflect on the difficulty of creating and validating data models(as discussed in Chapter 5), and you will have some idea of the amount of intellectual capital invested in a database design of 15,000 tables. Also, consider the magnitude of the task of filling such a database with users' data!

Although we did not discuss this database feature in Chapter 5, large organizational databases contain two types of program code. The first, called a **trigger**, is a computer program stored within the database that runs to keep the database consistent when certain conditions arise. The second, called a **stored procedure**, is a computer program stored in the database that is used to enforce business rules. An example of such a rule would be never to sell certain items at a discount. Triggers and stored procedures are also part of the ERP solution. Developers and business users need to configure the operation of such code during the ERP implementation as well.

Business Process Procedures

Another component of an ERP solution is a set of inherent procedures that implement standard business processes. ERP vendors develop hundreds, or even thousands, of procedures that enable the ERP customer organization to accomplish its work using the applications provided by the vendor. Figure 7-15 shows a part of the SAP ordering business process; this process implements a portion of the inbound logistics activities. Some ERP vendors call the inherent processes that are defined in the ERP solution **process blueprints**.

Without delving into the details, you should be able to understand the flow of work outlined in this process. Every function (rounded rectangles in Figure 7-15) consists of a set of procedures for accomplishing that function. Typically, these procedures require an ERP user to use application menus, screens, and reports to accomplish the activity.

As with application programs, ERP users must either adapt to the predefined, inherent processes and procedures or design new ones. In the latter case, the design of new procedures may necessitate changes to application programs and to database structures as well. Perhaps you can begin to understand why organizations attempt to conform to vendor standards.

Training and Consulting

Because of the complexity and difficulty of implementing and using ERP solutions, ERP vendors have developed training curricula and numerous classes. SAP operates universities, in which customers and potential customers receive training both before and after the ERP implementation. In addition, ERP vendors typically conduct classes on site. To reduce expenses, the vendors sometimes train the organization's employees, called Super Users, to become in-house trainers in training sessions called **train the trainer**.

ERP training falls into two broad categories. The first category is training about how to implement the ERP solution. This training includes topics such as obtaining top-level management support, preparing the organization for change, and dealing with the inevitable resistance that develops when people are asked to perform work in new ways. The second category is training on how to use the ERP application software; this training includes specific steps for using the ERP applications to accomplish the activities in processes such as those in Figure 7-15.

ERP vendors also provide on-site consulting for implementing and using the ERP system. Additionally, an industry of third-party ERP consultants has developed to support new ERP customers and implementations. These consultants provide knowledge gained through numerous ERP implementations. Such knowledge is valued because most organizations go through an ERP conversion only once. Ironically, having done so, they now know how to do it. Consequently, some employees, seasoned by an ERP conversion with their employer, leave that company to become ERP consultants.

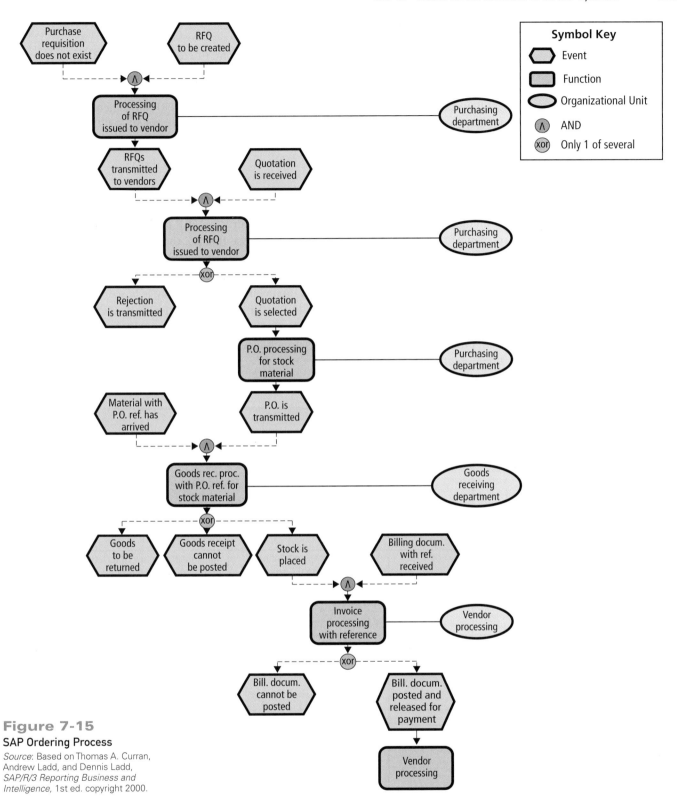

Figure 7-15

SAP Ordering Process

Source: Based on Thomas A. Curran, Andrew Ladd, and Dennis Ladd, *SAP/R/3 Reporting Business and Intelligence,* 1st ed. copyright 2000.

Industry-Specific Solutions

As you can tell, considerable work needs to be done to customize an ERP application to a particular customer. To reduce that work, ERP vendors provide starter kits for specific industries called **industry-specific solutions**. These solutions contain program and database configuration files as well as process blueprints that apply to ERP implementations in specific industries. Over time, SAP, which first provided such solutions, and other ERP vendors created dozens of such starter kits for manufacturing, sales and distribution, healthcare, and other major industries.

Which Companies Are the Major ERP Vendors?

Although more than 100 different companies advertise ERP products, not all of those products meet the minimal ERP criteria. Even of those that do, the bulk of the market is held by the five vendors shown in Figure 7-16. This figure shows market rank rather than market share because it is difficult to obtain comparable revenue numbers. Infor is owned by private equity investors and does not publish financial data. Its ranking is based on what little sales data is publicly available. Microsoft's ERP revenue is combined with its CRM revenue, and its true ERP revenue is unknown. Similarly, Oracle and SAP combine ERP revenue with revenue from other products. Sage revenue is an amalgam of ERP, CRM, and financial-oriented functional solutions.

Figure 7-16
SAP Characteristics of Top ERP Vendors
Source: Based on Louis Columbus. "Gartner's ERP Market Share Update Shows The Future Of Cloud ERP Is Now," *Forbes,* May 12, 2014. *http://www.forbes.com/sites/louiscolumbus/2014/05/12/gartners-erp-market-share-update-shows-the-future-of-cloud-erp-is-now/,* accessed April 9, 2015.

Company	ERP Market Rank	Remarks	Future
Microsoft Dynamics	5	Four products acquired: AX, Nav, GP, and Solomon. AX and Nav more comprehensive. Solomon on the way out? Large VAR channel.	Products not well integrated with Office. Not integrated at all with Microsoft development languages. Solutions not integrated and product direction uncertain. Microsoft Azure hosts Oracle and SAP products. Conflict with Azure hosting of Microsoft ERP products.
Sage	4	Offers ERP, CRM, and financial-oriented functional system solutions.	Sage adapted many of its legacy applications and solutions for the cloud and for mobile computing. Offers inexpensive, cloud-based solutions for startups and small businesses. Broad product suite.
Infor	3	Privately held corporation that acquired an ERP product named Baan, along with more than 20 others.	Many solutions, not integrated, particularly specialized for manufacturing and supply chain management. Evolving with revolution in 3D printing practices.
Oracle	2	Combination of in-house and acquired (PeopleSoft, Siebel) products. Expensive.	Intensely competitive company with strong technology base. Large customer base. Flexible SOA architecture. Will leverage strong technology base into innovative and effective cloud-based solutions. Strong challenge to SAP market leadership. Claims number 1 in CRM.
SAP	1	Led ERP success with client-server hardware. Largest vendor, most comprehensive solution. Largest customers. Expensive.	Technology older, but SAP is adapting to mobility and cloud trends. Expensive and seriously challenged by less expensive alternatives. Huge customer base. Future depends on effectively migrating traditional customers to the cloud. Claims number 1 in CRM.

What Are the Challenges of Implementing and Upgrading Enterprise Information Systems?

Implementing new enterprise systems, whether CRM, ERP, or EAI, is challenging, difficult, expensive, and risky. It is not unusual for enterprise system projects to be well over budget and a year or more late. In addition to new ERP implementations, numerous organizations implemented ERP 15 or 20 years ago and now need to upgrade their ERP installation to meet new requirements. If you work in an organization that is already using enterprise systems, you may find yourself engaged in a significant upgrade effort. Whether from a new implementation or an upgrade, expense and risks arise from five primary factors (see Figure 7-17).

Collaborative Management

Unlike departmental systems in which a single department manager is in charge, enterprise systems have no clear boss. Examine the discharge process in Figure 7-7; there is no manager of discharge. The discharge process is a collaborative effort among many departments (and customers).

With no single manager, who resolves the disputes that inevitably arise? All of these departments ultimately report to the CEO, so there is a single boss over all of them, but employees can't go to the CEO with a problem about, say, coordinating discharge activities between nursing and housekeeping. The CEO would throw them out of his or her office. Instead, the organization needs to develop some sort of collaborative management for resolving process issues.

Usually this means that the enterprise develops committees and steering groups for providing enterprise process management. Although this can be an effective solution, and in fact may be the *only* solution, the work of such groups is both slow and expensive.

Requirements Gaps

As stated in Q4, few organizations today create their own enterprise systems from scratch. Instead, they license an enterprise product that provides specific functions and features and that includes inherent procedures. But such licensed products are never a perfect fit. Almost always there are gaps between the organization's requirements and the application's capabilities.

The first challenge is identifying the gaps. To specify a gap, an organization must know both what it needs and what the new product does. However, it can be very difficult for an organization to determine what it needs; that difficulty is one reason organizations choose to license rather than to build. Further, the features and functions of complex products like CRM or ERP are not easy to identify. Thus, gap identification is a major task when implementing enterprise systems.

The second challenge is deciding what to do with gaps, once they are identified. Either the organization needs to change the way it does things to adapt to the new application, or the application must be altered to match what the organization does. Either choice is problematic. Employees will resist change, but paying for alterations is expensive, and, as noted in Chapter 4,

- Collaborative management

- Requirements gaps

- Transition problems

- Employee resistance

- New technology

Figure 7-17
Five Primary Factors

the organization is committing to maintaining those alterations as the application is changed over time. Here, organizations fill gaps by choosing their lesser regret.

Transition Problems

Transitioning to a new enterprise system is also difficult. The organization must somehow change from using isolated departmental systems to using the new enterprise system, while continuing to run the business. It's like having heart surgery while running a 100-yard dash.

Such transitions require careful planning and substantial training. Inevitably, problems will develop. Knowing this will occur, senior management needs to communicate the need for the change to the employees and then stand behind the new system as the kinks are worked out. It is an incredibly stressful time for all involved. We will discuss development techniques and implementation strategies further in Chapter 10.

Employee Resistance

People resist change. Change requires effort and engenders fear. Considerable research and literature exist about the reasons for change resistance and how organizations can deal with it. Here we will summarize the major principles.

First, senior-level management needs to communicate the need for the change to the organization and reiterate this, as necessary, throughout the transition process. Second, employees fear change because it threatens **self-efficacy**, which is a person's belief that he or she can be successful at his or her job. To enhance confidence, employees need to be trained and coached on the successful use of the new system. Word-of-mouth is a very powerful factor, and in some cases key users are trained ahead of time to create positive buzz about the new system. Video demonstrations of employees successfully using the new system are also effective.

Third, in many ways, the primary benefits of a new ERP system are felt by the accounting and finance departments and the senior management. Many of the employees who are asked to change their activities to implement ERP will not receive any direct benefit from it. Therefore, employees may need to be given extra inducement to change to the new system. As one experienced change consultant said, "Nothing succeeds like praise or cash, especially cash." Straight-out pay for change is bribery, but contests with cash prizes among employees or groups can be very effective at inducing change.

Implementing new enterprise systems can solve many problems and bring great efficiency and cost savings to an organization, but it is not for the faint of heart.

New Technology

Emerging, new technology affects all information systems, but it affects enterprise systems particularly because of their importance and their value. Consider, for example, the cloud. Because of the cost savings of cloud-based computing, organizations would like to move their enterprise systems to the cloud. But legal, risk, and business policy factors may make such a move infeasible. The organization may be required to keep physical control over its data. When moving it to the cloud, the cloud vendor controls the physical location of the data, and that location might not even be in the same country as the organization. So, some sort of hybrid model may need to be devised (see Q7-8).

Similar comments pertain to mobile technology. Employees want to use mobile devices to access and even modify enterprise system data. But mobile devices are just that—mobile. The enterprise system may be exposed to considerable risk while outside the control of the organization. And ERP data is a juicy target for crime (see "One Stop Shopping" on pages 314–315). These factors don't mean organizations cannot use new technology with enterprise systems, but they do add challenges.

Q7-7 How Do Inter-enterprise IS Solve the Problems of Enterprise Silos?

The discussion in Q7-4 illustrated the primary ways that enterprise systems solve the problems of workgroup information silos. In this question we will use the PRIDE example to show you how inter-enterprise systems can accomplish the same for enterprise silos. (The transition is shown by the lower arrow leading to the bottom row in Figure 7-6, page 293.)

Figure 7-18 shows the information silos that exist among healthcare providers, health clubs, and patients, the principal PRIDE users. Providers keep track of patient histories and maintain records of exercise recommendations, which are called exercise prescriptions in the PRIDE system. Health clubs maintain membership, class, personal trainer, and exercise performance data. At the club, the latter is gathered automatically from exercise equipment and member heart monitors and stored in a club database. At home, individuals generate exercise data on heart monitors and equipment; those data are recorded in mobile devices using exercise watches.

The isolation of this exercise data causes problems. For example, doctors would like to have reports on exercise data stored in patient devices and in health clubs. Patients would like to have prescription data from their providers as well as exercise data from their time at health clubs. Health clubs would like to have exercise prescriptions and home workout data to integrate with the data they have. All three entities would like to produce reports from the integrated data.

Figure 7-19 shows the structure of an inter-enterprise system that meets the goals of the three types of participant. In this figure, the labeled rectangles inside the cloud represent mobile applications that could be native, thin-client, or both. Some of the application processing might be done on cloud servers as well as on the mobile devices. Those design decisions are not shown. As illustrated, this system assumes that all users receive reports on mobile devices but, because of the large amount of keying involved, that healthcare providers submit and manage prescriptions using a personal computer.

As you can see, prescription and exercise data are integrated in the PRIDE database; that integrated data is processed by a reporting application (Chapter 9) to create and distribute the reports as shown.

Systems like that shown in Figure 7-19 are referred to as **distributed systems** because applications processing is distributed across multiple computing devices. Standards such as http, https, html5, css3, JavaScript, and SOA using Web services enable programs to receive data from, and display data to, a variety of mobile and desktop devices.

PRIDE data is requested and delivered using JSON.

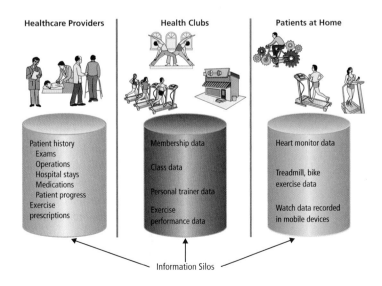

Figure 7-18
Information Silos Without PRIDE

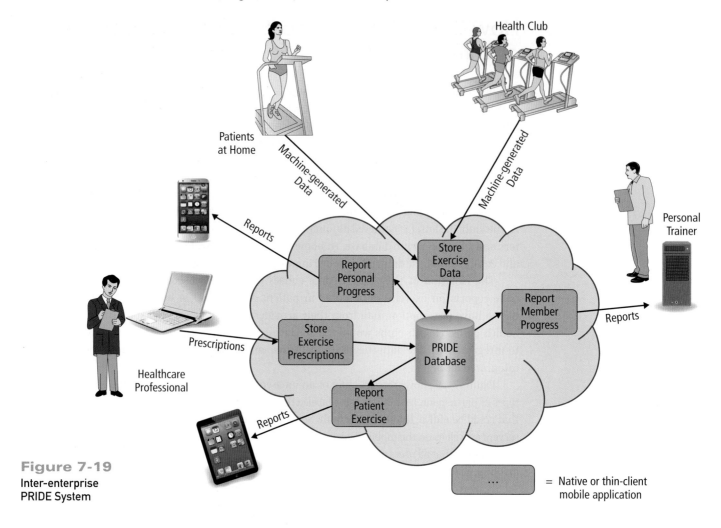

Figure 7-19
Inter-enterprise
PRIDE System

Q7-8   2026?

Within the next 10 years, ERP vendors and customers will have sorted out the problems of cloud-based ERP. In what is coming to be known as the **hybrid model**, ERP customers will store most of their data on cloud servers managed by cloud vendors and store sensitive data on servers that they manage themselves. Governmental agencies, financial analysts, and accountants will have defined standards against which organizations can be monitored for appropriate compliance. By the way, if you graduate as an accountant or financial analyst, this is interesting work in which you could be involved early in your career.

Mobility, however, will still present problems in 2026. Workers in the warehouse, loading dock, and shipping department will all carry mobile devices that enable them to process ERP and other enterprise applications from wherever they happen to be. Managers, decision makers, and other knowledge workers will have similar applications on their own phones or other mobile devices, devices that they can access from work, other offices, the street, or home.

However—and it's an enormous however—mobile devices are subject to severe security threats. It is one thing for criminals steal data about the past. As we learned from the Sony Entertainment data loss in late 2014, data loss is aggravating and embarrassing and damages the innocent. No one on the outside knows for sure, but it appears that Sony paid the hackers handsomely to call off the data releases. So, that loss was expensive in direct payoff as well as in the disruption of business operations.

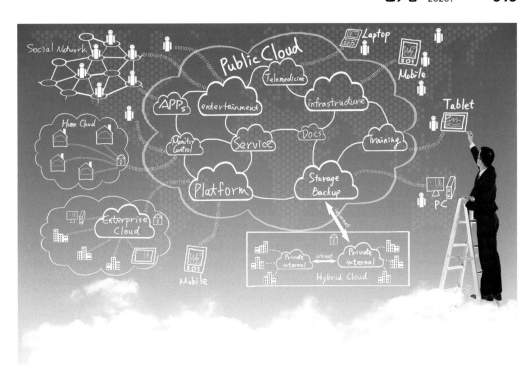

Figure 7-20
Designing a Future ERP System
Source: Tom Wang/Fotolia

Consider, however, what would happen if some criminal, perhaps a malicious insider, were to infiltrate an ERP system. It would be possible to wreak havoc in, say, supply chain orders and inventories or in the operation of machinery on the factory floor. The hacked organization would have to shut down its ERP system, and thus its company, to sort out the mess. But allowing users mobile access to the ERP system will enable organizations to make significant improvements in process quality. So, in the next 10 years, organizations must engage in a delicate balancing act between risk of loss and improvement to processes. We will discuss such trade-offs further in Chapter 10.

Consider also the effect of the Internet of Things. Future users of ERP systems will be not just people but also devices and machines. ERP vendors are adapting their software to the particular requirements of 3D printing. In the future, when a salesperson enters an order, he or she may be starting a machine to make that part on demand. In addition, factory automation will also add to process quality improvements. Inventory-picking robots are one example, but self-driving cars and trucks are likely to have an even larger effect. And within the next 10 years, machines will be able to employ the ERP system to schedule their own maintenance. For example, on the factory floor a milling machine will be able to order a replacement for a dull cutter, one possibly made by a 3D printer. Machines will schedule both routine and emergency maintenance for themselves, thus carrying factory automation to a new level.

As we have stated many times so far, the future belongs not to those who specialize in existing methods, technology, and processes but rather to those who can find and implement innovative applications of emerging trends. Technology's effect on enterprise systems will be widespread because enterprise systems are widespread. Many opportunities will occur in the early years of your career.

Security Guide

ONE-STOP SHOPPING

In this chapter, you've learned how the problems of information silos shown in Figure 7-5 can be eliminated by increasing the scope of information systems: Workgroup-induced silos can be eliminated by developing enterprise IS, and enterprise-induced silos can be eliminated by developing inter-enterprise IS. Nowhere in this discussion, however, have we thought about security.

In fact, while removing information silos does have the advantages discussed, moving data into a single, centralized facility creates a potential security problem. Namely, fraudsters can find all the data they want in one convenient location. It's one-stop shopping. So, data integration can make organizations more vulnerable.

On the other hand, centralizing data in one location enables the organization to focus security measures on a single resource. The IS support staff need not manage security over several, possibly many, distributed databases, but rather can focus security management on a single database. So, assuming appropriate security management, the two factors counterbalance one another: Risk of loss is higher, but security against such loss can be focused and ultimately result in less actual risk.

Consider how a large-scale integrated IS like the PRIDE system discussed at the start of this chapter can create unique security concerns. To start, for the purpose of this guide, let's assume that client privacy is appropriately protected. Clients only share the data with each of the PRIDE entities (employers, health clubs, equipment manufacturers, insurance companies, and healthcare providers) that they want to.

Even with that assumption, however, there are significant privacy and security issues. Clients, personal trainers, and healthcare providers need to see a client's complete exercise data. This means, however, that competing personal trainers (and health clubs) view data on their competitors' practices. Is this a problem? It's likely to be perceived as a problem even if there is no real danger, and that perception could limit PRIDE sales and use.

This example underlines some of the management problems of inter-enterprise IS. Unlike an enterprise system, where everyone works for the same employer and, except for inter-departmental rivalry, has the same incentive to protect data, an inter-enterprise system can connect competitors with different incentives and agendas. This fact not only increases security risk, it takes away one of the major ways of dealing with security flaws: procedures. In an enterprise system, it's possible for the organization to set up manual procedures that compensate for security weaknesses in programs or data controls. However, in an inter-enterprise system, if system users compete, they may have an incentive not to follow the compensating procedures.

Sources: © zentilia/Shutterstock and © andreiorlov/Fotolia

PRIDE's use of the cloud brings up another important security concern, one that exists at both the enterprise and inter-enterprise levels: How secure is the cloud vendor? The more important the information you store, the more attractive a target you become for attackers. The simplest example of this comes in the form of **bitcoins**.

In February 2014, Mt. Gox, the largest bitcoin exchange at the time, lost about 850,000 bitcoins valued at $460 million.[4] Mt. Gox declared bankruptcy and wouldn't, or couldn't, explain where all the bitcoins and cash had gone. Essentially, bitcoins represented a large cloud-based monetary system that was supposed to replace national currencies. It was, and still could be, a revolutionary idea.

The downside of Mt. Gox was that its very nature made it a perfect target. It was centrally located and accessible from anywhere, and it had a very large sum of money that could be electronically stolen. Hackers from around the world would never stop trying to steal from Mt. Gox. Gold is hard to steal because it's so heavy. But bits are light and easy to transport. Healthcare records, personal identities, financial records, and credit card information are all in digital form now, too.

The fall of Mt. Gox should cause one to wonder about the security of cloud storage. Most of the time, we don't even know the physical location of cloud data, let alone how well the data center is secured, who works there, what procedures and policies are in place, and so on. We will return to this question in Chapter 10; for now, just understand that this issue exists.

DISCUSSION QUESTIONS

1. Summarize why security risk is higher for integrated databases than for information silos. Describe a factor that can compensate for this increased risk.

2. Using PRIDE as an example, explain how users' incentives to protect data differ between an enterprise system and an inter-enterprise system. How does the use of security procedures differ between the two types of system?

3. Suppose you are a health club owner and you are approached by a PRIDE salesperson who says, "The PRIDE database is located in an XYZ cloud facility," where XYZ is the name of a large, reputable company, such as Amazon, Oracle, Microsoft, or IBM. You ask about data security, and the salesperson says, "You and I don't know anything about their security, but it has to be better than the security you have on that server you're operating in the closet down the hallway." How do you respond?

4. If you were a personal trainer at a health club, explain the value to you of having competitors' data about clients you share. Explain the value to you of obtaining, if you can, data about competitors' PRIDE clients who you have never trained.

5. Suppose you are a personal trainer at a health club and you are approached by a PRIDE salesperson who says, "Our system's security ensures that no one can see your clients' data." How do you respond?

6. Suppose the salesperson in question 5 says, "Only others who are coaching the same clients as you can see your client data." How can you verify the truth of this statement?

7. Suppose that a personal trainer at a health club uses a trivial password, such as *dog*. One of that health club's members watches the personal trainer sign in, obtains that password, and later steals all of the data on the clients who use that club.
   a. Who is responsible for the data theft?
   b. How do you respond if you are the personal trainer using the trivial password?
   c. If you are the club owner, how will you likely learn about this theft? How do you respond when you do learn of it?
   d. If you are a participating healthcare provider, how will you likely learn about this theft? How do you respond when you do learn of it?
   e. If you are a client who is using this system, whom do you hold accountable, and why?

8. Where was Mt. Gox physically located? Is the physical location of where your data is being stored important? Why or why not?

Guide

ERP AND THE STANDARD, STANDARD BLUEPRINT

Designing business processes is difficult, time consuming, and very expensive. Highly trained experts conduct seemingly countless interviews with users and domain experts to determine business requirements. Then even more experts join those people, and together this team invests thousands of labor hours to design, develop, and implement effective business processes that meet those requirements. All of this is a very high-risk activity, prone to failure. And it all must be done before IS development can even begin.

ERP vendors such as SAP have invested millions of labor hours into the business blueprints that underlie their ERP solutions. Those blueprints consist of hundreds or thousands of different business processes. Examples are processes for hiring employees, acquiring fixed assets, acquiring consumable goods, and custom "one-off" (a unique product with a unique design) manufacturing, to name just a few.

Additionally, ERP vendors have implemented their business processes in hundreds of organizations. In so doing, they have been forced to customize their standard blueprint for use in particular industries. For example, SAP has distribution-business blueprints that are customized for the auto parts industry, for the electronics industry, and for the aircraft industry. Hundreds of other customized solutions exist as well.

Even better, the ERP vendors have developed software solutions that fit their business-process blueprints. In theory, no software development is required at all if the organization can adapt to the standard blueprint of the ERP vendor.

As described in this chapter, when an organization implements an ERP solution, it identifies any differences that exist between its business processes and the standard blueprint. Then the organization must remove that difference, which can be done in one of two ways: It changes business processes to fit the standard blueprint; or the ERP vendor or a consultant modifies the standard blueprint (and software solution that matches that blueprint) to fit the unique requirements.

In practice, such variations from the standard blueprint are rare. They are difficult and expensive to implement, and they require the using organization to maintain the variations from the standard as new versions of the ERP software are developed. Consequently, most organizations choose to *modify*

their processes to meet the blueprint, rather than the other way around. Although such process changes are also difficult to implement, once the organization has converted to the standard blueprint, they need no longer support a "variation."

So, from a standpoint of cost, effort, risk, and avoidance of future problems, there is a huge incentive for organizations to adapt to the standard ERP blueprint.

Initially, SAP was the only true ERP vendor, but in the meantime other companies have developed and acquired ERP solutions as well. Because of competitive pressure across the software industry, all of these products are beginning to

Sources: Magdalena Kucova/Fotolia

have the same sets of features and functions. ERP solutions are becoming a commodity.

All of this is fine, as far as it goes, but it introduces a nagging question: If, over time, every organization tends to implement the standard ERP blueprint, and if, over time, every software company develops essentially the same ERP features and functions, then won't every business, worldwide, come to look just like every other business, worldwide? How will organizations gain a competitive advantage if they all use the same business processes?

If every auto parts distributor uses the same business processes, based on the same software, are they not all clones of one another? How will one distinguish itself? How will innovation occur? Even if one parts distributor does successfully innovate a business process that gives it a competitive advantage, will the ERP vendors be conduits to transfer that innovation to competitors? Does the use of "commoditized" standard blueprints mean that no company can sustain a competitive advantage?

 DISCUSSION QUESTIONS

1. Explain in your own words why an organization might choose to change its processes to fit the standard blueprint. What advantages accrue by doing so?

2. Explain how competitive pressure among software vendors will cause the ERP solutions to become commodities. What does this mean to the ERP software industry?

3. If two businesses use exactly the same processes and exactly the same software, can they be different in any way at all? Explain why or why not.

4. Explain the following statement: An ERP software vendor can be a conduit to transfer innovation. What are the consequences to the innovating company? To the software company? To the industry? To the economy?

5. In theory, such standardization might be possible, but worldwide, there are so many different business models, cultures, people, values, and competitive pressures, can any two businesses ever be exactly alike?

ACTIVE REVIEW

Use this Active Review to verify that you understand the ideas and concepts that answer the chapter's study questions.

Q7-1 What are the basic types of processes?

Define *structured* and *dynamic processes* and compare and contrast them. Define *workgroup processes, enterprise processes,* and *inter-enterprise processes* and explain their differences and challenges. Define those same levels of information systems. Define *functional systems* and *functional applications.*

Q7-2 How can information systems improve process quality?

Name, define, and give an example of two dimensions of process quality. Name and describe three ways that organizations can improve process quality. Name and describe three ways that information systems can be used to improve process quality.

Q7-3 How do information systems eliminate the problems of information silos?

Define *information silo* and explain how such silos come into existence. When do such silos become a problem? Describe the two types of silos in Figure 7-6 and explain the meaning implied by the two arrows.

Q7-4 How do CRM, ERP, and EAI support enterprise processes?

Define *business process reengineering* and explain why it is difficult and expensive. Explain two major reasons why developing enterprise information systems in-house is expensive. Explain the advantages of inherent processes. Define and differentiate among *CRM, ERP,* and *EAI.* Explain how the nature of CRM and ERP is more similar to each other than that of EAI.

Q7-5 What are the elements of an ERP system?

Describe the minimum capability of a true ERP product. Explain the nature of each of the following ERP solution components: programs, data, procedures, and training and consulting. For each, summarize the work that customers must perform. List the top five ERP vendors in decreasing order of market share.

Q7-6 What are the challenges of implementing and upgrading enterprise information systems?

Name and describe five sources of challenges when implementing enterprise systems. Describe why enterprise systems management must be collaborative. Explain two major tasks required to identify requirements gaps. Summarize the challenges of transitioning to an enterprise system. Explain why employees resist change and describe three ways of responding to that resistance. Discuss the challenges that new technology poses for enterprise systems.

Q7-7 How do inter-enterprise IS solve the problems of enterprise silos?

Describe information silos that exist among healthcare providers, health clubs, and individuals with regard to patient exercise data. Describe problems that those silos create. Explain how the system shown in Figure 7-19 will solve the problems caused by those silos. Define *distributed systems* and explain the benefits of SOA using Web services when implementing such systems.

Q7-8 2026?

Describe how the cloud, mobility, and the Internet of Things will affect enterprise systems in the next 10 years. Explain how these factors will create opportunities for business professionals. Explain how they will create opportunities for you!

Using Your Knowledge with PRIDE

Knowledge of this chapter will help you understand the fundamental value offered by solutions like PRIDE; namely, the elimination of the problems of enterprise-level information silos. As you now know, silos caused by workgroup processes can be eliminated (or managed, in the case of EAI) with enterprise systems. Similarly, silos caused by enterprise processes can be eliminated with inter-enterprise systems like PRIDE. Also, the knowledge of this chapter prepares you to understand the difficulty of adapting and of managing inter-enterprise systems. Finally, Figure 7-19 helps you understand how mobile devices and a cloud database can be used to implement an inter-enterprise system.

KEY TERMS AND CONCEPTS

MyMISLab™

To complete the problems with the ⭐, go to EOC Discussion Questions in the MyLab.

USING YOUR KNOWLEDGE

⭐ **7-1.** Using the example of your university, give examples of information systems for each of the three levels of scope (workgroup, enterprise, and inter-enterprise) discussed in Q7-1. Describe three departmental information systems likely to duplicate data. Explain how the characteristics of these systems relate to your examples.

⭐ **7-2.** In your answer to question 7-1, explain how the three workgroup information systems create information silos. Describe the kinds of problems these silos are likely to cause. Refer to the discussion in Q7-3 as a guide.

⭐ **7-3.** Using your answer to question 7-2, describe an enterprise information system that will eliminate the silos. Would the implementation of your system require business process reengineering? Explain why or why not.

7-4. a. ERP systems include "best industry practices" in the software. Explain what "best industry practices" means.

 b. In a feasibility study, suppose that a company finds conversion from its current stand alone systems to ERP system infeasible. The company is thus looking at alternate ways to eliminate the problems associated with its isolated systems. What solution would you recommend to this company?

7-5. a. What are the major components of a CRM application? How do they support the customer life cycle?

 b. Suppose that an insurance company wishes to implement a CRM system. Describe two ways in which a CRM system can be used in the insurance company, and what benefits will it obtain from it.

COLLABORATION EXERCISE 7

Using the collaboration IS you built in Chapter 2 (page 110), collaborate with a group of students to answer the following questions.

The county planning office issues building permits, septic system permits, and county road access permits for all building projects in a county in an eastern state. The planning office issues permits to homeowners and builders for the construction of new homes and buildings and for any remodeling projects

that involve electrical, gas, plumbing, and other utilities, as well as the conversion of unoccupied spaces, such as garages, into living or working space. The office also issues permits for new or upgraded septic systems and permits to provide driveway entrances to county roads.

Figure 7-21 shows the permit process that the county used for many years. Contractors and homeowners found this

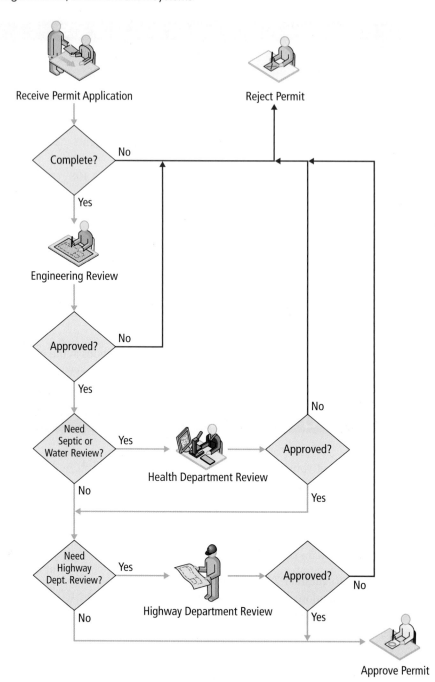

Figure 7-21
Building Permit Process,
Old Version

process slow and very frustrating. For one, they did not like its sequential nature. Only after a permit had been approved or rejected by the engineering review process would they find out that a health or highway review was also needed. Because each of these reviews could take 3 or 4 weeks, applicants requesting permits wanted the review processes to be concurrent rather than serial. Also, both the permit applicants and county personnel were frustrated because they never knew where a particular application was in the permit process. A contractor would call to ask how much longer, and it might take an hour or longer just to find which desk the permits were on.

Accordingly, the county changed the permit process to that shown in Figure 7-22. In this second process, the permit office

made three copies of the permit and distributed one to each department. The departments reviewed the permits in parallel; a clerk would analyze the results and, if there were no rejections, approve the permit.

Unfortunately, this process had a number of problems, too. For one, some of the permit applications were lengthy; some included as many as 40 to 50 pages of large architectural drawings. The labor and copy expense to the county was considerable.

Second, in some cases departments reviewed documents unnecessarily. If, for example, the highway department rejected an application, then neither the engineering nor health departments needed to continue their reviews. At first, the county

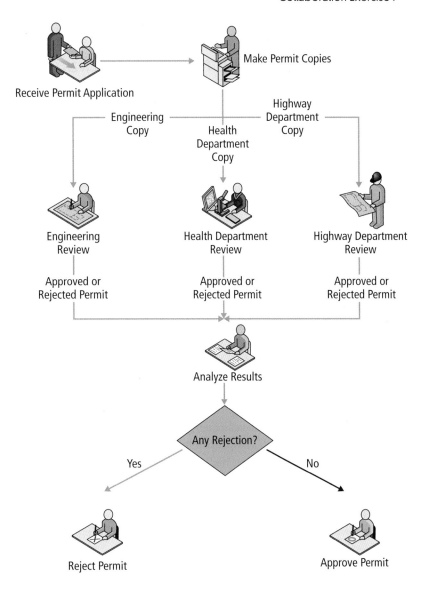

Figure 7-22
**Building Permit Process,
Revised Version**

responded to this problem by having the clerk who analyzed results cancel the reviews of other departments when a rejection was received. However, that policy was exceedingly unpopular with the permit applicants, because once the problem in a rejected application was corrected, the permit had to go back through the other departments. The permit would go to the end of the line and work its way back into the departments from which it had been pulled. Sometimes this resulted in a delay of 5 or 6 weeks.

Cancelling reviews was unpopular with the departments as well, because permit-review work had to be repeated. An application might have been nearly completed when it was cancelled due to a rejection in another department. When the application came through again, the partial work results from the earlier review were lost.

7-6. Explain why the processes in Figures 7-21 and 7-22 are classified as enterprise processes rather than departmental processes. Why are these processes not interorganizational processes?

7-7. Using Figure 7-8 as an example, redraw Figure 7-21 using an enterprise information system that processes a shared database. Explain the advantages of this system over the paper-based system in Figure 7-21.

7-8. Using Figure 7-10 as an example, redraw Figure 7-22 using an enterprise information system that processes a shared database. Explain the advantages of this system over the paper-based system in Figure 7-22.

7-9. Assuming that the county has just changed from the system in Figure 7-21 to the one in Figure 7-22, which of your answers in questions 7-7 and 7-8 do you think is better? Justify your answer.

7-10. Assume your team is in charge of the implementation of the system you recommend in your answer to question 7-9. Describe how each of the five challenges discussed in Q7-6 pertain to this implementation. Explain how your team will deal with those challenges.

Interorganizational IS – The National Programme for IT in the NHS Experience

The National Health Service (NHS) is the United Kingdom's publically funded healthcare system which serves the healthcare needs of its people, and proudly boasts its 'cradle-to-grave' and 'free-at-point-of-contact' credentials when compared to some other countries' similarly funded systems. It was founded in 1948 and continues to evolve organizationally, clinically, and in its development and use of information technologies, just like its publicly and privately funded counterparts in Europe, Africa, Asia, the Middle East, Australia, and the U.S. Although overall control lies with the Department of Health, the NHS is divided into a number of regional centers, including London, North, and South, each of which has semi-autonomous control of healthcare provision in an organizational structure, which includes Trusts, Community Health Services, and General Practices.

The National Programme for IT in the NHS (NPfIT) was established to develop systems to electronically administer patient information throughout the regions and their organizations. This required the development of interorganizational information systems. These parallel developments over an extended period of time provide us with an opportunity to learn from the experience of similar projects that had very different outcomes.

Consider, for example, the development of the shared X-rays system and the electronic patient records system. The shared X-rays system was delivered on time and on budget, and because of its success, is used nationally throughout the different NHS regions of England and in the organizational units, including Trusts and General Practices. By contrast, the electronic patient records system, which was being developed for each of the regions and organizational components of the NHS, was cancelled after a long period of investment and beyond what had originally been planned, and as such, is considered a failure. The electronic patient record system was never put into operation completely, despite having cost 6.40 billion GB Pounds (NAO, 2011). Although the programme in its original form was cancelled after the National Audit Office report of 2011, it was estimated that the expected total expenditure would have been 11.40 billion GB Pounds by 2015–16, if it had been implemented.

The two projects started at about the same time, and although they were of different scales, they had proportionately the same scope, goals, funding (the electronic patient records system eventually ended up overspending by several billions of GB Pounds) and the same required date of completion. In terms of the population sizes of Trust regions of England, the two systems would have potentially served the same number of patients. What then caused the outcomes to vary so much?

The National Programme for IT in the NHS

In 2002, the National Programme for IT in the NHS (NPfIT) was launched to reform the way information was used in England and transform services and the quality of patient care. This was to be realized by developing a number of national systems, including a broadband network and a system to share X-rays. The central aim was to develop a fully integrated electronic patient records database that would encompass the entire patient records system. This was to be designed to reduce reliance on paper files and make accurate patient records available continuously across the different parts of the NHS, and allow the rapid transmission of information.

The system was intended to be made up of two components representing each NHS patient: the Detailed Care Record (DCR) and the Summary Care Record (SCR). The DCR would contain complete details of the patient's medical history and treatment that would be accessible to a patient's General Practitioner and local community, and hospital care settings, for example, in the event of the patient being referred for hospital treatment. The SCR would contain key medical information, such as allergies, made available across England to NHS staff involved in treating the patient.

Figure 7-23 shows some of the organizations involved in the NPfIT in the NHS. Clearly, an interorganizational information system was needed. As you know from this chapter, such projects are often difficult to develop and manage, and it is not surprising that some providers failed to deliver the systems needed, most notably the electronic patient records system.

Electronic Sharing of X-rays System

The electronic sharing of X-rays system was part of the Picture Archive and Communications system (PAC). This was one of the national systems being developed for the NPfIT. From the outset, the involvement of health professionals gave evidence of the organization and planning of this project. This meant that the requirements for the system were clear and unambiguous, and thus grounded in clinical necessity versus political ambition. Importantly, an integral part of the programme involved the specification and implementation of a high-speed computer network linking all parts of the NHS organization, which enabled the relatively straightforward implementation of the X-rays sharing application.

As was noted by Campion-Awwad in 2014, "The computer accessible X–ray system was delivered smoothly on budget and on time. The X-ray system was a rare product of consultation with health professionals, and was also assisted by plans that

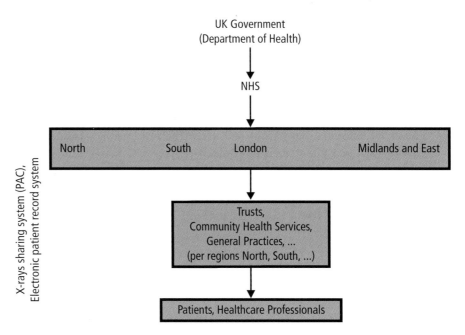

Figure 7-23
NPfIT Interorganizational IS

preceded the NPfIT. This system was added to the NPfIT well after the original specifications were approved, following a meeting between NPfIT and health professionals."

By 2007, the system had been successfully rolled out and delivered to all parts of the NHS organization with full buy-in with respect of all stakeholders, with their requirements in respect of the system being fully met clinically as well as organizationally. In these respects, the X-ray sharing system was an exemplar for other projects and systems within the NPfIT.

Electronic Patient Record System

The Electronic Patient Record System, on the other hand, was still far from completion by 2011 when the NAO reported on its progress in that year, some four years after the implementation of the X-rays sharing system. According to estimates given then, the work would have required a substantial further investment and would not have been complete until 2015–2016. Even after reducing the functional specification so as to bring forward the delivery of the system at reduced cost to the NHS organization, it became evident that timescales and cost savings would have been largely unaffected. By the time of the report, the Department of Health, and ultimately the government decided to dismantle and effectively cancel the programme in its NPfIT form.

Since the cancellation of the project, a forensic examination of the causes of the budget and time over-runs has taken place and the consensus is that at least four factors contributed to the abject failure of the programme: motives, buy-in, haste, and multi-sourcing. These could have been mitigated against had an interorganizational information system development – ERP, CRM,

EAI - been undertaken from the start of the project Although praise-worthy in its ambition, the programme was motivated by government in a top-down fashion without fully consulting IT experts, who would have been able to bring their project management skills and experience to bear. The lack of involvement of health professionals was found to be a major impediment as once systems and processes were being evaluated, there was a lack of buy-in from these end-users. Also, the speed with which contracts were awarded for the development of the system meant that planning, scope and deliverables among other crucial project parameters fell seriously short. Having many contactors develop the system for different parts of the NHS organization meant that, in-theory, if any one contractor failed to deliver at any point in the programme, they could be substituted with another. However, in hindsight, this multi-sourcing approach proved to be near impossible to operate effectively, moving too far away from the tried-and-tested 'one customer, one service provider' model of delivery.

Any one of these factors may have been recoverable if identified in reasonable time during the original project schedule. Unfortunately, this wasn't the case and when taken together, the seeds of the programme's failure were sown at an early stage.

QUESTIONS

7-11. Summarize the purpose and intended benefits of the NHS Programme for IT patient record system.

7-12. Explain why the NHS Programme for IT patient record system requires an interorganizational information system.

7-13. Using knowledge gained from this chapter, summarize the difficulties and challenges of developing interorganizational information systems, making references to how ERP, CRM and EAI systems may offer solutions to minimize these.

7-14. Systems in the NHS Programme for IT must use personal and confidential data about patients. Write a one-paragraph policy that stipulates responsible processing and storage of this data.

7-15. Explain what you believe are the reasons for the X-rays sharing system's success.

7-16. Read the summary of the National Audit Office's Executive Summary of the NHS Programme for IT (https://www.nao.org.uk/wp-content/uploads/2011/05/1012888es.pdf.) and summarize the report's findings.

7-17. Using the facts described in this case and your answer to question 7-16, list five key lessons that you can take from the NHS Programme for IT's X-rays sharing and Electronic Patient Records projects.

MyMISLab™

Go to the Assignments section of your MyLab to complete these writing exercises.

7-18. Processes tend to be either structured or dynamic. Clearly outline the key characteristics of structured and dynamic processes. Suggest a series of applications or circumstances in which either structured or dynamic processes could be used.

7-19. Go to www.microsoft.com and search for Microsoft Dynamics. Ignore Dynamics CRM. Have any important changes occurred in Microsoft's ERP product offerings since this edition was written? Has Microsoft brought a cloud-based ERP solution to market? Have any of the four ERP systems described in the chapter been better integrated with Office or the Microsoft Developer's platform? Using your knowledge guided by experience, what do you think are Microsoft's intentions with regard to ERP?

ENDNOTES

1. See *www.thisisant.com*.
2. The subject of this chapter is structured processes, and we will discuss process quality in terms of them. Note, however, that all of the concepts in this question pertain equally well to dynamic processes.
3. D. Peak, "An Interview with John Halamka, MD, Chief Information Officer, Harvard Medical School and CareGroup Health System, USA," *Journal of IT Case and Application Research*, 10, no. 1 (2008): 70.
4. Robert McMillian, "The Inside Story of Mt. Gox, Bitcoin's $460 Million Disaster," *Wired*, March 3, 2014, accessed June 2, 2014, *www.wired.com/2014/03/bitcoin-exchange*.

Social Media Information Systems

"**It's all about** eyeballs." Nicki Jensen is PRIDE Systems' new marketing director, and she's exploring ways to generate revenue from clicks on online ads. Zev Friedman, PRIDE Systems' new owner, asked her to do so in their last meeting (page 283).

"What do you mean?" James Wu is PRIDE's manager of information systems. He was with the company when it was owned by Dr. Flores. When Friedman bought the company, he brought James along.

"I mean, the number of eyeballs we get to look at our ads," Nicki responds.

"Well, not quite. It's about clicks, too." Michele Wilson is PRIDE Systems' new sales director. Her job is to ask vendors to sign up for ads for display on PRIDE's competitions and events.

Nicki looks at James. "We get as many eyes to look at our ads as we can. Then we motivate them to click."

She continues, "So how many people can we get into a virtual race? When we have the cloud connecting the data, we can get people spinning from their homes, their health clubs, wherever, worldwide, to race against each other."

Michele jumps in. "It could be 10,000 at one time, no?" She's looking for something to sell to vendors.

James shakes his head. "Maybe so, but we're getting way ahead of ourselves. PRIDE was designed to support eight to twelve people in an exercise class. People who were in treatment following a heart attack or something like that. Now you're saying, 'Let's have a class of 10,000.' Whoa. We're not there with our systems."

Nicki's heard this kind of talk in the past. "But we *could* support 10,000 in an event, no?"

"In theory, sure. But the devil's in the details. In this case, the details are the requirements. What kind of a user experience do you want? You can't put 10,000 little dots on a cell phone to show people where they are in the race. Well, let me correct myself: Of course we can put 10,000 little dots in the middle of a cell phone screen; we do it all the time, in fact. But what possible meaning would that have to anyone? They would see only a blur."

"Well, we can figure that out," Nicki says. "Couldn't we just show them the five or so people in front of them?"

"Sure we could. We could do anything. It's just bits. We can build anything you want. How much money and time have you got?" James is trying to sound positive.

He pauses to think, then continues, "And, like I said, the devil's in the details. Let's say the person in front of a particular user is 0.00000005 seconds ahead. How do we display that? Scale it up so it appears the person is way ahead? Or what if the person in front of this user is 10 minutes ahead, what then? And what if the user is the leader? What do we show? A blank screen?"

"Ah, we can figure that out. That doesn't seem so hard."

"No, it's not. It's just bits. We can do it, just like we could build a 20-story building to replace this old relic of a warehouse we're in. But we can't do it tomorrow, and it won't be free."

"So, what do you want to tell Zev, James?" Nicki is frustrated.

"I don't want to tell him anything. But he bought a company that had software that supported 10 people in an exercise class, and now he has you two telling me that we should multiply that by 1,000. All doable. Nothing wrong with the idea. But we are not there right now."

"Well," presses Nicki, "how long will it take? And what will it cost?"

"Let me try again. I want you to build a 20-story building to replace this one. How long will it take? How much will it cost?"

"It's all about eyeballs."

Image source: jiris/Fotolia

STUDY QUESTIONS

Q8-1 What is a social media information system (SMIS)?

Q8-2 How do SMIS advance organizational strategy?

Q8-3 How do SMIS increase social capital?

Q8-4 How do (some) companies earn revenue from social media?

Q8-5 How do organizations develop an effective SMIS?

Q8-6 What is an enterprise social network (ESN)?

Q8-7 How can organizations address SMIS security concerns?

Q8-8 2026?

"I have no idea; I need an architect, I need a contractor, and I need to know how much it costs to tear this building down." Nicki smiles at his analogy.

"OK. You've got it now."

As Michele listens to this, she wishes she hadn't left her last job. "Well, I'm telling you two, I can't sell anything with 10 people at an event. That's crazy."

"Well, what about 1,000 events with 10 people? You'll still get your 20,000 eyes … well, that assumes everyone has two eyes; probably a few less than 20,000." James likes accuracy.

"Come on, James, no vendor's gonna ask me how many one-eyed racers we've got."

"Stop it, you two! Michele, James is on to something. Think about it. How many people are in an online chess game?"

"Two, and let's assume that means four eyes, OK?" Michele is disgusted at James's comment.

"Let it go, Michele. But those online chess vendors make money. What if we did heats of races of 10 people each, then let the winner of each heat compete in the next round? We'd have continuing events and be able to sell between events … " Nicki trails off as she considers the possibilities.

CHAPTER PREVIEW

Changes to social media are happening so rapidly that we all struggle to keep up with the latest developments. We revise this textbook every year, and even still, writing in August, we know that by the time you read this in January or later, a good portion of it will be obsolete. Unfortunately, we don't know which parts they will be.

In our experience, the best response to rapid technological change is to learn and understand underlying principles. Rather than show you Facebook or Google+ features that we know will change before the ink on this page is dry, let's instead focus on principles, conceptual frameworks, and models that will be useful when you address the opportunities and risks of social media systems in the early years of your professional career.

This knowledge will also help you avoid mistakes. Every day, you hear businesspeople saying, "We're using Twitter" and "We've connected our Facebook page to our Web site." Or they mention that they are creating ads and news releases that say, "Follow us on Twitter." The important question is, for what purpose? To be modern? To be hip? And do they have a social media strategy? Will using social media affect their bottom line?

We'll begin in Q8-1 by defining and describing the components of a social media information system, which will help you understand the commitment that organizations make when they use social media. As you've learned, the purpose of information systems is to help organizations achieve their strategy, and, in Q8-2, we'll consider how social media information systems facilitate organizational strategies. Next, in Q8-3, we will address how social media information systems increase social capital. Q8-4 will address how some companies earn revenue from social media; Q8-5 will look at how you can develop an effective social media strategy; and Q8-6 will look at enterprise social networks. We will then describe in Q8-7 how organizations can address security concerns related to the use of social media. We'll wrap up in Q8-8 with an odd analogy about the change in the relationship between individuals and organizations heading into 2026.

Q8-1 What Is a Social Media Information System (SMIS)?

Social media (SM) is the use of information technology to support the sharing of content among networks of users. Social media enables people to form **communities of practice**, or simply **communities**, which are groups of people related by a common interest. A **social media information system (SMIS)** is an information system that supports the sharing of content among networks of users.

As illustrated in Figure 8-1, social media is a convergence of many disciplines. In this book, we will focus on the MIS portion of Figure 8-1 by discussing SMIS and how they contribute to organizational strategy. If you decide to work in the SM field as a professional, you will need some knowledge of all these disciplines, except possibly computer science.

Three SMIS Roles

Before discussing the components of an SMIS, we need to clarify the roles played by three organizational units:

*   Social media providers
*   Users
*   Communities

Social Media Providers

Social media providers such as Facebook, Google+, LinkedIn, Twitter, Instagram, and Pinterest provide platforms that enable the creation of **social networks**, or social relationships among people with common interests. The growth of SM over the past few years has been tremendous. Figure 8-2 shows the size of some well-known SM providers. In terms of the number of active users, several of these sites exceed the total population of the United States.[1] The growth of SM has generated extraordinary interest from businesses, advertisers, and investors. Social media providers compete with one another for the attention of users and for the associated advertising dollars.

Users

Users include both individuals *and* organizations that use SM sites to build social relationships. More than 73 percent of people with Internet access use SM, and 40 percent of people access SM via their mobile phones.[2] Social media providers are attracting, and targeting, certain

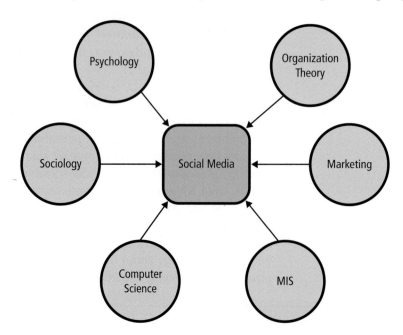

Figure 8-1

Social Media Is a Convergence of Disciplines

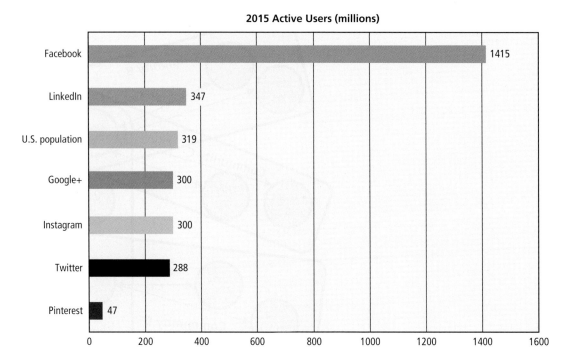

2015 Active Users (millions)

Figure 8-2
Number of Social Media
Active Users

demographic groups. For example, about 70 percent of Pinterest users are female.[3] On LinkedIn, 84 percent of users are 25 or older.[4]

Organizations are SM users too. You may not think of an organization as a typical user, but in many ways it is. Organizations create and manage SM accounts just like you do. It's estimated that 77 percent of *Fortune* 500 companies maintain active Twitter accounts, 70 percent have Facebook pages, and 69 percent have YouTube accounts.[5] These companies hire staff to maintain their SM presence, promote their products, build relationships, and manage their image.

Depending on how organizations want to use SM, they can be users, providers, or both. For example, larger organizations are big enough to create and manage their own internal social media platforms such as wikis, blogs, and discussion boards. In this case, the organization would be a social media provider. We'll look at the ways social media can be used within organizations later in this chapter.

Communities

Forming communities is a natural human trait; anthropologists claim that the ability to form them is responsible for the progress of the human race. In the past, however, communities were based on family relationships or geographic location. Everyone in the village formed a community. The key difference of SM communities is that they are formed based on mutual interests and transcend familial, geographic, and organizational boundaries.

Because of this transcendence, most people belong to several, or even many, different user communities. Google+ recognized this fact when it created user circles that enable users to allocate their connections (*people*, using Google+ terminology) to one or more community groups. Facebook and other SM application providers are adapting in similar ways.

To better understand the concept of communities, take a look at Figure 8-3. This figure shows that, from the point of view of the SM site, Community A is a first-tier community. It consists of users who have a direct relationship to that site. User 1, in turn, belongs to three communities: A, B, and C (these could be, say, classmates, professional contacts, and friends). From the point of view of the SM site, Communities B–E are second-tier communities because the relationships in those communities are intermediated by first-tier users. The number of second- and third-tier community members grows exponentially. If each community had, for example, 100 members,

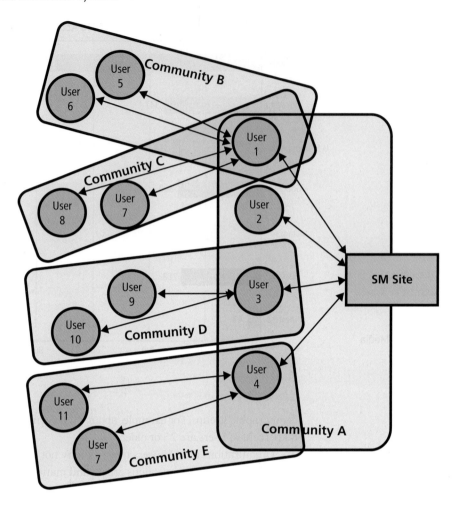

Figure 8-3
SM Communities

then the SM site would have 100×100, or 10,000, second-tier members and $100 \times 100 \times 100$, or 1 million, third-tier members. However, that statement is not quite true because communities overlap; in Figure 8-3, for example, User 7 belongs to Communities C and E. Thus, these calculations reveal the maximum number of users, as opposed to the actual number.

How the SM site chooses to relate to these communities depends on its goals. If the SM site is interested in pure publicity, it will want to relate to as many tiers of communities as it can. If so, it will create a **viral hook**, which is some inducement, such as a prize or other reward, for passing communications along through the tiers. If, however, the purpose of the SM site is to solve an embarrassing problem, say, to fix a product defect, then it would endeavor to constrain, as much as it can, the communications to Community A.

The exponential nature of relationships via community tiers offers organizations both a blessing and a curse. An employee who is a member of Community A can share her sincere and legitimate pride in her organization's latest product or service with hundreds or thousands of people in her communities. However, she can also blast her disappointment at some recent development to that same audience or, worse, inadvertently share private and proprietary organizational data with someone in that audience who works for the competition.

Social media is a powerful tool, and to use it well, organizations must know their goals and plan accordingly, as you'll learn.

SMIS Components

Because they are information systems, SMIS have the same five components as all IS: hardware, software, data, procedures, and people. Consider each component for the roles shown in Figure 8-4.

Component	Role	Description
Hardware	Social media providers	Elastic, cloud-based servers
	Users and communities	Any user computing device
Software	Social media providers	Application, NoSQL or other DBMS, Analytics
	Users and communities	Browser, IOS, Android, Windows 10, and other applications
Data	Social media providers	Content and connection data storage for rapid retrieval
	Users and communities	User-generated content, connection data
Procedures	Social media providers	Run and maintain application (beyond the scope of this text)
	Users and communities	Create and manage content, informal, copy each other
People	Social media providers	Staff to run and maintain application (beyond the scope of this text)
	Users and communities	Key users, adaptive, can be irrational

Figure 8-4
Five Components of SMIS

Hardware

Both users and organizations process SM sites using desktops, laptops, and mobile devices. In most cases, social media providers host the SM presence using elastic servers in the cloud.

Software

Users employ browsers and client applications to communicate with other users, send and receive content, and add and remove connections to communities and other users. These applications can be desktop or mobile applications for a variety of platforms, including iOS, Android, and Windows.

Social media providers develop and operate their own custom, proprietary, social networking application software. As you learned in Chapter 4, supporting custom software is expensive over the long term; SM application vendors must do so because the features and functions of their applications are fundamental to their competitive strategy. They can do so because they spread the development costs over the revenue generated by millions of users.

Many social networking vendors use a NoSQL database management system to process their data, though traditional relational DBMS products are used as well. Facebook began development of its own in-house DBMS (Cassandra), but later donated it to the open source community when it realized the expense and commitment of maintaining it. In addition to custom applications and databases, SM providers also invest in analytic software to understand how users interact with their site and application software.

Data

SM data falls into two categories: content and connections. **Content data** is data and responses to data that are contributed by users. You provide the source content data for your Facebook site, and your friends provide response content when they write on your wall, make comments, tag you, or otherwise publish on your site.

Connection data is data about relationships. On Facebook, for example, the relationships to your friends are connection data. The fact that you've liked particular organizations is also connection data. Connection data differentiates SMIS from Web site applications. Both Web sites and social networking sites present user and responder content, but only social networking applications store and process connection data.

SM providers store and retrieve SM data on behalf of users. They must do so in the presence of network and server failures, and they must do so rapidly. The problem is made somewhat easier, however, because SM content and connection data have a relatively simple structure.

Procedures

For social networking users, procedures are informal, evolving, and socially oriented. You do what your friends do. When the members of your community learn how to do something new and interesting, you copy them. SM Software is designed to be easy to learn and use.

Such informality makes using SMIS easy, but it also means that unintended consequences are common. The most troubling examples concern user privacy. Many people have learned not to post pictures of themselves in front of their house numbers on the same publicly accessible site on which they're describing their new high-definition television. Many others, alas, have not.

For organizations, social networking procedures are more formalized and aligned with the organization's strategy. Organizations develop procedures for creating content, managing user responses, removing obsolete or objectionable content, and extracting value from content. For example, setting up an SMIS to gather data on product problems is a wasted expense unless procedures exist to extract knowledge from that social networking data. Organizations also need to develop procedures to manage SM risk, as described in Q8-7.

Procedures for operating and maintaining the SM application are beyond the scope of this text.

People

Users of social media do what they want to do depending on their goals and their personalities. They behave in certain ways and observe the consequences. They may or may not change their behavior. By the way, note that SM users aren't necessarily rational, at least not in purely monetary ways. See, for example, the study by Vernon Smith in which people walked away from free money because they thought someone else was getting more![6]

Organizations cannot be so casual. Anyone who uses his or her position in a company to speak for an organization needs to be trained on both SMIS user procedures and the organization's social networking policy. We will discuss such procedures and policies in Q8-7.

Social media is creating new job titles, new responsibilities, and the need for new types of training. For example, what makes a good tweeter? What makes an effective wall writer? What type of people should be hired for such jobs? What education should they have? How does one evaluate candidates for such positions? How do you find these types of people? All of these questions are being asked and answered today.

Q8-2 How Do SMIS Advance Organizational Strategy?

In Chapter 3, Figure 3-1 (page 119), you learned the relationship of information systems to organizational strategy. In brief, strategy determines value chains, which determine business processes, which determine information systems. Insofar as value chains determine *structured* business processes, such as those discussed in Chapter 7, this chain is straightforward. However, social media is by its very nature *dynamic*; its flow cannot be designed or diagrammed, and if it were, no sooner would the diagram be finished than the SM process would have changed.

Therefore, we need to back up a step and consider how value chains determine dynamic processes and thus set SMIS requirements. As you will see, social media fundamentally changes the balance of power among users, their communities, and organizations.

Figure 8-5 summarizes how social media contributes to the five primary value chain activities and to the human resources support activity. Consider each row of this table.

Activity	Focus	Dynamic process	Risks
Sales and marketing	Outward to prospects	Social CRM Peer-to-peer sales	Loss of credibility Bad PR
Customer service	Outward to customers	Peer-to-peer support	Loss of control
Inbound logistics	Upstream supply chain providers	Problem solving	Privacy
Outbound logistics	Downstream supply chain shippers	Problem solving	Privacy
Manufacturing and operations	Outward for user design; Inward to operations and manufacturing	User-guided design Industry relationships Operational efficiencies	Efficiency/effectiveness
Human resources	Employment candidates; Employee communications	Employee prospecting, recruiting, and evaluation SharePoint for employee-to-employee communication	Error Loss of credibility

Figure 8-5
SM in Value Chain Activities

Social Media and the Sales and Marketing Activity

In the past, organizations controlled their relationships with customers using structured processes and related information systems. In fact, the primary purpose of traditional CRM was to manage customer touches. Traditional CRM ensured that the organization spoke to customers with one voice and that it controlled the messages, the offers, and even the support that customers received based on the value of a particular customer. In 1990, if you wanted to know something about an IBM product, you'd contact its local sales office; that office would classify you as a prospect and use that classification to control the literature, the documentation, and your access to IBM personnel.

Social CRM is a dynamic, SM-based CRM process. The relationships between organizations and customers emerge in a dynamic process as both parties create and process content. In addition to the traditional forms of promotion, employees in the organization create wikis, blogs, discussion lists, frequently asked questions, sites for user reviews and commentary, and other dynamic content. Customers search this content, contribute reviews and commentary, ask more questions, create user groups, and so forth. With social CRM, each customer crafts his or her own relationship with the company.

Social CRM flies in the face of the structured and controlled processes of traditional CRM. Because relationships emerge from joint activity, customers have as much control as companies. This characteristic is anathema to traditional sales managers who want structured processes for controlling what the customer reads, sees, and hears about the company and its products.

Further, traditional CRM is centered on lifetime value; customers that are likely to generate the most business get the most attention and have the most effect on the organization. However, with social CRM, the customer who spends 10 cents but who is an effective reviewer, commentator, or blogger can have more influence than the quiet customer who purchases $10M a year. Such imbalance is incomprehensible to traditional sales managers.

However, traditional sales managers *are* happy to have loyal customers sell their products using peer-to-peer recommendations. A quick look at products and their reviews on Amazon.com will show how frequently customers are willing to write long, thoughtful reviews of products they like or do not like. Amazon.com and other online retailers also allow readers to rate the helpfulness of reviews. In that way, substandard reviews are revealed for the wary.

Today, many organizations are struggling to make the transition from controlled, structured, traditional CRM processes to wide-open, adaptive, dynamic social CRM processes; this struggle represents a significant job opportunity for those interested in IS, sales, and social media.

Social Media and Customer Service

Product users are amazingly willing to help each other solve problems. Even more, they will do so without pay; in fact, payment can warp and ruin the support experience as customers fight with one another. SAP, for example, learned that it was better to reward its SAP Developer Network with donations on their behalf to charitable organizations than to give them personal rewards.

Not surprisingly, organizations whose business strategy involves selling to or through developer networks have been the earliest and most successful at SM-based customer support. In addition to SAP, Microsoft has long sold through its network of partners. Its MVP (Most Valuable Professional) program is a classic example of giving praise and glory in exchange for customer-provided customer assistance (*http://mvp.support.microsoft.com*). Of course, the developers in these networks have a business incentive to participate because that activity helps them sell services to the communities in which they participate.

However, users with no financial incentive are also willing to help others. For instance, Amazon.com supports a program called Vine by which customers can be selected to give prerelease and new product reviews to the buyer community.[7] You'll need your psychology course to explain what drives people to strive for such recognition. MIS just provides the platform!

The primary risk of peer-to-peer support is loss of control. Businesses may not be able to control peer-to-peer content. Negative comments about cherished products and recommendations for competitor's products are a real possibility. We address these risks in Q8-7.

Social Media and Inbound and Outbound Logistics

Companies whose profitability depends on the efficiency of their supply chain have long used information systems to improve both the effectiveness and efficiency of structured supply chain processes. Because supply chains are tightly integrated into structured manufacturing processes, there is less tolerance for the unpredictability of dynamic, adaptive processes. Solving problems is an exception; social media can be used to provide numerous solution ideas and rapid evaluation of them. The Japanese earthquake in the spring of 2011 created havoc in the automotive supply chain when major Japanese manufacturers lacked power and, in some cases, facilities to operate. Social media was used to dispense news, allay fears of radioactive products, and address ever-changing needs and problems.

SM communities may provide better and faster problem solutions to complex supply chain problems. Social media is designed to foster content creation and feedback among networks of users, and that characteristic facilitates the iteration and feedback needed for problem solving, as described in Chapter 2.

Loss of privacy is, however, a significant risk. Problem solving requires the open discussion of problem definitions, causes, and solution constraints. Because suppliers and shippers work with many companies, supply chain problem solving via social media may be problem solving in front of your competitors.

Social Media and Manufacturing and Operations

Operations and manufacturing activities are dominated by structured processes. The flexibility and adaptive nature of social media would result in chaos if applied to the manufacturing line or to the warehouse. However, social media does play a role in designing products, developing supplier relationships, and improving operational efficiencies.

Crowdsourcing is the dynamic social media process of employing users to participate in product design or product redesign. eBay often solicits customers to provide feedback on their eBay experience. As its site says, "There's no better group of advisors than our customers." User-guided design has been used to create video games, shoes, and many other products.

Social media has been widely used in **businesses-to-consumer (B2C)** relationships to market products to end users. Now manufacturers are starting to use social media to become industry leaders, promote brand awareness, and generate new **business-to-business (B2B)** leads to retailers. Manufacturers can use social media by starting a blog that discusses the latest industry-related news, posts interviews with experts, and comments on new product innovations. They can also create a YouTube channel and post videos of product reviews and testing and factory walk-throughs. Facebook and Twitter accounts are useful to promote positive consumer stories, announce new products, and follow competitors. Retailers view manufacturers who engage in such SM efforts as industry leaders.

Operations can use social media to improve communication channels within the organization and externally with consumers. For example, an enterprise social networking service like Yammer can be used to provide managers with real-time feedback about how to resolve internal operational inefficiencies. Externally, a retailer could monitor its corporate Twitter account and respond to product shortages or spikes in demand for new products around holidays.

Social Media and Human Resources

The last row in Figure 8-5 concerns the use of social media in human resources. As previously mentioned, social media is used for finding employee prospects, for recruiting candidates, and—in some organizations—for candidate evaluation.

Organizations use social media sites like LinkedIn to hire the best people more quickly and at a lower cost. For about $750 a month, recruiters can search through 350 million LinkedIn members to find the perfect candidate.[8] That $750 a month may sound like a lot to you, but to corporate customers, it's peanuts. The cost of hiring just one new employee runs around $4,000.[9] If an independent recruiting company is involved, that cost can be as high as 10 percent of the new employee's salary. LinkedIn also gives employers access to *passive* candidates who might not be looking for a job but are a perfect fit for a particular position. Once the employee is hired, the employer can leverage that new employee's social network to hire more candidates just like him or her.

Reppler, a social networking image management company, reports that 93 percent of employers it surveyed used social media to screen candidates. Furthermore, 55 percent of survey respondents reported that they had reconsidered a candidate because of what he or she had on social media sites. The good news is that 39 percent of those were positive reconsiderations. The bad news is that 61 percent were negative reconsiderations based on finding profanity; spelling or grammar mistakes; and references to sex, drugs, alcohol, or guns.[10]

Social media is also used for employee communications, using internal personnel sites such as MySite and MyProfile in SharePoint or other similar enterprise systems. SharePoint provides a place for employees to post their expertise in the form of "Ask me about" questions. When employees are looking for an internal expert, they can search SharePoint for people who have posted the desired expertise. SharePoint 2013 greatly extends support for social media beyond that in earlier SharePoint versions.

The risks of social media in human resources concern the possibility of error when using sites such as Facebook to form conclusions about employees. A second risk is that the SM site becomes too defensive or is obviously promulgating an unpopular management message.

Study Figure 8-5 to understand the general framework by which organizations can accomplish their strategy via a dynamic process supported by SMIS. We will now turn to an economic perspective on the value and use of SMIS.

Q8-3 How Do SMIS Increase Social Capital?

Business literature defines three types of capital. Karl Marx defined **capital** as the investment of resources for future profit. This traditional definition refers to investments into resources such as factories, machines, manufacturing equipment, and the like. **Human capital** is the investment in human knowledge and skills for future profit. By taking this class, you are investing in your own human capital. You are investing your money and time to obtain knowledge that you hope will differentiate you from other workers and ultimately give you a wage premium in the workforce.

According to Nan Lin, **social capital** is the investment in social relations with the expectation of returns in the marketplace.[11] You can see social capital at work in your personal life. You strengthen your social relationships when you help someone get a job, set a friend up on a date, or introduce a friend to someone famous. You weaken the strength of your social relationships by continually freeloading, declining requests for help, and failing to spend time with friends.

In your professional life, you are investing in your social capital when you attend a business function for the purpose of meeting people and reinforcing relationships. Similarly, you can use social media to increase your social capital by recommending or endorsing someone on LinkedIn, liking a picture on Facebook, retweeting a tweet, or commenting on an Instagram picture.

What Is the Value of Social Capital?

According to Lin, social capital adds value in four ways:

- Information
- Influence
- Social credentials
- Personal reinforcement

First, relationships in social networks can provide *information* about opportunities, alternatives, problems, and other factors important to business professionals. On a personal level, this could come in the form of a friend telling you about a new job posting or the best teacher to take for Business Law. As a business professional, this could be a friend introducing you to a potential new supplier or letting you know about the opening of a new sales territory.

Second, relationships provide an opportunity to *influence* decision makers at your employer or in other organizations who are critical to your success. For example, playing golf every Saturday with the CEO of the company you work for could increase your chances of being promoted. Such influence cuts across formal organizational structures, such as reporting relationships.

Third, being linked to a network of highly regarded contacts is a form of *social credential.* You can bask in the glory of those with whom you are related. Others will be more inclined to work with you if they believe critical personnel are standing with you and may provide resources to support you.

Finally, being linked into social networks *reinforces* a professional's identity, image, and position in an organization or industry. It reinforces the way you define yourself to the world (and to yourself). For example, being friends with bankers, financial planners, and investors may reinforce your identity as a financial professional.

As mentioned, a social network is a network of social relationships among individuals with a common interest. Each social network differs in value. The social network you maintain with your high school friends probably has less value than the network you have with your business associates, but not necessarily so. According to Henk Flap, the **value of social capital** is determined by the number of relationships in a social network, by the strength of those relationships, and by the resources controlled by those related.[12] If your high school friends happened to have been Mark Zuckerberg or Cameron and Tyler Winklevoss and if you maintain strong relations with them via your high school network, then the value of that social network far exceeds any you'll have at work. For most of us, however, the network of our current professional contacts provides the most social capital.

So, when you use social networking professionally, consider these three factors. You gain social capital by adding more friends and by strengthening the relationships you have with existing friends. Further, you gain more social capital by adding friends and strengthening relationships with people who control resources that are important to you. Such calculations may seem cold, impersonal, and possibly even phony. When applied to the recreational use of social networking, they may be. But when you use social networking for professional purposes, keep them in mind.

When it comes to social capital, one tool you might find particularly useful is *Klout.com.* This site searches social media activity on Facebook, Twitter, and other sites and creates what it calls a Klout score, which is a measure of an individual's social capital. Klout scores vary from 0 to 100; the more that others respond to your content, the higher your score. Also, responses from people who seldom respond are valued more than responses from those who respond frequently.[13]

How Do Social Networks Add Value to Businesses?

Organizations have social capital just as humans do. Historically, organizations created social capital via salespeople, customer support, and public relations. Endorsements by high-profile people are a traditional way of increasing social capital, but there are tigers in those woods.

Today, progressive organizations maintain a presence on Facebook, LinkedIn, Twitter, and possibly other sites. They include links to their social networking presence on their Web sites and make it easy for customers and interested parties to leave comments.

To understand how social networks add value to businesses, consider each of the elements of social capital: number of relationships, strength of relationships, and resources controlled by "friends."

Using Social Networking to Increase the Number of Relationships

In a traditional business relationship, a client (you) has some experience with a business, such as a restaurant or resort. Traditionally, you may express your opinions about that experience by word of mouth to your social network. If you are an **influencer** in your social network, your opinion may force a change in others' behavior and beliefs.

However, such communication is unreliable and brief: You are more likely to say something to your friends if the experience was particularly good or bad; but, even then, you are likely only to say something to those friends whom you encounter while the experience is still recent. And once you have said something, that's it; your words don't live on for days or weeks.

However, what if you could use SM to communicate your experience using text, pictures, and video instantly to everyone in your social network? For example, suppose a wedding photographer uses social media to promote her business by asking a recent client (user 1) to "like" her Facebook page and the wedding photos posted there (Figure 8-6). She also tags people in the client's pictures on Facebook. She may even ask the client to tweet about her experience.

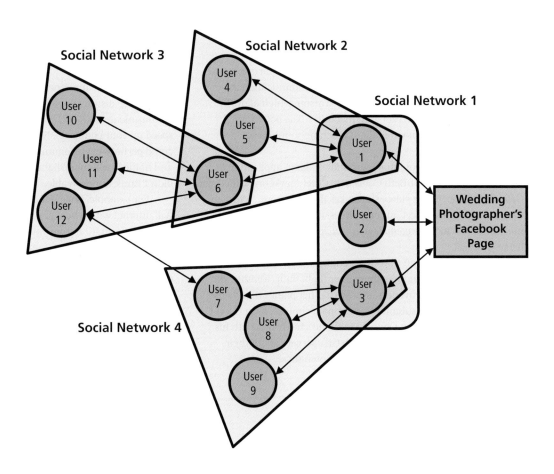

Figure 8-6
Growing Social Networks

SO WHAT?

Facebook for Organizations... and Machines

Social media is fun and entertaining for individuals, but what about commerce?

For example, what would happen if you took Facebook functionality and created an enterprise social network? How would the organization change if everyone was talking with everyone? That's exactly what Salesforce.com did when it created Chatter.

Chatter can be used to connect employees and customers via social media. For example, retail salespeople can communicate directly with managers to give instant feedback about a new sales promotion. Chatter can also connect salespeople with presale support personnel or customer service personnel with customers.

With Chatter, or its rival Yammer, organizational communities of practice identify and solve problems more quickly and more effectively than before. With social media, communities of practice readily find needed experts within the organization and recruit them to help solve problems. Organizations become more responsive because of faster project collaboration. Internal-facing communities of practice use all the things you like about your personal social media to make organizations better.

Enterprise social media is taking off, and consumer social media is an established success. But what lies ahead? Where will social media be applied next? Well, there's one player that's been left out of this scenario—the machines.

Machines have helped facilitate communication, but they haven't really been treated as communication partners. We're starting to see human-to-computer communication in applications like Apple's Siri and IBM's Watson, which allow humans to naturally interact with machines. The potential here is tremendous. But what about machine-to-machine communication?

A startling, and potentially groundbreaking, application is mentioned in a video of Beth Comstock, Chief Marketing Officer for General Electric. In the video, she makes the statement, "We want to use Chatter to connect our employees, our customers, and our machines." Go to *www.youtube.com/watch?v=nHaBCcn-9BU* and listen yourself.

Did Comstock mean that GE jet engines are going to be social media users? Will jet engines share their flight data (weather, air speed, chop, pilot effectiveness, etc.) with other planes that fly the same route? Will they submit reviews on mechanics, as in "Don't accept maintenance from Charlie Smith; he's too rough with his tools"? Will GE's jet engines chat with GE's servers about their performance and need for scheduled maintenance?

Source: Tuomas Kujansuu/iStock/Getty Images.

From a consumer perspective, social media among machines might have distinct advantages. For example, your car could communicate with each traffic light along your route to work to speed up your commute. No more sitting at red lights. Your car could perhaps even communicate with your phone, watch, tablet, and home (appliances, lights, doors, etc.) to solve problems you didn't think were solvable.

For example, once self-driving cars become widely used, they will interact with a host of different devices. Your self-driving car will get information from your health monitor indicating that you haven't eaten in 5 hours. Your car will also know, via your online calendar, that you have a meeting across town in an hour. Your car could then map out a route with a stop at your favorite bistro, pick up an electronic coupon, call in your order, send the dietary information to your health monitor, and get you to your meeting on time.

Social machines will change the way organizations operate and the way people live their lives. Embrace the change.

Questions

1. Visit *www.salesforce.com/chatter* to learn about Chatter's features and applications. How could Chatter affect value chain activities?

2. How might Chatter help Apple Inc. create better products?

3. Why would employees, managers, and owners like to use Chatter? Consider each individually.

4. One example of social media for machines is having machines report operational status data (say, speed, temperature, fuel usage, and so on, depending on the type of machine) to a Chatter or other SM site. How can an organization use such reporting in the context of machine, customer, and employee social media?

5. How might machines use foursquare (location-based social networking)? Consider machine-to-machine interactions as well as human-to-machine interactions.

6. Could machine-to-machine social interactions lead to security or privacy concerns? How?

All of the people in the client's social network (users 4–6) see the likes, tags, and tweets. If user 6 likes the pictures, they might be seen by users 10–12. It's possible that one of those users is looking for a wedding photographer. Using social media, the photographer has thus grown her social network to reach potential clients who she wouldn't have otherwise had access to. She also used SM to grow the number of relationships she has with clients. Depending on the number, strength, and value of those relationships, her social capital within those networks could substantially increase.

Such relationship sales have been going on by word of mouth for centuries; the difference here is that SMIS allow such relationships to scale to levels not possible in the past. In fact, the photographer in our example might even consider *paying* the client for the opportunity to take the wedding pictures if the client were a famous celebrity with hundreds of thousands of followers. In this way, social media may allow users to convert social capital into financial capital. Some famous celebrities get paid more than $10,000 for a single 140-character tweet![14]

Using Social Networks to Increase the Strength of Relationships

To an organization, the **strength of a relationship** is the likelihood that the other entity (person or other organization) in the relationship will do something that benefits the organization. An organization may have a strong relationship with you if you write positive reviews about it, post pictures of you using the organization's products or services, tweet about upcoming product releases, and so on.

In the previous example, the photographer asked a client to like her Facebook page and wedding photos. To the photographer, the number of friends the client has in her social network is important, but equally important is the strength of the relationships. Will the client's friends like the photographer's page and photos? Will they retweet the client's success story? If none of the client's friends like the photographer's page and photos, then the strength of the relationships is weak. If all of the client's friends like the photographer's page and photos, then the strength of the relationships in the client's social network is strong.

In his autobiography, Benjamin Franklin provided a key insight.[15] He said that if you want to strengthen your relationship with someone in power, ask him to do you a favor. Before Franklin invented the public library, he would ask powerful strangers to lend him their expensive books. In that same sense, organizations have learned that they can strengthen their relationships with you by asking you to do them a favor. When you provide that favor, it strengthens your relationship with the organization.

Traditional capital depreciates. Machines wear out, factories get old, technology and computers become obsolete, and so forth. Does social capital also depreciate? Do relationships wear out from use? So far, the answer seems to be both yes and no.

Clearly, there are only so many favors you can ask of someone in power. And there are only so many times a company can ask you to review a product, post pictures, or provide connections to your friends. At some point, the relationship deteriorates due to overuse. So, yes, social capital can be spent.

However, frequent interactions strengthen relationships and hence increase social capital. The more you interact with a company, the stronger your commitment and allegiance. But continued frequent interactions occur only when both parties see value in continuing the relationship. Thus, at some point, the organization must provide you an incentive to continue to do it a favor.

So, social capital can be spent, but it can also be earned by adding something of value to the interaction. If an organization can induce those in its relationships to provide more influence, information, social credentials, or personal reinforcement, it has strengthened those relationships. And, continuing a successful relationship over time substantially increases relationship strength.

Using Social Networks to Connect to Those with More Resources

Buying automated bot followers is a questionable practice. Read more about it in the Ethics Guide on pages 344–345.

The third measure of the value of social capital is the value of the resources controlled by those in the relationships. An organization's social capital is thus partly a function of the social capital of those to whom it relates. The most visible measure is the number of relationships. Someone with 1,000 loyal Twitter followers is usually more valuable than someone with 10. But the calculation is more subtle than that; for example, if those 1,000 followers are college students and if the organization's product is adult diapers, then the value of the relationship to the followers is low. A relationship with 10 Twitter followers who are in retirement homes would be more valuable.

To illustrate this point, Figure 8-7 shows the top five most popular YouTube channels in the beauty and style category and the food and cooking category.[16] In general, the more views a channel gets, the more the content creator gets paid. However, notice that the food and cooking channels have higher earnings than the beauty and style channels. The number of views is not the only factor influencing earnings. The resources (i.e., money) controlled by the viewers of the food and cooking channels may be higher than the viewers of the beauty and style channels.

Top 5 Beauty and Style Channels	Monthy Views (millions)	Est. Monthly Earnings
Yuya	35.8	$41,476
grav3yardgirl	27.7	$32,292
Zoella	23.5	$27,375
Cute Girls Hairstyles	18.4	$21,078
Rclbeauty101	17.8	$20,960

Top 5 Food and Cooking Channels	Monthy Views (millions)	Est. Monthly Earnings
CharlisCraftyKitchen	29.1	$127,777
Mosogourmet	22.9	$100,031
CookiesCupcakesandCardio	17.1	$79,309
How To Cook That	16.4	$77,773
MyCupcakeAddiction	13.5	$64,268

Figure 8-7
Top YouTube Channels
Source: Data from Nat Ives, "What a YouTube Celeb Pulls In," Adage .com, April 15, 2015, accessed May 5, 2015, *http://adage.com/article/ news/a-youtube-celeb-pulls/298015.*

There is no formula for computing social capital, but the three factors would seem to be more multiplicative than additive. Or, stated in other terms, the value of social capital is more in the form of

$$Social\ Capital = Number\ of\ Relationships \times Relationship\ Strength \times Entity\ Resources$$

than in the form of

$$Social\ Capital = Number\ of\ Relationships + Relationship\ Strength + Entity\ Resources$$

Again, do not take these equations literally; take them in the sense of the multiplicative interaction of the three factors.

This multiplicative nature of social capital means that a huge network of relationships with people who have few resources may be of less value than a smaller network of relationships with people who have substantial resources. Furthermore, those resources must be relevant to the organization. Students with pocket change are relevant to Pizza Hut; they are irrelevant to a BMW dealership.

This discussion brings us to the brink of social networking practice. Most organizations today ignore the value of entity assets and simply try to connect to more people with stronger relationships. This area is ripe for innovation. Data aggregators such as ChoicePoint and Acxiom maintain detailed data about people worldwide. It would seem that such data could be used by information systems to calculate the potential value of a relationship to a particular individual. This possibility would enable organizations to better understand the value of their social networks as well as guide their behavior with regard to particular individuals.

Stay tuned; many possibilities exist, and some ideas—maybe yours—will be very successful.

Q8-4 How Do (Some) Companies Earn Revenue from Social Media?

Having a large social network with strong relationships may not be enough. Facebook, for example, has more than 1.4 billion active users that generate 4.5 billion likes each day. YouTube has more than 1 billion active users that watch more than 6 billion hours of video each month.[17] Both companies have extremely large numbers of active users. The only problem is that they give it away for free. Billions of anything multiplied by zero is zero. Do all those users really matter if Facebook and YouTube can't make a single penny off of them?

As a business student, you know that nothing is free. Processing time, data communication, and data storage may be cheap, but they still cost something. Who pays for the hardware? Social media companies like Facebook, Twitter, and LinkedIn also need to pay people to develop, implement, and manage the SMIS. And where does Web content come from? *Fortune* pays authors for the content that it offers for free. Who is paying those authors? And from what revenue?

You Are the Product

Social media has evolved in such a way that users expect to use SM applications without paying for them. SM companies want to build up a large network of users quickly, but they have to offer a free product in order to attract users. The dilemma then becomes how do they **monetize**, or make money from, their application, service, or content.

The answer is by making *users* the product. That may sound strange at first. You don't want to think of yourself as a product. But try to look at it from the company's point of view. When a company runs an advertisement, it's essentially being paid to put the ad in front of its users. In a way, it's renting your eyeballs to an advertiser for a short period of time. Google is paid to target users with ads by using their search terms, sites they visit, and "scans" of their emails to place targeted ads in front of them. In essence, then, users are the product being sold to advertisers. As the old saying says, "If you're not paying, you're the product."

Revenue Models for Social Media

The two most common ways SM companies generate revenue are advertising and charging for premium services. On Facebook, for example, creating a company page is free, but Facebook charges a fee to advertise to communities that "like" that page.

Advertising

Most SM companies earn revenue through advertising. Facebook made 94 percent of its 2015 first quarter earnings ($3.5B) from advertising.[18] About 90 percent of Twitter's $436M first quarter earnings came from advertising as well.[19] Advertising on SM can come in the form of paid search, display or banner ads, mobile ads, classifieds, or digital video ads.

Google led the way in making digital advertising revenue with search, followed by Gmail and then YouTube. Today, it doesn't seem like any great insight to realize that if someone is searching for information about an Audi A5 Cabriolet, then that person may be interested in ads from local Audi dealers and BMW and Mercedes dealers as well. Or if someone is watching a soccer game on YouTube, maybe he or she likes soccer? While not mind-boggling to imagine, Google was the first to turn this notion into substantial revenue streams. Other tech companies followed.

Advertisers like digital ads because, unlike traditional media such as newspapers, users can respond directly to Web ads by clicking on them. Run an ad in the print version of *The Wall Street Journal,* and you have no idea of who responds to that ad and how strongly. But place an ad for that same product in the newspaper's online version, and you'll soon know the percentage of viewers who clicked that ad and what action they took next. This knowledge led to the **pay-per-click** revenue model, in which advertisers display ads to potential customers for free and pay only when the customer clicks.

Another way to grow ad revenue is to increase site value with user contributions. The term **use increases value** means the more people use a site, the more value it has, and the more people will visit. Furthermore, the more value a site has, the more existing users will return. This phenomenon led to user comments and reviews, blogging, and, within a few years, social media. If you can get people to connect their community of practice to a site, you will get more users, they will add more value, existing users will return more frequently, and, all things considered, the more ad clicks there will be.

Freemium

The **freemium** revenue model offers users a basic service for free and then charges a premium for upgrades or advanced features. LinkedIn earns part of its revenue by selling upgrades to its standard SaaS (Software as a Service) product. As of May 2015, regular users access LinkedIn for free; individual upgrades range from $29 to $79 a month and offer advanced search capabilities, greater visibility of user profiles, and more direct email messages to LinkedIn users outside one's network. Businesses that want to use LinkedIn for recruiting can purchase a Recruiter Corporate account for $120 to $750 a month. LinkedIn's revenue consists of about 19 percent from premium subscriptions, 62 percent from online recruitment, and 19 percent from advertising.[20]

By diversifying its revenue streams, LinkedIn has reduced its dependence on fluctuating ad revenue and lessened the negative impact of ad-blocking software. A recent report by PageFair indicated that 27.6 percent of Web surfers use **ad-blocking software** to filter out advertising content and rarely, if ever, see Internet ads.[21] It also reported that the use of ad-blocking software grew by 69 percent over the past year. SM companies that rely solely on ad revenue may see their share prices plummet if the use of ad-blocking software becomes widespread.

Other ways of generating revenue on SM sites include the sale of apps and virtual goods, affiliate commissions, and donations. In 2012 Facebook generated more than $810M in revenue from virtual goods. Wikipedia took in about \$52.8M in donations during 2014.[22] Interestingly some SM companies, like Pinterest, don't generate any revenue at all. They just focus on building a large network of users now and figuring out how to make money later.

Social media is the ultimate expression of use increasing value. The more communities of practice there are, the more people, and the more incentive people will have to come back again and again. So, social media would seem to be the next great revenue generator, except, possibly, for the movement from PCs to mobile devices.

Does Mobility Reduce Online Ad Revenue?

The ad click revenue model successfully emerged on PC devices where there is plenty of space for lots of ads. However, as users move from PCs to mobile devices, particularly small-screen smartphones, there is much less ad space. Does this mean a reduction in ad revenue?

On the surface, yes. According to eMarketer, mobile ad spending increased more than 100 percent in 2014 to \$42B accounting for 29 percent of total digital ad spending.[23] By 2019, as shown in Figure 8-8, mobile ad spending should reach \$195B and account for 70 percent of total digital ad spending. However, growth in the number of mobile devices far exceeds PC growth. In 2014, global mobile data traffic increased by 69 percent, and the number of mobile devices worldwide exceeded 7 billion. By 2019, the number of mobile devices is expected to reach 10 billion, which will exceed the world's population.[24] Cisco predicts that by 2019, smartphones will account for 75 percent of total global mobile traffic.[25] So, even though the revenue per device may be lower for mobile devices than PCs, the sheer number of mobile devices may swamp the difference in revenue.

Furthermore, the number of devices is not the whole story. According to Marin Software the average click-through rate of smartphones is 3.75 percent, while that same rate on PCs is 2.29 percent.[26] So, mobile users click ads more often and hence generate more revenue. This is especially true in Facebook's case. In the first quarter of 2015, 87 percent of Facebook users visited from a mobile device, and 73 percent of its total ad revenue came from mobile ads.[27]

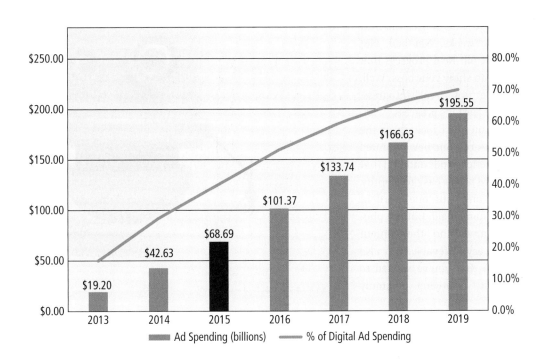

Figure 8-8
Mobile Ad Spending

Ethics Guide

SYNTHETIC FRIENDS

You've just been hired as a marketing manager for a national clothing retailer. Your boss has made it crystal clear that your predecessor was fired because she couldn't get any traction with the company's social media campaign. He wants results—soon. This is your dream job, and you don't want to lose it.

You read an online news article about a person who bought an army of bots that would follow him on Instagram. This could immediately inflate your follower count and show your boss that you're making real progress. Of course, the bots wouldn't be real followers, but if your follower count goes up, it might be easier to attract real human followers. People like popular people.

You do some searching and find an online forum where users are bragging about how realistic their bots are. You even find Web sites (click farms) that advertise Facebook "likes" for sale. You decide to spend $100 and see what happens. You end up getting 15,000 followers that slowly trickle in over the next couple weeks. Not bad. Not bad at all. Real progress that you can show your boss. Well, maybe not "real" progress. But at least it's progress.

You start looking at the profiles of your newly minted synthetic friends and find that they're pretty easy to identify. They only put one word in their name field. But the photos, names, and other content look very believable. You also notice that you've started to attract annoying spammy accounts that leave URLs and discount codes in their comments. This is buggy, but it helps push up your follower count, and that might mean more real followers.

Then comes the purge. Only a few months into your campaign, Instagram starts deleting bots! You lose about 2,000 followers overnight. Ouch. But you still have loads of fictitious followers left. Justin Bieber had the worst hit—3.5 million followers deleted in one day.[28] Other celebrities lost millions of followers as well. You check the news, and it looks like nearly every company, actor, singer, politician, and popular user on Instagram lost followers. You immediately get a sinking feeling in the pit of your stomach. What if you're not the only one who bought followers?

Source: gilbertc/Fotolia

344

DISCUSSION QUESTIONS

1. Consider your decision to use company funds to buy an army of bot followers.
   a. Is your action ethical according to the categorical imperative (pages 56–57)?
   b. Is your action ethical according to the utilitarian perspective (pages 92–93)?
   c. What would your boss say if he found out that all of the company's new corporate followers and Facebook likes are fake?
2. Consider Instagram's action to purge bot accounts.
   a. Is it ethical for Instagram to delete followers? Consider both the categorical imperative and utilitarian perspectives.
   b. Is it ethical for Instagram to allow any bots at all? Consider both the categorical imperative and utilitarian perspectives.
3. How hard should Instagram, or any other social media company, work to eliminate bots?
4. Suppose a social media startup decides to become a publicly traded company. It hasn't been profitable—yet. The number of average monthly users is one of the primary means of valuing the company.

   a. Does it have a *legal* obligation to find out how many of its users are bots?
   b. Does it have an *ethical* obligation to find out how many of its users are bots?
   c. Is there any way for investors to determine how many users are bots? How?
5. Consider the position of an advertising agency or social media company that sells your firm advertising.
   a. Suppose your company is charged based on the number of ads shown to users and the number of clicks on those ads. Does the advertising agency have an ethical obligation to find out how many of the ads it sells are seen by actual humans—not bots?
   b. The advertising agency offers to sell you "likes" for a new product line you're launching. It tells you that buying likes is just like hiring actors for a TV commercial. You're paying them to say they like your product. Is it ethical to buy or sell likes? Consider both the categorical imperative and utilitarian perspectives.

However, clicks aren't the final story either. Because ads take up so much more space on mobile devices than they do on PCs, many of the mobile clicks could have been accidental. **Conversion rate** measures the frequency that someone who clicks on an ad makes a purchase, "likes" a site, or takes some other action desired by the advertiser. According to Monetate, conversion rates for PCs (3.41 percent) are higher than those for tablets (2.86 percent) or smartphones (0.92 percent). So, on average, PC ad clicks are more effective than mobile clicks.[29]

Clickstream data is easy to gather, and as we have seen, analyses of it are widespread. It's possible, for example, to measure click and conversion rates by type of mobile device. According to Moovweb, iOS users have higher conversion rates than Android users, 1.18 percent versus 1.04 percent.[30] But why? Is it the device? Is it the way the ads are integrated into the user experience? Is it the user? Are iOS users more curious than Android users? Or do they have more spendable income? We do not know for sure.

What we can conclude from this morass of confusing data, however, is that mobile devices are most unlikely to spell the death of the Web/social media revenue model. The users are there, the interest is there, and what remains is a design problem: how best to configure the mobile experience to obtain legitimate clicks and conversions. The computer industry is superb at solving design problems; given the current dynamic evolution of mobile interfaces and USX, active, interesting, and compelling ways of presenting ads in iOS/Android/Windows 10 environments are just around the corner.

Q8-5 How Do Organizations Develop an Effective SMIS?

Users forget that digital content on social media can last forever. Read more about this in the Security Guide on pages 358–359.

At this point in your reading, you know what SMIS are, why they are important, and how they generate revenue. Now you need to know how to develop an effective SMIS that is strategically aligned with your organization's goals. In Q8-2, you saw that SM can be used to benefit an organization, but how do you get to that point? We're not talking about a recipe for turning your organization into the next Facebook. Rather, the steps shown in Figure 8-9 walk you through the process of developing a practical plan to effectively use existing social media platforms.

Many companies are still unsure how to use SM. They want to use it, but they're unsure how to facilitate their existing competitive strategy. Think back to Porter's model for

Figure 8-9
Social Media Plan Development

competitive strategies from Chapter 3 (Figure 3-5). Organizations can focus their strategies on being the cost leader or on differentiating their products from the competition. Organizations can then employ the chosen strategy across an entire industry or focus on a particular segment within that industry. Depending on an organization's strategy, it will use different SM platforms in different ways. Again, the key is premeditated alignment of the SMIS with the organization's strategy.

Organizations know SM is popular and could be strategically beneficial. They hear about it constantly in the news. It's not entirely their fault if they want to jump on board. Social media is a relatively new development with a dizzying array of companies, platforms, and services. It's constantly changing, too.

It's important to understand the development process presented in Figure 8-9 because you may be the "social media expert" at your future job. You may be called in to help develop the organization's SMIS. In order to be successful, take a few minutes to consider the steps in the process.

Step 1: Define Your Goals

It may sound clichéd, but the first step in developing an SMIS is to clearly define what the organization wants to achieve with SM. As previously mentioned, your goals must be clear, deliberate, and aligned with the organization's competitive strategy. Without clearly defined goals, you won't know whether your SM effort was successful.

As you learned in Chapter 3, the goals for each organization are different. For organizations that choose a differentiation strategy, SM goals could include better employee recruiting, quicker product development, becoming an industry product leader, or increasing customer loyalty. In general, most organizations include increased brand awareness, conversion rates, Web site traffic, or user engagement as goals. Figure 8-10 gives you examples of how these might manifest themselves in social media.

Step 2: Identify Success Metrics

After you know what you want to accomplish using SM, you need to identify metrics that will indicate when you've achieved your goals. These are referred to as **success metrics** or **key performance indicators (KPI)**. **Metrics** are simply measurements used to track performance. Every organization has different metrics for success. For example, a law firm may measure billable hours, a hospital may measure patients seen or procedures performed, and a manufacturer may look at units produced or operational efficiency.

The hard part in identifying success metrics is identifying the right ones. The right metrics help you make better decisions; the wrong metrics are meaningless and don't positively affect your decision making. For example, measuring the number of registered users on your site may be interesting but not really meaningful. What really matters is the number of *active* users on your

Goal	Description	Example
Brand awareness	Extent that users recognize a brand	Organization's brand mentioned in a tweet
Conversion rates	Measures the frequency that someone takes a desired action	Likes the organization's Facebook page
Web site traffic	Quantity, frequency, duration, and depth of visits to a Web site	Traffic from Google+ post mentioning the organization's site
User engagement	Extent to which users interact with a site, application, or other media	User regularly comments on organization's LinkedIn posts

Figure 8-10
Common SM Strategic Goals

Goal	Metrics
Brand awareness	Total Twitter followers, audience growth rate, brand mentions in SM, Klout or Kred score
Conversion rates	Click rate on your SM content, assisted social conversions
Web site traffic	Visitor frequency rate, referral traffic from SM
User engagement	Number of SM interactions, reshares of SM content

Figure 8-11
Common SM Metrics

site each month. Twitter, for example, had 938 million total registered users in 2014 but only 241 million monthly active users.[31] Metrics that don't improve your decision making are commonly referred to as **vanity metrics.**

Figure 8-11 shows examples of possible success metrics for the goals mentioned in Figure 8-10. Remember, in some circumstances you want to maximize the metric, while in others you want to minimize the metric. It's similar to sports in that respect: Sometimes you want a high score (basketball), and other times you want a low score (golf). It just depends on what you're measuring. Whereas you may want to maximize a metric like conversion rate,[32] or the percent of people who achieve a certain result, you will probably want to minimize other metrics like **bounce rate**, or the percent of people who visit your Web site and then immediately leave."

Step 3: Identify the Target Audience

The next step in creating an effective SMIS is to clearly identify your target audience. Chances are, it's not going to be everyone. For example, if you're Caterpillar Inc. trying to use social media to sell more D11 dozers, your target audience probably won't include many teenagers. Organizations go to great lengths to identify their target audience because it helps them focus their marketing efforts.

Once you've identified your target audience, you need to find out which SM platforms they use. Certain social media platforms attract certain audiences. For example, over 70 percent of Pinterest users are women,[33] 46 percent of Tumblr users are between 16 and 24,[34] 90 percent of Instagram users are under the age of 35,[35] and 84 percent of LinkedIn users are over 25.[36] Your target audience will influence which SM platforms you use.

Step 4: Define Your Value

After pinpointing your target audience, you'll need to define the value you'll provide your audience. Why should these users listen to you, go to your Web site, like your posts, or tweet about your products? Are you providing news, entertainment, education, employee recruiting, or information? In essence, you need to define what you are going to give your audience in exchange for making a connection with you.

When cultivating a personal social media presence, always think about your personal brand. For more information, see the Guide on pages 360–361.

Shopping is a good metaphor to explain how you can do this. When you go shopping, you see something of value and you exchange your *financial* capital (money) with the business for the item you value. The same is true of social media. Your audience members are constantly browsing for things of value, and they have *social* capital to spend. They may eventually spend financial capital at your Web site, but it's the social capital that is most important. You need to define what you're going to offer users in exchange for their social capital.

Take LinkedIn as an example. It helps users find jobs, build a professional network, join special interest groups, get introduced to prospective clients, and reconnect with past colleagues. From an organizational perspective, LinkedIn allows recruiters to quickly identify and contact potential hires from a large pool of candidates. This lowers hiring costs and improves the quality of new hires.

If you're unsure how your organization could add value, start by performing a **competitive analysis** to identify the strengths and weaknesses in your competitors' use of social media. Look at what they're doing right and what they're doing wrong.

Step 5: Make Personal Connections

The true value of social media can be achieved only when organizations use social media to interact with customers, employees, and partners in a more personal, humane, relationship-oriented way.

According to recent studies, younger users are more skeptical of organizational messages and may no longer listen to them. A 2014 CivicScience study found that 58 percent of younger consumers ages 18 through 29 were more influenced by social media chatter than either TV ads or Internet ads.[37] Interestingly, the study also found that only 29 percent of consumers over age 55 thought social media chatter was more influential than TV or Internet advertising. Such skepticism by younger consumers is understandable. They grew up with more sources of information and feel comfortable using social media. Skepticism of organizational messages gives a competitive advantage to organizations that can make personal connections with users via social media.

Today, people want informed, useful interactions that help them solve particular problems and satisfy unique needs. They increasingly ignore prepackaged organizational messages that tout product benefits. This requires you to engage audience members, ask them questions, and respond to their posts. It also means you must avoid hard-selling products, overwhelming audience members with content, and contacting them too often.

The sales force in Apple stores is an excellent example of how to make personal connections. Team members have been trained to act as customer problem-solving consultants and not as sellers of products. An organization's use of social media needs to mirror this behavior; otherwise, social media is nothing more than another channel for classic advertising.

Step 6: Gather and Analyze Data

Finally, when creating a social media strategy, you need to gather the right amount of data necessary to make the most informed decision you can. You can use online analystical tools like Google Analytics, Facebook Page Insights, Clicky, or KISSmetrics to measure the success metrics you defined earlier. These tools will show you statistical information such as which tweets get the most attention, which posts generate the most traffic, and which SM platform generates the most referrals.

Then you can refine your use of social media based on the performance of your success metrics. Be sure to rely on analysis of hard data, not anecdotes from friends. Also, remember that the SM landscape is changing rapidly, and today's winners could be tomorrow's losers. MySpace, for example, was the top SM site in late 2007 valued at $65B, but then succumbed to Facebook's success and was sold for $35M in 2011.[38] Users may shift away from current SM giants like Facebook toward a group of more customized applications like Instagram, Twitter, Snapchat, and WhatsApp.[39] Allow your use of social media to be flexible enough to change with the times.

Senior managers need to see regular progress reports about how SM is affecting the organization. They also need to be educated about changes in social media landscape. Watch for SM success stories and communicate them with upper management.

Q8-6 What Is an Enterprise Social Network (ESN)?

An **enterprise social network (ESN)** is a software platform that uses social media to facilitate cooperative work of people *within* an organization. Instead of using outward-facing SM platforms like Facebook and Twitter, it uses specialized enterprise social software designed to be used inside the organization. These applications may incorporate the same functionality used by traditional social media, including blogs, microblogs, status updates, image and video sharing, personal sites, and wikis. The primary goal of enterprise social networks is to improve communication, collaboration, knowledge sharing, problem solving, and decision making.

Enterprise 2.0

In 2006, Andrew McAfee wrote an article about how dynamic user-generated content systems, then termed **Web 2.0**, could be used in an enterprise setting. He described **Enterprise 2.0** as the use of emergent social software platforms within companies.[40] In other words, the term *Enterprise 2.0* refers to the *use* of enterprise social networks.

McAfee defined six characteristics that he refers to with the acronym **SLATES** (see Figure 8-12).[41] First, workers want to be able to *search* for content inside the organization just like they do on the Web. Most workers find that searching is more effective than navigating content structures such as lists and tables of content. Second, workers want to access organizational content via *links*, just as they do on the Web. They also want to *author* organizational content using blogs, wikis, discussion groups, published presentations, and so on.

According to McAfee, a fourth characteristic of ESNs is that their content is *tagged*, just like content on the Web, and these tags are organized into structures, as is done on the Web at sites like Delicious (*www.delicious.com*). These structures organize tags as a taxonomy does, but, unlike taxonomies, they are not preplanned; they emerge organically. In other words, ESNs employ a **folksonomy**, or a content structure that emerges from the processing of many user tags. Fifth, workers want applications that enable them to rate tagged content and to use the tags to predict content that will be of interest to them (as with Pandora), a process McAfee refers to as *extensions*. Finally, workers want relevant content pushed to them; or, in McAfee's terminology, they want to be *signaled* when something of interest to them happens in organizational content.

The potential problem with ESNs is the quality of their dynamic process. Because the benefits of an ESN result from emergence, there is no way to control for either effectiveness or efficiency. It's a messy process about which little can be predicted.

Changing Communication

Prior to 1980, communication in the United States was restricted to a few **communication channels**, or means of delivering messages. There were three major national TV networks and no more than a half-dozen major national newspapers. Consumers got their news twice a day: from

Figure 8-12
McAfee's SLATES Model
Source: Based on Andrew McAfee, "Enterprise 2.0: The Dawn of Emergent Collaboration," *MIT Sloan Management Review*, Spring 2006, accessed *http://sloanreview.mit.edu/article/enterprise-the-dawn-of-emergent-collaboration.*

Enterprise 2.0 Component	Remarks
Search	People have more success searching than they do in finding from structured content.
Links	Links to enterprise resources (like on the Web).
Authoring	Create enterprise content via blogs, wikis, discussion groups, presentations, etc.
Tags	Flexible tagging (like Delicious) results in folksonomies of enterprise content.
Extensions	Using usage patterns to offer enterprise content via tag processing (like the style of Pandora).
Signals	Pushing enterprise content to users based on subscriptions and alerts.

the morning paper and the evening news. A small number of people decided which stories were told. You got what you were given with few alternatives.

Communication within organizations was similarly restricted. Employees could communicate with their immediate supervisor and coworkers in their vicinity. It was difficult for employees of large corporations to get private meetings with the CEO or to communicate with their counterparts in other countries. If an employee had a good idea, it was passed up through his or her boss to senior management. As a result, it was common for bosses to claim subordinates' ideas as their own.

In recent decades, the Internet, Web sites, social networking, email, cable TV, and smartphones have radically altered existing communication channels. At the societal level, you can now get your news instantly from hundreds of different sources. Traditional news organizations have struggled to adapt to changes in traditional communication channels.

Communication channels within corporations have changed in equally dramatic ways. Using ESNs, employees can now bypass managers and post ideas directly for the CEO to read. They can also quickly identify internal subject matter experts to solve unforeseen problems. In addition, ESNs also enable collaboration with teams dispersed across the globe.

To better understand the potential impacts of ESNs, let's consider an example. In 2012, Yammer (a Microsoft subsidiary) conducted a case study analyzing how restaurant chain Red Robin used an ESN to transform its business.[42] The CIO of Red Robin Chris Laping rolled out Yammer to Red Robin's 26,000 employees across 450 restaurants in an effort to give line employees a voice. This effort yielded more than just stronger employee engagement.

When Red Robin rolled out its new Pig Out Style Double Tavern Burger, for instance, the customer response was disappointing. Employees used Yammer to give management immediate feedback about how the Pig Out recipe could be fixed. Within 4 months, the new-and-improved burger was ready to go. Here, using Yammer to improve internal communication resulted in an increase in organizational responsiveness. The result was a reduction in the amount of time needed to revamp the menu from 12 to 18 months to just 4 months.

In another example, Red Robin's CFO offered a $1,000 employee bonus for the best cost-saving idea. The winning idea was reusable kids' cups that saved hundreds of thousands of dollars. Laping attributes the cost savings to the ESN, stating, "I'm convinced that idea would never have surfaced if we didn't have a social network."[43]

Deploying Successful Enterprise Social Networks

The use of ESNs in organizations is new, and organizations are still learning how to use ESNs successfully (creating fascinating job opportunities for you, by the way.) Before deploying an ESN, organizations should develop a strategic plan for using SM *internally* via the same process they used for their *external* social media use. Once a strategic plan has been created, an ESN can then be implemented.

Deploying new systems—including ESNs—can be problematic, so the organization's strategic plan should be sure to address possible challenges, including the likelihood of employee resistance. Will employees adopt the new system? Not everyone uses every social media platforms in their personal lives, so why should they use them at work?

In order to ensure a successful implementation of an ESN, organizations can also follow industry **best practices**, or methods that have been shown to produce successful results in prior implementations. You'll learn more about systems implementation in Chapter 12. When implementing an ESN, successful companies follow a process of four stages having the elements shown in Figure 8-13. Read through the items and reflect on what you went through when you first started using SM. Think about how important your friends were in your decision to start using SM. Having an internal champion or defender of your internal ESN is equally important.

	ESN Deployment Best Practices
Strategy	1. Define how ESN supports the organization's existing goals and objectives. 2. Define success metrics. 3. Communicate the ESN strategy to all users. 4. Convey an expectation of organization-wide ESN adoption.
Sponsorship	5. Identify an executive sponsor to promote the ESN. 6. Identify ESN champions within each organizational unit. 7. Encourage champions to recruit users. 8. Identify groups that would benefit most from the ESN.
Support	9. Provide all users access to the ESN. 10. Mandate processes to be used within the ESN. 11. Provide incentives for ESN adoption and use. 12. Provide employee training and ESN demonstrations.
Success	13. Measure ESN effectiveness via success metrics. 14. Evaluate how ESN supports the organization's strategy. 15. Promote ESN success stories. 16. Continuously look for ways to use the ESN more effectively.

Figure 8-13
ESN Implementation Best Practices

Q8-7 How Can Organizations Address SMIS Security Concerns?

As you have seen, social media revolutionizes the ways that organizations communicate. Twenty years ago, most organizations managed all public and internal messaging with the highest degree of control. Every press conference, press release, public interview, presentation, and even academic paper needed to be preapproved by both the legal and marketing departments. Such approval could take weeks or months.

Today, progressive organizations have turned that model on its head. Employees are encouraged to engage with communities and, in most organizations, to identify themselves with their employer while doing so. All of this participation, all of this engagement, however, comes with risks. In this question, we will discuss the need for a social media policy, consider risks from nonemployee user-generated content, and look at risks from employee use of social media.

Managing the Risk of Employee Communication

The first step that any organization should take is to develop and publicize a **social media policy**, which is a statement that delineates employees' rights and responsibilities. You can find an index to 100 different policies at the Social Media Today Web site.[44] In general, the more technical the organization, the more open and lenient the social policies. The U.S. military has, perhaps surprisingly, endorsed social media with enthusiasm, tempered by the need to protect classified data.

Intel Corporation has pioneered open and employee-trusting SM policies, policies that continue to evolve as the company gains more experience with employee-written social media. The three key pillars of Intel's policy in 2015 are:

- Disclose
- Protect
- Use Common Sense[45]

Those policies are further developed as shown in Figure 8-14. Visit *www.intel.com/content/www/us/en/legal/intel-social-media-guidelines.html* to read Intel's social media guidelines in full. Be sure to read carefully, as the guidelines contain great advice and considerable wisdom.

Disclose	Be transparent—use your real name and employer Be truthful—point out if you have a vested interest Be yourself—stick to your expertise and write what you know
Protect	Don't tell secrets Don't slam the competition Don't overshare
Use Common Sense	Add value—make your contribution worthwhile Keep it cool—don't inflame or respond to every criticism Admit mistakes—be upfront and quick with corrections

Figure 8-14

Intel's Rules of Social Media Engagement

Source: Used with permission from Intel Corporation.

Two elements in this list are particularly noteworthy. The first is the call for transparency and truth. As an experienced and wise business professional once shared, "Nothing is more serviceable than the truth." Truth may not be convenient, but it is serviceable over the long term. Second, SM contributors and their employers should be open and candid. If you make a mistake, don't obfuscate; instead, correct it, apologize, and make amends. The SM world is too open, too broad, and too powerful to fool.

In 2013, Justine Sacco, a PR executive at IAC, was boarding a plane headed to South Africa and tweeted, "Going to Africa. Hope I don't get AIDS. Just kidding. I'm white." When she landed, she found out that she had been fired in flight and had elicited thousands of hostile posts.

The best way to avoid these types of missteps is to include an SM awareness module in users' annual security training. Social media is still new to many users. Honestly, they may be unaware a policy even exists. When cell phones first became popular, they were constantly ringing in movie theaters. Over time, people learned to mute their phones before entering a crowded theater. It just takes time for society to catch up to technology. Training helps.

Managing the Risk of Inappropriate Content

As with any relationship, comments can be inappropriate or excessively negative in tone or be otherwise problematic. Organizations need to determine how they will deal with such content before engaging in social media. This is done by designating a single individual to be responsible for official organizational SM interactions and by creating a process to monitor and manage SM interactions. This allows the organization to have a clear, coordinated, and consistent message.

User-generated content (UGC), which simply means content on your SM site that is contributed by users, is the essence of SM relationships. Below are a few examples of inappropriate UGC that can negatively affect organizations.

Problems from External Sources

The major sources of UGC problems are:

- Junk and crackpot contributions
- Inappropriate content
- Unfavorable reviews
- Mutinous movements

When a business participates in a social network or opens its site to UGC, it opens itself to misguided people who post junk unrelated to the site's purpose. Crackpots may also use the network or UGC site as a way of expressing passionately held views about unrelated topics, such as UFOs, government cover-ups, fantastic conspiracy theories, and so forth. Because of the possibility of such content, organizations should regularly monitor the site and remove objectionable material immediately. Monitoring can be done by employees or by companies such as Bazaarvoice, which offer services not only to collect and manage ratings and reviews, but also to monitor sites for irrelevant content.

Unfavorable reviews are another risk. Research indicates that customers are sophisticated enough to know that few, if any, products are perfect. Most customers want to know the disadvantages of a product before purchasing it so they can determine whether those disadvantages are important for their application. However, if every review is bad, if the product is rated 1 star out of 5, then the company is using social media to publish its problems. In this case, some action must be taken, as described next.

Mutinous movements are an extension of bad reviews. In January 2012, McDonald's opened a Twitter campaign to promote customer stories. Within a few hours, it was clear that disgruntled customers were hijacking the campaign. McDonald's pulled the Twitter hashtag, and within a few hours, negative conversations stopped. To be able to respond promptly, McDonald's created a contingency plan for dealing with unwanted results in all of its social media marketing.[46]

Responding to Social Networking Problems

Part of managing social networking risk is knowing the sources of potential problems and monitoring sites for problematic content. Once such content is found, however, organizations need to respond appropriately. Three possibilities in such situations are:

- Leave it
- Respond to it
- Delete it

If the problematic content represents reasonable criticism of the organization's products or services, the best response may be to leave it where it is. Such criticism indicates that the site is not just a shill for the organization but contains legitimate user content. Such criticism also serves as a free source of product reviews, which can be useful for product development. For the criticism to be useful, the development team needs to know about it, so, as stated, processes to ensure the criticism is found and communicated to the team are necessary.

A second alternative is to respond to the problematic content. However, this alternative is dangerous. If the response can be construed in any way as patronizing or insulting to the content contributor, it can enrage the community and generate a strong backlash. Also, if the response appears defensive, it can become a public relations negative.

In most cases, responses are best reserved for when the problematic content has caused the organization to do something positive as a result. For example, suppose a user publishes that he or she was required to hold for customer support for 45 minutes. If the organization has done something to reduce wait times, then an effective response to the criticism is to recognize it as valid and to state, nondefensively, what has been done to reduce wait times.

If a reasoned, nondefensive response generates continued and unreasonable UGC from that same source, it is best for the organization to do nothing. Never wrestle with a pig; you'll get dirty, and the pig will enjoy it. Instead, allow the community to constrain the user. It will.

Deleting content should be reserved for contributions that are inappropriate because they are contributed by crackpots, have nothing to do with the site, or contain obscene or otherwise inappropriate content. Deleting legitimate negative comments can result in a strong user backlash. In the early days of social media, Nestlé created a PR nightmare on its Facebook account with its response to criticism it received about its use of palm oil. Someone altered the Nestlé logo, and in response Nestlé decided to delete all Facebook contributions that used that altered logo and did so in an arrogant, heavy-handed way. The result was a negative firestorm on Twitter.[47]

A sound principle in business is to never ask a question to which you do not want the answer. We can extend that principle to social networking; never set up a site that will generate content for which you have no effective response!

Internal Risks from Social Media

The increased adoption of social media has created new risks within organizations as well. These risks include threats to information security, increased organizational liability, and decreased employee productivity.

First, the use of social media can directly affect the ability of an organization to secure its information resources. For example, suppose a senior-level employee tweets, "Married 20 years ago today in Dallas," or "Class of 1984 reunion at Central High School was awesome," or "Remembering my honeymoon to Hawaii." All of these tweets provide attackers with the answers to password reset questions. Once attackers reset the user's passwords, they could have full access to internal systems. Thus, seemingly innocuous comments can inadvertently leak information used to secure access to organizational resources. Unfortunately, it turns out that it's not a good idea to tell everyone it's your birthday because your date of birth (DOB) can be used to steal your identity.

Employees using social media also can unintentionally (or intentionally) leak information about intellectual property, new marketing campaigns, future products, potential layoffs, budget woes, product flaws, or upcoming mergers. It's not just information leakage, either. Employees may install unauthorized apps that deliver content using SM that bypasses existing security measures. Or worse, they may use their corporate password at less secure SM sites.

Second, employees may inadvertently increase corporate liability when they use social media. For example, suppose a coworker regularly looks at SM content with questionable sexual content on his or her own smartphone. The organization could be slapped with a sexual harassment lawsuit. Other organizations may face legal issues if employees leak information via social media. Schools, healthcare providers, and financial institutions must all follow specific guidelines to protect user data and avoid regulatory compliance violations. Thus, tweeting about students, patients, or customer accounts could have legal consequences.

Finally, increased use of social media can be a threat to employee productivity. Posts, tweets, pins, likes, comments, and endorsements all take time. This is time employers are paying for but not benefiting from. *Forbes* notes that 64 percent of employees visit non-work-related Web sites each day. Among the SM sites that are most detrimental to employee productivity are Tumblr (57 percent), Facebook (52 percent), Twitter (17 percent), Instagram (11 percent), and SnapChat (4 percent).[48]

From an employee's point of view, you might think a little lost productivity is OK. But imagine you're the employer or manager, which hopefully you'll be at some point. Would you mind if your employees spend their days using SM to look for another job, chat with friends, or look at vacation pictures when your paycheck is tied to their productivity? What if SM is being used for interoffice gossip that creates HR problems, morale issues, and possible lawsuits? Smart managers will understand that, like any technology, SM comes with both benefits and costs.

Q8-8   2026?

So much change is in the air: social media, Web 2.0, Enterprise 2.0. Is there an Enterprise 3.0 around the corner? Will social media become more unified on a single platform or become more fragmented across many different platforms? We don't know. However, new mobile devices with innovative mobile-device UX, coupled with dynamic and agile information systems based on cloud computing and dynamic virtualization, guarantee that monumental changes will continue to occur between now and 2026. (See Figure 8-15.)

Figure 8-15
Redesigning Enterprises for
Social Media

Source: Stephen VanHorn/Fotolia

Organizations like Harvard, Microsoft, and Starbucks are concerned enough with SM that they have hired Chief Digital Officers (CDOs), a position responsible for developing and managing innovative social media programs.[49]

Advance the clock 10 years. You're now the marketing manager for an important new product series for your company...the latest in a line of, say, intelligent home appliances. How are you going to promote your products? Will your machines do SM with family members? Will your refrigerators publish what kids are eating after school on the family's social media site? And what even more creative ideas will you need to have by then?

Think about your role as a manager in 2026. Say your team has 10 people, three of whom report to you; two report to other managers, and five work for different companies. Your company uses OpenGizmo 2026 with integrated mobile video, augmented by Google/Facebook's Whammo++ Star, all of which have many features that enable employees and teams to instantly publish their ideas in blogs, wikis, videos, and whatever other means have become available. Your employees no longer are assigned computers at work; a liberal, yet secure, BYOD policy enables them to use their own devices, often in their own, unique way. Of course, your employees have their own accounts on whatever Facebook, Twitter, LinkedIn, foursquare, and other social networking sites have become popular, and they regularly contribute to them.

How do you manage this team? If "management" means to plan, organize, and control, how can you accomplish any of these functions in this emergent network of employees? If you and your organization follow the lead of tech-savvy companies such as Intel, you'll know you cannot close the door on your employees' SM lives, nor will you want to. Instead, you'll harness the power of the social behavior of your employees and partners to advance your strategy.

In the context of CRM, the vendor might lose control of the customer relationship. Customers use all the vendor's touch points they can find to craft their own relationships. Emergence in the context of management means loss of control of employees. Employees craft their own relationships with their employers, whatever that might mean by 2026. Certainly it means a loss of control, one that is readily made public to the world.

In the 1960s, when someone wanted to send a letter to Don Draper at Sterling Cooper, his or her secretary addressed the envelope to Sterling Cooper and down at the bottom added, "Attention: Don Draper." The letter was to Sterling Cooper—and, oh, by the way—also to Don Draper. Email changed that. Today, someone would send an email to *DonDraper@SterlingCooper.com* or even just to *Don@SterlingCooper.com*. The email address is to a person first, and then to the company.

Social media changes addresses even further. When Don Draper creates his own blog, for example, people who respond to Don's blog only incidentally notice in the "About Don" section of the blog that Don works for Sterling Cooper. In short, the focus has moved in 50 years from organizations covering employee names to employees covering organization names.

Does this mean that organizations will go away by 2026? Hardly. Organizations are needed to raise and conserve capital and to organize vast groups of people and projects. No group of loosely affiliated people can envision, design, develop, manufacture, market, sell, and support an iPad. Organizations are required.

So what, then? Maybe we can take a lesson from biology. Crabs have an external exoskeleton. Deer, much later in the evolutionary chain, have an internal endoskeleton. When crabs grow, they must endure the laborious and biologically expensive process of shedding a small shell and growing a larger one. They are also vulnerable during the transition. When deer grow, the skeleton is inside and it grows with the deer. No need for vulnerable molting. And, considering agility, would you take a crab over a deer? In the 1960s, organizations were the exoskeleton around employees. By 2026, organizations will be the endoskeleton, supporting the work of people on the exterior.

What all of this means for you is that mobility + cloud + social media will create fascinating opportunities for your nonroutine cognitive skills in the next 10 years!

Security Guide

DIGITAL IS FOREVER

Have you ever told a friend something and asked him or her to keep it private? Most people have. Unfortunately, at some point, the person you confided in violated your trust. He or she shared that information with someone else. If so, you can probably recall the horrible feeling that accompanied the thought of other people knowing things you wanted kept private.

This is how several A-list celebrities felt when scores of their personal and highly sensitive photos stored in iCloud were hacked and subsequently plastered all over the Internet. You may be wondering how this could happen—how could cybercriminals access the private data of someone else stored on an iCloud account?

It turns out there was a security vulnerability associated with Apple's Find My iPhone application. Safeguards had not been implemented by Apple to limit the number of login attempts permitted before an account would be locked, a common security practice used to prevent hackers from entering endless combinations of usernames and passwords in an exhaustive attempt to guess the correct set of credentials (referred to as a brute-force attack).[50]

The celebrities affected by these attacks are still trying to remove their private data from the Web. The sad truth is that their private data will never completely be removed. Even more sobering is the fact that anyone who chooses to transmit any personal information using an Internet connection (i.e., send something via email, post something on a social media site, etc.) can become a victim, too.

Privacy? What's That?

Once you click the button to send an email, post a photo, or share a video, you lose control over that data. It can be copied, shared, and copied again. Your data will travel through numerous servers until it is delivered to the intended recipient. It will also be stored on a data farm owned by the company whose app you're using. You can *never* withdraw this information—and once it is transmitted, it is nearly impossible (and in most cases, impossible) to delete.

Think about it this way. Have you ever heard the saying that "two can keep a secret if one of them is dead"? Well, from a technology perspective, "two *can't* keep a secret if one of them is the Internet." Anything shared over the Internet morphs into a digital zombie, destined to wander the far reaches of cyberspace forever!

You may think that as long as you are sharing messages or photos with a trusted party you have nothing to worry about. Unfortunately, our digital world is rife with cybercriminals who spend countless hours trying to steal data from both companies and everyday citizens (just ask the Apple iCloud victims).

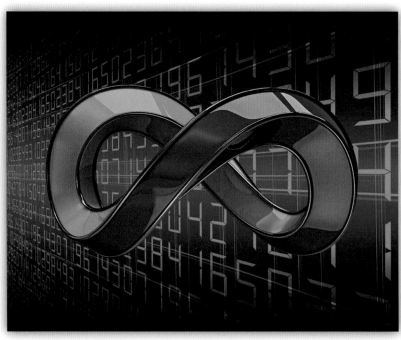

Source: valdis torms/Fotolia and vilisov/Fotolia

And cybercriminals aren't the only ones trying to take advantage of your personal data. Companies see the value in accessing and running various analyses on everything you digitally say or do. Google, for example, scans the contents of your emails sent through Gmail so it can serve you targeted ads. Google looks at more than just your emails, too. Google also looks at your search queries, the sites you visit, and your Google profile in an effort to make its ads more relevant.[51]

Big Data = Big Money

Taking into account the actions of both cybercriminals and corporations, we can infer one thing—accessing the private data of Internet users equals big money as personal data can be (1) illegally accessed by criminals and sold on the black market to other nefarious characters or (2) legally accessed by companies and sold to other companies. The good news is that high-profile privacy breaches like the iCloud incident raise awareness for everyone concerning the risks of storing or sharing personal information online.

For example, a recent poll conducted by the Pew Research Center found that "86% of Internet users have taken steps online to remove or mask their digital footprints—ranging from clearing cookies to encrypting their email, from avoiding using their name to using virtual networks that mask their internet protocol (IP) address."[52] This is encouraging, but they can do more. Rather than spending time trying to erase their digital footprint, users need to keep from making tracks in the first place. Think before you click, share, or post. Digital is forever.

QUESTIONS

1. The guide emphasizes that criminals and corporations both seek out the private data of Internet users for their own gains, but they are not the only ones trying to access your data. Why do you think employers might seek out data about applicants when making their hiring decisions?

2. You likely heard news reports about the iCloud and Sony breaches, both of which resulted in private photos and emails being shared with the masses on the Internet. But can you recall hearing about the perpetrators being brought to justice? If not, why do you think this is the case?

3. Stolen or compromised devices can also be used to access your private data. Even if that data has been deleted. Search the Web for information about software used to recover deleted files. Does normal deletion permanently remove a file from the memory of your device? Can it be recovered? How?

4. Take a few minutes to reflect on your online habits. Have you sent emails or posted messages or images that could be perceived as controversial in nature? Are there posts that you wouldn't want a future employer to see? How might your emails or posts affect your career?

Guide

DEVELOPING YOUR PERSONAL BRAND

The Security Guide (on the previous two pages) discusses ways to avoid making mistakes with social media that will interfere with your ability to obtain a job. Follow that guide to minimize the long-term effect of the errors and indiscretions of your college years. Now consider the other side of that coin. Instead of attempting to minimize the bad, suppose we ask: How can you use social media to maximize the good?

Leading professionals use social media to build their personal brand. You may be too young, too inexperienced, and not yet unique enough to have a personal brand, but, then again, maybe not. And even if now isn't the right time to build a personal brand, you will need to have, build, and maintain your personal brand at some point in the future if you want to be a business leader.

So, what is "building a personal brand"? It's not embarrassing self-promotion. It's not self-advertising, and it's not a resume of your recent experience. It is, instead, the means by which you conduct authentic relationships with the market for your talents and abilities. That market might be your professional colleagues, your employer, your fellow employees, your competition, or anyone who cares about what you care about.

As a business professional, how do you create authentic relationships that are less transactional and more personal? You start by realizing that the people who consume your services are not just bosses and colleagues, but rather full-fledged human beings with the rich stew of complexity that all humans have. With this idea in mind, can you use social media to transform your relationships from being transactional in nature to being more personal?

Such a transformation is possible but difficult. You don't want to share every detail of your personal life on your professional blog; few readers will care about your vacation in the Bahamas. However, they might want to know what you read while lying on the beach, why you read it, and what you learned from it—or perhaps how disappointed you were about what you didn't learn. But your report has to be authentic. If you're reading Kierkegaard or Aristotle for the purpose of showing erudition on your personal blog, you

missed the point. But if Kierkegaard has something interesting to say about the ethics of the latest business scandal that affects your professional interests, many readers who share those interests will want to know. And they will then have a way to approach you on a common interest. That common interest may lead to an exciting new job opportunity, or maybe it will lead to a fulfilling new relationship, or maybe it will go nowhere. You just don't know.

Be aware, however, that maintaining a professional brand can become all consuming. Just like personal Facebook

Source: Fergregory/Fotolia

use can suck up most of your free time, so, too, can maintaining your professional brand. To help avoid this situation, start modestly and work up from there.

When engaging in personal branding efforts, always be guided by your personal strategy. Consider Figure 3-12 again, in light of your personal competitive strategy. What is your personal competitive advantage? Why would someone choose you, your expertise, or your work products over others? Then, with answers to these questions in mind, start building your personal brand. Again, be sure your

efforts focus on creating authentic relationships and not on shameless advertising.

Realize, too, that a strong personal brand is essential to some careers. For example, if you want to be an independent consultant, say, an expert on privacy and control for cloud data storage, you'll need to invest considerable time developing and maintaining your professional brand. But whether or not it's essential, having a strong personal brand is an asset in any field, in any job. And you can be sure that if you don't have a good personal brand, one of your competitors will.

 DISCUSSION QUESTIONS

1. Using your own words, define and describe a personal brand.
2. Describe how you could use social media to make an existing professional contact more personal in nature while still maintaining your privacy.
3. Pick a contemporary topic of interest in your major field of study. For example, if you're an operations major, pick something like *3D printing*. If you're an accounting major, choose something like *auditing in the cloud*. (Read question 4, however, before you pick.)
   a. Search the Web for opinions about the realities, contemporary uses, big issues and problems, or other interesting dimensions of your topic.
   b. Find two or three experts in that topic, and go to their professional brand sites. That brand might be a blog, a Web page, a collection of articles, an SM site on Facebook or LinkedIn, or some other public statement of their professionalism.
   c. Which of the sites is the best? Explain why you think so.

4. Suppose you become an expert in the topic you used in your answer to question 3. Think about your experiences in the past year that relate to that topic. It could be experiences in class, out of class with fellow students, or in conversations with roommates. It could be something that happened at your job at McDonald's. Whatever.
   a. Make a list of 10 such experiences.
   b. Describe how you could use social media, including blogs, to present five of the best of those 10 experiences in a way that helps build your professional brand.
5. Reflect on your answers to questions 1–4.
   a. Do you think having a personal brand is important for you? Explain why or why not. (The answer to this question may not be *yes*, and for good reasons.)
   b. What was the most difficult task for you when formulating your answers to question 4?
   c. Summarize what you have learned from this exercise about how you might get more value from your college experiences.

ACTIVE REVIEW

Use this Active Review to verify that you understand the ideas and concepts that answer this chapter's study questions.

Q8-1 What is a social media information system (SMIS)?

Define *social media, communities of practice, social media information systems, social media provider,* and *social networks.* Name and describe three SMIS organizational roles. Explain the elements of Figure 8-3. In your own words, explain the nature of the five components of SMIS for each of the three SMIS organizational roles.

Q8-2 How do SMIS advance organizational strategy?

Summarize how social media contributes to sales and marketing, customer support, inbound logistics, outbound logistics, manufacturing and operations, and human resources. Name SM risks for each activity. Define *social CRM,* and *crowdsourcing.*

Q8-3 How do SMIS increase social capital?

Define *capital, human capital,* and *social capital.* Explain four ways that social capital adds value. Name three factors that determine social capital and explain how "they are more multiplicative than additive." Define *influencer* and describe how you could use social media to increase the number and strength of your social relationships.

Q8-4 How do (some) companies earn revenue from social media?

Define *monetize* and describe why it's difficult for social media companies to generate revenue. Give examples of how social media companies generate revenue from advertising and charging for premium services. Define *pay-per-click, conversion rate,* and *freemium.* Define *ad blocking* and explain how it hurts online companies' ability to generate revenue. Summarize how growth in mobile devices affects revenue streams. Explain why concerns about mobile devices limiting ad revenue are overreactions.

Q8-5 How do organizations develop an effective SMIS?

Discuss why aligning the development of SMIS with the organization's strategy is important. Describe the process of developing an effective SMIS. List four common social media goals and describe why they are important. Define *metrics, success metrics,* and *vanity metrics* and give examples of metrics that could be

measured for the four goals mentioned above. Describe the importance of making personal connections with users.

Q8-6 What is an enterprise social network (ESN)?

Define *enterprise social network (ESN)* and describe the primary goal of an ESN. Define *Web 2.0* and *Enterprise 2.0.* Explain each element of the SLATES model. Explain how changes in communication channels have changed the way organizations communicate with employees. Give an example of how an ESN could benefit an organization. Define *best practices* and explain how the ESN implementation best practices listed in Figure 8-13 could improve adoption of the ESN.

Q8-7 How can organizations address SMIS security concerns?

Name and describe two sources of SM risk. Describe the purpose of an SM policy and summarize Intel's guiding principles. Describe an SM mistake, other than one in this text, and explain the wise response to it. Name four sources of problems of UGC; name three possible responses and give the advantages and disadvantages of each. Explain how internal use of social media can create risks to information security, organizational liability, and employee productivity.

Q8-8 2026?

Describe ways in which the use of social media is changing today. Summarize possible management challenges when controlling employees in 2026. Describe the text's suggested response. How does the change in forms of address since the 1960s indicate a change in the relationship of employees and organizations to the business world? Explain the relationship of the differences between crab and deer to this change.

Using Your Knowledge with PRIDE

This chapter has given you several important models for assessing the PRIDE system's social media program. You can apply the components of SMIS to understand the commitment that Zev Friedman and developers must make. You can use organizational strategy and social capital models to assess the desirability of social media to companies that participate in PRIDE. You can also consider whether PRIDE might want to generate revenue via a freemium model or by placing ads within the application. You can help craft an effective social media strategy for PRIDE and help Zev manage the risks of using social media.

KEY TERMS AND CONCEPTS

MyMISLab™

To complete the problems with the ⭐, go to EOC Discussion Questions in the MyLab.

USING YOUR KNOWLEDGE

⭐ **8-1.** There are two approaches given in the chapter regarding the effect of mobility on online ad revenue. The first approach is regarding the size of screen versus the sheer number of mobile phones, and the second is regarding the number of the conversion rate versus effectiveness of conversion rate. Which approach do you think is more appropriate and why? If you don't agree with these views, suggest some other measure to know the effect of mobility on online ad revenue.

⭐ **8-2.** According to Nan Lin, social capital can benefit a person in following ways:
  a. Information
  b. Influence
  c. Social credentials
  d. Personal Reinforcement

Do you agree with the findings of Nan Lin. If yes, which benefit do you weigh more and why? If no, suggest some new ways in which social capital can benefit a person.

⭐ **8-3.** Several actors, these days, are promoting their forthcoming movies on social media. In your opinion, what are the perils of using social media as a promotional platform for films. Answer this question by keeping in mind the problems from internal sources regarding social media. In case your favorite actor gets some inappropriate comments, according to you what should that actor do i.e. whether ignore, respond or delete it.

8-4. Find out whether your institution's HR is using social media for HR processes and managing the internal staff, i.e. teaching as well as non-teaching staff, and also figure out its effectiveness. If your college/university is not using social media to manage the human resource then list the possible benefits of using social media to manage the internal staff.

8-5. Suppose that your college/university wants to develop SMIS (even if has already developed SMIS, frame a new SMIS), for this purpose refer to Figure 8-9 and answer the following:
  a. Define its goals
  b. Identify its success metrics
  c. Identify the target audiences

COLLABORATION EXERCISE 8

Using the collaboration IS you built in Chapter 2 (page 110), collaborate with a group of students to answer the following questions.

Twitter's IPO on November 7, 2013, was one of the biggest tech IPOs in history. The social media giant's stock closed that day at $44.90 a share, making the company worth an estimated $25B.[53] Not bad for a company that had never made a profit. In fact, Twitter posted a $70M loss the quarter before listing! How could a company be worth $25B and never have made any money?

Analysts argue that tech companies, like those shown in Figure 8-16, should be valued based on growth potential, user base, consumer engagement, and market size. It turns out that Amazon.com, Instagram, and Pinterest weren't profitable when they went public, either.

Traditional IPO valuations focus on measures of profitability. This means investors look at revenues, profits, assets, liabilities, and new products. Figure 8-16 shows price-to-earnings ratios (P/E) for several well-known traditional and tech companies.

Using iteration and feedback, answer the following questions:

8-6. Compare the tech companies' P/E ratios to the traditional companies' P/E ratios. Note that some of the tech companies have very high P/E ratios. (A low P/E is good; a high P/E is bad.) Some don't even have a P/E ratio because they didn't turn a profit. As a group, list the reasons why the tech companies have such high P/E ratios. Are the prices of these companies' stocks justified given the earnings? Why?

8-7. Identify public tech stocks you believe are undervalued (not limited to this list). Design an investment portfolio consisting solely of tech stocks that you believe will be profitable. Justify your decision with regard to risk and return on those stocks.

8-8. Currently many organizations are using social media data to analyze the current trends in technology. Make a twitter handler of #Roleofsocialmediainjudgingcurrenttrends

Tech Companies	Market Cap ($)	P/E
Apple	721.63B	16.96
Google	368.92B	25.82
Facebook	219.51B	75.63
Amazon.com	198.24B	N/A
Netflix	34.20B	147.31
LinkedIn	25.35B	N/A
Twitter	24.68B	N/A

Traditional Companies	Market Cap ($)	P/E
General Electric	272.23B	N/A
Wal-Mart Stores	251.73B	15.45
Verizon Comm.	202.80B	20.88
Toyota	216.92B	12.91
BP	126.88B	34.17
Johnson & Johnson	277.11B	17.48
Ford	61.65B	19.44

Figure 8-16
Tech Company Valuations

and take the opinion of your network on this issue. Summarize your discussion in a couple of paragraphs.

8-9. Analyze the social buzz created by Twitter before the launching of its initial public offering (IPO). Make a report highlighting the steps taken by Twitter to create a positive social buzz regarding its IPO. If you were handling Twitter's IPO campaign as its the social media manager, what steps would you have taken to create a greater impact on social media regarding the forthcoming IPO.

CASE STUDY 8

Sedona Social

Sedona, Arizona, is a city of 10,000 people surrounded by Coconino National Forest. At an elevation of 4,500 feet, Sedona is considerably higher than the valley cities of Phoenix and Tucson but 2,000 feet below the altitude of Flagstaff. This middle elevation provides a moderate climate that is neither too hot in the summer nor too cold in the winter. Sedona is surrounded

by gorgeous sandstone red-orange rocks and stunning red rock canyons, as shown in Figure 8-17.

This beautiful city was the location for more than 60 movies, most of them westerns, between the 1930s and the 1950s. If you've ever watched an old black-and-white western, it was likely situated in Sedona. Among the well-known movies located

Figure 8-17
Sedona Red Rocks
Sources: © David Kroenke

in Sedona are *Stagecoach, Johnny Guitar, Angel and the Badman,* and *3:10 to Yuma.*

Many who visit Sedona believe there is something peaceful yet energizing about the area, especially in certain locations known as *vortices.* According to VisitSedona.com, "Vortex sites are enhanced energy locations that facilitate prayer, meditation, mind/body healing, and exploring your relationship with your Soul and the divine. They are neither electric nor magnetic."[54]

Tests with scientific instruments have failed to identify any unusual readings of known energy types, and yet many people, of all religions and religious persuasions, believe there is something about Sedona that facilitates spiritual practice. For a city of its size, Sedona has many more churches than one might

expect, including the Catholic Chapel of the Holy Cross (shown in Figure 8-18), Protestant churches of many dominations, a Latter-Day Saints (Mormon) church, a local synagogue, and the new-age Sedona Creative Life Center.

Because it is situated in the middle of a national forest, Sedona is surrounded by hundreds of miles of hiking trails; it is possible to hike every day for a year and not use all the trails. The area was home to Native Americans in the 12th and 13th centuries, and there are numerous cliff dwellings and other native sites nearby.

As a relatively young modern city, Sedona does not have the cultural history of Santa Fe or Taos, New Mexico. Nonetheless, there is a burgeoning arts community centered

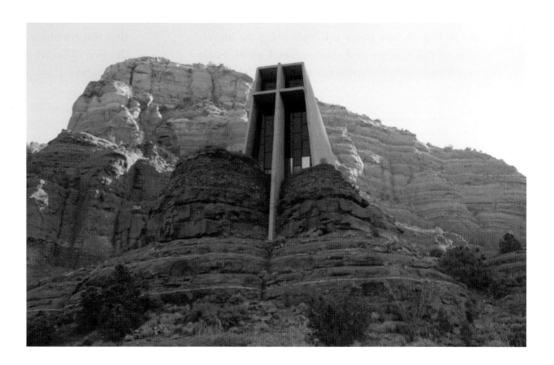

Figure 8-18
Chapel of the Holy Cross
Sources: © David Kroenke

around Tlaquepaque, a 1980s-built shopping area modeled on a Mexican city of the same name.

As with many tourist destinations, there are tensions. Pink Jeep Tours runs daily trips of raucous tourists past vortices occupied by meditating spiritual practitioners. With its Hollywood past, Sedona is home to many Los Angeles expatriates, and at the local health food store, it's possible to see 50-something blond women wearing tight pants and jewel-studded, fresh-from-Rodeo-Drive sandals fighting for the last pound of organic asparagus with aging male hippies shaking their white-gray ponytails off the shoulders of their tie-dyed shirts.

The emerging arts community wants to be serious; the uptown jeep-riding tourists (see Figure 8-19) want to have fun with four-wheel thrills and margaritas (we hope in that sequence). Hikers want to visit petroglyphs, while nature pre-servers don't want the locations of those sites to be known. Those seeking spiritual guidance want enlightenment in silence, while the locals want to shut out everyone, just as long, that is, as their property values increase at a steady pace, year by year. Meanwhile, the Learjets and Citations fly in and out carrying who-knows-who Hollywood celebrity from her home behind the walls of Seven Canyons Resort. And businesses in town want to have reliable, year-round revenue and not too much competition.

Given all that, let's suppose that the Sedona Chamber of Commerce has just hired you as its first-ever manager of community social media. It wants you to provide advice and assistance to local businesses in the development of their social media sites, and it wants you to manage its own social media presence as well.

QUESTIONS

8-10. Search Facebook for *Sedona, Arizona*. Examine a variety of Sedona-area pages you find. Using the knowledge of this chapter and your personal social media experience, evaluate these pages and list several positive and negative features of each. Make suggestions on ways they could be improved.

8-11. Repeat question 8-10 for another social media provider. As of this writing, possibilities include Twitter, LinkedIn, and Pinterest, but choose another social media provider if you wish.

8-12. The purpose of a Chamber of Commerce is to foster a healthy business climate for all of the businesses in the community. Given that purpose, your answers to questions 8-10 and 8-11, and the knowledge of this chapter, develop a set of 7 to 10 guidelines for local businesses to consider when developing their social media presence.

8-13. Sedona has quite a number of potentially conflicting community groups. Explain three ways the Chamber of Commerce can use social media to help manage conflict so as to maintain a healthy business environment.

8-14. Examine Figure 8-5, and state how the focus of each of the primary value chain activities pertains to the Chamber of Commerce. If one does not pertain, explain why. In your answer, be clear about who the Chamber's customers are.

8-15. Given your answer to question 8-14 and considering your responsibility to manage the Chamber's social media presences, state how each applicable row of Figure 8-5 guides the social media sites you will create.

8-16. Using your answers to these questions, write a job description for yourself.

8-17. Write a two-paragraph summary of this exercise that you could use to demonstrate your knowledge of the role of social media in commerce in a future job interview.

Figure 8-19
Pink Jeep Tours
Sources: © David Kroenke

MyMISLab™

Go to the Assignments section of your MyLab to complete these writing exercises.

8-18. According to Paul Greenberg, Amazon.com is the master of the 2-minute relationship, and Boeing is the master of the 10-year relationship.[55] Visit *www.boeing.com* and *www.amazon.com*. From Greenberg's statement and from the appearance of these Web sites, it appears that Boeing is committed to traditional CRM and Amazon.com to social CRM. Give evidence from each site that this might be true. Explain why the products and business environment of both companies cause this difference. Is there any justification for traditional CRM at Amazon.com? Why or why not? Is there any justification for social CRM at Boeing? Why or why not? Based on these companies, is it possible that a company might endorse enterprise social networks but not endorse social CRM? Explain.

8-19. Suppose you are hired by a local farming cooperative to develop a SMIS. The cooperative wants to promote eating healthy foods, increase awareness about its weekly farmer's market, increase traffic to its Web site, and sell more of its products directly to consumers. Which success metrics would indicate that the cooperative has achieved its goals? Who would be the cooperative's target audience? What value would the cooperative's SMIS provide to its customers? How could the cooperative make personal connections with its customers? Which SM platform(s) would you recommend the cooperative use? Justify your recommendations.

ENDNOTES

1. Shea Bennett, "Pinterest, Twitter, Facebook, Instagram, Google+, LinkedIn—Social Media Stats 2014," All Twitter on *MediaBistro.com*, January 20, 2014, accessed June 17, 2014, *www.mediabistro.com/alltwitter/social-media-stats-2014_b54243*.
2. Pew Research Internet Project, "Social Networking Fact Sheet," Pew Research, February 27, 2014, accessed May 5, 2015, *www.pewinternet.org/fact-sheets/social-networking-fact-sheet/*.
3. John McDermott, "Pinterest: The No-bro Zone," Digiday.com, February 20, 2014, accessed May 5, 2015, *http://digiday.com/platforms/why-pinterest-is-still-a-predominantly-female-platform/*.
4. Quantcast, *LinkedIn.com* profile, accessed May 5, 2015, *www.quantcast.com/linkedin.com*.
5. Amy Gesenhues, "Social Media Use Growing Among *Fortune* 500 List with 77% Tweeting & 70% on Facebook," Marketing Land, July 23, 2013, accessed May 5, 2015, *http://marketingland.com/fortune-500-companys-social-media-use-on-the-rise-52726*.
6. Vernon Smith, *Rationality in Economics: Constructivist and Ecological Forms* (Cambridge, UK: Cambridge University Press, 2007), pp. 247–250.
7. "About Customer Ratings," Amazon.com, accessed July 30, 2013, *www.amazon.com/gp/help/customer/display.html/ref=hp_200791020_vine?nodeId=200791020#vine*.
8. LinkedIn Talent Solutions, "Recruiter," accessed May 5, 2015, *http://business.linkedin.com/talent-solutions/products/recruiter.html*.
9. Erika Welz Prafder, "Hiring Your First Employee," *Entrepreneur.com*, accessed May 26, 2014, *www.entrepreneur.com/article/83774*.
10. Jobvite Inc., "2014 Social Recruiting Survey," *Jobvite.com*, August 2014, accessed July 23, 2015, *https://www.jobvite.com/wp-content/uploads/2014/10/Jobvite_SocialRecruiting_Survey2014.pdf*.
11. Nan Lin, *Social Capital: The Theory of Social Structure and Action* (Cambridge, UK: Cambridge University Press, 2002), Kindle location 310.
12. Henk D. Flap, "Social Capital in the Reproduction of Inequality," *Comparative Sociology of Family, Health, and Education*, Vol. 20 (1991), pp. 6179–6202. Cited in Nan Lin, *Social Capital: The Theory of Social Structure and Action* (Cambridge, UK: Cambridge University Press, 2002), Kindle location 345.
13. Accessed May 5, 2015, *http://klout.com/corp/how-it-works*.
14. *SponsoredTweets.com* maintains a list of celebrities, number of their followers, and their price for a sponsored tweet.
15. Founding father of the United States. Author of *Poor Richard's Almanac*. Successful businessman; owner of a chain of print shops. Discoverer of groundbreaking principles in the theory of electricity. Inventor of bifocals, the potbelly stove, the lightning rod, and much more. Founder of the public library and the postal service. Darling of the French court and salons and, now, contributor to social network theory!
16. Nat Ives, "What a YouTube Celeb Pulls In," *Adage.com*, April 15, 2015, accessed May 5, 2015, *http://adage.com/article/news/a-youtube-celeb-pulls/298015*.
17. "YouTube Press Statistics," YouTube.com, accessed May 5, 2015, *www.youtube.com/yt/press/statistics.html*.
18. Josh Constine, "Facebook Has Mixed Q1 Earnings with Miss on $3.54B Revenue, Beat on $0.42 EPS, User Growth Up to Hit 1.44B," *TechCrunch.com*, April 22, 2015, accessed May 5, 2015 *http://techcrunch.com/2015/04/22/facebook-q1-2015-earnings*.
19. Twitter Inc., "Twitter Reports First Quarter 2015 Results," *Twitterinc.com*, April 28, 2015, accessed May 5, 2015, *https://investor.twitterinc.com/results.cfm*.
20. LinkedIn Corporation, "LinkedIn Announces First Quarter 2015 Results," *LinkedIn Investor Relations*, April 30, 2015, accessed May 5, 2015, *http://investors.linkedin.com*.
21. Sean Blanchfield, "Adblocking Goes Mainstream," *PageFair*, August 2014, accessed May 5, 2015, *http://blog.pagefair.com/2014/adblocking-report*.
22. Wikimedia Foundation, "2013–2014 Annual Plan Questions and Answers," WikimediaFoundation.org, accessed June 19, 2014, *https://meta.wikimedia.org/wiki/Wikimedia_Foundation/Annual_Report/2013-2014*.

23. eMarketer, "Mobile Ad Spend to Top $100 Billion Worldwide in 2016, 51% of Digital Market," *eMarketer.com*, April 2, 2015 accessed May 6, 2015, *http://www.emarketer.com/Article/Mobile-Ad-Spend-Top-100-Billion-Worldwide-2016-51-of-Digital-Market/1012299*.

24. Cisco, "Cisco Visual Networking Index: Global Mobile Data Traffic Forecast Update, 2014–2019," Cisco.com, February 3, 2015, accesssed May 6, 2015, *www.cisco.com/c/en/us/solutions/collateral/service-provider/visual-networking-index-vni/vni-forecast-qa.pdf*.

25. Ibid.

26. Marin Software, "Mobile Search Advertising Around The Globe: 2014 Annual Report," MarinSoftware.com, March 2014, accessed May 6, 2015, *www.marinsoftware.com/resources/whitepapers*.

27. Facebook Inc., "Facebook Reports First Quarter 2015 Results," *Facebook.com*, April 22, 2015, accessed May 6, 2015, *http://investor.fb.com/releasedetail.cfm?ReleaseID=908022*.

28. Monetate, "Ecommerce Quarterly EQ4 2014: The Gift of Personalization," *Monetate.com*, February 2015, accessed May 6, 2015, *www.monetate.com/resources/research/#ufh-i-48179143-ecommerce-quarterly-q4-2014*.

29. Rex Santus, "Justin Bieber Dethroned as King of Instagram in Massive Follower Purge," *Mashable*, December 19, 2013, accessed April 2, 2015, *http://mashable.com/2014/12/19/instagram-purge*.

30. Moovweb, "Android vs. iOS, Are iOS Shoppers More Valuable than Android Shoppers," *Moovweb.com*, December 9, 2014, accessed May 6, 2015, *www.moovweb.com/blog/android-vs-ios*.

31. Jim Edwards, "Here's the Vast Number of People Who Abandon Twitter That Dick Costolo Refuses to Talk About," *Business Insider*, February 6, 2014, accessed May 5, 2015, *www.businessinsider.com/number-of-users-who-abandon-twitter-2014-2*.

32. While a conversion is having someone take a desired action, as assisted social conversion is when social media helps the conversion take place.

33. Sarah Perez, "Pinterest Goes After the Male Demographic with Debut of New Search Filters," TechCrunch, January 23, 2015, accessed May 7, 2015, *http://techcrunch.com/2015/01/23/pinterest-goes-after-the-male-demographic-with-debut-of-new-search-filters*.

34. Hilary Heino, "Social Media Demographics—Instagram, Tumblr, and Pinterest," Agile Impact, March 13, 2014, accessed May 7, 2015, *http://agileimpact.org/social-media-demographics-instagram-tumblr-and-pinterest*

35. Cooper Smith, "LinkedIn May Not Be the Coolest Social Network, but It's Only Becoming More Valuable to Businesses," Business Insider, May 1, 2014, accessed May 7, 2015, *www.businessinsider.com/demographic-data-and-social-media-2014-2*.

36. Ibid.

37. CivicScience, "Social Media Now Equals TV Advertising in Influence Power on Consumption Decisions," CivicScience.com, September 2014, accessed May 5, 2015, *https://civicscience.com/library/insightreports/social-media-equals-tv-advertising-in-influence-power-on-consumption-decisions*.

38. Nicholas Jackson, "As MySpace Sells for $35 Million, a History of the Network's Valuation," *The Atlantic*, June 29, 2011, accessed June 18, 2015, *www.theatlantic.com/technology/archive/2011/06/as-myspace-sells-for-35-million-a-history-of-the-networks-valuation/241224/*.

39. Gene Marks, "Why Facebook Is in Decline," *Forbes*, August 19, 2013, accessed June 18, 2015, *www.forbes.com/sites/quickerbettertech/2013/08/19/why-facebook-is-in-decline/*.

40. Andrew McAfee, "Enterprise 2.0, version 2.0," AndrewMcAfee.org, May 27, 2006, accessed May 5, 2015, *http://andrewmcafee.org/2006/05/enterprise_20_version_20/*.

41. Andrew McAfee, "Enterprise 2.0: The Dawn of Emergent Collaboration," *MIT Sloan Management Review*, Spring 2006, accessed May 5, 2015, *http://sloanreview.mit.edu/article/enterprise-the-dawn-of-emergent-collaboration*.

42. Yammer, "Empowering Employees for Improved Customer Service and a Better Bottom Line," Yammer.com, accessed June 25, 2014, *https://about.yammer.com/assets/Yammer-Case-Study-Red-Robin.pdf*.

43. Ibid.

44. Ralph Paglia, "Social Media Employee Policy Examples from Over 100 Organizations," July 3, 2010, *Social Media Today*, accessed May 7, 2015, *http://socialmediatoday.com/ralphpaglia/141903/social-media-employee-policy-examples-over-100-companies-andorganizations*.

45. "Intel Social Media Guidelines," *Intel*, accessed May 7, 2015, *www.intel.com/content/www/us/en/legal/intel-social-media-guidelines.html*.

46. Marissa Brassfield, "McDonald's McDStories Twitter Promotion Sparks Huge Backlash," *Foodista*, last modified January 24, 2012, *www.foodista.com/blog/2012/01/24/mcdonalds-mcdstories-twitter-promotion-sparks-huge-backlash*.

47. Bernhard Warner, "Nestlé's 'No Logo' Policy Triggers Facebook Revolt," *Social Media Influence*, March 19, 2010, *http://socialmediainfluence.com/2010/03/19/nestles-no-logo-policy-triggers-facebook-revolt/*.

48. Cheryl Conner, "Who Wastes the Most Time at Work," *Forbes*, September 7, 2014, accessed May 7, 2015, *www.forbes.com/sites/cherylsnappconner/2013/09/07/who-wastes-the-most-time-at-work/*.

49. Jennifer Wolfe, "How Marketers Can Shape the Chief Digital Officer Role," CMO.com, March 21, 2013, accessed May 7, 2015, *www.cmo.com/articles/2013/3/20/how_marketers_can_shape.html*.

50. Mohit Kumar, "Apple Patches 'Find My iPhone' Vulnerability Which May Caused Celebrities Photo Leak," *The Hacker News*, September 4, 2014, accessed April 24, 2015, *http://thehackernews.com/2014/09/apple-patches-find-my-iphone.html*.

51. Google, "Ads in Gmail," *Gmail Help*, accessed April 26, 2015, *https://support.google.com/mail/answer/6603?hl=en*.

52. Lee Rainie, Sara Kiesler, Ruogu Kang, and Mary Madden, "Anonymity, Privacy, and Security Online," September 5, 2013, The Pew Research Center, accessed April 26, 2015, *www.pewinternet.org/2013/09/05/anonymity-privacy-and-security-online*.

53. Olivia Oran and Gerry Shih, "Twitter Shares Soar in Frenzied NYSE Debut," Reuters, November 7, 2013, accessed May 7, 2015, *www.reuters.com/article/2013/11/07/us-twitter-ipo-idUSBRE99N1AE20131107*.

54. Sedona Chamber of Commerce, accessed July 30, 2013, *www.visitsedona.com/article/151*.

55. Paul Greenberg, *CRM at the Speed of Light*, 4th ed. (New York: McGraw-Hill, 2010), p. 105.

Business Intelligence Systems

"What'd you get for lunch, Nicki?" James asks as they walk back to the office together.

"That five-spice beef thing they do at Hong's. You?"

"Oh, pot stickers and stuff from New China."

"That place has good food; I should have gone there with you. Hey, James, I'm wondering if you can help me with something."

"I'll try. What's up?"

"Well, we're tracking winners and runners-up from each of our spinning events, and we're having unbelievable success selling products to them."

"Ah, competition. Participants want something to gain an advantage in the next heat?"

"Right. But I know there's more we can do if we can link in personal trainers somehow. Maybe go after the losers, the people who didn't win their heat. I'd like to send them to a trainer and earn a referral fee back to us … or maybe take a percent of the training fees."

"OK. Makes sense. So, where do you need my help?"

"Where do they live? The racers, I mean. Where are they? Are they clustered geographically? I mean, we don't want to send the name of a trainer in Minneapolis to someone living in San Diego."

"Well, we could ask them for their address when they sign up for the event?"

"Yeah, maybe, justify it by saying we need it for some sort of map we could display. They might like that. But I hate to ask them for anything that distracts them from the races."

"We could use their connection IP addresses. That would tell us where the bikes are that they're using…might not be where they live, though."

"I don't mean where they sleep; I mean where they work out. That would do."

"What if they're traveling?"

"I don't care…most people won't be. I'm not quite sure what I want, and I know that drives you crazy."

"It does for operational things; it's typical for BI."

"What's BI?"

"Business intelligence. Data analysis, where you don't know the second question to ask until you see the answer to the first one."

"Yeah. That's it exactly! That's where I am right now."

"Suppose we start with this. I'll sample a bunch of our data, maybe 5,000 racers, and locate them with the connection IP. Then I'll give it to you in an Excel pivot table."

"Yeah, so what?"

"Well, then you can look at it by state, city, and ZIP code and see what we've got."

"How come you're not asking me for budget?"

"I might, but this part is easy. We've got the data, and I can deliver it with Excel. And I've got just one user: *you*. So I don't have to make the UI easy, write documentation, develop procedures, etcetera. Besides, you're a pretty smart user."

"Thanks for the praise … "

"On the other hand, if you take off with this in some crazy way and you want to use it to build something for users or do some serious data mining, set up a data mart, then you'll need to come up with some money for my budget."

"Data analysis, where you don't know the second question to ask until you see the answer to the first one."

STUDY QUESTIONS

Q9-1 How do organizations use business intelligence (BI) systems?

Q9-2 What are the three primary activities in the BI process?

Q9-3 How do organizations use data warehouses and data marts to acquire data?

Q9-4 How do organizations use reporting applications?

Q9-5 How do organizations use data mining applications?

Q9-6 How do organizations use BigData applications?

Q9-7 What is the role of knowledge management systems?

Q9-8 What are the alternatives for publishing BI?

Q9-9 2026?

"You mean this Excel thing is sort of a taste teaser."

"Yeah, but you've got to like the taste."

"Hope it's better than that five-spice thing."

"See you later."

"When do I get my report?"

"Friday?"

"That soon?"

"It's just a teaser, Nicki."

CHAPTER·PREVIEW

The information systems described in Chapters 7 and 8 generate enormous amounts of data. The systems in Chapter 7 generate structured data that is used for operational purposes, such as tracking orders, inventories, payables, and so forth. This data has a potential windfall: It contains patterns, relationships, and clusters and can be used to classify, forecast, and predict. Social media data, from systems discussed in Chapter 8, is unstructured but also provides that same windfall. However, there is so much social media data that it results in BigData collections, which need specialized processing.

This chapter considers business intelligence (BI) systems: information systems that can produce patterns, relationships, and other information from organizational structured and unstructured social data as well as from external, purchased data. In addition to this data, another rich source of knowledge is employees themselves. Employees come to the organization with expertise, and as they gain experience in the organization they add to that expertise. Vast amounts of collective knowledge exist in every organization's employees. How can that knowledge be shared?

As a future business professional, business intelligence is a critical skill. According to a recent survey by PricewaterhouseCoopers, 50 percent of U.S. CEOs see *very high value* of digital technology in data analytics (business intelligence). Eighty percent reported that data mining and analytics were strategically important to their organizations.[1] In 2014, Gartner found that CEOs believe digital marketing (of which business intelligence is the core) to be the number-one priority for technology investment. Foundation Capital estimates that marketing technology expenditures will grow from $12B in 2014 to $120B by 2026. As you will learn, business intelligence is the key technology supporting such marketing technology.[2]

This chapter begins by summarizing the ways organizations use business intelligence. It then describes the three basic activities in the BI process and illustrates those activities using a parts selection problem. We then discuss the role of data warehouses and data marts followed by survey reporting, data mining, BigData, and knowledge management BI applications. After that, you'll learn alternatives for publishing the results of BI applications. We will wrap up the chapter with a 2026 observation that many people find frightening.

Q9-1 How Do Organizations Use Business Intelligence (BI) Systems?

Business intelligence (BI) systems are information systems that process operational, social, and other data to identify patterns, relationships, and trends for use by business professionals and other knowledge workers. These patterns, relationships, trends, and predictions are referred to as

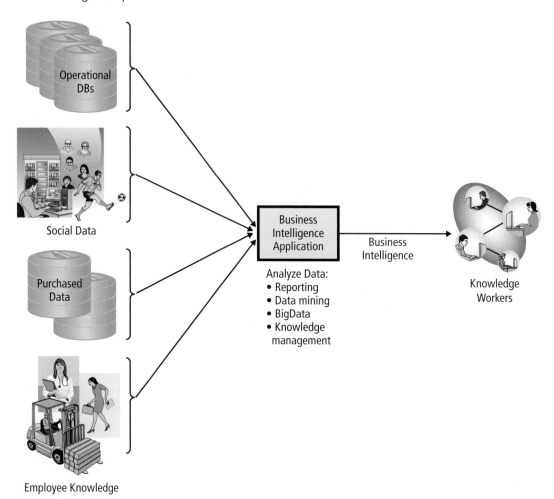

Figure 9-1

Components of a Business
Intelligence System

business intelligence. As information systems, BI systems have the five standard components: hardware, software, data, procedures, and people. The software component of a BI system is called a **BI application**.

In the context of their day-to-day operations, organizations generate enormous amounts of data. AT&T, for example, processes 1.9 trillion call records in its database and Google stores a database with over 33 trillion entries.[3] Business intelligence is buried in that data, and the function of a BI system is to extract it and make it available to those who need it.

The boundaries of BI systems are blurry. In this text, we will take the broad view shown in Figure 9-1. Source data for a BI system can be the organization's own operational data, social media data, data that the organization purchases from data vendors, or employee knowledge. The BI application processes the data with reporting applications, data mining applications, BigData applications, and knowledge management applications to produce business intelligence for knowledge workers. Today such workers include not only analysts in the home office but also operations and field personnel who use BI to approve loans, order goods, and decide when to prescribe, to take a few examples.

How Do Organizations Use BI?

As shown in Figure 9-2, organizations use BI for all four of the collaborative tasks described in Chapter 2. Starting with the last row of Figure 9-2, business intelligence can be used just for informing. Personal trainers can use PRIDE to learn how clients are using the new system. At the time of the analysis, the trainers may not have any particular purpose in mind, but are just browsing the BI results for some future, unspecified purpose. At Falcon Security, the company we

Task	PRIDE Example	Faclon Security Example
Project Management	Create a partnership program between PRIDE competitors and local health clubs.	Expand geographically.
Problem Solving	How can we increase ad revenue from competitions?	How can we save money by rerouting drone flights?
Deciding	Which competitions generate the most ad revenue? Develop more of the best competitions.	Which drones and related equipment are in need of maintenance?
Informing	In what ways are clients using the new system?	How do sales compare to our sales forecast?

Figure 9-2

Example Uses of Business Intelligence

studied in Chapters 1– 6, Mateo may just want to know how Falcon's current sales compare to the forecast. He may have no particular purpose in mind; he just wants to know "how we're doing."

Moving up a row in Figure 9-2, some managers use BI systems for decision making. PRIDE Systems could use BI on its competitive events to determine characteristics of the events that generate the most revenue, and it could then conduct more of that type of event. Falcon Security could use a BI analysis of flight failures to decide when it is time to service drones and related camera equipment.

(By the way, some authors define BI systems as supporting decision making only, in which case they use the older term **decision support systems** as a synonym for decision-making BI systems. We take the broader view here to include all four of the tasks in Figure 9-2 and will avoid the term *decision support systems*.)

Problem solving is the next category of business intelligence use. Again, a problem is a perceived difference between what is and what ought to be. Business intelligence can be used for both sides of that definition: determining *what is* as well as *what should be*. If revenue is below expectations, PRIDE Systems can use BI to learn what factors to change to obtain more event attendance and more ad revenue. Falcon Security could use BI to determine whether it could save costs by rerouting its drone flights.

Finally, business intelligence can be used during project management. PRIDE can be used to support a project to create a partnership with local health clubs. When Falcon Security wants to expand to new geographic locations, it can use business intelligence to determine which locations will be the most advantageous.

As you study Figure 9-2, recall the hierarchical nature of these tasks. Deciding requires informing; problem solving requires deciding (and informing); and project management requires problem solving (and deciding [and informing]).

What Are Typical BI Applications?

This section summarizes three BI applications that will give you a flavor of what is possible. Because *business intelligence* and the related term *BigData* are hot topics today, a Web search will produce dozens of similar examples. After you read this chapter, search for more applications that appeal to your particular interests.

Identifying *Changes* in Purchasing Patterns

Most students are aware that business intelligence is used to predict purchasing patterns. Amazon made the phrase "Customers who bought . . . also bought" famous; when we buy something today, we expect the e-commerce application to suggest what else we might want. Later in this chapter, you'll learn some of the techniques that are used to produce such recommendations.

More interesting, however, is identifying *changes* in purchasing patterns. Retailers know that important life events cause customers to change what they buy and, for a short interval, to form new loyalties to new brands. Thus, when people start their first professional job, get married, have a baby, or retire, retailers want to know. Before BI, stores would watch the local newspapers for graduation, marriage, and baby announcements and send ads in response. That is a slow, labor-intensive, and expensive process.

Target wanted to get ahead of the newspapers and in 2002 began a project to use purchasing patterns to determine that someone was pregnant. By applying business intelligence techniques to its sales data, Target was able to identify a purchasing pattern of lotions, vitamins, and other products that reliably predicts pregnancy. When Target observed that purchasing pattern, it sent ads for diapers and other baby-related products to those customers.

Its program worked—too well for one teenager who had told no one she was pregnant. When she began receiving ads for baby items, her father complained to the manager of the local Target store, who apologized. It was the father's turn to apologize when he learned that his daughter was, indeed, pregnant.[4]

BI for Entertainment

Amazon, Netflix, Pandora, Spotify, and other media-delivery organizations generate billions of bytes of data on consumer media preferences. Using that data, Amazon has begun to produce its own video and TV, basing plots and characters and selecting actors on the results of its BI analysis.[5]

Netflix decided to buy *House of Cards*, starring Kevin Spacey, based on its analysis of customers' viewing patterns. Similarly, Spotify processes data on customers' listening habits to determine locations where particular bands' songs are heard most often. Using that data, it then recommends the best cities for popular bands and other musical groups to perform.[6]

A popular adage among marketing professionals is that "buyers are liars," meaning they'll say they want one thing but purchase something else. That characteristic reduces the efficacy of marketing focus groups. BI produced from data on watching, listening, and rental habits, however, determines what people actually want, not what they say. Will this enable data miners like Amazon to become the new Hollywood? We will see.

Just-in-Time Medical Reporting

Practice Fusion Inc., a medical record startup, provides injection notification services to doctors during exams. As the doctor enters data, the software analyzes patient's records, and if injections are needed, it recommends that the doctor prescribe them as the exam progresses. It seems to work, too. During a 4-month study period, patients whose doctors were using the recommendation service prescribed 73 percent more vaccinations than those in a control group who did not use the service.[7]

The service is free to doctors. Practice Fusion is paid by Merck, a pharmaceutical company. While Practice Fusions software recommends many products that are not sold by Merck, it also recommends many that are. Hence, the service stands on the blurry edge of medical ethics. Should a drug company provide software that recommends its products to doctors "for free"? If the injections are truly needed, who could object? On the other hand, how unbiased is the Practice Fusion software?

Setting the ethical issues aside, Practice Fusion provides an excellent example of data mining and reporting in real time. During your career, there likely will be many examples of middle-of-the-sales-call sales assistance.

Given these examples, we next consider the process used to create business intelligence.

Q9-2 What Are the Three Primary Activities in the BI Process?

Figure 9-3 shows the three primary activities in the BI process: acquire data, perform analysis, and publish results. These activities directly correspond to the BI elements in Figure 9-1. **Data acquisition** is the process of obtaining, cleaning, organizing, relating, and cataloging source

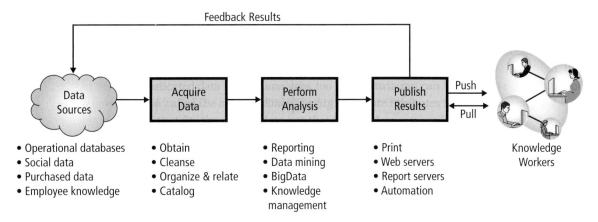

Figure 9-3
Three Primary
Activities in the
BI Process

data. We will illustrate a simple data acquisition example later in this question and discuss data acquisition in greater detail in Q9-3.

BI analysis is the process of creating business intelligence. The four fundamental categories of BI analysis are reporting, data mining, BigData, and knowledge management. We will illustrate a simple example of a reporting system later in this question and describe each of the categories of BI analysis in greater detail in Q9-4 through Q9-7, respectively.

Publish results is the process of delivering business intelligence to the knowledge workers who need it. **Push publishing** delivers business intelligence to users without any request from the users; the BI results are delivered according to a schedule or as a result of an event or particular data condition. **Pull publishing** requires the user to request BI results. Publishing media include print as well as online content delivered via Web servers, specialized Web servers known as *report servers*, and BI results that are sent via automation to other programs. We will discuss these publishing options further in Q9-8. For now, consider a simple example of the use of business intelligence.

Using Business Intelligence to Find Candidate Parts

3D printing offers the possibility for customers to print parts they need rather than order them from a retailer or distributor. One large distributor of bicycle parts wanted to stay on top of this potential change in demand and decided to investigate the possibility of selling 3D printing files for the parts rather than the parts themselves. Accordingly, it created a team to examine past sales data to determine which part designs it might sell. To do so, the company needed to identify qualifying parts and compute how much revenue potential those parts represent.

To address this problem, the team obtained an extract of sales data from its IS department and stored it in Microsoft Access. It then created five criteria for parts that might quality for this new program. Specifically, it looked for parts that were:

1. Provided by certain vendors (starting with just a few vendors that had already agreed to make part design files available for sale)
2. Purchased by larger customers (individuals and small companies would be unlikely to have 3D printers or the needed expertise to use them)
3. Frequently ordered (popular products)
4. Ordered in small quantities (3D printing is not suited for mass production)
5. Simple in design (easier to 3D print)

The team knew that the fifth criterion would be difficult to evaluate because the company doesn't store data on part complexity per se. After some discussion, the team decided to use part weight and price as surrogates for simplicity, operating under the assumption that "If it doesn't weigh very much or cost very much, it probably isn't complex." At least, the team decided to start that way and find out. Accordingly, the team asked the IS department to include part weight in the extract.

Island Biking	John Steel	Marketing Manager	2014		14	59	$438.81	Internet
Island Biking	John Steel	Marketing Manager	2014		21	55	$255.96	AWS
Island Biking	John Steel	Marketing Manager	2015		4	11	$85.55	Internet
Kona Riders	Renate Messne	Sales Representative	2012		43	54	$349.27	Internet
Kona Riders	Renate Messne	Sales Representative	2013		30	53	$362.45	Internet
Kona Riders	Renate Messne	Sales Representative	2014		1	2	$14.34	Internet
Lone Pine Crafters	Jaime Yorres	Owner	2015		4	14	$108.89	Internet
Lone Pine Crafters	Jaime Yorres	Owner	2015		2	2	$15.56	Internet
Lone Pine Crafters	Jaime Yorres	Owner	2016		2	2	$15.56	Internet
Moab Mauraders	Carlos Gonzále	Accounting Manager	2015		2	4	$4,106.69	Internet
Moab Mauraders	Carlos Gonzále	Accounting Manager	2015		3	7	$7,404.18	Internet
Moab Mauraders	Carlos Gonzále	Accounting Manager	2015		2	6	$6,346.44	Internet
Sedona Mountain Trails	Felipe Izquierc	Owner	2015		6	7	$73.46	Internet
Sedona Mountain Trails	Felipe Izquierc	Owner	2015		3	7	$39.14	Phone
Sedona Mountain Trails	Felipe Izquierc	Owner	2015		3	9	$74.59	Phone
Sedona Mountain Trails	Felipe Izquierc	Owner	2014		5	20	$153.00	Phone
Sedona Mountain Trails	Felipe Izquierc	Owner	2012		3	8	$37.14	Phone
Sedona Mountain Trails	Felipe Izquierc	Owner	2013		1	0	$89.30	Internet
Sedona Mountain Trails	Felipe Izquierc	Owner	2013		6	20	$73.13	Phone
Sedona Mountain Trails	Felipe Izquierc	Owner	2012		4	8	$67.41	Internet
Flat Iron Riders	Maria Anders	Sales Representative	2013		7	22	$11,734.25	Internet
Flat Iron Riders	Maria Anders	Sales Representative	2015		2	1	$595.00	Internet
Flat Iron Riders	Maria Anders	Sales Representative	2014		10	29	$16,392.25	Internet
Flat Iron Riders	Maria Anders	Sales Representative	2015		20	32	$12,688.80	AWS

Figure 9-4a

Sample Extracted Data: Order Extract Table

Source: © Access 2013, Microsoft Corporation

Acquire Data

As shown in Figure 9-3, acquiring data is the first step in the BI process. In response to the team's request for data, the IS department extracted operational data to produce the following two tables:

> Sales (CustomerName, Contact, Title, Bill Year, Number Orders, Units, Revenue, Source, PartNumber)
>
> Part (PartNumber, Shipping Weight, Vendor)

Sample data for these two tables is shown in Figure 9-4. As team members examined this data, they concluded they had what they needed and actually wouldn't need all of the data columns in the Sales table. They were surprised that the data was divided into different billing years, but because they planned to sum item sales over those years, that division wouldn't affect their analysis.

Part Data

ID	PartNumber	Shipping Weight	Vendor	Click to Add
9	200-219	7.28	DePARTures, Inc.	
22	200-225	3.61	DePARTures, Inc.	
23	200-227	5.14	DePARTures, Inc.	
11	200-207	9.23	DePARTures, Inc.	
28	200-205	4.11	DePARTures, Inc.	
29	200-211	4.57	DePARTures, Inc.	
10	200-213	1.09	DePARTures, Inc.	
37	200-223	3.61	DePARTures, Inc.	
45	200-217	1.98	DePARTures, Inc.	
2	200-209	10.41	DePARTures, Inc.	
3	200-215	1.55	DePARTures, Inc.	
47	200-221	10.85	DePARTures, Inc.	
42	200-203	3.20	DePARTures, Inc.	
17	300-1007	2.77	Desert Gear Supply	
13	300-1017	9.46	Desert Gear Supply	
50	300-1016	4.14	Desert Gear Supply	
27	300-1013	2.66	Desert Gear Supply	
8	300-1008	10.13	Desert Gear Supply	
30	300-1015	5.96	Desert Gear Supply	
15	300-1014	10.18	Desert Gear Supply	
7	300-1009	3.76	Desert Gear Supply	
6	300-1011	6.41	Desert Gear Supply	
43	300-1010	10.87	Desert Gear Supply	
31	300-1012	9.08	Desert Gear Supply	
1	500-2035	9.66	ExtremeGear	
41	500-2030	4.71	ExtremeGear	
40	500-2040	9.92	ExtremeGear	

Figure 9-4b

Sample Extracted Data: Part Data Table

Source: © Access 2013, Microsoft Corporation

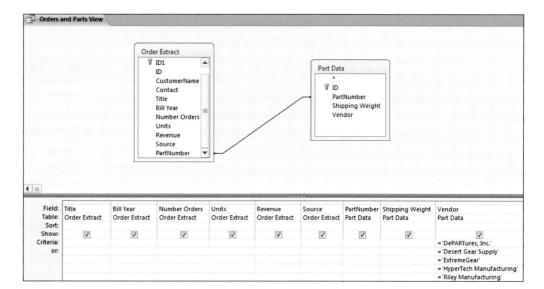

Figure 9-5

Joining *Orders Extract* and Filtered *Parts* Tables

Source: © Access 2013, Microsoft Corporation

Analyze Data

The team's first step was to combine the data in the two tables into a single table that contained both the sales and part data. Also, because team members had already selected certain vendors to work with (those they knew would agree to release 3D part design files), they set filtering criteria for those vendor names, as shown in Figure 9-5. In this Access query, the line between PartNumber in Order Extract and PartNumber in Part Data means that rows of the two tables are to be combined if they have matching values of PartNumber.

The result of this query is shown in Figure 9-6. Notice there are some missing and questionable values. Numerous rows have missing values of Contact and Title, and some of the rows have a value of zero for Units. The missing contact data and title data wasn't a problem. But the values of zero units might be problematic. At some point, the team might need to investigate what these values mean and possibly correct the data or remove those rows from the analysis. In the immediate term, however, the team decided to proceed even with these incorrect values. You will learn in Q9-3 that, for a number of reasons, such problematic data is common in data extracts.

The data in Figure 9-6 has been filtered for their first criterion, to consider parts only from particular vendors. For their next criterion, team members needed to decide how to identify

Figure 9-6

Sample *Orders* and *Parts View* Data

Source: © Access 2013, Microsoft Corporation

CustomerName	Contact	Title	Bill Year	Number Orders	Units	Revenue	Source	PartNumber	Shipping Weight	Vendor
Gordos Dirt Bikes	Sergio Gutiérrez	Sales Represe	2011	43	107	$26,234.12	Internet	100-108	3.32	Riley Manufacturing
Island Biking			2012	59	135	$25,890.62	Phone	500-2035	9.66	ExtremeGear
Big Bikes			2010	29	77	$25,696.00	AWS	700-1680	6.06	HyperTech Manufacturing
Lazy B Bikes			2009	19	30	$25,576.50	Internet	700-2280	2.70	HyperTech Manufacturing
Lone Pine Crafters	Carlos Hernández	Sales Represe	2012	1	0	$25,171.56	Internet	500-2030	4.71	ExtremeGear
Seven Lakes Riding	Peter Franken	Marketing M:	2009	15	50	$25,075.00	Internet	500-2020	10.07	ExtremeGear
Big Bikes			2012	10	40	$24,888.00	Internet	500-2025	10.49	ExtremeGear
B' Bikes	Georg Pipps	Sales Manage	2012	14	23	$24,328.02	Internet	700-1680	6.06	HyperTech Manufacturing
Eastern Connection	Isabel de Castro	Sales Represe	2012	48	173	$24,296.17	AWS	100-105	10.73	Riley Manufacturing
Big Bikes	Carine Schmitt	Marketing M:	2009	22	71	$23,877.48	AWS	500-2035	9.66	ExtremeGear
Island Biking	Manuel Pereira	Owner	2011	26	45	$23,588.86	Internet	500-2045	3.22	ExtremeGear
Mississippi Delta Riding	Rene Phillips	Sales Represe	2012	9	33	$23,550.25	Internet	700-2180	4.45	HyperTech Manufacturing
Uncle's Upgrades			2012	9	21	$22,212.54	Internet	700-1680	6.06	HyperTech Manufacturing
Big Bikes			2010	73	80	$22,063.92	Phone	700-1680	6.06	HyperTech Manufacturing
Island Biking			2012	18	59	$22,025.88	Internet	100-108	3.32	Riley Manufacturing
Uncle's Upgrades			2011	16	38	$21,802.50	Internet	500-2035	9.66	ExtremeGear
Hard Rock Machines			2012	42	57	$21,279.24	Internet	100-108	3.32	Riley Manufacturing
Kona Riders			2012	11	20	$21,154.80	Internet	700-1880	2.28	HyperTech Manufacturing
Moab Mauraders			2012	6	20	$21,154.80	Internet	700-2180	4.45	HyperTech Manufacturing
Lone Pine Crafters			2012	35	58	$21,016.59	Internet	100-106	6.23	Riley Manufacturing
Big Bikes	Carine Schmitt	Marketing M:	2010	9	36	$20,655.00	Internet	500-2035	9.66	ExtremeGear
East/West Enterprises			2011	14	60	$20,349.00	Internet	100-104	5.80	Riley Manufacturing
Jeeps 'n More	Yvonne Moncada	Sales Agent	2012	47	50	$20,230.00	AWS	500-2030	4.71	ExtremeGear
East/West Enterprises			2009	14	60	$20,178.15	AWS	500-2035	9.66	ExtremeGear
Lone Pine Crafters			2012	20	54	$20,159.28	Internet	100-106	6.23	Riley Manufacturing
Lone Pine Crafters	Carlos Hernández	Sales Represe	2012	1	0	$20,137.27	Internet	500-2030	4.71	ExtremeGear
Lazy B Bikes			2012	21	29	$19,946.78	AWS	700-1580	7.50	HyperTech Manufacturing
Eastern Connection	Isabel de Castro	Sales Represe	2012	42	173	$19,907.06	Phone	100-105	10.73	Riley Manufacturing
Lazy B Bikes			2012	8	30	$19,724.25	AWS	700-1580	7.50	HyperTech Manufacturing

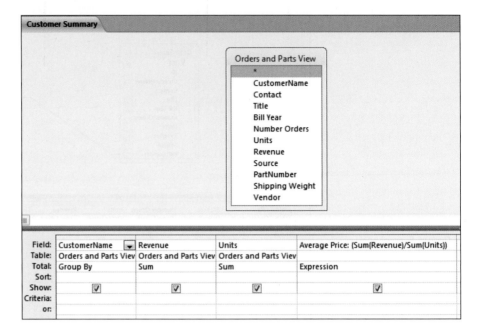

Figure 9-7
Creating the Customer Summary Query

Source: © Access 2013, Microsoft Corporation

large customers. To do so, they created the query in Figure 9-7, which sums the revenue, units, and average price for each customer. Looking at the query results in Figure 9-8, team members decided to consider only customers having more than $200,000 in total revenue; they created a query having just those customers and named that query Big Customers.

Next, team members discussed what they meant by frequent purchase and decided to include items ordered an average of once a week or roughly 50 times per year. You can see that they set that criterion for Number Orders in the query in Figure 9-9. To select only parts that are ordered in small quantities, they first created a column that computes average order size (Units / [Number Orders]) and then set a criterion on that expression that the average must be less than 2.5. Their last two criteria were that the part be relatively inexpensive and that it be lightweight. They decided to select parts with a unit price (computed as Revenue / Units) less than 100 and a shipping weight less than 5 pounds.

Figure 9-8
Customer Summary

Source: © Access 2013, Microsoft Corporation

CustomerName	SumOfRevenue	SumOfUnits	Average Price
Great Lakes Machines	$1,760.47	142	12.3976535211268
Seven Lakes Riding	$288,570.71	5848	49.3451963919289
Around the Horn	$16,669.48	273	61.0603611721612
Dewey Riding	$36,467.90	424	86.0092018867925
Moab Mauraders	$143,409.27	1344	106.7033234375
Gordos Dirt Bikes	$113,526.88	653	173.854335068913
Mountain Traders	$687,710.99	3332	206.395855432173
Hungry Rider Off-road	$108,602.32	492	220.736416056911
Eastern Connection	$275,092.28	1241	221.669848186946
Mississippi Delta Riding	$469,932.11	1898	247.593315542676
Island Biking	$612,072.64	2341	261.457770098249
Big Bikes	$1,385,867.98	4876	284.222310233798
Hard Rock Machines	$74,853.22	241	310.594267219917
Lone Pine Crafters	$732,990.33	1816	403.629038215859
Sedona Mountain Trails	$481,073.82	1104	435.755269474638
Flat Iron Riders	$85,469.20	183	467.044808743169
Bottom-Dollar Bikes	$72,460.85	154	470.52502012987
Uncle's Upgrades	$947,477.61	1999	473.975794047024
Ernst Handel Mechanics	$740,951.15	1427	519.236962438683
Kona Riders	$511,108.05	982	520.476624439919
Lazy B Bikes	$860,950.72	1594	540.119648619824
Jeeps 'n More	$404,540.62	678	596.667583185841
French Riding Masters	$1,037,386.76	1657	626.063224984912
B' Bikes	$113,427.06	159	713.377735849057
East/West Enterprises	$2,023,402.09	2457	823.525474074074
Bon App Riding	$65,848.90	60	1097.48160833333

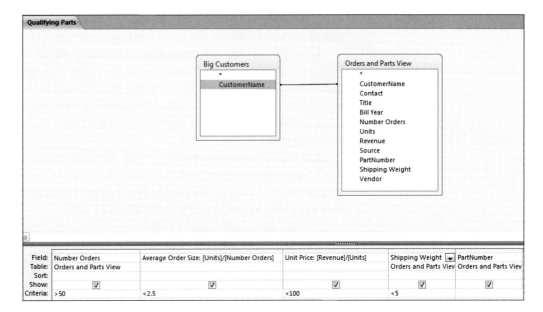

Figure 9-9
Qualifying Parts Query Design
Source: © Access 2013, Microsoft Corporation

The results of this query are shown in Figure 9-10. Of all the parts that the company sells, these 12 fit the criteria that the team created.

The next question was how much revenue potential these parts represent. Accordingly, the team created a query that connected the selected parts with their past sales data. The results are shown in Figure 9-11.

Publish Results

Publish results is the last activity in the BI process shown in Figure 9-3. In some cases, this means placing BI results on servers for publication to knowledge workers over the Internet or other networks. In other cases, it means making the results available via a Web service for use by other applications. In still other cases, it means creating PDFs or PowerPoint presentations for communicating to colleagues or management.

In this case, the team reported these results to management in a team meeting. Judging just by the results in Figure 9-11, there seems to be little revenue potential in selling designs for these

Qualifying Parts

Number Orders	Average Order Size	Unit Price	Shipping Weight	PartNumber
275	1	9.14173854545455	4.14	300-1016
258	1.87596899224806	7.41284524793388	4.14	300-1016
110	1.18181818181818	6.46796923076923	4.11	200-205
176	1.66477272727273	12.5887211604096	4.14	300-1016
139	1.0431654676259	6.28248965517241	1.98	200-217
56	1.83928571428571	6.71141553398058	1.98	200-217
99	1.02020202020202	7.7775	3.20	200-203
76	2.17105263157895	12.0252206060606	2.66	300-1013
56	1.07142857142857	5.0575	4.57	200-211
73	1.15068493150685	5.0575	4.57	200-211
107	2.02803738317757	6.01096405529954	2.77	300-1007
111	2.07207207207207	6.01096434782609	2.77	300-1007

Figure 9-10
Qualifying Parts Query Results
Source: © Access 2013, Microsoft Corporation

Revenue Potential

Total Orders	Total Revenue	PartNumber
3987	$84,672.73	300-1016
2158	$30,912.19	200-211
1074	$23,773.53	200-217
548	$7,271.31	300-1007
375	$5,051.62	200-203
111	$3,160.86	300-1013
139	$1,204.50	200-205

Figure 9-11
Sales History for Selected Parts
Source: © Access 2013, Microsoft Corporation

parts. The company would earn minimal revenue from the parts themselves; the designs would have to be priced considerably lower, and that would mean almost no revenue.

In spite of the low revenue potential, the company might still decide to offer 3D designs to customers. It might decide to give the designs away as a gesture of goodwill to its customers; this analysis indicates it will be sacrificing little revenue to do so. Or it might do it as a PR move intended to show that it's on top of the latest manufacturing technology. Or it might decide to postpone consideration of 3D printing because it doesn't see that many customers ordering the qualifying parts.

Of course, there is the possibility that the team members chose the wrong criteria. If they have time, it might be worthwhile to change their criteria and repeat the analysis. Such a course is a slippery slope, however. They might find themselves changing criteria until they obtain a result they want, which yields a very biased study.

This possibility points again to the importance of the human component of an IS. The hardware, software, data, and query-generation procedures are of little value if the decisions that the team made when setting and possibly revising criteria are poor. Business intelligence is only as intelligent as the people creating it!

With this example in mind, we will now consider each of the activities in Figure 9-3 in greater detail.

Q9-3 How Do Organizations Use Data Warehouses and Data Marts to Acquire Data?

Although it is possible to create basic reports and perform simple analyses from operational data, this course is not usually recommended. For reasons of security and control, IS professionals do not want data analysts processing operational data. If an analyst makes an error, that error could cause a serious disruption in the company's operations. Also, operational data is structured for fast and reliable transaction processing. It is seldom structured in a way that readily supports BI analysis. Finally, BI analyses can require considerable processing; placing BI applications on operational servers can dramatically reduce system performance.

For these reasons, most organizations extract operational data for BI processing. For small organizations, the extraction may be as simple as an Access database. Larger organizations, however, typically create and staff a group of people who manage and run a **data warehouse**, which is a facility for managing an organization's BI data. The functions of a data warehouse are to:

- Obtain data
- Cleanse data
- Organize and relate data
- Catalog data

Figure 9-12 shows the components of a data warehouse. Programs read operational and other data and extract, clean, and prepare that data for BI processing. The prepared data is stored in a data warehouse database using a data warehouse DBMS, which can be different from the organization's operational DBMS. For example, an organization might use Oracle for its operational processing, but use SQL Server for its data warehouse. Other organizations use SQL Server for operational processing, but use DBMSs from statistical package vendors such as SAS or SPSS in the data warehouse.

Collecting and selling data about consumer shopping habits is big business. But what information about you is being collected? And how is it being used? The Ethics Guide on pages 384–385 considers these questions.

Data warehouses include data that is purchased from outside sources. The purchase of data about organizations is not unusual or particularly concerning from a privacy standpoint. However, some companies choose to buy personal consumer data (e.g., marital status) from data vendors such as Acxiom Corporation. Figure 9-13 lists some of the consumer data that can be readily purchased. An amazing (and, from a privacy standpoint, frightening) amount of data is available.

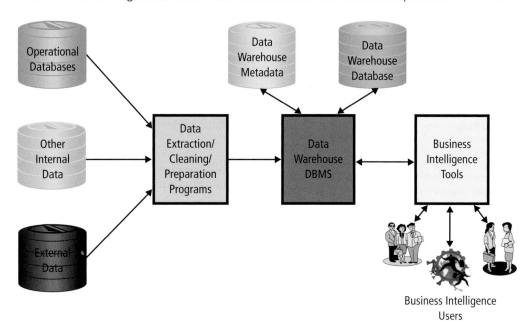

Figure 9-12
Components of a Data Warehouse

Metadata concerning the data—its source, its format, its assumptions and constraints, and other facts about the data—is kept in a data warehouse metadata database. The data warehouse DBMS extracts and provides data to BI applications.

The term *business intelligence users* is different from *knowledge workers* in Figure 9-1. BI users are generally specialists in data analysis, whereas knowledge workers are often nonspecialist users of BI results. A loan approval officer at a bank is a knowledge worker, but not a BI user.

Problems with Operational Data

Most operational and purchased data has problems that inhibit its usefulness for business intelligence. Figure 9-14 lists the major problem categories. First, although data that is critical for successful operations must be complete and accurate, marginally necessary data need not be. For example, some systems gather demographic data in the ordering process. But, because such data is not needed to fill, ship, and bill orders, its quality suffers.

Security concerns about access to data are problematic. See the Security Guide on pages 406–407 for more information.

Problematic data is termed dirty data. Examples are a value of B for customer gender and of 213 for customer age. Other examples are a value of 999–999–9999 for a U.S. phone number, a part color of "gren," and an email address of WhyMe@GuessWhoIAM.org. The value of zero for Units in Figure 9-6 is dirty data. All of these values can be problematic for BI purposes.

Purchased data often contains missing elements. The contact data in Figure 9-6 is a typical example; orders can be shipped without contact data, so its quality is spotty and has many missing values. Most data vendors state the percentage of missing values for each attribute in the data

- Name, address, phone
- Age
- Gender
- Ethnicity
- Religion
- Income
- Education
- Voter registration
- Home ownership
- Vehicles
- Magazine subscriptions
- Hobbies
- Catalog orders
- Marital status, life stage
- Height, weight, hair and eye color
- Spouse name, birth date
- Children's names and birth dates

Figure 9-13
Examples of Consumer Data That Can Be Purchased

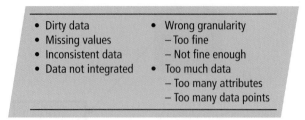

- Dirty data
- Missing values
- Inconsistent data
- Data not integrated
- Wrong granularity
  - Too fine
  - Not fine enough
- Too much data
  - Too many attributes
  - Too many data points

Figure 9-14
Possible Problems with
Source Data

they sell. An organization buys such data because for some uses, some data is better than no data at all. This is especially true for data items whose values are difficult to obtain, such as Number of Adults in Household, Household Income, Dwelling Type, and Education of Primary Income Earner. However, care is required here because for some BI applications a few missing or erroneous data points can seriously bias the analysis.

Inconsistent data, the third problem in Figure 9-14, is particularly common for data that has been gathered over time. When an area code changes, for example, the phone number for a given customer before the change will not match the customer's number afterward. Likewise, part codes can change, as can sales territories. Before such data can be used, it must be recoded for consistency over the period of the study.

Some data inconsistencies occur from the nature of the business activity. Consider a Web-based order-entry system used by customers worldwide. When the Web server records the time of order, which time zone does it use? The server's system clock time is irrelevant to an analysis of customer behavior. Coordinated Universal Time (formerly called Greenwich Mean Time) is also meaningless. Somehow, Web server time must be adjusted to the time zone of the customer.

Another problem is nonintegrated data. A particular BI analysis might require data from an ERP system, an e-commerce system, and a social networking application. Analysts may wish to integrate that organizational data with purchased consumer data. Such a data collection will likely have relationships that are not represented in primary key/foreign key relationships. It is the function of personnel in the data warehouse to integrate such data somehow.

Data can also have the wrong **granularity**, a term that refers to the level of detail represented by the data. Granularity can be too fine or too coarse. For the former, suppose we want to analyze the placement of graphics and controls on an order-entry Web page. It is possible to capture the customers' clicking behavior in what is termed *clickstream data*. Those data, however, include everything the customer does at the Web site. In the middle of the order stream are data for clicks on the news, email, instant chat, and a weather check. Although all of that data may be useful for a study of consumer browsing behavior, it will be overwhelming if all we want to know is how customers respond to an ad located differently on the screen. To proceed, the data analysts must throw away millions and millions of clicks.

Data can also be too coarse. For example, a file of regional sales totals cannot be used to investigate the sales in a particular store in a region, and total sales for a store cannot be used to determine the sales of particular items within a store. Instead, we need to obtain data that is fine enough for the lowest-level report we want to produce.

In general, it is better to have too fine a granularity than too coarse. If the granularity is too fine, the data can be made coarser by summing and combining. This is what team members did with the sales data in Figure 9-6. Sales by Bill Year were too fine for their needs, so they summed sales data over those years. If the granularity is too coarse, however, there is no way to separate the data into constituent parts.

The final problem listed in Figure 9-14 is to have too much data. As shown in the figure, we can have either too many attributes or too many data points. Think back to the discussion of tables in Chapter 5. We can have too many columns or too many rows.

Consider the first problem: too many attributes. Suppose we want to know the factors that influence how customers respond to a promotion. If we combine internal customer data with purchased customer data, we will have more than a hundred different attributes to consider. How do we select among them? In some cases, analysts can ignore the columns they don't need. But in more sophisticated data mining analyses, too many attributes can be problematic. Because of a phenomenon called the *curse of dimensionality*, the more attributes there are, the easier it is to build a model that fits the sample data but that is worthless as a predictor. There are other good reasons for reducing the number of attributes, and one of the major activities in data mining concerns efficient and effective ways of selecting attributes.

The second way to have an excess of data is to have too many data points—too many rows of data. Suppose we want to analyze clickstream data on CNN.com. How many clicks does that site receive per month? Millions upon millions! In order to meaningfully analyze such data we need to reduce the amount of data. One good solution to this problem is statistical sampling. Organizations should not be reluctant to sample data in such situations.

Data Warehouses Versus Data Marts

To understand the difference between data warehouses and data marts, think of a data warehouse as a distributor in a supply chain. The data warehouse takes data from the data manufacturers (operational systems and other sources), cleans and processes the data, and locates the data on the shelves, so to speak, of the data warehouse. The data analysts who work with a data warehouse are experts at data management, data cleaning, data transformation, data relationships, and the like. However, they are not usually experts in a given business function.

A **data mart** is a data collection, smaller than the data warehouse, that addresses the needs of a particular department or functional area of the business. If the data warehouse is the distributor in a supply chain, then a data mart is like a retail store in a supply chain. Users in the data mart obtain data that pertain to a particular business function from the data warehouse. Such users do not have the data management expertise that data warehouse employees have, but they are knowledgeable analysts for a given business function.

Figure 9-15 illustrates these relationships. In this example, the data warehouse takes data from the data producers and distributes the data to three data marts. One data mart is used to analyze clickstream data for the purpose of designing Web pages. A second analyzes store sales data and determines which products tend to be purchased together. This information is used to

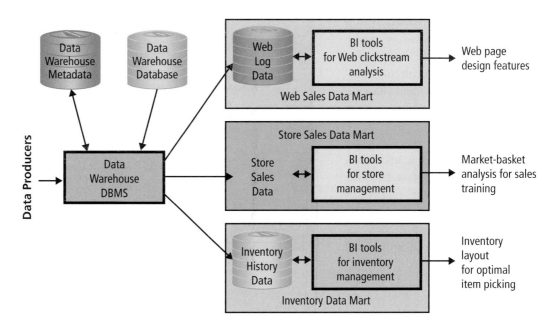

Figure 9-15
Data Mart Examples

Ethics Guide

UNSEEN CYBERAZZI

A data broker or **data aggregator** is a company that acquires and purchases consumer and other data from public records, retailers, Internet cookie vendors, social media trackers, and other sources and uses it to create business intelligence that it sells to companies and the government. Two prominent data brokers are Datalogix and Acxiom Corporation.

Data brokers gather vast amounts of data. According to *The New York Times*, as of June 2012, Acxiom Corporation had used 23,000 servers to process data of 50 trillion transactions on 500 million consumers. It stores more than 15,000 data points on some consumers.[8]

So, what do data brokers do with all this data? If you buy pizza online on Friday nights only when you receive a substantial discount, a data broker (or the broker's customer) knows to send you a discount pizza coupon Friday morning. If you use a customer loyalty card at your local grocery store and regularly buy, say, large bags of potato chips, the data broker or its customer will send you coupons for more potato chips or for a second snack product that is frequently purchased by potato chip consumers. Or, as discussed in Q1, if you suddenly start buying certain lotions and vitamins, the data broker will know you're pregnant.

Federal law provides strict limits on gathering and using medical and credit data. For other data, however, the possibilities are unlimited. In theory, data brokers enable you to view the data that is stored about you, but in practice it is difficult to learn how to request your data. Further, the process for doing so is torturous, and ultimately, the data that is released is limited to innocuous data such as your name, phone numbers, and current and former addresses.[9] Without an easy means for viewing all of your data, it is impossible to verify its accuracy.

Of even greater concern, however, is the unknown processing of such data. What business intelligence techniques are employed by these companies? What are the accuracy and reliability of those techniques? If the data broker errs in predicting that you'll buy a pizza on Friday night, who cares? But if the data broker errs in predicting that you're a terrorist, it matters. Data brokers are silent on these questions.

Source: Sergey Nivens/Shutterstock

1. We've used Kant's categorical imperative as one criterion for assessing ethical behavior: *Act as if you would have your behavior be a universal law.* As a litmus test of this principle, we've said that if you're willing to publish your behavior in *The New York Times*, then your behavior conforms to the categorical imperative.

   a. Consider the inverse of that litmus test. Is it true that if you're not willing to publish your behavior in *The New York Times*, it is unethical? (You might find it easier to consider this question in a different but equivalent form: Your behavior is ethical *if and only if* you're willing to publish it in *The New York Times*.)

   b. Considering your answer to question a, if data brokers are unwilling to say what data they are collecting and how they are processing it, is it reasonable to conclude their behavior is unethical? Explain your answer.

2. Using business intelligence applied to consumer purchasing data for targeted marketing seems innocuous enough. However, is it? Using both the categorical imperative (pages 56–57) and utilitarian (pages 92–93) perspectives, assess the ethics of the following:

   a. Some people, whether from genetic factors, habit, lack of education, or other factors, are prone to overeating junk food. By focusing junk food sales offers at this market segment, data brokers or their customers are promoting obesity. Is their behavior ethical?

   b. Data brokers claim they can reliably infer ethnicity from consumer behavior data. Suppose they also determine that one ethnic group is more likely to attend college than others. Accordingly, they focus the marketing for college-prep materials, scholarships, and university admissions applications on this ethnic group. Over time, that group will be guided into positive (assuming you believe college is positive) decisions that other groups will not. Is this behavior different from ethnic profiling? Is it ethical?

3. Suppose a data broker correctly identifies that your grandmother is addicted to playing online hearts. From its business intelligence, it knows that frequent hearts players are strong prospects for online gambling. Accordingly, the data broker refers your grandmother's data to an online gambling vendor, one of its customers. Grandma gets hooked and loses all of her savings, including money earmarked for your college tuition.

   a. Is the data broker's behavior ethical?

   b. Assume the data broker says, "Look, it's not us, it's our customer, the online gambling vendor, that's causing the problem." Does the broker's posture absolve it of ethical considerations for Grandma's losses?

   c. Assume the online gambling vendor says, "Look, it's not us; it's Grandma. We provide fair and honest games. If Grandma likes to play games where the odds of winning are low, talk to Grandma." Assume in your answer that the gaming company has gone to great lengths to provide the elderly with an emotionally rewarding UX for games with low winning odds. Does the vendor's posture absolve it of any ethical considerations for Grandma's losses?

4. If all of your behavior is ethical, then, according to the categorical imperative, you are willing to have your life story printed in *The New York Times*. Thus, you needn't be concerned about the data and business intelligence created about you. However, consider the following:

   a. Suppose, as the most junior member of a club, you are required to purchase beer for your club's bi-monthly beer fest. To obtain a substantial discount from the vendor, you use your customer loyalty card for these purchases. A data aggregator obtains your purchase history and classifies you as a heavy drinker. Unknown to you, the data aggregator informs your medical insurance company of its classification. Your insurance premiums increase, and you never know why. Using either the categorical imperative or utilitarianism, is there an ethical problem here?

   b. Do you think something should be done to reduce the likelihood of situations like that in question a? If so, what?

   c. Suppose you have a personal medical problem that you wish to keep private. Your condition requires you to purchase a particular set of off-the-shelf products from the pharmacy at your grocery store. A data aggregator observes your purchasing pattern, infers your problem, and sends you coupons and other promotional products that clearly identify your condition. Against your strongest wishes, your roommates become aware of your medical problem. Using either the categorical imperative or utilitarianism, is there an ethical problem here?

   d. Do you think something should be done to reduce the likelihood of situations like that in question c? If so, what?

5. According to the Privacy Act of 1974, the U.S. government is prohibited from storing many types of data about U.S. citizens. The act does not, however, prohibit it from purchasing business intelligence from data brokers. If the government purchases business intelligence that is based, in part, on data that it is prohibited from storing, is the government's behavior ethical? Use both the categorical imperative and utilitarian perspectives in your answer.

train salespeople on the best way to up-sell to customers. The third data mart is used to analyze customer order data for the purpose of reducing labor for item picking from the warehouse. A company like Amazon, for example, goes to great lengths to organize its warehouses to reduce picking expenses.

As you can imagine, it is expensive to create, staff, and operate data warehouses and data marts. Only large organizations with deep pockets can afford to operate a system like that shown in Figure 9-12. Smaller organizations operate subsets of this system, but they must find ways to solve the basic problems that data warehouses solve, even if those ways are informal.

Q9-4 How Do Organizations Use Reporting Applications?

A **reporting application** is a BI application that inputs data from one or more sources and applies reporting operations to that data to produce business intelligence. We will first summarize reporting operations and then illustrate two important reporting applications: RFM analysis and OLAP.

Basic Reporting Operations

Reporting applications produce business intelligence using five basic operations:

- Sorting
- Filtering
- Grouping
- Calculating
- Formatting

None of these operations is particularly sophisticated; they can all be accomplished using SQL and basic HTML or a simple report writing tool.

The team that analyzed parts in Q9-3 used Access to apply all five of these operations. Examine, for example, Figure 9-11 (page 379). The results are *sorted* by Total Revenue, *filtered* for particular parts, sales are *grouped by* PartNumber, Total Orders and Total Revenue are *calculated*, and the calculations for Total Revenue are *formatted* correctly as dollar currency.

These simple operations can be used to produce complex and highly useful reports. Consider RFM analysis and Online Analytical Processing as two prime examples.

RFM Analysis

RFM analysis, a technique readily implemented with basic reporting operations, is used to analyze and rank customers according to their purchasing patterns.[10] RFM considers how *recently* (R) a customer has ordered, how *frequently* (F) a customer ordered, and how much *money* (M) the customer has spent.

To produce an RFM score, the RFM reporting tool first sorts customer purchase records by the date of their most recent (R) purchase. In a common form of this analysis, the tool then divides the customers into five groups and gives customers in each group a score of 1 to 5. The 20 percent of the customers having the most recent orders are given an R score of 1, the 20 percent of the customers having the next most recent orders are given an R score of 2, and so forth, down to the last 20 percent, who are given an R score of 5.

The tool then re-sorts the customers on the basis of how frequently they order. The 20 percent of the customers who order most frequently are given an F score of 1, the next 20 percent of most frequently ordering customers are given a score of 2, and so forth, down to the least frequently ordering customers, who are given an F score of 5.

Customer	RFM Score		
Big 7 Sports	1	1	3
St. Louis Soccer Club	5	1	1
Miami Municipal	5	4	5
Central Colorado State	3	3	3

Figure 9-16
Example RFM Scores

Finally, the tool sorts the customers again according to the amount spent on their orders. The 20 percent who have ordered the most expensive items are given an M score of 1, the next 20 percent are given an M score of 2, and so forth, down to the 20 percent who spend the least, who are given an M score of 5.

Figure 9-16 shows sample RFM results. The first customer, Big 7 Sports, has ordered recently and orders frequently. Big 7 Sports' M score of 3 indicates, however, that it does not order the most expensive goods. From these scores, the sales team can conclude that Big 7 Sports is a good, regular customer and that it should attempt to up-sell more expensive goods to Big 7 Sports.

The second customer in Figure 9-16 could represent a problem. St. Louis Soccer Club has not ordered in some time, but when it did order in the past, it ordered frequently, and its orders were of the highest monetary value. This data suggests that St. Louis Soccer Club might have taken its business to another vendor. Someone from the sales team should contact this customer immediately.

No one on the sales team should even think about the third customer, Miami Municipal. This company has not ordered for some time; it did not order frequently; and, when it did order, it bought the least expensive items and not many of them. Let Miami Municipal go to the competition; the loss will be minimal.

The last customer, Central Colorado State, is right in the middle. Central Colorado State is an OK customer, but probably no one in sales should spend much time with it. Perhaps sales can set up an automated contact system or use the Central Colorado State account as a training exercise for an eager departmental assistant or intern.

Online Analytical Processing (OLAP)

Online analytical processing (OLAP), a second type of reporting application, is more generic than RFM. OLAP provides the ability to sum, count, average, and perform other simple arithmetic operations on groups of data. The defining characteristic of OLAP reports is that they are dynamic. The viewer of the report can change the report's format, hence the term *online*.

An OLAP report has measures and dimensions. A **measure** is the data item of interest. It is the item that is to be summed or averaged or otherwise processed in the OLAP report. Total sales, average sales, and average cost are examples of measures. A **dimension** is a characteristic of a measure. Purchase date, customer type, customer location, and sales region are all examples of dimensions.

Figure 9-17 shows a typical OLAP report. Here, the measure is *Store Sales Net*, and the dimensions are *Product Family* and *Store Type*. This report shows how net store sales vary by product family and store type. Stores of type *Supermarket* sold a net of $36,189 worth of nonconsumable goods, for example.

Figure 9-17

Example Grocery Sales
OLAP Report

Source: © Access 2013, Microsoft
Corporation

	A	B	C	D	E	F	G
1							
2							
3	Store Sales Net	Store Type					
4	Product Family	Deluxe Supermarket	Gourmet Supermarket	Mid-Size Grocery	Small Grocery	Supermarket	Grand Total
5	Drink	$8,119.05	$2,392.83	$1,409.50	$685.89	$16,751.71	$29,358.98
6	Food	$70,276.11	$20,026.18	$10,392.19	$6,109.72	$138,960.67	$245,764.87
7	Non-Consumable	$18,884.24	$5,064.79	$2,813.73	$1,534.90	$36,189.40	$64,487.05
8	Grand Total	$97,279.40	$27,483.80	$14,615.42	$8,330.51	$191,901.77	$339,610.90

A presentation like that in Figure 9-17 is often called an **OLAP cube**, or sometimes simply a *cube*. The reason for this term is that some software products show these displays using three axes, like a cube in geometry. The origin of the term is unimportant here, however. Just know that an *OLAP cube* and an *OLAP report* are the same thing.

The OLAP report in Figure 9-17 was generated by Microsoft SQL Server Analysis Services and is displayed in an Excel pivot table. The data was taken from a sample instructional database, called Food Mart, that is provided with SQL Server.

It is possible to display OLAP cubes in many ways besides with Excel. Some third-party vendors provide more extensive graphical displays. For more information about such products, check for OLAP vendors and products at the Data Warehousing Review at *http://dwreview.com/OLAP/index.html*. For an example of a superb, easy-to-use OLAP tool, visit *www.TableauSoftware.com*. Tableau has a liberal student-use policy as well.

As stated earlier, the distinguishing characteristic of an OLAP report is that the user can alter the format of the report. Figure 9-18 shows such an alteration. Here, the user added another dimension, *Store Country* and *Store State*, to the horizontal display. Product-family sales are now broken out by store location. Observe that the sample data only includes stores in the United States, and only in the western states of California, Oregon, and Washington.

With an OLAP report, it is possible to **drill down** into the data. This term means to further divide the data into more detail. In Figure 9-19, for example, the user has drilled down into the stores located in California; the OLAP report now shows sales data for the four cities in California that have stores.

Notice another difference between Figures 9-18 and 9-19. The user has not only drilled down, she has also changed the order of the dimensions. Figure 9-18 shows *Product Family* and then store location within *Product Family*. Figure 9-19 shows store location and then *Product Family* within store location.

Both displays are valid and useful, depending on the user's perspective. A product manager might like to see product families first and then store location data. A sales manager might like to see store locations first and then product data. OLAP reports provide both perspectives, and the user can switch between them while viewing the report.

Unfortunately, all of this flexibility comes at a cost. If the database is large, doing the necessary calculating, grouping, and sorting for such dynamic displays will require substantial computing power. Although standard commercial DBMS products do have the features and functions required to create OLAP reports, they are not designed for such work. They are designed, instead, to provide rapid response to transaction-processing applications, such as order entry or manufacturing planning. Consequently, some organizations tune DBMS products on dedicated servers for this purpose. Today, many OLAP servers are being moved to the cloud.

Figure 9-18

Example of Expanded Grocery Sales OLAP Report

Source: © Access 2013, Microsoft Corporation

	A	B	C	D	E	F	G	H	I
1									
2									
3	Store Sales Net			Store Type					
4	Product Family	Store Country	Store State	Deluxe Superma	Gourmet Supermar	Mid-Size Groce	Small Grocery	Supermarket	Grand Total
5	Drink	USA	CA		$2,392.83		$227.38	$5,920.76	$8,540.97
6			OR	$4,438.49				$2,862.45	$7,300.94
7			WA	$3,680.56		$1,409.50	$458.51	$7,968.50	$13,517.07
8		USA Total		$8,119.05	$2,392.83	$1,409.50	$685.89	$16,751.71	$29,358.98
9	Drink Total			$8,119.05	$2,392.83	$1,409.50	$685.89	$16,751.71	$29,358.98
10	Food	USA	CA		$20,026.18		$1,960.53	$47,226.11	$69,212.82
11			OR	$37,778.35				$23,818.87	$61,597.22
12			WA	$32,497.76		$10,392.19	$4,149.19	$67,915.69	$114,954.83
13		USA Total		$70,276.11	$20,026.18	$10,392.19	$6,109.72	$138,960.67	$245,764.87
14	Food Total			$70,276.11	$20,026.18	$10,392.19	$6,109.72	$138,960.67	$245,764.87
15	Non-Consumable	USA	CA		$5,064.79		$474.35	$12,344.49	$17,883.63
16			OR	$10,177.89				$6,428.53	$16,606.41
17			WA	$8,706.36		$2,813.73	$1,060.54	$17,416.38	$29,997.01
18		USA Total		$18,884.24	$5,064.79	$2,813.73	$1,534.90	$36,189.40	$64,487.05
19	Non-Consumable Total			$18,884.24	$5,064.79	$2,813.73	$1,534.90	$36,189.40	$64,487.05
20	Grand Total			$97,279.40	$27,483.80	$14,615.42	$8,330.51	$191,901.77	$339,610.90

Figure 9-19

	A	B	C	D	E	F	G	H	I	J
1										
2										
3	Store Sales Net				Store Type ▼					
4	Store Country ▼	Store Sta ▼	Store City	Product Family ▼	Deluxe Super	Gourmet Supermar	Mid-Size Groce	Small Grocery	Supermarket	Grand Total
5	USA	CA	Beverly Hills	Drink		$2,392.83				$2,392.83
6				Food		$20,026.18				$20,026.18
7				Non-Consumable		$5,064.79				$5,064.79
8			Beverly Hills Total			$27,483.80				$27,483.80
9			Los Angeles	Drink					$2,870.33	$2,870.33
10				Food					$23,598.28	$23,598.28
11				Non-Consumable					$6,305.14	$6,305.14
12			Los Angeles Total						$32,773.74	$32,773.74
13			San Diego	Drink					$3,050.43	$3,050.43
14				Food					$23,627.83	$23,627.83
15				Non-Consumable					$6,039.34	$6,039.34
16			San Diego Total						$32,717.61	$32,717.61
17			San Francisco	Drink				$227.38		$227.38
18				Food				$1,960.53		$1,960.53
19				Non-Consumable				$474.35		$474.35
20			San Francisco Total					$2,662.26		$2,662.26
21		CA Total				$27,483.80		$2,662.26	$65,491.35	$95,637.41
22		OR		Drink	$4,438.49				$2,862.45	$7,300.94
23				Food	$37,778.35				$23,818.87	$61,597.22
24				Non-Consumable	$10,177.89				$6,428.53	$16,606.41
25		OR Total			$52,394.72				$33,109.85	$85,504.57
26		WA		Drink	$3,680.56		$1,409.50	$458.51	$7,968.50	$13,517.07
27				Food	$32,497.76		$10,392.19	$4,149.19	$67,915.69	$114,954.83
28				Non-Consumable	$8,706.36		$2,813.73	$1,060.54	$17,416.38	$29,997.01
29		WA Total			$44,884.68		$14,615.42	$5,668.24	$93,300.57	$158,468.91
30	USA Total				$97,279.40	$27,483.80	$14,615.42	$8,330.51	$191,901.77	$339,610.90
31	Grand Total				$97,279.40	$27,483.80	$14,615.42	$8,330.51	$191,901.77	$339,610.90

Figure 9-19

Example of Drilling Down into Expanded Grocery Sales OLAP Report

Source: © Access 2013, Microsoft Corporation

Q9-5   How Do Organizations Use Data Mining Applications?

Data mining is the application of statistical techniques to find patterns and relationships among data for classification and prediction. As shown in Figure 9-20, data mining resulted from a convergence of disciplines. Data mining techniques emerged from statistics and mathematics and from artificial intelligence and machine-learning fields in computer science. As a result, data mining terminology is an odd blend of terms from these different disciplines. Sometimes people use the term *knowledge discovery in databases (KDD)* as a synonym for data mining.

Data mining and other business intelligence systems are useful, but they are not without their problems, as discussed in the Guide on pages 408–409.

Most data mining techniques are sophisticated, and many are difficult to use well. Such techniques are valuable to organizations, however, and some business professionals, especially those in finance and marketing, have become expert in their use. In fact, today there are many interesting and rewarding careers for business professionals who are knowledgeable about data mining techniques.

Data mining techniques fall into two broad categories: unsupervised and supervised. We explain both types in the following sections.

Unsupervised Data Mining

With **unsupervised data mining**, analysts do not create a model or hypothesis before running the analysis. Instead, they apply a data mining application to the data and observe the results. With this method, analysts create hypotheses *after the analysis*, in order to explain the patterns found.

One common unsupervised technique is **cluster analysis**. With it, statistical techniques identify groups of entities that have similar characteristics. A common use for cluster analysis is to find groups of similar customers from customer order and demographic data.

For example, suppose a cluster analysis finds two very different customer groups: One group has an average age of 33, owns four Android phones and three iPads, has an expensive home entertainment system, drives a Lexus SUV, and tends to buy expensive children's play equipment. The second group has an average age of 64, owns Arizona vacation property, plays golf, and buys expensive wines. Suppose the analysis also finds that both groups buy designer children's clothing.

These findings are obtained solely by data analysis. There is no prior model about the patterns and relationships that exist. It is up to the analyst to form hypotheses, after the fact, to explain why two such different groups are both buying designer children's clothes.

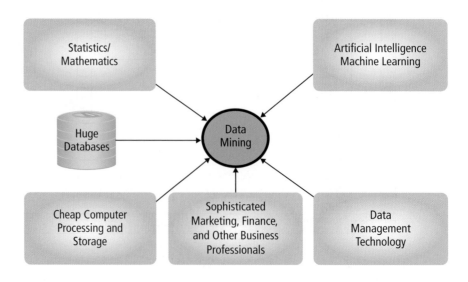

Figure 9-20
Source Disciplines of Data Mining

Supervised Data Mining

With **supervised data mining**, data miners develop a model *prior to the analysis* and apply statistical techniques to data to estimate parameters of the model. For example, suppose marketing experts in a communications company believe that cell phone usage on weekends is determined by the age of the customer and the number of months the customer has had the cell phone account. A data mining analyst would then run an analysis that estimates the effect of customer and account age.

One such analysis, which measures the effect of a set of variables on another variable, is called a **regression analysis**. A sample result for the cell phone example is:

$$\text{CellphoneWeekendMinutes} = 12 + (17.5 \times \text{Customer Age}) \\ + (23.7 \times \text{NumberMonthsOfAccount})$$

Using this equation, analysts can predict the number of minutes of weekend cell phone use by summing 12, plus 17.5 times the customer's age, plus 23.7 times the number of months of the account.

As you will learn in your statistics classes, considerable skill is required to interpret the quality of such a model. The regression tool will create an equation, such as the one shown. Whether that equation is a good predictor of future cell phone usage depends on statistical factors, such as *t* values, confidence intervals, and related statistical techniques.

Neural networks are another popular supervised data mining application used to predict values and make classifications such as "good prospect" or "poor prospect" customers. The term *neural networks* is deceiving because it connotes a biological process similar to that in animal brains. In fact, although the original *idea* of neural nets may have come from the anatomy and physiology of neurons, a neural network is nothing more than a complicated set of possibly nonlinear equations. Explaining the techniques used for neural networks is beyond the scope of this text. If you want to learn more, search *http://kdnuggets.com* for the term *neural network*.

In the next sections, we will describe and illustrate two typical data mining tools—market-basket analysis and decision trees—and show applications of those techniques. From this discussion, you can gain a sense of the nature of data mining. These examples should give you, a future manager, a sense of the possibilities of data mining techniques. You will need additional coursework in statistics, data management, marketing, and finance, however, before you will be able to perform such analyses yourself.

Market-Basket Analysis

Suppose you run a dive shop, and one day you realize that one of your salespeople is much better at up-selling to your customers. Any of your sales associates can fill a customer's order, but this one salesperson is especially good at selling customers items *in addition* to those for which they ask. One day, you ask him how he does it.

"It's simple," he says. "I just ask myself what is the next product they would want to buy. If someone buys a dive computer, I don't try to sell her fins. If she's buying a dive computer, she's already a diver and she already has fins. But these dive computer displays are hard to read. A better mask makes it easier to read the display and get the full benefit from the dive computer."

A **market-basket analysis** is an unsupervised data mining technique for determining sales patterns. A market-basket analysis shows the products that customers tend to buy together. In marketing transactions, the fact that customers who buy product X also buy product Y creates a **cross-selling** opportunity; that is, "If they're buying X, sell them Y" or "If they're buying Y, sell them X."

Figure 9-21 shows hypothetical sales data from 400 sales transactions at a dive shop. The number on the diagonal (shaded) in the first set of rows is the total number of times an item was

	Mask	Tank	Fins	Weights	Dive Computer
Mask	270	10	250	10	90
Tank	10	200	40	130	30
Fins	250	40	280	20	20
Weights	10	130	20	130	10
Dive Computer	90	30	20	10	120
	Support				
Num Trans	400				
Mask	0.675	0.025	0.625	0.025	0.225
Tank	0.025	0.5	0.1	0.325	0.075
Fins	0.625	0.1	0.7	0.05	0.05
Weights	0.025	0.325	0.05	0.325	0.025
Dive Computer	0.225	0.075	0.05	0.025	0.3
	Confidence				
Mask	1	0.05	0.892857143	0.076923077	0.75
Tank	0.037037037	1	0.142857143	1	0.25
Fins	0.925925926	0.2	1	0.153846154	0.166666667
Weights	0.037037037	0.65	0.071428571	1	0.083333333
Dive Computer	0.333333333	0.15	0.071428571	0.076923077	1
	Lift (Improvement)				
Mask		0.074074074	1.322751323	0.113960114	1.111111111
Tank	0.074074074		0.285714286	2	0.5
Fins	1.322751323	0.285714286		0.21978022	0.238095238
Weights	0.113960114	2	0.21978022		0.256410256
Dive Computer	1.111111111	0.5	0.238095238	0.256410256	

Figure 9-21
Market-Basket Analysis at a Dive Shop
Source: © Access 2013, Microsoft Corporation

sold. For example, the 270 on the diagonal cell for Masks means that 270 of the 400 transactions included masks. The 120 in the diagonal cell for Dive Computer means that 120 of the 400 transactions included dive computers.

We can use the number of times an item sold to estimate the probability that a customer will purchase an item. Because 270 of the 400 transactions were masks, we can estimate the probability that a customer will buy a mask to be 270/400, or .675. The probabilty of selling a dive computer is .3.

In market-basket terminology, **support** is the probability that two items will be purchased together. To estimate that probability, we examine sales transactions and count the number of times that two items occurred in the same transaction. For the data in Figure 9-21, fins and masks appeared together 250 times, and thus the support for fins and a mask is 250/400, or .625. Similarly, the support for fins and weights is 20/400, or .05.

These data are interesting by themselves, but we can refine the analysis by taking another step and considering additional probabilities. For example, what proportion of the customers who bought a mask also bought fins? Masks were purchased 270 times, and of those individuals who bought masks, 250 also bought fins. Thus, given that a customer bought a mask, we can estimate the probability that he or she will buy fins to be 250/270, or .926. In market-basket terminology, such a conditional probability estimate is called the **confidence**.

Reflect on the meaning of this confidence value. The likelihood of someone walking in the door and buying fins is 250/400, or .625. But the likelihood of someone buying fins, given that he or she bought a mask, is .926. Thus, if someone buys a mask, the likelihood that he or she will also buy fins increases substantially, from .625 to .926. Thus, all sales personnel should be trained to try to sell fins to anyone buying a mask.

Now consider dive computers and fins. Of the 400 transactions, fins were sold 280 times, so the probability that someone walks into the store and buys fins is .7. But of the 120 purchases of dive computers, only 20 appeared with fins. So the likelihood of someone buying fins, given he or she bought a dive computer, is 20/120, or .1666. Thus, when someone buys a dive computer, the likelihood that he or she will also buy fins falls from .625 to .1666.

The ratio of confidence to the base probability of buying an item is called **lift**. Lift shows how much the base probability increases or decreases when other products are purchased. The lift of fins and a mask is the confidence of fins given a mask, divided by the base probability of fins. In Figure 9-21, the lift of fins and a mask is .926/.7, or 1.32. Thus, the likelihood that people buy fins when they buy a mask increases by 32 percent. Surprisingly, it turns out that the lift of fins and a mask is the same as the lift of a mask and fins. Both are 1.32.

We need to be careful here, though, because this analysis shows only shopping carts with two items. We cannot say from this data what the likelihood is that customers, given that they bought a mask, will buy both weights and fins. To assess that probability, we need to analyze shopping carts with three items. This statement illustrates, once again, that we need to know what problem we're solving before we start to build the information system to mine the data. The problem definition will help us decide if we need to analyze three-item, four-item, or some other sized shopping cart.

Many organizations are benefiting from market-basket analysis today. You can expect that this technique will become a standard CRM analysis during your career.

Decision Trees

A **decision tree** is a hierarchical arrangement of criteria that predict a classification or a value. Here we will consider decision trees that predict classifications. Decision tree analyses are an unsupervised data mining technique: The analyst sets up the computer program and provides the data to analyze, and the decision tree program produces the tree.

A common business application of decision trees is to classify loans by likelihood of default. Organizations analyze data from past loans to produce a decision tree that can be converted to loan-decision rules. A financial institution could use such a tree to assess the default risk on a new loan. Sometimes, too, financial institutions sell a group of loans (called a *loan portfolio*) to one another. An institution considering the purchase of a loan portfolio can use the results of a decision tree program to evaluate the risk of a given portfolio.

Figure 9-22 shows an example provided by Insightful Corporation, a vendor of BI tools. This example was generated using its Insightful Miner product. This tool examined data from 3,485 loans. Of those loans, 72 percent had no default and 28 percent did default. To perform the analysis, the decision tree tool examined six different loan characteristics.

In this example, the decision tree program determined that the percentage of the loan that is past due (*PercPastDue*) is the best first criterion. Reading Figure 9-22, you can see that of the 2,574 loans with a *PercPastDue* value of 0.5 or less (amount past due is less than half the loan amount), 94 percent were not in default. Reading down several lines in this tree, 911 loans had a value of *PercPastDue* greater than 0.5; of those loans, 89 percent were in default.

These two major categories are then further subdivided into three classifications: *CreditScore* is a creditworthiness score obtained from a credit agency; *MonthsPastDue* is the number of months since a payment; and *CurrentLTV* is the current ratio of outstanding balance of the loan to the value of the loan's collateral.

With a decision tree like this, the financial institution can develop decision rules for accepting or rejecting the offer to purchase loans from another financial institution. For example:

- If percent past due is less than 50 percent, then accept the loan.
- If percent past due is greater than 50 percent *and*
- If *CreditScore* is greater than 572.6 *and*
- If *CurrentLTV* is less than .94, then accept the loan.
- Otherwise, reject the loan.

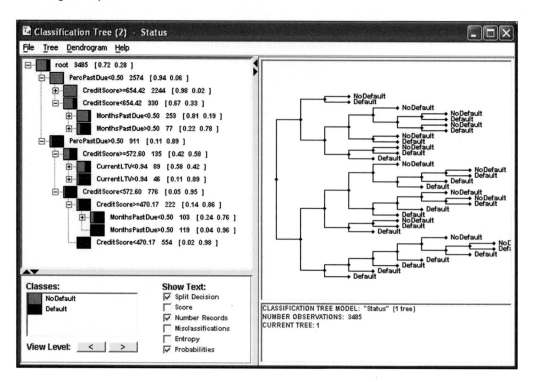

Figure 9-22
Credit Score Decision Tree
Source: Used with permission of
TIBCO Software Inc. Copyright ©
1999–2005 TIBCO Software Inc. All
rights reserved.

Of course, the financial institution will need to combine this risk data with an economic analysis of the value of each loan to determine which loans to take.

Decision trees are easy to understand and, even better, easy to implement using decision rules. They also can work with many types of variables, and they deal well with partial data. Organizations can use decision trees by themselves or combine them with other techniques. In some cases, organizations use decision trees to select variables that are then used by other types of data mining tools. For example, decision trees can be used to identify good predictor variables for neural networks.

Q9-6 How Do Organizations Use BigData Applications?

BigData (also spelled Big Data) is a term used to describe data collections that are characterized by huge *volume*, rapid *velocity*, and great *variety*. In general, the following statements are true of BigData:

- BigData data sets are at least a petabyte in size, and usually larger.
- BigData is generated rapidly.
- BigData has structured data, free-form text, log files, possibly graphics, audio, and video.

MapReduce

Because BigData is huge, fast, and varied, it cannot be processed using traditional techniques. **MapReduce** is a technique for harnessing the power of thousands of computers working in parallel. The basic idea is that the BigData collection is broken into pieces, and hundreds or thousands of independent processors search these pieces for something of interest. That process is

SO WHAT?   BI for Securities Trading?

Since the 1970s there have been rumors of large computers buried in nondescript offices near Wall Street, cranking out analyses for smart stock trading. Do they work? Who knows? If you found a correlation between, say, a decrease in the dollar-to-euro exchange rate that influenced the price of 3M stock, would you publish it? No, you'd trade on it and hope that no one else noticed that correlation. Or if your hedge fund developed a model that failed miserably, would you publish that failure? No. So, due to a lack of data, no controlled study of the success and failure of model-based trading has been done (nor is likely to be done).

Still, it is known that traders such as Alexander Migdal, a former Soviet physicist, made millions of dollars in a high-frequency trading firm[11] that he started. The firm and others like it earn small gains on hundreds of thousands of automated transactions.[12] Unfortunately, such high-frequency trading places severe stresses on the market and was responsible for the near melt-downs in 2007 and 2008.[13] Still such trading continues, if with a bit more control.

Critics say there is far too much noise in the market for any reliable-over-time predictive analysis to work. Consider, for example, the factors that influence the price of 3M stock: global exchange rates, oil prices, the overall stock market, recent patent filings, patents that are about to expire, employee and customer tweets, product failures—the list goes on and on. No model can account for such complexity.

Or can it?

Today a new class of quantitative applications is using BigData and business intelligence to analyze immense amounts of data over a broad spectrum of sources. These applications both build and evaluate investment strategies. Two Sigma (*www.twosigma.com*) is in the forefront of this new style of quantitative analysis. According to the firm, it analyzes vast amounts of data, including corporate financial statements, developing news, Twitter activity, weather reports, and other data sources. From those analyses, it develops and tests investment strategies.[14] They could, in theory, model all of the factors that influence stocks like 3M.

Two Sigma uses a five-step process:

1. Acquire data
2. Create models
3. Evaluate models

Source: tonsnoei/Fotolia

4. Analyze risks
5. Place trades[15]

Does it work? Two Sigma and other firms claim it does. We will see.

We can, however, make one important observation: It has never been easy, some would say even possible, for regular investors to *time the market* by buying just before an upturn or selling just before a downturn. But today, if you try that, you're not only trying to beat the market, you're competing with Two Sigma, with its hundreds of PhDs and massive computing power, and with a slew of similar companies. For most of us, John Bogle, founder of Vanguard, had it right. Buy an index fund, take your 6 percent, and be happy. And, over 30 years, that 6 percent will net a near sixfold increase.

Questions

1. Consider two publicly traded companies: Apple and Alaska Airlines. List 10 factors that you believe influence the price of those two stocks. The factors may be different.

2. Pick one of the two companies in your answer to question 1. Briefly explain how each of the 10 factors influences the price of the stock.

3. For the factors in your answer to question 2, list sources of data for measuring each of the 10 factors. What role would BigData play in processing that data?

4. If you had the data in your answer to question 3, how would you go about determining how much each of the factors influences the price of the stock? What kinds of BI techniques would you employ?

5. Assuming you had used BI to answer question 4 and now had a model of how your 10 factors influence the price of that stock, how would you determine how good your model is? How would you know that the 10 factors you choose were the right 10 factors?

6. Suppose it is possible to obtain the data needed and to build a model to predict with 51 percent accuracy the price of a stock. Is that a usable model? What do you need to make such a model effective?

7. Suppose you've misjudged your model and it predicts with only 49 percent accuracy. What is likely to happen?

8. Summarize what you have learned from this exercise.

referred to as the *Map* phase. In Figure 9-23, for example, a data set having the logs of Google searches is broken into pieces, and each independent processor is instructed to search for and count search keywords. Figure 9-23, of course, shows just a small portion of the data; here you can see a portion of the keywords that begin with *H*.

As the processors finish, their results are combined in what is referred to as the *Reduce* phase. The result is a list of all the terms searched for on a given day and the count of each. The process is considerably more complex than described here, but this is the gist of the idea.

By the way, you can visit Google Trends to see an application of MapReduce. There you can obtain a trend line of the number of searches for a particular term or terms. Figure 9-24 compares the search trends for the terms *Web 2.0* and *Hadoop*. Go to *www.google.com/trends* and enter the terms *Big Data*, *BigData*, and *data analytics* to see why learning about them is a good use of your time.

Hadoop

Hadoop is an open source program supported by the Apache Foundation[16] that implements MapReduce on potentially thousands of computers. Hadoop could drive the process of finding and counting the Google search terms, but Google uses its own proprietary version of MapReduce to do so instead.

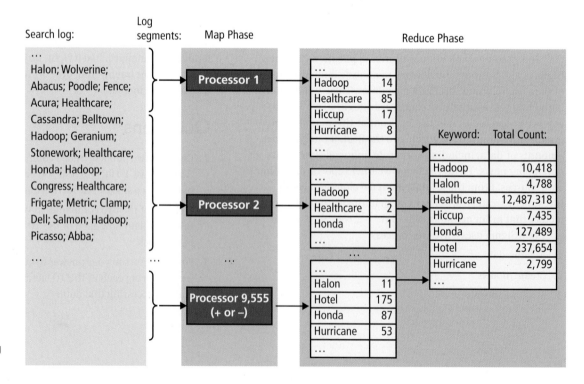

Figure 9-23

MapReduce Processing Summary

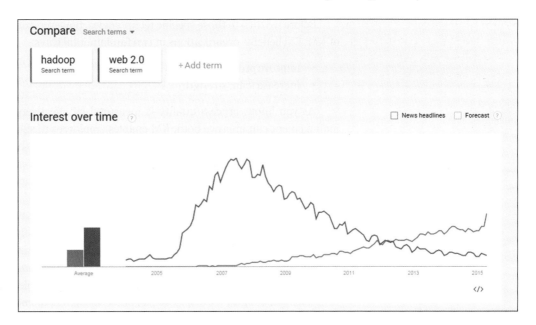

Figure 9-24

Google Trends on the Terms
Web 2.0 and *Hadoop*

Source: Google and the Google logo are
registered trademarks of Google Inc.,
Used with permission.

Hadoop began as part of Cassandra, but the Apache Foundation split it off to become its own product. Hadoop is written in Java and originally ran on Linux. Some companies implement Hadoop on server farms they manage themselves, and others run Hadoop in the cloud. Amazon.com supports Hadoop as part of its EC3 cloud offering. Microsoft offers Hadoop on its Azure platform as a service named HDInsight. Hadoop includes a query language titled **Pig**.

At present, deep technical skills are needed to run and use Hadoop. Judging by the development of other technologies over the years, it is likely that higher-level, easier-to-use query products will be implemented on top of Hadoop. For now, understand that experts are required to use it; you may be involved, however, in planning a BigData study or in interpreting results.

BigData analysis can involve both reporting and data mining techniques. The chief difference is, however, that BigData has volume, velocity, and variation characteristics that far exceed those of traditional reporting and data mining.

Q9-7 What Is the Role of Knowledge Management Systems?

Nothing is more frustrating for a manager to contemplate than the situation in which one employee struggles with a problem that another employee knows how to solve easily. Or to learn of a customer who returns a large order because the customer could not perform a basic operation with the product that many employees (and other customers) can readily perform. Even worse, someone in the customer's organization may know how to use the product, but the people who bought it didn't know that.

Knowledge management (KM) is the process of creating value from intellectual capital and sharing that knowledge with employees, managers, suppliers, customers, and others who need that capital. The goal of knowledge management is to prevent the kinds of problems just described.

Knowledge management was done before social media, and we discuss two such KM systems. However, notice in the first sentence of this paragraph that the scope of KM (employees, managers, suppliers, customer, and others...) is the same scope as that of the use of SM in hyper-social organizations. In fact, modern knowledge management ascribes to hyper-social organization theory, as we will discuss.

Before we turn to those specific technologies, however, consider the overall goals and benefits of KM. KM benefits organizations in two fundamental ways:

- Improve process quality
- Increase team strength

As you know, process quality is measured by effectiveness and efficiency, and knowledge management can improve both. KM enables employees to share knowledge with each other and with customers and other partners. By doing so, it enables the employees in the organization to better achieve the organization's strategy. At the same time, sharing knowledge enables employees to solve problems more quickly and to otherwise accomplish work with less time and other resources, hence improving process efficiency.[17]

Additionally, recall from Chapter 2 that successful teams not only accomplish their assigned tasks, they also grow in capability, both as a team and as individuals. By sharing knowledge, team members learn from one another, avoid making repetitive mistakes, and grow as business professionals.

For example, consider the help desk at any organization, say, one that provides support for electronic components like iPhones. When a user has a problem with an iPhone, he or she might contact Apple support for help. The customer service department has, collectively, seen just about any problem that can ever occur with an iPhone. The organization, as a whole, knows how to solve the user's problem. However, that is no guarantee that a particular support representative knows how to solve that problem. The goal of KM is to enable employees to be able to use knowledge possessed collectively by people in the organization. By doing so, both process quality and team capability improve.

What Are Expert Systems?

The earliest KM systems, called expert systems, attempted to directly capture employee expertise. They existed long before social media and in fact were in use long before the Internet.

Expert systems are rule-based systems that encode human knowledge in the form of **If/Then rules**. Such rules are statements that specify if a particular condition exists, then to take some action. Figure 9-25 shows an example of a few rules that could be part of a medical expert system for diagnosing heart disease. In this set of rules, the system examines various factors for heart disease and computes a *CardiacRiskFactor*. Depending on the value of that risk factor, other variables are given values.

The set of rules shown here may need to be processed many times because it is possible that *CardiacRiskFactor* is used on the If side of a rule occurring before these rules. Unlike this example, an operational expert system may consist of hundreds, if not thousands, of rules.

The programs that process a set of rules are called **expert systems shells**. Typically, the shell processes rules until no value changes. At that point, the values of all the variables are reported as results.

```
Other rules here...

IF CardiacRiskFactor = 'Null' THEN Set CardiacRiskFactor = 0
IF PatientSex = 'Male' THEN Add 3 to CardiacRiskFactor
IF PatientAge >55 THEN Add 2 to CardiacRiskFactor
IF FamilyHeartHistory = 'True' THEN Add 5 to CardiacRiskFactor
IF CholesterolScore = 'Problematic' THEN Add 4 to CardiacRiskFactor
IF BloodPressure = 'Problematic' THEN Add 3 to CardiacRiskFactor
IF CardiacRiskFactor >15 THEN Set EchoCardiagramTest = 'Schedule'
...
Other rules here...
```

Figure 9-25
Example of If/Then Rules

To create the system of rules, the expert system development team interviews human experts in the domain of interest. The rules in Figure 9-25 would have been obtained by interviewing cardiologists who are known to be particularly adept at diagnosing cardiac disease. Such a system encodes the knowledge of those highly skilled experts and makes it available to less-skilled or less-knowledgeable professionals.

Many expert systems were created in the late 1980s and early 1990s, but only a few have enjoyed success. They suffer from three major disadvantages. First, they are difficult and expensive to develop. They require many labor hours from both experts in the domain under study and designers of expert systems. This expense is compounded by the high opportunity cost of tying up domain experts. Such experts are normally some of the most sought-after employees in an organization.

Second, expert systems are difficult to maintain. Because of the nature of rule-based systems, the introduction of a new rule in the middle of hundreds of others can have unexpected consequences. A small change can cause very different outcomes. Unfortunately, such side effects cannot be predicted or eliminated. They are the nature of complex rule-based systems.

Finally, expert systems were unable to live up to the high expectations set by their name. Initially, proponents of expert systems hoped to be able to duplicate the performance of highly trained experts, like doctors. It turned out, however, that no expert system has the same diagnostic ability as knowledgeable, skilled, and experienced doctors. Even when expert systems were developed that came close in ability, changes in medical technology required constant changing of the expert system, and the problems caused by unexpected consequences made such changes very expensive.

The few expert systems that have been successful have addressed more restricted problems than duplicating a doctor's diagnostic ability. They address problems such as checking for harmful prescription drug interactions and configuring products to meet customer specifications. These systems require many fewer rules and are therefore more manageable to maintain. However, unless expert systems technology gets a boost from massively parallel computing (think MapReduce and Hadoop), their problems will cause them to fade from use.

What Are Content Management Systems?

Another form of knowledge management concerns knowledge that is encoded in documents. **Content management systems (CMS)** are information systems that support the management and delivery of documents including reports, Web pages, and other expressions of employee knowledge.

Typical users of content management systems are companies that sell complicated products and want to share their knowledge of those products with employees and customers. Someone at Toyota, for example, knows how to change the timing belt on the four-cylinder 2015 Toyota Camry. Toyota wants to share that knowledge with car owners, mechanics, and Toyota employees.

What Are the Challenges of Content Management?

Content management systems face serious challenges. First, most content databases are huge; some have thousands of individual documents, pages, and graphics. Second, CMS content is dynamic. Imagine the frequency of Web page changes at Apple or Google or Amazon.com that must occur each day!

Another complication for content management systems is that documents do not exist in isolation from each other. Documents refer to one another, and when one changes, others must change as well. To manage these connections, content management systems must maintain linkages among documents so that content dependencies are known and used to maintain document consistency.

A fourth complication is that document contents are perishable. Documents become obsolete and need to be altered, removed, or replaced. Consider, for example, what happens when a new product is announced. Figure 9-26 shows the main page for Microsoft.com less than 2 hours

Figure 9-26
Microsoft.com Main Page Less than 2 Hours After Surface Announcement
Source: © Access 2013, Microsoft Corporation

after its announcement of Surface. We can only wonder how many other pages on Microsoft.com needed to be changed within those 2 hours.

Finally, content is provided in many languages. 3M has tens of thousands of products, some of which are harmful when used improperly. 3M must publish product safety data for all such products in all the languages shown. Every document, in whatever language it was authored, must be translated into all languages before it can be published on 3M's site. And when one of them changes, all of the translated versions must change as well.

What Are Content Management Application Alternatives?

Three common alternatives for content management applications are:

- In-house custom
- Off-the-shelf
- Public search engine

In the past, organizations developed their own *in-house content management applications*. A customer support department, for example, might develop in-house database applications to track customer problems and their resolution. Operations might develop an in-house system to track machine maintenance procedures. Like all custom applications, however, custom content management applications are expensive to develop and maintain. Unless the domain of the content management is crucial to the organization's strategy and no off-the-shelf solution is available, most organizations today choose not to support a custom CMS application.

Because of the expense of custom applications, many organizations today use *off-the-shelf* software. Horizontal market products like Microsoft SharePoint provide generalized facilities to manage documents and other content types. Some organizations choose vertical market off-the-shelf applications. An accounting firm, for example, may license a vertical market application to manage document flow for the processing of tax returns or the management of audit documents.

Such off-the-shelf products have considerably more functionality than most in-house systems, and they are far less expensive to maintain. Keep in mind, however, that organizations need to develop data structures and procedures for managing their content; they also need to train users.

Some organizations just rely on *Internet search engines*, such as Google or Bing, to manage their content. Because these engines search through all public sites of all organizations, they are usually the fastest and easiest way to find public documents, even within the organization. It may be easier, for example, for a General Motors employee to find a General Motors document using Google than using an in-house search engine.

This is content management on the cheap. Just put documents on a public server and let Google or Bing do the rest! However, documents that reside behind a corporate firewall are not publicly accessible and will not be reachable by Google or other search engines. Organizations must index their own proprietary documents and provide their own search capability for them.

How Do Hyper-Social Organizations Manage Knowledge?

In recent years, social media has changed the orientation of knowledge management. In the past, the focus was on structured systems such as expert systems and content management systems. These KM techniques relied on planned and prestructured content management and delivery methods. Social media fosters emergence. In the KM context, employees and others express their knowledge in a variety of modes and media, and the mechanisms for managing and delivering that knowledge emerge from usage.

Hyper-social knowledge management is the application of social media and related applications for the management and delivery of organizational knowledge resources. Progressive organizations encourage their employees to Tweet, post on Facebook or other social media sites, write blogs, and post videos on YouTube and any of the other sites. Of course, as discussed in Chapter 8, such organizations need to develop and publish an employee social media policy as well.

Hyper-organization theory provides a framework for understanding this new direction in KM. In this frame, the focus moves from the knowledge and content per se to the fostering of authentic relationships among the creators and the users of that knowledge.

Blogs provide an obvious example. An employee in customer support who writes a daily blog on current, common customer problems is expressing authentic opinions on the company's products, positive and possibly negative. If perceived as authentic, customers will comment upon blog entries and, in the process, teach others how they solved those problems themselves.

The open airing of product use issues may make traditional marketing personnel uncomfortable, but this KM technique does insert the company in the middle of customer conversations about possible product problems, and, while it does lose control, the organization is at least a party to those conversations. As stated in Chapter 8, hyper-social organizations move from controlled processes to messy ones.

Hyper-Social KM Alternative Media

Figure 9-27 lists common hyper-social KM alternative media, whether each medium is used for public, private, or either, and the best group type. Except for rich directories, you know what each of these is already, and we need not discuss them further.

A **rich directory** is an employee directory that includes not only the standard name, email, phone, and address but also organizational structure and expertise. With a rich directory, it is possible to determine where in the organization someone works, who is the first common manager between two people, and what past projects and expertise an individual has. For international organizations, such directories also include languages spoken. Microsoft's product Active Directory is the most popular rich directory.

Rich directories are particularly useful in large organizations where people with particular expertise are unknown. For example, who at 3M knows which 3M product is the best to use to glue teak wood to fiberglass? Probably dozens, but who are they and who is the closest to a factory in Brazil? If no one is near Brazil, is there anyone who speaks Portuguese?

Media	Public or Private	Best for:
Blogs	Either	Defender of belief
Discussion groups (including FAQ)	Either	Problem solving
Wikis	Either	Either
Surveys	Either	Problem solving
Rich directories, (e.g., Active Directory)	Private	Problem solving
Standard SM (Facebook, Twitter, etc.)	Public	Defender of belief
YouTube	Public	Either

Figure 9-27
Hyper-Social KM Media

Resistance to Knowledge Sharing

Two human factors inhibit knowledge sharing in organizations. The first is that employees can be reluctant to exhibit their ignorance. Out of fear of appearing incompetent, employees may not submit entries to blogs or discussion groups. Such reluctance can sometimes be reduced by the attitude and posture of managers. One strategy for employees in this situation is to provide private media that can be accessed only by a smaller group of people who have an interest in a specific problem. Members of that smaller group can then discuss the issue in a less-inhibiting forum.

The other inhibiting human factor is employee competition. "Look," says the top salesperson. "I earn a substantial bonus from being the top salesperson. Why would I want to share my sales techniques with others? I'd just be strengthening my competition." This understandable perspective may not be changeable. A hyper-social KM application may be ill-suited to a competitive group. Or the company may be able to restructure rewards and incentives to foster sharing of ideas among employees (e.g., giving a bonus to the group that develops the best idea).

If these two factors are limiting knowledge sharing, strong management endorsement can be effective, especially if that endorsement is followed by strong positive feedback. As we stated in Chapter 7, concerning employee resistance, "Nothing wrong with praise or cash…especially cash."

Q9-8 What Are the Alternatives for Publishing BI?

The previous discussions have illustrated the power and utility of reporting, data mining, and knowledge management BI applications. But, for BI to be actionable, it must be published to the right user at the right time. In this question, we will discuss the primary publishing alternatives and the functionality of BI servers, a special type of Web server.

Characteristics of BI Publishing Alternatives

Figure 9-28 lists four server alternatives for BI publishing. **Static reports** are BI documents that are fixed at the time of creation and do not change. A printed sales analysis is an example of a static report. In the BI context, most static reports are published as PDF documents.

Dynamic reports are BI documents that are updated at the time they are requested. A sales report that is current at the time the user accessed it on a Web server is a dynamic report. In almost all cases, publishing a dynamic report requires the BI application to access a database or other data source at the time the report is delivered to the user.

Server	Report Type	Push Options	Skill Level Needed
Email or collaboration tool	Static	Manual	Low
Web server	Static/Dynamic	Alert/RSS	Low for static High for dynamic
SharePoint	Static/Dynamic	Alert/RSS Workflow	Low for static High for dynamic
BI server	Dynamic	Alert/RSS Subscription	High

Figure 9-28
BI Publishing Alternatives

Pull options for each of the servers in Figure 9-28 are the same. The user goes to the site, clicks a link (or opens an email), and obtains the report. Because they're the same for all four server types, they are not shown in Figure 9-28.

Push options vary by server type. For email or collaboration tools, push is manual; someone, say, a manager, an expert, or an administrator, creates an email with the report as an attachment (or URL to the collaboration tool) and sends it to the users known to be interested in that report. For Web servers and SharePoint, users can create alerts and RSS feeds to have the server push content to them when the content is created or changed, with the expiration of a given amount of time, or at particular intervals. SharePoint workflows can also push content.

A BI server extends alert/RSS functionality to support user **subscriptions**, which are user requests for particular BI results on a particular schedule or in response to particular events. For example, a user can subscribe to a daily sales report, requesting that it be delivered each morning. Or the user might request that RFM analyses be delivered whenever a new result is posted on the server, or a sales manager might subscribe to receive a sales report whenever sales in his region exceed $1M during the week. We explain the two major functions of a BI server in the next section.

The skills needed to create a publishing application are either low or high. For static content, little skill is needed. The BI author creates the content, and the publisher (usually the same person) attaches it to an email or puts it on the Web or a SharePoint site, and that's it. Publishing dynamic BI is more difficult; it requires the publisher to set up database access when documents are consumed. In the case of a Web server, the publisher will need to develop or have a programmer write code for this purpose. In the case of SharePoint and BI servers, program code is not necessarily needed, but dynamic data connections need to be created, and this task is not for the technically faint of heart. You'll need knowledge beyond the scope of this class to develop dynamic BI solutions. You should be able to do this, however, if you take a few more IS courses or major in IS.

What Are the Two Functions of a BI Server?

A **BI server** is a Web server application that is purpose-built for the publishing of business intelligence. The Microsoft SQL Server Report manager (part of Microsoft SQL Server Reporting Services) is the most popular such product today, but there are other products as well.

BI servers provide two major functions: management and delivery. The management function maintains metadata about the authorized allocation of BI results to users. The BI server tracks what results are available, what users are authorized to view those results, and the schedule upon which the results are provided to the authorized users. It adjusts allocations as available results change and users come and go.

As shown in Figure 9-29, all management data needed by any of the BI servers is stored in metadata. The amount and complexity of such data depends, of course, on the functionality of the BI server.

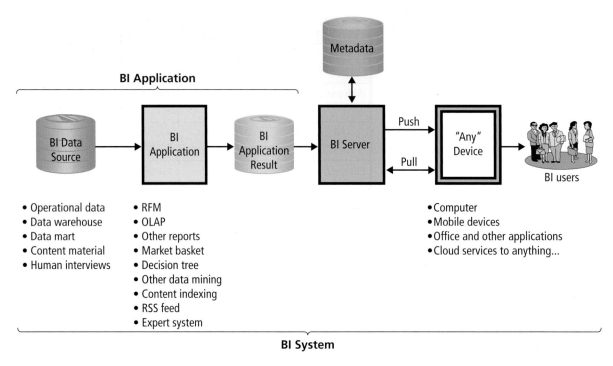

Figure 9-29
Elements of a BI System

BI servers use metadata to determine what results to send to which users and, possibly, on which schedule. Today, the expectation is that BI results can be delivered to "any" device. In practice, *any* is interpreted to mean computers, smartphones, tablets, applications such as Microsoft Office, and SOA Web services.

Q9-9   2026?

BI systems truly add value. As described in the Guide on pages 408–409, not every system is a success, but simple ones like RFM and OLAP often are, and even complicated and expensive data mining applications can generate tremendous return if they are applied to appropriate problems and are well designed and implemented.

For example, suppose you never buy expensive jewelry on your credit card. If you travel to South America and attempt to buy a $5,000 diamond bracelet using that credit card, watch what happens! Especially if you make the attempt on a credit card other than the one for which you paid for the travel. A data mining application integrated into the credit card agency's purchase-approval process will detect the unusual pattern, on the spot, and require you to personally verify the purchase on the telephone or in some other way before it will accept the charge. Such applications are exceedingly accurate because they are well designed and implemented by some of the world's best data miners.

How will this change by 2026? We know that data storage is free, that CPU processors are becoming nearly so, that the world is generating and storing exponentially more information about customers, and that data mining techniques are only going to get better. It is likely that by 2026 some companies will know more about your purchasing psyche than you, your mother, or your analyst.

In fact, it may be important to ask the question: How unsupervised do we want unsupervised data mining to be? Today, a data miner extracts a data set and inputs it into an unsupervised data mining application for analysis. The application finds patterns, trends, and other business intelligence and reports the results to the human analyst. The BI analyst examines the results and possibly iterates by finding more data and running more analyses.

But what happens when BI applications become sophisticated enough to replace the BI analyst? What happens when the unsupervised data mining application has features and functions to find its own data sets and to evaluate those data sets based on the results of a prior BI analysis? And then decides which BI analysis to perform next?

Machines work faster than humans, and they work 24/7. At some point, will machines know so much about us that we are incapable of understanding the results? What happens when, because of complexity, such BI machines can only communicate with other BI machines?

Ray Kurzweil developed a concept he calls **the Singularity**, which is the point at which computer systems become sophisticated enough that they can adapt and create their own software and hence adapt their behavior without human assistance. Apply this idea to unsupervised data mining.[18] What happens when machines can direct their own data mining activities? There will be an accelerating positive feedback loop among the BI machines. Then what will they know about us? Is it important that at that date we will lack the capacity to know what the machines will know?

This line of thinking exposes a future flaw that runs through this text. We've defined information as something possessed only by humans. If it's on a piece of paper or on a screen, it's data. If it's in the mind of a human, it is (or can be) information. When we're talking about simple reporting operations such as grouping and filtering, and so on, that's legitimate. But, in the day when unsupervised data mining truly is unsupervised, machines will possess and create information for themselves.

Do you know what your data mining application is doing tonight?

Security Guide

SEMANTIC SECURITY

Security is a very difficult problem—and risks grow larger every year. Not only do we have cheaper, faster computers (remember Moore's Law), we also have more data, more systems for reporting and querying that data, and easier, faster, and broader communication. We have organizational data in the cloud that is not physically under our control. All of these combine to increase the chances that private or proprietary information is inappropriately divulged.

Access security is hard enough: How do we know that the person (or program) who signs on as Megan Cho really is Megan Cho? We use passwords, but files of passwords can be stolen. Setting that issue aside, we need to know that Megan Cho's permissions are set appropriately. Suppose Megan works in the HR department, so she has access to personal and private data of other employees. We need to design the reporting system so that Megan can access all of the data she needs to do her job, and no more.

Also, the delivery system must be secure. A BI server is an obvious and juicy target for any would-be intruder. Someone can break in and change access permissions. Or a hacker could pose as someone else to obtain reports. Application servers help the authorized user, resulting in faster access to more information. But without proper security reporting, servers also ease the intrusion task for unauthorized users.

All of these issues relate to access security. Another dimension to security is equally serious and far more problematic: **semantic security**. Semantic security concerns the unintended release of protected information through the release of a combination of reports or documents that are independently not protected. The term **data triangulation** is also used for this same phenomenon.

Take an example from class. Suppose I assign a group project, and I post a list of groups and the names of students assigned to each group. Later, after the assignments have been completed and graded, I post a list of grades on the Web site. Because of university privacy policy, I cannot post the

Source: Freshidea/Fotolia

grades by student name or identifier, so instead I post the grades for each group. If you want to get the grades for each student, all you have to do is combine the list from Lecture 5 with the list from Lecture 10. You might say that the release of grades in this example does no real harm—after all, it is a list of grades from one assignment.

But go back to Megan Cho in HR. Suppose Megan evaluates the employee compensation program. The COO believes salary offers have been inconsistent over time and that they vary too widely by department. Accordingly, the COO authorizes Megan to receive a report that lists *SalaryOfferAmount* and *OfferDate* and a second report that lists *Department* and *AverageSalary*.

Those reports are relevant to her task and seem innocuous enough. But Megan realizes that she could use the information they contain to determine individual salaries—information she does not have and is not authorized to receive. She proceeds as follows.

Like all employees, Megan has access to the employee directory on the Web portal. Using the directory, she can obtain a list of employees in each department, and using the facilities of her ever-so-helpful report-authoring system she combines that list with the department and average-salary report. Now she has a list of the names of employees in a group and the average salary for that group.

Megan's employer likes to welcome new employees to the company. Accordingly, each week the company publishes an article about new employees who have been hired. The article makes pleasant comments about each person and encourages employees to meet and greet them.

Megan, however, has other ideas. Because the report is published on SharePoint, she can obtain an electronic copy of it. It's an Acrobat report, and using Acrobat's handy Search feature, she soon has a list of employees and the week they were hired.

She now examines the report she received for her study, the one that has *SalaryOfferAmount* and the offer date, and she does some interpretation. During the week of July 21, three offers were extended: one for $35,000, one for $53,000, and one for $110,000. She also notices from the "New Employees" report that a director of marketing programs, a product test engineer, and a receptionist were hired that same week. It's unlikely that they paid the receptionist $110,000; that sounds more like the director of marketing programs. So, she now "knows" (infers) that person's salary.

Next, going back to the department report and using the employee directory, she sees that the marketing director is in the marketing programs department. There are just three people in that department, and their average salary is $105,000. Doing the arithmetic, she now knows that the average salary for the other two people is $102,500. If she can find the hire week for one of those other two people, she can find out both the second and third person's salaries.

You get the idea. Megan was given just two reports to do her job. Yet she combined the information in those reports with publicly available information and was able to deduce salaries, for at least some employees. These salaries are much more than she is supposed to know. This is a semantic security problem.

 # DISCUSSION QUESTIONS

1. In your own words, explain the difference between access security and semantic security.
2. Why do reporting systems increase the risk of semantic security problems?
3. What can an organization do to protect itself against accidental losses due to semantic security problems?

4. What legal responsibility does an organization have to protect against semantic security problems?
5. Suppose semantic security problems are inevitable. Do you see an opportunity for new products from insurance companies? If so, describe such an insurance product. If not, explain why.

Guide

DATA MINING IN THE REAL WORLD

"I'm not really opposed to data mining. I believe in it. After all, it's my career. But data mining in the real world is a lot different from the way it's described in textbooks, for many reasons.

"One is that the data are always dirty, with missing values, values way out of the range of possibility, and time values that make no sense. Here's an example: Somebody sets the server system clock incorrectly and runs the server for a while with the wrong time. When they notice the mistake, they set the clock to the correct time. But all of the transactions that were running during that interval have an ending time before the starting time. When we run the data analysis, and compute elapsed time, the results are negative for those transactions.

"Missing values are a similar problem. Consider the records of just 10 purchases. Suppose that two of the records are missing the customer number, and one is missing the year part of the transaction date. So you throw out three records, which is 30 percent of the data. You then notice that two more records have dirty data, and so you throw them out, too. Now you've lost half your data.

"Another problem is that you know the least when you start the study. So you work for a few months and learn that if you had another variable— say, the customer's ZIP code, or age, or something else—you could do a much better analysis. But those other data just aren't available. Or maybe they are available, but to get the data you have to reprocess millions of transactions, and you don't have the time or budget to do that.

"Overfitting is another problem, a huge one. I can build a model to fit any set of data you have. Give me 100 data points and in a few minutes, I can give you 100 different equations that will predict those 100 data points. With neural networks, you can create a model of any level of complexity you want, except that none of those equations will predict new cases with any accuracy at all. When using neural nets, you have to be very careful not to overfit the data.

"Then, too, data mining is about probabilities, not certainty. Bad luck happens. Say I build a model that predicts the probability that a customer will make a purchase. Using the model on new customer data, I find three customers who have a .7 probability of buying something. That's a good number, well over a 50–50 chance, but it's still possible that none of them will buy. In fact, the probability that none of them will buy is .3 x .3 x .3, or .027, which is 2.7 percent.

"Now suppose I give the names of the three customers to a salesperson who calls on them, and sure enough, we have a stream of bad luck and none of them buys. This bad result doesn't mean the model is wrong. But what does the salesperson think? He thinks the model is worthless, and he can do better on his own. He tells his manager who tells her associate, who tells everyone in the Northeast Region, and sure enough, the model has a bad reputation all across the company.

"Another problem is seasonality. Say all your training data are from the summer. Will your model be valid for the winter? Maybe, but maybe not. You might even know that it won't be valid for predicting winter sales, but if you don't have winter data, what do you do?

"When you start a data mining project, you never know how it will turn out. I worked on one project for 6 months, and when we finished, I didn't think our model was any good. We had too many problems with data: wrong, dirty, and missing. There was no way we could know ahead of time that it would happen, but it did.

"When the time came to present the results to senior management, what could we do? How could we say we took 6 months of our time and substantial computer resources to create a bad model? We had a model, but I just didn't think it would make accurate predictions. I was a junior member of the team, and it wasn't for me to decide. I kept my mouth shut, but I never felt good about it. Fortunately, the project was cancelled later for other reasons.

"However, I'm only talking about my bad experiences. Some of my projects have been excellent. On many, we found interesting and important patterns and information, and a few times I've created very accurate predictive models. It's not easy, though, and you have to be very careful. Also, lucky!"

 DISCUSSION QUESTIONS

1. Summarize the concerns expressed by this data analyst.
2. Do you think the concerns raised here are sufficient to avoid data mining projects altogether?
3. If you were a junior member of a data mining team and you thought that the model that had been developed was ineffective, maybe even wrong, what would you do? If your boss disagrees with your beliefs, would you go higher in the organization? What are the risks of doing so? What else might you do?

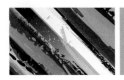

ACTIVE REVIEW

Use this Active Review to verify that you understand the ideas and concepts that answer the chapter's study questions.

Q9-1   How do organizations use business intelligence (BI) systems?

Define *business intelligence* and *BI system*. Explain the components in Figure 9-1. Give an example, other than one in this text, of one way that an organization could use business intelligence for each of the four collaborative tasks in Figure 9-2. Describe one use of BI in retailing, entertainment, and medicine.

Q9-2   What are the three primary activities in the BI process?

Name and describe the three primary activities in the BI process. Using Figure 9-3 as a guide, describe the major tasks for each activity. Summarize how the team at the parts distribution company used these activities to produce BI results. Explain the role of Figures 9-4 through 9-11.

Q9-3   How do organizations use data warehouses and data marts to acquire data?

Describe the need and functions of data warehouses and data marts. Name and describe the role of data warehouse components. List and explain the problems that can exist in data used for data mining and sophisticated reporting. Use the example of a supply chain to describe the differences between a data warehouse and data mart.

Q9-4   How do organizations use reporting applications?

Name and describe five basic reporting operations. Define *RFM analysis* and explain the actions that should be taken with customers who have the following scores: [1, 1, 1,], [5, 1, 1,], [1, 1, 3], and [1, 4, 1]. Explain OLAP and describe its unique characteristics. Explain the roles for measure and dimension in an OLAP cube. Illustrate an OLAP cube with a single measure and five dimensions, two dimensions on one axis and three on another. Show how drill down applies to your example.

Q9-5   How do organizations use data mining applications?

Define *data mining* and explain how its use typically differs from reporting applications. Explain why data mining tools are difficult to use well. Describe the differences between unsupervised and supervised data mining. Use an example to illustrate cluster analysis and regression analysis. Define *neural networks* and explain why the term is a misnomer. Define *support, confidence,* and *lift* and describe these terms using the data in Figure 9-21. Describe a good application for market-basket analysis results. Describe the purpose of decision trees and explain how the data in Figure 9-22 is used to evaluate loans for possible purchase.

Q9-6   How do organizations use BigData applications?

Name and explain the three v's of BigData. Describe the general goal of MapReduce and explain, at a conceptual level, how it works and how it could generate the data for Figure 9-24. Explain the purpose of Hadoop and describe its origins. Describe the ways organizations can deploy Hadoop. Define *Pig*.

Q9-7   What is the role of knowledge management systems?

Define *knowledge management*. Explain five key benefits of KM. Briefly describe three types of KM systems. Define *expert systems, If/Then rules,* and *expert system shell*. Explain how expert system rules are created. Differentiate expert system If/Then rules from decision tree If/Then rules. Summarize the three major disadvantages of expert systems and assess their future. Define *content management system (CMS)*. Describe five challenges organizations face for managing content. Name three CMS application alternatives and explain the use of each.

Explain how social media has changed the orientation of knowledge management. Define *hyper-social knowledge management*. Explain the hyper-social KM use of each medium in Figure 9-28. Explain the entries in the second and third columns of this figure. Define *rich directory* and explain three uses for it. Summarize possible employee resistance to hyper-social knowledge sharing and name two management techniques for reducing it.

Q9-8 What are the alternatives for publishing BI?

Name four alternative types of server used for publishing business intelligence. Explain the difference between static and dynamic reports; explain the term *subscription*. Describe why dynamic reports are difficult to create.

Q9-9 2026?

Summarize the function of the credit card approval application. Explain how you think that application uses data. Summarize the way that unsupervised data mining could spiral out of the control of humans. In your opinion, is this a problem? Why or why not? Describe how Kurzweil's singularity pertains to data

mining applications. Explain the potential flaw in the use of the term *information* that runs throughout this text.

Using Your Knowledge with PRIDE

From this chapter, you know the three phases of BI analysis, and you have learned common techniques for acquiring, processing, and publishing business intelligence. This knowledge will enable you to imagine innovative uses for data that your employer generates and also to know some of the constraints of such use. At PRIDE, the knowledge of this chapter will help you understand possible uses for competition and exercise data to increase ad revenue, the critical driver for the success of PRIDE Systems.

KEY TERMS AND CONCEPTS

BI analysis   375
BI application   372
BI server   403
BigData   403
Business intelligence (BI)   372
Business intelligence (BI) systems   371
Cluster analysis   390
Confidence   392
Content management systems (CMS)   399
Cookie   413
Cross-selling   391
Data acquisition   374
Data aggregator   384
Data broker   384
Data mart   383
Data mining   390
Data triangulation   406

Data warehouse   380
Decision support systems   373
Decision tree   393
Dimension   387
Drill down   388
Dynamic reports   402
Expert systems   398
Expert systems shells   398
Granularity   382
Hadoop   396
Hyper-social knowledge management   401
If/Then rules   398
Knowledge management (KM)   397
Lift   393
MapReduce   394
Market-basket analysis   391
Measure   387
Neural networks   391

OLAP cube   388
Online analytical processing (OLAP)   387
Pig   397
Publish results   375
Pull publishing   375
Push publishing   375
Regression analysis   391
Reporting application   386
RFM analysis   386
Rich directory   401
Semantic security   406
Static reports   402
Subscriptions   403
Supervised data mining   391
Support   392
The Singularity   405
Third-party cookie   413
Unsupervised data mining   390

MyMISLab™
To complete the problems with the ✪, go to EOC Discussion Questions in the MyLab.

USING YOUR KNOWLEDGE

⭐ **9-1.** Using the knowledge gained from Q.9-1 about the different uses of Business Intelligence, provide an instance where you have been recommended a certain type of product based on your viewing pattern on a particular shopping website. Also, state which BI application it corresponds to.

⭐ **9-2.** In your opinion, is it ethical to collect and disseminate personal data by various mobile apps or other apps on Facebook. In the era of smart phones and smart cars, etc. do you think we are more secure or are we faced with a greater threat?

⭐ **9-3.** Other than Microsoft power BI software, list ten other BI apps that allow businesses and customers to explore dashboards and reports, etc.

9-4. Explain the role of Business intelligence in increasing admissions to universities? How can BI assist universities to gain competitive advantage? What is the role of data warehouses in the education industry?

9-5. Suppose you work at Costco or another major, national big-box store; you do a market-basket analysis and identify the 25 pairs of items in the store that have the highest lift and the 25 pairs that have the lowest lift. What would you do with this knowledge? Costco (or your big-box store) doesn't have

salespeople, so up-selling is not an option. What else might you do with information about these items' lift? Consider advertising, pricing, item location in stores, and any other factor that you might adjust. Do you think the lift calculations are valid for all stores in the United States (or other country)? Why or why not? Are the 50 pairs of products with the highest and lowest lift the best place to focus your attention? What other 50 pairs of products might you want to consider? Explain.

9-6. What do you understand by operational data? What problems does it have? What did you come to know about inconsistency and missing values in the data after reading Q 9-3. Based on that understanding, give an example of database taken from your university/ institute and highlight the problems of the operational data, missing values and inconsistency in data taken.

9-7. Using Google search, identify the patterns of Predictive Analytics and Business Intelligence, and show the results. Also analyze the extent to which is BI is being used in prediction and how organizations are monitoring your online activities.

9-8. Recently Google Cloud Platform (GCP) was launched. As a student, how can you optimise the benefits of GCP?

COLLABORATION EXERCISE 9

Using the collaboration IS you built in Chapter 2 (page 110), collaborate with a group of students to answer the following questions.

Read Case Study 9 (pages 413–414) if you have not already done so. Undeniably, third-party cookies offer advantages to online sellers. They also increase the likelihood that consumers will receive online ads that are close to their interests; thus, third-party cookies can provide a consumer service as well. But at what cost to personal privacy? And what should be done about them? Working with your team, answer the following questions:

9-9. Summarize the ways that third-party cookies are created and processed. Even though cookies are not supposed to contain personally identifying data, explain how such data can readily be obtained. (See question 9-19, page 415.)

9-10. Numerous browser features, add-ins, and other tools exist for blocking third-party cookies. Search the Web for *block third-party cookies for xxx*, and fill in the *xxx*

with the name and version of your browser. Read the instructions, and summarize the procedures that you need to take to view the cookies issued from a given site.

9-11. In large measure, ads pay for the free use of Web content and even Web sites themselves. If, because of a fear of privacy, many people block third-party cookies, substantial ad revenue will be lost. Discuss with your group how such a movement would affect the valuation of Facebook and other ad-revenue–dependent companies. Discuss how it would affect the delivery of free online content such as that supplied by *Forbes* or other providers.

9-12. Many companies have a conflict of interest with regard to third-party cookies. On the one hand, such cookies help generate revenue and pay for Internet content. On the other hand, trespassing on users' privacy could turn out to be a PR disaster. As you learned in your answer to question 9-10, browsers include options to block third-party cookies. However, in most cases, those options are turned off in the default browser installation. Discuss why that might be so. If sites were required to obtain your permission before installing third-party cookies, how would you determine whether to grant it? List criteria that your team thinks you would actually use (as opposed to what the team thinks you *should* do). Assess the effectiveness of such a policy.

9-13. The processing of third-party cookies is hidden; we don't know what is being done behind the scenes with the data about our own behavior. Because there is so much of it and so many parties involved, the possibilities are difficult to comprehend, even if the descriptions were available. And if your privacy is compromised by the interaction of seven different companies working independently, which is to be held accountable? Summarize consequences of these facts on consumers.

9-14. Summarize the benefits of third-party cookies to consumers.

9-15. Using the decision tree developed in the Figure in 9-22, make a decision tree to classify the students into weak, average, and good, based on their class performance, attendance, surprise tests, and assignment marks.

CASE STUDY 9

Hadoop the Cookie Cutter

A **cookie** is data that a Web site stores on your computer to record something about its interaction with you. The cookie might contain data such as the date you last visited, whether you are currently signed in, or something else about your interaction with that site. Cookies can also contain a key value to one or more tables in a database that the server company maintains about your past interactions. In that case, when you access a site, the server uses the value of the cookie to look up your history. Such data could include your past purchases, portions of incomplete transactions, or the data and appearance you want for your Web page. Most of the time cookies ease your interaction with Web sites.

Cookie data includes the URL of the Web site of the cookie's owner. Thus, for example, when you go to Amazon, it asks your browser to place a cookie on your computer that includes its name, *www.amazon.com*. Your browser will do so unless you have turned cookies off.

A **third-party cookie** is a cookie created by a site other than the one you visited. Such cookies are generated in several ways, but the most common occurs when a Web page includes content from multiple sources. For example, Amazon designs its pages so that one or more sections contain ads provided by the ad-servicing company, DoubleClick. When the browser constructs your Amazon page, it contacts DoubleClick to obtain the content for such sections (in this case, ads). When it responds with the content, DoubleClick instructs your browser to store a DoubleClick cookie. That cookie is a third-party cookie. In general, third-party cookies do not contain the name or any value that identifies a particular user. Instead, they include the IP address to which the content was delivered.

On its own servers, when it creates the cookie, DoubleClick records that data in a log, and if you click on the ad, it will add that fact of that click to the log. This logging is repeated every time DoubleClick shows an ad. Cookies have an expiration date, but that date is set by the cookie creator, and they can last many years. So, over time, DoubleClick and any other third-party cookie owner will have a history of what they've shown, what ads have been clicked, and the intervals between interactions.

But the opportunity is even greater. DoubleClick has agreements not only with Amazon, but also with many others, such as Facebook. If Facebook includes any DoubleClick content on its site, DoubleClick will place another cookie on your computer. This cookie is different from the one that it placed via Amazon, but both cookies have your IP address and other data sufficient to associate the second cookie as originating from the same source as the first. So, DoubleClick now has a record of your ad response data on two sites. Over time, the cookie log will contain data to show not only how you respond to ads, but also your pattern of visiting various Web sites on all those sites in which it places ads.

You might be surprised to learn how many third-party cookies you have. The browser Firefox has an optional feature called *Lightbeam* that tracks and graphs all the cookies on your computer. Figure 9-30 shows the cookies that were placed on my computer as I visited various Web sites. As you can see, in Figure 9-30a, when I started my computer and browser, there were no cookies. The cookies on my computer after I visited *www.msn.com* are shown in Figure 9-30b. At this point, there are already eight third-party cookies tracking. After I visited five sites I had 27 third-party cookies, and after I visited seven sites I had 69, as shown in Figures 9-30c and d.

a. Display on Startup

b. After MSN.com and Gmail

c. Five Sites Visited Yield 27 Third Parties

d. Sites Connected to DoubleClick

Figure 9-30
Third-Party Cookie Growth
Source: © Mozilla Corporation

Who are these companies that are gathering my browser behavior data? If you hold your mouse over one of the cookies, Lightbeam will highlight it in the data column on the right. As you can see in Figure 9-30d, after visiting seven sites, DoubleClick was connected to a total of 16 other sites, only seven of which can be sites I visited. So, DoubleClick is connecting to sites I don't even know about and on my computer. Examine the connection column on the right. I visited MSN, Amazon, MyNorthwest, and WSJ, but who are Bluekai and Rubiconproject? I never heard of them until I saw this display. They, apparently, have heard of me, however!

Third-party cookies generate incredible volumes of log data. For example, suppose a company, such as DoubleClick, shows 100 ads to a given computer in a day. If it is showing ads to 10 million computers (possible), that is a total of 1 billion log entries per day, or 365 billion a year. Truly this is BigData.

Storage is essentially free, but how can they possibly process all that data? How do they parse the log to find entries just for your computer? How do they integrate data from different cookies on the same IP address? How do they analyze those entries to determine which ads you clicked on? How do they then characterize differences in ads to determine which characteristics matter most to you? The answer, as you learned in Q9-6, is to use parallel processing. Using a MapReduce algorithm, they distribute the work to thousands of processors that work in parallel. They then aggregate the results of these independent processors and then, possibly, move to a second phase of analysis where they do it again. Hadoop, the open-source program that you learned about in Q9-6, is a favorite for this process.

(See the collaboration exercise on pages 412–413 for a continuation of the discussion: third-party cookies—problem? Or opportunity?)

QUESTIONS

9-16. Using your own words, explain how third-party cookies are created.

9-17. Suppose you are an ad-serving company, and you maintain a log of cookie data for ads you serve to Web pages for a particular vendor (say, Amazon).
  a. How can you use this data to determine which are the best ads?
  b. How can you use this data to determine which are the best ad formats?
  c. How could you use records of past ads and ad clicks to determine which ads to send to a given IP address?
  d. How could you use this data to determine how well the technique you used in your answer to question c was working?

e. How could you use this data to determine that a given IP address is used by more than one person?

f. How does having this data give you a competitive advantage vis-à-vis other ad-serving companies?

9-18. Suppose you are an ad-serving company, and you have a log of cookie data for ads served to Web pages of all your customers (Amazon, Facebook, etc.).

a. Describe, in general terms, how you can process the cookie data to associate log entries for a particular IP address.

b. Explain how your answers to question 9-10 change, given that you have this additional data.

c. Describe how you can use this log data to determine users who consistently seek the lowest price.

d. Describe how you can use this log data to determine users who consistently seek the latest fashion.

e. Explain why uses like those in c and d above are only possible with MapReduce or a similar technique.

9-19. As stated, third-party cookies usually do not contain, in themselves, data that identifies you as a particular person. However, Amazon, Facebook, and other first-party cookie vendors know who you are because you signed in. Only one of them needs to reveal your identity to the ad-server, and your identity can then be correlated with your IP address. At that point, the ad-server and potentially all of its clients know who you are. Are you concerned about the invasion of your privacy that third-party cookies enable? Explain your answer.

MyMISLab™

Go to the Assignments section of your MyLab to complete these writing exercises.

9-20. Reflect on the differences among reporting systems, data mining systems, and BigData systems. What are their similarities and differences? How do their costs differ? What benefits does each offer? How would an organization choose among them?

9-21. Install Firefox, if you do not already have it, and then install the Lightbeam add-on. Visit the sites you normally visit first thing in your day.

a. How many third-party sites are you connected to?

b. Find DoubleClick in the Lightbeam display. List the companies that DoubleClick is connected to that you did not visit.

c. Choose one of the companies in your answer to question 9-21b. Google it and describe what it does.

9-22. Suppose you work for an online sporting goods retailer. You've been hired as a business analyst with the task of increasing sales. Describe how you could use RFM and market-basket analysis to increase the sales of sporting goods. If used effectively, how could RFM and market-basket analysis affect customer satisfaction?

ENDNOTES

1. PricewaterhouseCoopers. *2015 U.S. CEO Survey,* accessed April 3, 2015, *www.pwc.com/us/en/ceo-survey/index.html.*
2. Mary K. Pratt, "Data in a Blender," *CIO,* April 1, 2015, p. 12.
3. Nipun Gupta, "Top 10 Databases in the World," May 4, 2014, accessed April 2, 2015, csnipuntech.blogspot.com/2014/05/top-10-largest-databases-in-world.html.
4. Charles Duhigg, "How Companies Learn Your Secrets," *The New York Times,* last modified February 16, 2012, *www.nytimes.com/2012/02/19/magazine/shopping-habits.html?_r=2&hp=&pagewanted=all&.*
5. Alistair Barr, "Crowdsourcing Goes to Hollywood as Amazon Makes Movies," *Reuters,* last modified October 10, 2012, *www.reuters.com/article/2012/10/10/us-amazon-hollywood-crowd-idUSBRE8990JH20121010.*
6. Martin U. Müller, Marcel Rosenbach, and Thomas Schulz, "Living by the Numbers: Big Data Knows What Your Future Holds," *Der Spiegel,* accessed July 31, 2013, *www.spiegel.de/international/business/big-data-enables-companies-and-researchers-to-look-into-the-future-a-899964.html.*
7. Elizabeth Dwoskin, "The Next Marketing Frontier: Your Medical Records," *Wall Street Journal,* March 3, 2015, accessed April 3, 2015, *www.wsj.com/articles/the-next-marketing-frontier-your-medical-records-1425408631?mod=WSJ_hpp_MIDDLENexttoWhatsNewsFifthhttp.*

8. Natasha Singer, "Mapping, and Sharing, the Consumer Genome," *The New York Times*, last modified June 16, 2012, *www.nytimes.com/2012/06/17/technology/acxiom-the-quiet-giant-of-consumer-database-marketing.html*.

9. Lois Beckett, "What Data Brokers Know About You," *RealClearTechnology*, last modified March 8, 2013, *www.realcleartechnology.com/articles/2013/03/08/what_data_brokers_know_about_you_326.html*.

10. Arthur Middleton Hughes, "Boosting Response with RFM," *Marketing Tools*, May 1996. See also *http://dbmarketing.com*.

11. Bradley Hope, "5 Things to Know about High Frequency Trading," *Wall Street Journal*, April 2, 2014, accessed April 2, 2015, *http://blogs.wsj.com/briefly/2014/04/02/5-things-to-know-about-high-frequency-trading/*.

12. Bradley Hope, "How Computers Troll a Sea of Data for Stock Picks, *Wall Street Journal*, April 2, 2015, accessed April 2, 2015, *www.wsj.com/articles/how-computers-trawl-a-sea-of-data-for-stock-picks-1427941801?mod=WSJ_hp_RightTopStories*.

13. Scott Patterson. *The Quants* (New York: Crown Business, 2011).

14. accessed April 2, 2015, *www.twosigma.com/about.html*.

15. Hope, "How Computers Troll a Sea of Data for Stock Picks."

16. A nonprofit corporation that supports open source software projects, originally those for the Apache Web server, but today for a large number of additional major software projects.

17. Meridith Levinson, "Knowledge Management Definition and Solutions," *CIO Magazine*, accessed May 2012, *www.cio.com/article/40343/Knowledge_Management_Definition_and_Solutions?page=2*.

18. "The Singularity Is Near," accessed June 3, 2014, *www.singularity.com*.

Information Systems Management

Part 4 addresses the management of information systems security, development, and resources. We begin with security because of its great importance today. With the Internet, the interconnectivity of systems, and the rise of inter-organizational IS, security problems in one organization become security problems in connected organizations as well. You'll see how that affects PRIDE in the Chapter 10 opener.

While you can readily understand that IS security is important to you as a future manager, it may be more difficult for you to appreciate why you need to know about IS development. As a business professional, you will be the customer of development projects. You need basic knowledge of development processes to be able to assess the quality of the work being done on your behalf. As a manager, you may allocate budget and release funds for IS development. You need knowledge that allows you to be an active and effective participant in such projects.

Finally, you need to know how IS resources are managed so that you can better relate to your IS department. IS managers can sometimes seem rigid and overly protective of IS assets, but usually they have important reasons for their concerns. You need to understand the IS department's perspective and know both your rights and responsibilities as a user of IS resources within your organization. Having such knowledge is key to success for any business professional today.

Collaboration

FBA

Office 365

Jobs!

Google+ vs. Facebook

Source: Nongkran_ch/iStock/Thinkstock/Getty Images; Christopher Futcher/E+/Getty Images

Information Systems Management

Information Systems Security

James and Michele are videoconferencing with Sam Ide, the manager of security for San Diego Sports, a large sports equipment vendor that Michele wants to involve in race events. Mr. Ide's job is to determine if PRIDE Systems provides an acceptable level of security. Michele has gone over this several times with San Diego Sports personnel, and they asked to speak with someone outside of sales who has direct knowledge of PRIDE Systems' security. Michele asked James to participate in the videoconference with Mr. Ide.

"Sam, I have James Wu, our IS manager here, on our videoconference line. Why don't I let you explain your concerns and I'll ask James to respond?"

"Sure. James, thanks for taking the time to speak with me."

"Happy to do it, Mr. Ide."

"Please, call me Sam. OK, we at SDS…that's how we refer to ourselves…we at SDS have always been concerned with security. But, given the recent troubles at Target and Adobe, our senior management team has asked us to be even more careful. It appears that criminals have begun to focus attacks on interorganizational systems, and so we address security with all of our partners."

"I understand, Sam. Although in this case, we're not talking about any connection between your systems and ours. As I understand it, we just want to feature San Diego Sports in a major way in our advertising and promotion of events." James is careful as he gains a sense of his interests.

"Thanks, James, that's my understanding as well. All the same, we don't want to become affiliated in the mind of our market with any company that does have a major security problem, and that's the reason for this call."

"Got it. Do you have specific matters you'd like me to address?"

"Actually, I do. Michele has explained to me the basics of your security program, and she said that, given the fact that your systems were originally designed to store medical data, you have designed security deep into your systems." Sam sounds like he's reading from notes.

"Correct." James nods at Michele as he says this.

"I wonder if you could explain that to me with some specifics."

"Sure, but first, may I ask if you have a technical background?" James isn't sure how much detail to provide him.

"I'm not a developer, not by a long shot, but I was closely involved as a systems analyst in the development of many of our systems." Sam's actually quite a bit more technical than he reveals.

"Great. Let me dive in then, and if the dive is too deep, just let me know." There's not the least bit of condescension in James's voice as he speaks.

"Will do."

"Each user is in charge of the distribution of his or her data. Initially, users' data is not shared at all. But we provide a simple-to-use UI that allows users to change their security settings."

"OK. Michele told me that. But how do you implement that security?" Sam wants to dive deeper.

"Because we have thousands and thousands of users, we store all privacy settings in a database and we have elaborate security on that database that I can go into later, if you want." James wants to focus on specific PRIDE features.

"Maybe. Just keep explaining."

"It turns out that event participants have a many-to-many relationship with all of our major players. Thus, for example, a participant may belong to several health clubs, and of course a health club has a relationship to many of our participants. Similarly, a participant has a relationship to potentially many insurance companies, and each company can have a relationship to many of our participants. Are you with me?"

"Yes, keep going." Sam sounds curious.

"But how do you implement that security?"

Image source: jiris/Fotolia

STUDY QUESTIONS

Q10-1 What is the goal of information systems security?

Q10-2 How big is the computer security problem?

Q10-3 How should you respond to security threats?

Q10-4 How should organizations respond to security threats?

Q10-5 How can technical safeguards protect against security threats?

Q10-6 How can data safeguards protect against security threats?

Q10-7 How can human safeguards protect against security threats?

Q10-8 How should organizations respond to security incidents?

Q10-9 2026?

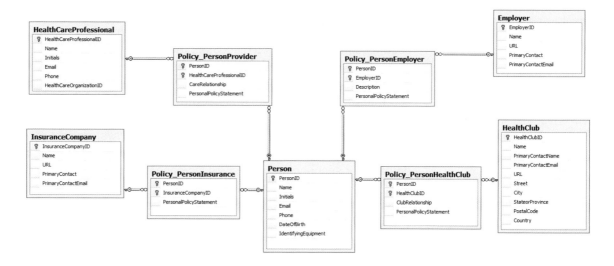

"So, as you know, to represent a many-to-many relationship we create an intersection or bridge table. And we store the security preferences for each person and his or her relationship to the external agent in that intersection table."

Michele jumps in at this point. "Sam, let me see if I can bring up an illustration onto your screen. Do you see the table diagram?"

"Just a second. Something's loading. Ah, yes, there it is."

James continues, "OK, the data for each participant is stored in the Person table in the center. Actually, we store quite a bit more data than shown here, but this will give you the idea of what we do. The security allowed is stored in attributes called *PolicyStatements* in the intersection tables. By default, the value is 'None.' However, if someone decides to share his or her data with, say, a health club, then he or she uses a form to specify what he or she wants, and we store the result of that decision in the PolicyStatement attribute. All of our code uses the value of that attribute to limit data access."

"That makes sense; it's a clean design. But what about SQL injection?"

"Good question. There are four types of access allowed: None, which is the default; Non-identifying; Summary; and Full Access. The last two include the person's identity. In the form, those four are presented with radio buttons and the user picks. There's no place for SQL injection to occur."

The meeting continues in this vein for another 15 minutes. Sam seems satisfied with James's responses. Afterward, James and Michele walk back to their offices together.

"James, that was the best meeting I've had with him. He's so impatient with me, but he related to you really well."

"Michele, I'm glad you're happy with it. I couldn't tell what he thought, but his questions were good and ones that we've thought about a lot."

"Well, James, you're good at explaining things. Ever think about going into sales?"

"Heavens, no, Michele. But I'll take that as a compliment."

"Thanks again."

CHAPTER PREVIEW

This chapter provides an overview of the major components of information systems security. We begin in Q10-1 by defining the goals of IS security and then, in Q10-2, discuss the size of the computer security problem. Next, in Q10-3, we address how you, both as a student today and as a business professional in the future, should respond to security threats. Then, in Q10-4, we ask what organizations need to do to respond to security threats. After that, Q10-5 through Q10-7 address security safeguards. Q10-5 discusses technical safeguards that involve hardware and software components, Q10-6 addresses data safeguards, and Q10-7 discusses human safeguards that involve procedure and people components. Q10-8 then summarizes what organizations need to do when they incur a security incident, and we wrap up the chapter with a preview of IS security in 2026.

Unfortunately, threats to data and information systems are increasing and becoming more complex. In fact, the U.S. Bureau of Labor Statistics estimates that demand for security specialists will increase by more than 37 percent between 2012 and 2022 with a median salary of $86,170. This is strong growth considering computer occupations are projected to grow at 18 percent and all occupations at 11 percent.[1] If you find this topic attractive, majoring in information systems with a security specialty would open the door to many interesting jobs.

Q10-1 What Is the Goal of Information Systems Security?

Information systems security is really about trade-offs. In one sense, it's a trade-off between security and freedom. For example, organizations can increase the security of their information systems by taking away users' freedom to choose their own passwords and force them to choose stronger passwords that are difficult for hackers to crack.

Another way to look at information systems security, and the primary focus of this chapter, is that it's a trade-off between cost and risk. To understand the nature of this trade-off, we begin with a description of the security threat/loss scenario and then discuss the sources of security threats. Following that, we'll state the goal of information systems security.

The IS Security Threat/Loss Scenario

Figure 10-1 illustrates the major elements of the security problem that individuals and organizations confront today. A **threat** is a person or organization that seeks to obtain or alter data or other IS assets illegally, without the owner's permission and often without the owner's knowledge. A **vulnerability** is an opportunity for threats to gain access to individual or organizational assets. For example, when you buy something online, you provide your credit card data; when that data

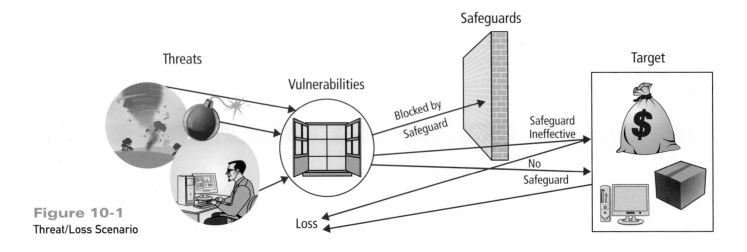

Figure 10-1
Threat/Loss Scenario

Threat/Target	Vulnerability	Safeguard	Result	Explanation
Hacker wants to steal your bank login credentials	Hacker creates a phishing site nearly identical to your online banking site	Only access sites using https	No loss	Effective safeguard
		None	Loss of login credentials	Ineffective safeguard
Employee posts sensitive data to public Google + group	Public access to not-secure group	Passwords Procedures Employee training	Loss of sensitive data	Ineffective safeguard

Figure 10-2
Examples of Threat/Loss

is transmitted over the Internet, it is vulnerable to threats. A **safeguard** is some measure that individuals or organizations take to block the threat from obtaining the asset. Notice in Figure 10-1 that safeguards are not always effective; some threats achieve their goal despite safeguards. Finally, the **target** is the asset that is desired by the threat.

Figure 10-2 shows examples of threats/targets, vulnerabilities, safeguards, and results. In the first two rows, a hacker (the threat) wants your bank login credentials (the target) to access your bank account. If you click on links in emails you can be directed to phishing sites that look identical to your bank's Web site. Phishing sites don't typically use https. If, as shown in the first row of Figure 10-2, you always access your bank's site using https rather than http (discussed in Q10-5), you will be using an effective safeguard, and you will successfully counter the threat.

If, however, as described in the second row of Figure 10-2, you access what appears to be your bank's site without using https (i.e., an unsecured site), you have no safeguard at all. Your login credentials can be quickly recorded and resold to other criminals.

The bottom row of Figure 10-2 shows another situation. Here an employee at work obtains sensitive data and posts it on what he thinks is a work-only Google+ group. However, the employee errs and instead posts it to a public group. The target is the sensitive data, and the vulnerability is public access to the group. In this case, there are several safeguards that should have prevented this loss; the employee needed passwords to obtain the sensitive data and to join the private, work-only group. The employer has procedures that state employees are not to post confidential data to any public site, such as Google+, but these procedures were either unknown or ignored. A third safeguard is the training that all employees are given. Because the employee ignores the procedures, though, all of those safeguards are ineffective and the data is exposed to the public.

What Are the Sources of Threats?

Figure 10-3 summarizes the sources of security threats. The type of threat is shown in the columns, and the type of loss is shown in the rows.

Human Error

Human errors and mistakes include accidental problems caused by both employees and nonemployees. An example is an employee who misunderstands operating procedures and accidentally deletes customer records. Another example is an employee who, in the course of backing up a database, inadvertently installs an old database on top of the current one. This category also includes poorly written application programs and poorly designed procedures. Finally, human errors and mistakes include physical accidents, such as driving a forklift through the wall of a computer room.

		Threat		
		Human Error	**Computer Crime**	**Natural Disasters**
Loss	**Unauthorized data disclosure**	Procedural mistakes	Pretexting Phishing Spoofing Sniffing Hacking	Disclosure during recovery
	Incorrect data modification	Procedural mistakes Incorrect procedures Ineffective accounting controls System errors	Hacking	Incorrect data recovery
	Faulty service	Procedural mistakes Development and installation errors	Usurpation	Service improperly restored
	Denial of service (DoS)	Accidents	DoS attacks	Service interruption
	Loss of infrastructure	Accidents	Theft Terrorist activity	Property loss

Figure 10-3
Security Problems and Sources

Computer Crime

The second threat type is *computer crime*. This threat type includes employees and former employees who intentionally destroy data or other system components. It also includes hackers who break into a system and virus and worm writers who infect computer systems. Computer crime also includes terrorists and those who break into a system to steal for financial gain.

Natural Events and Disasters

Natural events and disasters are the third type of security threat. This category includes fires, floods, hurricanes, earthquakes, tsunamis, avalanches, and other acts of nature. Problems in this category include not only the initial loss of capability and service, but also losses stemming from actions to recover from the initial problem.

What Types of Security Loss Exist?

Five types of security loss exist: unauthorized data disclosure, incorrect data modification, faulty service, denial of service, and loss of infrastructure. Consider each.

Unauthorized Data Disclosure

Unauthorized data disclosure occurs when a threat obtains data that is supposed to be protected. It can occur by human error when someone inadvertently releases data in violation of policy. An example at a university is a department administrator who posts student names, identification numbers, and grades in a public place, when the releasing of names and grades violates state law and Federal law. Another example is employees who unknowingly or carelessly release proprietary data to competitors or to the media. WikiLeaks is a famous example of unauthorized disclosure; the situation described in the third row of Figure 10-2 is another example.

The popularity and efficacy of search engines have created another source of inadvertent disclosure. Employees who place restricted data on Web sites that can be reached by search engines might mistakenly publish proprietary or restricted data over the Web.

Of course, proprietary and personal data can also be released and obtained maliciously. **Pretexting** occurs when someone deceives by pretending to be someone else. A common scam involves a telephone caller who pretends to be from a credit card company and claims to be checking the validity of credit card numbers: "I'm checking your MasterCard number; it begins with 5491. Can you verify the rest of the number?" Thousands of MasterCard numbers start with 5491; the caller is attempting to steal a valid number.

Phishing compromises legitimate brands and trademarks. See the Guide (pages 452–453) for more.

Phishing is a similar technique for obtaining unauthorized data that uses pretexting via email. The **phisher** pretends to be a legitimate company and sends an email requesting confidential data, such as account numbers, Social Security numbers, account passwords, and so forth.

Spoofing is another term for someone pretending to be someone else. If you pretend to be your professor, you are spoofing your professor. **IP spoofing** occurs when an intruder uses another site's IP address to masquerade as that other site. **Email spoofing** is a synonym for phishing.

Sniffing is a technique for intercepting computer communications. With wired networks, sniffing requires a physical connection to the network. With wireless networks, no such connection is required: **Wardrivers** simply take computers with wireless connections through an area and search for unprotected wireless networks. They can monitor and intercept traffic on unsecured wireless networks. Even protected wireless networks are vulnerable, as you will learn. Spyware and adware are two other sniffing techniques discussed later in this chapter.

Other forms of computer crime include **hacking**, which is breaking into computers, servers, or networks to steal data such as customer lists, product inventory data, employee data, and other proprietary and confidential data.

Finally, people might inadvertently disclose data during recovery from a natural disaster. During a recovery, everyone is so focused on restoring system capability that they might ignore normal security safeguards. A request such as "I need a copy of the customer database backup" will receive far less scrutiny during disaster recovery than at other times.

Incorrect Data Modification

The second type of security loss in Figure 10-3 is *incorrect data modification*. Examples include incorrectly increasing a customer's discount or incorrectly modifying an employee's salary, earned days of vacation, or annual bonus. Other examples include placing incorrect information, such as incorrect price changes, on a company's Web site or company portal.

Incorrect data modification can occur through human error when employees follow procedures incorrectly or when procedures have been designed incorrectly. For proper internal control on systems that process financial data or control inventories of assets, such as products and equipment, companies should ensure separation of duties and authorities and have multiple checks and balances in place.

A final type of incorrect data modification caused by human error includes *system errors*. An example is the lost-update problem discussed in Chapter 5 (page 211).

Computer criminals can make unauthorized data modifications by hacking into a computer system. For example, hackers could hack into a system and transfer people's account balances or place orders to ship goods to unauthorized locations and customers.

Finally, faulty recovery actions after a disaster can result in incorrect data changes. The faulty actions can be unintentional or malicious.

Faulty Service

The third type of security loss, *faulty service*, includes problems that result because of incorrect system operation. Faulty service could include incorrect data modification, as just described. It also could include systems that work incorrectly by sending the wrong goods to a customer or the ordered goods to the wrong customer, inaccurately billing customers, or sending the wrong information to employees. Humans can inadvertently cause faulty service by making procedural mistakes. System developers can write programs incorrectly or make errors during the installation of hardware, software programs, and data.

Usurpation occurs when computer criminals invade a computer system and replace legitimate programs with their own, unauthorized ones that shut down legitimate applications and substitute their own processing to spy, steal and manipulate data, or achieve other purposes. Faulty service can also result when service is improperly restored during recovery from natural disasters.

Denial of Service

Human error in following procedures or a lack of procedures can result in **denial of service (DoS)**, the fourth type of loss. For example, humans can inadvertently shut down a Web server or corporate gateway router by starting a computationally intensive application. An OLAP application that uses the operational DBMS can consume so many DBMS resources that order-entry transactions cannot get through.

Computer criminals can launch an intentional denial-of-service attack in which a malicious hacker floods a Web server, for example, with millions of bogus service requests that so occupy the server that it cannot service legitimate requests. Also, computer worms can infiltrate a network with so much artificial traffic that legitimate traffic cannot get through. Finally, natural disasters may cause systems to fail, resulting in denial of service.

Loss of Infrastructure

Many times, human accidents cause loss of infrastructure, the last loss type. Examples are a bull-dozer cutting a conduit of fiber-optic cables and a floor buffer crashing into a rack of Web servers.

Theft and terrorist events also cause loss of infrastructure. For instance, a disgruntled, terminated employee might walk off with corporate data servers, routers, or other crucial equipment. Terrorist events also can cause the loss of physical plants and equipment.

Natural disasters present the largest risk for infrastructure loss. A fire, flood, earthquake, or similar event can destroy data centers and all they contain.

You may be wondering why Figure 10-3 does not include terms such as viruses, worms, and Trojan horses. The answer is that viruses, worms, and Trojan horses are techniques for causing some of the problems in the figure. They can cause a denial-of-service attack, or they can be used to cause malicious, unauthorized data access or data loss.

Finally, a new threat term has come into recent use. An **Advanced Persistent Threat (APT)** is a sophisticated, possibly long-running computer hack that is perpetrated by large, well-funded organizations such as governments. APTs can be a means to engage in cyberwarfare and cyber-espionage. An example of an APT is a group called "APT1" based out of Shanghai. In 2014, the U.S. Department of Justice indicted five individuals involved with APT1 for theft of intellectual property from U.S. firms. Mandiant, a U.S. security firm, released a detailed report about APT1's attacks on nearly 150 victims over a 7-year period. It provided detailed descriptions of APT1's tools, tactics, and procedures.[2] More recently, an APT group named "Deep Panda" was identified by forensic experts as the group behind the Anthem healthcare data breach that resulted in the loss of sensitive data for 80 million people. If you work in the military or for intelligence agencies, you will certainly be concerned, if not involved, with APTs. We return to this topic in Q10-9.

Goal of Information Systems Security

As shown in Figure 10-1, threats can be stopped, or if not stopped, the costs of loss can be reduced by creating appropriate safeguards. Safeguards are, however, expensive to create and maintain. They also reduce work efficiency by making common tasks more difficult, adding additional labor expense. The goal of information security is to find an appropriate trade-off between the risk of loss and the cost of implementing safeguards.

Business professionals need to consider that trade-off carefully. In your personal life, you should certainly employ antivirus software. You should probably implement other safeguards that you'll learn about in Q10-3. Some safeguards, such as deleting browser cookies, will make using your computer more difficult. Are such safeguards worth it? You need to assess the risks and benefits for yourself.

Similar comments pertain to organizations, though they need to go about it more systematically. The bottom line is not to let the future unfold without careful analysis and action as indicated by that analysis. Get in front of the security problem by making the appropriate trade-off for your life and your business.

Q10-2 How Big Is the Computer Security Problem?

We do not know the full extent of the financial and data losses due to computer security threats. Certainly, the losses due to human error are enormous, but few organizations compute those losses, and even fewer publish them. However, a recent security report by Risk Based Security called 2014 a record-breaking year due to the loss of 1.1 billion personal records in 3,014 security incidents. Some of the more notable data breaches included the loss of user accounts at Home Depot (56 million), JPMorgan (83 million), and eBay (145 million).[3] And that's not even counting the loss of more than 100TB of corporate data from Sony or the loss of hundreds of nude celebrity photos from Apple's iCloud. The majority of user records stolen (83 percent) were taken by external hackers targeting businesses. These are only the companies that made the news and reported estimated losses.

Losses due to natural disasters are also enormous and impossible to compute. The 2011 earthquake in Japan, for example, shut down Japanese manufacturing, and losses rippled through the supply chain from the Far East to Europe and the United States. One can only imagine the enormous expense for Japanese companies as they restored their information systems.

Furthermore, no one knows the cost of computer crime. For one, there are no standards for tallying crime costs. Does the cost of a denial-of-service attack include lost employee time, lost revenue, or long-term revenue losses due to lost customers? Or, if an employee loses a $2,000 laptop, does the cost include the value of the data that was on it? Does it include the cost of the time of replacing it and reinstalling software? Or, if someone steals next year's financial plan, how is the cost of the value that competitors glean determined?

Second, all the studies on the cost of computer crime are based on surveys. Different respondents interpret terms differently, some organizations don't report all their losses, and some won't report computer crime losses at all. Absent standard definitions and a more accurate way of gathering crime data, we cannot rely on the accuracy of any particular estimate. The most we can do is look for trends by comparing year-to-year data, assuming the same methodology is used by the various types of survey respondents.

Figure 10-4 shows the results of a survey done over 5 years.[4] It was commissioned by Hewlett-Packard and performed by the Ponemon Institute, a consulting group that specializes in computer crime. It shows the average cost and percent of total incidents of the six most

	2010	2011	2012	2013	2014
Denial of Service	NA	$187,506 (17%)	$172,238 (20%)	$243,913 (21%)	$166,545 (18%)
Malicous Insiders	$100,300 (11%)	$105,352 (9%)	$166,251 (8%)	$198,769 (8%)	$213,542 (8%)
Web-based Attacks	$143,209 (15%)	$141,647 (12%)	$125,795 (13%)	$125,101 (12%)	$116,424 (14%)
Malicous Code	$124,083 (26%)	$126,787 (23%)	$109,533 (26%)	$102,216 (21%)	$91,500 (23%)
Phishing & Social Engineering	$35,514 (12%)	$30,397 (9%)	$18,040 (7%)	$21,094 (11%)	$45,959 (13%)
Stolen Devices	$25,663 (17%)	$24,968 (13%)	23,541 (12%)	$20,070 (9%)	$43,565 (10%)

Figure 10-4

Average Computer Crime Cost and Percent of Attacks by Type (Six Most Expensive Types)

Source: Data from Ponemon Institute. *2014 Cost of Cyber Crime Study: United States*, October 2014, p. 12.

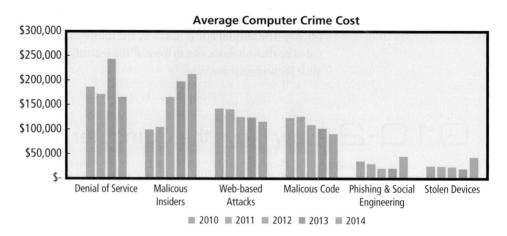

Figure 10-5
Computer Crime Costs

expensive types of attack. Without tests of significance, it's difficult to determine if the differences shown are random; they could be. But taking the data at face value, it appears the source of most of the increase in computer crime costs is malicious insiders. The number of attacks of this type is slightly decreasing, but the average cost of such attacks is increasing, possibly dramatically (Figure 10-5). Apparently, insiders are getting better at stealing more. The study, by the way, defined an insider as an employee, temporary employee, contractor, or business partner. The average costs of the remaining categories are slightly decreasing.

In addition to this data, Ponemon also surveyed losses by type of asset compromised. It found that business disruption was the single most expensive consequence of computer crime, accounting for 38 percent of costs in 2014. Information loss was the second highest cost, at 35 percent in 2014. Equipment losses and damages were only 4 percent of the lost value. Clearly, value lies in data and not in hardware!

Looking to the future, in a separate study,[5] Ponemon reported that 78 percent of its respondents believe that negligent or careless employees not following security policies pose a significant risk to their organizations. The next most worrisome concerns were personal devices connected to the corporate network (68 percent) and employee use of commercial cloud-based applications at work (66 percent).

The *2014 Cost of Computer Crime Study* includes an in-depth analysis of the effect of different security policies on the savings in computer crime. The bottom line is that organizations that spend more to create the safeguards discussed in Q10-4 through Q10-7 (later in this chapter) experience less computer crime and suffer smaller losses when they do. Security safeguards do work!

If you search for the phrase *computer crime statistics* on the Web, you will find numerous similar studies. Some are based on dubious sampling techniques and seem to be written to promote a particular safeguard product or point of view. Be aware of such bias as you read.

Using the Ponemon study, the bottom line, as of 2014, is:

- Malicious insiders are an increasingly serious security threat.
- Business disruption and data loss are principal costs of computer crime.
- Survey respondents believe negligent employees, personal devices connecting to the corporate network, and the use of commercial cloud-based applications pose a significant security threat.
- Security safeguards work.

Q10-3 How Should You Respond to Security Threats?

As stated at the end of Q10-1, your personal IS security goal should be to find an effective trade-off between the risk of loss and the cost of safeguards. However, few individuals take security as seriously as they should, and most fail to implement even low-cost safeguards.

- Take security seriously
- Create strong passwords
- Use multiple passwords
- Send no valuable data via email or IM
- Use https at trusted, reputable vendors
- Remove high-value assets from computers
- Clear browsing history, temporary files, and cookies (CCleaner or equivalent)
- Regularly update antivirus software
- Demonstrate security concern to your fellow workers
- Follow organizational security directives and guidelines
- Consider security for all business initiatives

Figure 10-6
Personal Security Safeguards

Figure 10-6 lists recommended personal security safeguards. The first safeguard is to take security seriously. You cannot see the attempts that are being made, right now, to compromise your computer. However, they are there.

Unfortunately, the first sign you receive that your security has been compromised will be bogus charges on your credit card or messages from friends complaining about the disgusting email they just received from your email account. Computer security professionals run intrusion detection systems to detect attacks. An **intrusion detection system (IDS)** is a computer program that senses when another computer is attempting to scan or access a computer or network. IDS logs can record thousands of attempts each day. If these attempts come from outside the country, there is nothing you can do about them except use reasonable safeguards.

If you decide to take computer security seriously, the single most important safeguard you can implement is to create and use strong passwords. We discussed ways of doing this in Chapter 1 (pages 60–61). To summarize, do not use any word, in any language, as part of your password. Use passwords with a mixture of upper- and lowercase letters and numbers and special characters.

Such nonword passwords are still vulnerable to a **brute force attack** in which the password cracker tries every possible combination of characters. John Pozadzides, a security researcher, estimates that a brute force attack can crack a six-character password of either upper- or lowercase letters in about 5 minutes. However, brute force requires 8.5 days to crack that length password having a mixture of upper- and lowercase letters, numbers, and special characters. A 10-digit password of only upper- and lowercase letters takes 4.5 years to crack, but one using a mix of letters, numbers, and special characters requires nearly 2 million years. A 12-digit, letter-only password requires 3 million years, and a 12-digit mixed password will take many, many millions of years.[6] All of these estimates assume, of course, that the password contains no word in any language. The bottom line is this: Use long passwords with no words, 10 or more characters, and a mix of letters, numbers, and special characters.

In addition to using long, complex passwords, you should also use different passwords for different sites. That way, if one of your passwords is compromised, you do not lose control of all of your accounts. Make sure you use very strong passwords for important sites (like your bank's site), and do not reuse those passwords on less important sites (like your social networking sites). Some sites are focused on innovating products and may not allocate the same amount of resources to protect your information. Guard your information with a password it deserves.

Management sets security policies to ensure compliance with security law, as discussed in the Ethics Guide on pages 434–435.

Never send passwords, credit card data, or any other valuable data in email or IM. As stated numerous times in this text, most email and IM is not protected by encryption (see Q10-5), and you should assume that anything you write in email or IM could find its way to the front page of *The New York Times* tomorrow.

Buy only from reputable online vendors using a secure https connection. If the vendor does not support https in its transactions (look for *https://* in the address line of your browser), do not buy from that vendor.

You can reduce your vulnerability to loss by removing high-value assets from your computers. Now, and especially later as a business professional, make it your practice not to travel out of your office with a laptop or other device that contains any data that you do not need. In general, store proprietary data on servers or removable devices that do not travel with you. (Office 365, by the way, uses https to transfer data to and from SharePoint. You can use it or a similar application for processing documents from public locations such as airports while you are traveling.)

Your browser automatically stores a history of your browsing activities and temporary files that contain sensitive data about where you've visited, what you've purchased, what your account names and passwords are, and so forth. It also stores **cookies**, which are small files that your browser receives when you visit Web sites. Cookies enable you to access Web sites without having to sign in every time, and they speed up processing of some sites. Unfortunately, some cookies also contain sensitive security data. The best safeguard is to remove your browsing history, temporary files, and cookies from your computer and to set your browser to disable history and cookies.

CCleaner is a free, open source product that will do a thorough job of securely removing all such data (*http://download.cnet.com/ccleaner/*). You should make a backup of your computer before using CCleaner, however.

Removing and disabling cookies presents an excellent example of the trade-off between improved security and cost. Your security will be substantially improved, but your computer will be more difficult to use. You decide, but make a conscious decision; do not let ignorance of the vulnerability of such data make the decision for you.

We will address the use of antivirus software in Q10-5. The last three items in Figure 10-6 apply once you become a business professional. With your coworkers, and especially with those whom you manage, you should demonstrate a concern and respect for security. You should also follow all organizational security directives and guidelines. Finally, consider security in all of your business initiatives.

Q10-4 How Should Organizations Respond to Security Threats?

Q10-3 discussed ways that you as an individual should respond to security threats. In the case of organizations, a broader and more systematic approach needs to be taken. To begin, senior management needs to address two critical security functions: security policy and risk management.

Considering the first, senior management must establish company-wide security policies. Take, for example, a data security policy that states the organization's posture regarding data that it gathers about its customers, suppliers, partners, and employees. At a minimum, the policy should stipulate:

- What sensitive data the organization will store
- How it will process that data
- Whether data will be shared with other organizations
- How employees and others can obtain copies of data stored about them
- How employees and others can request changes to inaccurate data

The specifics of a policy depend on whether the organization is governmental or nongovernmental, on whether it is publically held or private, on the organization's industry, on the relationship of management to employees, and on other factors. As a new hire, seek out your employer's security policy if it is not discussed with you in new-employee training.

New from Black Hat 2014

Hackers, security professionals, and government agents flock to Las Vegas each year to attend an important security conference: Black Hat. Black Hat caters to hackers, security professionals, corporations, and government entities.

Each year, speakers make briefings on how things can be hacked. Presenters show exactly how to exploit weaknesses in hardware, software, protocols, or systems. One session may show you how to hack your smartphone, while another may show you how to empty the cash out of an ATM.

Presentations encourage companies to fix product vulnerabilities and serve as an educational forum for hackers, developers, manufacturers, and government agencies. The following are highlights from the 2014 Black Hat conference:

Keynote by Dan Geer: The most talked-about event at Black Hat was the keynote speech by In-Q-Tel CISO Dan Geer. In-Q-Tel is a venture capital firm that invests in technologies that support the missions of the Central Intelligence Agency and the U.S. Intelligence Community. In his talk, Geer discussed 10 policy proposals he believed would greatly improve information security.[7] Some of his more notable policy proposals included:

1. Mandatory reporting of security vulnerabilities similar to the way disease outbreaks are reported to the Centers for Disease Control and Prevention.
2. Software makers need to be liable for the damage their code may cause after they abandon it or allow users to see their source code and choose to cut out the code they don't want to run.
3. Internet service providers (ISP) need to be liable for harmful content going over their networks if they inspect the data being sent. If they don't inspect users' data, they could still be protected as a common carrier.
4. The European Union's laws that guarantee an individual's "right to be forgotten" are appropriate and advantageous.

End-to-End Encrypted Email: Yahoo!'s CISO Alex Stamos revealed that consumers will be able to use end-to-end encrypted email through Yahoo! Mail by 2015.[8] This would mean that only the original sender and final receiver of a message would be able to read it. This announcement was the highlight of the conference for most conference goers who saw it as a first step at bringing back individual privacy. Edward Snowden's revelations about the complicit relationship between government

Source: Rawpixel/Fotolia

and tech industry giants designed to monitor consumers was still fresh in the minds of security professionals and civil libertarians at the conference.

Hacking Smart Things: Some of the more eye-catching briefings at Black Hat were about hacking smart things like smartphones, TVs, webcams, thermostats, and cars. Security researchers Charlie Miller (Twitter©) and Chris Valasek (IOActive©) looked at potential vulnerabilities for 24 different cars.[9] They found that automobiles with wireless features (i.e., Bluetooth, Wi-Fi, and cellular connectivity) and poor internal systems architecture may allow hackers to access automated driving functions through seemingly innocuous features like a car's radio.

Another security researcher, Jesus Molina, talked about security vulnerabilities at the St. Regis Shenzhen hotel in China.[10] On a recent stay at the hotel, Molina discovered that he was able to control the lights, thermostats, televisions, and blinds in more than 200 rooms by reverse-engineering a home automation protocol called KNX/IP. These briefings illustrate the importance of companies developing secure software for IP-enabled smart things. In a recent study looking at vulnerabilities of smart devices, HP noted that 70 percent of the smart devices they tested used unencrypted network services, and six out of 10 devices were vulnerable to persistent XSS (cross-site scripting) and weak credentials.[11]

Questions

1. How could mandatory reporting of vulnerabilities make systems more secure?

2. Dan Geer suggested that software makers be held liable for damage caused by their software after they abandon it or freed from liability by making the source code open source so it can be "fixed." What impact would this policy have on Microsoft?

3. How would a "right to be forgotten" rule affect online businesses like Google or Facebook?

4. Who might be harmed by end-to-end encrypted email?

5. Why are vulnerabilities in smart devices so important?

The second senior management security function is to manage risk. Risk cannot be eliminated, so *manage risk* means to proactively balance the trade-off between risk and cost. This trade-off varies from industry to industry and from organization to organization. Financial institutions are obvious targets for theft and must invest heavily in security safeguards. On the other hand, a bowling alley is unlikely to be much of a target, unless, of course, it stores credit card data on computers or mobile devices (a decision that would be part of its security policy and that would seem unwise, not only for a bowling alley but also for most small businesses).

To make trade-off decisions, organizations need to create an inventory of the data and hardware they want to protect and then evaluate safeguards relative to the probability of each potential threat. Figure 10-3 is a good source for understanding categories and frequencies of threat. Given this set of inventory and threats, the organization needs to decide how much risk it wishes to take or, stated differently, which security safeguards it wishes to implement.

A good analogy of using safeguards to protect information assets is buying car insurance. Before buying car insurance you determine how much your car is worth, the likelihood of incurring damage to your car, and how much risk you are willing to accept. Then you transfer some of your risk to the insurer by buying a safeguard called an insurance policy. Instead of buying just one insurance policy, organizations implement a variety of safeguards to protect their data and hardware.

An easy way to remember information systems safeguards is to arrange them according to the five components of an information system, as shown in Figure 10-7. Some of the safeguards involve computer hardware and software. Some involve data; others involve procedures and people. We will consider technical, data, and human safeguards in the next three questions.

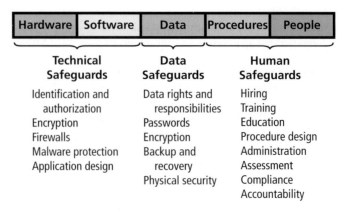

Hardware	Software	Data	Procedures	People

Technical Safeguards	Data Safeguards	Human Safeguards
Identification and authorization	Data rights and responsibilities	Hiring
Encryption	Passwords	Training
Firewalls	Encryption	Education
Malware protection	Backup and recovery	Procedure design
Application design	Physical security	Administration
		Assessment
		Compliance
		Accountability

Figure 10-7

Security Safeguards as They Relate to the Five Components

Q10-5 How Can Technical Safeguards Protect Against Security Threats?

Technical safeguards involve the hardware and software components of an information system. Figure 10-8 lists primary technical safeguards. Consider each.

Identification and Authentication

Every information system today should require users to sign on with a username and password. The username *identifies* the user (the process of **identification**), and the password *authenticates* that user (the process of **authentication**).

Passwords have important weaknesses. In spite of repeated warnings (don't let this happen to you!), users often share their passwords, and many people choose ineffective, simple passwords. In fact, a 2014 Verizon report states, "Passwords, usernames, emails, credit/debit card and financial account information, and Social Security Numbers are being compromised at a staggering rate, endangering the identities of consumers nationwide."[12] Because of these problems, some organizations choose to use smart cards and biometric authentication in addition to passwords.

Smart Cards

A **smart card** is a plastic card similar to a credit card. Unlike credit, debit, and ATM cards, which have a magnetic strip, smart cards have a microchip. The microchip, which holds far more data than a magnetic strip, is loaded with identifying data. Users of smart cards are required to enter a **personal identification number (PIN)** to be authenticated.

Biometric Authentication

Biometric authentication uses personal physical characteristics such as fingerprints, facial features, and retinal scans to authenticate users. Biometric authentication provides strong authentication, but the required equipment is expensive. Often, too, users resist biometric identification because they feel it is invasive.

Biometric authentication is in the early stages of adoption. Because of its strength, it likely will see increased usage in the future. It is also likely that legislators will pass laws governing the use, storage, and protection requirements for biometric data. For more on biometrics, search for *biometrics* at *http://searchsecurity.techtarget.com*.

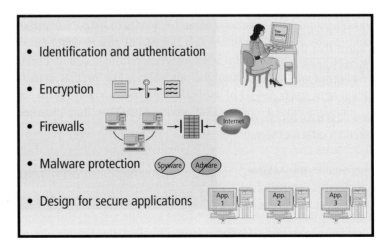

Figure 10-8
Technical Safeguards

Ethics Guide

SECURING PRIVACY

Some organizations have legal requirements to protect the customer data they collect and store, but the laws may be more limited than you think. The **Gramm-Leach-Bliley (GLB) Act**, passed by Congress in 1999, protects consumer financial data stored by financial institutions, which are defined as banks, securities firms, insurance companies, and organizations that supply financial advice, prepare tax returns, and provide similar financial services.

The **Privacy Act of 1974** provides protections to individuals regarding records maintained by the U.S. government, and the privacy provisions of the **Health Insurance Portability and Accountability Act (HIPAA)** of 1996 give individuals the right to access health data created by doctors and other healthcare providers. HIPAA also sets rules and limits on who can read and receive your health information.

The law is stronger in other countries. In Australia, for example, the Privacy Principles of the Australian Privacy Act of 1988 govern not only government and healthcare data, but also records maintained by businesses with revenues in excess of AU$3 million.

Most consumers would say, however, that online retailers have an ethical requirement to protect a customer's credit card and other data, and most online retailers would agree. Or at least the retailers would agree that they have a strong business reason to protect that data. A substantial loss of credit card data by any large online retailer would have detrimental effects on both sales and brand reputation.

Data aggregators like Acxiom Corporation further complicate the risk to individuals because they develop a complete profile of households and individuals. And no federal law prohibits the U.S. government from buying information products from the data accumulators.

But let's bring the discussion closer to home. What requirements does your university have on the data it maintains about you? State law or university policy may govern those records, but no federal law does. Most universities consider it their responsibility to provide public access to graduation records. Anyone can determine when you graduated, your degree, and your major. (Keep this service in mind when you write your resume.)

Most professors endeavor to publish grades by student number and not by name, and there may be state law that requires that separation. But what about your work? What about the papers you write, the answers you give on exams? What about the emails you send to your professor? The data are not protected by federal law, and they are probably not protected by state law. If your professor chooses to cite your work in research, she will be subject to copyright law, but not privacy law. What you write is no longer your personal property; it belongs to the academic community. You can ask your professor

what she intends to do with your coursework, emails, and office conversations, but none of these data are protected by law.

The bottom line is this: Be careful where you put your personal data. Large, reputable organizations are likely to endorse ethical privacy policy and to have strong and effective safeguards to effectuate that policy. But individuals and small organizations might not. If in doubt, don't give the data.

DISCUSSION QUESTIONS

1. As stated in the case feature, when you order from an online retailer, the data you provide is not protected by U.S. privacy law. Does this fact cause you to reconsider setting up an account with a stored credit card number? What is the advantage of storing the credit card number? Do you think the advantage is worth the risk? Are you more willing to take the risk with some companies than with others? If so, state the criteria you use for choosing to take the risk.

2. Suppose you are the treasurer of a student club and you store records of club members' payments in a database. In the past, members have disputed payment amounts; therefore, when you receive a payment, you scan an image of the check or credit card invoice and store the scanned image in a database. Unfortunately, you have placed that database into a shared folder.

    One day, you are using your computer in a local coffee shop. A malicious student watches you sign in. Your name is visible, and your password is very short so it's easy for that student to see what it is. While you're enjoying your coffee, the malicious student learns the name of your computer from the coffee shop's wireless device, uses your login and password to connect to your shared folder, and then copies the club database. You know nothing about this until the next day, when a club member complains that a popular student Web site has published the names, bank names, and bank account numbers for everyone who has given you a check.

    What liability do you have in this matter? Could you be classified as a financial institution because you are taking students' money? (You can find the GLB at *www.ftc.gov/privacy/privacyinitiatives/glbact.html*.) If so, what liability do you have? If not, do you have any other liability? Does the coffee shop have liability?

    Even if you have no legal liability, was your behavior ethical? Explain your answer. In this and in questions 3, 4, and 5, use either the categorical imperative or utilitarianism in your answer.

3. Suppose you are asked to fill out a study questionnaire that requires you to enter identifying data, as well as answers to personal questions. You hesitate to provide the data, but the top part of the questionnaire states, "All responses will be strictly confidential." So, you fill out the questionnaire.

    Unfortunately, the person who is managing the study visits that same wireless coffee shop that you visited (in question 2), but this time the malicious student is sniffing packets to see what might turn up.

    The study manager joins the coffee shop's wireless network and starts her email. Her first message is from a small online Web store at which she has just opened an account. The email says, in part, "Welcome! Your account name is *Emily100* and your password is Jd5478IaE$%$55."

    "Eureka!" says the packet-sniffing, malicious student to himself as the packets carrying that email appear on his screen. "That looks like a pretty good password. Well, Emily100, I'll bet you use it on other accounts, like maybe your email?" The malicious student signs into email using Emily100 and password Jd5478IaE$%$55 and, sure enough, he's in. First thing he reads are emails to the study monitors, emails that contain attachments containing all of the study results. The next day, your name and all of your "confidential" responses appear on the public student Web site.

    Did the person conducting the study violate a law? Did she do anything unethical? What mistake(s) did she make?

4. In question 3, does the online Web site that sent the email have any legal liability for this loss? Did it do anything unethical?

5. In question 2, did the malicious student do anything illegal? Unethical? In question 3, did the malicious student do anything illegal? Unethical?

6. Given these two scenarios, describe good practice for computer use at public wireless facilities.

7. Considering your answers to the above questions, state three to five general principles to guide your actions as you disseminate and store data.

Note that authentication methods fall into three categories: what you know (password or PIN), what you have (smart card), and what you are (biometric).

Single Sign-on for Multiple Systems

Information systems often require multiple sources of authentication. For example, when you sign on to your personal computer, you need to be authenticated. When you access the LAN in your department, you need to be authenticated again. When you traverse your organization's WAN, you will need to be authenticated to even more networks. Also, if your request requires database data, the DBMS server that manages that database will authenticate you yet again.

It would be annoying to enter a name and password for every one of these resources. You might have to use and remember five or six different passwords just to access the data you need to perform your job. It would be equally undesirable to send your password across all of these networks. The further your password travels, the greater the risk it can be compromised.

Instead, today's operating systems have the capability to authenticate you to networks and other servers. You sign on to your local computer and provide authentication data; from that point on your operating system authenticates you to another network or server, which can authenticate you to yet another network and server, and so forth. Because this is so, your identity and passwords open many doors beyond those on your local computer; remember this when you choose your passwords!

Encryption

Encryption is the process of transforming clear text into coded, unintelligible text for secure storage or communication. Considerable research has gone into developing **encryption algorithms** (procedures for encrypting data) that are difficult to break. Commonly used methods are DES, 3DES, and AES; search the Web for these terms if you want to know more about them.

A **key** is a string of bits used to encrypt the data. It is called a *key* because it unlocks a message, but it is a string of bits, expressed as numbers or letters, used with an encryption algorithm. It's not a physical thing like the key to your apartment.

To encrypt a message, a computer program uses the encryption method (say, AES) combined with the key (say, the word "key") to convert a plaintext message (in this case the word "secret") into an encrypted message. The resulting coded message ("U2FsdGVkX1+b637aTP80u+y2WYl UbqUz2XtYcw4E8m4=") looks like gibberish. Decoding (decrypting) a message is similar; a key is applied to the coded message to recover the original text. With **symmetric encryption**, the same key is used to encode and to decode. With **asymmetric encryption**, two keys are used; one key encodes the message, and the other key decodes the message. Symmetric encryption is simpler and much faster than asymmetric encryption.

A special version of asymmetric encryption, **public key encryption**, is used on the Internet. With this method, each site has a *public key* for encoding messages and a *private key* for decoding them. Before we explain how that works, consider the following analogy.

Suppose you send a friend an open combination lock (like you have on your gym locker). Suppose you are the only one who knows the combination to that lock. Now, suppose your friend puts something in a box and locks the lock. Now, neither your friend nor anyone else can open that box. That friend sends the locked box to you, and you apply the combination to open the box.

A *public key* is like the combination lock, and the *private key* is like the combination. Your friend uses the public key to code the message (lock the box), and you use the private key to decode the message (open the lock).

Now, suppose we have two generic computers, A and B. Suppose B wants to send an encrypted message to A. To do so, A sends B its public key (in our analogy, A sends B an open combination lock). Now B applies A's public key to the message and sends the resulting coded message back to A.

At that point, neither B nor anyone other than A can decode that message. It is like the box with a locked combination lock. When A receives the coded message, A applies its private key (the combination in our analogy) to unlock or decrypt the message.

Again, public keys are like open combination locks. Computer A will send a lock to anyone who asks for one. But A never sends its private key (the combination) to anyone. Private keys stay private.

Most secure communication over the Internet uses a protocol called **https**. With https, data are encrypted using a protocol called the **Secure Sockets Layer (SSL)**, which is also known as **Transport Layer Security (TLS)**. SSL/TLS uses a combination of public key encryption and symmetric encryption.

The basic idea is this: Symmetric encryption is fast and is preferred. But the two parties (say, you and a Web site) don't share a symmetric key. So, the two of you use public key encryption to share the same symmetric key. Once you both have that key, you use symmetric encryption for the remainder of the communication.

Figure 10-9 summarizes how SSL/TLS works when you communicate securely with a Web site:

1. Your computer obtains the *public* key of the Web site to which it will connect.
2. Your computer generates a key for symmetric encryption.
3. Your computer encodes that key using the Web site's public key. It sends the encrypted symmetric key to the Web site.
4. The Web site then decodes the symmetric key using its *private* key.
5. From that point forward, your computer and the Web site communicate using symmetric encryption.

At the end of the session, your computer and the secure site discard the keys. Using this strategy, the bulk of the secure communication occurs using the faster symmetric encryption. Also, because keys are used for short intervals, there is less likelihood they can be discovered.

Use of SSL/TLS makes it safe to send sensitive data such as credit card numbers and bank balances. Just be certain that you see *https://* in your browser and not just *http://*. Most browsers have additional plug-ins or add-ons (like HTTPS Everywhere) that can force https connections when available.

Firewalls

A **firewall** is a computing device that prevents unauthorized network access. A firewall can be a special-purpose computer, or it can be a program on a general-purpose computer or on a router. In essence, a firewall is simply a filter. It can filter traffic in a variety of ways including where

1. Your computer obtains public key of Web site.

Web Site Public Key

2. Your computer generates key for symmetric encryption.

You

3. Your computer encrypts symmetric key using Web site's public key.

Symmetric Key Encrypted Using Web Site's Public Key

Web Site

4. Web site decodes your message using its private key. Obtains key for symmetric encryption.

Communications Using Symmetric Encryption

5. All communications between you and Web site use symmetric encryption.

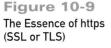

Figure 10-9
The Essence of https
(SSL or TLS)

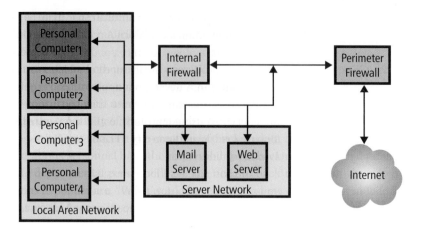

Figure 10-10
Use of Multiple Firewalls

network traffic is coming from, what types of packets are being sent, the contents of the packets, and if the packets are part of an authorized connection.

Organizations normally use multiple firewalls. A **perimeter firewall** sits outside the organizational network; it is the first device that Internet traffic encounters. In addition to perimeter firewalls, some organizations employ **internal firewalls** inside the organizational network. Figure 10-10 shows the use of a perimeter firewall that protects all of an organization's computers and a second internal firewall that protects a LAN.

A **packet-filtering firewall** examines each part of a message and determines whether to let that part pass. To make this decision, it examines the source address, the destination address(es), and other data.

Packet-filtering firewalls can prohibit outsiders from starting a session with any user behind the firewall. They can also disallow traffic from particular sites, such as known hacker addresses. They can prohibit traffic from legitimate, but unwanted, addresses, such as competitors' computers, and filter outbound traffic as well. They can keep employees from accessing specific sites, such as competitors' sites, sites with pornographic material, or popular news sites. As a future manager, if you have particular sites with which you do not want your employees to communicate, you can ask your IS department to enforce that limit via the firewall.

Packet-filtering firewalls are the simplest type of firewall. Other firewalls filter on a more sophisticated basis. If you take a data communications class, you will learn about them. For now, just understand that firewalls help to protect organizational computers from unauthorized network access.

No computer should connect to the Internet without firewall protection. Many ISPs provide firewalls for their customers. By nature, these firewalls are generic. Large organizations supplement such generic firewalls with their own. Most home routers include firewalls, and Microsoft Windows has a built-in firewall as well. Third parties also license firewall products.

Malware Protection

The next technical safeguard in our list in Figure 10-8 concerns malware. **Malware** is a broad category of software that includes viruses, spyware, and adware.

- A **virus** is a computer program that replicates itself. Unchecked replication is like computer cancer; ultimately, the virus consumes the computer's resources. Furthermore, many viruses also take unwanted and harmful actions. The program code that causes the unwanted actions is called the payload. The **payload** can delete programs or data—or, even worse, modify data in undetected ways.
- **Trojan horses** are viruses that masquerade as useful programs or files. The name refers to the gigantic mock-up of a horse that was filled with soldiers and moved into Troy during

the Trojan War. A typical Trojan horse appears to be a computer game, an MP3 music file, or some other useful, innocuous program.

- A **worm** is a virus that self-propagates using the Internet or other computer network. Worms spread faster than other virus types because they can replicate by themselves. Unlike nonworm viruses, which must wait for the user to share a file with a second computer, worms actively use the network to spread. Sometimes, worms can propagate so quickly that they overload and crash a network.

- **Spyware** programs are installed on the user's computer without the user's knowledge or permission. Spyware resides in the background and, unknown to the user, observes the user's actions and keystrokes, monitors computer activity, and reports the user's activities to sponsoring organizations. Some malicious spyware, called **key loggers**, captures keystrokes to obtain usernames, passwords, account numbers, and other sensitive information. Other spyware supports marketing analyses such as observing what users do, Web sites visited, products examined and purchased, and so forth.

- **Adware** is similar to spyware in that it is installed without the user's permission and resides in the background and observes user behavior. Most adware is benign in that it does not perform malicious acts or steal data. It does, however, watch user activity and produce pop-up ads. Adware can also change the user's default window or modify search results and switch the user's search engine.

- **Ransomware** is malicious software that blocks access to a system or data until money is paid to the attacker. Some forms of ransomware encrypt your data (CryptoLocker), prevent you from running applications, or even lock you out of your operating system (Reveton). Attackers demand to be paid before they will allow access to your data or system.

Figure 10-11 lists some of the symptoms of adware and spyware. Sometimes these symptoms develop slowly over time as more malware components are installed. Should these symptoms occur on your computer, remove the spyware or adware using antimalware programs.

Malware Safeguards

Fortunately, it is possible to avoid most malware using the following malware safeguards:

1. *Install antivirus and antispyware programs on your computer.* Your IS department will have a list of recommended (perhaps required) programs for this purpose. If you choose a program for yourself, choose one from a reputable vendor. Check reviews of antimalware software on the Web before purchasing.

2. *Set up your antimalware programs to scan your computer frequently.* You should scan your computer at least once a week and possibly more often. When you detect malware code, use the antimalware software to remove it. If the code cannot be removed, contact your IS department or antimalware vendor.

3. *Update malware definitions.* **Malware definitions**—patterns that exist in malware code—should be downloaded frequently. Antimalware vendors update these definitions continuously, and you should install these updates as they become available.

- Slow system startup
- Sluggish system performance
- Many pop-up advertisements
- Suspicious browser homepage changes
- Suspicious changes to the taskbar and other system interfaces
- Unusual hard-disk activity

Figure 10-11
Spyware and Adware Symptoms

4. *Open email attachments only from known sources.* Also, even when opening attachments from known sources, do so with great care. With a properly configured firewall, email is the only outside-initiated traffic that can reach user computers.

Most antimalware programs check email attachments for malware code. However, all users should form the habit of *never* opening an email attachment from an unknown source. Also, if you receive an unexpected email from a known source or an email from a known source that has a suspicious subject, odd spelling, or poor grammar, do not open the attachment without first verifying with the known source that the attachment is legitimate.

5. *Promptly install software updates from legitimate sources.* Unfortunately, all programs are chock full of security holes; vendors are fixing them as rapidly as they are discovered, but the practice is inexact. Install patches to the operating system and application programs promptly.

6. *Browse only reputable Web sites.* It is possible for some malware to install itself when you do nothing more than open a Web page. You can use the Web of Trust (WOT) browser plug-in to help you know which Web sites might be harmful. Recently, malware writers have been paying for banner ads on legitimate sites that have malware embedded in the ad. One click and you're infected.

Design for Secure Applications

The final technical safeguard in Figure 10-8 concerns the design of applications. As you learned in the opening vignette, Michele and James are designing PRIDE with security in mind; PRIDE will store users' privacy settings in a database, and it will develop all applications to first read the privacy settings before revealing any data in exercise reports. Most likely, PRIDE will design its programs so that privacy data is processed by programs on servers; that design means that such data need be transmitted over the Internet only when it is created or modified.

By the way, a **SQL injection attack** occurs when users enter a SQL statement into a form in which they are supposed to enter a name or other data. If the program is improperly designed, it will accept this code and make it part of the database command that it issues. Improper data disclosure and data damage and loss are possible consequences. A well-designed application will make such injections ineffective.

As a future IS user, you will not design programs yourself. However, you should ensure that any information system developed for you and your department includes security as one of the application requirements.

Q10-6 How Can Data Safeguards Protect Against Security Threats?

Data safeguards protect databases and other organizational data. Two organizational units are responsible for data safeguards. **Data administration** refers to an organization-wide function that is in charge of developing data policies and enforcing data standards.

Database administration refers to a function that pertains to a particular database. ERP, CRM, and MRP databases each have a database administration function. Database administration develops procedures and practices to ensure efficient and orderly multiuser processing of the database, to control changes to the database structure, and to protect the database. Database administration was summarized in Chapter 5.

Both data and database administration are involved in establishing the data safeguards in Figure 10-12. First, data administration should define data policies such as "We will not share identifying customer data with any other organization" and the like. Then data administration and

> • Define data policies
> • Data rights and responsibilities
> • Rights enforced by user accounts
>   authenticated by passwords
> • Data encryption
> • Backup and recovery procedures
> • Physical security

Figure 10-12
Data Safeguards

database administration(s) work together to specify user data rights and responsibilities. Third, those rights should be enforced by user accounts that are authenticated at least by passwords.

The organization should protect sensitive data by storing it in encrypted form. Such encryption uses one or more keys in ways similar to that described for data communication encryption. One potential problem with stored data, however, is that the key might be lost or that disgruntled or terminated employees might destroy it. Because of this possibility, when data are encrypted, a trusted party should have a copy of the encryption key. This safety procedure is sometimes called **key escrow**.

Another data safeguard is to periodically create backup copies of database contents. The organization should store at least some of these backups off premises, possibly in a remote location. Additionally, IT personnel should periodically practice recovery to ensure that the backups are valid and that effective recovery procedures exist. Do not assume that just because a backup is made that the database is protected.

Physical security is another data safeguard. The computers that run the DBMS and all devices that store database data should reside in locked, controlled-access facilities. If not, they are subject not only to theft, but also to damage. For better security, the organization should keep a log showing who entered the facility, when, and for what purpose.

When organizations store databases in the cloud, all of the safeguards in Figure 10-12 should be part of the cloud service contract.

Q10-7 How Can Human Safeguards Protect Against Security Threats?

Human safeguards involve the people and procedure components of information systems. In general, human safeguards result when authorized users follow appropriate procedures for system use and recovery. Restricting access to authorized users requires effective authentication methods and careful user account management. In addition, appropriate security procedures must be designed as part of every information system, and users should be trained on the importance and use of those procedures. In this section, we will consider the development of human safeguards for employees. According to the survey of computer crime discussed in Q10-2, crime from malicious insiders is increasing in frequency and cost. This fact makes safeguards even more important.

Read more about how to secure the security system in the Security Guide on pages 450–451.

Human Safeguards for Employees

Figure 10-13 lists security considerations for employees. Consider each.

Position Definitions

Effective human safeguards begin with definitions of job tasks and responsibilities. In general, job descriptions should provide a separation of duties and authorities. For example, no single individual should be allowed to both approve expenses and write checks. Instead, one person should

- Position definition
  - Separate duties and authorities
  - Determine least privilege
  - Document position sensitivity

"OK to pay this."

- Hiring and screening

"Where did you last work?"

- Dissemination and enforcement
  - Responsibility
  - Accountability
  - Compliance

"Let's talk security..."

- Termination
  - Friendly

"Congratulations on your new job."

  - Unfriendly

"We've closed your accounts. Goodbye."

Figure 10-13
Security Policy for In-House Staff

approve expenses, another pay them, and a third should account for the payment. Similarly, in inventory, no single person should be allowed to authorize an inventory withdrawal and also to remove the items from inventory.

Given appropriate job descriptions, user accounts should be defined to give users the *least possible privilege* needed to perform their jobs. For example, users whose job description does not include modifying data should be given accounts with read-only privileges. Similarly, user accounts should prohibit users from accessing data their job description does not require. Because of the problem of semantic security, even access to seemingly innocuous data may need to be limited.

Finally, the security sensitivity should be documented for each position. Some jobs involve highly sensitive data (e.g., employee compensation, salesperson quotas, and proprietary marketing or technical data). Other positions involve no sensitive data. Documenting *position sensitivity* enables security personnel to prioritize their activities in accordance with the possible risk and loss.

Hiring and Screening

Security considerations should be part of the hiring process. Of course, if the position involves no sensitive data and no access to information systems, then screening for information systems security purposes will be minimal. When hiring for high-sensitivity positions, however, extensive interviews, references, and background investigations are appropriate. Note, too, that security screening applies not only to new employees, but also to employees who are promoted into sensitive positions.

Dissemination and Enforcement

Employees cannot be expected to follow security policies and procedures that they do not know about. Therefore, employees need to be made aware of the security policies, procedures, and responsibilities they will have.

Employee security training begins during new-employee training, with the explanation of general security policies and procedures. That general training must be amplified in accordance with the position's sensitivity and responsibilities. Promoted employees should receive security training that is appropriate to their new positions. The company should not provide user accounts and passwords until employees have completed required security training.

Enforcement consists of three interdependent factors: responsibility, accountability, and compliance. First, the company should clearly define the security *responsibilities* of each position. The design of the security program should be such that employees can be held *accountable* for security violations. Procedures should exist so that when critical data are lost, it is possible to determine how the loss occurred and who is accountable. Finally, the security program should encourage security *compliance*. Employee activities should regularly be monitored for compliance, and management should specify the disciplinary action to be taken in light of noncompliance.

Management attitude is crucial: Employee compliance is greater when management demonstrates, both in word and deed, a serious concern for security. If managers write passwords on staff bulletin boards, shout passwords down hallways, or ignore physical security procedures, then employee security attitudes and employee security compliance will suffer. Note, too, that effective security is a continuing management responsibility. Regular reminders about security are essential.

Termination

Companies also must establish security policies and procedures for the termination of employees. Many employee terminations are friendly and occur as the result of promotion or retirement or when the employee resigns to take another position. Standard human resources policies should ensure that system administrators receive notification in advance of the employee's last day so that they can remove accounts and passwords. The need to recover keys for encrypted data and any other special security requirements should be part of the employee's out-processing.

Unfriendly termination is more difficult because employees may be tempted to take malicious or harmful actions. In such a case, system administrators may need to remove user accounts and passwords prior to notifying the employee of his or her termination. Other actions may be needed to protect the company's data assets. A terminated sales employee, for example, may attempt to take the company's confidential customer and sales-prospect data for future use at another company. The terminating employer should take steps to protect those data prior to the termination.

The human resources department should be aware of the importance of giving IS administrators early notification of employee termination. No blanket policy exists; the information systems department must assess each case on an individual basis.

Human Safeguards for Nonemployee Personnel

Business requirements may necessitate opening information systems to nonemployee personnel—temporary personnel, vendors, partner personnel (employees of business partners), and the public. Although temporary personnel can be screened, to reduce costs the screening will be abbreviated from that for employees. In most cases, companies cannot screen either vendor or partner personnel. Of course, public users cannot be screened at all. Similar limitations pertain to security training and compliance testing.

In the case of temporary, vendor, and partner personnel, the contracts that govern the activity should call for security measures appropriate to the sensitivity of the data and the IS resources involved. Companies should require vendors and partners to perform appropriate screening and security training. The contract also should mention specific security responsibilities that are particular to the work to be performed. Companies should provide accounts and passwords with the least privilege and remove those accounts as soon as possible.

The situation differs with public users of Web sites and other openly accessible information systems. It is exceedingly difficult and expensive to hold public users accountable for security violations. In general, the best safeguard from threats from public users is to *harden* the Web site or other facility against attack as much as possible. **Hardening** a site means to take extraordinary measures to reduce a system's vulnerability. Hardened sites use special versions of the operating system, and they lock down or eliminate operating systems features and functions that are not required by the application. Hardening is actually a technical safeguard, but we mention it here as the most important safeguard against public users.

Finally, note that the business relationship with the public, and with some partners, differs from that with temporary personnel and vendors. The public and some partners use the information system to receive a benefit. Consequently, safeguards need to protect such users from internal company security problems. A disgruntled employee who maliciously changes prices on a Web site potentially damages both public users and business partners. As one IT manager put it, "Rather than protecting ourselves from them, we need to protect them from us." This is an extension of the fifth guideline in Figure 10-7.

Account Administration

The administration of user accounts, passwords, and help-desk policies and procedures is another important human safeguard.

Account Management

Account management concerns the creation of new user accounts, the modification of existing account permissions, and the removal of unneeded accounts. Information system administrators perform all of these tasks, but account users have the responsibility to notify the administrators of the need for these actions. The IS department should create standard procedures for this purpose. As a future user, you can improve your relationship with IS personnel by providing early and timely notification of the need for account changes.

The existence of accounts that are no longer necessary is a serious security threat. IS administrators cannot know when an account should be removed; it is up to users and managers to give such notification.

Password Management

Passwords are the primary means of authentication. They are important not just for access to the user's computer, but also for authentication to other networks and servers to which the user may have access. Because of the importance of passwords, the National Institute of Standards and Technology (NIST) recommends that employees be required to sign statements similar to those shown in Figure 10-14.

Figure 10-14

Sample Account Acknowledgment Form

Source: National Institute of Standards and Technology, U.S. Department of Commerce. Introduction to Computer Security: The NIST Handbook, Publication 800–812

> I hereby acknowledge personal receipt of the system password(s) associated with the user IDs listed below. I understand that I am responsible for protecting the password(s), will comply with all applicable system security standards, and will not divulge my password(s) to any person. I further understand that I must report to the Information Systems Security Officer any problem I encounter in the use of the password(s) or when I have reason to believe that the private nature of my password(s) has been compromised.

When an account is created, users should immediately change the password they are given to one of their own. In fact, well-constructed systems require the user to change the password on first use.

Additionally, users should change passwords frequently thereafter. Some systems will require a password change every 3 months or perhaps more frequently. Users grumble at the nuisance of making such changes, but frequent password changes reduce not only the risk of password loss, but also the extent of damage if an existing password is compromised.

Some users create two passwords and switch back and forth between those two. This strategy results in poor security, and some password systems do not allow the user to reuse recently used passwords. Again, users may view this policy as a nuisance, but it is important.

Help-Desk Policies

In the past, help desks have been a serious security risk. A user who had forgotten his password would call the help desk and plead for the help-desk representative to tell him his password or to reset the password to something else. "I can't get this report out without it!" was (and is) a common lament.

The problem for help-desk representatives is, of course, that they have no way of determining that they are talking with the true user and not someone spoofing a true user. But they are in a bind: If they do not help in some way, the help desk is perceived to be the "unhelpful desk."

To resolve such problems, many systems give the help-desk representative a means of authenticating the user. Typically, the help-desk information system has answers to questions that only the true user would know, such as the user's birthplace, mother's maiden name, or last four digits of an important account number. Usually, when a password is changed, notification of that change is sent to the user in an email. Email is sent as plaintext, however, so the new password itself ought not to be emailed. If you ever receive notification that your password was reset when you did not request such a reset, immediately contact IT security. Someone has compromised your account.

All such help-desk measures reduce the strength of the security system, and, if the employee's position is sufficiently sensitive, they may create too large a vulnerability. In such a case, the user may just be out of luck. The account will be deleted, and the user must repeat the account-application process.

Systems Procedures

Figure 10-15 shows a grid of procedure types—normal operation, backup, and recovery. Procedures of each type should exist for each information system. For example, the order-entry system will have procedures of each of these types, as will the Web storefront, the inventory

	System Users	Operations Personnel
Normal operation	Use the system to perform job tasks, with security appropriate to sensitivity.	Operate data center equipment, manage networks, run Web servers, and do related operational tasks.
Backup	Prepare for loss of system functionality.	Back up Web site resources, databases, administrative data, account and password data, and other data.
Recovery	Accomplish job tasks during failure. Know tasks to do during system recovery.	Recover systems from backed up data. Perform role of help desk during recovery.

Figure 10-15
Systems Procedures

system, and so forth. The definition and use of standardized procedures reduces the likelihood of computer crime and other malicious activity by insiders. It also ensures that the system's security policy is enforced.

Procedures exist for both users and operations personnel. For each type of user, the company should develop procedures for normal, backup, and recovery operations. As a future user, you will be primarily concerned with user procedures. Normal-use procedures should provide safeguards appropriate to the sensitivity of the information system.

Backup procedures concern the creation of backup data to be used in the event of failure. Whereas operations personnel have the responsibility for backing up system databases and other systems data, departmental personnel have the need to back up data on their own computers. Good questions to ponder are, "What would happen if I lost my computer or mobile device tomorrow?" "What would happen if someone dropped my computer during an airport security inspection?" "What would happen if my computer was stolen?" Employees should ensure that they back up critical business data on their computers. The IS department may help in this effort by designing backup procedures and making backup facilities available.

Finally, systems analysts should develop procedures for system recovery. First, how will the department manage its affairs when a critical system is unavailable? Customers will want to order and manufacturing will want to remove items from inventory even though a critical information system is unavailable. How will the department respond? Once the system is returned to service, how will records of business activities during the outage be entered into the system? How will service be resumed? The system developers should ask and answer these questions and others like them and develop procedures accordingly.

Security Monitoring

Security monitoring is the last of the human safeguards we will consider. Important monitoring functions are activity log analyses, security testing, and investigating and learning from security incidents.

Many information system programs produce *activity logs*. Firewalls produce logs of their activities, including lists of all dropped packets, infiltration attempts, and unauthorized access attempts from within the firewall. DBMS products produce logs of successful and failed log-ins. Web servers produce voluminous logs of Web activities. The operating systems in personal computers can produce logs of log-ins and firewall activities.

None of these logs adds any value to an organization unless someone looks at them. Accordingly, an important security function is to analyze these logs for threat patterns, successful and unsuccessful attacks, and evidence of security vulnerabilities.

Today, most large organizations actively investigate their security vulnerabilities. They may employ utilities such as Tenable's Nessus or IBM's Security AppScan to assess their vulnerabilities.

Many companies create **honeypots**, which are false targets for computer criminals to attack. To an intruder, a honeypot looks like a particularly valuable resource, such as an unprotected Web site, but in actuality the only site content is a program that determines the attacker's IP address. Organizations can then trace the IP address back using free online tools, like DNSstuff, to determine who has attacked them.[13] If you are technically minded, detail-oriented, and curious, a career as a security specialist in this field is almost as exciting as it appears on *CSI*. To learn more, check out DNSstuff, Nessus, or Security AppScan. See also *Applied Information Security*, 2nd ed.[14]

Another important monitoring function is to investigate security incidents. How did the problem occur? Have safeguards been created to prevent a recurrence of such problems? Does the incident indicate vulnerabilities in other portions of the security system? What else can be learned from the incident?

Security systems reside in a dynamic environment. Organization structures change. Companies are acquired or sold; mergers occur. New systems require new security measures. New technology changes the security landscape, and new threats arise. Security personnel must constantly monitor the situation and determine if the existing security policy and safeguards are adequate. If changes are needed, security personnel need to take appropriate action.

Security, like quality, is an ongoing process. There is no final state that represents a secure system or company. Instead, companies must monitor security on a continuing basis.

Q10-8 How Should Organizations Respond to Security Incidents?

The last component of a security plan that we will consider is incident response. Figure 10-16 lists the major factors. First, every organization should have an incident-response plan as part of the security program. No organization should wait until some asset has been lost or compromised before deciding what to do. The plan should include how employees are to respond to security problems, whom they should contact, the reports they should make, and steps they can take to reduce further loss.

Consider, for example, a virus. An incident-response plan will stipulate what an employee should do when he notices the virus. It should specify whom to contact and what to do. It may stipulate that the employee should turn off his computer and physically disconnect from the network. The plan should also indicate what users with wireless computers should do.

The plan should provide centralized reporting of all security incidents. Such reporting will enable an organization to determine if it is under systematic attack or whether an incident is isolated. Centralized reporting also allows the organization to learn about security threats, take consistent actions in response, and apply specialized expertise to all security problems.

When an incident does occur, speed is of the essence. The longer the incident goes on, the greater the cost. Viruses and worms can spread very quickly across an organization's networks, and a fast response will help to mitigate the consequences. Because of the need for speed, preparation pays. The incident-response plan should identify critical personnel and their off-hours contact information. These personnel should be trained on where to go and what to do when they get there. Without adequate preparation, there is substantial risk that the actions of well-meaning people will make the problem worse. Also, the rumor mill will be alive with all sorts of nutty ideas about what to do. A cadre of well-informed, trained personnel will serve to dampen such rumors.

Finally, organizations should periodically practice incident response. Without such practice, personnel will be poorly informed on the response plan, and the plan itself may have flaws that only become apparent during a drill.

- Have plan in place
- Centralized reporting
- Specific responses
  - Speed
  - Preparation pays
  - Don't make problem worse
- Practice

Figure 10-16

Factors in Incident Response

Q10-9 2026?

What will be the status of information security by 2026? Will we have found a magic bullet to eliminate security problems? No. Human error is a constant; well-managed organizations will plan better for it and know how to respond better when it does occur, but as long as we have humans, we'll have error. Natural disasters are similar. The horrific events surrounding Hurricane Katrina in 2005 and the Japanese tsunami in 2011, as well as Hurricane Sandy in 2012, have alerted the world that we need to be better prepared, and more companies will set up hot or cold sites and put more data in well-prepared clouds. So, we'll be better prepared, but natural disasters are natural, after all.

Unfortunately, it is likely that sometime in the next 10 years some new, major incidents of cyberwarfare will have occurred. APTs will become more common, if indeed, they are not already common but we don't know it. Will some new nation or group enter the cyberwar picture? That also seems likely. Unless you're in the security and intelligence business, there isn't much you can do about it. But don't be surprised if some serious damage is inflicted somewhere in the world due to APTs.

As of June 2015, privacy advocates were outraged at the existence of **PRISM**, the intelligence program by which the National Security Agency (NSA) requested and received data about Internet activities from major Internet providers. They claimed their **privacy**, or freedom from being observed by other people, was being destroyed in the name of **security**, or state of being free from danger. After the initial hullabaloo, it appears that Internet providers did not allow the government direct access to their servers but rather delivered only data about specific individuals, as legally requested according to security laws enacted after 9/11. If so, then PRISM represents a legal governmental request for data, different only in scale from a governmental request for banking data about an organized crime figure.

As of June 2015, Edward Snowden, the man who exposed the PRISM program, appears to be either an advocate for Internet freedom and privacy or a traitor who sold government secrets to China and Russia for private gain. Regardless of the reasons for the leak, the episode raises the question of what governmental intrusion should be allowed into private data. We can hope the revelation of the existence of PRISM will spark a public conversation on the balance of national security and data privacy.

What about computer crime? It is a game of cat and mouse. Computer criminals find a vulnerability to exploit, and they exploit it. Computer security experts discover that vulnerability and create safeguards to thwart it. Computer criminals find a new vulnerability to exploit, computer security forces thwart it, and so it goes. The next major challenges will likely be those affecting mobile devices. But security on these devices will be improved as threats emerge that exploit their vulnerabilities. This cat-and-mouse game is likely to continue for at least the next 10 years. No super-safeguard will be devised to prevent computer crime, nor will any particular computer crime be impossible to thwart. However, the skill level of this cat-and-mouse activity is likely to increase, and substantially so. Because of increased security in operating systems and other software, and because of improved security procedures and employee training, it will become harder and harder for the lone hacker to find some vulnerability to exploit. Not impossible, but vastly more difficult.

So, what will happen? Cloud vendors and major organizations will continue to invest in safeguards; they'll hire more people (maybe you), train them well, and become ever more difficult to infiltrate. Although some criminals will continue to attack these fortresses, most will turn their attention to less protected, more vulnerable, midsized and smaller organizations and to individuals. You can steal $50M from one company or $50 from a million people with the same cash result. And, in the next 10 years, because of improved security at large organizations, the difficulty and cost of stealing that $50M will be much higher than stealing $50 a million times.

Part of the problem is porous national borders. People can freely enter the United States electronically without a passport. They can commit crimes with little fear of repercussions. There are no real electronic IDs. Cyber-gangs are well organized, financially motivated, and possibly state-sponsored. Electronic lawlessness is the order of the day. If someone in Romania steals from Google, Apple, Microsoft, or Boeing and then disappears into a cloud of networks in Uzbekistan, do those large organizations have the resources, expertise, and legal authority to pursue the attackers? What if that same criminal steals from you in Nashville? Can your local or state law enforcement authorities help? And, if your portion of the crime is for $50, how many calls to Uzbekistan do they want to make?

At the federal level, finances and politics take precedence over electronic security. The situation will likely be solved as it was in the past. Strong local "electronic" sheriffs will take control of their electronic borders and enforce existing laws. It will take at least a couple decades for this to happen. Technology is moving faster than either the public or elected officials can educate themselves.

Take another look at Figure 10-6. Send a copy to your loved ones.

Security Guide

EMV TO THE RESCUE

Have you traveled abroad recently? If so, you may have noticed that retailers in foreign countries now prefer, and in many cases require, that you make purchases using EMV chip-and-PIN technology. EMV stands for Europay, MasterCard®, and Visa®, the first three financial institutions involved in developing this technology.[15] If you didn't have an EMV card, you probably had to show your passport or use an alternative method of payment.

EMV has the potential to make companies more secure because it means they won't have to store credit card data that hackers want to steal. EMV changes the way cards are verified. With a traditional magnetic stripe card the *account* associated with that card is verified. With EMV, the chip embedded in the card verifies the authenticity of the physical *card*, and the PIN (or signature) entered by the customer verifies the identity of the *cardholder*. Without the physical card and the associated PIN, stolen account data cannot be used to make purchases. EMV makes credit card fraud much more difficult.

Let's take a look at a recent data breach to see what EMV can do to protect you!

Data Breach at Home Depot

Home Depot suffered a major data breach in 2014 that resulted in the loss of 56 million customer credit card records and 53 million customer email addresses.[16] When viewed in conjunction with the Target (98 million accounts) and JPMorgan Chase (83 million accounts) data breaches, all three of which occurred within less than a year, these incidents formed a tipping point. The prevalence and severity of cybercrimes occurring in corporate America have become more visible.

Hackers gained access to Home Depot's internal network using stolen credentials from a third-party vendor. They then distributed malware to internal point-of-sale (POS) terminals that would "scrape" credit card data from the random-access memory of the terminals. From there the stolen account data was collected and moved out of Home Depot's network.

After reviewing the details of the data breach, analysts found that Home Depot was using an older version of anti-virus software, and lacked encryption between point-of-sale (POS) systems and central servers. However, even though the software wasn't the latest version, the virus signature files (used to identify specific viruses) were up to date. The malware used by the hackers was likely new and undetectable. The lack of encryption didn't directly contribute to the data breach either.

Source: nobeastsofierce/Fotolia

The credit card numbers were stolen from the POS systems directly, not hijacked en route to a central server.[17]

The real security weakness was the access to the residual credit card data being stored in the memory of the POS. This could have been prevented through the adoption of EMV chip-and-PIN (or chip-and-signature) technology because the credit card data wouldn't have been stored in memory. Only transaction ID numbers are processed using EMV. Memory scraping malware, like the one used in the Home Depot data breach, wouldn't be able to recover any credit card data at all if Home Depot and its customers used EMV.

Building Adoption Momentum

Adoption of EMV chip-and-PIN is widespread in Western Europe (99.9 percent), Canada (84.7 percent), and Asia (71.4 percent).[18] But only 0.3 percent of transactions in the United States are completed using a chip-and-PIN card.

Consequently, about 50 percent of credit card fraud worldwide occurs in the United States. This is because the United States is one of the last places that still allows purchases with older magnetic stripe card technology.

But there is good news on the horizon. Major credit card issuers and some large banks in the United States have announced adoption deadlines for chip-and-PIN technology by October 2015. At that point, merchants will start to become liable for credit card fraud occurring at their location if their POS terminals do not support EMV. But all benefits come with costs. In this case, the cost of the cards themselves will rise from $0.25 per card to between $1.25 and 2.50 per card.[19] And the cost of upgrading each card reader will rise from $20 per card reader to between $40 and $100 per card reader. By the end of 2015, nearly 575 million new credit cards will be reissued to cardholders in the United States.

DISCUSSION QUESTIONS

1. Why would EMV chip-and-PIN cards be more secure than older magnetic stripe cards?
2. How have the data breaches discussed in this article (Home Depot, Target, and JPMorgan Chase) influenced your perception of cyberattacks and cybercrimes? Have you changed your behavior to help protect your own systems and data because of these breaches?
3. This article discusses how Home Depot's antivirus software program was out of date but that the virus signature files used by the software were current. Explain why

security experts would argue that out-of-date antivirus software would not have played a role in the Home Depot breach.
4. The cybercriminals responsible for the Home Depot breach stole residual credit card data from self-checkout POS systems. What does it mean to access residual data?
5. When a breach of this magnitude is reported, there are often lawsuits filed against the company that was attacked. Do you think companies should be legally responsible for securing customer data? Why or why not?

Guide

PHISHING FOR CREDIT CARDS, IDENTIFYING NUMBERS, BANK ACCOUNTS

A phisher is an individual or organization that spoofs legitimate companies in an attempt to illegally capture personal data such as credit card numbers, email accounts, and driver's license numbers. Some phishers install malicious program code on users' computers as well.

Phishing is usually initiated via email. Phishers steal legitimate logos and trademarks and use official-sounding words in an attempt to fool users into revealing personal data or clicking a link. Phishers do not bother with laws about trademark use. They place names and logos like Visa, MasterCard, Discover, and American Express on their Web pages and use them as bait. In some cases, phishers copy the entire look and feel of a legitimate company's Web site.

In this exercise, you and a group of your fellow students will be asked to investigate phishing attacks. If you search the Web for *phishing*, be aware that your search may bring the attention of an active phisher. Therefore, do not give any data to any site that you visit as part of this exercise!

Source: Carlos_bcn/Fotolia

Your Order ID: "17152492"
Order Date: "09/07/12"
Product Purchased: "Two First Class Tickets to Cozumel"
Your card type: "CREDIT"
Total Price: "$349.00"

Hello, when you purchased your tickets you provided an incorrect mailing address.

See more details here

Please follow the link and modify your mailing address or cancel your order. If you have questions, feel free to contact us account@usefulbill.com

Figure 1
Fake Phishing Email

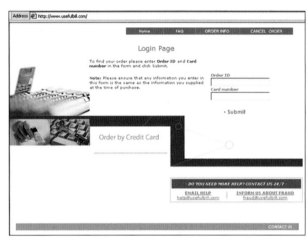

Figure 2
Fake Phishing Screen

DISCUSSION QUESTIONS

1. To learn the fundamentals of phishing, visit the following site: *www.microsoft.com/protect/fraud/phishing/symptoms.aspx*. To see recent examples of phishing attacks, visit *www.fraudwatchinternational.com/phishing/*.

   a. Using examples from these Web sites, describe how phishing works.

   b. Explain why a link that appears to be legitimate, such as *www.microsoft.mysite.com* may, in fact, be a link to a phisher's site.

   c. List five indicators of a phishing attack.

   d. Write an email that you could send to a friend or relative who is not well versed in technical matters that explains what phishing is and how that person can avoid it.

2. Suppose you received the email in Figure 1 and mistakenly clicked *See more details here*. When you did so, you were taken to the Web page shown in Figure 2.

List every phishing symptom that you find in these two figures and explain why it is a symptom.

3. Suppose you work for an organization that is being phished.

   a. How would you learn that your organization is being attacked?

   b. What steps should your organization take in response to the attack?

   c. What liability, if any, do you think your organization has for damages to customers that result from a phishing attack that carries your brand and trademarks?

4. Summarize why phishing is a serious problem to commerce today.

5. Describe actions that industry organizations, companies, governments, or individuals can take to help reduce phishing.

ACTIVE REVIEW

Use this Active Review to verify that you understand the ideas and concepts that answer the chapter's study questions.

Q10-1 What is the goal of information systems security?

Define *threat*, *vulnerability*, *safeguard*, and *target*. Give an example of each. List three types of threats and five types of security losses. Give different examples for the three rows of Figure 10-2. Summarize each of the elements in the cells of Figure 10-3. Explain why it is difficult to know the true cost of computer crime. Explain the goal of IS security.

Q10-2 How big is the computer security problem?

Explain why it is difficult to know the true size of the computer security problem in general and of computer crime in particular. List the takeways in this question and explain the meaning of each.

Q10-3 How should you respond to security threats?

Explain each of the elements in Figure 10-6. Define *IDS*, and explain why the use of an IDS program is sobering, to say the least. Define *brute force attack*. Summarize the characteristics of a strong password. Explain how your identity and password do more than just open doors on your computer. Define *cookie* and explain why using a program like CCleaner is a good example of the computer security trade-off.

Q10-4 How should organizations respond to security threats?

Name and describe two security functions that senior management should address. Summarize the contents of a security policy. Explain what it means to manage risk. Summarize the steps that organizations should take when balancing risk and cost.

Q10-5 How can technical safeguards protect against security threats?

List five technical safeguards. Define *identification* and *authentication*. Describe three types of authentication. Explain how SSL/TLS works. Define *firewall*, and explain its purpose. Define

malware and name six types of malware. Describe six ways to protect against malware. Summarize why malware is a serious problem. Explain how PRIDE is designed for security.

Q10-6 How can data safeguards protect against security threats?

Define *data administration* and *database administration*, and explain their difference. List data safeguards.

Q10-7 How can human safeguards protect against security threats?

Summarize human safeguards for each activity in Figure 10-12. Summarize safeguards that pertain to nonemployee personnel. Describe three dimensions of safeguards for account administration. Explain how system procedures can serve as human safeguards. Describe security monitoring techniques.

Q10-8 How should organizations respond to security incidents?

Summarize the actions that an organization should take when dealing with a security incident.

Q10-9 2026?

What, in the opinion of the author, is likely to happen regarding cyberwarfare in the next 10 years? Explain how the phrase *cat and mouse* pertains to the evolution of computer crime. Describe the types of security problems that are likely to occur in the next 10 years. Explain how the focus of computer criminals will likely change in the next 10 years. Explain how this is likely to impact smaller organizations, and you.

Using Your Knowledge with PRIDE

As an employee, investor, or advisor to PRIDE Systems, you can use the knowledge of this chapter to understand the security threats to which any business is subject. You know the need to trade off cost versus risk. You also know three categories of safeguards and the major types of safeguards for each. And, Zev Friedman you know what it means to design for security. You can also help ensure that PRIDE Systems employees and PRIDE users create and use strong passwords.

KEY TERMS AND CONCEPTS

MyMISLab™

To complete the problems with the ⭐, go to EOC Discussion Questions in the MyLab.

USING YOUR KNOWLEDGE

⭐ **10-1.** Visit the website of WeTransfer (https://www.wetransfer.com/documents/cookiepolicy.pdf) and examine its cookie policy.

    a. What's a cookie? Why does WeTransfer uses cookies?

    b. What type of cookies does WeTransfer use?

    c. What type of information is stored in cookies?

    d. Does the cookie policy include information on blocking or deleting cookies? What will be the impact if you decide to block or delete WeTransfer cookies?

⭐ **10-2.** Briefly describe DDOS attack and its purpose. What harm does it cause to the organization?

⭐ **10-3.** Suppose that you receive an email from your bank asking for your personal information in order to verify your account and your account will be deactivated if that information is not provided.

    a. What is this type of attack called? What harm does it cause?

    b. Search the web for "Social Engineering". What does it mean? How is it related to this type of attack?

c. What security measures will you take to prevent yourself from becoming a victim of this attack?

d. What security measures should be taken by a bank in order to minimize such attacks?

e. Is this a type of identity theft? List two other ways in which identity theft can occur.

f. Search the web for Vishing. List one similarity and difference between Vishing and this type of attack.

COLLABORATION EXERCISE 10

Using the collaboration IS you built in Chapter 2 (page 110), collaborate with a group of students to answer the following questions.

The purpose of this activity is to assess the current state of computer crime.

10-4. Search the Web for the term *computer crime* and any related terms. Identify what you and your teammates think are the five most serious recent examples. Consider no crime that occurred more than 6 months ago. For each crime, summarize the loss that occurred and the circumstances surrounding the loss, and identify safeguards that were not in place or were ineffective in preventing the crime.

10-5. Every college/university has its website, which provides vital information to both outsiders as well to insiders (teachers and for students).
   a. Find out who is the in-charge of managing your college/university website.
   b. List the possible security threats faced by your college/university website.
   c. Enlist the security measures taken by your college/university in order to overcome the above mentioned threats.

10-6. Go to *www.ponemon.org/blog/ponemon-institute-releases-2014-cost-of-data-breach-global-analysis* and download

the 2014 report (or a more recent report if one is available).
   a. Summarize the survey with regard to safeguards and other measures that organizations use.
   b. Summarize the study's conclusions with regard to the efficacy of organizational security measures.
   c. Does your team agree with the conclusions in the study? Explain your answer.

10-7. Suppose that you are asked by your boss for a summary of what your organization should do with regard to computer security. Using the knowledge of this chapter and your answer to questions 10-4 through 10-6 above, create a PowerPoint presentation for your summary. Your presentation should include, but not be limited to:
   a. Definition of key terms
   b. Summary of threats
   c. Summary of safeguards
   d. Current trends in computer crime
   e. What senior managers should do about computer security
   f. What managers at all levels should do about computer security

CASE STUDY 10

Hitting the Target

On December 18, 2013, Target Corporation announced that it had lost 40 million credit and debit card numbers to attackers. Less than a month later Target announced an additional 70 million customer accounts were stolen that included names, emails, addresses, phone numbers, and so on.

After accounting for some overlap between the two data losses, it turns out that about 98 million customers were affected.[20] That's 31 percent of all 318 million people in the United States (including children and those without credit cards). This was one of the largest data breaches in U.S. history.

These records were stolen from point-of-sale (POS) systems at Target retail stores during the holiday shopping season

(November 27 to December 15, 2013). If you were shopping at a Target during this time, it's likely your data was lost. Below is a short summary of how attackers got away with that much data.

How Did They Do It?

The attackers first used spear-phishing to infect a Target third-party vendor named Fazio Mechanical Services (refrigeration and HVAC services).[21] Attackers placed a piece of malware called Citadel to gather keystrokes, login credentials, and screenshots from Fazio users.[22] The attackers then used the stolen login credentials from Fazio to access a vendor portal (server)

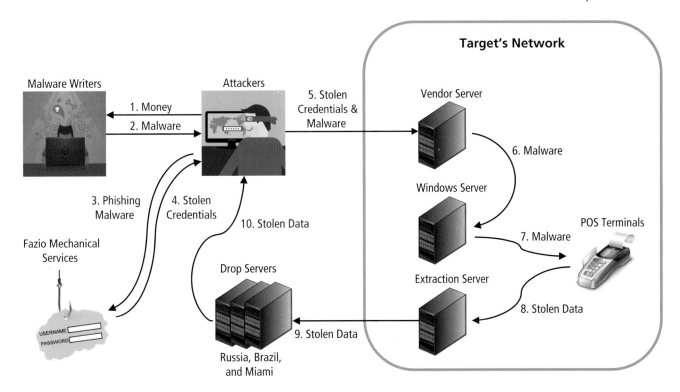

Figure 10-18
Target Data Breach

on Target's network. The attackers escalated privileges on that server and gained access to Target's internal network.

Once in, the attackers compromised an internal Windows file server. From this server the attackers used malware named Trojan.POSRAM (a variant of BlackPOS) to extract information from POS terminals. BlackPOS was developed by a 17-year-old from St. Petersburg, Russia, and can be purchased from underground sites for about $2,000.[23]

The customer data was continuously sent from the POS terminals to an extraction server within Target's network. It was then funneled out of Target's network to drop servers in Russia, Brazil, and Miami. From there the data was taken and sold on the black market.

The Damage

For the attackers, the "damage" was great. It's estimated that the attackers sold about 2 million credit cards for about $26.85 each for a total profit of $53.7M.[24] Not bad for a few weeks of work. Incentives for this type of criminal activity are substantial. Payoffs like these encourage even more data breaches.

Target, on the other hand, incurred much greater losses than the hacker's gains. It was forced to upgrade its payment terminals to support chip-and-PIN enabled cards (to prevent cloning cards from stolen information), which cost more than $100M. In 2015, Target lost a legal battle with banks over reimbursement of costs associated with the data breach, which

could exceed $160M. It also had to pay increased insurance premiums, pay legal fees, pay for consumer credit monitoring, and pay regulatory fines.

Target faced a loss of customer confidence and a drop in its revenues (a 46 percent loss for that quarter). Analysts put the direct loss to Target as high at $450M.[25] The company lost its CIO Beth Jacob and paid its CEO Gregg Steinhafel $16M to leave.[26]

The data breach affected more than just Target. The amount of media coverage related to the Target data breach likely accelerated the shift from magnetic swipe cards to EMV-compliant smart cards set to happen in 2015. This shift will force the replacement of 800 million payment cards and 14 million POS terminals at a cost of $7B.[27]

The good news is that the adoption of EMV-compliant smart cards will greatly reduce the $10B in credit card fraud that occurs each year. It will also likely reduce the amount of credit card theft by hackers because stolen credit card numbers would be of little value without the physical card.

Just like car accidents, data breaches may not be viewed as important until *after* they occur. The data breach affected Target enough that it upgraded its infrastructure, changed internal systems, and hired a Chief Information Security Officer (CISO).[28]

Will there be a more severe data breach in the future? Probably. Are organizations ready for it? Based on past performance, we won't be ready for it until *after* it happens.

QUESTIONS

10-8. Why did the attackers spear-phish a contractor to Target?

10-9. Explain how a third-party contractor could weaken an organization's overall security.

10-10. Describe how data was stolen from Target.

10-11. How might a data loss at one organization affect other organizations?

10-12. Explain why large organizations are attractive targets for attackers.

10-13. Why might chip-and-pin cards reduce this type of theft?

10-14. Why didn't Target have a CISO before the data breach?

MyMISLab™

Go to the Assignments section of your MyLab to complete these writing exercises.

10-15. Suppose you need to terminate an employee who works in your department. Summarize security protections you must take. How would you behave differently if this termination were a friendly one?

10-16. Suppose you were just notified that your company has experienced a major data breach. You've lost customer records, including usernames, email addresses, passwords, addresses, and phone numbers for all 500,000 of your customers. Estimate the direct costs for notification, detection, escalation, remediation, and legal fees. Suppose the attackers contact you and offer to destroy all records, tell no one about the data breach, and show you how to patch the security hole. The only trick is they want to be hired as a "consultant" and have $600,000 deposited into their European bank account. Would you pay the "consulting" fee? Justify your decision.

ENDNOTES

1. Bureau of Labor Statistics, U.S. Department of Labor, *2014–2015 Occupational Outlook Handbook*, accessed June 6, 2014, *www.bls.gov/ooh/*. Information about information security analysts can be found in the Computer and Information Technology section.
2. Mandiant (2013), APT1: Exposing One of China's Cyber Espionage Units. February 18, 2013, accessed July 24, 2015, http://intelreport.mandiant.com/Mandiant_APT1_Report.pdf.
3. Risk Based Security, "2014 Data Breach Trends," February 2015, RiskedBasedSecurity.com, accessed May 8, 2015, *www.riskbasedsecurity.com/reports/2014-YEDataBreachQuickView.pdf*.
4. Ponemon Institute, 2014 *Cost of Cyber Crime Study: United States*, October 2014.
5. Ponemon Institute, "2014 Global Report on the Cost of Cyber Crime," October 2014, accessed July 24, 2015, www.ponemon.org/library/2014-global-report-on-the-cost-of-cyber-crime.
6. John Pozadzides, "How I'd Hack Your Weak Passwords." *One Man's Blog*, last modified March 26, 2007, http://onemansblog.com/2007/03/26/how-id-hack-your-weak-passwords/. When Pozadzides wrote this in 2007, it was for a personal computer. Using 2013 technology, these times would be half or less. Using a cloud-based network of servers for password cracking would cut these times by 90 percent or more.
7. Dan Geer, "Cybersecurity as Realpolitik," *Black Hat USA 2014*, accessed April 1, 2015, *www.blackhat.com/us-14/video/cybersecurity-as-realpolitik.html*.
8. Violet Blue, "Yahoo CISO: End-to-End Mail Encryption by 2015," ZDNet.com, August 7, 2014, accessed April 1, 2015, *www.zdnet.com/article/yahoo-ciso-end-to-end-mail-encryption-by-2015*.

9. Andy Greenberg, "How Hackable Is Your Car?," *Wired.com*, August 6, 2014, accessed April 1, 2015, *www.wired.com/2014/08/car-hacking-chart*.
10. Danielle Walker, "Black Hat: Researcher Demonstrates How He Controlled Room Devices in Luxury Hotel," *SC Magazine*, August 6, 2014, accessed April 1, 2015, *www.scmagazine.com/black-hat-researcher-demonstrates-how-he-controlled-room-devices-in-luxury-hotel/article/365038*.
11. Hewlett-Packard Development Company, *Internet of Things Research Study*, September 2014, accessed April 1, 2015, *http://h20195.www2.hp.com/V2/GetDocument.aspx?docname=4AA5-4759ENW*.
12. *Verizon 2014 Data Breach Investigations Report*, accessed June 2014, *www.verizonenterprise.com/DBIR/2014/*.
13. For this reason, do *not* attempt to scan servers for fun. It won't take the organization very long to find you, and it will not be amused!
14. Randall Boyle and Jeffrey Proudfoot, *Applied Information Security*, 2nd ed. (Upper Saddle River, NJ: Pearson Education, 2014).
15. Accessed July 24, 2015, *www.chasepaymentech.com/faq_emv_chip_card_technology.html*.
16. Brian Krebs, "Home Depot: Hackers Stole 53M Email Addresses," *Krebs On Security*, November 7, 2014, accessed April 28, 2015, *http://krebsonsecurity.com/2014/11/home-depot-hackers-stole-53m-email-addresses*.
17. Mathew Schwartz, "Analysis: Home Depot Breach Details: Why Anti-Virus Didn't Stop POS Malware Attack," *Bank Info Security*, September 16, 2014, accessed April 28, 2015, *www.bankinfosecurity.com/analysis-home-depot-breach-details-a-7323/op-1*.
18. Accessed July 24, 2015, *www.paypal.com/webapps/mpp/emv*.

19. Tom Groenfeldt, "American Credit Cards Improving Security with EMV, At Last," *Forbes*, January 28, 2014, accessed April 28, 2015, *www.forbes.com/sites/tomgroenfeldt/2014/01/28/ american-credit-cards-improving-security-with-emv-at-last.*

20. Ben Elgin, "Three New Details from Target's Credit Card Breach," *Bloomberg Business*, March 26, 2014, accessed June 23, 2015, *www.bloomberg.com/bw/articles/2014-03-26/ three-new-details-from-targets-credit-card-breach.*

21. Brian Krebs, "Target Hackers Broke In via HVAC Company," *KrebsonSecurity.com*, February 5, 2014, accessed June 23, 2015, *http://krebsonsecurity.com/2014/02/ target-hackers-broke-in-via-hvac-company.*

22. Chris Poulin, "What Retailers Need to Learn from the Target Data Breach to Protect Against Similar Attacks," Security Intelligence, January 31, 2014, accessed June 23, 2015, *http://securityintelligence. com/target-breach-protect-against-similar-attacks-retailers/#. VYngl_lVikr.*

23. Swati Khandelwal, "BlackPOS Malware Used in Target Data Breach Developed by 17-Year-Old Russian Hacker," The Hacker News, January 17, 2014, accessed May 8, 2015, *http://thehackernews. com/2014/01/BlackPOS-Malware-russian-hacker-Target.html.*

24. Brian Krebs, "The Target Breach, by the Numbers," KrebsonSecurity. com, May 6, 2014, accessed May 8, 2015, *http://krebsonsecurity. com/2014/05/the-target-breach-by-the-numbers.*

25. Bruce Horovitz, "Data Breach Takes Toll on Target Profit," *USA Today*, February 26, 2014, accessed May 8, 2015, *www.usatoday.com/story/ money/business/2014/02/26/target-earnings/5829469.*

26. Fred Donovan, "Target Breach: A Timeline," FierceITSecurity.com, February 18, 2014, accessed May 8, 2015, *www.fierceitsecurity.com/ story/target-breach-timeline/2014-02-18.*

27. Dick Mitchell, "The EMV Migration Will Be a Rough, Risky Ride," PaymentSource.com, January 14, 2015, accessed May 23, 2015, *www.paymentssource.com/news/paythink/the-emv-migration-will-be-a- rough-risky-ride-randstad-exec-3020311-1.html.*

28. Dune Lawrence, "Target Taps an Outsider to Revamp IT Security After Massive Hack," *BusinessWeek*, April 29, 2014, accessed May 8, 2015, *www.businessweek.com/articles/2014-04-29/target-turns-to-an- outsider-for-cio-bob-derodes-to-revamp-it-security-after-massive-hack.*

Information Systems Management

"I've worked with him before, but not on an Android project." James Wu and Jared Cooper are discussing the pros and cons of outsourcing Amazon Fire phone development to India.

"But it was a phone application?" Jared trusts James to do his homework, but he wants to understand his risks in outsourcing.

"Right, and in native iOS. I'm not sure about his skills developing on Android."

"So tell me what you know about this guy."

"His name is Ajit Barid. At least that's the name of his company." James looks a little sheepish.

"That's not his name?"

"I don't know. Maybe. You know what Ajit Barid means?" He starts to smile…

"No. What?"

"Invincible cloud."

"Umm…probably not the name his mother gave him…or she was prophetic. James, this makes me nervous. I don't know anything about doing business in India. The guy takes our money and runs, what do we do?" Jared is down to business now.

"Well, we don't pay him until he delivers...or at least not much. But I've had a positive experience with him, and his references are good on a recent game development project."

"India is a long way away. What if he gives our code to somebody else? Or our ideas? What if we find some horrible bug in his code, and we can't find him to fix it? What if he just disappears? What if he gets two-thirds done and then loses interest...or goes to work on someone else's project?" Jared is on a roll.

"All are risks, I agree. But it will cost you four to six times as much to develop over here." James starts to list risks on the whiteboard.

"Well, it's been my experience that you get what you pay for in this life..."

"You want me to find some local developers we can outsource to?" James thinks local development is a poor choice but wants Jared to feel comfortable with the decision they reach.

"Yes, no, I mean no. I don't think so. How'd you meet him?"

"At a conference when he was working for Microsoft in its Hyderabad facility. He was programming SharePoint cloud features. When the iPad took off, he left Microsoft and started his own company. That's when I hired him to build the iOS app."

"That worked out OK?" Jared wants to be convinced.

"Yes, but it was one of his first jobs...he had to get it right for us."

"What do you think? What do you want to do?"

James ponders the questions. "Well, I think the biggest risk is his success. You know, the restaurant that gets the great reviews and then is buried in new customers and the kitchen falls apart."

"Doesn't he have more employees now?"

"Yes, he does, and I know he's a good developer, but I don't know whether he's a good manager."

"OK, what else?" Jared is all business.

"Well, Android development is different from iOS, which is what he used for the iPad. I guess I'd say inexperience with this dev environment would be another risk factor."

"What about money?"

"Well, like I said, we structure the agreement so we don't pay much until we know it all works."

"So what else do you worry about?" Jared wants to get all of James's concerns on the table.

"Loss of time. Maybe he gets distracted, doesn't finish the app, or hires someone else to do it, and they can't. And September rolls around and we find that, while we're not out any real money, we've lost most of a year of time."

"I don't like the sound of that."

"I don't know anything about doing business in India."

Image source: jiris/Fotolia

STUDY QUESTIONS

Q11-1 What are the functions and organization of the IS department?

Q11-2 How do organizations plan the use of IS?

Q11-3 What are the advantages and disadvantages of outsourcing?

Q11-4 What are your user rights and responsibilities?

Q11-5 2026?

"Neither do I," James responds while he adds schedule risk to the list.

"You think maybe we should bite the bullet and hire our own programmers?"

"Good heavens, no! No way! That would be incredibly expensive, we couldn't keep them busy, not yet, anyway, and I don't have the time to manage a software project nor the money to hire someone who does." James is certain about this.

"But what about long term?"

"Long term, maybe. We'll have to see what we have for budget and what our long-term dev needs are. That's a big step. We need to build infrastructure we don't have like testing facilities, hire developers, QA personnel, and managers. If we make PRIDE Systems the success we hope, we'll do that. But not yet."

"So?" Jared's tone shows he wants to wrap up this conversation.

James summarizes, "Let me finish the requirements document and then get a proposal and bid from Ajit as well as a local, domestic developer. We'll look at the proposals and bids and then make a decision. One problem, though..."

"What's that?"

"The local developer may outsource it anyway."

"You mean we pay the local developer to hire Ajit or his cousin?" Jared shakes his head.

"Something like that."

Jared gets up from the table to show James out of his office. "That's crazy."

"Maybe not. Let's see what we get."

CHAPTER PREVIEW

Information systems are critical to organizational success and, like all critical assets, need to be managed responsibly. In this chapter, we will survey the management of IS and IT resources. We begin by discussing the major functions and the organization of the IS department. Then we will consider planning the use of IT/IS. Outsourcing is the process of hiring outside vendors to provide business services and related products. For our purposes, outsourcing refers to hiring outside vendors to provide information systems, products, and applications. We will examine the pros and cons of outsourcing and describe some of its risks. Finally, we will conclude this chapter by discussing the relationship of users to the IS department. In this last section, you will learn both your own and the IS department's rights and responsibilities. We continue this discussion in 2026 with a new challenge: mobile devices at work.

Q11-1 What Are the Functions and Organization of the IS Department?

The major functions of the information systems department[1] are as follows:

- Plan the use of IS to accomplish organizational goals and strategy.
- Manage outsourcing relationships.
- Protect information assets.
- Develop, operate, and maintain the organization's computing infrastructure.
- Develop, operate, and maintain applications.

We will consider the first two functions in Q11-2 and Q11-3 of this chapter. The protection function was the topic of Chapter 10. The last two functions are important for IS majors, but less so for other business professionals; therefore, we will not consider them in this text. To set the stage, consider the organization of the IS department.

How Is the IS Department Organized?

Figure 11-1 shows typical top-level reporting relationships. As you will learn in your management classes, organizational structure varies depending on the organization's size, culture, competitive environment, industry, and other factors. Larger organizations with independent divisions will have a group of senior executives such as those shown here for each division. Smaller companies may combine some of these departments. Consider the structure in Figure 11-1 as typical.

The title of the principal manager of the IS department varies from organization to organization. A common title is **chief information officer, or CIO**. Other common titles are *vice president of information services, director of information services*, and, less commonly, *director of computer services*.

In Figure 11-1, the CIO, like other senior executives, reports to the *chief executive officer* (CEO), though sometimes these executives report to the *chief operating officer* (COO), who, in turn, reports to the CEO. In some companies, the CIO reports to the *chief financial officer* (CFO). That reporting arrangement might make sense if the primary information systems support only accounting and finance activities. In organizations such as manufacturers that operate significant nonaccounting information systems, the arrangement shown in Figure 11-1 is more common and effective.

The structure of the IS department also varies among organizations. Figure 11-1 shows a typical IS department with four groups and a data administration staff function.

Most IS departments include a *Technology* office that investigates new information systems technologies and determines how the organization can benefit from them. For example, today many organizations are investigating social media and elastic cloud opportunities and planning how they can use those capabilities to better accomplish their goals and objectives. An individual called the **chief technology officer, or CTO**, often heads the technology group. The CTO evaluates new technologies, new ideas, and new capabilities and identifies those that are most relevant to the organization. The CTO's job requires deep knowledge of information technology and the ability to envision and innovate applications for the organization.

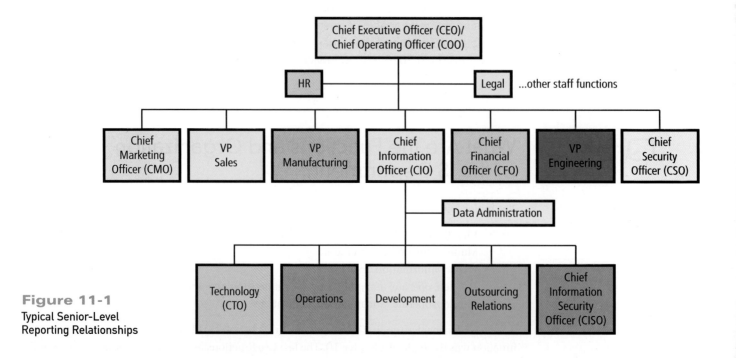

Figure 11-1
Typical Senior-Level
Reporting Relationships

The next group in Figure 11-1, *Operations*, manages the computing infrastructure, including individual computers, in-house server farms, networks, and communications media. This group includes system and network administrators. As you will learn, an important function for this group is to monitor the user experience and respond to user problems.

The third group in the IS department in Figure 11-1 is *Development*. This group manages the process of creating new information systems as well as maintaining existing ones.

The size and structure of the development group depend on whether programs are developed in-house. If not, this department will be staffed primarily by business and systems analysts who work with users, operations, and vendors to acquire and install licensed software and to set up the system components around that software. If the organization develops programs in-house, then this department will include programmers, test engineers, technical writers, and other development personnel.

The last IS department group in Figure 11-1 is *Outsourcing Relations*. This group exists in organizations that have negotiated outsourcing agreements with other companies to provide equipment, applications, or other services. You will learn more about outsourcing later in this chapter.

Figure 11-1 also includes a *Data Administration* staff function. The purpose of this group is to protect data and information assets by establishing data standards and data management practices and policies.

There are many variations on the structure of the IS department shown in Figure 11-1. In larger organizations, the operations group may itself consist of several different departments. Sometimes, there is a separate group for data warehousing and data marts.

As you examine Figure 11-1, keep the distinction between IS and IT in mind. *Information systems (IS)* exist to help the organization achieve its goals and objectives. Information systems have the five components we have discussed throughout this text. *Information technology (IT)* is simply technology. It concerns the products, techniques, procedures, and designs of computer-based technology. IT must be placed into the structure of an IS before an organization can use it.

Security Officers

After Target Corp. lost 98 million customer accounts, it created a new C-level security position to help prevent these type of losses.[2] Many organizations reeling from large-scale data breaches are creating similar executive security positions. A **chief security officer, or CSO**, manages security for all of the organization's assets: physical plant and equipment, employees, intellectual property, and digital. The CSO reports directly to the CEO. A **chief information security officer, or CISO**, manages security for the organization's information systems and information. The CISO reports to the CIO.

Both positions involve the management of staff, but they also call for strong diplomatic skills. Neither the CSO nor the CISO has line authority over the management of the activities he or she is to protect and cannot enforce compliance with the organization's security program by direct order. Instead, they need to educate, encourage, even cajole the organization's management into the need for compliance with the security program (discussed in Chapter 10, page 447).

What IS-Related Job Positions Exist?

IS departments provide a wide range of interesting and well-paying jobs. Many students enter the MIS class thinking that the IS departments consist only of programmers and tech support engineers. If you reflect on the five components of an information system, you can understand why this cannot be true. The data, procedures, and people components of an information system require professionals with highly developed interpersonal communications skills.

Figure 11-2 summarizes the major job positions in the IS industry. With the exception of tech support engineers and possibly test QA engineers, all of these positions require a 4-year degree. Furthermore, with the exception of programmer and test QA engineer, they all require business

Title	Responsibilities	Knowledge, Skill, and Characteristics Requirements
Business analyst, IT	Work with business leaders and planners to develop processes and systems that implement business strategy and goals.	Knowledge of business planning, strategy, process management, and technology. Can deal with complexity. See big picture but work with details. Strong interpersonal and communications skills needed.
Systems analyst	Work with users to determine system requirements, design and develop job descriptions and procedures, help determine system test plans.	Strong interpersonal and communications skills. Knowledge of both business and technology. Adaptable.
Programmer	Design and write computer programs.	Logical thinking and design skills, knowledge of one or more programming languages.
Test QA engineer	Develop test plans, design and write automated test scripts, perform testing.	Logical thinking, basic programming, superb organizational skills, eye for detail.
Technical writer	Write program documentation, help text, procedures, job descriptions, training materials.	Quick learner, clear writing skills, high verbal communications skills.
Tech support engineer	Help users solve problems, provide training.	Communications and people skills. Product knowledge. Patience.
Network administrator	Monitor, maintain, fix, and tune computer networks.	Diagnostic skills, in-depth knowledge of communications technologies and products.
Consultant, IT	Wide range of activities: programming, testing, database design, communications and networks, project management, security and risk management, social media, strategic planning.	Quick learner, entrepreneurial attitude, communication and people skills. Respond well to pressure. Particular knowledge depends on work.
Technical sales	Sell software, network, communications, and consulting services.	Quick learner, knowledge of product, superb professional sales skills.
Project manager, IT	Initiate, plan, manage, monitor, and close down projects.	Management and people skills, technology knowledge. Highly organized.
Manager, IT	Manage teams of technical workers and manage the implementation of new systems	Management and people skills, critical thinking, very strong technical skills.
Database administrator	Manage and protect database.	Diplomatic skills, database technology knowledge.
Business intelligence analyst	Collaborate with cross-functional teams on projects, analyze organizational data.	Excellent analytical, presentation, collaboration, database, and decision-making skills.
Chief technology officer (CTO)	Advise CIO, executive group, and project managers on emerging technologies.	Quick learner, good communications skills, business background, deep knowledge of IT.
Chief information officer (CIO)	Manage IT departments, communicate with executive staff on IT- and IS-related matters. Member of the executive group.	Superb management skills, deep knowledge of business and technology, and good business judgment. Good communicator. Balanced and unflappable.
Chief information security officer (CISO)	Manage IS security program, protect the organization's information systems and information, manage IS security personnel.	Deep knowledge of security threats, protections, and emerging security threat trends. Excellent communication and diplomacy skills. Good manager.

Figure 11-2

Job Positions in the Information Systems Industry

knowledge. In most cases, successful professionals have a degree in business. Note, too, that most positions require good verbal and written communications skills. Business, including information systems, is a social activity.

Median salaries and approximate salary ranges for the positions discussed in Figure 11-2 are shown in Figure 11-3.[3] According to the U.S. Social Security Administration, the median salary in 2013 for the average U.S. worker was $28,031.[4] Salary ranges for CTO, CIO, and CISO are higher than the other positions because they require many more years of experience.

Salaries for information systems jobs have a wide range. Higher salaries are for professionals with more experience, working for larger companies, and living in larger cities.[5] Do not expect to begin your career at the high end of these ranges. As noted, all salaries are for positions in the United States and are shown in U.S. dollars.

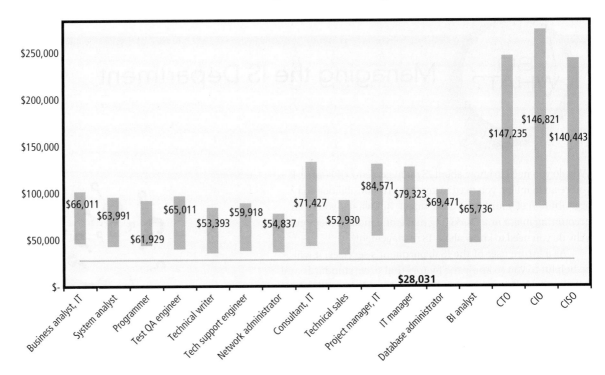

Figure 11-3
Salaries for Information
Systems Jobs

(By the way, for all but the most technical positions, knowledge of a business specialty can add to your marketability. If you have the time, a dual major can be an excellent choice. Popular and successful dual majors are accounting and information systems, marketing and information systems, and management and information systems.)

Q11-2 How Do Organizations Plan the Use of IS?

We begin our discussion of IS functions with planning. Figure 11-4 lists the major IS planning functions.

Align Information Systems with Organizational Strategy

The purpose of an information system is to help the organization accomplish its goals and objectives. In order to do so, all information systems must be aligned with the organization's competitive strategy.

Recall the four competitive strategies from Chapter 3. The first two strategies are that an organization can be a cost leader either across an industry or within an industry segment. Alternatively, for the second two strategies, an organization can differentiate its products or services either across the industry or within a segment. Whatever the organizational strategy, the CIO and the IS department must constantly be vigilant to align IS with it.

- Align information systems with organizational strategy; maintain alignment as organization changes.
- Communicate IS/IT issues to executive group.
- Develop/enforce IS priorities within the IS department.
- Sponsor steering committee.

Figure 11-4
Planning the Use of IS/IT

SO WHAT? Managing the IS Department

Why do you need to know about IS management? Of course, if you're an IS major, you need to know the responsibilities and organization of your future department. But what if you're an accounting major or a marketing major or a management major? Why do you need to know about IS management?

As a future user of the IS department's services, it will be helpful to you to know the factors that drive standards and policies. And, if you're a manager, this knowledge will help you guide your employees' behavior vis-à-vis the IS department. But let's take it a step further. Suppose you work for Zev at PRIDE Systems. Zev brought James over when he bought PRIDE Systems from Dr. Flores. Suppose Zev has some misgivings about James and asks you to help him. Zev would likely say something like "Do you think James knows his job?" or "Is James the right guy for us?"

If you had that assignment, how would you proceed? Answering the following questions will help you.

Source: Peshkova/Shutterstock

Questions

1. State the major functions of this new IS department. Explain how each of the functions defined in this chapter pertain to PRIDE.

2. Assume James hired Ajit Barid and, so far, he's worked out well. Even still, Zev, as PRIDE Systems' owner, and you, as a key employee, might be nervous about the risks of this decision. Describe those risks. Assess how significant they are. Explain how the decision to use an offshore contractor influences your assessment of James.

3. Assume that James decided to use a cloud vendor to provide PaaS functionality. Explain what this means and how it reflects on James's competence.

4. Given the decisions (in questions 1–3) that James has made,
   a. What will be the function and goals of the Operations group (see Figure 11-1)?
   b. What will be the function and goals of the Development group? What job descriptions will this group need to staff?
   c. What will be the function and goals of the Outsourcing Relations group?
   d. Assume James has not specified the need for a CTO. Is this a mistake?

5. Given your answers to questions 1–4, how would you respond to Zev's question "Is James right for us?"

Maintaining alignment between IS direction and organizational strategy is a continuing process. As strategies change, as the organization merges with other organizations, as divisions are sold, IS must evolve along with the organization. As you will learn in Chapter 12, maintaining that alignment is an important role for BPM and for COBIT, in particular.

Unfortunately, however, adapting IS to new versions of business processes is neither easy nor quick. For example, switching from in-house hosting to cloud hosting requires time and resources. Such a change must also be made without losing the organization's computing infrastructure. The difficulty of adapting IS is often not appreciated in the executive suite. Without a persuasive CIO, IS can be perceived as a drag on the organization's opportunities.

Communicate IS Issues to the Executive Group

This last observation leads to the second IS planning function in Figure 11-4. The CIO is the representative for IS and IT issues within the executive staff. The CIO provides the IS perspective during discussions of problem solutions, proposals, and new initiatives.

For example, when considering a merger, it is important that the company consider integration of information systems in the merged entities. This consideration needs to be addressed during the evaluation of the merger opportunity. Too often, such issues are not considered until after the deal has been signed. Such delayed consideration is a mistake; the costs of the integration need to be factored into the economics of the purchase. Involving the CIO in high-level discussions is the best way to avoid such problems.

Develop Priorities and Enforce Them Within the IS Department

The next IS planning function in Figure 11-4 concerns priorities. The CIO must ensure that priorities consistent with the overall organizational strategy are developed and then communicated to the IS department. At the same time, the CIO must also ensure that the department evaluates proposals and projects for using new technology in light of those communicated priorities.

Technology is seductive, particularly to IS professionals. The CTO may enthusiastically claim, "By moving all our reporting services to the cloud, we can do this and this and this..." Although true, the question that the CIO must continually ask is whether those new possibilities are consistent with the organization's strategy and direction.

Thus, the CIO must not only establish and communicate such priorities, but enforce them as well. The department must evaluate every proposal, at the earliest stage possible, as to whether it is consistent with the organization's goals and aligned with its strategy.

Furthermore, no organization can afford to implement every good idea. Even projects that are aligned with the organization's strategy must be prioritized. The objective of everyone in the IS department must be to develop the most appropriate systems possible, given constraints on time and money. Well-thought-out and clearly communicated priorities are essential.

Sponsor the Steering Committee

The final planning function in Figure 11-4 is to sponsor the steering committee. A **steering committee** is a group of senior managers from the major business functions that works with the CIO to set the IS priorities and decide among major IS projects and alternatives.

The steering committee serves an important communication function between IS and the users. In the steering committee, information systems personnel can discuss potential IS initiatives and directions with the user community. At the same time, the steering committee provides a forum for users to express their needs, frustrations, and other issues they have with the IS department.

One other task related to planning the use of IT is establishing the organization's computer-use policy. For more on computer-use issues, read the Ethics Guide on pages 470–471.

Typically, the IS department sets up the steering committee's schedule and agenda and conducts the meetings. The CEO and other members of the executive staff determine the membership of the steering committee.

Q11-3 What Are the Advantages and Disadvantages of Outsourcing?

Outsourcing is the process of hiring another organization to perform a service. Outsourcing is done to save costs, to gain expertise, and to free management time.

The father of modern management, Peter Drucker, is reputed to have said, "Your back room is someone else's front room." For instance, in most companies, running the cafeteria is not an essential function for business success; thus, the employee cafeteria is a "back room." Google wants to be the worldwide leader in search and mobile computing hardware and applications, all

Ethics Guide

PRIVACY VERSUS PRODUCTIVITY: THE BYOD DILEMMA?

I'm Justin, I work in operations. My boss asked me to meet with a committee the IS department created. The purpose of the committee is to determine our company's BYOD policy. Well, that's not quite right. The IS department will determine the policy, but they want to hear from active mobile users before they do so.

The first meeting we had was a real eye-opener. I thought we would be discussing which devices we could use and when. I see a few coworkers constantly checking social media, browsing the Web, or messaging their friends. They obviously need some guidance on what is and is not acceptable. No doubt, this needs to be addressed. But on my team, we live on our smartphones. We use them for everything, and they really do make us more productive. We're not giving them up.

I thought the meeting was going to be a discussion about how to restrict these devices to improve productivity. Boy, was I wrong. The IS folks started right into security issues. They worried about how they were going to secure company data from leaking out through new devices. They wanted to discuss the possibility of "configuring" people's personal devices. I was shocked. I get that they want to protect the company's data. I agree with that 100 percent. But, honestly, I thought they were being a little too cynical. From what I've seen, our people may be a little unfocused, but they're not criminal.

It's strange how fast things change. My grandfather worked for IBM in the 1960s. I saw him last weekend, and when I told him about this committee, he laughed. He said when he was working at IBM, he wanted to take an adding machine home once. I guess all it did was add and subtract; it didn't even multiply. Anyway, he wanted to take it home for the weekend to work on budgets, but to get it past security on the way out of the building, he had to have a permission slip signed by his boss and by the facilities department head. I guess the thing weighed 40 pounds. He said there was no way he could take a computer home then; it weighed a couple of tons and needed special power and an air-conditioned room.

"BYOD!" he said, "They want you to bring your own computer to work? Crazy. I couldn't even take an adding machine out, and they want you to bring your computer in?" Then he asked, "What keeps you from taking all of their secret data?"

"That's one of the things we talked about."

"I'll bet you did."

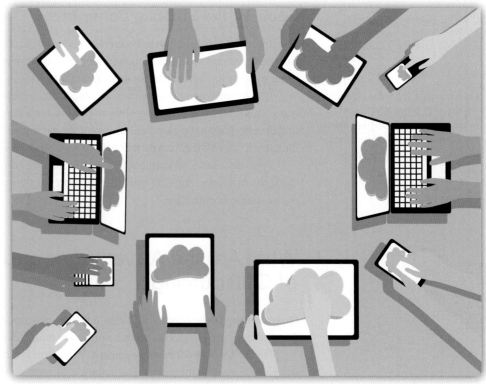

His story got me wondering when the data security problem started. Long before mobile devices, I think. Twenty years ago, you could copy data onto a CD and take it out of the office. Later, you could use a thumb drive or take it home on your laptop and, if you wanted to steal it, copy it onto one of your home computers. Now, we can take data on our own mobile devices if we want. So, mobile devices aren't a new data security threat.

Now that I think about it, maybe it isn't what I'm taking *out* that's a threat; maybe it's what I'm bringing *in*. The IS department doesn't know what apps I've got on my mobile device. That must be why they want to "configure" it. Maybe they want to make sure I'm not using an app to steal data. Or maybe they want to see that I don't have malware that could damage the corporate network. But they did mention that they want to add apps of their own to it as well.

That part makes me nervous. I heard that one company installs *key loggers*, you know, a program that records all the user's keystrokes into a file. The IS department regularly checks what owners are doing with *their own devices*. What prevents them from looking at my personal messages or pictures or seeing whom I talk to? This sounds like a big privacy issue. People won't like this at all.

Plus, on the committee, I've learned one plan is to install a program that IS can use to remotely wipe all the programs off mobile devices at their command. They say they need it in case we lose our devices. OK, I get that. But what if someone makes a mistake? Wipes out my device by accident? Or what if I quit? Or they fire me? Will they wipe all the programs off my mobile device then? Will they take my own programs?

Right now, I'm not sure what to do. I told my boss that our productivity and morale would tank if our personal devices were banned. I also told him that there would be a full-scale revolt if the IS department loaded any type of monitoring software on our devices. Honestly, I doubt they'll be able to get anything loaded onto any personal device. The most talented people we've got might just quit.

But from the IS perspective, they don't trust the programs I put on my mobile device. They've also got some legitimate concerns about data walking out the door. Maybe they should just buy me a smartphone and computer to use at work. Their hardware costs would go up, but they'd be able to control their devices. I'll still bring my mobile device to work, but I'll use my own wireless network, not theirs, and I won't do work with it. Is that why my boss wants me on this committee?

 # DISCUSSION QUESTIONS

1. Consider the decision to install monitoring software on an employee's personal device.
   a. Is this decision ethical according to the categorical imperative (pages 56–57)?
   b. Is this decision ethical according to the utilitarian perspective (pages 92–93)?
   c. How could monitoring software be used unethically by the IS department?
   d. How would users react if they found out that the IS department was reading their personal text messages or viewing their browsing history?
2. The IS department is concerned about data theft by employees. But employees are concerned about the IS department using monitoring software to violate their privacy.
   a. Which do you think is more likely to happen?
   b. Which do you think would cause more harm to the organization? Why?
3. In your opinion, which is the greater threat of mobile devices at work: the data the employees take *out* or the programs they bring *in*? Explain your answer.
4. Is it ethical for an organization to monitor its employees' behavior if it purchased the devices for them? Consider both the categorical imperative and utilitarian perspectives.

supported by ever-increasing ad revenue. It does not want to be known for how well it runs cafeterias. Using Drucker's sentiment, Google is better off hiring another company, one that specializes in food services, to run its cafeterias.

Because food service is some company's "front room," that company will be better able to provide a quality product at a fair price. Outsourcing to a food vendor will also free Google's management from attention on the cafeteria. Food quality, chef scheduling, plastic fork acquisition, waste disposal, and so on, will all be another company's concern. Google can focus on search, mobile computing, and advertising-revenue growth.

Outsourcing Information Systems

Many companies today have chosen to outsource portions of their information systems activities. Figure 11-5 lists popular reasons for doing so. Consider each major group of reasons.

Management Advantages

First, outsourcing can be an easy way to gain expertise. As you'll learn in Chapter 12, PRIDE Systems wants to build an Xbox prototype, but no one on their staff knows the particulars of coding for that device. Outsourcing can be an easy and quick way to obtain that expertise.

Another reason for outsourcing is to avoid management problems. At PRIDE Systems, building a large development and test team may be more than the company needs and require management skills that neither James nor Jared have. Outsourcing the development function saves them from needing this expertise.

Similarly, some companies choose to outsource to save management time and attention. Toshio at Falcon Security has the skills to manage a new software development project, but he may choose to not invest the time.

Note, too, that it's not just Toshio's time. It is also time from more senior managers who approve the purchase and hiring requisitions for that activity. And those senior managers, like Joni, will need to devote the time necessary to learn enough about server infrastructure to approve or reject the requisitions. Outsourcing saves both direct and indirect management time.

Cost Reduction

Other common reasons for choosing to outsource concern cost reductions. With outsourcing, organizations can obtain part-time services. Another benefit of outsourcing is to gain economies of scale. If 25 organizations develop their own payroll applications in-house, then when the tax law changes 25 different groups will have to learn the new law, change their software to meet the law, test the changes, and write the documentation explaining the changes. However, if those

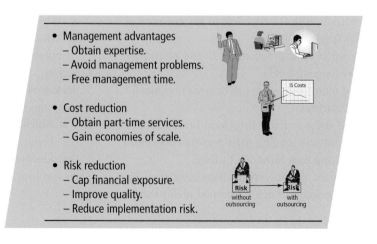

Figure 11-5

Popular Reasons for Outsourcing
IS Services

same 25 organizations outsource to the same payroll vendor, then that vendor can make all of the adjustments once, and the cost of the change can be amortized over all of them (thus lowering the cost that the vendor must charge).

Risk Reduction

Another reason for outsourcing is to reduce risk. First, outsourcing can cap financial risk. In a typical outsourcing contract, the outsource vendor will agree to a fixed price contract for services. This occurs, for example, when companies outsource their hardware to cloud vendors. Another way to cap financial risk is as James recommends: delay paying the bulk of the fee until the work is completed and the software (or other component) is working. In the first case, it reduces risk by capping the total due; in the second, it ensures that little money need be spent until the job is done.

Second, outsourcing can reduce risk by ensuring a certain level of quality or avoiding the risk of having substandard quality. A company that specializes in food service knows what to do to provide a certain level of quality. It has the expertise to ensure, for example, that only healthy food is served. So, too, a company that specializes in, say, cloud-server hosting knows what to do to provide a certain level of reliability for a given workload.

Note that there is no guarantee that outsourcing will provide a certain level of quality or quality better than could be achieved in-house. If it doesn't outsource the cafeteria, Google might get lucky and hire only great chefs. James might get lucky and hire the world's best software developer. But, in general, a professional outsourcing firm knows how to avoid giving everyone food poisoning or how to develop new mobile applications. And, if that minimum level of quality is not provided, it is easier to hire another vendor than it is to fire and rehire internal staff.

Finally, organizations choose to outsource IS in order to reduce implementation risk. Hiring an outside cloud vendor reduces the risk of picking the wrong brand of hardware or the wrong virtualization software or implementing tax law changes incorrectly. Outsourcing gathers all of these risks into the risk of choosing the right vendor. Once the company has chosen the vendor, further risk management is up to that vendor.

International Outsourcing

Choosing to use an outsourcing developer in India is not unique to PRIDE. Many firms headquartered in the United States have chosen to outsource overseas. Microsoft and Dell, for example, have outsourced major portions of their customer support activities to companies outside the United States. India is a popular source because it has a large, well-educated, English-speaking population that will work for 20 to 30 percent of the labor cost in the United States. China and other countries are used as well. In fact, with modern telephone technology and Internet-enabled service databases, a single service call can be initiated in the United States, partially processed in India, then Singapore, and finalized by an employee in England. The customer knows only that he has been put on hold for brief periods of time.

International outsourcing is particularly advantageous for customer support and other functions that must be operational 24/7. Amazon.com, for example, operates customer service centers in the United States, Costa Rica, Ireland, Scotland, Germany, Italy, Beijing, Japan, and India. During the evening hours in the United States, customer service reps in India, where it is daytime, can handle the calls. When night falls in India, customer service reps in Ireland or Scotland can handle the early morning calls from the east coast of the United States. In this way, companies can provide 24/7 service without requiring employees to work night shifts.

By the way, as you learned in Chapter 1, the key protection for your job is to become someone who excels at nonroutine symbolic analysis. Someone with the ability to find innovative applications of new technology is also unlikely to lose his or her job to overseas workers.

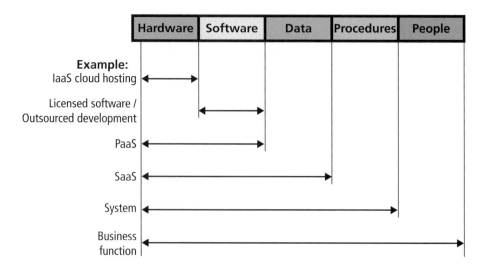

Figure 11-6
IS/IT Outsourcing Alternatives

What Are the Outsourcing Alternatives?

Organizations have found hundreds of different ways to outsource information systems and portions of information systems. Figure 11-6 organizes the major categories of alternatives according to information systems components.

Some organizations outsource the acquisition and operation of computer hardware. Electronic Data Systems (EDS) has been successful for more than 30 years as an outsource vendor of hardware infrastructure. Figure 11-6 shows another alternative: outsourcing the computers in the cloud via IaaS.

Acquiring licensed software, as discussed in Chapters 4 and 12, is a form of outsourcing. Rather than develop the software in-house, an organization licenses it from another vendor. Such licensing allows the software vendor to amortize the cost of software maintenance over all of the users, thus reducing that cost for all who use it. Another option is Platform as a Service (PaaS), which is the leasing of hardware with preinstalled operating systems as well as possibly DBMS systems. Microsoft's Azure is one such PaaS offering.

Some organizations choose to outsource the development of software. Such outsourcing might be for an entire application, as with PRIDE, or it could also be for making customizations to licensed software, as is frequently done with ERP implementations.

Yet another alternative is Software as a Service (SaaS), in which hardware and both operating system and application software are leased. Salesforce.com is a typical example of a company that offers SaaS.

It is also possible to outsource an entire system. PeopleSoft (now owned by Oracle) attained prominence by providing the entire payroll function as an outsourced service. In such a solution, as the arrow in Figure 11-6 implies, the vendor provides hardware, software, data, and some procedures. The company need provide only employee and work information; the payroll outsource vendor does the rest.

Finally, some organizations choose to outsource an entire business function. For years, many companies have outsourced to travel agencies the function of arranging for employee travel. Some of these outsource vendors even operate offices within the company facilities. Such agreements are much broader than outsourcing IS, but information systems are key components of the applications that are outsourced.

What Are the Risks of Outsourcing?

With so many advantages of outsourcing and so many different outsourcing alternatives, you might wonder why any company has in-house IS/IT functions. In fact, outsourcing presents significant risks, as listed in Figure 11-7.

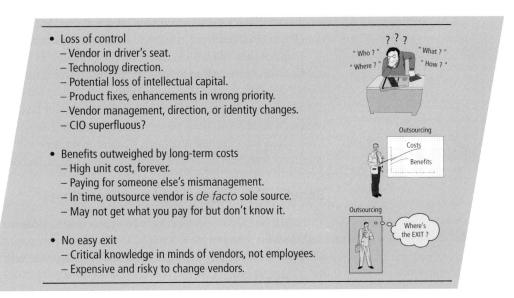

Figure 11-7
Outsourcing Risks

Loss of Control

Not everyone agrees on the desirability of outsourcing. For potential pitfalls, read the example in the Guide on pages 480–481.

The first risk of outsourcing is a loss of control. For PRIDE, once James contracts with Ajit, Ajit is in control. At least for several weeks or months. If he makes PRIDE a priority project and devotes his attention and that of his employees as needed, all can work out well. On the other hand, if he obtains a larger, more lucrative contract soon after he starts PRIDE, schedule and quality problems can develop. Neither Jared nor James has any control over this eventuality. If they pay at the end, they may not lose money, but they can lose time.

For service-oriented outsourcing, say, the outsourcing of IT infrastructure, the vendor is in the driver's seat. Each outsource vendor has methods and procedures for its service. The organization and its employees will have to conform to those procedures. For example, a hardware infrastructure vendor will have standard forms and procedures for requesting a computer, for recording and processing a computer problem, or for providing routine maintenance on computers. Once the vendor is in charge, employees must conform.

When outsourcing the cafeteria, employees have only those food choices that the vendor provides. Similarly, when obtaining computer hardware and services, the employees will need to take what the vendor supports. Employees who want equipment that is not on the vendor's list will be out of luck.

Unless the contract requires otherwise, the outsource vendor can choose the technology that it wants to implement. If the vendor, for some reason, is slow to pick up on a significant new technology, then the hiring organization will be slow to attain benefits from that technology. An organization can find itself at a competitive disadvantage because it cannot offer the same IS services as its competitors.

Another concern is a potential loss of intellectual capital. The company may need to reveal proprietary trade secrets, methods, or procedures to the outsource vendor's employees. As part of its normal operations, that vendor may move employees to competing organizations, and the company may lose intellectual capital as that happens. The loss need not be intellectual theft; it could simply be that the vendor's employees learned to work in a new and better way at your company, and then they take that learning to your competitor.

Similarly, all software has failures and problems. Quality vendors track those failures and problems and fix them according to a set of priorities. When a company outsources a system, it no longer has control over prioritizing those fixes. Such control belongs to the vendor. A fix that might be critical to your organization might be of low priority to the outsource vendor.

Other problems are that the outsource vendor may change management, adopt a different strategic direction, or be acquired. When any of those changes occur, priorities may change, and an outsource vendor that was a good choice at one time might be a bad fit after it changes direction. It can be difficult and expensive to change an outsource vendor when this occurs.

The final loss-of-control risk is that the company's CIO can become superfluous. When users need a critical service that is outsourced, the CIO must turn to the vendor for a response. In time, users learn that it is quicker to deal directly with the outsource vendor, and soon the CIO is out of the communication loop. At that point, the vendor has essentially replaced the CIO, who has become a figurehead. However, employees of the outsource vendor work for a different company, with a bias toward their employer. Critical managers will thus not share the same goals and objectives as the rest of the management team. Biased, bad decisions can result.

Benefits Outweighed by Long-Term Costs

The initial benefits of outsourcing can appear huge. A cap on financial exposure, a reduction of management time and attention, and the release of many management and staffing problems are all possible. (Most likely, outsource vendors promise these very benefits.) Outsourcing can appear too good to be true.

In fact, it *can be* too good to be true. For one, although a fixed cost does indeed cap exposure, it also removes the benefits of economies of scale. If PRIDE demand takes off and it suddenly needs 200 servers instead of 20, the using organization will pay 200 times the fixed cost of supporting one server. It is possible, however, that because of economies of scale, the costs of supporting 200 servers are far less than 10 times the costs of supporting 20 servers. If they were hosting those servers in-house, they and not the vendor would be the beneficiary.

Also, the outsource vendor may change its pricing strategy over time. Initially, an organization obtains a competitive bid from several outsource vendors. However, as the winning vendor learns more about the business and as relationships develop between the organization's employees and those of the vendor, it becomes difficult for other firms to compete for subsequent contracts. The vendor becomes the *de facto* sole source and, with little competitive pressure, might increase its prices.

Another problem is that an organization can find itself paying for another organization's mismanagement, with little knowledge that that is the case. If PRIDE outsources its servers, it is difficult for it to know if the vendor is well managed. The PRIDE investors may be paying for poor management; even worse, PRIDE may suffer the consequences of poor management, such as lost data. It will be very difficult for PRIDE to learn about such mismanagement.

No Easy Exit

The final category of outsourcing risk concerns ending the agreement. There is no easy exit. For one, the outsource vendor's employees have gained significant knowledge of the company.

They know the server requirements in customer support, they know the patterns of usage, and they know the best procedures for downloading operational data into the data warehouse. Consequently, lack of knowledge will make it difficult to bring the outsourced service back in-house.

Also, because the vendor has become so tightly integrated into the business, parting company can be exceedingly risky. Closing down the employee cafeteria for a few weeks while finding another food vendor would be unpopular, but employees would survive. Shutting down the enterprise network for a few weeks would be impossible; the business would not survive. Because of such risk, the company must invest considerable work, duplication of effort, management time, and expense to change to another vendor. In truth, choosing an outsource vendor can be a one-way street.

At PRIDE, if, after the initial application development, the team decides to change development vendors, it may be very difficult to do. The new vendor will not know the application code as well as the current one who created it. It may become infeasible in terms of time and money to consider moving to another, better, lower-cost vendor.

Choosing to outsource is a difficult decision. In fact, the correct decision might not be clear, but time and events could force the company to decide.

Q11-4 What Are Your User Rights and Responsibilities?

As a future user of information systems, you have both rights and responsibilities in your relationship with the IS department. The items in Figure 11-8 list what you are entitled to receive and indicate what you are expected to contribute.

Your User Rights

You have a right to have the computing resources you need to perform your work as proficiently as you want. You have a right to the computer hardware and programs that you need. If you process huge files for data-mining applications, you have a right to the huge disks and the fast processor that you need. However, if you merely receive email and consult the corporate Web portal, then your right is for more modest requirements (leaving the more powerful resources for those in the organization who require them).

You have a right to reliable network and Internet services. *Reliable* means that you can process without problems almost all of the time. It means that you never go to work wondering, "Will the network be available today?" Network problems should be a rare occurrence.

You also have a right to a secure computing environment. The organization should protect your computer and its files, and you should not normally even need to think about security. From time to time, the organization might ask you to take particular actions to protect your computer and files, and you should take those actions. But such requests should be rare and related to specific outside threats.

You have a right to participate in requirements meetings for new applications that you will use and for major changes to applications that you currently use. You may choose to delegate this right to others, or your department may delegate that right for you, but if so, you have a right to contribute your thoughts through that delegate.

You have a right to reliable systems development and maintenance. Although schedule slippages of a month or 2 are common in many development projects, you should not have to endure schedule slippages of 6 months or more. Such slippages are evidence of incompetent systems development.

Additionally, you have a right to receive prompt attention to your problems, concerns, and complaints about information services. You have a right to have a means to report problems and to know that your problem has been received and at least registered with the IS department. You have a right to have your problem resolved, consistent with established priorities. This means that

Figure 11-8
User Information Systems
Rights and Responsibilities

You have a right to:
- Computer hardware and programs that allow you to perform your job proficiently
- Reliable network and Internet connections
- A secure computing environment
- Protection from viruses, worms, and other threats
- Contribute to requirements for new system features and functions
- Reliable systems development and maintenance
- Prompt attention to problems, concerns, and complaints
- Properly prioritized problem fixes and resolutions
- Effective training

You have a responsibility to:
- Learn basic computer skills
- Learn standard techniques and procedures for the applications you use
- Follow security and backup procedures
- Protect your password(s)
- Use computers and mobile devices according to your employer's computer-use policy
- Make no unauthorized hardware modifications
- Install only authorized programs
- Apply software patches and fixes when directed to do so
- When asked, devote the time required to respond carefully and completely to requests for requirements for new system features and functions
- Avoid reporting trivial problems

an annoying problem that allows you to conduct your work will be prioritized below another's problem that interferes with his ability to do his job.

Finally, you have a right to effective training. It should be training that you can understand and that enables you to use systems to perform your particular job. The organization should provide training in a format and on a schedule that is convenient to you.

Your User Responsibilities

Recent news articles have focused on digital monitoring. You must understand your organization's internal and external privacy policies. See the Security Guide on pages 480–481.

You also have responsibilities toward the IS department and your organization. Specifically, you have a responsibility to learn basic computer skills and to learn the techniques and procedures for the applications you use. You should not expect hand-holding for basic operations. Nor should you expect to receive repetitive training and support for the same issue.

You have a responsibility to follow security and backup procedures. This is especially important because actions that you fail to take might cause problems for your fellow employees and your organization as well as for you. In particular, you are responsible for protecting your password(s). This is important not only to protect your computer but, because of intersystem authentication, also to protect your organization's networks and databases.

You have a responsibility for using your computer resources in a manner that is consistent with your employer's policy. Many employers allow limited email for critical family matters while at work but discourage frequent and long casual email. You have a responsibility to know your employer's policy and to follow it. Further, if your employer has a policy concerning use of personal mobile devices at work, you are responsible for following it.

You also have a responsibility to make no unauthorized hardware modifications to your computer and to install only authorized programs. One reason for this policy is that your IS department constructs automated maintenance programs for upgrading your computer. Unauthorized hardware and programs might interfere with these programs. Additionally, the installation of unauthorized hardware or programs can cause you problems that the IS department will have to fix.

You have a responsibility to install computer updates and fixes when asked to do so. This is particularly important for patches that concern security and backup and recovery. When asked for input to requirements for new and adapted systems, you have a responsibility to take the time necessary to provide thoughtful, complete responses. If you do not have that time, you should delegate your input to someone else.

Finally, you have a responsibility to treat information systems professionals professionally. Everyone works for the same company, everyone wants to succeed, and professionalism and courtesy will go a long way on all sides. One form of professional behavior is to learn basic computer skills so that you avoid reporting trivial problems.

Q11-5 2026?

Many changes and developments will have a major effect on the organizational management of IS and IT resources in the next 10 years. Most organizations will move their internal hardware infrastructure into the cloud. Sure, some companies will be concerned enough about security that they'll keep some data on their own, privately controlled servers, but vast amounts of hardware infrastructure will migrate to the cloud. Running a computer center for anyone other than a cloud vendor is not a promising career.

We will most certainly see the rise in the use of mobile devices at work. Mobile devices will become cheaper, more powerful, with dynamic, maybe even gamelike user experiences. They will be ubiquitous. Organizations will develop BYOD policies that meet their needs and strategies, and many will encourage employees to bring their own devices to work. Meanwhile, IoT (the Internet of Things) will offer the opportunity for innovation in operations, manufacturing, and supply chain management.

By 2026, organizations will use social media inside the organization in true Enterprise 2.0 style. Organizational knowledge management will be done using social media, and most projects will have a social media component. Social media sites will have a project component.

Meanwhile, organizations will continue to lose control, as summarized in the Ethics Guide on pages 470–471, while mobile devices are becoming even more popular. When employees come to work with their own computing devices that are just as powerful as any computer they have at work, and when those devices access networks that are paid for by the employees, how will the IS department maintain control?

For a few years, organizations may be able to maintain some semblance of control with restrictive BYOD policies. That policy will work for a while, but ultimately it's doomed. For one, at some point that policy will put employees at a competitive disadvantage. Employees will want to access the network using whatever hardware they have, wherever they happen to be. If they can't, their competitors will.

But there's a second reason that limiting access to the corporate network won't work. Employees will move off the network! "Ah, we can't access SharePoint from our iPads, so let's use my Google Drive instead of the corporate SharePoint site. I'll share my folder with the whole team, and then we can get to it using our own mobile devices. Here, I'll copy the data from the computer at work onto my Drive, and we can take it from there." Or "Let's create a Google+ circle." Or...

Now, all the corporate data is out on someone's Google Drive or Google+ account or somewhere else and has been shared with, well, who knows? Employee Jones made a mistake; instead of sharing her Google+ circle with her teammates at work, she shared it on a public circle. Now, anyone, or any crawler, that stumbles over that data has access to it.

By 2026, the most important change to the IS department in organizations will be cultural. With the increasing IS sophistication of senior management, the CIO will become, finally, a full-fledged member of the executive suite, and IS will be seen no longer as a hindrance on organizational strategy and growth but as a key player for gaining competitive advantage. The ubiquity of social media and mobile devices will focus attention on the role that IS can play in achieving organizational goals.

Security Guide

SELLING PRIVACY

When was the last time you cleared your Web browser history? We have all done it, and the reason for doing so varies from person to person. Most people would feel uncomfortable with others knowing about their online behavior, however benign it may be. In other words, we all want *privacy*, or the freedom from being observed by other people. All of us want the right to conceal or disclose information about ourselves as we see fit.

In a non-digital world, personal privacy breaches were limited to the unauthorized disclosure of physical documents or sharing of information via word-of-mouth conversations. Sharing documents was limited to how fast you could write and send letters. Nowadays, almost everything we do digitally can be tracked, traced, recorded, and distributed around the world in a matter of seconds. Your personal information can be disclosed to thousands, or even millions, of people instantaneously.

For example, if you tweet that you turned 21 years old last Friday, you've unwittingly given out your date of birth to everyone. This knowledge could then be used by unscrupulous attackers to commit financial fraud or identity theft. But that's not all. It turns out that data about you is valuable to other people. It's gathered, packaged, and sold just like any other commodity. That's right, not only can your privacy be violated fairly quickly, but your private data can also be collected and sold for a quick profit.

Who Watches the Watchers

Internet service providers (ISPs) have a tremendous amount of power. A relatively small number of ISPs provide Internet access to the vast majority of both private and commercial customers.

Unbeknownst to most consumers, ISPs have been known to aggregate and analyze the Web activities of their users. This practice is often frowned-upon by paying customers. A recent survey of users' feelings toward online privacy found that "80% of Americans are concerned about advertisers gaining access to their social media data; 61% said they would like to do more to keep their data secure."[6] Service providers are recognizing this new push for personal privacy and are looking for new ways to monetize it.

AT&T recently announced a new fiber-based service called GigaPower. GigaPower customers have the option to sign up for this speedy Internet service at a reduced rate (roughly $30 less) if they are willing to have their browsing activities monitored, compiled, and sold to other companies for marketing purposes. An AT&T representative recently made the following comment about this service: "We can offer a lower price to customers participating in AT&T Internet Preferences, because advertisers will pay us for the opportunity to deliver relevant advertising and offers tailored to our

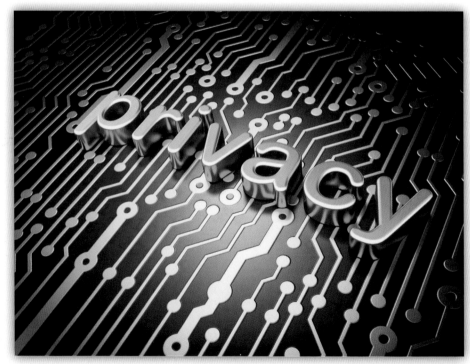

Source: Maksim Kabakou/Fotolia

customer's interests."[7] Some GigaPower consumers may find comfort in the fact that they *chose* to sell their data in the form of reduced Internet costs. Others will be irate that they have to pay more to protect what they see as their own personal and private data.

More Than Meets the ISP

Unauthorized analysis of users' Web traffic patterns isn't the only thing users have to worry about. Email is another major privacy concern. Several well-known email providers openly admit that they analyze the contents of their users' emails and share that data with government agencies. Yahoo!, for example, is attempting to reassure users that it values their email privacy by offering a complete end-to-end encrypted email service.[8] Social media sites are also rife with the scraping, packaging, and sale of user data to third parties. Interestingly, ISPs, email providers, and social media companies aren't the only ones aggregating information about people.

In a disturbing revelation, a new *60 Minutes* segment looked at data brokers and the sale of personal information; Steve Kroft stated, "No one even knows how many companies there are trafficking in our data. But it's certainly in the thousands, and would include research firms, all sorts of Internet companies, advertisers, retailers and trade associations. The largest data broker is Acxiom, a marketing giant that brags it has, on average, 1,500 pieces of information on more than 200 million Americans."[9]

What does that mean to you? It means that Acxiom has about 1,500 data points for two out of every three people you know.

Promoting Privacy

So what can you do to protect your privacy? You have already read about a few solutions. You can seek out email providers that offer encrypted end-to-end email service. If you want to protect your online privacy you could try to find an ISP, like AT&T, that is offering a premium privacy service. Or you could choose to use a public computer provided by your university or municipality (e.g., the local library).

If you are more tech-savvy, you may have heard of Tor (The Onion Router) networks, which allow you to connect your computer to a series of network relays and send your Internet traffic "through a series of virtual tunnels rather than making a direct connection, thus allowing both organizations and individuals to share information over public networks without compromising their privacy."[10] Alternatively, if you've got an entrepreneurial spirit, you could throw caution to the wind and find a company that will pay *you* to access your data and sell it for you![11]

 # DISCUSSION QUESTIONS

1. How do you feel about AT&T's strategy of offering customers cheaper Internet service in exchange for the sale of personal data to marketing companies? If you were an AT&T customer, would you choose this cheaper service in exchange for your privacy? Why?

2. Think about your email and social media activity for a 24-hour period. Identify all of the different types of data you send using these platforms. Try to identify all of the marketing opportunities that a company could exploit if it could access your data.

3. Tor networks are increasingly mentioned in the news as more and more Internet users attempt to maintain their privacy. Spend some time browsing the Tor Web site at *www.torproject.org* to learn more about the functionality of this service. Would you ever consider using Tor? Why or why not?

4. The quote in this guide from the *60 Minutes* story states that there are thousands of companies working to access and use private data for commercial purposes. Imagine that 5 or 10 years from now you are a manager at a company working to take advantage of this flood of user data. Would you feel comfortable accessing other people's personal data for commercial purposes knowing that they were probably unaware they were being tracked? How would you feel if it was your own personal data?

IS OUTSOURCING FOOL'S GOLD?

"People are kidding themselves. It sounds so good—just pay a fixed, known amount to some vendor for your computer infrastructure, and all your problems go away. Everyone has the computers they need, the network never goes down, and you never have to endure another horrible meeting about network protocols, https, and the latest worm. You're off into information systems nirvana....

"Except it doesn't work that way. You trade one set of problems for another. Consider the outsourcing of computer infrastructure. What's the first thing the outsource vendor does? It hires all of the employees who were doing the work for you. Remember that lazy, incompetent network administrator the company had—the one who never seemed to get anything done? Well, he's baaaaack, as an employee of your outsource company. Only this time he has an excuse, 'Company policy won't allow me to do it that way.'

"So the outsourcers get their first-level employees by hiring the ones you had. Of course, the outsourcer says it will provide management oversight, and if the employees don't work out, they'll be gone. What you're really outsourcing is middle-level management of the same IT personnel you had. But there's no way of knowing whether the managers they supply are any better than the ones you had.

"Also, you think you had bureaucratic problems before? Every vendor has a set of forms, procedures, committees, reports, and other management 'tools.' They will tell you that you have to do things according to the standard blueprint. They have to say that

because if they allowed every company to be different, they'd never be able to gain any leverage themselves, and they'd never be profitable.

"So now you're paying a premium for the services of your former employees, who are now managed by strangers who are paid by the outsource vendor, who evaluates those managers on how well they follow the outsource vendor's profit-generating procedures. How quickly can they turn your operation into a clone of all their other clients? Do you really want to do that?

"Suppose you figure all this out and decide to get out of it. Now what? How do you undo an outsource agreement? All the critical knowledge is in the minds of the outsource vendor's employees, who have no incentive to work for you. In fact, their employment contract probably prohibits it. So now you have to take an existing operation within your own

Source: AlexRoz/Shutterstock

company, hire employees to staff that function, and relearn everything you ought to have learned in the first place.

"Gimme a break. Outsourcing is fool's gold, an expensive leap away from responsibility. It's like saying, 'We can't figure out how to manage an important function in our company, so you do it!' You can't get away from IS problems by hiring someone else to manage them for you. At least you care about *your* bottom line."

 # DISCUSSION QUESTIONS

1. Hiring an organization's existing IS staff is common practice when starting a new outsourcing arrangement. What are the advantages of this practice to the outsource vendor? What are the advantages to the organization?

2. Suppose you work for an outsource vendor. How do you respond to the charge that your managers care only about how they appear to their employer (the outsource vendor), not how they actually perform for the organization?

3. Consider the statement "We can't figure out how to manage an important function in our company, so you do it!" Do you agree with the sentiment of this statement? If this is true, is it necessarily bad? Why or why not?

4. Explain how it is possible for an outsource vendor to achieve economies of scale that are not possible for the hiring organization. Does this phenomenon justify outsourcing? Why or why not?

5. In what ways is outsourcing IS infrastructure like outsourcing the company cafeteria? In what ways is it different? What general conclusions can you make about infrastructure outsourcing?

6. This guide assumes that the outsourcing agreement is for the organization's computing infrastructure. Outsourcing for software development, as PRIDE is doing, involves less direct involvement with the contractor. Explain how your answers to questions 1–5 would be different for software outsourcing.

7. How do your answers to questions 1–5 differ if the outsourcing agreement is just for PaaS resources?

ACTIVE REVIEW

Use this Active Review to verify that you understand the ideas and concepts that answer the chapter's study questions.

Q11-1 What are the functions and organization of the IS department?

List the five primary functions of the IS department. Define *CIO* and explain the CIO's typical reporting relationships. Name the four groups found in a typical IS department and explain the major responsibilities of each. Define *CTO* and explain typical CTO responsibilities. Explain the purpose of the data administration function. Define *CSO* and *CISO* and explain the differences in their responsibilities.

Q11-2 How do organizations plan the use of IS?

Explain the importance of strategic alignment as it pertains to IS planning. Explain why maintaining alignment can be difficult. Describe the CIO's relationship to the rest of the executive staff. Describe the CIO's responsibilities with regard to priorities. Explain challenges to this task. Define *steering committee* and explain the CIO's role with regard to it.

Q11-3 What are the advantages and disadvantages of outsourcing?

Define *outsourcing*. Explain how Drucker's statement "Your back room is someone else's front room" pertains to outsourcing. Summarize the management advantages, cost advantages, and risks of outsourcing. Differentiate among IaaS, PaaS, and SaaS, and give an example of each. Explain why international outsourcing can be particularly advantageous. Describe skills you can develop that will protect you from having your job outsourced. Summarize the outsourcing risks concerning control, long-term costs, and exit strategy.

Q11-4 What are your user rights and responsibilities?

Explain in your own words the meaning of each of your user rights as listed in Figure 11-8. Explain in your own words the meaning of each of your user responsibilities in Figure 11-8.

Q11-5 2026?

List the changes and developments that will have an effect on an organization's management of IS and IT. Summarize the predictions for mobile devices and IoT. Explain why loss of data control is inevitable and discuss why restrictive BYOD policies are not viable. Describe how employees may move off that network and discuss the security threat that occurs. Explain the organizational cultural change that will affect the IS department.

Using Your Knowledge with PRIDE

You now know the primary responsibilities of the IS department and can understand why it may implement the standards and policies that it does. You know the planning functions of IS and how they relate to the rest of your organization. You also know the reasons for outsourcing IS services, the most common and popular outsource alternatives, and the risks of outsourcing. Finally, you know your rights and responsibilities with regard to services provided by your IS department.

The knowledge of this chapter will help you understand what needs to be done, whether you work for PRIDE Systems, are a potential investor in PRIDE Systems, or are an advisor to a potential investor.

KEY TERMS AND CONCEPTS

Chief information officer (CIO)   464
Chief information security officer
  (CISO)   465
Chief security officer (CSO)   465
Chief technology officer (CTO)   464
  Green computing   485
Outsourcing   469
Steering committee   469

USING YOUR KNOWLEDGE

⭐ **11-1.** Refer to Figure 11-1. Find out who is in-charge of the information system department at your college/university. Also, find out about the levels of hierarchy in the department and the role played by each of them. How is the information system helping it to achieve its goals and objectives?

⭐ **11-2.** Suppose that you are working as Chief Technology Officer (CTO) for your college/university. What advice would you give regarding the implementation of new technologies, like social media or cloud computing, to gain competitive advantage. Also state if you would suggest outsourcing to the third party or develop an in-house team to implement the same.

⭐ **11-3.** Refer to Figure 11-2. As a student of MIS, what role do you expect to play in your professional life and why?

COLLABORATION EXERCISE 11

Using the collaboration IS you built in Chapter 2 (page 110), collaborate with a group of students to answer the following questions.

Green computing is environmentally conscious computing consisting of three major components: power management, virtualization, and e-waste management. In this exercise, we focus on power.

You know, of course, that computers (and related equipment, such as printers) consume electricity. That burden is light for any single computer or printer. But consider all the computers and printers in the United States that will be running tonight, with no one in the office. Proponents of green computing encourage companies and employees to reduce power and water consumption by turning off devices when not in use.

Is this issue important? Is it just a concession to environmentalists to make computing professionals appear virtuous? Form a team and develop your own, informed opinion by considering computer use at your campus.

11-4. Search the Internet to determine the power requirements for typical computing and office equipment. Consider laptop computers, desktop computers, CRT monitors, LCD monitors, and printers. For this exercise, ignore server computers. As you search, be aware that a *watt* is a measure of electrical power. It is *watts* that the green computing movement wants to reduce.

11-5. Estimate the number of each type of device in use on your campus. Use your university's Web site to determine the number of colleges, departments, faculty, staff, and students. Make assumptions about the number of computers, copiers, and other types of equipment used by each.

11-6. Using the data from items 11-4 and 11-5, estimate the total power used by computing and related devices on your campus.

11-7. A computer that is in screensaver mode uses the same amount of power as one in regular mode. Computers that are in sleep mode, however, use much less power, say, 6 watts per hour. Reflect on computer use on your campus and estimate the amount of time that computing devices are in sleep versus screensaver or use mode. Compute the savings in power that result from sleep mode.

11-8. Computers that are automatically updated by the IS department with software upgrades and patches cannot be allowed to go into sleep mode because if they are sleeping they will not be able to receive the upgrade. Hence, some universities prohibit sleep mode on university computers (sleep mode is never used on servers, by the way). Determine the cost, in watts, of such a policy.

11-9. Calculate the monthly cost, in watts, if:

   a. All user computers run full time night and day.

   b. All user computers run full time during work hours and in sleep mode during off-hours.

   c. All user computers are shut off during nonwork hours.

11-10. Refer to Figure 11-8 and ask your subject teacher as to what are his/ her rights and responsibilities as a user in your institution's information systems. Make a table and find out if there are any gaps between the rights and the responsibilities. If there is any gap, give suggestions to overcome the same.

CASE STUDY 11

iApp$$$$ 4 U

Let's suppose that you have a great idea for an iOS application. It doesn't matter what it is; it could be something to make life easier for college students or your parents or something to track healthcare expenses and payments for your grandparents. Whatever it is, let's assume that the idea is a great one.

First, what is the value of that idea? According to Raven Zachary, writing on the O'Reilly blog, it is zero.[12]

Nada. According to Zachary, no professional iPhone developer (he wrote this in 2008 about iPhone apps) will take equity or the promise of future revenue sharing in exchange for cash. There is too much cash-paying work. And ideas are only as good as their implementation, a fact that is true for every business project, not just iOS applications.

So, how can you go about getting your iOS application developed? You have three basic choices. You can go to a professional developer, one with a series of successes behind it. It will provide developers, designers, and project management. The cost depends, of course, on the requirements of your app, but according to Ryan Matzner, who manages fueled.com, a typical mobile commerce application will cost about $150K.[13]

If that's too high, your choices are either to attempt to do some of the work yourself, perhaps by managing an offshore developer, or to reduce your requirements. If you choose the former, you're engaging in a risky endeavor.

First, do as much work as you can. Read the stages in the systems development life cycle in Chapter 12. Determine how many of those stages you can do yourself. Unless you are already a skilled object-oriented programmer and comfortable writing in Objective-C or Apple's new language Swift, you cannot do the coding yourself. You might, however, be able to reduce development costs if you design the user interface and specify the ways that your users will employ it. You can also develop at least the skeleton of a test plan. You might also perform some of the testing tasks yourself.

If you have, let's round up, say, $30,000 that you're willing to invest, then you could outsource the development to a developer in the United States. If not, you have two other possible choices: outsource offshore or hire a computer science student. Elance is a clearinghouse for development experts; it lists developers, their locations, typical costs, and ratings provided by previous customers.[14] As you can see, you can hire developers in India, Russia, the Ukraine, Romania, and other countries. Costs start at $2,000 for a simple app, but again, that estimate does not include costs for design, graphics, and project management—nor the costs you will incur getting your application into the App Store.

What about hiring a local computer science student? The price might be right, certainly far less than a professional developer, but this alternative is fraught with problems. First, good students are in high demand, and, second, good students are, well, students. They need to study and don't have as much time to devote to your app. And, hard as it is to believe, some students are flakes. However, if you have a friend whom you trust, you might make this option work.

One other option is to divide and conquer. Break your really great idea up into smaller apps. Pick one that is sure to be a hit, and sell it cheaply, say, for $.99. Use the money that you earn from that application to fund the next application, one that you might sell for more.

QUESTIONS

11-11. What characteristics make a mobile application great? Describe at least five characteristics that compel you to buy applications. What characteristics would make an application easy and cheap to develop? Difficult and expensive?

11-12. Visit www.elance.com and identify five potential outsource vendors that you could use to develop an iOS app. Describe criteria you would use for selecting one of these vendors.

11-13. Explain why the costs of application coding are a third or less of mobile application development costs. Name other major cost sources.

11-14. Summarize the risks of hiring an offshore developer to write a mobile application. Explain ways to reduce those risks.

11-15. According to the Gartner Group, by 2018, less than .01 percent of consumer mobile applications will be considered a financial success by their developers.[15] Using your own knowledge and experience, explain three major reasons this might be so.

11-16. Explain how you think Google's purchase of Motorola Mobility changes the opportunity for iOS apps. In theory, does this purchase cause you to believe it would be wiser for you to develop on the Android or on the Windows 10 phone?

11-17. Search the Web for "Android developers" and related terms. Does it appear that the process of creating an Android app is easier, cheaper, or more desirable than creating an iOS app?

11-18. This case assumes that you have made the decision to develop an iOS application. Take an opposing view that developing a thin-client browser application would be a better decision. Explain how you would justify a thin-client app as a better decision.

11-19. Prepare a 1-minute summary of your experience with this exercise that you could use in a job interview to demonstrate innovative thinking. Give your summary to the rest of your class.

MyMISLab™

Go to the Assignments section of your MyLab to complete these writing exercises.

11-20. Consider the following statement: "In many ways, choosing an outsource vendor is a one-way street." Explain what this statement means. Do you agree with it? Why or why not? Does your answer change depending on what systems components are being outsourced? Why or why not?

11-21. A large multinational corporation experiences a severe data breach that results in the loss of customer data for nearly 250 million customers. The lost data included names, addresses, email addresses, passwords, credit card numbers, and dates of birth. During the first week, the entire company is in damage control mode. About 2 weeks after the data breach, the company's board of directors starts asking who was responsible. Heads are going to roll. They want to show their customers that they are taking steps so this won't happen again. Should they fire the CEO, CIO, CISO, CTO, database administrators, or line workers? Justify your choices.

ENDNOTES

1. Often, the department we are calling the *IS department* is known in organizations as the *IT department*. That name is a misnomer, however, because the IT department manages systems as well as technology. If you hear the term *IT department* in industry, don't assume that the scope of that department is limited to technology.
2. Kristin Burnham, "Target Hires GM Exec as First CISO," *InformationWeek*, June 11, 2014, accessed May 11, 2015, *www.informationweek.com/strategic-cio/team-building-and-staffing/target-hires-gm-exec-as-first-ciso/d/d-id/1269600*.
3. PayScale Inc., "Salary Data & Career Research Center (United States)," PayScale.com, accessed May 12, 2015, *www.payscale.com/research/US/Country=United_States/Salary*.
4. U.S. Social Security Administration, "Measures of Central Tendency For Wage Data," SSA.gov, accessed May 12, 2015, *www.ssa.gov/oact/cola/central.html*.
5. DHI Group Inc., "Dice Tech Salary Survey," Dice.com, January 22, 2015, accessed May 12, 2015, *http://marketing.dice.com/pdf/Dice_TechSalarySurvey_2015.pdf*.
6. Leo Mirani, "People Are Finally Worrying About Online Privacy—and Tech Firms Are Already Cashing In," QZ.com, March 5, 2015, accessed April 28, 2015, from *http://qz.com/350812/people-are-finally-worrying-about-online-privacy-and-tech-firms-are-already-cashing-in*.
7. Chris Neiger, "AT&T Inc. Now Wants You to Pay for Privacy—Here's How Much," *The Motley Fool*, February 22, 2015, accessed April 27,

2015, *www.fool.com/investing/general/2015/02/22/att-now-wants-you-to-pay-for-privacy-heres-how-muc.aspx*.
8. Swati Khandelwal, "End-to-End Encryption for Yahoo Mail Coming Next Year," *The Hacker News*, August 7, 2014, accessed April 28, 2015, *http://thehackernews.com/2014/08/end-to-end-encryption-for-yahoo-mail.html*.
9. Steve Kroft, "The Data Brokers: Selling Your Personal Information," *CBS News*, March 9, 2014, accessed April 28, 2015, *www.cbsnews.com/news/the-data-brokers-selling-your-personal-information*.
10. Accessed July 24, 2015, *www.torproject.org/about/overview.html.en*.
11. Laura Palet, "Privacy or Profit? These Firms Want to Help You Sell Your Data," NPR.org, September 9, 2014, accessed April 27, 2015, *www.npr.org/2014/09/09/346981606/privacy-or-profit-these-firms-want-to-help-you-sell-your-data*.
12. Raven Zachary, "Turning Ideas into iPhone Applications," *O'Reilly Media*, last modified November 21, 2008, *http://blogs.oreilly.com/iphone/2008/11/turning-ideas-into-application.html*.
13. Mary Hurd, "How Much Does It Cost to Develop an App?," Fueled.com, February 24, 2015, accessed May 12, 2015, *http://fueled.com/blog/how-much-does-it-cost-to-develop-an-app*.
14. "iPhone Development Experts Group," Elance, accessed May 12, 2015, *www.elance.com/groups/iPhone_Development_Experts/1115*.
15. accessed May 15, 2015, *www.gartner.com/newsroom/id/2648515*.

Information Systems Development

"Thanks for coming over on a Saturday morning. I just finished tennis, and the game went on longer than I expected. Anyway, forgive my appearance." Zev Friedman looks around the table.

"You must have won, Mr. Friedman. You look pleased." Michele is just getting to know PRIDE Systems' owner.

"Call me Zev. These other folks do. And yes, we won."

"Yes, sir." Michele is still a bit formal.

"OK, so, Jared, I understand you want to spend some real money. This morning you're going to tell me why, right?"

"That's why we're here, Zev. We've got a couple of options for you to consider. Here's a copy. I'm going to let James take you through it."

"I can hardly wait." Zev's mood is upbeat, but his demeanor and sleepy-eyed posture don't fool anyone. They know he's poised to detect errors or poor preparation.

"OK, Zev, you know that we were able to adjust our systems in order to support the new focus on multi-heat races." James is a little nervous as he starts.

"Yes, I do. And I understand that was your idea." Zev wants to make James comfortable with that compliment, and it works.

"It was a team discussion. Anyway, we were able to do that, and thanks to every-one's hard work, we're having success." James looks around the table as he speaks.

"It's a start, anyway." Zev knows they have a long way to go to establish a sustainable business.

"As you know, we only run on Apple and Android devices. We've done OK ignoring Surface and Windows phones."

"Yeah. I just don't understand Microsoft. They've blown every opportunity at mobile devices."

"Except, well, we think we can open the doors to an entirely new market if we start developing for the Xbox."

"The Xbox?"

"Yes, because these contests are very game-like. I'm spinning on my bike in my basement against 10 other players. They happen to be real people, but why don't we push the UI and use the Xbox to make it more visually exciting?"

"Interesting. Could be. So you want funds for Xbox development?"

"Yes, but take a look at the third page of the document we gave you. There are two ways to go. One is to develop using tools and technology specific to the Xbox. That would give us three separate code bases: Apple, Android, and Xbox."

"So?"

"We'll have essentially three different projects under way at the same time, with a lot of duplicated effort." From his voice and expression it's clear James hates the idea of duplicated effort.

"Hmph."

"But if we use—and I'll spare you the details—but if we use another, more ge-neric type of technology, called *html5* and *css3*, we can have a lot of common code. Not all, but a lot."

"Do spare me the details. I'll let Jared be my guide there. So have you got costs on this?"

"As shown on the third page, for the first—the Xbox only—somewhere between $100K and $175K."

"Big range." Zev sounds dubious.

"And, as shown on the fourth page, for reengineering all of our interfaces with html5, something between $225K and $300K." James sits back to watch Zev's reaction.

"We think we can open the doors to an entirely new market"

Image source: jiris/Fotolia

STUDY QUESTIONS

Q12-1 How are business processes, IS, and applications developed?

Q12-2 How do organizations use business process management (BPM)?

Q12-3 How is business process modeling notation (BPMN) used to model processes?

Q12-4 What are the phases in the systems development life cycle (SDLC)?

Q12-5 What are the keys for successful SDLC projects?

Q12-6 How can scrum overcome the problems of the SDLC?

Q12-7 2026?

"Jared, what do you think?" Zev looks at Jared.

"It's a question of how much we want to spend to position ourselves for the future, Zev." Jared knows its Zev's money and his decision.

"That it is, that it is," Zev ponders.

"Nicki, what's your thinking?" Zev moves in his seat to get a better look at her face.

"Xbox is a big market, no doubt about it. And we'd be the first to really get into that market space."

"Can you sell this, Michele?"

"Without a doubt. It would be huge. It has to be incredibly exciting, though. People expect Wow/Now on game devices."

Zev sits silently for a minute or two. Then he looks back at the group, each person at a time, as he speaks.

"Nope. I don't want to do either one. We're not ready for it. But what I do want to do is develop an Xbox prototype. Use whatever technology will get you there fastest. Then I want to try it out … not with all the bells and whistles, but enough that we can see how well this gamer direction will work. Jared, bring me back a plan to do that. James, I want you there too. Questions?"

Silence around the table until Jared speaks, "Thanks, Zev, we'll do just that."

CHAPTER PREVIEW

As a future business professional, you will be involved in the development of new technology applications to your business. You may take the lead, as Jared has been doing in developing PRIDE, or you might be an office manager who implements procedures and trains people in the use of systems such as PRIDE. Or you might become a business analyst and work as a liaison between users and technical staff. If nothing else, you may be asked to provide requirements and to test the system to ensure those requirements have been met. Whatever your role, it is important that you understand how processes and systems are developed and managed.

We begin in Q12-1 by clarifying what we're developing and introducing three different development processes. Then, in the next series of questions, we'll go into more detail for each. In Q12-2, we'll discuss business process management, and in Q12-3 you'll learn how to interpret process diagrams that you may be called upon to evaluate during your career. Next, we'll discuss the stages of the systems development life cycle in Q12-4, and then in Q12-5 summarize the keys to successful SDLC project management. Q12-6 then presents a newer, possibly superior development process known as scrum, and we'll wrap up this chapter in Q12-7 with a discussion of how information systems careers are likely to change between now and 2026.

Q12-1 How Are Business Processes, IS, and Applications Developed?

Many business professionals become confused when discussing business processes, information systems, and applications. You can avoid this confusion by understanding that they are different, by knowing those differences, and by realizing how they relate to each other. That knowledge will make it easier for you to appreciate the ways that processes, systems, and applications are developed and, in turn, help you be more effective as a team member on development projects.

How Do Business Processes, Information Systems, and Applications Differ and Relate?

As you learned in Chapter 3, a business process consists of one or more activities. For example, Figure 12-1 shows activities in an ordering business process: A quotation is prepared and, assuming the customer accepts those terms, the order is processed. Inventory availability is verified, customer credit is checked, special terms, if any, are approved, and then the order is processed and shipped. Each of these activities includes many tasks, some of which involve processing exceptions (only part of the order is available, for example), but those exceptions are not shown.

The activities in a business process often involve information systems. In Figure 12-1, for example, all of the activities except Approve Special Terms use an information system. (For this example, we'll assume that special terms are rare and approved by having a salesperson walk down the hallway to the sales manager.) Each of these information systems has the five components that we've repeatedly discussed. The actors or participants in the business process are the users of the information systems. They employ IS procedures to use information systems to accomplish tasks in process activities.

Each of these information systems contains a software component. Developing software nearly always involves the data component, and it often involves the specification and characteristics of hardware (e.g., mobile devices). Consequently, we define the term **application** to mean a combination of hardware, software, and data components that accomplishes a set of requirements. In Figure 12-1, the Customer Credit IS contains an application that processes a customer database to approve or reject credit requests.

As you can see from the example in Figure 12-1, this one business process uses four different IS. In general, we can say that a single business process relates to one or more information systems. However, notice that not all process activities use an IS; some require just manual tasks. In Figure 12-1, the Approve Special Terms activity uses no IS. Instead, as stated, salespeople walk down the hallway to ask their manager if terms are acceptable. In some cases (not in this example, however), it is possible for none of the activities to use an IS, in which case the entire business process is manual.

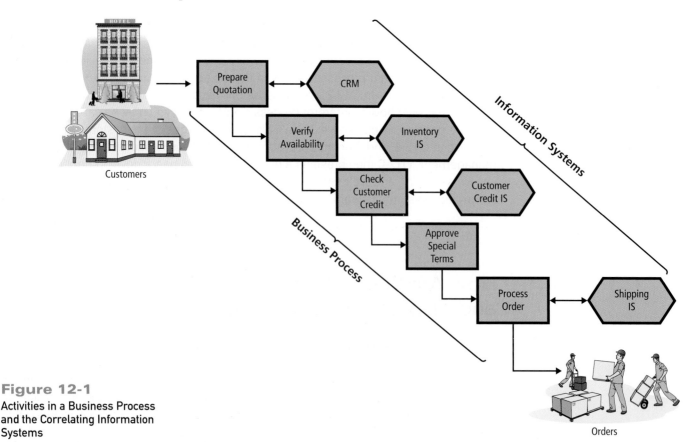

Figure 12-1

Activities in a Business Process and the Correlating Information Systems

Figure 12-2

Relationship of Business Processes and Information Systems

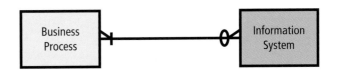

Now, consider any of the information systems in Figure 12-1, say, the Inventory IS. In addition to providing features and functions to verify item availability, that IS has other features that support additional business processes. For example, the Inventory IS supports the item ordering process, the item stocking process, the item backorder process, and more. So, even though we cannot see it from Figure 12-1, we can correctly infer that IS supports many business processes. Further, every IS supports at least one business process; if it did not, it would have little utility to the organization that pays for it.

We can use the terminology of Chapter 5 to summarize these statements and state that the relationship of business processes and information systems is many-to-many. One business process can potentially use many IS, and a single IS can support potentially many business processes. Furthermore, a business process is not required to use an IS, but every IS supports at least one business process. Figure 12-2 shows the process/information system relationship using an entity-relationship diagram.

Every information system has at least one application because every IS includes a software component. We could further investigate the relationship between IS and applications, but that relationship is beyond the scope of this text.

So, to summarize:

1. Business processes, information systems, and applications have different characteristics and components.
2. The relationship of business processes to information systems is many-to-many, or N:M. A business process need not relate to any information system, but an information system relates to at least one business process.
3. Every IS has at least one application because every IS has a software component.

When you participate in development meetings, you'll sometimes hear people confuse these terms. They'll quickly switch back and forth among processes, systems, and applications without knowing that they've changed terms and contexts. With these understandings, you can add value to your team simply by clarifying these differences.

Which Development Processes Are Used for Which?

A fourth way to develop applications is to steal them. Read the Security Guide on pages 526–527 to learn more.

Over the years, many different processes have been tried for the development of processes, IS, and applications. In this chapter, we'll investigate three: business process management (BPM), systems development life cycle (SDLC), and scrum.

Business process management is a technique used to create new business processes and to manage changes to existing processes. Except for start-ups, organizations already have processes, in one form or another, in varying levels of quality. If they did not, they wouldn't be able to operate. Therefore, BPM is, in most cases, used to manage the evolution of existing business processes from one version to an improved version. We'll discuss BPM in Q12-2 and Q12-3.

As shown in Figure 12-3, the systems development life cycle (SDLC) is a process that can be used to develop both information systems and applications. The SDLC achieved prominence in the 1980s when the U.S. Department of Defense required that it be used on all software and systems development projects. It is common, well-known, and often used but, as you'll learn, frequently problematic. You need to know what it is and when and when not to use it. We'll discuss the SDLC in Q12-4 and Q12-5.

Scrum is a new development process that was created, in part, to overcome the problems that occur when using the SDLC. Scrum is generic enough that it can be used for the development (and adaptation) of business processes, information systems, and applications. We'll discuss scrum in Q12-6.

Figure 12-3
Scope of Development
Processes

		Development Processes		
		BPM	**SDLC**	**Scrum**
Scope	Business Processes	✓		✓
	Information Systems		✓	✓
	Applications		✓	✓

Personnel that take the most active and important role for each of these processes are shown in Figure 12-4. A **business analyst** is someone who is well versed in Porter's models (see Chapter 3) and in the organization's strategies and who focuses, primarily, on ensuring that business processes and information systems meet the organization's competitive strategies. As you would expect, the primary focus of a business analyst is business processes.

Systems analysts are IS professionals who understand both business and information technology. They focus primarily on IS development, but are involved with business analysts on the management of business processes as well. Systems analysts play a key role in moving development projects through the SDLC or scrum development process.

Applications are developed by technical personnel such as programmers, database designers, test personnel, hardware specialists, and other technical staff. Systems analysts play a key role in developing applications requirements and in facilitating the work of the programmers, testers, and users.

Because applications development involves technical details that are beyond the scope of this introductory class, we will only be peripherally concerned with applications development here. If you have a technical bent, however, you should consider these jobs because they are absolutely fascinating and are in extremely high demand.

Q12-2 How Do Organizations Use Business Process Management (BPM)?

For the purposes of this chapter, we will extend the definition of business processes that we used in Chapter 3. Here we will define a **business process** as a network of activities, repositories, roles, resources, and flows that interact to accomplish a business function. As stated in Chapter 3,

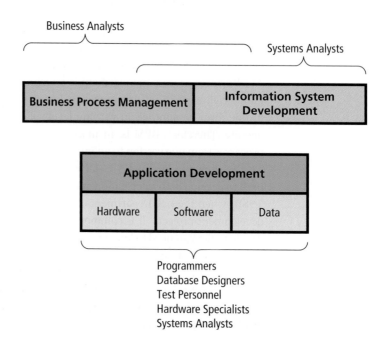

Figure 12-4
Role of Development Personnel

activities are collections of related tasks that receive inputs and produce outputs. A *repository* is a collection of something; an inventory is a physical repository and a database is a data repository. The new terms in this definition are **roles**, which are collections of activities, and **resources**, which are people or computer applications that are assigned to roles. Finally, a flow is either a **control flow** that directs the order of activities or a **data flow** that shows the movement of data among activities and repositories.

To clarify these terms, think of roles as job titles. Example roles are *salesperson, credit manager, inventory supervisor*, and the like. Thus, an organization might assign three people (resources) to the salesperson role, or it might create an information system (resource) to perform the credit manager role.

Why Do Processes Need Management?

Business processes are not fixed in stone; they always evolve. To understand why, suppose you are a salesperson working at the company having the ordering process shown in Figure 12-1. When you joined the firm, they taught you to follow this process, and you've been using for it 2 years. It works fine as far as you know, so why does it need to be managed? Fundamentally, there are three reasons: to improve process quality, to adapt to changes in technology, and to adapt to changes in business fundamentals. Consider each.

Improve Process Quality

As you learned in Chapter 7, process quality has two dimensions: efficiency (use of resources) and effectiveness (accomplish strategy). The most obvious reason for changing a process is that it has efficiency or effectiveness problems. Consider a sales process. If the organization's goal is to provide high-quality service, then if the process takes too long or if it rejects credit inappropriately, it is ineffective and needs to be changed.

With regard to efficiency, the process may use its resources poorly. For example, according to Figure 12-1, salespeople verify product availability before checking customer credit. If checking availability means nothing more than querying an information system for inventory levels, that sequence makes sense. But suppose that checking availability means that someone in operations needs not only to verify inventory levels, but also to verify that the goods can be shipped to arrive on time. If the order delivery is complex, say, the order is for a large number of products that have to be shipped from three different warehouses, an hour or two of labor may be required to verify shipping schedules.

After verifying shipping, the next step is to verify credit. If it turns out the customer has insufficient credit and the order is refused, the shipping-verification labor will have been wasted. So, it might make sense to check credit before checking availability.

Similarly, if the customer's request for special terms is disapproved, the cost of checking availability and credit is wasted. If the customer has requested special terms that are not normally approved, it might make sense to obtain approval of special terms before checking availability or credit. However, your boss might not appreciate being asked to consider special terms for orders in which the items are not available or for customers with bad credit.

As you can see, it's not easy to determine what process structure is best. The need to monitor process quality and adjust process design, as appropriate, is one reason that processes need to be managed.

Change in Technology

Changing technology is a second reason for managing processes. For example, suppose the equipment supplier who uses the business process in Figure 12-1 invests in a new information system that enables it to track the location of trucks in real time. Suppose that with this capability the company can provide next-day availability of goods to customers. That capability will be of limited value, however, if the existing credit-checking process requires 2 days. "I can get the goods to you tomorrow, but I can't verify your credit until next Monday" will not be satisfying to either customers or salespeople.

Thus, when new technology changes any of a process's activities in a significant way, the entire process needs to be evaluated. That evaluation is another reason for managing processes.

Change in Business Fundamentals

A third reason for managing business processes is a change in business fundamentals. A substantial change in any of the following factors might result in the need to modify business processes:

- Market (e.g., new customer category, change in customer characteristics)
- Product lines
- Supply chain
- Company policy
- Company organization (e.g., merger, acquisition)
- Internationalization
- Business environment

To understand the implications of such changes, consider just the sequence of verifying availability and checking credit in Figure 12-1. A new category of customers could mean that the credit-check process needs to be modified; perhaps a certain category of customers is too risky to be extended credit. All sales to such customers must be cash. A change in product lines might require different ways of checking availability. A change in the supply chain might mean that the company no longer stocks some items in inventory but ships directly from the manufacturer instead.

Or the company might make broad changes to its credit policy. It might, for example, decide to accept more risk and sell to companies with lower credit scores. In this case, approval of special terms becomes more critical than checking credit, and the sequence of those two activities might need to be changed.

Of course, a merger or acquisition will mean substantial change in the organization and its products and markets, as does moving portions of the business offshore or engaging in international commerce. Finally, a substantial change in the business environment, say, the onset of a recession, might mean that credit checking becomes vitally important and needs to be moved to first in this process.

What Are BPM Activities?

The factors just discussed will necessitate changes in business processes, whether the organization recognizes that need or not. Organizations can either plan to develop and modify business processes, or they can wait and let the need for change just happen to them. In the latter case, the business will continually be in crisis, dealing with one process emergency after another.

Figure 12-5 shows the basic activities in **business process management (BPM)**, a cyclical process for systematically creating, assessing, and altering business processes. This cycle begins by creating a model of the existing business process, called an **as-is model**. Then business users who are involved in the process (this could be you!) and business and systems analysts evaluate that model and make improvements. As you learned in Chapter 7, business processes can be improved by changing the structure of the process, by adding resources, or both. If the process structure is to be changed, a model of the changed process is constructed. Two common ways of adding resources to a process are to assign more people to process activities and to create or modify information systems.

The second activity in the BPM process is to create components. In this activity, the team designs changes to the business process at a depth sufficient for implementation. If the business process involves new information systems or changes to existing information systems then systems development projects are created and managed at this stage. Again, some activities involve IS, and some do not. For those that do, information systems procedures need to be created to enable users to accomplish their process tasks.

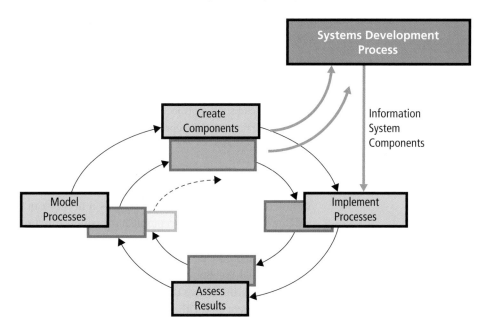

Figure 12-5
Four Stages of BPM

Implementing the new or changed process is the third activity in BPM. Here process actors are trained on the activities that they will perform and on the IS procedures that they will use. Converting from an existing process to a new or revised one usually meets with employee resistance, as you learned with regard to ERP implementations in Chapter 7. Thus, an important activity for you during implementation is softening that resistance. We will discuss four different conversion alternatives in Q12-4, when we discuss the SDLC. These four strategies pertain equally well to process implementation.

Once the process has been implemented, well-managed organizations don't stop there. Instead, they create policy, procedures, and committees to continually assess business process effectiveness. The Information Systems Audit and Control Association has created a set of standard practices called **COBIT (Control Objectives for Information and related Technology)** that are often used in the assessment stage of the BPM cycle. Explaining these standards is beyond the scope of this discussion, but you should know that they exist. See *www.isaca.org/cobit* for more information.

When the assessment process indicates that a significant need for change has arisen, the BPM cycle is repeated and adjusted. New process models are developed, and components are created, implemented, and assessed.

Effective BPM enables organizations to attain continuous process improvement. Like quality improvement, process improvement is never finished. Process effectiveness is constantly monitored, and processes are adjusted as and when required.

By the way, do not assume that business process management applies only to commercial, profit-making organizations. Nonprofit and government organizations have business processes just as commercial ones do, but most of these processes are service-oriented rather than revenue-oriented. Your state's Department of Labor, for example, has a need to manage its processes, as does the Girl Scouts of America. BPM applies to all types of organizations.

Q12-3 How Is Business Process Modeling Notation (BPMN) Used to Model Processes?

One of the four stages of BPM, and arguably the most important stage, is to model business processes. Such models are the blueprint for understanding the current process and for designing new versions of processes. They also set the stage for the requirements for any information systems and applications that need to be created or adapted. If models are incomplete and incorrect, follow-on components cannot be created correctly. In this question, you will learn standard notation for creating process documentation.

Learning this standard notation is important to you because, as a business professional, you may be involved in modeling projects. Unless you become a business or systems analyst, you are unlikely to lead such a project, but as a user, you may be asked to review and approve models and you may participate as a representative of your department or area of expertise in the creation of new models.

Need for Standard for Business Processing Notation

As stated, we define a *business process* as a network of activities, repositories, roles, resources, and flows that interact to accomplish a business function. This definition is commonly accepted, but unfortunately dozens of other definitions are used by other authors, industry analysts, and software products. For example, IBM, a key leader in business process management, has a product called WebSphere Business Modeler that uses a different set of terms. It has activities and resources, but it uses the term *repository* more broadly than we do, and it uses the term *business item* for *data flow*. Other business-modeling software products use still other definitions and terms. These differences and inconsistencies can be problematic, especially when two different organizations with two different sets of definitions must work together.

Accordingly, a software-industry standards organization called the **Object Management Group (OMG)** created a standard set of terms and graphical notations for documenting business processes. That standard, called **Business Process Modeling Notation (BPMN)**, is documented at *www.bpmn.org*. A complete description of BPMN is beyond the scope of this text. However, the basic symbols are easy to understand, and they work naturally with our definition of business process. Hence, we will use the BPMN symbols in the illustrations in the chapter. All of the diagrams in this chapter were drawn using Microsoft Visio, which includes several BPMN symbol templates. Figure 12-6 summarizes the basic BPMN symbols.

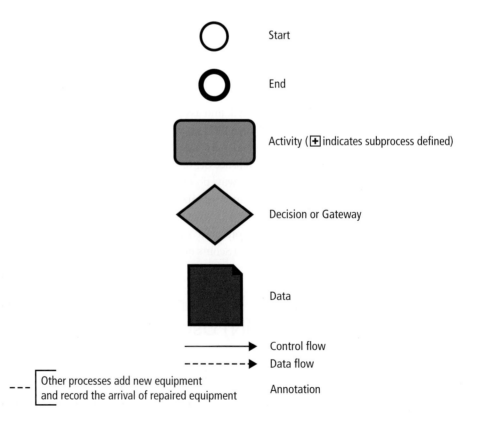

Figure 12-6
Business Process Management
Notation (BPMN) Symbols

Documenting the As-Is Business Order Process

Figure 12-7 shows the as-is, or existing, order process introduced in Figure 12-1. First, note that this process is a model, an abstraction that shows the essential elements of the process but omits many details. If it were not an abstraction, the model would be as large as the business itself. This diagram is shown in **swim-lane layout**. In this format, each role in the business process is given its own swim lane. In Figure 12-7, there are five roles, hence five swim lanes. All activities for a given role are shown in that role's swim lane. Swim-lane layout simplifies the process diagram and draws attention to interactions among components of the diagram.

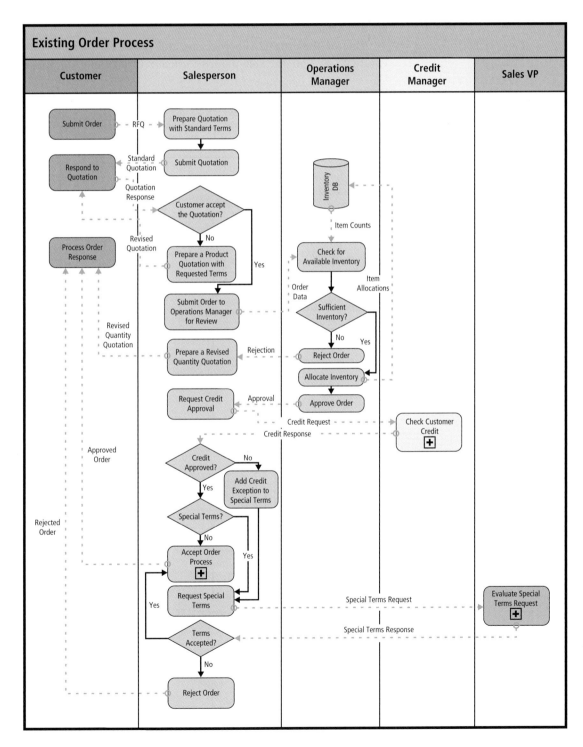

Figure 12-7
Existing Order Process

Two kinds of arrows are shown. Dotted arrows depict the flow of messages and data flows. Solid arrows depict the flow or sequence of the activities in the process. Some sequence flows have data associated with them as well. According to Figure 12-7, the customer sends an RFQ (request for quotation) to a salesperson (dotted arrow). That salesperson prepares a quotation in the first activity and then (solid arrow) submits the quotation back to the customer. You can follow the rest of the process in Figure 12-7. Allocate inventory means that if the items are available, they are allocated to the customer so that they will not be sold to someone else.

Diamonds represent decisions and usually contain a question that can be answered with yes or no. Process arrows labeled Yes and No exit two of the points of the diamond. Three of the activities in the as-is diagram contain a square with a plus (+) sign. This notation means that the activity is considered to be a subprocess of this process and that it is defined in greater detail in another diagram.

One of these three subprocesses, the Check Customer Credit subprocess, is shown in Figure 12-8. Note the role named *Customer Credit IS* in this subprocess. In fact, this role is

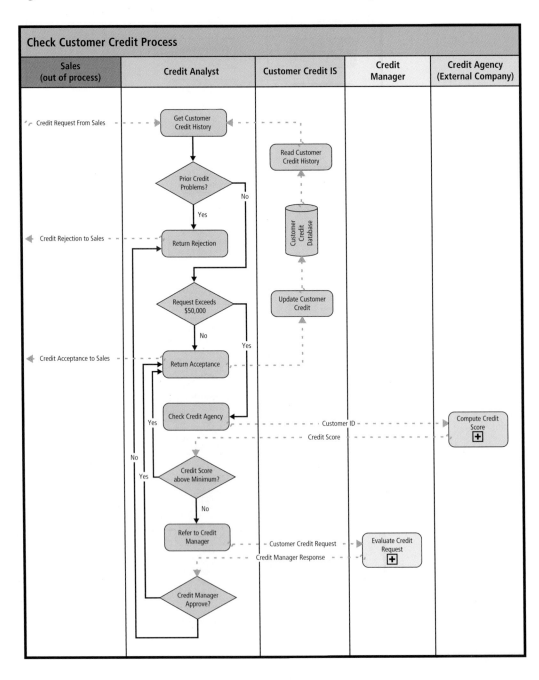

Figure 12-8
Check Customer Credit Process

performed entirely by an information system, although we cannot determine that fact from this diagram. Again, each role is fulfilled by some set of resources, either people or information systems or both.

Once the as-is model has been documented, that model can then be analyzed for problems or for improvement opportunities. For example, the process shown in Figure 12-7 has a serious problem. Before you continue, examine these figures and see if you can determine what they are.

The problem involves allocations. The Operations Manager role allocates inventory to the orders as they are processed, and the Credit Manager role allocates credit to the customer of orders in process. These allocations are correct as long as the order is accepted. However, if the order is rejected, these allocations are not freed. Thus, inventory is allocated that will not be ordered, and credit is extended for orders that will not be processed.

One fix (many are possible) is to define an independent process for Reject Order (in Figure 12-7 that would mean placing a box with a + in the Reject Order activity) and then designing the Reject Order subprocess to free allocations. Creating such a diagram is part of Exercise 12-3 in Using Your Knowledge (page 531).

Sometimes, BPMN diagrams are used to define process alternatives for discussion and evaluation. Another use is to document processes for employee training, and yet another use is to provide process requirements documentation for systems and application development. As a business professional, you may be asked to interpret and approve BPMN diagrams for any of these purposes.

Q12-4 What Are the Phases in the Systems Development Life Cycle (SDLC)?

The **systems development life cycle (SDLC)** is the traditional process used to develop information systems and applications. The IT industry developed the SDLC in the "school of hard knocks." Many early projects met with disaster, and companies and systems developers sifted through the ashes of those disasters to determine what went wrong. By the 1970s, most seasoned project managers agreed on the basic tasks that need to be performed to successfully build and maintain information systems. These basic tasks are combined into phases of systems development. As stated, SDLC rose to prominence when the U.S. Department of Defense required it on government contracts.

Different authors and organizations package the tasks into different numbers of phases. Some organizations use an eight-phase process, others use a seven-phase process, and still others use a five-phase process. In this book, we will use the following five-phase process:

1. Define System
2. Determine Requirements
3. Design System Components
4. Implement System
5. Maintain System

Figure 12-9 shows how these phases are related. Development begins when a business-planning process identifies a need for a new system. This need may come from a BPM design activity, or it might come from some other business planning process. For now, suppose that management has determined, in some way, that the organization can best accomplish its goals and objectives by constructing a new information system.

For the potential PRIDE Xbox system, Zev, the owner of the business, directs his team to create a prototype. That directive will start a systems development project.

Developers in the first SDLC phase—system definition—use management's statement of the system needs in order to begin to define the new system (for the Xbox version of PRIDE, this statement is based on experience with the prototype). The resulting project plan is the input to the

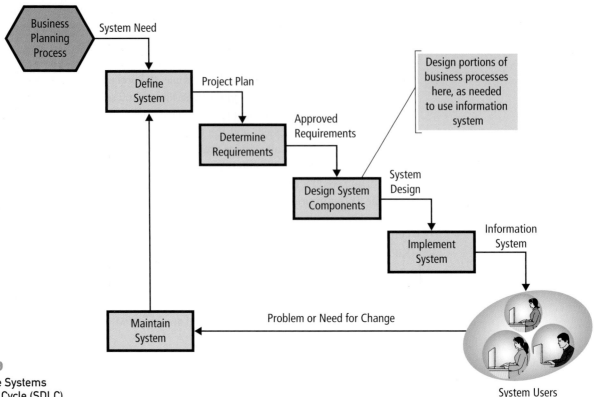

Figure 12-9
Five Phases of the Systems
Development Life Cycle (SDLC)

second phase—**requirements analysis**. Here, developers identify the particular features and functions of the new system. The output of that phase is a set of approved user requirements, which become the primary input used to design system components. In phase 4, developers implement, test, and install the new system.

Over time, users will find errors, mistakes, and problems. They will also develop new requirements. The description of fixes and new requirements is input into a system maintenance phase. The maintenance phase starts the process all over again, which is why the process is considered a cycle.

In the following sections, we will consider each phase of the SDLC in more detail.

Define the System

In response to the need for the new system, the organization will assign a few employees, possibly on a part-time basis, to define the new system, assess its feasibility, and plan the project. In a large organization, someone from the IS department leads the initial team, but the members of that initial team are both users and IS professionals. For small organizations, and for startups like PRIDE, the team will be led by IS-savvy managers like Jared.

Define System Goals and Scope

As Figure 12-10 shows, the first step is to define the goals and scope of the new information system. Information systems exist to facilitate an organization's competitive strategy by improving the quality of business processes. At this step, the development team defines the goal and purpose of the new system in terms of these reasons.

Consider PRIDE. The current systems are working for competitions, but the team wants an Xbox application. What, exactly, does that mean? What kind of an application? How fancy of a user interface is needed? In broad strokes, what is the Xbox application to do?

In other systems, the scope might be defined by specifying the users, or the business processes, or the plants, offices, and factories that will be involved.

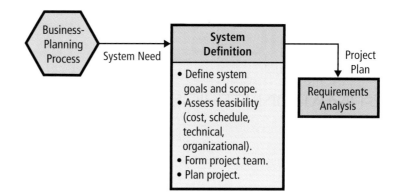

Figure 12-10
SDLC: System Definition Phase

Assess Feasibility

Once we have defined the project's goals and scope, the next step is to assess feasibility. This step answers the question "Does this project make sense?" The aim here is to eliminate obviously non-sensible projects before forming a project development team and investing significant labor.

Feasibility has four dimensions: *cost, schedule, technical,* and *organizational.* Because IS development projects are difficult to budget and schedule, cost and schedule feasibility can be only an approximate, back-of-the-envelope analysis. The purpose is to eliminate any obviously infeasible ideas as soon as possible.

Cost feasibility is an assessment of whether the anticipated benefits of the system are likely to justify the estimated development and operational costs. In some cases, it also means whether the project can realistically be done within the budget provided. Clearly, costs depend on the scope of the project. Saying we're going to build an Xbox prototype with a game-like interface doesn't provide much for the team to go on. So, at this point, all the team can do is to make rough estimates. Given those estimates, the team can then ask, "Does this project make sense? Will we obtain sufficient return to justify these estimated costs?" At PRIDE, Zev most likely asked for a prototype because he didn't like the $100K to $300K range for developing the full system.

For a discussion of the ethical issues relating to cost estimates, see the Ethics Guide on pages 504–505.

Like cost feasibility, **schedule feasibility** is difficult to determine because it is hard to estimate the time it will take to build the system. However, if James and his team determine that it will take, say, no less than 6 months to develop the system and put it into operation, Jared and Zev can then decide if they can accept that minimum schedule. At this stage of the project, the organization should not rely on either cost or schedule estimates; the purpose of these estimates is simply to rule out any obviously unacceptable projects.

Technical feasibility refers to whether existing information technology is likely to be able to meet the needs of the new system. With regard to the Xbox prototype, the team would assess technical differences between the mobile devices it currently supports and the Xbox. For example, can an Xbox effectively connect to exercise equipment using the Ant protocol?

Finally, **organizational feasibility** concerns whether the new system fits within the organization's customs, culture, charter, or legal requirements. Dr. Flores, who developed the initial, medical application for PRIDE, did not sufficiently consider medical customs and culture. As a consequence, doctors avoided using it and he eventually had to sell the system to be used for a different purpose.

Form a Project Team

If the defined project is determined to be feasible, the next step is to form the project team. Normally the team consists of both IS professionals and user representatives. The project manager and IS professionals can be in-house personnel or outside contractors as described in Chapter 11.

Typical personnel on a development team are a manager (or managers for larger projects), business analysts, systems analysts, programmers, software testers, and users.

Ethics Guide

ESTIMATION ETHICS

A *buy-in* occurs when a company agrees to produce a system or product for less money than it knows the project will require. For example, when a vendor of development services agrees to build a system for, say, $50,000, when good estimating techniques indicate it would take $75,000. If the contract for the system or product is written for "time and materials," the project's sponsors will ultimately pay the $75,000 for the finished system. Or the project will fail once the true cost is known. If the contract for the system or product is written for a fixed cost, then the developer will absorb the extra costs. A vendor would use the latter strategy if the contract opens up other business opportunities that are worth the $25,000 loss.

Buy-ins always involve deceit. Most would agree that buying-in on a time-and-materials project, planning to stick the customer with the full cost later, is wrong. Opinions on buying-in on a fixed-priced contract vary. You know you'll take a loss, but why? To build intellectual capital for sale elsewhere? For a favor down the road? Or for some other unethical reason?

What about in-house projects? Do the ethics change if an in-house development team is building a system for use in-house? If team members know there is only $50,000 in the budget, should they start the project if they believe that its true cost is $75,000? If they do start, at some point senior management will either have to admit a mistake and cancel the project with a loss or find the additional $25,000. Project sponsors can state all sorts of reasons for such buy-ins. For example, "I know

the company needs this system. If management doesn't realize it and fund it appropriately, then we'll just force their hand."

These issues become even stickier if team members disagree about how much the project will cost. Suppose one faction of the team believes the project will cost $35,000, another faction estimates $50,000, and a third thinks $65,000. Can the project sponsors justify taking the average? Or should they describe the range of estimates?

Other buy-ins are more subtle. Suppose you are a project manager of an exciting new project that is possibly a career-maker for you. You are incredibly busy, working 6 days a week and long hours each day. Your team has developed an estimate for $50,000 for the project. A little voice in the back of your mind says that maybe not all costs for every aspect

Source: Gigra/Fotolia

504

of the project are included in that estimate. You mean to follow up on that thought, but more pressing matters in your schedule take precedence. Soon you find yourself in front of management, presenting the $50,000 estimate. You probably should have found the time to investigate the estimate, but you didn't. Is there an ethical issue here?

Or suppose you approach a more senior manager with your dilemma. "I think there may be other costs, but I know that $50,000 is all we've got. What should I do?" Suppose the senior manager says something like, "Well, let's go forward. You don't know of anything else, and we can always find more budget elsewhere if we have to." How do you respond?

You can buy-in on schedule as well as cost. If the marketing department says, "We have to have the new product for the trade show," do you agree, even if you know it's highly unlikely that you'll make the deadline? What if marketing says, "If we don't have it by then, we should just cancel the project." Suppose it's not impossible to make that schedule; it's just highly unlikely. How do you respond?

 DISCUSSION QUESTIONS

1. Assess the ethics of buying-in on a cost-and-materials project from both the perspective of the categorical imperative (pages 56–57) and utilitarianism (pages 92–93).
2. Are there circumstances in which buying-in on a cost-and-materials contract could be illegal? If so, state them.
3. Suppose you learn through the grapevine that your opponents in a competitive bid are buying-in on a time-and-materials contract. Does this change your answer to question 1?
4. Suppose you are a project manager who is preparing a request for a proposal on a cost-and-materials systems development project. What can you do to prevent buy-ins?
5. Under what circumstances do you think buying-in on a fixed-price contract is ethical? Use either the categorical imperative or utilitarian perspective or both. What are the dangers of this strategy?

6. Explain why in-house development projects are always time-and-materials projects.
7. Given your answer to question 5, assess the ethics of buying-in on an in-house project from the perspective of the categorical imperative and utilitarianism. Are there circumstances that will change your ethical assessment? If so, state what they are and why.
8. Suppose you ask a senior manager for advice as described in the guide. Does the manager's response absolve you of ethical responsibility? Suppose you ask the manager and then do not follow her guidance. What problems could result?
9. Explain how you can buy-in on schedule as well as costs.
10. For an in-house project, what is an ethical response to the marketing manager who says the project should be canceled if it will not be ready for the trade show? In your answer, suppose that you disagree with this opinion because you know the system has value regardless of whether it is done by the trade show.

Systems analysts are closer to IT and are a bit more technical than business analysts, though, as stated, there is considerable overlap in their duties and responsibilities. Both are active throughout the systems development process and play a key role in moving the project through it. Business analysts work more with managers and executives; systems analysts integrate the work of the programmers, testers, and users. Depending on the nature of the project, the team may also include hardware and communications specialists, database designers and administrators, and other IT specialists.

The team composition changes over time. During requirements definition, the team will be heavy with business and systems analysts. During design and implementation, it will be heavy with programmers, testers, and database designers. During integrated testing and conversion, the team will be augmented with testers and business users.

User involvement is critical throughout the system development process. Depending on the size and nature of the project, users are assigned to the project either full or part time. Sometimes users are assigned to review and oversight committees that meet periodically, especially at the completion of project phases and other milestones. Users are involved in many different ways. *The important point is for users to have active involvement and to take ownership of the project throughout the entire development process.*

The first major task for the assembled team is to plan the project. Team members specify tasks to be accomplished, assign personnel, determine task dependencies, and set schedules.

Determine Requirements

Determining the system's requirements is the most important phase in the SDLC process. If the requirements are wrong, the system will be wrong. If the requirements are determined completely and correctly, then design and implementation will be easier and more likely to result in success.

Sources of Requirements

Examples of requirements are the contents and the format of Web pages and the functions of buttons on those pages, or the structure and content of a report, or the fields and menu choices in a data entry form. Requirements include not only what is to be produced, but also how frequently and how fast it is to be done. Some requirements specify the volume of data to be stored and processed.

If you take a course in systems analysis and design, you will spend weeks learning techniques for determining requirements. Here, we will just summarize that process. Typically, systems analysts interview users and record the results in some consistent manner. Good interviewing skills are crucial; users are notorious for being unable to describe what they want and need. Users also tend to focus on the tasks they are performing at the time of the interview. Tasks performed at the end of the quarter or end of the year are forgotten if the interview takes place mid-quarter. Seasoned and experienced systems analysts know how to conduct interviews to bring such requirements to light.

As listed in Figure 12-11, sources of requirements include existing systems as well as the Web pages, forms, reports, queries, and application features and functions desired in the new system. Security is another important category of requirements.

If the new system involves a new database or substantial changes to an existing database, then the development team will create a data model. As you learned in Chapter 5, that model must reflect the users' perspective on their business and business activities. Thus, the data model is constructed on the basis of user interviews and must be validated by those users.

Sometimes, the requirements determination is so focused on the software and data components that other components are forgotten. Experienced project managers ensure consideration of requirements for all five IS components, not just for software and data. Regarding hardware, the team might ask: Are there special needs or restrictions on hardware? Is there an organizational

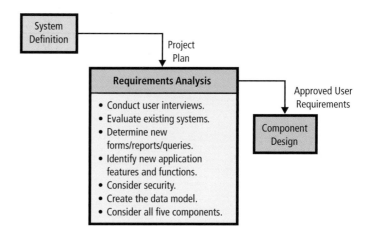

Figure 12-11
SDLC: Requirements
Analysis Phase

standard governing what kinds of hardware may or may not be used? Must the new system use existing hardware? What requirements are there for communications and network hardware?

Similarly, the team should consider requirements for procedures and personnel: Do accounting controls require procedures that separate duties and authorities? Are there restrictions that some actions can be taken only by certain departments or specific personnel? Are there policy requirements or union rules that restrict activities to certain categories of employees? Will the system need to interface with information systems from other companies and organizations? In short, requirements for all of the components of the new information system need to be considered.

These questions are examples of the kinds of questions that must be asked and answered during requirements analysis.

Role of a Prototype

Because requirements are difficult to specify, building a working prototype, as is being done for the PRIDE Xbox prototype, can be quite beneficial. Whereas future systems users often struggle to understand and relate to requirements expressed as word descriptions and sketches, working with a prototype provides direct experience. As they work with a prototype, users will assess usability and remember features and functions they have forgotten to mention. Additionally, prototypes provide evidence to assess the system's technical and organizational feasibility. Further, prototypes create data that can be used to estimate both development and operational costs.

To be useful, a prototype needs to work; mock-ups of forms and reports, while helpful, will not generate the benefits just described. The prototype needs to put the user into the experience of employing the system to do his or her tasks.

Prototypes can be expensive to create; however, this expense is often justified not only for the greater clarity and completeness of requirements, but also because parts of the prototype can often be reused in the operational system. Much of the code created for the Xbox prototype at PRIDE can be reused for the operational system, if that system is created. The cloud helps in that hardware and storage can be leased cheaply for a short term and need not be purchased and installed.

Unfortunately, systems developers face a dilemma when funding prototypes; the cost of the prototype occurs early in the process, sometimes well before full project funding is available. A common complaint is "We need the prototype to get the funds, and we need the funds to get the prototype." Unfortunately, no uniform solution to this dilemma exists, except applying experience guided by intuition. Again we see the need for nonroutine problem-solving skills.

Approve Requirements

Once the requirements have been specified, the users must review and approve them before the project continues. The easiest and cheapest time to alter the information system is in the requirements phase. Changing a requirement at this stage is simply a matter of changing a description.

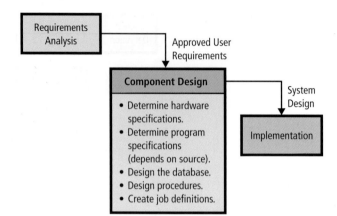

Figure 12-12
SDLC: Component Design Phase

Changing a requirement in the implementation phase may require weeks of reworking applications components and the database structure.

Design System Components

Each of the five components is designed in this stage. Typically, the team designs each component by developing alternatives, evaluating each of those alternatives against the requirements, and then selecting from among those alternatives. Accurate requirements are critical here; if they are incomplete or wrong, then they will be poor guides for evaluation.

Figure 12-12 shows that design tasks pertain to each of the five IS components. For hardware, the team determines specifications for what the system will need. (The team is not designing hardware in the sense of building a CPU or a disk drive.) Program design depends on the source of the programs. For off-the-shelf software, the team must determine candidate products and evaluate them against the requirements. For off-the-shelf with alteration programs, the team identifies products to be acquired off-the-shelf and then determines the alterations required. For custom-developed programs, the team produces design documentation for writing program code.

If the project includes constructing a database, then during this phase database designers convert the data model to a database design using techniques such as those described in Chapter 5. If the project involves off-the-shelf programs, then little database design needs to be done; the programs will have been coded to work with a preexisting database design.

Procedure design differs, depending on whether the project is part of a BPM process or part of a systems development process. If the former, then business processes will already be designed, and all that is needed is to create procedures for using the application. If the latter, then procedures for using the system need to be developed, and it is possible that business processes that surround the system will be needed as well.

With regard to people, design involves developing job descriptions for the various roles. These descriptions will detail responsibilities, skills needed, training required, and so forth.

System Implementation

The term **implementation** has two meanings for us. It could mean to implement the information systems components only, or it could mean to implement the information system and the business processes that use the system. As you read the following task descriptions, keep in mind that the tasks can apply to both interpretations of implementation. Tasks in the implementation phase are to build and test system components and to convert users to the new system and possibly new business processes (see Figure 12-13).

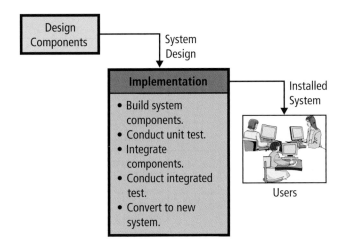

Figure 12-13
SDLC: Implementation Phase

Testing

Developers construct each of the components independently. They obtain, install, and test hardware. They license and install off-the-shelf programs; they write adaptations and custom programs as necessary. They construct a database and fill it with data. They document, review, and test procedures, and they create training programs. Finally, the organization hires and trains needed personnel. Once each component has been tested independently, the entire system is tested as an integrated whole.

Testing is important, time consuming, and expensive. A **test plan**, which is a formal description of the system's response to use and misuse scenarios, is written. Professional test engineers, called product quality assurance (PQA) test engineers, are hired for this task. Often, teams of these engineers are augmented by users as well.

System Conversion

Once the system has passed testing, the organization installs the new system. The term **system conversion** is often used for this activity because it implies the process of *converting* business activity from the old system to the new. Again, conversion can be to the new system only, or it can be to the new system, including new business processes.

Four types of conversion are possible: pilot, phased, parallel, and plunge. Any of the first three can be effective. In most cases, companies should avoid "taking the plunge"!

With **pilot installation**, the organization implements the entire system/business processes on a limited portion of the business, say, a single department. The advantage of pilot implementation is that if the system fails, the failure is contained within a limited boundary.

As the name implies, with **phased installation** the new system/business processes are installed in phases across the organization(s). Once a given piece works, then the organization installs and tests another piece of the system, until the entire system has been installed. Some systems are so tightly integrated that they cannot be installed in phased pieces. Such systems must be installed using one of the other techniques.

With **parallel installation**, the new system/business processes run parallel with the old one until the new system is tested and fully operational. Parallel installation is expensive because the organization incurs the costs of running both the existing and the new system/business processes. Users must work double-time, if you will, to run both systems. Then considerable work is needed to reconcile the results of the new with the old.

The final style of conversion is **plunge installation** (sometimes called *direct installation*). With it, the organization shuts off the old system/business processes and starts the new one. If the new system/business processes fail, the organization is in trouble: Nothing can be done until either the

	Hardware	Software	Data	Procedures	People
Design	Determine hardware specifications.	Select off-the-shelf programs. Design alterations and custom programs as necessary.	Design database and related structures.	Design user and operations procedures.	Develop user and operations job descriptions.
Implementation	Obtain, install, and test hardware.	License and install off-the-shelf programs. Write alterations and custom programs. Test programs.	Create database. Fill with data. Test data.	Document procedures. Create training programs. Review and test procedures.	Hire and train personnel.
	Integrated Test and Conversion				

Unit test each component

Note: Cells shaded gray represent software development.

Figure 12-14

Design and Implementation for the Five Components

new system/business processes are fixed or the old ones are reinstalled. Because of the risk, organizations should avoid this conversion style if possible. The one exception is if the new system is providing a new capability that will not disrupt the operation of the organization if it fails.

Figure 12-14 summarizes the tasks for each of the five components during the design and implementation phases. Use this figure to test your knowledge of the tasks in each phase.

Maintain System

With regard to information systems, **maintenance** is a misnomer; the work done during this phase is either to *fix* the system so that it works correctly or to *adapt* it to changes in requirements.

Figure 12-15 shows tasks during the maintenance phase. First, there needs to be a means for tracking both failures[1] and requests for enhancements to meet new requirements. For small systems, organizations can track failures and enhancements using word processing documents.

As systems become larger, however, and as the number of failure and enhancement requests increases, many organizations find it necessary to develop a tracking database. Such a database contains a description of the failure or enhancement. It also records who reported the problem,

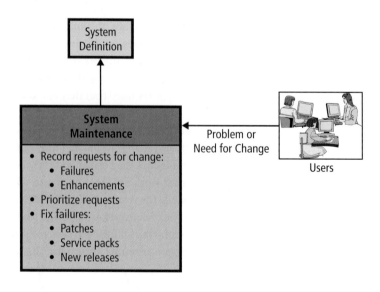

Figure 12-15

SDLC: System Maintenance Phase

who will make the fix or enhancement, what the status of that work is, and whether the fix or enhancement has been tested and verified by the originator.

Typically, IS personnel prioritize system problems according to their severity. They fix high-priority items as soon as possible, and they fix low-priority items as time and resources become available.

Because an enhancement is an adaptation to new requirements, developers usually prioritize enhancement requests separate from failures. The decision to make an enhancement includes a business decision that the enhancement will generate an acceptable rate of return.

Q12-5 What Are the Keys for Successful SDLC Projects?

SDLC projects are difficult to manage. In this question we will consider five keys to success:

- Create a work breakdown structure.
- Estimate time and costs.
- Create a project plan.
- Adjust the plan via trade-offs.
- Manage development challenges.

Create a Work Breakdown Structure

The key strategy for SDLC projects is to divide and conquer. Most such projects are too large, too complicated, and the duration too long to attempt to manage them as one piece. Instead, successful project managers break the project into smaller and smaller tasks until each task is small enough to estimate and to manage. Every task should culminate in one or more results called **deliverables**. Examples of deliverables are documents, designs, prototypes, data models, database designs, working data entry screens, and the like. Without a defined deliverable, it is impossible to know if the task was accomplished.

Tasks are interrelated, and to prevent them from becoming a confusing morass, project teams create a **work breakdown structure (WBS)**, which is a hierarchy of the tasks required to complete a project. The WBS for a large project is huge; it might entail hundreds or even thousands of tasks. Figure 12-16 shows the WBS for the system definition phase for a typical IS project.

In Figure 12-16, the overall task, *System definition*, is divided into *Define goals and scope*, *Assess feasibility*, *Plan project*, and *Form project team*. Each of those tasks is broken into smaller tasks until the work has been divided into small tasks that can be managed and estimated.

Estimate Time and Costs

As stated, it is exceedingly difficult to determine duration and labor requirements for many development tasks. Fred Brooks[2] defined software as "logical poetry." Like poetry, software is not made of wood or metal or plastic; it is pure thought-stuff. Some years ago, when I pressed a seasoned software developer for a schedule, he responded by asking me, "What would Shakespeare have said if someone asked him how long it would take him to write *Hamlet?*" Another popular rejoinder is, "What would a fisherman say if you ask him how long it will take to catch three fish? He doesn't know, and neither do I."

Organizations take a variety of approaches to this challenge. One is to avoid scheduling problems altogether and never develop systems and software in-house. Instead, they license packages, such as ERP systems, that include both business processes and information systems components. As stated in Chapter 7, even if the vendor provides workable processes, those processes will need to be integrated into the business. However, the schedule risk of integration activities is far less than those for developing processes, programs, databases, and other components.

```
System definition
1.1             Define goals and scope
                1.1.1               Define goals
                1.1.2               Define system boundaries
                1.1.3               Review results
                1.1.4               Document results
1.2             Assess feasibility
                1.2.1               Cost
                1.2.2               Schedule
                1.2.3               Technical
                1.2.4               Organizational
                1.2.5               Document feasibility
                1.2.6               Management  review and go/no-go decision
1.3             Plan project
                1.3.1               Establish milestones
                1.3.2               Create WBS
                                    1.3.2.1               Levels 1 and 2
                                    1.3.2.2               Levels 3+
                1.3.3               Document WBS
                                    1.3.3.1               Create WBS baseline
                                    1.3.3.2               Input to Project
                1.3.4               Determine resource requirements
                                    1.3.4.1               Personnel
                                    1.3.4.2               Computing
                                    1.3.4.3               Office space
                                    1.3.4.4               Travel and Meeting Expense
                1.3.5               Management review
                                    1.3.5.1               Prepare presentation
                                    1.3.5.2               Prepare background documents
                                    1.3.5.3               Give presentation
                                    1.3.5.4               Incorporate feedback into plan
                                    1.3.5.5               Approve project
1.4             Form project team
                1.4.1               Meet with HR
                1.4.2               Meet with IT Director
                1.4.3               Develop job descriptions
                1.4.4               Meet with available personnel
                1.4.5               Hire personnel
```

Figure 12-16

Example Work Breakdown Structure (WBS)

But what if no suitable package exists? In this case, companies can admit the impossibility of scheduling a date for the completion of the entire system and take the best result they can get.

Only the loosest commitments are made regarding the date of complete and final system functionality. Project sponsors dislike this approach because they feel like they are signing a blank check, and in fact, they are. But this approach doesn't treat fictional estimates and schedules as if they were real, which may be the only other alternative.

The third approach is to attempt to schedule the development project in spite of all the difficulties. Several different estimation techniques can be used. If the project is similar to a past project, the schedule data from that past project can be used for planning. When such similar past projects exist, this technique can produce quality schedule estimates. If there is no such past project, managers must make the best estimates they can. For computer coding, some managers estimate the number of lines of code that will need to be written and apply industry or company averages to estimate the time required. Other coding estimation techniques exist; visit *http://sunset.usc.edu/csse/research/COCOMOII/cocomo_main.html*. Of course, lines of code and other advanced techniques estimate schedules only for software components. The schedules for processes, procedures, databases, and the other components must be estimated using different methods.

Create a Project Plan

A project plan is a list of WBS tasks, arranged to account for task dependencies, with durations and resources applied. Some tasks cannot be started or finished until other tasks are completed. You can't, for example, put electrical wires in a house until you've built the walls. You can define task dependencies in planning software such as Microsoft Project, and it will arrange the plan accordingly.

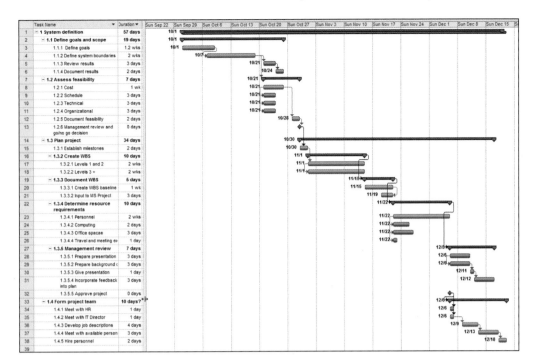

Figure 12-17
Gantt Chart of the WBS for the Definition Phase of a Project
Source: © Access 2013, Microsoft Corporation

Given dependencies, estimates for task duration and resource requirements are then applied to the WBS to form a project plan. Figure 12-17 shows the WBS as input to Microsoft Project, with task dependencies and durations defined. The display below, called a **Gantt chart**, shows tasks, dates, and dependencies.

The user has entered all of the tasks from the WBS and has assigned each task a duration. She has also specified task dependencies, although the means she used are beyond our discussion. The two red arrows emerging from task 4, *Define system boundaries*, indicate that neither the *Review results* task nor the *Assess feasibility* task can begin until *Define system boundaries* is completed. Other task dependencies are also shown; you can learn about them in a project management class.

The **critical path** is the sequence of activities that determine the earliest date by which the project can be completed. Reflect for a moment on that statement: The *earliest date* is the date determined by considering the *longest path* through the network of activities. Paying attention to task dependencies, the planner will compress the tasks as much as possible. Those tasks that cannot be further compressed lie on the critical path. Microsoft Project and other project-planning applications can readily identify critical path tasks.

Figure 12-17 shows the tasks on the critical path in red. Consider the first part of the WBS. The project planner specified that task 4 cannot begin until 2 days before task 3 ends. (That's the meaning of the red arrow emerging from task 3.) Neither task 5 nor task 8 can begin until task 4 is completed. Task 8 will take longer than tasks 5 and 6, and so task 8—not tasks 5 or 6—is on the critical path. Thus, the critical path to this point is tasks 3, 4, and 8. You can trace the critical path through the rest of the WBS by following the tasks shown in red, though the entire WBS and critical path are not shown.

Using Microsoft Project or a similar product, it is possible to assign personnel to tasks and to stipulate the percentage of time that each person devotes to a task. Figure 12-18 shows a Gantt chart for which this has been done. The notation means that Eleanore works only 25 percent of the time on task 3; Lynda and Richard work full time. Additionally, one can assign costs to personnel and compute a labor budget for each task and for the overall WBS. One can assign resources to tasks and use Microsoft Project to detect and prevent two tasks from using the same resources. Resource costs can be assigned and summed as well.

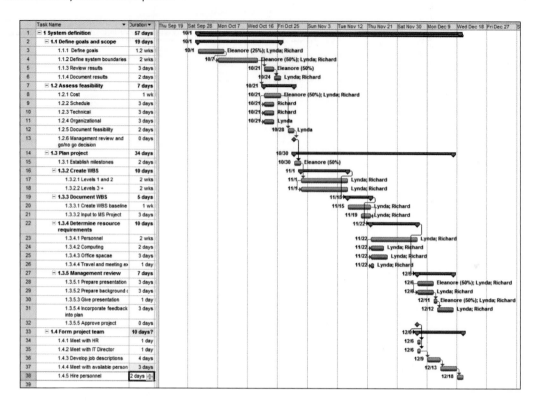

Figure 12-18

Gantt Chart with Resources (People) Assigned

Source: © Access 2013, Microsoft Corporation

Managers can use the critical path to perform critical path analysis. First, note that if a task is on the critical path, and if that task runs late, the project will be late. Hence, tasks on the critical path cannot be allowed to run late if the project is to be delivered on time. Second, tasks not on the critical path can run late to the point at which they would become part of the critical path. Hence, up to a point, resources can be taken from noncritical path tasks to shorten tasks on the critical path. **Critical path analysis** is the process by which project managers compress the schedule by moving resources, typically people, from noncritical path tasks onto critical path tasks.

Adjust Plan via Trade-offs

The project plan for the entire project results in a finish date and a total cost. In our experience in more than a dozen major development projects, the first response to a completed project plan is always "Good heavens! No way! We can't wait that long or pay that much!" And our experience is not unusual.

Thus, the first response to a project plan is to attempt to reduce time and costs. Reductions can be made, but not out of thin air. An old adage in planning development projects is "Believe your first number." Believe what you have estimated before your desires and wishes cloud your judgment.

So, how can schedules and costs be responsibly reduced? By considering trade-offs. A **trade-off** is a balancing of three critical factors: requirements, cost, and time. To understand this balancing challenge, consider the construction of something relatively simple—say, a piece of jewelry, such as a necklace, or the deck on the side of a house. The more elaborate the necklace or the deck, the more time it will take. The less elaborate, the less time it will take. Further, if we embellish the necklace with diamonds and precious gems, it will cost more. Similarly, if we construct the deck from old crates, it will be cheaper than if we construct it of clear-grained, prime Port Orford cedar.

We can summarize this situation as shown in Figure 12-19. We can *trade off* requirements against time and against cost. If we make the necklace simpler, it will take less time. If we eliminate the diamonds and gems, it will be cheaper. The same trade-offs exist in the construction of anything: houses, buildings, ships, furniture, *and* information systems.

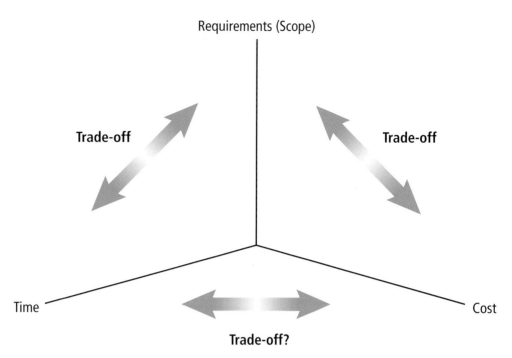

Figure 12-19
Primary Drivers of Systems
Development

The relationship between time and cost is more complicated. Normally, we can reduce time by increasing cost *only to a point.* For example, we can reduce the time it takes to produce a deck by hiring more laborers. At some point, however, there will be so many laborers working on the deck that they will get in one another's way, and the time to finish the deck will actually increase. At some point, adding more people creates **diseconomies of scale**, the situation that occurs when adding more resources creates inefficiencies. A famous adage in the software industry is **Brooks' Law** (named for the Fred Brooks discussed earlier), which states that adding more people to a late project makes it later. This occurs, in part, because new team members need to be trained by existing team members, who must be taken off productive tasks.

In some projects, we can reduce costs by increasing time. If, for example, we are required to pay laborers time-and-a-half for overtime, we can reduce costs by eliminating overtime. If finishing the deck—by, say, Friday—requires overtime, then it may be cheaper to avoid overtime by completing the deck sometime next week. This trade-off is not always true, however. Extending the project interval means that we need to pay labor and overhead for a longer period; thus, adding more time can also increase costs.

Consider how these trade-offs pertain to information systems. We specify a set of requirements for the new information system, and we schedule labor over a period of time. Suppose the initial schedule indicates the system will be finished in 3 years. If business requirements necessitate the project be finished in 2 years, we must shorten the schedule. We can proceed in two ways: reduce the requirements or add labor. For the former, we eliminate functions and features. For the latter, we hire more staff or contract with other vendors for development services. Deciding which course to take will be difficult and risky.

Using trade-offs, the WBS plan can be modified to shorten schedules or reduce costs. But they cannot be reduced by management fiat.

Manage Development Challenges

Given the project plan and management's endorsement and approval, the next stage is to do it. The final WBS plan is denoted as the **baseline WBS**. This baseline shows the planned tasks, dependencies, durations, and resource assignments. As the project proceeds, project managers can input actual dates, labor hours, and resource costs. At any point in time, planning applications can be used to determine whether the project is ahead of or behind schedule and how the actual project costs compare to baseline costs.

However, nothing ever goes according to plan, and the larger the project and the longer the development interval, the more things will violate the plan. Four critical factors need to be considered:

1. Coordination
2. Diseconomies of scale
3. Configuration control
4. Unexpected events

Development projects, especially large-scale projects, are usually organized into a variety of development groups that work independently. Coordinating the work of these independent groups can be difficult, particularly if the groups reside in different geographic locations or different countries. An accurate and complete WBS facilitates coordination, but no project ever proceeds exactly in accordance with the WBS. Delays occur, and unknown or unexpected dependencies develop among tasks.

The coordination problem is increased because software, as stated, is just thought-stuff. When constructing a new house, electricians install wiring in the walls as they exist; it is impossible to do otherwise. No electrician can install wiring in the wall as designed 6 months ago, before a change. In software, such physical constraints do not exist. It is entirely possible for a team to develop a set of application programs to process a database using an obsolete database design. When the database design was changed, all involved parties should have been notified, but this may not have occurred. Wasted hours, increased cost, and poor morale are the result.

Another problem is diseconomies of scale. The number of possible interactions among team members rises exponentially with the number of team members. Ultimately, no matter how well managed a project is, diseconomies of scale will set in.

As the project proceeds, controlling the configuration of the work product becomes difficult. Consider requirements, for example. The development team produces an initial statement of requirements. Meetings with users produce an adjusted set of requirements. Suppose an event then occurs that necessitates another version of requirements. After deliberation, assume the development team decides to ignore a large portion of the requirements changes resulting from the event. At this point, there are four different versions of the requirements. If the changes to requirements are not carefully managed, changes from the four versions will be mixed up, and confusion and disorder will result. No one will know which requirements are the correct, current ones.

Similar problems occur with designs, program code, database data, and other system components. The term **configuration control** refers to a set of management policies, practices, and tools that developers use to maintain control over the project's resources. Such resources include documents, schedules, designs, program code, test suites, and any other shared resource needed to complete the project. Configuration control is vital; a loss of control over a project's configuration is so expensive and disruptive that it can result in termination for senior project managers.

The last major challenge to large-scale project management is unexpected events. The larger and longer the project, the greater the chance of disruption due to an unanticipated event. Critical people can change companies; even whole teams have been known to pack up and join a competitor. A hurricane may destroy an office; the company may have a bad quarter and freeze hiring just as the project is staffing up; technology will change; competitors may do something that makes the project more (or less) important; or the company may be sold and new management may change requirements and priorities.

Because software is thought-stuff, team morale is crucial. Author David Kroenke once managed two strong-headed software developers who engaged in a heated argument over the design of a program feature. The argument ended when one threw a chair at the other. The rest of the team divided its loyalties between the two developers, and work came to a standstill as subgroups sneered and argued with one another when they met in hallways or at the coffee pot. How do you schedule that event into your WBS? As a project manager, you never know what strange event is heading your way. Such unanticipated events make project management challenging, but also incredibly fascinating!

Q12-6 How Can Scrum Overcome the Problems of the SDLC?

The systems development life cycle (SDLC) process is falling out of favor in the systems development community, primarily for two reasons. First, the nature of the SDLC denies what every experienced developer knows to be true: systems requirements are fuzzy and always changing. They change because they need to be corrected, or more is known, or users change their minds about what they want after they use part of the system, or business needs change, or technology offers other possibilities.

According to the SDLC, however, progress goes in a linear sequence from requirements to design to implementation. Sometimes this is called the **waterfall method** because the assumption is that once you've finished a phase, you never go back; you go over the waterfall into the pool of the next stage. Requirements are done. Then you do design. Design is done; then you implement. However, experience has shown that it just doesn't work that way.

In the beginning, systems developers thought the SDLC might work for IS and applications because processes like the SDLC work for building physical things. If you're going to build a runway, for example, you specify how long it needs to be, how much airplane weight the surface must support, and so forth. Then you design it, and then you build it. Here waterfall processes work.

However, business processes, information systems, and applications are not physical; as stated, they're made of thought-stuff. They're also social; they exist for people to inform themselves and achieve their goals. But people and social systems are incredibly malleable; they adapt. That characteristic enables humans to do many amazing things, but it also means that requirements change and the waterfall development process cannot work.

The second reason that the SDLC is falling out of favor is that it is very risky. The people for whom the system is being constructed cannot see what they have until the very end. At that point, if something is wrong, all the money and time has already been spent. Furthermore, what if, as frequently happens, the project runs out of money or time before it is completed? The result is a form of management blackmail in which the developers say, "Well, it's not done yet, but give us another $100,000 and another 6 months, and *then* we'll have it done." If management declines, which it might because at that point, the time and money are sunk, it is left not only with the loss but also with the unmet need that caused it to start the SDLC in the first place.

In short, the SDLC assumes that requirements don't change, which everyone who has ever been within 10 feet of a development project knows is false, and it's very risky for the business that sponsors it.

What Are the Principles of Agile Development Methodologies?

Over the past 40 years, numerous alternatives to the SDLC have been proposed, including *rapid application development*, the *unified process*, *extreme programming*, *scrum*, and others. All of these techniques addressed the problems of the SDLC, and by the turn of the last century, their

Using This Knowledge for Your Number-One Priority

Source: Daniel A. Leifheit/Moment Open/Getty Images

Examine the picture of the dog team. Those dogs are starting a 1,049-mile race in which they will sometimes run 20 hours a day. They can't qualify for this race unless they've succeeded at similar events, so they know what they're in for. But, clearly, they like their jobs.

That should be you. No, not a musher on the Iditarod, but that's the way you should feel at the start of your workweek. You will spend at least a third of your life at work; work will be one of the biggest sources of personal satisfaction; and your job will determine the quality of your life in money, in friends and associates, and in interesting experiences. So between now and graduation, finding and getting that job should be the *number-one priority* in your life. Don't wait.

So, how will you do that? Haphazardly sign up for whatever recruiters happen to come to campus? That's one approach, and you can hope that your competitors use it. But what about you? Can you find a way to apply what you've learned in this chapter to finding that job? It's worth taking 20 minutes to think about it, no? And, hey, you might get to wear booties, too!

Questions

1. Examine Figure 12-9 and the following figures that detail tasks in each of the five phases. Interpret each of the activities in the SDLC not as they pertain to systems development but rather as they could pertain to finding your job. Briefly summarize the tasks you can perform at each stage.

2. Finding a job is a process. Like all processes, job-acquiring processes vary in quality. State two dimensions of process and quality and explain how they pertain to job acquisition.

3. Sketch the job-acquisition process you are currently using. Use whatever BPMN symbols from Figure 12-6 that you find relevant.

4. Examine the quality of your current job-acquisition process. Explain two ways you could improve the quality of that process.

5. Write the requirements for the job-acquisition process using scrum-like requirements statements. Break the requirements into sufficient detail so that you can satisfy each one in 2 hours or less. Rather than start every requirement with "As a student," start them with the role you will use. "As an interviewee, I will . . ." or "As a prospect-seeker, I will." (See pages 521–522.)

6. Consider your answers to questions 1–5. Explain how those answers inform you about how to obtain that perfect job.

7. Start tonight!

philosophy had coalesced into what has come to be known as **agile development**, which means a development process that conforms to the principles in Figure 12-20. Scrum is an agile technique and conforms to these principles.

First, scrum and the other agile techniques expect and even welcome change. Given the nature of social systems, *expect* is not a surprise, but why *welcome*? Isn't welcoming requirements change a bit like welcoming a good case of the flu? No, because systems are created to help organizations and people achieve their strategies, and the more the requirements change, the closer they come to facilitating strategies. The result is better and more satisfying for both the users and the development team.

- Expect, even welcome, changes in requirements.
- Frequently deliver *working* version of the product.
- Work closely with customer for the duration.
- Design as you go.
- Test as you go.
- Team knows best how it's doing/how to change.
- Can be used for business processes, information systems, and applications development.

Figure 12-20
Principles of Agile (Scrum) Development

Second, scrum and other agile development processes are designed to frequently deliver a *working* version of some part of the product. Frequently means 1 to 8 weeks, not longer. This frequency means that management is at risk only for whatever costs and time have been consumed in that period. And, at the end of the period, they will have some usable product piece that has at least some value to the business.

Thus, unlike the SDLC, agile techniques deliver benefits early and often. The initial benefits might be small, but they are positive and increase throughout the process. With the SDLC, no value is generated until the very end. Considering the time value of money, this characteristic alone makes agile techniques more desirable.

The third principle in Figure 12-20 is that the development team will work closely with the customer until the project ends. Someone who knows the business requirements must be available to the development team and must be able and willing to clearly express, clarify, and elaborate on requirements. Also, customers need to be available to test the evolving work product and provide guidance on how well new features work.

The fourth principle is a tough one for many developers to accept. Rather than design the complete, overall system at the beginning, only those portions of the design that are needed to complete the current work are done. Sometimes this is called **just-in-time design**. Designing in this way means that the design is constantly changing, and existing designs may need to be revised, along with substantial revision to the work product produced so far. On the surface, it is inefficient. However, experience has shown that far too many teams have constructed elaborate, fanciful, and complete designs that turned out to be glamorous fiction as the requirements changed.

Test as you go, the next principle, is obvious if the team is going to be delivering working versions. Testing is initially conducted among members of the team but involves the business customer as well.

Development teams know how well they're doing. You could go into any development environment today and ask the team how it's doing and, once team members understood you were not about to inflict a new management program on them, you would find they know their strengths, weaknesses, bottlenecks, and process problems quite well. That principle is part of agile development methodologies. At the end of every deliverable or some other (short) milestone, the team meets to assess how it's doing and how it can improve.

Finally, agile development methodologies are generic. They can be applied to the creation of business processes, information systems, and applications. They are applicable to other team projects as well, but that subject is beyond the scope of this text.

What Is the Scrum Process?

Scrum is an agile development methodology developed by Jeff Sutherland, Jeff McKenna, and John Scumniotales for a project at the Easel Corporation[3] and extended by others over the past 15 years. *Scrum* is a rugby term and was first used for teamwork in a *Harvard Business Review*

> - Requirements list drives process
> - Each work period (1 to 4–8 weeks):
>   - Select requirements to consider
>   - Determine tasks to perform—select requirements to deliver
>   - Team meets daily for 15 min (stand-up)
>   - What I did yesterday
>   - What I'm going to do today
>   - What's blocking me
>   - Test frequently
>   - Paired work possible
>   - Minimal documentation
>   - Deliver (something) that works
>   - Evaluate team's work process at end of period (and say thanks)
> - Rinse and repeat until
>   - Customer says we're done
>   - Out of time
>   - Out of money
> - Three principal roles
>   - Product owner (business professional who represents customer)
>   - Scrum master
>   - Team members (7 ± 2 people)

Figure 12-21
Scrum Essentials

article written by Hirotaka Takeuchi and Ikujiro Nonaka.[4] In rugby, a *scrum* is a gathering of a team into a circle to restart play after a foul or other interruption. Think of it as a huddle in American football.

Scrum Essentials

As stated, scrum is one type of agile development process having the specific characteristics shown in Figure 12-21. First, the process is driven by a prioritized list of requirements that is created by the users and business sponsors of the new system. Scrum work periods can be as short as 1 week but, as with all agile processes, never longer than 8. Two to 4 weeks is recommended. Each work period, the team selects the top priority items that it will commit to delivering that period. Each workday begins with a **stand-up**, which is a 15-minute meeting in which each team member[5] states:

- What he or she has done in the past day
- What he or she will do in the coming day
- Any factors that are blocking his or her progress

The purpose of the stand-up is to achieve accountability for team members' progress and to give a public forum for blocking factors. Oftentimes one team member will have the expertise to help a blocked team member resolve the blocking issue.

Testing is done frequently, possibly many times per day. Sometimes the business owner of the project is involved in daily testing as well. In some cases, team members work in pairs; in **paired programming**, for example, two team members share the same computer and write a computer program together. Sometimes, one programmer will provide a test, and the other will either demonstrate that the code passes that test or alter the code so that it will. Then the two members switch roles. Other types of paired work are possible as well.

Minimal documentation is prepared. The result of the team's work is not design or other documents but, rather, a working version of the requirements that were selected at the start of the scrum period.

At the end of the scrum period, the working version of the product is delivered to the customer, who can, if desired, put it to use at that time, even in its not-fully-finished state. After the product is delivered, the team meets to evaluate its own process and to make changes as needed.

Team members are given an opportunity to express thanks and receive recognition for superior work at these meetings. (Review the criteria for team success in Chapter 2, and you will see how scrum adheres to the principles of a successful team.)

Figure 12-22 summarizes the scrum process.

When Are We Done?

Work continues in a repeating cycle of scrum periods until one of three conditions is met:

- The customer is satisfied with the product created and decides to accept the work product, even if some requirements are left unsatisfied.
- The project runs out of time.
- The project runs out of money.

Unlike the SDLC, if a scrum project terminates because of time or budget limitations, the customer will have some useful result for the time and money expended. It may not be the fully functioning version that was desired, but it is something that, assuming requirements are defined and prioritized correctly, can generate value for the project sponsors.

How Do Requirements Drive the Scrum Process?

Scrum is distinguished from other agile development methodologies, in part, by the way that it uses requirements to drive planning and scheduling. First, requirements are specified in a particular manner. One common format is to express requirements in terms of *who* does *what* and *why*.

For example, in the doctor's version of the PRIDE system, a requirement was expressed as:

"As a doctor, I want to view a patient's exercise records so I can make sure he is not doing too much."

Or,

"As a doctor, I want to view a patient's exercise records so I can make sure she is following her prescription."

Each of these requirements specifies who (the doctor) does what (view a patient's exercise data) and why (make sure she is following her prescription). It's not surprising that the requirement includes *who* and *what*, but the need for *why* may surprise you. The purpose of the *why* clause of the requirement is to set a context for the value that will be delivered by the requirement. Including it increases the likelihood that the product will deliver business value and not just blindly meet the requirement.

As stated, the product owner creates requirements and prioritizes them. For example, one of the two requirements above will be judged higher in importance than the other. All other

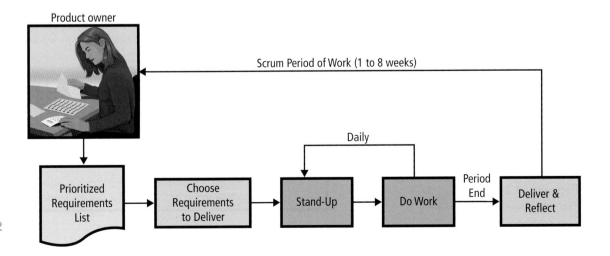

Figure 12-22
Scrum Process

things being equal, the team will satisfy the higher priority requirement first. This means, too, that if the project runs out of time or money, the highest priority requirements will have been completed first.

Creating Requirements Tasks

Given a requirement, the team meets to create tasks that must be accomplished to meet that requirement. In Figure 12-22, this work is done in the *Choose requirements to deliver* activity.

Figure 12-23 shows eight tasks that need to be done to accomplish an example requirement. In the *Choose requirements to deliver* activity, tasks for additional requirements that might also be implemented in this scrum period are created.

Tasks are created in a team meeting because the team as a whole can iterate and allow members to give feedback. One team member will think of a task that needs to be done, of which other members are not aware. Or the team member will realize that a particular task is incomplete, or is doable in some other way, or doesn't really need to be done.

Scheduling Tasks

As described so far, scrum is a good idea, one of many agile processes that might be used. What makes scrum particularly innovative, however, is the way that tasks are scheduled.

Scrum methodology recognizes that developers are terrible, even wretched, at determining how long a task will take. However, developers are quite good at determining how long something will take in comparison to something else. So, while a developer may be poor at estimating the time required to do, say, Task 2 in Figure 12-23, he or she will likely be accurate when saying that Task 2 will take twice as long as Task 1, or some other ratio.

So, according to the scrum process, once the tasks are known for a given set of requirements, the next step is to assign each task a difficulty score, called *points*. The easiest task has a point score of 1. A task that will take five times longer is given a point score of 5, etc. For reasons that are beyond the scope of this discussion, points are expressed in values from a sequence of integers known as the Fibonacci sequence: {1, 2, 3, 5, 8, 13, 21, 34, 55, 89, 144, and?}. The question mark is used because any number larger than 144 is meaningless. Most likely 89 and 144 are meaningless as well. Tasks with such large point scores need to be subdivided into multiple requirements. When all tasks have received points, the points are summed to a total for the requirement.

Scrum includes several different techniques for assigning points. Team estimation and planning poker are two. You can learn more about them in *The Elements of Scrum*.[6] The gist of these techniques is to obtain team scores by applying the team's expertise in an iterative, feedback-generating process.

Figure 12-23
Example Requirement and Tasks

Requirement:
"As a doctor, I want to view the patient's exercise records so I can make sure she is following her prescription."

Tasks:
1. Authenticate the doctor.
2. Obtain patient identifying data from doctor.
3. Determine this doctor is authorized to view this patient's records.
4. Read the database to obtain exercise records.
5. Read the database to obtain most recent prescription record.
6. Format the data into a generic format.
7. Determine the type of mobile device the doctor is using.
8. Format the generic report into a report for that mobile device.

1. Team assigns 1 point to simplest task.
2. Times to deliver working tasks are compared to each other and assigned points (points are Fibonacci numbers). Use:
   a. Team estimation
   b. Planning poker
   c. Other
3. Using past experience, team computes its velocity ... number of points it can accomplish per scrum period.
4. Working with product owner, team selects tasks for the upcoming scrum period, constrained by its velocity.

Figure 12-24
Summary of Scrum Estimation Techniques

Committing to Finish Tasks

As teams work together, they will learn the total number of points of work they can accomplish each scrum period. That term is called the team's **velocity**. The team uses its velocity to determine how many requirements it can commit to accomplishing in the next scrum period. Of course, during the first period, the team will not know its velocity. In that case, senior members will need to make a guess. That guess may be far off, but it will get better as the team gains experience. Unlike the SDLC, there is at least well-founded hope that, over time, estimating will improve.

Suppose the five requirements on a team's prioritized requirements list total 125 points. If a team knows its velocity is 100 points per scrum period, it knows it cannot do all five. However, if the top four total, say, 80 points, it can commit to doing those four, plus something else. In this case, the team would go back to the product owner and ask if there is a requirement lower on the priority list that can be done for the available 20 points of capacity. This estimation technique is summarized in Figure 12-24.

Hocus-Pocus?

If you haven't participated in software or systems development, this process may sound like so much hocus-pocus. However, it has two very important characteristics that make it not so. First, scrum is a methodology that incorporates team iteration and feedback for scheduling and tasking, which, as you know by now, is a way for a team to create something together that exceeds what each member can do individually. Second, scrum provides a framework for process learning. As a team works more and more scrum periods together, it learns better and better how to assign points, and it learns more and more what its true velocity is.

But scrum isn't a magic bullet. It can't guarantee that the project will produce a high quality product, on time, and under budget. But, as an alternative to the traditional SDLC, it can limit potential financial losses and produce substantial results in just a few weeks.

Q12-7 2026?

You will be involved in a systems development project between now and 2026; that's almost a sure bet. If, as stated in Chapter 9, technical marketing expenditures increase from \$12B to \$120B, then every marketing and sales professional will become involved. Given robots, drones, driverless cars, and 3D printing, how will anyone in manufacturing or operations not be involved in systems development? Finance and accounting? Where are the great opportunities? And how are they to be funded? And, of course, all management grads are going to play strong roles in developing new systems strategies and priorities as well as managing the projects.

Furthermore, your generation is computer-competent and interested. Although these skills are second nature to you, your ability to use Facebook, Twitter, Pinterest, and so on, has given you hours of experience dealing with computer-based systems. You also know that user interfaces can be easy or difficult to use, depending on their design. You've experienced the frustration of working with a poor interface, and you won't put up with one in your organization. When someone says, "We've got to improve our customers' experience on our website," you know intuitively what that means. In fact, you're probably the one making that statement. Your knowledge will enable you to help create a closer alignment between processes and IS and business strategy, goals, and objectives. And later, you won't sit in your c-level job and complacently leave systems development to others.

In the next 10 years, applications will be more easily changed and adapted. Software vendors know that the key to their future growth is not having the single best solution, but rather having a solution that is readily tailored to their customers' idiosyncrasies. When ERP was new, customers were willing to adapt their business processes to those of the vendors because there was no other choice. But, as indicated by the popularity of ERP industry–specific solution templates, ERP customers want more. They want to be able to do whatever it is they do to gain a competitive advantage, and adapting their business processes to the same processes used by everyone else isn't going to get them there. So, software vendors will find ways to make their solutions more agile using SOA and Web services, and, as a result, systems and processes will be more agile and better able to adapt to changing needs.

In the next 10 years, application development speed will accelerate. That will occur, in part, through the use of improved development processes such as scrum, but it will also occur because applications will become better at creating other applications. Whether we will reach Kurzweil's singularity before 2026, as he predicts, we do not know (visit *http://TheSingularity.com* to learn more). We can depend, however, on applications that generate other applications far more effectively, and frequently, than they do now. New systems will come online fast, and the limiting factor will be humans' ability to cope. Business professionals have a key role in solving those coping problems.

Finally, between now and 2026, the nature of the industry will change. First, as you learned in Chapter 5, the NoSQL DBMS products were not developed by existing DBMS vendors. They were developed by organizations that had unique needs and that developed software to meet those needs. The DBMS vendors caught on after the fact. In the next 10 years, we will see similar stories repeated again and again.

Another industry change is the emergence of new business models based on loosely coupled partnerships. The Firm (*www.thefirmmpls.com*), a workout studio in Minneapolis, pays almost nothing in license fees for the full-service operations application it obtains from the SaaS vendor MindBody, Inc. Instead, all of the credit card charges made by The Firm customers are processed by MindBody, Inc. This processing enables MindBody to earn a small amount on every customer transaction. MindBody supports more than 6,000 studios and trainers in the United States. Its software is a veritable money machine.

A key element of this new business model is the alignment of the goals of the loose coupling of workout studios and MindBody. Both make more money when customers purchase. Therefore, MindBody's software includes features and functions that enable studio managers to determine which products, classes, trainers, and even ads and marketing campaigns are the most successful. Furthermore, MindBody has a window on the best practices in the industry. To motivate studios to adapt to new practices that will create more revenue, MindBody provides comparative statistics on any given studio's performance against that of similar companies in its region.

That's it! You've reached the end of this text. Take a moment to consider how you will use what you learned, as described in the Guide on pages 528–529.

But there is one stumbling block in the middle of these positive trends. We have known for more than 40 years that the key factor in information systems development success is active involvement by users. We've seen billion-dollar disasters play out for a lack of control over requirements.

So, have we learned? Not yet. Reread Case Study 7 and ask what single factor was responsible for the debacle in the Cover Oregon health exchange. The governor didn't get involved and didn't have anyone else manage the project, and the users fought with the development organization over requirements, which were never stabilized.

So, it all comes down to the users. The future environment is positive, but unless senior management and users are actively involved in systems development projects, we will have many new million- and billion-dollar disasters on our hands. You and your classmates can make a difference.

Security Guide

PSST. THERE'S ANOTHER WAY, YOU KNOW...

"All this talk about BPM, and SDLC, and scrum is really unnecessary. There's another way, you know. We just download a copy of their source code, and we're in business. I have a friend who knows how to do that. We'd have the application in seconds, and it would save so much time and agony, no?"

Industrial espionage is as old as commerce. Infiltrating your competitors with spies and stealing whatever you can is nothing new. It's a way to save hundreds of labor years, maybe more. Of course, if you're so stupid as to steal the designs of an iPad, and next month bring your own iPad to market, the jig will be up. Apple, the FBI, and who knows who else will be upon you.

So, instead, you can just learn from the stolen designs and apply your new knowledge to build similar devices, doing it much faster than you could without the theft. Use what you learn from, say, iPad touch-screen design to build your own auto navigation touch screen.

Or choose a company less prominent than Apple. For example, find out where Jared and his team keep the PRIDE source code and take it. Then build your own PRIDE system in another country... say, New Zealand or Singapore. How likely is it for Jared to know you're running his code in New Zealand? Not likely, and, if he does learn of it, how much does he want to pay the one attorney in Austin, Texas, who knows New Zealand law and prosecution? Plus, how would he prove you got the code from him?

Sound far-fetched? In June 2012, ESET, the antivirus software vendor based in Bratislava, Slovakia, detected a big spike in infections of a worm named ACAD/Medre.A.[7] Initially the spike was in Peru, but the malware soon spread. Investigation revealed that this worm copies itself into file folders containing drawings produced using AutoCAD, the world's most popular computer-based design software. Once there, it installs code to send copies of engineering drawings it finds on the host machine to one of several email servers in China. If Outlook is installed on the infected computer, it also sends copies of the computer's contact list and other email data.

ACAD/Medre.A was spread by unsuspecting engineers. An AutoCAD design consists of many files, and to transfer a design to a collaborator, engineers routinely compress the files in an AutoCAD design directory into a zip file and send it to legitimate recipients. Once the worm gets into a design directory, it's compressed with the legitimate files and rides along in the compressed file. When the recipient decompresses the zip file, ACAD/Medre.A is decompressed as well. It then runs its payload to steal designs and email data.

Why Peru? Apparently, the original infection was on a server of a Peruvian manufacturer whose suppliers needed the manufacturer's engineering designs to create component parts. When suppliers copied the manufacturer's drawings,

Source: © Eliane SULLE/Alamy

526

they copied the worm as well. Soon the worm was on its way around the world.

Was it serious? According to the ESET, tens of thousands of engineering drawings were leaked. ESET says, however, that when it notified the providers of those email servers in China, the providers shut those server sites down, so the damage is supposed to be stopped. Autodesk, the vendor of AutoCAD, took corrective and protective action as well.

 DISCUSSION QUESTIONS

1. If, in your absence, your roommate opens your desk and eats the top layer of your 2-pound box of chocolates, you'll know it; at least you'll know they're gone. But, if in your absence, your roommate uses your computer to copy your MIS term project onto his flash drive, do you know? If so, how? If not, why not?

2. Of course *your* roommate wouldn't steal your term project. So, instead, suppose the person across the hall obtains the name of your computer and your logon name (the name you enter when your computer starts). She could surreptitiously watch you enter your password and learn it, too. But let's say instead that she notices the 75 pictures of your family basset hound, Fido, taped to your desk and correctly guesses that your password is *Fido*. With that data and a little knowledge, she uses your dorm's network to access shared folders on your computer *from her computer*. (Search the Internet for *How to share a folder in Windows (or Mac)* if you don't know what shared folders are.) When she finds your MIS term paper in one of your shared folders and copies it to her computer, do you know? Why or why not?

3. How does the situation in question 2 differ from packet sniffing? (Reread the Guide in Chapter 6, pages 272–273 if necessary.) What's required for her to steal your paper from a shared folder? What's required to steal that paper using packet sniffing? Which is easier?

4. As a student, you're unlikely to share many folders, but once you start work, you're likely to do so. Is the scenario in question 2 possible at work? Does it matter if your employer has strong network security? What is the one thing you can do to protect yourself from the person in the cubicle down the hallway accessing your shared folders?

5. Now consider the suppliers in this guide who had their designs stolen. Will they know their designs were stolen? How will they find out? How will they know which designs were taken? How can they assess their damages?

6. It's possible for companies to configure their network so that email can only be sent to their own Internet service provider. Such a configuration would thwart the ACAD/Medre.A worm, and indeed it did, for all the companies that had such security. Companies with large, knowledgeable IS departments (see Chapter 11) most likely will, but in this case hundreds did not. If you're the owner of a small business, what can you do?

7. Search the Internet for the term *industrial espionage*. Find one example of espionage that has been conducted using malware. Summarize the problem and the damages. What could the companies involved have done to avoid losses?

Guide

THE FINAL, FINAL WORD

Congratulations! You've made it through the entire book. With this knowledge, you are well prepared to be an effective user of information systems. And with work and imagination, you can be much more than that. Many interesting opportunities are available to those who can apply information in innovative ways. Your professor has done what she can do, and the rest, as they say, is up to you.

So what's next? In Chapter 1, we claimed that Introduction to MIS is the most important course in the business curriculum today. That claim was based on the organization's innovative use of nearly free data communications and data storage. By now, you've learned many of the ways that businesses and organizations use these resources and information systems based upon those resources. You've also seen how businesses like Falcon Security use information systems to solve problems and further their competitive strategies. With PRIDE, you've investigated the use of mobile and cloud technology for an inter-enterprise system.

How can you use that knowledge? Chapter 1 claimed that future business professionals must be able "to assess, evaluate, and apply emerging information technology to business." Have you learned how to do that? At least, are you better able to do that than you were before this class? You probably know the meaning of many more terms than you did when you started, and such knowledge is important. But even more important is the ability to use that knowledge to apply MIS to your business interests.

Chapter 1 also reviewed the work of the RAND Corporation and that of Robert Reich on what professional workers in the 21st century need to know. Those sources state that such workers need to know how to innovate the use of technology and how to "collaborate, reason abstractly, think in terms of systems, and experiment." Have you learned those behaviors? Or, at least, are you better at them than you were when you started this course?

Overall, job prospects have been improving in recent years, but good jobs, and the perfect job for you, will not be easy to obtain. You need to apply every asset you have. One of those assets is the knowledge you've gained in this class. (See the So What? on page 518.) Take the time to do the exercises at the end of this guide, and then use the answers in your job interviews!

Look for the job you truly want to do, get that job, and work hard. In the movie *Glass: A Portrait of Philip in Twelve Parts*, the composer Philip Glass claimed he knew the secret to success. It was, he said, "Get up early and work hard all day." That quotation seems obvious and hardly worth stating, except that it has the ring of truth. And, if you can find a job you truly love, it isn't even hard. Actually, it's fun, most of the time. So, use what you've learned in this class to obtain the job you really want!

Source: Hoda Bogdan/Fotolia

DISCUSSION QUESTIONS

1. Reflect on what you have learned from this course. Write two paragraphs about how the knowledge you have gained will help you to "assess, evaluate, and apply emerging information technology to business." Shape your writing around the kind of job that you want to obtain upon graduation.

2. Write two paragraphs about how the knowledge and experiences you've had in this class will help you "collaborate, reason abstractly, think in terms of systems, and experiment." Again, shape your writing around the kind of job you wish to obtain.

3. Using your answer to question 1, extract three or four sentences about yourself that you could use in a job interview.

4. Using your answer to question 2, extract three or four sentences about yourself that you could use in a job interview.

5. Practice using your answers to questions 3 and 4 in a job interview with a classmate, roommate, or friend.

ACTIVE REVIEW

Use this Active Review to verify that you understand the ideas and concepts that answer the chapter's study questions.

Q12-1 How are business processes, IS, and applications developed?

Using your own words, explain the differences among business processes, information systems, and applications. State the components of each. Using the terminology from Chapter 5, describe the relationship of business processes and IS. Name three development processes and state which processes are used for the development of business processes, information systems, and applications. Explain the primary roles of business and systems analysts.

Q12-2 How do organizations use business process management (BPM)?

State the definition of business process used in this chapter and define *roles, resources,* and *data flows.* Explain three reasons why business processes need to be managed. Describe the need for BPM and explain why it is a cycle. Name the four stages of the BPM process and summarize the activities in each. Define *as-is model.* Explain the role of COBIT.

Q12-3 How is business process modeling notation (BPMN) used to model processes?

Explain the need for a process documentation standard. Describe swim-lane layout. Explain each of the symbols in Figures 12-7 and 12-8 and describe the relationship of these two diagrams. Describe the problems in the process in Figure 12-7 and suggest one solution. Name three uses for BPMN diagrams.

Q12-4 What are the phases in the systems development life cycle (SDLC)?

Describe the origins of the SDLC and how it came to prominence. Name five basic systems development activities. Describe tasks required for the definition, requirements, and design steps. Explain the tasks required to implement a system and describe four types of system conversion. State specific activities for each of the five components during the design and implementation stages. Explain why the term *maintenance* is a misnomer when applied to information systems; state tasks performed during systems maintenance.

Q12-5 What are the keys for successful SDLC projects?

Name five keys for successful development projects. Explain the purpose of a work breakdown structure. Summarize the difficulties of development estimation and describe three ways of addressing it. Explain the elements in the Gantt chart in Figure 12-17. Define *critical path* and explain critical path analysis. Summarize requirements, cost, and schedule trade-offs. List and explain four critical factors for development project management.

Q12-6 How can scrum overcome the problems of the SDLC?

Explain two reasons that the SDLC is falling out of favor. In your own words, explain the meaning and importance of each of the principles in Figure 12-23. Explain how each of the scrum essential items in Figure 12-24 is implemented in the scrum process shown in Figure 12-25. Name three elements in a scrum requirement. Describe what is unique about the way that scrum determines the time required to accomplish a task. Define *velocity* and explain how it is used in scheduling. Explain how scrum provides a framework for process learning.

Q12-7 2026?

Explain why you will be involved in systems development projects during your professional career. How does the knowledge of your generation of businesspeople influence systems development? Explain why systems will be more easily adapted. Using the example of MindBody, explain how new business models will enable software to be delivered to customers in innovative ways. Describe a key requirement for avoiding systems development disaster.

Using Your Knowledge with PRIDE

Jared, James, and even Zev need to know the basics of development processes, which to use for what, and the advantages of using the SDLC and scrum. Before spending any money, they need to understand the difficulties and risks of developing processes, IS, and applications, particularly inter-enterprise systems, such as PRIDE.

At some point in your career, you will need this knowledge as well.

KEY TERMS AND CONCEPTS

MyMISLab™

To complete the problems with the ⭐, go to EOC Discussion Questions in the MyLab.

USING YOUR KNOWLEDGE

⭐ **12-1.** Suppose that you are appointed as business and system analyst of a newly constructed hotel. Identify the key business processes and the respective information systems that need to be implemented to manage the daily operations.

⭐ **12-2.** Suppose that the hotel in the previous question has identified the required business processes and information systems. The front desk executive receives a call for booking a banquet hall. As per the hotel's rules, in addition to checking the availability of the hall, the occupancy of rooms also has to be checked for arrangements of food and service. Since booking can also be refused on grounds of insufficient credit, the customer's credit limit is also verified. These require considerable time and may result in loss of customers for the hotel. As a manager of information system, how would you tackle this problem?

⭐ **12-3.** As a student of MIS, would you like to play the role of a business analyst, system analyst, or both in your dream organization. Give reasons to justify your choice. Also, segregate the role of a business analyst from that of a system analyst, based on the responsibilities that need to be performed for each of the roles.

12-4. Suppose you are working as the business and system analyst for your college/university. As a business and system analyst, design the BPM (refer to Figure 12-5) for your campus placement process.. In this BPM, enlist three stages. For the first stage take the option of your classmates and seniors. Then accordingly create components for each identified process in the second stage. In the third stage, identify process actors who will play key role in this process.

12-5. a. Your college/university wants to shift from Conventional CRM to Social CRM. As a business and system analyst, prepare a complete plan using SDLC approach to implement the Social CRM. Try to be elaborate in as many stages as possible in SDLC approach.

   b. Enlist the problems you might encounter if you adopt SDLC approach for Social CRM plan.

   c. Prepare the same plan, i.e. Social CRM plan, applying SCRUM approach.

   d. Compare these two plans and find out which approach yields better results and why.

COLLABORATION EXERCISE 12

Using the collaboration IS you built in Chapter 2 (page 110), collaborate with a group of students to answer the following questions.

Wilma Baker, Jerry Barker, and Chris Bickel met in June 2015 at a convention of resort owners and tourism operators. They sat next to each other by chance while waiting for a presentation; after introducing themselves and laughing at the odd sound of their three names, they were surprised to learn that they managed similar businesses. Wilma Baker lives in Santa Fe, New Mexico, and specializes in renting homes and apartments to visitors to Santa Fe. Jerry Barker lives in Whistler Village, British Columbia, and specializes in renting condos to skiers and other visitors to the Whistler/Blackcomb Resort. Chris Bickel lives in Chatham, Massachusetts, and specializes in renting homes and condos to vacationers to Cape Cod.

The three agreed to have lunch after the presentation. During lunch, they shared frustrations about the difficulty of obtaining new customers, especially given the numerous travel opportunities available via the Internet today. Further, the rise in value of the dollar over the euro has created substantial competition for North American tourism.

As the conversation developed, they began to wonder if there was some way to combine forces (i.e., they were seeking a competitive advantage from an alliance). So, they decided to skip one of the next day's presentations and meet to discuss ways to form an alliance. Ideas they wanted to discuss further were sharing customer data, developing a joint reservation service, and exchanging property listings.

As they talked, it became clear they had no interest in merging their businesses; each wanted to stay independent. They also discovered that each was very concerned, even paranoid, about protecting their existing customer base from poaching. Still, the conflict was not as bad as it first seemed. Barker's business was primarily the ski trade, and winter was his busiest season; Bickel's business was mostly Cape Cod vacations, and she was busiest during the summer. Baker's high season was the summer and fall. So, it seemed there was enough difference in their high seasons that they would not necessarily cannibalize their businesses by selling the others' offerings to their own customers.

The question then became how to proceed. Given their desire to protect their own customers, they did not want to develop a common customer database. The best idea seemed to be to share data about properties. That way they could keep control of their customers but still have an opportunity to sell time at the others' properties.

They discussed several alternatives. Each could develop her or his own property database, and the three could then share those databases over the Internet. Or they could develop a centralized property database that they would all use. Or they could find some other way to share property listings.

Because we do not know Baker, Barker, and Bickel's detailed requirements, you cannot develop a plan for a specific system. In general, however, they first need to decide how elaborate an information system they want to construct. Consider the following two alternatives:

a. They could build a simple system centered on email. With it, each company sends property descriptions to the others via email. Each independent company then forwards these descriptions to its own customers, also using email. When a customer makes a reservation for a property, that request is then forwarded back to the property manager via email.

b. They could construct a more complex system using a Web-based, shared database that contains data on all their properties and reservations. Because reservations tracking is a common business task, it is likely that they can license an existing application with this capability.

In your answers to 12-6 and 12-7, use Microsoft Visio and BPMN templates to construct your diagram. If you don't have those templates, use the cross-functional and basic flowchart templates. If you do not have access to Visio, use PowerPoint instead.

12-6. Create a process diagram for alternative a, using Figure 12-8 as a guide. Each company will need to have a role for determining its available properties and sending emails to the other companies that describe them. They will also need to have a role for receiving emails and a role for renting properties to customers. Assume the companies have from three to five agents who can fulfill these roles. Create a role for the email system if you think it is appropriate. Specify roles, activities, repositories, and data flows.

12-7. Create a process diagram for alternative b, using Figure 12-8 as a guide. Each company will need to have a role for determining its available properties and adding them to the reservation database. They will also need a role for renting properties that accesses the shared database. Assume the companies have from three to five agents who can fulfill these roles. Create a role for the property database application. Specify roles, activities, repositories, and data flows.

12-8. Compare and contrast your answers in questions 12-6 and 12-7. Which is likely to be more effective in generating rental income? Which is likely to be more expensive to develop? Which is likely to be more expensive to operate?

12-9. After answering above question, make a development plan (applying SDLC approach) of the alternative that you think may be more effective in generating the income.

CASE STUDY 12

When Will We Learn?

When David Kroenke, one of the authors of this text, was teaching at Colorado State in 1974, he participated in a study that investigated the primary causes of information systems development failures. The findings? The number one reason for failure was a lack of user involvement in creating and managing system requirements.

Technology has made enormous strides since that study. In 1974, computers consumed large rooms, and neither the minicomputer nor the personal computer had been invented. Alas, the development of information systems has not kept up; in fact, one can argue that nothing has changed.

Consider Case Study 7 (pages 288–290). The state of Oregon wasted more than $248M attempting to develop an information system to support its healthcare exchange. And very early in the project, Maximus Company, an independent consulting firm that had been hired to provide quality assurance, warned that requirements were vague, changing, and inconsistent. Those warnings made no difference. Why?

Why Are Requirements Not Managed?

In 1974, it might have been that managers were computer illiterate and thus couldn't know how to manage requirements. However, everyone involved in Cover Oregon has a cell phone and probably an iPad or Kindle, so they are hardly computer illiterate. So today, at least, computer literacy isn't the problem.

Does the problem of *managing requirements* lie with *management?* Or with *requirements?* In Case Study 7, you learned that Access CT, the Connecticut healthcare project, succeeded. Was it because the project was closely managed by the lieutenant governor? A woman with future political ambitions? Oregon has no lieutenant governor, but surely there was someone to manage the project. One indication of management problems in Oregon is that the information system was to be used by one healthcare agency (Cover Oregon) but developed by a different healthcare agency (Oregon Health Administration). The two agencies fought battles over requirements. Due to lack of senior-level management, not only were requirements unmanaged, they were fought over by two competing governmental agencies.

That might be the prime cause for Cover Oregon's failure. But is there something else? Even in well-managed organizations, is there something about requirements that makes them hard to manage? Fred Brooks provided one insight when he said that software is logical poetry. It's made of pure thought-stuff. If two governmental agencies were to construct a building and if they fought over, say, how many stories that building was to have, then their disagreement would be visible for all to see.

People would notice one group of contractors adding a floor while another group is tearing it down.

So part of the problem is that the requirements are requirements for pure thought-stuff. But what else?

How do you know if the requirements are complete? If the blueprints for a building don't include any provisions for electrical systems, that omission is obvious. Less so with software and systems. For example, what if no one considers the need to do something when a client forgets his username or password and has no record of policy numbers? Software or procedures need to be developed for this situation, but if no one thinks to specify that requirement, then nothing will be done. The system will fail when such a client need appears.

And how do you know the quality of the requirements statements? A requirement like "Select a qualifying insurance policy for this client" is written at such a high level that it is useless. One of the reasons for building a prototype is to flush out missing and incomplete requirements.

Assess Feasibility and Make Trade-offs

But there's more we can learn from this example. All of the state and federal healthcare exchanges needed to be operating by October 1, 2013. So, the schedule was fixed with no chance for an adjustment. Considering cost, while funds were not fixed, they were not easily changed. The states initially provided some funding, as did the U.S. government. Once those financial allocations were made, it was difficult to obtain more money. Not impossible, but difficult.

Examine Figure 12-19 again. If schedule is fixed and if funding is nearly fixed, what is the one factor that can be traded off to reduce project difficulty and risk? The requirements. Reduce them to the bare minimum and get the system running. Then, after some success, add to the project. That seems to be the strategy that Access CT followed.

But this principle exposes another of the problems in Oregon. It wanted everything. It embarked on a policy called "No Wrong Door,"[8] a policy that would leave no person nor problem behind. Cover Oregon should provide a solution for all. Such statements make wonderful political messaging, but if the schedule is fixed and the funding is nearly so, how are those goals to be accomplished? Tell your roommate that you have 1 week between semesters and nearly no money and you plan to take a first-class, 2-month jungle excursion in Africa. Hello? Anyone home?

Software and systems are made of pure thought-stuff. Easy to imagine a glorious future of amazing capability. But they are constructed by costly human labor, and nine women can't make a baby in 1 month. Remember that sentence when you are asked to help determine requirements for your new information system.

Will this case still be relevant 40 years from now? It's up to you and your classmates.

QUESTIONS

12-10. Describe three reasons why cases like this will remain relevant 40 years from now. Describe three developments that could make these cases obsolete. Which will pertain? Will such cases be relevant 40 years from now? Justify your opinion.

12-11. Read the Executive Summary of the First Data report located at *www.oregon.gov/DAS/docs/co_assessment.pdf*. Applying your knowledge about the SDLC, describe what you think are the three major reasons that Cover Oregon failed.

12-12. In Case Study 7 (pages 322–324), you learned that three vendors had been considered as outside contractors, but two of them bowed out of the competition. Describe three reasons that they may have done so.

12-13. The project was known to be in trouble, but it seemed to have a life of its own. Ying Kwong, a technology analyst at Oregon's Department of Administrative Services, said in May 2013 that the Cover Oregon project reminded him of the science fiction movie *The Blob:* "You simply don't know how to shoot this beast, because it does not have a known anatomy with the normal vital organs that make it tick."[9] Had you been a senior manager at Cover Oregon, what would you have done when the problems became apparent?

12-14. In a June 2014 survey, a majority of Oregonians held Governor Kitzhaber responsible. But in that same survey, 48 percent say they would vote for his reelection.[10] Bruce Goldberg, former head of OHA and acting head of Cover Oregon, was fired on March 18, 2014, yet by May 15 was back on full salary with OHA.[11] Given these results, does it seem likely that anyone will bear the consequences for these mistakes? Consider who that might be.

MyMISLab™

Go to the Assignments section of your MyLab to complete these writing exercises.

12-15. Assume that your company has just licensed a cloud-based SaaS CRM system. Your boss asks you what needs to be done to make it operational. Using the SDLC, summarize on one page the work to do to transform that SaaS into a working IS.

12-16. Suppose you work for a medium-sized oil and natural gas company as a systems developer. The CEO is interested in developing an application that will give him information about the amount of natural gas passing through pumping stations located around North America. He wants it to work on his desktop, iPad, and smartphone. The features he wants on the application seem to change every time you talk with him, and you're still in the planning phase. Now he's asked for a schedule. Why might it be difficult to develop a schedule for this project? How would you explain this to the CEO? Describe a metaphor you could use to explain how difficult it will be to accurately predict when the application will be completed.

ENDNOTES

1. A *failure* is a difference between what the system does and what it is supposed to do. Sometimes, you will hear the term *bug* used instead of failure. As a future user, call failures *failures* because that's what they are. Don't have a *bugs list*; have a *failures list*. Don't have an *unresolved bug*; have an *unresolved failure*. A few months of managing an organization that is coping with a serious failure will show you the importance of this difference in terms.

2. Fred Brooks was a successful executive at IBM in the 1960s. After retiring from IBM, he authored a classic book on IT project management called *The Mythical Man-Month*. Published by Addison-Wesley in 1975,

the book is still pertinent today and should be read by every IS manager. It's informative and quite enjoyable to read as well.

3. Chris Sims and Hillary Louise Johnson, *The Elements of Scrum* (Dymaxcon, 2011), pp. 65, 66.

4. Hirotaka Takeuchi and Ikujiro Nonaka, "New New Product Development Game," *Harvard Business Review*, Jan. 1, 1986. Available for purchase at *http://hbr.org*.

5. Some scrum teams have the rule that only *pigs* can speak at stand-ups. The term comes from the joke about the difference between eggs and ham: The chicken is interested, but the pig is committed.

6. Chris Sims and Hillary Louise Johnson, *The Elements of Scrum* (Dymaxcon, 2011), pp. 125–133.

7. *www.eset.com/fileadmin/Images/US/Docs/Business/white_Papers/ESET_ACAD_Medre_A_whitepaper.pdf*.

8. Maria L. La Ganga, "Oregon Dumps Its Broken Healthcare Exchange for Federal Website," *Los Angeles Times*, April 15, 2014, accessed June 14, 2014, *www.latimes.com/nation/politics/politicsnow/la-pn-oregon-drops-broken-healthcare-exchange-20140425-story.html*.

9. Nick Budnick, "Cover Oregon: Health Exchange Failure Predicted, but Tech Watchdogs' Warnings Fell on Deaf Ears," *The Oregonian*, January 18, 2014, accessed June 14, 2014, *www.oregonlive.com/health/index.ssf/2014/01/cover_oregon_health_exchange_f.html*.

10. Hillary Lake, "Exclusive Poll: Majority Holds Kitzhaber Accountable for Cover Oregon Failure," *KATU News*, June 11, 2014, accessed June 14, 2014, *www.katu.com/politics/Exclusive-poll-Majority-holds-Kitzhaber-accountable-for-Cover-Oregon-failure-262818611.html*.

11. Nick Budnick, "Long after Announced 'Resignation,' Ex-Cover Oregon Director Bruce Goldberg Draws $14,425 Monthly Salary," *The Oregonian*, May 21, 2014, accessed June 14, 2014, *www.oregonlive.com/politics/index.ssf/2014/05/long_after_publicized_resignat.html*.

The International Dimension

INTERNATIONAL MIS

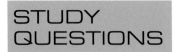
QID-1 How Does the Global Economy Affect Organizations and Processes?

Today's businesses compete in a global market. International business has been sharply increasing since the middle of the 20th century. After World War II, the Japanese and other Asian economies exploded when those countries began to manufacture and sell goods to the West. The rise of the Japanese auto industry and the semiconductor industry in southeastern Asia greatly expanded international trade. At the same time, the economies of North America and Europe became more closely integrated.

Since then, a number of other factors have caused international business to mushroom. The fall of the Soviet Union opened the economies of Russia and Eastern Europe to the world market. Even more important, the telecommunications boom during the dot-com heyday caused the world to be encircled many times over by optical fiber that can be used for data and voice communications.

After the dot-com bust, optical fiber was largely underused and could be purchased for pennies on the dollar. Plentiful, cheap telecommunications enabled people worldwide to participate in the global economy. Before the advent of the Internet, if a young Indian professional wished to participate in the Western economy, he or she had to migrate to the West—a process that was politicized and limited. Today, that same young Indian professional can sell his or her goods or services over the Internet without leaving home. The Chinese economy has also benefitted from plentiful, cheap telecommunications and has become more open to the world.

All of these developments led columnist and author Thomas Friedman to claim, now famously, that "the world is flat," implying seamless integration among the world's economies. That claim and the popular book[1] of the same name fit with the business press's biases and preconceptions, and it seemed to make intuitive sense. A general sense that the world's economies were integrated came to pervade most business thinking.

However, Harvard professor Pankaj Ghemawat decided to look deeper, and the data he found prompted him to write a *Foreign Policy* article titled "Why the World Isn't Flat."[2] His article was published in 2007; the fact that it took such solid research and more than 8 years to gain widespread attention is a testament to the power of bias and preconception.

Some of Ghemawat's data is summarized in Figure ID-1. Notice that, even including cross-border telecommunications, Internet and voice averages less than 17 percent. Even international commerce, which most people think is a large factor in all economies, is less than 23 percent, when corrected for double-counting.[3]

536

Figure ID-1

Percent of Cross-Border Commerce

Source: Pankaj Ghemawat and Steven Altman, *www.dhl.com/content/dam/ Campaigns/gci2014/downloads/dhl_ gci_2014_study_high.pdf*

Commerce Type	Cross-Border Percent
Telecommunication	Voice: 2 percent Internet and voice: 17 percent
Immigration	3 percent immigrants
Investment	8 percent direct investment
Exports	23 percent commerce

Does this mean that international business is not important to you? No, it does not. What it does mean, as Ghemawat points out, is that most of the opportunity of international commerce is ahead of us. The world is not (yet) flat. While information systems have already played a key role in international commerce, their effect in the future is likely to be larger. As Web services become more widespread, it becomes easier to link information systems together. As mobile devices continue their exploding growth in developing countries, even more users will enter the world economy via the Internet. And as collaboration tools become more powerful, it becomes possible to provide services as well as products on the international stage. Opportunity abounds.

How Does the Global Economy Change the Competitive Environment?

To understand the effect of globalization, consider each of the elements in Figure ID-2.

The enlarging Internet-supported world economy has altered every one of the five competitive forces. Suppliers have to reach a wider range of customers, and customers have to consider a wider range of vendors. Suppliers and customers benefit not just from the greater size of the economy, but from the ease with which businesses can learn about each other using tools such as Google and Bing and, in China, Baibu.com.

Because of the data available on the Internet, customers can also learn of substitutions more easily. The Internet has made it substantially easier for new market entrants, although not in all cases. Amazon.com, Apple, and Google, for example, have garnered such a large market share that it would be difficult for any new entrant to challenge them. Still, in other industries,

Figure ID-2

Organizational Strategy Determines Information Systems

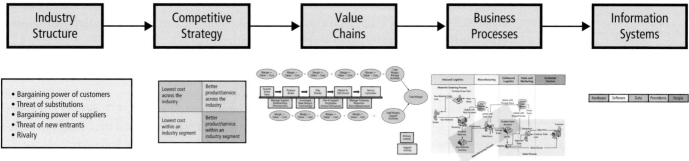

537

the global economy facilitates new entrants. Finally, the global economy has intensified rivalry by increasing product and vendor choices and by accelerating the flow of information about price, product, availability, and service.

How Does the Emerging Global Economy Change Competitive Strategy?

The emerging global economy changes thinking about competitive strategies in two major ways: product localization and product differentiation. First, the sheer size and complexity of the global economy means that any organization that chooses a strategy allowing it to compete industry-wide is taking a very big bite! Competing in many different countries, with products localized to the language and culture of those countries, is an enormous and expensive task.

For example, to promote Windows worldwide, Microsoft must produce versions of Windows in dozens of different languages. Even in English, Microsoft produces a UK version, a U.S. version, an Australian version, and so forth. The problem for Microsoft is even greater because different countries use different character sets. In some languages, writing flows from left to right. In other languages, it flows from right to left. When Microsoft set out to sell Windows worldwide, it embarked on an enormous project.

The second major way today's world economy changes competitive strategies is that its size, combined with the Internet, enables unprecedented product differentiation. If you choose to produce the world's highest quality and most exotic oatmeal—and if your production costs require you to sell that oatmeal for $350 a pound—your target market might contain only 200 people worldwide. The Internet allows you to find them—and them to find you. The decision involving a global competitive strategy requires the consideration of these two changing factors.

How Does the Global Economy Change Value Chains and Business Processes?

Because of information systems, any or all of the value chain activities in Figure ID-2 can be performed anywhere in the world. An international company can conduct sales and marketing efforts locally, for every market in which it sells. 3M divisions, for example, sell in the United States with a U.S. sales force, in France with a French sales force, and in Argentina with an Argentinean sales force. Depending on local laws and customs, those sales offices may be owned by 3M, or they may be locally owned entities with which 3M contracts for sales and marketing services. 3M can coordinate all of the sales efforts of these entities using the same CRM system. When 3M managers need to roll up sales totals for a sales projection, they can do so using an integrated, worldwide system.

Manufacturing of a final product is frequently distributed throughout the world. Components of the Boeing 787 are manufactured in Italy, China, England, and numerous other countries and delivered to Washington and South Carolina for final assembly. Each manufacturing facility has its own inbound logistics, manufacturing, and outbound logistics activity, but those activities are linked via information systems.

For example, Rolls-Royce manufactures an engine and delivers that engine to Boeing via its outbound logistics activity. Boeing receives the engine using its inbound logistics activity. All of this activity is coordinated via shared, inter-enterprise information systems. Rolls-Royce's CRM is connected with Boeing's supply processes, using techniques such as CRM and enterprise resource planning (ERP). We discuss global supply chains further in QID-3.

Because of the abundance of low-cost, well-educated, English-speaking professionals in India, many organizations have chosen to outsource their service and support functions to India. Some accounting functions are outsourced to India as well.

World time differences enable global virtual companies to operate 24/7. Boeing engineers in Los Angeles can develop a design for an engine support strut and send that design to Rolls-Royce in England at the end of their day. The design will be waiting for Rolls-Royce engineers at the start of their day. They review the design, make needed adjustments, and send it back to

Boeing in Los Angeles, where the reviewed, adjusted design arrives at the start of the workday in Los Angeles. The ability to work around the clock by moving work into other time zones increases productivity.

QID-2 What Are the Characteristics of International IS Components?

To understand the effect of internationalization on information systems, consider the five components. Computer hardware is sold worldwide, and most vendors provide documentation in at least the major languages, so it has always been possible to obtain local hardware and set up local networks. Today, however, the emergence of the international cloud makes it even easier for any company, anywhere in the world, to obtain the latest in server technology. It does need to know how to do so, however, pointing to a possible future role for you as an international IS major.

Regarding software, consider the user interface for an international information system. Does it include a local-language version of Windows? What about the software application itself? Does an inventory system used worldwide by Boeing suppose that each user speaks English? If so, at what level of proficiency? If not, what languages must the user interface support?

Next, consider the data component. Suppose that the inventory database has a table for parts data, and that table contains a column named Remarks. Further suppose Boeing needs to integrate parts data from three different vendors: one in China, one in India, and one in England. What language is to be used for recording remarks? Does someone need to translate all of the remarks into one language? Into three languages?

The human components—procedures and people—are obviously affected by language and culture. As with business processes, information systems procedures need to reflect local cultural values and norms. For systems users, job descriptions and reporting relationships must be appropriate for the setting in which the system is used. We will say more about this in QID-5.

What's Required to Localize Software?

The process of making a computer program work in a second language is called **localizing** software. It turns out to be surprisingly hard to do. To localize a document or the content of a Web page, all you need to do is hire a translator to convert your document or page from one language to another. The situation is much more difficult for a computer program, however.

Consider a program you use frequently—say, Microsoft Word—and ask what would need to be done to translate it to a different language. The entire user interface needs to be translated. The menu bar and the commands on it will need to be translated. It is possible that some of the icons will need to be changed because some graphic symbols that are harmless in one culture are confusing or offensive in another.

What about an application program such as CRM that includes forms, reports, and queries? The labels on each of these will require translation. Of course, not all labels translate into words of the same length, and so the forms and reports may need to be redesigned. The questions and prompts for queries, such as "Enter part number for back order," must also be translated.

All of the documentation will need to be translated. That should be just a matter of hiring a translator, except that all of the illustrations in the documentation will need to be redrawn in the second language.

Think, too, about error messages. When someone attempts to order more items than there are in inventory, the application produces an error message. All of those messages will need to be translated. There are other issues as well. Sorting order is one. Spanish uses accents on certain letters, and it turns out that an accented *ó* will sort after *z* when you use the computer's default sort ordering. Figure ID-3 summarizes the factors to address when localizing software.

Figure ID-3
Factors to Address When
Localizing a Computer Program

- Translate the user interface, including menu bars and commands.
- Translate, and possibly redesign, labels in forms, reports, and query prompts.
- Translate all documentation and help text.
- Redraw and translate diagrams and examples in help text.
- Translate all error messages.
- Translate text in all message boxes.
- Adjust sorting order for different character set.
- Fix special problems in Asian character sets and in languages that read and write from right to left.

Programming techniques can be used to simplify and reduce the cost of localization. However, those techniques must be used in design, long before any code is written. For example, suppose that when a certain condition occurs, the program is to display the message "Insufficient quantity in stock." If the programmer codes all such messages into the computer program, then, to localize that program, a programmer will have to find every such message in the code and then ask a translator to change that code. A preferred technique is to give every error message a unique identifier and to create a separate error file that contains a list of identifiers and their associated text. Then, when an error occurs, program code uses the identifier to obtain the text of the message to be displayed from the error file. During localization, translators simply translate the file of error messages into the second language.

The bottom line for you, as a future manager, is to understand two points: (1) Localizing computer programs is much more difficult, expensive, and time consuming than translating documents. (2) If a computer program is likely to be localized, then plan for that localization from the beginning, during design. In addition, when considering the acquisition of a company in a foreign country, be sure to budget time and expense for the localization of information systems.

IBM's Watson Learns Japanese

A good example of the inherent problems with localization can be seen in the recent partnership between IBM and the large Japanese telecommunications provider Softbank.[4] Softbank wants to use IBM's Watson, an artificial intelligence platform able to answer questions using a person's natural language, to improve customer service in its education, banking, healthcare, insurance, and retail sectors. In order to do this, Watson has started learning Japanese.

This is no easy task. The Japanese language uses different characters (kanji), doesn't use spaces between words, and, relative to English, can be contextually difficult to decipher. Watson uses an iterative process to learn Japanese. It processes some text in Japanese, gets feedback from humans who speak Japanese, and then processes more text. It continues this process until it learns how to speak Japanese.

The localization of IBM's Watson won't be easy, but the *potential* benefits are tremendous. Watson doesn't forget, sleep, or take vacations. It's continually learning and processing more information. It could potentially provide customer service to billions of customers worldwide across many different industries at the same time. And it could do it in the customer's native language, not a secondary language (Figure ID-4).[5]

What Are the Problems and Issues of Global Databases?

When we discussed CRM and ERP in Chapter 7, you learned the advantage of having all data stored in a single database. In brief, a single database reduces data integrity problems and makes it possible to have an integrated view of the customer or the operations of the organization.

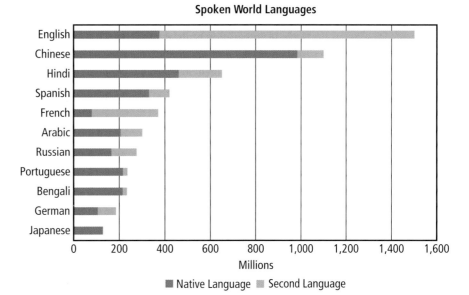

Figure ID-4

Spoken World Languages

Based on the source: "The Most Spoken Languages Worldwide," Statista.com, May 13, 2015, *http:// www.statista.com/statistics/266808/ the-most-spoken-languages-worldwide.*

International companies that have a single database must, however, declare a single language for the company. Every Remark or Comment or other text field needs to be in a single language. If not, the advantages of a single database disappear. This is not a problem for companies that commit to a single company language.

A single database is not possible, however, for companies that use multiple languages. Such companies often decide to give up on the benefits of a single database to let divisions in different countries use different databases, with data in local languages. For example, an international manufacturer might allow a component manufacturing division in South Korea to have a database in Korean and a final assembly division in Brazil to have a different database in Portuguese. In this scenario, the company needs applications to export and import data among the separate databases.

Besides language, performance is a second issue that confronts global databases. When using a single database, data transmission speeds are often too slow to process data from a single geographic location. If so, companies sometimes distribute their database to locations around the world.

Distributed database processing refers to the processing of a single database that resides in multiple locations. If the distributed database contains copies of the same data items, it is called a **replicated database**. If the distributed database does not contain copies of the same data, but rather divides the database into nonoverlapping segments, it is called a **partitioned database**. In most cases, querying either type of distributed database can improve performance without too much development work. However, updating a replicated database so that changes are correctly made to all copies of the data is full of challenges that require highly skilled personnel to solve. Still, companies like Amazon. com, which operates call centers in the United States, India, and Ireland, have invested in applications that are able to successfully update distributed databases worldwide. Given this infrastructure, Amazon.com then made this distributed database technology available via its Web services, as you learned in Chapters 5 and 6. The cloud has made the international distribution of data much easier.

Challenges of International Enterprise Applications?

As you learned in Chapter 7, workgroup business processes and functional applications support particular activities within a single department or business activity. Because the systems operate independently, the organization suffers from islands of automation. Sales and marketing data, for example, are not integrated with operations or manufacturing data.

You learned that many organizations eliminate the problems of information silos by creating enterprise systems. With international IS, however, such systems may not be worthwhile.

Advantages of Functional Systems

Lack of integration is disadvantageous in many situations, but it has *advantages* for international organizations and international systems. For example, if an order-processing functional system located in the United States is independent from the manufacturing systems located in Taiwan, it becomes unnecessary to accommodate language, business, and cultural differences within a single system. U.S. order-processing systems can operate in English and reflect the practices and culture of the United States. Taiwanese manufacturing information systems can operate in Chinese and reflect the business practices and culture of Taiwan. As long as there is an adequate data interface between the two systems, they can operate independently, sharing data when necessary.

Enterprise systems, such as ERP, solve the problems of data isolation by integrating data into a database that provides a comprehensive and organization-wide view. However, that advantage requires that the company standardize on a single language and, most likely, place that database in a single location. Otherwise, separated, functional databases are needed.

Problems of Inherent Processes

Processes inherent in ERP and other applications are even more problematic. Each software product assumes that the software will be used by people filling particular roles and performing their actions in a certain way. ERP vendors justify this standardization by saying that their procedures are based on industry-wide best practices and that the organization will benefit by following these standard processes. That statement may be true, but some inherent processes may conflict with cultural norms. If they do, it will be very difficult for management to convince the employees to follow those processes. Or at least it will be difficult in some cultures to do so.

Differences in language, culture, norms, and expectations compound the difficulties of international process management. Just creating an accurate as-is model is difficult and expensive; developing alternative international processes and evaluating them can be incredibly challenging. With cultural differences, it can be difficult just to determine what criteria should be used for evaluating the alternatives, let alone performing the evaluation.

Because of these challenges, in the future it is likely that international business processes will be developed more like inter-enterprise business processes. A high-level process will be defined to document the service responsibilities of each international unit. Then Web services will be used to connect those services into an integrated, enterprise, international system. Because of encapsulation, the only obligation of an international unit will be to deliver its defined service. One service can be delivered using procedures based on autocratic management policies, and another can be delivered using procedures based on collaborative management policies. The differences will not matter in a Web service-based enterprise system.

QID-3   How Do Inter-enterprise IS Facilitate Global Supply Chain Management?

A **supply chain** is a network of organizations and facilities that transforms raw materials into products delivered to customers. Figure ID-5 shows a generic supply chain. Customers order from retailers, who in turn order from distributors, who order from manufacturers, who order from suppliers. In addition to the organizations shown here, the supply chain also includes transportation companies, warehouses, and inventories and some means for transmitting messages and information among the organizations involved.

Because of disintermediation, not every supply chain has all of these organizations. Some companies sell directly to the customer. Both the distributor and retailer organizations are omitted from their supply chains. In other supply chains, manufacturers sell directly to retailers and omit the distribution level.

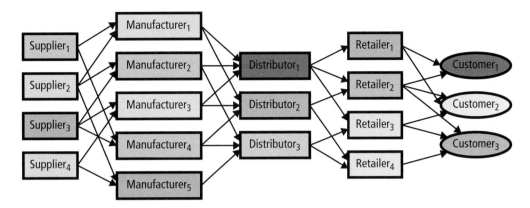

Figure ID-5
Supply Chain Relationships

The term *chain* is misleading. *Chain* implies that each organization is connected to just one company up the chain (toward the supplier) and down the chain (toward the customer). That is not the case. Instead, at each level an organization can work with many organizations both up and down the supply chain. Thus, a supply chain is a *network*.

To appreciate the international dimension of a supply chain, consider Figure ID-6. Suppose you decide to take up cross-country skiing. You go to REI (by visiting either one of its stores or its Web site) and purchase skis, bindings, boots, and poles. To fill your order, REI removes those items from its inventory of goods. Those goods have been purchased, in turn, from distributor/importers.

According to Figure ID-6, REI purchases the skis, bindings, and poles from one distributor/importer and the boots from a second. The distributor/importers, in turn, purchase the required items from the manufacturers, which, in turn, buy raw materials from their suppliers.

In Figure ID-6, notice the national flags on the suppliers and manufacturers. For example, the pole manufacturer is located in Brazil and imports plastic from China, aluminum from Canada, and fittings from Italy. The poles are then imported to REI in the United States by the Importer/Distributor.

The only source of revenue in a supply chain is the customer. In the REI example, you spend your money on the ski equipment. From that point all the way back up the supply chain to the raw materials suppliers, there is no further injection of cash into the system. The money you spend on the ski equipment is passed back up the supply chain as payments for goods or raw materials. Again, the customer is the only source of revenue.

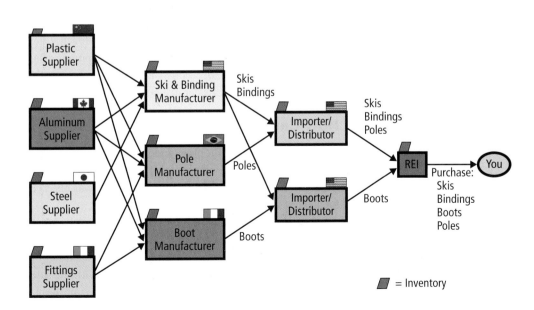

Figure ID-6
Supply Chain Example

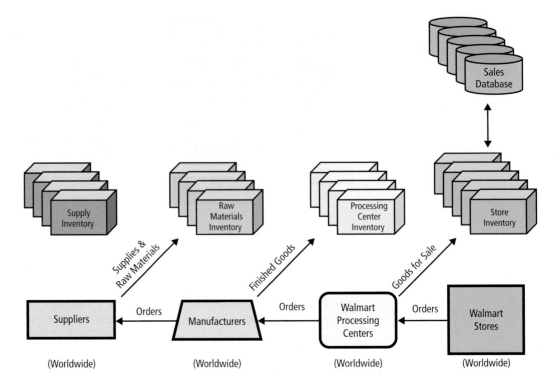

Figure ID-7

Example Walmart Supply Chain

The Importance of Information in the Supply Chain

In order to stay competitive, the focus of many businesses, worldwide, is to reduce costs. Supply chain costs are a primary target for such reductions, especially among companies that have a global supply chain. Figure ID-7 illustrates how Walmart overhauled its supply chain to eliminate distributors and other intermediaries, enabling it to buy directly from manufacturers. Walmart's goal is to increase sales and revenues from its private-label goods. At the same time, it also has consolidated purchasing and warehousing into four global merchandising centers, such as the one near Mexico City that processes goods for emerging markets.[6]

As you'll learn in your production and supply chain courses, many different factors determine the cost and performance of a supply chain. However, information is one of the most important. Consider, for example, inventory management at each of the companies in Figure ID-7. How do those companies decide when and how much to purchase? How does the new Walmart processing center in Mexico City determine how many pairs of jeans, ice chests, or bottles of vitamin C to order? How large should the orders be? How frequently should orders be placed? How are those orders tracked? What happens when a shipment disappears? Information is a major factor in making each of those decisions, along with dozens of others. To provide insight into the importance of information, consider just one example, the bullwhip effect.

How Can Information Relieve the Bullwhip Effect?

The **bullwhip effect** is a phenomenon in which the variability in the size and timing of orders increases at each stage up the supply chain, from customer to supplier. Figure ID-8 depicts the situation. In a famous study, the bullwhip effect was observed in Procter & Gamble's supply chain for diapers.[7]

Except for random variation, diaper demand is constant. Diaper use is not seasonal; the requirement for diapers does not change with fashion or anything else. The number of babies determines diaper demand, and that number is constant or possibly slowly changing.

Retailers do not order from the distributor with the sale of every diaper package. The retailer waits until the diaper inventory falls below a certain level, called the *reorder quantity*. Then the

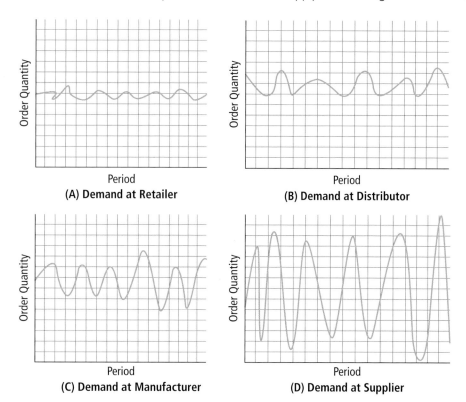

Figure ID-8

The Bullwhip Effect

Source: Adapted from Hau L. Lee, V. Padmanabhan, and S. Whang, "The Bullwhip Effect in Supply Chains," *Sloan Management Review,* Spring 1997, pp. 93–102.

retailer orders a supply of diapers, perhaps ordering a few more than it expects to sell to ensure that it does not have an outage.

The distributor receives the retailer's order and follows the same process. It waits until its supply falls below the reorder quantity, and then it reorders from the manufacturer, with perhaps an increased amount to prevent outages. The manufacturer, in turn, uses a similar process with the raw-materials suppliers.

Because of the nature of this process, small changes in demand at the retailer are amplified at each stage of the supply chain. As shown in Figure ID-8, those small changes become quite large variations on the supplier end.

The bullwhip effect is a natural dynamic that occurs because of the multistage nature of the supply chain. It is not related to erratic consumer demand, as the study of diapers indicated. You may have seen a similar effect while driving on the freeway. One car slows down, the car just behind it slows down a bit more abruptly, which causes the third car in line to slow down even more abruptly, and so forth, until the thirtieth car or so is slamming on its brakes.

The large fluctuations of the bullwhip effect force distributors, manufacturers, and suppliers to carry larger inventories than should be necessary to meet the real consumer demand. Thus, the bullwhip effect reduces the overall profitability of the supply chain. Eliminating or at least reducing the bullwhip effect is particularly important for international supply chains where logistics costs are high and shipping times are long.

One way to eliminate the bullwhip effect is to give all participants in the supply chain access to consumer-demand information from the retailer. Each organization can thus plan its inventory or manufacturing based on the true demand (the demand from the only party that introduces money into the system) and not on the observed demand from the next organization up the supply chain. Of course, an *inter-enterprise information system* is necessary to share such data.

Consider the Walmart example in Figure ID-9. Along the bottom, each entity orders from the entity up the supply chain (the entity to its left in Figure ID-9). Thus, for example, the Walmart processing centers order finished goods from manufacturers. Without knowledge of the true

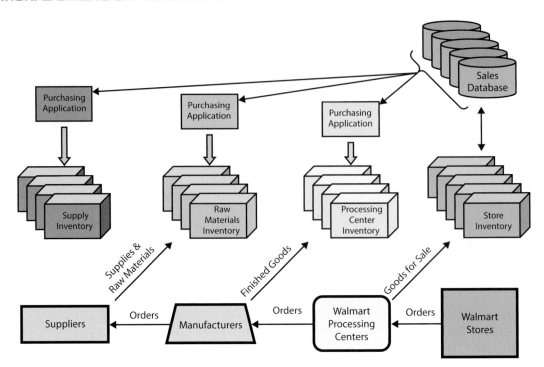

Figure ID-9
Eliminate Bullwhip Effect with
True Demand Information

demand, this supply chain is vulnerable to bullwhip effects. However, if each entity can, via an information system, obtain data about the true demand—that is, the demand from the retail customers who are the source of funds for this chain—then each can anticipate orders. The data about true demand will enable each entity to meet order requirements, while maintaining a smaller inventory.

QID-4 What Are the Security Challenges of International IS?

Managing international systems creates unique security challenges that derive from differences in legal systems, physical environments, and cultural norms. These security challenges represent very real threats to an organization's ability to operate in another country.

Legal Environment

First, differences in legal environments between countries have a direct impact on the daily operation of information systems. The legal differences related to the use of encryption, distribution of content, and personal privacy protections can substantially affect international IS.

Most people are unaware that encryption is *illegal* or highly restricted in many countries. Yes, you read that correctly, illegal. In Russia and China, a license is required to import or export encryption products.[8] The use of any encryption product requires a license. Other countries like England, India, and Australia have laws that can force decryption. In fact, in 2015 British Prime Minister David Cameron suggested that back doors be placed in all software that would effectively circumvent all encryption. Companies that use encryption need to be aware that encryption laws differ between countries and may affect their ability to operate effectively.

Laws regarding the legality of the nature of the content stored in an organization's systems are also different between countries. For example, in 2010 Google moved its search engine service from China to Hong Kong over censorship problems. The People's Republic of China (PRC) regularly forced Google to remove content that the PRC found unacceptable. Google subsequently saw its search market share drop from 12 percent to about 1.7 percent in 2013.[9]

In fact, dozens of countries regularly block access to certain Internet companies. Iraq blocked Twitter, Facebook, and YouTube during a 2014 insurgency. Turkey's government blocked Twitter and YouTube once in 2014 to suppress an embarrassing video showing officials talking about starting a war and then again in 2015 to block a YouTube video of a prosecutor being held hostage.[10]

Variations in privacy laws can also affect the operation of an organization's international systems. For example, in parts of Europe employers cannot read their workers' emails, personal data cannot be collected without an individual's permission, organizations must provide individuals with the ability to correct inaccuracies in the data they collect, and personal data cannot be shared by companies without express permission. None of these apply to organizations in the United States.

Differences in privacy laws may become even more pronounced. In 2014, Google lost a legal battle and was forced to provide European users with the "right to be forgotten." Individuals can request references of them to be removed from search results. As of 2015, Google had received more than 250,000 removal requests for more than 920,000 URLs. It has removed 41.3 percent of the requested URLs.[11]

This ruling will likely be applied to other service providers like Bing, Yahoo!, and Ask.com as well. Unfortunately, none of these privacy protections apply to U.S. citizens. In fact, Google assembled its own panel of advisers, which recommended that the "right to be forgotten" rule not apply to any of Google's properties outside the EU. This means EU users can still see their removed URLs if they visit *www.google.com* rather than *www.google.co.uk*.

Organizations need to be aware that laws related to privacy, content, and encryption will affect the way they collect, process, and store data. Consider how these laws might affect organizations that use cloud-based services to store data. Organizations could operate in a country with loose content laws and then store all of their data and applications in another country with stricter privacy laws in order to protect their users. In other words, the intersection of international law and technology is forcing organizations to carefully evaluate how they manage their information systems, in particular, the location of their data.

Physical Security

Second, operating information systems internationally can be problematic because of different physical environments. This includes threats to infrastructure in the form of natural disasters, geopolitical risks, civil unrest, and terrorist attacks.

Place your data center in Kansas, and it's subject to tornados. Place your data center internationally, and it's potentially subject to typhoons/hurricanes, earthquakes, floods, volcanic eruptions, or mudslides. For example, the data centers in Japan survived the terrible effects of the 2011 earthquake, tsunami, and nuclear reactor meltdowns. They survived the shaking, flooding, and widespread power outages because they were housed in special facilities with shock-absorbing structures and had backup power generators.

An organization's physical infrastructure is also vulnerable to outright seizure. In 2011, the FBI seized several racks of servers from a data center in Reston, Virginia, that belonged to a Switzerland-based company named DigitalOne.[12] DigitalOne's owner, Sergej Ostroumow, said the seizure knocked several sites offline, but declined to say which one of his clients was being targeted.

Employees who run critical infrastructure can be targeted as well. In 2014, Russian president Vladimir Putin revoked visas for nearly 1,000 foreign workers when tensions flared between Russia and Western countries. Deloitte & Touche's local chief operating officer, Quentin O'Toole, was deported for his wife's speeding tickets.

Cultural Norms

Finally, cultural norms can affect the way organizations manage their international information systems. For example, bribery is generally considered unacceptable in the United States, but in other countries it is accepted as a normal way of doing business.

In 2012, Walmart became embroiled in a bribery scandal that showed that local Walmart executives in Mexico used bribes to get building permits and expedite its expansion in Mexico. The fallout from the scandal resulted in departures of several key executives and $439 million spent on investigations and a new compliance program. It's important to note that this is just one example. Graft is a worldwide problem. This example points out how differences in cultural norms can affect an organization's daily operations.

Apply these cultural differences to the management of international information systems. Can an organization depend on the control of separation of duties and authorities in a culture for which graft is an accepted norm? Could an organization lose valuable intellectual property in such an environment? Or what is the utility of a personal reference in a culture in which it is considered exceedingly rude to talk about someone when he or she is not present?

Organizations need to carefully examine how the deployment of international information systems might be affected by cultural norms. Because of differences in cultural norms, safeguards need to be chosen and evaluated on a culture-by-culture basis. Additional safeguards may be needed, but the technical and data safeguards described in Chapter 10 still apply to international systems.

QID-5 What Are the Challenges of International IS Management?

In addition to security, size and complexity make international IS management challenging. The components of international information systems are larger and more complex. Projects to develop them are larger and more complicated to manage. International IS departments are bigger and composed of people from many cultures with many different native languages. International organizations have more IS and IT assets, and those assets are exposed to more risk and greater uncertainty. Because of the complexity of international law, security incidents are more complicated to investigate.

Why Is International IS Development More Challenging?

The factors that affect international information systems development are more challenging than those that affect international software development. If the *system* is truly international, if many people from many different countries will be using the system, then the development project is exceedingly complicated.

To see why, consider the five components. Running hardware in different countries is not a problem, especially using the cloud, and localizing software is manageable, assuming programs were designed to be localized. Databases pose more difficulties. First, is a single database to be used, and if so, is it to be distributed? If so, how will updates be processed? Also, what language, currency, and units of measure will be used to store data? If multiple databases are to be used, how are data going to be transported among them? Some of these problems are difficult, but they are solvable, and cloud-based databases make them more so.

The same cannot be said for the procedure and people components. An international system is used by people who live and work in cultures that are vastly different from one another. The way customers are treated in Japan differs substantially from the way customers are treated in Spain, which differs substantially from the way they are treated in the United States. Therefore, the procedures for using a CRM will be correspondingly different.

Consider the relationship of business processes and information systems as discussed in Chapter 12. Information systems are supposed to facilitate the organization's competitive strategy and support business processes. But what if the underlying business processes differ? Customer support in Japan and customer support in Spain may involve completely different processes and activities.

Even if the purpose and scope can be defined in some unified way, how are requirements to be determined? Again, if the underlying business processes differ, then the specific requirements for the information system will differ. Managing requirements for a system in one culture is difficult, but managing requirements for international systems can be many times more difficult.

There are two responses to such challenges: (1) either define a set of standard business processes or (2) develop alternative versions of the system that support different processes in different countries. Both responses are problematic. The first response requires conversion of the organization to different work processes, and, as you learned in Chapter 7, such conversion can be exceedingly difficult. People resist change, and they will do so with vehemence if the change violates cultural norms.

The second response is easier to implement, but it creates system design challenges. It also means that, in truth, there is not one system, but many.

In spite of the problems, both responses are used. For example, SAP, Oracle, and other ERP vendors define standard business processes via the inherent procedures in their software products. Many organizations attempt to enforce those standard procedures. When it becomes organizationally infeasible to do so, organizations develop exceptions to those inherent procedures and develop programs to handle the exceptions. This choice means high maintenance expense.

What Are the Challenges of International Project Management?

Managing a global IS development project is difficult because of project size and complexity. Requirements are complex, many resources are required, and numerous people are involved. Team members speak different languages, live in different cultures, work in different time zones, and seldom meet face to face.

One way to understand how these factors affect global project management is to consider each of the project management knowledge areas as set out by the International Project Management Institute's document, the *PMBOK*® *Guide* (*www.pmi.org/PMBOK-Guide-and-Standards.aspx*). Figure ID-10 summarizes challenges for each knowledge area. Project integration

Knowledge Areas	Challenge
Project integration	Complex integration of results from distributed work groups. Management of dependencies of tasks from physically and culturally different work groups.
Requirements (scope)	Need to support multiple versions of underlying business processes. Possibly substantial differences in requirements and procedures.
Time	Development rates vary among cultures and countries.
Cost	Cost of development varies widely among countries. Two members performing the same work in different countries may be paid substantially different rates. Moving work among teams may dramatically change costs.
Quality	Quality standards vary among cultures. Different expectations of quality may result in an inconsistent system.
Human resources	Worker expectations differ. Compensation, rewards, work conditions vary widely.
Communications	Geographic, language, and cultural distance among team members impedes effective communication.
Risk	Development risk is higher. Easy to lose control.
Procurement	Complications of international trade.

Figure ID-10

Challenges for International IS Project Management

is more difficult because international development projects require the complex integration of results from distributed work groups. Also, task dependencies can span teams working in different countries, increasing the difficulty of task management.

The scope and requirements definition for international IS is more difficult, as just discussed. Time management is more difficult because teams in different cultures and countries work at different rates. Some cultures have a 35-hour workweek, and some have a 60-hour workweek. Some cultures expect 6-week vacations, and some expect 2 weeks. Some cultures thrive on efficiency of labor, and others thrive on considerate working relationships. There is no standard rate of development for an international project.

In terms of cost, different countries and cultures pay vastly different labor rates. Using critical path analysis, managers may choose to move a task from one team to another. Doing so, however, may substantially increase costs. Thus, management may choose to accept a delay rather than move work to an available (but more expensive) team. The complex trade-offs that exist between time and cost become even more complex for international projects.

Quality and human resources are also more complicated for international projects. Quality standards vary among countries. The IT industry in some nations, such as India, has invested heavily in development techniques that increase program quality. Other countries, such as the United States, have been less willing to invest in quality. In any case, the integration of programs of varying quality results in an inconsistent system.

Worker expectations vary among cultures and nations. Compensation, rewards, and worker conditions vary, and these differences can lead to misunderstandings, poor morale, and project delays.

Because of these factors, effective team communication is exceedingly important for international projects, but because of language and culture differences and geographic separation, such communication is difficult. Effective communication is also more expensive. Consider, for example, just the additional expense of maintaining a team portal in three or four languages.

If you consider all of the factors in Figure ID-10, it is easy to understand why project risk is high for international IS development projects. So many things can go wrong. Project integration is complex; requirements are difficult to determine; cost, time, and quality are difficult to manage; worker conditions vary widely; and communication is difficult. Finally, project procurement is complicated by the normal challenges of international commerce.

What Are the Challenges of International IS Management?

Chapter 11 defined the four primary responsibilities of the IS department: plan, operate, develop, and protect information systems and supporting infrastructure. Each of these responsibilities becomes more challenging for international IS organizations.

Regarding planning, the principal task is to align IT and IS resources with the organization's competitive strategy. The task does not change character for international companies; it just becomes more complex and difficult. Multinational organizations and operations are complicated; thus, the business processes that support their competitive strategies also tend to be complicated. Furthermore, changes in global economic factors can mean dramatic changes in processes and necessitate changes in IS and IT support. Technology adoption can also cause remarkable change. The increasing use of cell phones in developing countries, for example, changes the requirements for local information systems. The price of oil and energy can change international business processes. For these reasons, planning tasks for international IS are larger and more complex.

Three factors create challenges for international IS operations. First, conducting operations in different countries, cultures, and languages adds complexity. Go to the Web site of any multinational corporation, say, *www.3m.com* or *www.dell.com*, and you'll be asked to click on the country in which you reside. When you click, you are likely to be directed to a Web server running in some other country. Those Web servers need to be managed consistently, even though they are operated by people living in different cultures and speaking various languages.

The second operational challenge of international IS is the integration of similar, but different, systems. Consider inventory. A multinational corporation might have dozens of different inventory systems in use throughout the world. To enable the movement of goods, many of these systems need to be coordinated and integrated.

Or consider customer support that operates from three different support centers in three different countries. Each center may have its own information system, but the data among those systems will need to be exported or otherwise shared. If not, then a customer who contacts one center will be unknown to the others.

The third complication for operations is outsourcing. Many organizations have chosen to outsource customer support, training, logistics, and other backroom activities. International outsourcing is particularly advantageous for customer support and other functions that must be operational 24/7. Many companies outsource logistics to UPS because doing so offers comprehensive, worldwide shipping and logistical support. The organization's information systems usually need to be integrated with outsource vendors' information systems, and this may need to be done for different systems, all over the world.

The fourth IS department responsibility is protecting IS and IT infrastructure. We consider that function next.

Setting Up Information Systems in Foreign Offices

The fourth IS department responsibility is protecting IS and IT infrastructure. To illustrate the challenges of international IS management, suppose that Falcon Security decides to open an office in Europe. How might it go about developing information systems for that office?

Before answering that question, consider how the Mahr Group, a midsized, multinational firm headquartered in Germany manages its foreign offices. The Mahr Group purchases its hardware and Internet access from local vendors but has its corporate employees install and configure the same software worldwide. It also has corporate employees perform standardized IT audits worldwide at each foreign office.[13]

Because it is a manufacturer, Mahr operates an ERP system, for which it maintains a centralized database in Germany that is accessed via its own leased communication lines worldwide. It also requires that the same computer-assisted-design (CAD) software be used worldwide. Doing so allows Mahr employees to exchange designs with offices around the world without worrying about compatibility problems.

ACTIVE REVIEW

Use this Active Review to verify that you understand the ideas and concepts that answer the study questions.

QID-1 How does the global economy affect organizations and processes?

Describe how the global economy has changed since the mid-20th century. Explain how the dot-com bust influenced the global economy and changed the number of workers worldwide. Summarize why the idea that the world is flat gained momentum and why that notion is incorrect. State how the lack of a "flat" world presents business opportunities. Summarize the ways in which today's global economy influences the five competitive forces. Explain how the global economy changes the way organizations assess industry structure. How does the global economy change competitive strategy? How do global information systems benefit the value chain? Using Figure 3-6 (page 124) as a guide, explain how each primary value chain activity can be performed anywhere in the world.

QID-2 What are the characteristics of international IS components?

Explain how internationalization affects the five components of an IS. What does it mean to localize software? Summarize the work required to localize a computer program. In your own words, explain why it is better to design a program to be localized rather than attempt to adapt an existing single-language program to a second language. Explain the problems of having a single database for an international IS. Define *distributed database, replicated database,* and *partitioned database.* State a source of problems for processing replicated databases.

Summarize the advantages of functional systems for international companies. Summarize the issues of inherent processes for multinational ERP. Explain how SOA services could be used to address the problems of international enterprise applications.

QID-3 How do inter-enterprise IS facilitate global supply chain management?

Define *supply chain,* and explain why the term *chain* is misleading. Under what circumstances are not all of the organizations in Figure ID-6 part of the supply chain? Name the only source of revenue in a supply chain. Explain how Walmart is attempting to reduce supply costs. Describe the bullwhip effect and explain why it adds costs to a supply chain. Explain how the system shown in Figure ID-9 can eliminate the bullwhip effect.

QID-4 What are the security challenges of international IS?

Explain legal differences between countries with respect to the use of encryption, distribution of content, and personal privacy protections. Describe how natural disasters, geopolitical risks, civil unrest, and terrorist attacks could threaten the physical security of international IS. Give an example of how differences in cultural norms may affect international IS.

QID-5 What are the challenges of international IS management?

State the two characteristics that make international IS management challenging.

Explain the difference between international systems development and international software development. Using the five-component framework, explain why international systems development is more difficult. Give an example of one complication for each knowledge area in Figure ID-10. State the four responsibilities for IS departments. Explain how each of these responsibilities is more challenging for international IS organizations. Describe three factors that create challenges for international IS operations. Summarize the strategy that Mahr uses when creating IS infrastructure in foreign offices.

KEY TERMS AND CONCEPTS

Bullwhip effect   544
Distributed database processing   541

Localizing   539
Partitioned database   541

Replicated database   541
Supply chain   542

MyMISLab™

To complete the problems with the ⭐, go to EOC Discussion Questions in the MyLab.

USING YOUR KNOWLEDGE

⭐ **ID-1.** Suppose you are about to have a job interview with a multinational company, such as 3M, Starbucks, or Coca-Cola. Further suppose you wish to demonstrate an awareness of the changes for international commerce that the Internet and modern information technology have made. Using the information in QID-1, create a list of three questions that you could ask the interviewer regarding the company's use of IT in its international business.

⭐ **ID-2.** Suppose you work for a business that has $100M in annual sales that is contemplating acquiring a company in Mexico. Assume you are a junior member of a team that is analyzing the desirability of this acquisition. Your boss, who is not technically savvy, has asked you to prepare a summary of the issues that she should be aware of in the merging of information systems of the two companies. She wants your summary to include a list of questions that she should ask of both your IS department and the IS department personnel in the prospective acquisition. Prepare that summary.

⭐ **ID-3.** Using the data in this module as well as in Chapter 7, summarize the strengths and weaknesses of functional systems, CRM, and ERP. How do the advantages and disadvantages of each change in an international setting? For your answer, create a table with strength and weakness columns and with one row for each of the four systems types.

ID-4. Suppose you are the CISO for a *Fortune* 500 company with offices in 15 different countries. Your company has substantial intellectual property to protect, and the CEO has suggested that the company move part of its R&D offshore to reduce costs. Using the information from QID-4, describe the potential threats that might arise from moving R&D to an offshore site.

MyMISLab™

Go to the Assignments section of your MyLab to complete these writing exercises.

ID-5. Suppose you are working for a well-known social media company based in the United States. You've been placed in charge of expanding the company internationally. The first day on the job the chief information security officer (CISO) informs you that there have been repeated intrusions into corporate servers located in Asia. The hackers targeted accounts of well-known political dissidents. And they continue to do so on a regular basis. They make little effort to cover their tracks. The problem is that they're based in the country in which you're focusing your expansion efforts. Explain how different legal and cultural norms may hamper your expansion plans. Why might foreign government officials be hesitant to help you catch the hackers? Why types of concessions or changes might the foreign government ask you to make to your social media platform before you're given permission to operate in the country?

ID-6. Assume you are Toshio at Falcon Security. Using your knowledge from QID-5, write a one-page memo to Joni explaining what needs to be done to set up information systems in a new European office. State and justify any assumptions you make.

ENDNOTES

1. Thomas L. Friedman, *The World Is Flat 3.0: A Brief History of the Twenty-First Century* (New York: Farrar, Strauss and Giroux, 2007).
2. "Pankaj Ghemawat, "Why the World Isn't Flat," *Foreign Policy*, March 2007, *www.foreignpolicy.com/articles/2007/02/14/why_the_world_isnt_flat*.
3. Pankaj Ghemawat and Steven Altman, "DHL Global Connectedness Index 2014," DHL International GmbH, October 2014, accessed May 12, 2015, *www.dhl.com/content/dam/Campaigns/gci2014/downloads/dhl_gci_2014_study_high.pdf*.
4. IBM Corporation, "IBM, SoftBank Alliance to Bring Watson to All of Japan," February 10, 2015, IBM.com, accessed May 13, 2015, *www-03.ibm.com/press/us/en/pressrelease/46045.wss*.
5. Statistia Inc., "The Most Spoken Languages Worldwide," Statista.com, May 13, 2015, *www.statista.com/statistics/266808/the-most-spoken-languages-worldwide*.
6. Jim Jubak, "China Feels Global Market Pain," *Jubak's Journal*, last updated August 12, 2010, *http://articles.moneycentral.msn.com/Investing/JubaksJournal/global-markets-pain-moves-to-china.aspx*.
7. Hau L. Lee, V. Padmanabhan, and S. Whang, "The Bullwhip Effect in Supply Chains," *Sloan Management Review*, Spring 1997, pp. 93–102.
8. Bert-Jaap Koops, "Crypto Law Survey," *Cryptolaw.org*, February 2013, *www.cryptolaw.org*, accessed May 13, 2015.
9. Paul Carsten, "Microsoft blocks censorship of Skype in China: advocacy group," *Reuters.com*, November 27, 2013, accessed May 14, 2015, *http://www.reuters.com/article/2013/11/27/us-microsoft-china-censorship-idUSBRE9AQ0Q520131127*.
10. Raziye Akkoc, "Turkey Blocks Access to Social Media and YouTube over Hostage Photos," *The Telegraph*, April 6, 2015, accessed May 14, 2015, *www.telegraph.co.uk/news/worldnews/europe/turkey/11518004/Turkey-blocks-access-to-Facebook-Twitter-and-YouTube.html*.
11. Google Inc., "European Privacy Requests for Search Removals," Google.com, May 13, 2015, accessed July 31, 2015, *www.google.com/transparencyreport/removals/europeprivacy*.
12. Verne Kopytoff, "FBI Seizes Web Servers, Knocking Sites Offline," *The New York Times*, June 21, 2011, accessed June 27, 2014, *http://bits.blogs.nytimes.com/2011/06/21/f-b-i-seizes-web-servers-knocking-sites-offline/*.
13. Private correspondence with the author, August 2011.

Application Exercises

All exercise files can be found on the following Web site: *www.pearsonglobaleditions.com/kroenke*.

Chapter 1

AE1-1. The spreadsheet in Microsoft Excel file **Ch01Ex01_U9e.xlsx** contains records of employee activity on special projects. Open this workbook and examine the data that you find in the three spreadsheets it contains. Assess the accuracy, relevancy, and sufficiency of this data to the following people and problems.

    a. You manage the Denver plant, and you want to know how much time your employees are spending on special projects.

    b. You manage the Reno plant, and you want to know how much time your employees are spending on special projects.

    c. You manage the Quota Computation project in Chicago, and you want to know how much time your employees have spent on that project.

    d. You manage the Quota Computation project for all three plants, and you want to know the total time employees have spent on your project.

    e. You manage the Quota Computation project for all three plants, and you want to know the total labor cost for all employees on your project.

    f. You manage the Quota Computation project for all three plants, and you want to know how the labor-hour total for your project compares to the labor-hour totals for the other special projects.

    g. What conclusions can you make from this exercise?

AE1-2. The database in the Microsoft Access file **Ch01Ex02_U9e.accdb** contains the same records of employee activity on special projects as in Application Exercise 1-1. Before proceeding, open that database and view the records in the Employee Hours table.

    a. Eight queries have been created that process this data in different ways. Using the criteria of accuracy, relevancy, and sufficiency, select the single query that is most appropriate for the information requirements in Application Exercise 1-1, parts a–f. If no query meets the need, explain why.

    b. What conclusions can you make from this exercise?

    c. Comparing your experiences on these two projects, what are the advantages and disadvantages of spreadsheets and databases?

Chapter 2

AE2-1. Suppose that you have been asked to assist in the managerial decision about how much to increase pay in the next year. Assume you are given a list of the departments in your company, along with the average salary for employees in each department for major companies in your industry. Additionally, you are given the names and salaries of 10 people in each of three departments in your company.

    Assume you have been asked to create a spreadsheet that shows the names of the 10 employees in each department, their current salary, the difference between their current salary and the industry average salary for their department, and the percent their salary would need to be increased to meet the industry average. Your spreadsheet should also compute the average increase needed to meet the industry average for each department and the average increase, company-wide, to meet industry averages.

a. Use the data in the file **Ch02Ex01_U9e.docx** and create the spreadsheet.

b. How can you use this analysis to contribute to the employee salary decision? Based on this data, what conclusions can you make?

c. Suppose other team members want to use your spreadsheet. Name three ways you can share it with them and describe the advantages and disadvantages of each.

AE2-2. Suppose that you have been asked to assist in the managerial decision about how much to increase pay in the next year. Specifically, you are tasked to determine if there are significant salary differences among departments in your company.

You are given an Access database with a table of employee data with the following structure:

EMPLOYEE (Name, Department, Specialty, Salary)

where *Name* is the name of an employee who works in a department, *Department* is the department name, *Specialty* is the name of the employee's primary skill, and *Salary* is the employee's current salary. Assume that no two employees have the same name. You have been asked to answer the following queries:

(1) List the names, department, and salary of all employees earning more than $100,000.

(2) List the names and specialties of all employees in the Marketing department.

(3) Compute the average, maximum, and minimum salary of employees in your company.

(4) Compute the average, minimum, and maximum salary of employees in the Marketing department.

(5) Compute the average, minimum, and maximum salary of employees in the Information Systems department.

(6) *Extra credit:* Compute the average salary for employees in every department. Use *Group By*.

a. Design and run Access queries to obtain the answers to these questions, using the data in the file **Ch02Ex02_U9e.accdb**.

b. Explain how the data in your answer contributes to the salary increase decision.

c. Suppose other team members want to use your Access application. Name three ways you can share it with them, and describe the advantages and disadvantages of each.

Chapter 3

AE3-1. Figure AE-1 shows an Excel spreadsheet that the resort bicycle rental business uses to value and analyze its bicycle inventory. Examine this figure to understand the meaning of the data. Now use Excel to create a similar spreadsheet. Note the following:

- The top heading is in 20-point Calibri font. It is centered in the spreadsheet. Cells A1 through H1 have been merged.
- The second heading, Bicycle Inventory Valuation, is in 18-point Calibri, italics. It is centered in cells A2 through H2, which have been merged.
- The column headings are set in 11-point Calibri, bold. They are centered in their cells, and the text wraps in the cells.

a. Make the first two rows of your spreadsheet similar to that in Figure AE-1. Choose your own colors for background and type, however.

b. Place the current date so that it is centered in cells C3, D3, and E3, which must be merged.

c. Outline the cells as shown in Figure AE-1.

	A	B	C	D	E	F	G	H
1				Resort Bicycle Rental				
2				*Bicycle Inventory Valuation*				
3				Saturday, May 27, 2017				
4	**Make of Bike**	**Bike Cost**	**Number on Hand**	**Cost of Current Inventory**	**Number of Rentals**	**Total Rental Revenue**	**Revenue per Bike**	**Revenue as Percent of Cost of Inventory**
5	Wonder Bike	$325	12	$3,900	85	$6,375	$531	163.5%
6	Wonder Bike II	$385	4	$1,540	34	$4,570	$1,143	296.8%
7	Wonder Bike Supreme	$475	8	$3,800	44	$5,200	$650	136.8%
8	LiteLift Pro	$655	8	$5,240	25	$2,480	$310	47.3%
9	LiteLift Ladies	$655	4	$2,620	40	$6,710	$1,678	256.1%
10	LiteLift Racer	$795	3	$2,385	37	$5,900	$1,967	247.4%

Figure AE-1
Excel Spreadsheet
Source: © Access 2013, Microsoft Corporation

d. Figure AE-1 uses the following formulas:

> **Cost of Current Inventory = Bike Cost × Number on Hand**
> **Revenue per Bike = Rental Revenue/Number on Hand**
> **Revenue as a Percent of Cost of Inventory = Total Rental Revenue/**
> **Cost of Current Inventory**

Use these formulas in your spreadsheet, as shown in Figure AE-1.

e. Format the cells in the columns, as shown.

f. Give three examples of decisions that management of the bike rental agency might make from this data.

g. What other calculation could you make from this data that would be useful to the bike rental management? Create a second version of this spreadsheet in your worksheet document that has this calculation.

AE3-2. In this exercise, you will learn how to create a query based on data that a user enters and how to use that query to create a data entry form.

a. Download the Microsoft Access file **Ch03Ex02_U9e.accdb**. Open the file and familiarize yourself with the data in the Customer table.

b. Click *Create* in the Access ribbon. Click the icon labeled *Query Design*. Select the Customer table as the basis for the query by double-clicking on *Customer*. Close the Show Table dialog. Drag CustomerName, CustomerEmail, DateOfLastRental, BikeLastRented, TotalNumberOfRentals, and TotalRentalRevenue into the columns of the query results pane (the table at the bottom of the query design window).

c. In the CustomerName column, in the row labeled Criteria, place the following text:

> **[Enter Name of Customer:]**

Type this exactly as shown, including the square brackets. This notation tells Access to ask you for a customer name to query.

d. In the ribbon, click the red exclamation mark labeled *Run*. Access will display a dialog box with the text "Enter Name of Customer:" (the text you entered in the query Criteria row). Enter the value *Maple, Rex* and click OK.

e. Save your query with the name *Parameter Query*.

f. Click the Home tab on the ribbon and click the Design View (upper left-hand button on the Home ribbon). Replace the text in the Criteria column of the CustomerName column with the following text. Type it exactly as shown:

> **Like "*" & [Enter part of Customer Name to search by:] & "*"**

g. Run the query by clicking Run on the ribbon. Enter *Maple* when prompted *Enter part of Customer Name to search by*. Notice that the two customers who have the name Maple are displayed. If you have any problems, ensure that you have typed the phrase above *exactly* as shown into the Criteria row of the CustomerName column of your query.

h. Save your query again under the name *Parameter Query*. Close the query window.

i. Click *Create* on the Access ribbon. Under the Forms group, choose *Form Wizard*. In the dialog that opens, in the Tables/Queries box, click the down arrow. Select *Query: Parameter Query*. Click the double chevron << symbol and all of the columns in the query will move to the Selected Fields area.

j. Click *Next* two times. In the box under *What title do you want for your form?* enter *Customer Query Form* and click *Finish*.

k. Enter *Maple* in the dialog box that appears. Access will open a form with the values for Maple, Rex. At the bottom of the form, click the right-facing arrow and the data for the second customer named Maple will appear. What is that customer's first name? will appear.

l. Close the form. Select *Object Type* and *Forms* in the Access Navigation Pane. Double-click the Customer Query Form and enter the value *Amanda*. Access will display data for all three customers having the value Amanda in their name.

Chapter 4

AE4-1. Sometimes you will have data in one Office application and want to move it to another Office application without rekeying it. Often this occurs when data was created for one purpose but then is used for a second purpose. For example, Figure AE-2 presents a portion of an Excel spreadsheet that shows the assignment of computers to employees.

Suppose you want to use this data to help you assess how to upgrade computers. Let's say, for example, that you want to upgrade all of the computers' operating systems to Windows 10. Furthermore, you want to first upgrade the computers that most need upgrading, but suppose you have a limited budget. To address this situation, you would like to query the data in Figure AE-2, find all computers that do not have Windows 10, and then select those with slower CPUs or smaller memory as candidates for upgrading. To do this, you need to move the data from Excel into Access.

Once you have analyzed the data and determined the computers to upgrade, you want to produce a report. In that case, you may want to move the data from Access back to Excel, or perhaps into Word. In this exercise, you will learn how to perform these tasks.

a. To begin, download the Excel file **Ch04Ex01_U9e.xlsx** into one of your directories. We will import the data in this file into Access, but before we do so, familiarize yourself with the data by opening it in Excel. Notice that there are three worksheets in this workbook. Close the Excel file.

	A	B	C	D	E	F	G	H
1	EmpLastName	EmpFirstName	Plant	Computer Brand	CPU (GHz)	Memory (GB)	Disk (TB)	OS
2	Ashley	Linda	Denver	Dell	3	8	2	Windows 8
3	Davidson	Victor	Denver	Dell	3	6	2	Windows 8
4	Ching	Diem Thi	Denver	HP	3	6	2.5	Windows 8
5	Collins	James	Denver	Dell	2.5	4	1	Windows 7
6	Corning	Haley	Denver	HP	3	6	2	Windows 8
7	Scott	Richard	Denver	HP	2.5	6	2.5	Windows 8
8	Corovic	Anna	Denver	Dell	4	2	3	Windows 10
9	Lane	Kathy	Denver	Lenovo	2.5	4	1	Windows 7
10	Wei	James	Denver	IBM	3	8	2	Windows 8
11	Dixon	Mary	Denver	IBM	2	4	1	Windows 7
12	Lee	Matthew	Denver	Dell	2.5	4	1	Windows 7
13	Duong	Steven	Denver	Dell	2	2	0.75	Vista
14	Bosa	William	Denver	HP	3	6	2.5	Windows 8
15	Drew	Tony	Denver	HP	3	8	2	Windows 8
16	Adams	Mark	Denver	HP	2.5	4	1	Windows 7
17	Lunden	Nicole	Denver	Lenovo	4	2	3	Windows 10
18	Utran	Bryan	Denver	Dell	3	6	2	Windows 8
19								
20		Primary Contact:	Kaye Davidson					

Figure AE-2

Sample Excel Data for Import

Source: © Access 2013, Microsoft Corporation

b. Create a blank Access database. Name the database Ch04Ex01_Answer. Place it in some directory; it may be the same directory into which you have placed the Excel file, but it need not be. Close the default table that Access creates and delete it.

c. Now, we will import the data from the three worksheets in the Excel file **Ch04Ex01_U9e.xlsx** into a single table in your Access database. On the ribbon, select *External Data* and in the Import & Link section, click *Excel*. Start the import. For the first worksheet (Denver), you should select *Import the source data into a new table in the current database*. Ignore the warning about the first row by clicking OK. Be sure to click *First Row Contains Column Headings* when Access presents your data. You can use the default Field types and let Access add the primary key. Name your table *Employees* and click *Finish*. There is no need to save your import script.

  For the Miami and Boston worksheets, again click *External Data, Import Excel*, but this time select *Append a copy of the records to the table Employees*. Select the Miami worksheet and click *Finish*. Repeat to import the Boston office employees.

d. Open the *Employee* table and examine the data. Notice that Access has erroneously imported a blank line and the *Primary Contact* data into rows at the end of each data set. This data is not part of the employee records, and you should delete it (in three places—once for each worksheet). The *Employee* table should have a total of 40 records.

e. Create a parameterized query on this data. Place all of the columns except *ID* into the query. In the *OS* column, set the criteria to select rows for which the value is not *Windows 10*. In the *CPU* (GHz) column, enter the criterion: <=[Enter cutoff value for CPU] and in the *Memory* (GB) column, enter the criterion: <=[Enter cutoff value for Memory]. Test your query. For example, run your query and enter a value of 4 for both CPU and memory. Verify that the correct rows are produced.

f. Use your query to find values of CPU and memory that give you as close to a maximum of 15 computers to upgrade as possible.

g. When you have found values of CPU and memory that give you 15, or nearly 15, computers to upgrade, leave your query open. Now, click *External data, Word*, and create a Word document that contains the results of your query. Adjust the column widths of the created table so that it fits on the page. Write a memo around this table explaining that these are the computers that you believe should be upgraded.

AE4-2.   Assume you have been asked to create a spreadsheet to help make a buy-versus-lease decision about the servers for your organization. Assume that you are considering the servers for a 5-year period, but you do not know exactly how many servers you will need. Initially, you know you will need five servers, but you might need as many as 50, depending on the success of your organization's e-commerce activity. (By the way, many organizations are still making these calculations. However, those that have moved to the cloud no longer need to do so!)

a. For the buy-alternative calculations, set up your spreadsheet so that you can enter the base price of the server hardware, the price of all software, and a maintenance expense that is some percentage of the hardware price. Assume that the percent you enter covers both hardware and software maintenance. Also assume that each server has a 3-year life, after which it has no value. Assume straight-line depreciation for computers used less than 3 years, and that at the end of the 5 years you can sell the computers you have used for less than 3 years for their depreciated value. Also assume that your organization pays 2 percent interest on capital expenses. Assume the servers cost $2,500 each, and the needed software costs $1250. Assume that the maintenance expense varies from 2 to 7 percent.

b. For the lease-alternative calculations, assume that the leasing vendor will lease the same computer hardware you can purchase. The lease includes all the software you need as well as all maintenance. Set up your spreadsheet so that you can enter various lease costs, which vary according to the number of years of the lease (1, 2, or 3). Assume the cost of a 3-year lease is $285 per machine per month, a 2-year lease is $335 per machine per month, and a 1-year lease is $415 per machine per month. Also, the lessor offers a 5 percent discount if you lease from 20 to 30 computers and a 10 percent discount if you lease from 31 to 50 computers.

c. Using your spreadsheet, compare the costs of buy versus lease under the following situations. (Assume you either buy or lease. You cannot lease some and buy some.) Make assumptions as necessary and state those assumptions.

(1) Your organization requires 20 servers for 5 years.

(2) Your organization requires 20 servers for the first 2 years and 40 servers for the next 3 years.

(3) Your organization requires 20 servers for the first 2 years, 40 servers for the next 2 years, and 50 servers for the last year.

(4) Your organization requires 10 servers the first year, 20 servers the second year, 30 servers the third year, 40 servers the fourth year, and 50 servers the last year.

(5) For the previous case, does the cheaper alternative change if the cost of the servers is $4,000? If it is $8,000?

AE4-3. As you read in Chapter 4, open source software is popular because it's stable, customizable, and free. But you may not have used open source software before. In this project, you will download an alternate to the Microsoft Office suite called LibreOffice. It has applications for making documents (Writer), spreadsheets (Calc), presentations (Impress), databases (Base), and graphics (Draw) similar to those in Microsoft Office.

If you're used to Microsoft Office, it will take some time to become familiar with the LibreOffice interface. LibreOffice can do just about everything Microsoft Office can do, but it does it in a slightly different way. The main benefit of using LibreOffice is that it's totally free. You can install it as many times as you'd like on as many computers as you'd like.

a. Browse to *www.libreoffice.org*.

b. Click on the Download menu and select LibreOffice Fresh.

c. Download and install the latest version of LibreOffice. (There are LibreOffice versions for Windows, Mac OS X, and Linux.)

d. Open LibreOffice Calc. (There will be a shortcut on your desktop.)

e. Enter your name, date, and time into the new spreadsheet in cells A1, A2, and A3, respectively.

f. Click Tools and Options.

g. Expand the Load/Save menu and click on General.

h. Change the "Always save as" dropdown from ODF Spreadsheet to Microsoft Excel 2007/2010/2013 XML and click OK. (You can do the same thing for documents and presentations.)

i. Click File, Save, and Save.

j. Take a screenshot with your name showing and paste it into your document. (You can take a screenshot by pressing Alt + Print Screen.)

k. Explain why more people don't use LibreOffice if it's free.

l. Explain why a systems administrator, who manages hundreds of servers (with Linux and Windows operating systems), might like using LibreOffice.

m. Explain why LibreOffice might be an important application for users or organizations in developing countries.

Chapter 5

AE5-1. In some cases, users want to use Access and Excel together. They process relational data with Access, import some of the data into Excel, and use Excel's tools for creating professional-looking charts and graphs. You will do exactly that in this exercise.

Download the Access file **Ch05Ex01_U9e.accdb**. Open the database and select *DATABASE TOOLS/Relationships*. As you can see, there are three tables: *Product*, *VendorProductInventory*, and *Vendor*. Open each table individually to familiarize yourself with the data.

For this problem, we will define *InventoryCost* as the product of *IndustryStandardCost* and *QuantityOnHand*. The query *InventoryCost* computes these values for every item in inventory for every vendor. Open that query and view the data to be certain you understand this computation. Open the other queries as well so that you understand the data they produce.

a. Sum this data by vendor and display it in a pie chart like that shown in Figure AE-3 (your totals will be different from those shown). Proceed as follows:

(1) Open Excel and create a new spreadsheet.

(2) Click *DATA* on the ribbon and select *From Access* in the *Get External Data* ribbon category.

(3) Navigate to the location in which you have stored the Access file **Ch05Ex01_U9e.accdb**.

(4) Select the query that contains the data you need for this pie chart.

(5) Import the data into a worksheet.

(6) Format the appropriate data as currency.

(7) Select the range that contains the data, press the Function key, and proceed from there to create the pie chart. Name the data and pie chart worksheets appropriately.

b. Follow a similar procedure to create the bar chart shown in Figure AE-4. Again, your data will be different. Place the data and the chart in separate worksheets and name them appropriately.

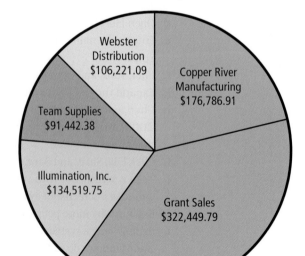

Figure AE-3

Data Displayed in Pie-Chart Format

Source: © Access 2013, Microsoft Corporation

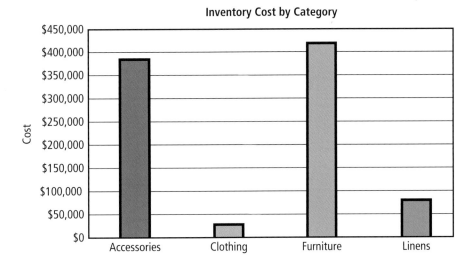

Inventory Cost by Category

Figure AE-4

Data Displayed in
Bar-Chart Format

Source: © Access 2013,
Microsoft Corporation

AE5-2. Read Case Study 5 on pages 230–234. A copy of Dean's database is stored in the Access file **Ch05Ex02_U9e.accdb.** Download a copy of this file and create queries to provide the following data:

   a. Sort the pianos from high quality to low.

   b. Sort the pianos from high quality to low and, within each quality, sort by Building and then by Location within that building.

   c. List the pianos in the shed and sort the results by manufacturer.

   d. List all of the pianos with a Type of 'Spinet.'

   e. Count the pianos for each value of quality (ranging from 1 to 5).

   f. Write a query to produce the report in Figure 5-36 on page 200.

AE5-3. In this exercise, you will create a two-table database, define relationships, create a form and a report, and use them to enter data and view results.

   a. Download the Excel file **Ch05Ex03_U9e.xlsx.** Open the spreadsheet and review the data in the *Employee* and *Computer* worksheets.

   b. Create a new Access database with the name *Ch05Ex03_Solution.* Close the table that Access automatically creates and delete it.

   c. Import the data from the Excel spreadsheet into your database. Import the *Employee* worksheet into a table named *Employee.* Be sure to check *First Row Contains Column Headings.* Select *Choose my own primary key* and use the ID field as that key.

   d. Import the *Computer* worksheet into a table named *Computer.* Check *First Row Contains Column Headings,* but let Access create the primary key.

   e. Open the relationships window and add both *Employee* and *Computer* to the design space. Drag ID from *Employee* and drop it on *EmployeeID* in *Computer.* Check *Enforce Referential Integrity* and the two checkmarks below. Ensure you know what these actions mean.

   f. Open the Form Wizard dialog box (under *Create, More Forms*) and add all of the columns for each of your tables to your form. Select *View your data by Employee.* Title your form *Employee* and your subform *Computer.*

   g. Open the *Computer* subform and delete *EmployeeID* and *ComputerID.* These values are maintained by Access, and it is just a distraction to keep them. Your form should appear like the one shown in Figure AE-5 (Your data will be different.).

   h. Use your form to add two new computers to *Michael Murphy.* Both computers are Dells, both use Windows 10, one costs $750, and the other costs $1,400.

   i. Delete the Lenovo computer for Stan Larsen.

Figure AE-5
Employee Computer Assignment Form
Source: © Access 2013, Microsoft Corporation

j. Use the Report Wizard (under *Create*) to create a report having all data from both the *Employee* and *Computer* tables. Adjust the report design until you find a design you like. Correct the label alignment if you need to.

Chapter 6

AE6-1. Numerous Web sites are available that will test your Internet data communications speed. You can find one good example at *www.speedtest.net*. (If that site is no longer active, Google or Bing "What is my Internet speed?" to find another speed-testing site. Use it.)

a. While connected to your university's network, go to Speedtest.net and test your speed against servers in Seattle, New York City, and Atlanta. Compute your average upload and download speeds.

b. Go home, or to a public wireless site, and run the Speedtest.net test again. Compute your average upload and download speeds. If you are performing this test at home, are you getting the performance you are paying for?

c. Contact a friend or relative in another state. Ask him or her to run the Speedtest.net test against those same three cities.

d. Compare the results in parts a–c. What conclusion, if any, can you draw from these tests?

AE6-2. Assume you have been asked to create an Office application to estimate cloud computing costs. You decide to create a spreadsheet into which your customers can provide their cloud computing needs and which you can then import into an Access database and use queries to compute cloud computing costs.

Figure AE-6 shows the structure of the spreadsheet into which your customers will input their requirements. You can download this spreadsheet in the Excel file **Ch06Ex02_U9e.xlsx**. Figure AE-7 shows an Access table that has costs corresponding to the requirements in Figure AE-6. You can download this database in the Access file **Ch06Ex02_U9e.accdb**.

a. Import the spreadsheet data into the Access database.

b. Write queries to compute the cost of each resource.

c. Create a report that shows the cost for each type of resource for each month. Show the total costs for the 6-month period for each resource as well. Include a grand total of all the costs.

	A	B	C	D	E	F	G
1		Jan-17	Feb-17	Mar-17	Apr-17	May-17	Jun-17
2	**Compute requirements (hours):**						
3							
4	Extra Small Instance	1200	1200	1200	1200	1200	1200
5	Small Instance	2000	2000	2400	2400	0	3000
6	Medium Instance	900	1800	2700	3600	3600	3600
7	Large Instance	0	500	1000	1500	2000	2000
8	Extra Large Instance	0	0	0	1000	1500	2000
9							
10	Storage requirements:						
11	Storage Required (GB)	30	35	40	45	50	55
12	Storage Transactions (1000s)	30	30	35	35	40	50
13							
14	Database requirements (number of instances)						
15	10GB Database	2	2	2	2	1	1
16	20GB Database	0	3	3	3	3	3
17	30GB Database		4	5	6	6	7
18	40GB Database	0	0	0	3	3	4
19	50GB Database	0	0	2	2	3	0

Figure AE-6
Worksheet for Inputting Cloud Computing Requirements
Source: © Access 2013, Microsoft Corporation

CloudCosts

ID	Resource Name	Units	Cost
1	Extra Small Instance	Hours	$0.03
2	Small Instance	Hours	$0.09
3	Medium Instance	Hours	$0.12
4	Large Instance	Hours	$0.37
5	Extra Large Instance	Hours	$0.55
6	StorageRequired	GB / month	$0.15
7	StorageTransactions	10,000	$0.01
8	10GB Database	Each	$9.99
9	20GB Database	Each	$149.98
10	30GB Database	Each	$199.97
11	40GB Database	Each	$299.96
12	50GB Database	Each	$399.95

Figure AE-7
Cloud Computing Costs
Source: © Access 2013, Microsoft Corporation

   d. Create a pie chart that breaks out the total costs by resource. *Hint:* You can import the query data back into Excel.

   e. Create a pie chart that breaks out the total costs by month. *Hint:* You can import the query data back into Excel.

   f. Assume that processing costs increase by 10 percent across the board. Repeat parts c, d, and e for the changed costs.

AE6-3.   There are a few problems with cloud-based storage. First, it seems like there's never enough of it. This is especially true if it's free. Second, you always wonder if it's really secure. Yes, your storage provider says your data is secure. But is it really? Is there some way to be sure?

   In this project, you will learn how to use 7-Zip to solve both of these problems. You'll learn how to compress and encrypt important files and directories. If you are storing confidential data in the cloud, it's important to make sure it's encrypted—by you. Using a third-party encryption tool like 7-Zip means only *you* can access your data. Trusting your cloud providers isn't necessary. 7-Zip is also a very efficient file archiver that will save you a lot of space.

    a. Browse to *www.7-zip.org*.

    b. Click on Download and install the latest version of 7-Zip for your operating system. (There are 7-Zip versions for Windows, Mac OS X, Linux, BSD, and UNIX.)

    c. Go to your Downloads folder. (You can go to any folder that contains large files.)

    d. Right-click on a large file.

    e. Click 7-Zip and Add to archive.

    f. Rename the file YourName.7z. (Replace "YourName" with your first and last names. If your name was John Doe, the file would be named JohnDoe.7z.)

    g. In the Encryption section, enter a password—twice. (Choose a simple password you can remember.)

    h. Take a screenshot and paste it into your document. (You can take a screenshot by pressing Alt + Print Screen.)

    i. Click OK. (Notice that your original file remains unchanged.)

    j. After your new YourName.7z file is compressed, right-click it and select 7-Zip and Extract to "YourName\".

    k. Enter the password you set, and click OK. (Your file should start extracting.)

    l. Explain why third-party encryption is important for highly confidential files.

    m. Explain why compressing large files is important when using cloud-based storage.

Chapter 7

AE7-1. Suppose your manager asks you to create a spreadsheet to compute a production schedule. Your schedule should stipulate a production quantity for seven products that is based on sales projections made by three regional managers at your company's three sales regions.

    a. Create a separate worksheet for each sales region. Use the data in the Word file **Ch07Ex01_U9e.docx**. This file contains each manager's monthly sales projections for the past year, actual sales results for those same months, and projections for sales for each month in the coming quarter.

    b. Create a separate worksheet for each manager's data. Import the data from Word into Excel.

    c. On each of the worksheets, use the data from the prior four quarters to compute the discrepancy between the actual sales and the sale projections. This discrepancy can be computed in several ways: You could calculate an overall average, or you could calculate an average per quarter or per month. You could also weight recent discrepancies more heavily than earlier ones. Choose a method that you think is most appropriate. Explain why you chose the method you did.

    d. Modify your worksheets to use the discrepancy factors to compute an adjusted forecast for the coming quarter. Thus, each of your spreadsheets will show the raw forecast and the adjusted forecast for each month in the coming quarter.

    e. Create a fourth worksheet that totals sales projections for all of the regions. Show both the unadjusted forecast and the adjusted forecast for each region and for the company overall. Show month and quarter totals.

    f. Create a bar graph showing total monthly production. Display the unadjusted and adjusted forecasts using different colored bars.

AE7-2. Figure AE-8 is a sample bill of materials (BOM), a form that shows the components and parts used to construct a product. In this example, the product is a child's wagon. Such bills of materials are an essential part of manufacturing functional applications as well as ERP applications.

      This particular example is a form produced using Microsoft Access. Creating such a form is a bit tricky, so this exercise will guide you through the steps required. You can

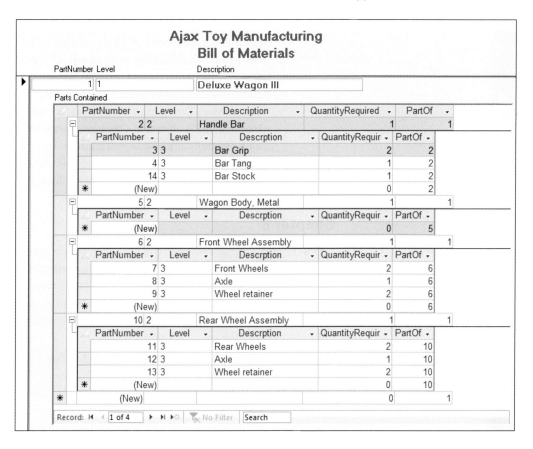

Figure AE-8
Bill of Materials Example
Source: © Access 2013,
Microsoft Corporation

then apply what you learn to produce a similar report. You can also use Access to experiment on extensions of this form.

a. Create a table named *PART* with columns *PartNumber, Level, Description, QuantityRequired,* and *PartOf. Description* and *Level* should be text, *PartNumber* should be AutoNumber, and *QuantityRequired* and *PartOf* should be numeric, long integer. Add the *PART* data shown in Figure AE-8 to your table.

b. Create a query that has all columns of *PART*. Restrict the view to rows having a value of 1 for *Level*. Name your query *Level1*.

c. Create two more queries that are restricted to rows having values of 2 or 3 for *Level*. Name your queries *Level2* and *Level3*, respectively.

d. Create a form that contains *PartNumber, Level,* and *Description* from *Level1*. You can use a wizard for this if you want. Name the form *Bill of Materials*.

e. Select the Subform/Subreport tool in the Controls section of the DESIGN ribbon and create a subform in your form in part d. Set the data on this form to be all of the columns of *Level2*. After you have created the subform, ensure that the Link Child Fields property is set to *PartOf* and that the Link Master Fields property is set to *PartNumber*. Close the *Bill of Materials* form.

f. Open the subform created in part e and create a subform on it using the Subform/Subreport control. Set the data on this subform to be all of the columns of *Level3*. After you have created the subform, ensure that the Link Child Fields property is set to *PartOf* and that the Link Master Fields property is set to *PartNumber*. Close the *Bill of Materials* form.

g. Open the *Bill of Materials* form. It should appear as in Figure AE-8. Open and close the form and add new data. Using this form, add sample BOM data for a product of your own choosing.

h. Following the process similar to that just described, create a *Bill of Materials Report* that lists the data for all of your products.

i. (**Optional, challenging extension**) Each part in the BOM in Figure AE-8 can be used in at most one assembly (there is space to show just one *PartOf* value). You can change your design to allow a part to be used in more than one assembly as follows: First, remove *PartOf* from PART. Next, create a second table that has two columns: *AssemblyPartNumber* and *ComponentPartNumber*. The first contains a part number of an assembly, and the second contains a part number of a component. Every component of a part will have a row in this table. Extend the views described above to use this second table and to produce a display similar to Figure AE-8.

Chapter 8

AE8-1.   Suppose you are the manager of social media policy for an organization having 1,000 employees with seven different offices throughout North America. Further suppose that the CEO has requested a report showing a list of all of the employees' blogs, the employees' job titles and departments, and the purpose and URL of each blog. She doesn't want to control employees; she just wants to know where they are.

a. Explain the conditions under which using a spreadsheet to track this data would be appropriate.

b. Suppose that employees can have more than one blog, but that a blog is only supported by a single employee. Further suppose that you decide that you need to track the dates on which a blog was first created and the date of the last posting, if the blog is no longer active. Design a database for these requirements.

c. Fill your database with the sample data in the Word document **Ch08Ex01_U9e. docx**. EmployeeID is a unique identifier; a null value for EndDate means the blog is still active. Do not retype this data; import it instead. You can either import it several times, each time to a different table, or you can import it once and use queries to fill the tables.

d. Create a report that you believe is suitable for the CEO's needs. Justify the content and structure of your report.

AE8-2.   Assume that you have been given the task of compiling evaluations that your company's purchasing agents make of their vendors. Each month, every purchasing agent evaluates all of the vendors that he or she has ordered from in the past month on three factors: price, quality, and responsiveness. Assume the ratings are from 1 to 5, with 5 being the best. Because your company has hundreds of vendors and dozens of purchasing agents, you decide to use Access to compile the results.

a. Create a database with three tables: VENDOR (*VendorNumber, Name, Contact*), PURCHASER (*EmpNumber, Name, Email*), and RATING (*EmpNumber, VendorNumber, Month, Year, Price Rating, QualityRating, ResponsivenessRating*). Assume that *VendorNumber* and *EmpNumber* are the keys of VENDOR and PURCHASER, respectively. Decide what you think is the appropriate key for RATING.

b. Create appropriate relationships.

c. Import the data in the Excel file **Ch08Ex02_U9e.xlsx**. Note that data for Vendor, Purchaser, and Rating are stored in three separate worksheets.

d. Create a query that shows the names of all vendors and their average scores.

e. Create a query that shows the names of all employees and their average scores. *Hint:* In this and in part f, you will need to use the *Group By* function in your query.

f. Create a parameterized query that you can use to obtain the minimum, maximum, and average ratings on each criterion for a particular vendor. Assume you will enter *VendorName* as the parameter.

g. Using the data created by your queries, what conclusions can you make about vendors or purchasers?

Chapter 9

AE9-1.   OLAP cubes are very similar to Microsoft Excel pivot tables. For this exercise, assume that your organization's purchasing agents rate vendors similar to the situation described in Application Exercise 8-2.

a. Open the Excel file **Ch09Ex01_U9e.xlsx**. The spreadsheet has the following column names: *VendorName, EmployeeName, Date, Year,* and *Rating.*

b. Under the *INSERT* ribbon in Excel, click *Pivot Table.*

c. When asked to provide a data range, drag your mouse over the column names and data values so as to select all of the data. Excel will fill in the range values in the open dialog box. Place your pivot table in a new worksheet. Click OK.

d. Excel will create a field list on the right-hand side of your spreadsheet. Underneath it, a grid labeled Drag fields between areas below: should appear. Drag and drop the field named *VendorName* into the area named ROWS. Observe what happens in the pivot table to the left (in column A). Now drag and drop *EmployeeName* on to COLUMNS and *Rating* on to VALUES. Again observe the effect of these actions in the pivot table to the left. Voilà! You have a pivot table.

e. To see how the pivot table works, drag and drop more fields onto the grid in the bottom right hand side of your screen. For example, drop *Year* just underneath *EmployeeName.* Then move *Year* above *Employee.* Now move *Year* below *Vendor.* All of this action is just like an OLAP cube, and, in fact, OLAP cubes are readily displayed in Excel pivot tables. The major difference is that OLAP cubes are usually based on thousands or more rows of data.

AE9-2.   It is surprisingly easy to create a market-basket report using table data in Access. To do so, however, you will need to enter SQL expressions into the Access query builder. Here, you can just copy SQL statements or type them in. If you take a database class, you will learn how to code SQL statements like those you will use here.

a. Create an Access database with a table named *Order_Data* having columns *OrderNumber, ItemName,* and *Quantity,* with data types Number (*LongInteger*), Short Text (50), and Number (*LongInteger*), respectively. Define the key as the composite (*OrderNumber, ItemName*). (You can do this in the table designer by highlighting both columns and clicking the Primary Key icon.)

b. Import the data from the Excel file **Ch09Ex02_U9e.xlsx** into the *Order_Data* table.

c. Now, to perform the market-basket analysis, you will need to enter several SQL statements into Access. To do so, click *CREATE/Query Design.* Click Close when the Show Table dialog box appears. Right-click in the gray section above the grid in the window. Select SQL View. Enter the following expression exactly as it appears here:

```
SELECT    T1.ItemName as FirstItem,
          T2.ItemName as SecondItem
FROM      Order_Data T1, Order_Data T2
WHERE     T1.OrderNumber =
          T2.OrderNumber
AND       T1.ItemName <> T2.ItemName;
```

Click the red exclamation point in the toolbar to run the query. Correct any typing mistakes and, once it works, save the query using the name TwoItem Basket.

d. Now enter a second SQL statement. Again, click *CREATE/Query Design*. Click Close when the Show Table dialog box appears. Right-click in the gray section above the grid in the window. Select SQL View. Enter the following expression exactly as it appears here:

```
SELECT     TwoItemBasket.FirstItem,
           TwoItemBasket.SecondItem,
           Count(*) AS SupportCount
FROM       TwoItemBasket
GROUP BY   TwoItemBasket.FirstItem,
           TwoItemBasket.SecondItem;
```

Correct any typing mistakes and, once it works, save the query using the name SupportCount.

e. Examine the results of the second query and verify that the two query statements have correctly calculated the number of times that two items have appeared together. Explain further calculations you need to make to compute support.

f. Explain the calculations you need to make to compute lift. Although you can make those calculations using SQL, you need more SQL knowledge to do it, and we will skip that here.

g. Explain, in your own words, what the query in part c seems to be doing. What does the query in part d seem to be doing? Again, you will need to take a database class to learn how to code such expressions, but this exercise should give you a sense of the kinds of calculations that are possible with SQL.

AE9-3. Suppose you work for the bicycle parts distributor mentioned in Q9-2 of Chapter 9. The team was investigating the possibility of selling 3D printable plans for bike parts rather than the parts themselves. The team needed to identify qualifying parts and compute how much revenue potential those parts represent. Download the Access file **Ch09Ex03_U9e.accdb**, which contains the data extract the team used.

    a. Suppose Desert Gear Supply decides not to release its 3D design files at any price. Remove parts provided by it from consideration and repeat the data analysis in Chapter 9.

    b. The team decides, in light of the absence of Desert Gear Supply's part designs, to repeat its analysis with different criteria as follows:
- Large customers are those who have ordered more than 900 parts.
- Frequent purchases occur at least 25 times per year.
- Small quantities have an average order size of 3 or less.
- Inexpensive parts cost less than $75.
- Shipping weight is less than 4 pounds.

Repeat the data analysis in Chapter 9.

    c. How does the second set of criteria change the results?

    d. What recommendations would you make in light of your analysis?

Chapter 10

AE10-1. Most of the Web sites you visit are not secure. Anyone between you and the Web site you are visiting can see the contents of the packets you are sending. Hypertext Transfer Protocol Secure (https) provides secure communication between hosts. It encrypts the traffic between the two hosts and provides Web server authentication.

In this exercise, you will install HTTPS Everywhere®, an add-on from *www.EFF.org*. This add-on checks to see if the Web site you are visiting offers an https connection. Larger Web sites do offer https connections if requested.

a. Open your Firefox Web browser. (If you don't already have Firefox, it can be downloaded from *www.mozilla.org*.)

b. Browse to *www.wikipedia.org*. (Note that it does not use an encrypted connection.)

c. Browse to *https://www.eff.org/https-everywhere*.

d. Download and install HTTPS Everywhere for Firefox, and then restart your Web browser. (You should see an HTTPS Everywhere icon in the top-right corner of your browser after it restarts.)

e. Browse to *www.wikipedia.org*. (Note that it is using an encrypted connection.)

f. Enter your name into the search box at the encrypted site.

g. Take a screenshot with your name showing and paste it into your document. (You can take a screenshot by pressing Alt + Print Screen simultaneously.)

h. Explain why all Web sites don't offer https connections.

i. Explain why an employer might not like you using https connections.

j. Specify what would you need in order to start offering https on a Web site.

AE10-2. Most users want an easy way to identify which Web sites are trustworthy and which Web sites they should avoid. Web of Trust® (WOT) provides a "scorecard" for each Web site you visit. This scorecard gives you a summary of four ratings: trustworthiness, vendor reliability, privacy, and child safety. The values shown on the scorecard are based on ratings from members of the WOT community who have contributed their evaluations of that Web site.

After installing WOT, you will notice a slight addition to the search results from major search engines (e.g., Google, Bing, and Yahoo!). You will see a WOT evaluation at the end of each search result. This evaluation provides a scorecard for each Web site displayed in the search results. The WOT evaluation can serve as a quick visual indicator of Web sites to avoid.

a. Open Firefox, click the Firefox menu, and click Add-ons.

b. Search for *WOT*.

c. Click Install (WOT) and Restart now. (You should see a small flag in the navigation bar.)

d. Browse to *www.google.com*, and search for your full name.

e. Take a screenshot of the results and paste it into your document. (You can take a screenshot by pressing Alt + Print Screen. Notice the WOT icons next to each of the search results.)

f. Click on the WOT icon for one of the search results. (This will show you the WOT scorecard for that specific Web site.)

g. Using *Google.com*, search for *warez keygen*. (You should get a few Web sites with red circles, meaning they have a poor reputation.)

h. Click on the WOT icon for one of the Web site's WOT scorecard.

i. Take a screenshot and paste it into your document.

j. Describe how WOT gets the values for their Web site scorecards.

k. Describe how you can evaluate Web sites using WOT.

l. Explain how WOT can protect users when surfing the Internet.

Chapter 11

AE11-1. Suppose you have just been appointed manager of a help desk with an IS department. You have been there for just a week, and you are amazed to find only limited data to help you manage your employees. In fact, the only data kept concerns the processing of particular issues, called *Tickets*. The following data are kept: *Ticket#*, *Date_Submitted*, *Date_Opened*, *Date_Closed*, *Type* (new or repeat), *Reporting_ Employee_Name*, *Reporting_Employee_Division*, *Technician_Name_Problem_ System*, and *Problem_Description*. You can find sample Ticket data in the Excel file **Ch11Ex01_U9e.xlsx**.

As a manager, you need information that will help you manage. Specifically, you need information that will help you learn who are your best- and worst-performing technicians, how different systems compare in terms of number of problems reported and the time required to fix those problems, how different divisions compare in terms of problems reported and the time required to fix them, which technicians are the best and worst at solving problems with particular systems, and which technicians are best and worst at solving problems from particular divisions.

a. Use either Access or Excel, or a combination of the two, to produce the information you need using the data in the Excel file **Ch11Ex01_U9e.xlsx**. In your answer, you may use queries, formulas, reports, forms, graphs, pivot tables, pivot charts, or any other type of Access or Excel display. Choose the best display for the type of information you are producing.

b. Explain how you would use these different types of information to manage your department.

c. Specify any additional information that you would like to have produced from this data to help you manage your department.

d. Use either Access or Excel, or a combination, to produce the information in part c.

Chapter 12

AE12-1. In this exercise, you will use Visio to create process diagrams in BPMN notation.

a. Download the Visio file **Ch12Ex01_U9e.vsd** from this text's support site. Open the file and familiarize yourself with this diagram, which is a copy of Figure 12-7.

b. Notice that Visio includes the BPMN shapes. Go to the Shape organizer to see other types of flowchart shapes that Visio supports.

c. Create a new Visio diagram. Add BPMN shapes that you may want to use.

d. Model the customer process Respond to Quotation. Make sure your process accepts the inputs shown in **Ch12Ex01_U9e.vsd** and produces the outputs shown in that figure. Create your process so that your company checks prices and delivery dates, and requests changes, if appropriate. Include other logic, if necessary.

e. Show your work by saving your document as a PDF file.

AE12-2. Suppose you are given the task of comparing labor costs of meetings for systems development projects to budgets. Download the Word file **Ch12Ex02_U9e.docx** and the Excel file with the same name. The Word file has records of meeting dates, times, and attendees. The document was created from informal notes taken at the meetings. The Excel file has the project budgets as well as labor costs for different categories of employees.

Assume your company uses the traditional systems-first process illustrated in Figure 12-12. Further assume that each SDLC step requires two types of meetings: *Working meetings* involve users, business analysts, systems analysts, programmers, and PQA test engineers. *Review meetings* involve all of those people, plus level-1 and level-2 managers of both user departments and the IS department.

    a. Using either Access or Excel, whichever you think is better suited to the task, import the Word data to a work file and compute the total labor for each type of employee for each meeting.

    b. Using the file you created in part a, compute the total labor for each type of employee for each phase of the project.

    c. Combine your answer in part b with the data in the Excel file **Ch12Ex02_U9e.xlsx** to compute the total cost of meetings of each phase of the project.

    d. Use a graphic chart of the type you think best to show the differences between meeting cost and budget.

    e. Comment on your choice of Excel or Access for your work file. If you were to do this exercise over, would you use that same tool again? Why or why not?

AE12-3.   Use Access to develop a failure-tracking database application. Use the sample data in the Excel file **Ch12Ex03_U9e.xlsx** for this exercise. The data includes columns for the following:

> *FailureNumber*
> *DateReported*
> *FailureDescription*
> *ReportedBy (the name of the PQA engineer reporting the failure)*
> *ReportedBy_email (the email address of the PQA engineer reporting the failure)*
> *FixedBy (the name of the programmer who is assigned to fix the failure)*
> *FixedBy_email (the email address of the programmer assigned to fix the failure)*
> *DateFailureFixed*
> *FixDescription*
> *DateFixVerified*
> *VerifiedBy (the name of the PQA engineer verifying the fix)*
> *VerifiedBy_email (the email address of the PQA engineer verifying the fix)*

    a. The data in the spreadsheet are not normalized. Normalize the data by creating a *Failure* table, a *PQA Engineer* table, and a *Developer* table. Assume problems are reported and verified by PQA engineers and problems are fixed by developers. Add other appropriate columns to each table. Create appropriate relationships.

    b. Create one or more forms that can be used to report a failure, to report a failure fix, and to report a failure verification. Create the form(s) so that the user can use a combo box to pull down the name of a PQA engineer or developer from the appropriate table to fill in the *ReportedBy*, *FixedBy*, and *VerifiedBy* fields.

    c. Construct a report that shows all failures sorted by reporting PQA engineer and then by *Date Reported*.

    d. Construct a report that shows only fixed and verified failures.

    e. Construct a report that shows only fixed but unverified failures.

Glossary

10/100/1000 Ethernet A type of Ethernet that conforms to the IEEE 802.3 protocol and allows for transmission at a rate of 10, 100, or 1,000 Mbps (megabits per second). 247

Abstract reasoning The ability to make and manipulate models. One of four key skills for nonroutine cognitive thinking. 44

Access A popular personal and small workgroup DBMS product licensed by Microsoft. Included with some versions of Microsoft Office. 204

ACID An acronym standing for atomic, consistent, isolated, and durable. Used to describe the processing of transactions such that all of the transaction is processed or none of it is (atomic), transactions are processed in the same manner (consistent) whether processed alone or in the presence of millions of other transactions (isolated), and that once a transaction is stored it never goes away—even in the presence of failure (durable). 222

Activity A business function that receives inputs and produces outputs. An activity can be performed by a human, by a computer system, or by both. 126

Ad-blocking software Software that filters out advertising content. 342

Advanced Persistent Threat (APT) A sophisticated, possibly long-running, computer hack that is perpetrated by large, well-funded organizations like governments. APTs are a means to engage in cyberwarfare. 426

Adware Programs installed on the user's computer without the user's knowledge or permission that reside in the background and, unknown to the user, observe the user's actions and keystrokes, modify computer activity, and report the user's activities to sponsoring organizations. Most adware is benign in that it does not perform malicious acts or steal data. It does, however, watch user activity and produce pop-up ads. 439

Agile development An adaptive project management process based on the principles listed in Figure 12-20. Can be used for the management of many types of projects, including processes, information systems, and applications. 518

Android A mobile operating system that is a version of Linux. Android runs on the Google Nexus 7 and the Amazon Kindle Fire as well as many other mobile devices. 163

Application (1) Synonym for application software. (2) A combination of hardware, software, and data that is to be developed for an information system. 492

Application software Programs that perform a business function. Some application programs are general purpose, such as Excel or Word. Other application programs are specific to a business function, such as accounts payable. 166

As-is model A model that represents the current situation and processes. 496

Asymmetric encryption An encryption method whereby different keys are used to encode and to decode the message; one key encodes the message, and the other key decodes the message. Asymmetric encryption is slower and more complicated than symmetric encryption. 436

Asynchronous communication Information exchange that occurs when all members of a work team do not meet at the same time, such as those who work different shifts. 84

Attributes Characteristics of an entity. Example attributes of Order are *OrderNumber, OrderDate, SubTotal, Tax, Total*, and so forth. Example attributes of Salesperson are *SalespersonName, Email, Phone*, and so forth. 213

Augmented reality (AR) The combination of the real world with virtual images or objects. 155

Authentication The process whereby an information system verifies (validates) a user. 433

Baseline WBS The initial work breakdown structure that shows the planned tasks, dependencies, durations, and resource assignments. 515

Bell's Law A new computer class forms roughly each decade, establishing a new industry. 40

Best practices Methods that have been shown to produce successful results in prior implementations. 351

BI analysis The process of creating business intelligence. The four fundamental categories of BI analysis are reporting, data mining, BigData, and knowledge management. 375

BI application The software component of a BI system. 372

BigData A term used to describe data collections that are characterized by huge volume, rapid velocity, and great variety. 394

Binary digits See *bits*. 153

Biometric authentication The use of personal physical characteristics, such as fingerprints, facial features, and retinal scans, to authenticate users. 433

BI server A Web server application that is purpose-built for the publishing of business intelligence. 403

Bitcoins A large cloud-based monetary system that was supposed to replace national currencies. 315

Bits The means by which computers represent data; also called binary digits. A bit is either a zero or a one. 153

BlackBerry OS One of the most successful early mobile operating systems; was primarily used by business users on BlackBerry devices. 163

Bluetooth A common wireless protocol designed for transmitting data over short distances, replacing cables. 247

Bounce rate Percent of people who visit your Web site and then immediately leave. 348

Bring your own device (BYOD) policy An official organizational policy that states employees' permissions and responsibilities when using personal mobile devices for organizational business. 181

Brooks' Law The adage that states: Adding more people to a late project makes the project later. Brooks' Law is true not only because a larger staff requires increased coordination, but also because new people need to be trained. The only people who can train the new employees are the existing team members, who are thus taken off productive tasks. The costs of training new people can overwhelm the benefit of their contributions. Named for Fred Brooks, author of *The Mythical Man-Month.* 515

Brute force attack A password-cracking program that tries every possible combination of characters. 429

Business analyst (1) A person who understands business strategies, goals, and objectives and who helps businesses develop and manage business processes and information systems. (2) Someone who is well versed in Porter's models, organizational strategy, and systems alignment theory, like COBIT, and who also understands technology sufficiently well to communicate with systems analysts and developers. Compare with systems analyst. 494

Business intelligence (BI) The processing of operational data, social data, purchased data, and employee knowledge to expose solutions, patterns, relationships, and trends of importance to the organization. 372

Business intelligence (BI) systems Information systems that produce business intelligence. 371

Business process (1) A network of activities that generate value by transforming inputs into outputs. (2) A network of activities, repositories, roles, resources, and flows that interact to achieve some business function; sometimes called a business system. 126, 494

Business process management (BPM) A cyclical process for systematically creating, assessing, and altering business processes. 127, 496

Business Process Modeling Notation (BPMN) Standard set of terms and graphical notations for documenting business processes. 498

Business process reengineering The activity of altering existing and designing new business processes to take advantage of the capabilities of new information systems technology. 295

Business-to-business (B2B) Relationships through which businesses generate new retail leads. 334

Business-to-consumer (B2C) Relationships through which businesses market their products to end users. 334

Bytes (1) 8-bit chunks of data. (2) Characters of data. 154

Cable line Cable television lines that provide high-speed data transmission. 249

Capital Resources that are invested with the expectation of future gain. 335

Carrier A telecommunications company that provides voice and data transportation services. 250

Central processing unit (CPU) The portion of a computer that selects instructions, processes them, performs arithmetic and logical comparisons, and stores results of operations in memory. 152

Chief information officer (CIO) The title of the principal manager of the IS department. Other common titles are vice president of information services, director of information services, and, less commonly, director of computer services. 464

Chief information security officer (CISO) The title of the person who manages security for the organization's information systems and information. 465

Chief security officer (CSO) The title of the person who manages security for all of the organization's assets: physical plant and equipment, employees, intellectual property, and digital. 465

Chief technology officer (CTO) The title of the head of the technology group. The CTO filters new ideas and products to identify those that are most relevant to the organization. The CTO's job requires deep knowledge of information technology and the ability to envision how new IT could affect an organization over time. 464

Client PCs, tablets, and smartphones that access servers via the cloud. 152

Closed source Source code that is highly protected and only available to trusted employees and carefully vetted contractors. 170

Cloud A term that refers to elastic leasing of pooled computer resources over the Internet. 239

Cluster analysis Unsupervised data mining using statistical techniques to identify groups of entities that have similar characteristics. A common use for cluster analysis is to find groups of similar customers in data about customer orders and customer demographics. 390

COBIT (Control Objectives for Information and related Technology) A set of standard practices, created by the Information Systems Audit and Control Association, that are used in the assessment stage of the BPM cycle to determine how well an information system complies with an organization's strategy. 497

Collaboration The activity of two or more people working together to achieve a common goal via a process of feedback and iteration. One of four key skills for nonroutine cognitive thinking. 44, 73

Collaboration information system An information system that supports collaboration. See also *collaboration system*. 82

Collaboration system See *collaboration information system*. 82

Columns Also called fields, or groups of bytes. A database table has multiple columns that are used to represent the attributes of an entity. Examples are PartNumber, EmployeeName, and SalesDate. 199

Commerce server An application program that runs on a server tier computer. A typical commerce server obtains product data from a database, manages items in users' shopping carts, and coordinates the checkout process. 255

Communication channels Means of delivering messages. 350

Communities See *communities of practice*. 328

Communities of practice Also called communities; groups of people related by a common interest. 328

Competitive analysis Process of identifying the strength and weaknesses in competitors' use of social media. 349

Competitive strategy The strategy an organization chooses as the way it will succeed in its industry. According to Porter, there are four fundamental competitive strategies: cost leadership across an industry or within a particular industry segment and product or service differentiation across an industry or within a particular industry segment. 121

Computer-based information system An information system that includes a computer. 48

Computer hardware Electronic components and related gadgetry that input, process, output, store, and communicate data according to the instructions encoded in computer programs or software. One of the five fundamental components of an information system. 48, 151

Confidence In market-basket terminology, the probability estimate that two items will be purchased together. 392

Configuration control A set of management policies, practices, and tools that systems developers use to maintain control over a project's resources. 516

Connection data In social media systems, data about relationships. 331

Content data In social media systems, data and responses to data that are contributed by users and SM sponsors. 331

Content delivery network (CDN) An information system that serves content to Web pages over the Internet. To reduce wait time, data is typically stored and served from many geographic locations. 260

Content management systems (CMS) Information systems that support the management and delivery of documentation including reports, Web pages, and other expressions of employee knowledge. 399

Control flow A BPMN symbol that documents the flow of activity in a business process. 495

Conversion rate Measures the frequency with which someone who clicks on an ad makes a purchase, "likes" a site, or takes some other action desired by the advertiser. 346

Cookie A small file that is stored on the user's computer by a browser. Cookies can be used for authentication, for storing shopping card contents and user preferences, and for other legitimate purposes. Cookies can also be used to implement spyware. 413, 430

Cooperation The process by which a group of people having the same skills work in parallel to shorten the time required to accomplish a job (e.g., four painters each painting one wall of a room). 73

Cost The cost of a business process is equal to the cost of the inputs plus the cost of activities. 126

Cost feasibility An assessment of the cost of an information system development project that compares estimated costs to the available budget. Can also refer to a comparison of development plus operational costs versus value delivered. 503

Critical path The sequence of activities that determine the earliest date by which the project can be completed. 513

Critical path analysis The process by which project managers compress a schedule by moving resources, typically people, from noncritical path tasks to critical path tasks. 514

Cross-selling The sale of related products to customers based on salesperson knowledge, market-basket analysis, or both. 391

Crowdsourcing The dynamic social media process of employing users to participate in product design or redesign. 334

Crow's feet Lines on an entity-relationship diagram that indicate a 1:N relationship between two entities. 214

Crow's-foot diagram A type of entity-relationship diagram that uses a crow's foot symbol to designate a 1:N relationship. 215

Custom-developed software Software tailor-made for a particular organization's requirements. 167

Customer life cycle Taken as a whole, the processes of marketing, customer acquisition, relationship management, and loss/churn that must be managed by CRM systems. 296

Customer relationship management (CRM) system A suite of applications, a database, and a set of inherent processes for managing all the interactions with the customer, from lead generation to customer service. 295

Data Recorded facts or figures. One of the five fundamental components of an information system. 48

Data acquisition In business intelligence systems, the process of obtaining, cleaning, organizing, relating, and cataloging source data. 374

Data administration An organization-wide function that develops and enforces data policies and standards. 440

Data aggregator See *data broker*. 384

Data broker Also called data aggregator; a company that acquires and purchases consumer and other data from public records, retailers, Internet cookie vendors, social media trackers, and other sources and uses it to create business intelligence that it sells to companies and the government. 384

Data flow A BPMN symbol that documents the movement of data among activities and repositories in a business process. 495

Data integrity In a database or a collection of databases, the condition that exists when data values are consistent and in agreement with one another. 292

Data integrity problem In a database, the situation that exists when data item values disagree with one another. An example is two different names for the same customer. 214

Data mart A data collection, smaller than a data warehouse, that addresses the needs of a particular department or functional area of a business. 383

Data mining The application of statistical techniques to find patterns and relationships among data for classification and prediction. 390

Data model A logical representation of the data in a database that describes the data and relationships that will be stored in the database. Akin to a blueprint. 212

Data safeguards Measures used to protect databases and other data assets from threats. Includes data rights and responsibilities, encryptions, backup and recovery, and physical security. 440

Data triangulation See *semantic security*. 406

Data warehouse A facility for managing an organization's BI data. 380

Database A self-describing collection of integrated records. 199

Database administration A person or department that develops procedures and practices to ensure efficient and orderly multiuser processing of the database, to control changes to database structure, and to protect the database. 206, 440

Database application A collection of forms, reports, queries, and application programs that facilitates users' processing of a database. A database can be processed by many different database applications. 206

Database management system (DBMS) A program for creating, processing, and administering a database. A DBMS is a large and complex program that is licensed like an operating system. Microsoft Access and Oracle Database are example DBMS products. 204

Database tier In the three-tier architecture, the tier that runs the DBMS and receives and processes requests to retrieve and store data. 252

DB2 A popular, enterprise-class DBMS product licensed by IBM. 204

Decision support systems Some authors define business intelligence (BI) systems as supporting decision making only, in which case they use this older term as a synonym for decision-making BI systems. 373

Decision tree A hierarchical arrangement of criteria that predict a classification or a value. 393

Deliverables Work products that are the result of the completion of tasks in a development project. 511

Denial of service (DoS) Security problem in which users are not able to access an information system; can be caused by human errors, natural disaster, or malicious activity. 426

Desktop virtualization Also called client virtualization and PC virtualization. The process of storing a user's desktop on a remote server. It enables users to run their desktop from many different client computers. 166

Digital Revolution The conversion from mechanical and analog devices to digital devices. 39

Digital subscriber line (DSL) A communications line that operates on the same lines as voice telephones but does so in such a manner that its signals to not interfere with voice telephone service. 248

Dimension A characteristic of an OLAP measure. Purchase date, customer type, customer location, and sales region are examples of dimensions. 387

Discussion forums Forms of asynchronous communication in which one group member posts an entry and other group members respond. A better form of group communication than email because it is more difficult for one person to monopolize the discussion or for the discussion to go off track. 86

Diseconomies of scale A principle that states as development teams become larger, the average contribution per worker decreases. 515

Distributed systems Systems in which application processing is distributed across multiple computing devices. 311

Domain name A worldwide unique name registered in the domain name system (DNS) and affiliated with a public IP address. 251

Drill down With an OLAP report, to further divide the data into more detail. 388

Dual processor A computer with two CPUs. 152

Dynamic processes Flexible, informal, and adaptive processes that normally involve strategic and less specific managerial decisions and activities. 286

Dynamic reports Business intelligence documents that are updated at the time they are requested. 402

Elastic In cloud computing, the situation that exists when the amount of resource leased can be dynamically increased or decreased, programmatically, in a short span of time, and organizations pay for just the resources that they use. This term was first used in this way by Amazon.com. 239

Email A form of asynchronous communication in which participants send comments and attachments electronically. As a form of group communication, it can be disorganized, disconnected, and easy to hide from. 85

Email spoofing A synonym for phishing. A technique for obtaining unauthorized data that uses pretexting via email. The phisher pretends to be a legitimate company and sends email requests for confidential data, such as account numbers, Social Security numbers, account passwords, and so forth. Phishers direct traffic to their sites under the guise of a legitimate business. 425

Encapsulated A characteristic of systems design in which the details of a process are hidden from users of that process. A formal interface is defined for the process that specifies how the process is to be accessed, what data it requires, and the data that it will produce. The means by which that process creates those results are never exposed, nor do they need to be. 255

Encryption The process of transforming clear text into coded, unintelligible text for secure storage or communication. 436

Encryption algorithms Algorithms used to transform clear text into coded, unintelligible text for secure storage or communication. 436

Enterprise 2.0 The use of emergent social software platforms within companies or between companies and their partners or customers. 350

Enterprise application integration (EAI) A suite of software applications that integrates existing systems by providing layers of software that connect applications together. 303

Enterprise information system Information systems that support cross-functional processes and activities in multiple departments. 288

Enterprise processes Processes that span an organization and support activities in multiple departments. 288

Enterprise resource planning (ERP) A suite of applications called modules, a database, and a set of inherent processes for consolidating business operations into a single, consistent,computing platform. 297

Enterprise social network (ESN) A software platform that uses social media to facilitate cooperative work of people within an organization. 349

Entity In the E-R data model, a representation of some thing that users want to track. Some entities represent a physical object; others represent a logical construct or transaction. 213

Entity-relationship (E-R) data model A tool for constructing data models that defines the entities stored in a database and the relationships among those entities. 212

Entity-relationship (E-R) diagrams A type of diagram used by database designers to document entities and their relationships to each other. 214

ERP system An information system based upon ERP technology. 297

Ethernet Another name for the IEEE 802.3 protocol, Ethernet is a communications standard that specifies how messages are to be packaged, processed, and transmitted for wired transmission over a LAN. 247

Exabyte (EB) 1,024 PB. 154

Experimentation A careful and reasoned analysis of an opportunity, envisioning potential products or solutions or applications of technology and then developing those ideas that seem to have the most promise, consistent with the resources you have. One of four key skills for nonroutine cognitive thinking. 45

Expert systems Rule-based systems that encode human knowledge in the form of If/Then rules. 398

Expert systems shells A program in an expert system that processes a set of rules, typically many times, until the values of the variables no longer change, at which point the system reports the results. 398

Fields Also called columns; groups of bytes in a database table. A database table has multiple columns that represent the attributes of an entity. Examples are PartNumber, EmployeeName, and SaleDate. 199

File A group of similar rows or records. In a database, sometimes called a table. 199

File server A networked computer that stores files. 89

File Transfer Protocol (ftp) An applications-layer protocol used to transfer files over the Internet. 257

Firewall Computing devices located between public and private networks that prevent unauthorized access to or from the internal network. A firewall can be a special-purpose computer, or it can be a program on a general-purpose computer or on a router. 437

Firmware Computer software installed into devices such as printers, print servers, and various types of communication devices. The software is coded just like other software, but it is installed into special, programmable memory of the printer or other device. 167

Five-component framework The five fundamental components of an information system—computer hardware, software, data, procedures, and people—present in every information system, from the simplest to the most complex. 48

Five forces model Model, proposed by Michael Porter, that assesses industry characteristics and profitability by means of five competitive forces—bargaining power of suppliers, threat of substitution, bargaining power of customers, rivalry among firms, and threat of new entrants. 120

Folksonomy A structure of content that emerges from the activity and processing of many users. 350

Foreign keys A column or group of columns used to represent relationships. Values of the foreign key match values of the primary key in a different (foreign) table. 201

Freemium A revenue model offering a basic service for free and charging a premium for upgrades or advanced features. 342

Functional application Software that provides features and functions necessary to support a particular business activity or department (function). 287

Functional information systems Workgroup information systems that support a particular business function. 287

Gantt chart A timeline graphical chart that shows tasks, dates, dependencies, and possibly resources. 513

Gigabyte (GB) 1,024 MB. 154

GNU A set of tools for creating and managing open source software. Originally created to develop an open source Unix-like operating system. 168

GNU general public license (GPL) agreement One of the standard license agreements for open source software. 168

Google Drive Cloud-based hardware used for sharing documents, spreadsheets, presentations, drawings, and other types of data. Includes version tracking. Used in conjunction with Google Docs. 89

Gramm-Leach-Bliley (GLB) Act Passed by Congress in 1999, this act protects consumer financial data stored by financial institutions, which are defined as banks, securities firms, insurance companies, and organizations that provide financial advice, prepare tax returns, and provide similar financial services. 434

Granularity The level of detail in data. Customer name and account balance is large granularity data. Customer name, balance, and details of all contacts with that customer, orders, and payments is smaller granularity. 382

Graphical queries Queries in which criteria are created when the user clicks on a graphic. 210

Green computing Environmentally conscious computing consisting of three major components: power management, virtualization, and e-waste management. 486

Hacking A form of computer crime in which a person gains unauthorized access to a computer system. Although some people hack for the sheer joy of doing it, other hackers invade systems for the malicious purpose of stealing or modifying data. 425

Hadoop An open source program supported by the Apache Foundation that manages thousands of computers and that implements MapReduce. 396

Hardening A term used to describe server operating systems that have been modified to make it especially difficult for them to be infiltrated by malware. 444

Health Insurance Portability and Accountability Act (HIPAA) The privacy provisions of this 1996 act give individuals the right to access health data created by doctors and other healthcare providers. HIPAA also sets rules and limits on who can read and receive a person's health information. 434

Honeypots False targets for computer criminals to attack. To an intruder, a honeypot looks like a particularly valuable resource, such as an unprotected Web site, but in actuality the only site content is a program that determines the attacker's IP address. 446

Hop In an internet, the movement from one network to another. 249

Horizontal-market application Software that provides capabilities common across all organizations and industries; examples include word processors, graphics programs, spreadsheets, and presentation programs. 166

Host operating system In virtualization, the operating system that hosts the virtual operating systems. 164

https An indication that a Web browser is using the SSL/TLS protocol to provide secure communication. 257, 437

Human capital The investment in human knowledge and skills with the expectation of future gain. 335

Human safeguards Steps taken to protect against security threats by establishing appropriate procedures for users to following during system use. 441

Hybrid model An enterprise system in which some of the data is stored in the cloud and managed by cloud vendors and other data is stored in the premises of the using organization and managed by it. 312

Hyper-social knowledge management The application of social media and related applications for the management and delivery of organizational knowledge resources. 401

Hypertext Transfer Protocol (http) An application-layer protocol used between browsers and Web servers. 257

ICANN (Internet Corporation for Assigned Names and Numbers) The organization responsible for managing the assignment of public IP addresses and domain names for use on the Internet. Each public IP address is unique across all computers on the Internet. 250

Identification The process whereby an information system identifies a user by requiring the user to sign on with a username and password. 433

Identifier An attribute (or group of attributes) whose value is associated with one and only one entity instance. 213

IEEE 802.3 protocol A standard for packaging and managing traffic on wired local area networks. 247

IEEE 802.11 protocol A standard for packaging and managing traffic on wireless local area networks. 247

If/Then rules Statements that specify that if a particular condition exists, then a particular action should be taken. Used in different ways, by both expert systems and decision tree data mining. 398

Implementation In the context of the systems development life cycle, the phase following the design phase consisting of tasks to build, test, and convert users to the new system. 508

Industry-specific solutions An ERP template designed to serve the needs of companies or organizations in specific industries. Such solutions save time and lower risk. The development of industry-specific solutions spurred ERP growth. 308

Influencer An individual in a social network whose opinion can force a change in others' behavior and beliefs. 337

Information (1) Knowledge derived from data, where *data* is defined as recorded facts or figures; (2) data presented in a meaningful context; (3) data processed by summing, ordering, averaging, grouping, comparing, or other similar operations; (4) a difference that makes a difference. Information exists only in the minds of humans. 53

Information Age A period in history where the production, distribution, and control of information is the primary driver of the economy. 39

Information silo A condition that exists when data are isolated in separated information systems. 291

Information system (IS) A group of hardware, software, data, procedure, and people components that interacts to produce information. 47

Information technology (IT) The products, methods, inventions, and standards used for the purpose of producing information. 47

Infrastructure as a service (IaaS) The cloud hosting of a bare server computer or data storage. 259

Inherent processes The procedures that must be followed to effectively use licensed software. For example, the processes inherent in ERP systems assume that certain users will take specified actions in a particular order. In most cases, the organization must conform to the processes inherent in the software. 295

In-memory DBMS DBMS products that process databases stored in (very large) memories. Usually such DBMS utilize or extend the relational model. ACID support is common. 222

Inter-enterprise information systems Information systems that support one or more inter-enterprise processes. 289

Inter-enterprise processes Processes that support activities in multiple, independent companies or other organizations. 289

Internal firewalls Firewalls that sit inside the organizational network. 438

Internet When spelled with a small i, as in *internet*, a private network of networks. When spelled with a capital I, as in *Internet*, the public internet known as the Internet. 246

Internet of Things (IoT) The idea that objects are becoming connected to the Internet so they can interact with other devices, applications, or services. 155

Internet service provider (ISP) An ISP provides users with Internet access. An ISP provides a user with a legitimate Internet address; it serves as the user's gateway to the Internet; and it passes communications back and forth between the user and the Internet. ISPs also pay for the Internet. They collect money from their customers and pay access fees and other charges on the users' behalf. 248

Intranet A private internet (note small i) used within a corporation or other organization. 246

Intrusion detection system (IDS) A computer program that senses when another computer is attempting to scan the disk or otherwise access a computer. 429

iOS The operating system used on the iPhone, iPod Touch, and iPad. 163

IP address A series of dotted decimals in a format like 192.168.2.28 that identifies a unique device on a network or internet. 250

IP spoofing A type of spoofing whereby an intruder uses another site's IP address as if it were that other site. 425

IPv4 The most commonly used Internet layer protocol; has a four-decimal dotted notation, such as 165.193.123.253. 251

IPv6 An Internet layer protocol that uses 128-bit addresses and is gradually replacing IPv4. 251

Just-in-time data Data delivered to the user at the time it is needed. 179

Just-in-time design Rather than design the complete, overall system at the beginning, only those portions of the design needed to complete the current work are done. Common for agile development techniques such as scrum. 519

Key (1) A column or group of columns that identifies a unique row in a table. Also referred to as a primary key. (2) A string of bits used to encrypt data. The encryption algorithm applies the key to the original message to produce the coded message. Decoding (decrypting) a message is similar; a key is applied to the coded message to recover the original text. 200, 436

Key escrow A control procedure whereby a trusted party is given a copy of a key used to encrypt database data. 441

Key logger Malicious spyware that captures keystrokes without the user's knowledge. Used to steal usernames, passwords, account numbers, and other sensitive data. 439

Key performance indicators (KPI) See *success metrics*. 347

Kilobyte (KB) 1,024 bytes. 154

Knowledge management (KM) The process of creating value from intellectual capital and sharing that knowledge with employees, managers, suppliers, customers, and others who need it. 397

Kryder's Law The storage density on magnetic disks is increasing at an exponential rate. 42

Libraries In SharePoint and other version-control collaboration systems, shared directories that allow access to various documents by means of permissions. 94

License A contract that stipulates how a program can be used. Most specify the number of computers on which the program can be installed; some specify the number of users who can connect to and use the program remotely. Such agreements also stipulate limitations on the liability of the software vendor for the consequences of errors in the software. 166

Lift In market-basket terminology, the ratio of confidence to the base probability of buying an item. Lift shows how much the base probability changes when other products are purchased. If the lift is greater than 1, the change is positive; if it is less than 1, the change is negative. 393

Linkages In Porter's model of business activities, interactions across value chain activities. 124

Linux A version of Unix developed by the open source community. The open source community owns Linux, and there is no fee to use it. Linux is a popular operating system for Web servers. 163

Local area network (LAN) A network that connects computers that reside in a single geographic location on the premises of the company that operates the LAN. The number of connected computers can range from two to several hundred. 246

Lost-update problem A problem that exists in database applications in which two users update the same data item, but only one of those changes is recorded in the data. Can be resolved using locking. 211

Machine code Code compiled from source code and ready to be processed by a computer. Cannot be understood by humans. 170

Mac OS An operating system developed by Apple Computer, Inc., for the Macintosh. The current version is Mac OS X El Capitan. Initially, Macintosh computers were used primarily by graphic artists and workers in the arts community, but today Macs are used more widely. 162

Main memory Memory that works in conjunction with the CPU. Stores data and instructions read by the CPU and stores the results of the CPU's computations. 152

Maintenance In the context of information systems, (1) to fix the system to do what it was supposed to do in the first place or (2) to adapt the system to a change in requirements. 510

Malware Viruses, worms, Trojan horses, spyware, and adware. 438

Malware definitions Patterns that exist in malware code. Antimalware vendors update these definitions continuously and incorporate them into their products in order to better fight against malware. 439

Management information systems (MIS) The management and use of information systems that help organizations achieve their strategies. 47

Managerial decisions Decisions that concern the allocation and use of resources. 78

Many-to-many (N:M) relationships Relationships involving two entity types in which an instance of one type can relate to many instances of the second type, and an instance of the second type can relate to many instances of the first. For example, the relationship between Student and Class is N:M. One student may enroll in many classes, and one class may have many students. Contrast with one-to-many relationships. 214

MapReduce A two-phase technique for harnessing the power of thousands of computers working in parallel. During the first phase, the Map phase, computers work on a task in parallel; during the second phase, the Reduce phase, the work of separate computers is combined, eventually obtaining a single result. 394

Margin The difference between the value that an activity generates and the cost of the activity. 124

Market-basket analysis A data mining technique for determining sales patterns. A market-basket analysis shows the products that customers tend to buy together. 391

Maximum cardinality The maximum number of entities that can be involved in a relationship. Common examples of maximum cardinality are 1:N, N:M, and 1:1. 215

M-commerce E-commerce transacted using mobile devices. 175

Measure The data item of interest on an OLAP report. It is the item that is to be summed, averaged, or otherwise processed in the OLAP cube. Total sales, average sales, and average cost are examples of measures. 387

Megabyte (MB) 1,024 KB. 154

Metadata Data that describes data. 201

Metcalfe's Law The value of a network is equal to the square of the number of users connected to it. 41

Metrics Measurements used to track performance. 347

Microsoft Windows The most popular nonmobile client operating system. Also refers to Windows Server, a popular server operating system that competes with Linux. 161

Minimum cardinality The minimum number of entities that must be involved on one side of a relationship, typically zero or one. 215

Mobile device A small, lightweight, power-conserving, computing device that is capable of wireless access. 175

Mobile device management (MDM) software Products that install and update mobile device software, back up and restore mobile devices, and wipe software and data from devices in the event the device is lost or the employee leaves the company. Such products also report usage and provide other mobile device management data. 181

Mobile systems Information systems that support users in motion. 174

Modern-style applications Windows applications that are touch-screen oriented and provide context-sensitive, popup menus. 162

Modules A suite of applications in an ERP system. 297

Monetize A social media company's ability to make money from its application, service, or content. 341

MongoDB An open source, document-oriented, nonrelational DBMS. 221

Moore's Law A law, created by Gordon Moore, stating that the number of transistors per square inch on an integrated chip doubles every 18 months. Moore's prediction has proved generally accurate in the 40 years since it was made. Sometimes this law is stated that the performance of a computer doubles every 48 months. Although not strictly true, this version gives the gist of the idea. 40

Multi-user processing The situation in which multiple users process the database at the same time. 211

MySQL A popular open source DBMS product that is license-free for most applications. 204

Native application A thick-client application designed to work with a particular operating system and sometimes further limited to work only with a particular mobile device that runs that operating system. 161

Net neutrality The idea that all data should be treated equally as it passes between networks regardless of its type, source, or quantity. 250

Network A collection of computers that communicate with one another over transmission lines. 243

Neural networks A popular supervised data mining technique used to predict values and make classifications, such as "good prospect" or "poor prospect." 391

NewSQL DBMS Relational DBMS with ACID support that provide processing speeds equivalent to those of NoSQL DBMS products. 222

Nielsen's Law Network connection speeds for high-end users will increase by 50 percent per year. 42

Nonvolatile Memory that preserves data contents even when not powered (e.g., magnetic and optical disks). With such devices, you can turn the computer off and back on, and the contents will be unchanged. 155

Normal forms Definitions of table characteristics that identify various problems to which a table is subject. 217

Normalization The process of converting poorly structured tables into two or more better-structured tables. 216

NoSQL DBMS Nonrelational DBMS that support very high transaction rates processing relatively simple data structures, replicated on many servers in the cloud. No ACID support. 222

Object Management Group (OMG) A software industry standards organization that created a standard set of terms and graphical notations for documenting business processes. 498

Object-oriented When referring to languages, ones that can be used to create difficult, complex applications and, if used properly, will result in high-performance code that is easy to alter when requirements change. 171

Off-the-shelf software Software used without making any changes. 167

Off-the-shelf with alterations software Software bought off the shelf but altered to fit an organization's specific needs. 167

OLAP cube A presentation of an OLAP measure with associated dimensions. The reason for this term is that some products show these displays using three axes, like a cube in geometry. Same as OLAP report 388

One-of-a-kind application Software developed for a specific, unique need, usually for a single company's requirements. 167

One-to-many (1:N) relationships Relationships involving two entity types in which an instance of one type can relate to many instances of the second type, but an instance of the second type can relate to at most one instance of the first. For example, in most businesses, the relationship between Department and Employee is 1:N. A department may relate to many employees, but an employee relates to at most one department. 214

Online analytical processing (OLAP) A dynamic type of reporting system that provides the ability to sum, count, average, and perform other simple arithmetic operations on groups of data. Such reports are dynamic because users can change the format of the reports while viewing them. 387

Open source (1) Source code available for a community to access. (2) A collaborative effort by which software developers create a product such as Linux; the developers often volunteer their time. In most cases, the jointly developed product can be used without paying a license fee. 168

Operating system (OS) A computer program that controls the computer's resources: It manages the contents of main memory, processes keystrokes and mouse movements, sends signals to the display monitor, reads and writes disk files, and controls the processing of other programs. 161

Operational decisions Decisions that concern the day-to-day activities of an organization. 78

Oracle Database A popular, enterprise-class DBMS product from Oracle Corporation. 204

Organizational feasibility Whether an information system fits within an organization's customer, culture, and legal requirements. 503

Outsourcing The process of hiring another organization to perform a service. Outsourcing is done to save costs, to gain expertise, and to free up management time. 469

Over the Internet When applied to cloud computing, the provisioning of worldwide servers over the Internet. 241

Packet A formatted message that passes through networks. 250

Packet-filtering firewall A firewall that examines each packet and determines whether to let the packet pass. To make this decision, it examines the source address, the destination addresses, and other data. 438

Packet sniffers A program that captures network traffic. 272

Paired programming The situation in which two computer programmers share the same computer and develop a computer program together. 520

Parallel installation A type of system conversion in which the new system runs in parallel with the old one and the results of the two are reconciled for consistency. Parallel installation is expensive because the organization incurs the costs of running both systems, but it is the safest form of installation. 509

Pay per click Revenue model in which advertisers display ads to potential customers for free and pay only when the customer clicks. 342

Payload The program codes of a virus that causes unwanted or hurtful actions, such as deleting programs or data, or even worse, modifying data in ways that are undetected by the user. 438

PC virtualization Synonym for desktop virtualization. 164

Peering Exchanging information between telecommunication providers without charging an access fee. 250

People As part of the five-component framework, one of the five fundamental components of an information system; includes those who operate and service the computers, those who maintain the data, those who support the networks, and those who use the system. Information exists only in the minds of people. 48

Perimeter firewall A firewall that sits outside the organizational network; it is the first device that Internet traffic encounters. 438

Personal area network (PAN) A network connecting devices located around a single person. 246

Personal computers Classic computing devices used by individuals. Examples of PCs include laptop or desktop computers. 152

Personal identification number (PIN) A form of authentication whereby the user supplies a number that only he or she knows. 433

Petabyte (PB) 1,024 TB. 154

Phased installation A type of system conversion in which the new system is installed in pieces across the organization(s). Once a given piece works, then the organization installs and tests another piece of the system, until the entire system has been installed. 509

Phisher An individual or organization that spoofs legitimate companies in an attempt to illegally capture personal data, such as credit card numbers, email accounts, and driver's license numbers. 425

Phishing A technique for obtaining unauthorized data that uses pretexting via email. The phisher pretends to be a legitimate company and sends an email requesting confidential data, such as account numbers, Social Security numbers, account passwords, and so forth. 425

Pig Query language used with Hadoop. 397

Pilot installation   A type of system conversion in which the organization implements the entire system on a limited portion of the business. The advantage of pilot implementation is that if the system fails, the failure is contained within a limited boundary. This reduces exposure of the business and also protects the new system from developing a negative reputation throughout the organizations. 509

PixelSense   The Microsoft product formerly known as Surface. It allows many users to process the same tabletop touch interface. Primarily used in hotels and entertainment centers. 190

Platform as a service (PaaS)   Vendors provide hosted computers, an operating system, and possibly a DBMS. 259

Plunge installation   A type of system conversion in which the organization shuts off the old system and starts the new system. If the new system fails, the organization is in trouble: Nothing can be done until either the new system is fixed or the old system is reinstalled. Because of the risk, organizations should avoid this conversion style if possible. Sometimes called direct installation. 509

Pooled   The situation in which many different organizations use the same physical hardware. 240

Power curve   A graph that shows the relationship of the power (the utility that one gains from a software product) as a function of the time using that product. 101

Pretexting   Deceiving someone over the Internet by pretending to be another person or organization. 425

Primary activities   Activities that contribute directly to the production, sale, or service of a product. In Porter's model they are inbound logistics, operations and manufacturing, outbound logistics, sales and marketing, and customer service. 124

Primary key   One or more columns in a relation whose values identify a unique row of that relation. Also known as a key. 200

PRISM   Code name for a secret global surveillance program by which the National Security Agency (NSA) requested and received data about Internet activities from major Internet providers. 448

Privacy   The freedom from being observed by other people. 448

Privacy Act of 1974   Federal law that provides protections to individuals regarding records maintained by the U.S. government. 434

Private cloud   In-house hosting, delivered via Web service standards, which can be dynamically configured. 264

Private IP address   A type of IP address used within private networks and internets. Private IP addresses are assigned and managed by the company that operates the private network or internet. 250

Problem   A *perceived* difference between what is and what ought to be. 80

Procedures   Instructions for humans. One of the five fundamental components of an information system. 48

Process blueprints   In an ERP application, comprehensive sets of inherent processes for all organizational activities, each of which is documented with diagrams that use a set of standardized symbols. 306

Process effectiveness   A measure of how well a process achieves organizational strategy. 289

Process efficiency   A measure of the ratio of process outputs to inputs. 289

Project data   Data that is part of a collaboration's work product. 82

Project metadata   Data that is used to manage a project. Schedules, tasks, budgets, and other managerial data are examples. 82

Protocol   A set of rules and data structures for organizing communication. 246

Public IP address   An IP address used to identify a particular device on the Internet. Such IP addresses are assigned to major institutions in blocks by the Internet Corporation for Assigned Names and Numbers (ICANN). Each IP address is unique across all computers on the Internet. 250

Public key encryption   A special version of asymmetric encryption that is popular on the Internet. With this method, each site has a public key for encoding messages and a private key for decoding them. 436

Publish results   The process of delivering business intelligence to the knowledge workers who need it. 375

Pull publishing   In business intelligence (BI) systems, the mode whereby users must request BI results 375

Push publishing   In business intelligence (BI) systems, the mode whereby the BI system delivers business intelligence to users without any request from the users, according to a schedule, or as a result of an event or particular data condition. 375

Quad processor   A computer with four CPUs. 152

Quick Launch   A menu with links to important content on a SharePoint site. 112

RAM   Random access memory. Another name for a computer's main memory. 152

Ransomware   Malicious software that blocks access to a system or data until money is paid to the attacker. 439

Records   Also called rows, groups of columns in a database table. 199

Regression analysis A type of supervised data mining that estimates the values of parameters in a linear equation. Used to determine the relative influence of variables on an outcome and also to predict future values of that outcome. 391

Relation A formal name for a database table. 201

Relational databases Databases that store data in the form of relations (tables with certain restrictions) and that represents record relationships using foreign keys. 201

Relationships Associations among entities or entity instances in an E-R model or an association among rows of a table in a relational database. 213

Remote action system An information system that provides action at a distance, such as telesurgery or telelaw enforcement. 268

Reporting application A business intelligence application that inputs data from one or more sources and applies reporting operations to that data to produce business intelligence. 386

Repository In a business process model, a collection of something; for example, a database is a repository of data. 124

Requirements analysis The second phase in the SDLC, in which developers conduct user interviews; evaluate existing systems; determine new forms/reports/queries; identify new features and functions, including security; and create the data model. 502

Resources People or information system applications that are assigned to roles in business processes. 495

RFM analysis A technique readily implemented with basic reporting operations to analyze and rank customers according to their purchasing patterns. 386

Rich directory An employee directory that includes not only the standard name, email, phone, and address but also expertise, organizational relationships, and other employee data. 401

Roles In a business process, collections of activities. 495

Rows Also called records, groups of columns in a database table. 199

Safeguard Any action, device, procedure, technique, or other measure that reduces a system's vulnerability to a threat. 423

Schedule feasibility Whether an information system can be developed within the time available. 503

Screen-sharing applications Applications that offer users the ability to view the same whiteboard, application, or other display over a network. 85

Secure Sockets Layer (SSL) A protocol that uses both asymmetric and symmetric encryption. When SSL is in use, the browser address will begin with https://. The most recent version of SSL is called TLS. 437

Security The state of being free from danger. 448

Self-driving car A driverless car that uses a variety of sensors to navigate like a traditional car but without human intervention. 157

Self-efficacy A person's belief that he or she can successfully perform the tasks required in his or her job. 310

Semantic security Also called data triangulation; concerns the unintended release of protected data through the release of a combination of reports or documents that are not protected independently. 406

Server A computer that provides some type of service, such as hosting a database, running a blog, publishing a Web site, or selling goods. Server computers are faster, larger, and more powerful than client computers. 152

Server farm A large collection of server computers organized to share work and compensate for one another's failures. 153

Server tier In the three-tier architecture, the tier that consists of computers that run Web servers for generating Web pages and responding to requests from browsers. Web servers also process application programs. 252

Server virtualization The process of running two or more operating system instances on the same server. The host operating system runs virtual operating system instances as applications. 164

Service-oriented architecture (SOA) A design philosophy that dictates that all interactions among computing devices are defined as services in a formal, standardized way. SOA makes the cloud possible. 253

Simple Mail Transfer Protocol (smtp) The protocol used for email transmission. 257

Site license A license purchased by an organization to equip all the computers on a site with certain software. 166

SLATES Acronym developed by Andrew McAfee that summarizes key characteristics of Enterprise 2.0: search, links, author, tagged, extensions, signaled. 350

Small office/home office (SOHO) A business office with usually fewer than 10 employees often located in the business professional's home. 246

Smart cards Plastic cards similar to credit cards that have microchips. The microchip, which holds much more data than a magnetic strip, is loaded with identifying data. Normally requires a PIN. 433

Smart device A device that has processing power, memory, network connectivity, and the ability to interconnect with other devices and applications. 155

Sniffing A technique for intercepting computer communications. With wired networks, sniffing requires a physical connection to the network. With wireless networks, no such connection is required. 425

Social capital The investment in social relations with expectation of future returns in the marketplace. 336

Social CRM CRM that includes social networking elements and gives the customer much more power and control in the customer/vendor relationship. 333

Social media (SM) The use of information technology to support the sharing of content among networks of users. 328

Social media information system (SMIS) An information system that supports the sharing of content among networks of users. 328

Social media policy A statement that delineates employees' rights and responsibilities when generating social media content. 352

Social media providers Companies that provide platforms that enable the creation of social networks. Facebook, Twitter, LinkedIn, and Google are all social media providers. 328

Social networks The social relationships among people with common interests. 328

Software Instructions for computers. One of the five fundamental components of an information system. 48

Software as a service (SaaS) Leasing hardware infrastructure, operating systems, and application programs to another organization. 259

Source code Computer code written by humans and understandable by humans. Source code must be translated into machine code before it can be processed. 168

Spoofing When someone pretends to be someone else with the intent of obtaining unauthorized data. If you pretend to be your professor, you are spoofing your professor. 425

Spyware Programs installed on the user's computer without the user's knowledge or permission that reside in the background and, unknown to the user, observe the user's actions and keystrokes, modify computer activity, and report the user's activities to sponsoring organizations. Malicious spyware captures keystrokes to obtain usernames, passwords, account numbers, and other sensitive information. Other spyware is used for marketing analyses, observing what users do, Web sites visited, products examined and purchased, and so forth. 439

SQL injection attack The situation that occurs when a user obtains unauthorized access to data by entering a SQL statement into a form in which one is supposed to enter a name or other data. If the program is improperly designed, it will accept this statement and make it part of the SQL command that it issues to the DBMS. 440

SQL Server A popular enterprise-class DBMS product licensed by Microsoft. 204

Stand-up In scrum, a 15-minute meeting in which each team member states what he or she has done in the past day, what he or she will do in the coming day, and any factors that are blocking his or her progress. 520

Static reports Business intelligence documents that are fixed at the time of creation and do not change. 402

Steering committee A group of senior managers from a company's major business functions that works with the CIO to set the IS priorities and decide among major IS projects and alternatives. 469

Storage hardware Hardware that saves data and programs. Magnetic disks are by far the most common storage device, although optical disks, such as CDs and DVDs, also are popular. 152

Strategic decisions Decisions that concern broad-scope, organizational issues. 79

Strength of a relationship In social media, the likelihood that a person or other organization in a relationship will do something that will benefit the organization. 339

Strong password A password with the following characteristics: at least 10 characters; does not contain the user's username, real name, or company name; does not contain a complete dictionary word in any language; is different from the user's previous passwords; and contains both upper- and lowercase letters, numbers, and special characters. 60

Structured decisions A type of decision for which there is a formalized and accepted method for making the decision. 79

Structured processes Formally defined, standardized processes that involve day-to-day operations; accepting a return, placing an order, and purchasing raw materials are common examples. 286

Structured Query Language (SQL) An international standard language for processing database data. Can also be used to create and modify database structure. 205

Subscriptions User requests for particular business intelligence results on a stated schedule or in response to particular events. 403

Success metrics Also called key performance indicators (KPI); measures that indicate when you've achieved your goals. 347

Supervised data mining A form of data mining in which data miners develop a model prior to the analysis and apply statistical techniques to determine the validity of that model and to estimate values of the parameters of the model. 391

Support In market-basket terminology, the probability that two items will be purchased together. 392

Support activities In Porter's value chain model, the activities that contribute indirectly to value creation: procurement, technology, human resources, and the firm's infrastructure. 124

Swift Apple's new programming language for OS X and iOS applications. 171

Swim-lane layout A process diagram layout similar to swim lanes in a swimming pool; each role in the process is shown in its own horizontal rectangle, or lane. 499

Switching costs Business strategy of locking in customers by making it difficult or expensive to change to another product or supplier. 131

Symbian A mobile client operating system popular on phones in Europe and the Far East but less so in North America. 163

Symmetric encryption An encryption method whereby the same key is used to encode and to decode the message. 436

Synchronous communication Information exchange that occurs when all members of a work team meet at the same time, such as face-to-face meeting or conference calls. 84

System A group of components that interacts to achieve some purpose. 48

System conversion The process of converting business activity from the old system to the new. 509

Systems analyst IS professionals who understand both business and technology. They are active throughout the systems development process and play a key role in moving the project from conception to conversion and, ultimately, maintenance. Systems analysts integrate the work of the programmers, testers, and users. Compare with business analyst. 494

Systems development life cycle (SDLC) The classical process used to develop information systems. The basic tasks of systems development are combined into the following phases: system definition, requirements analysis, component design, implementation, and system maintenance (fix or enhance). 501

Systems thinking The mental activity of making one or more models of the components of a system and connecting the inputs and outputs among those components into a sensible whole, one that explains the phenomenon observed. One of four key skills for nonroutine cognitive thinking. 44

Table Also called files, groups of similar rows or records in a database. 199

Tablets Computing devices that allow interaction through a flat touch screen. 152

Target The asset that is desired by a security threat. 423

TCP/IP protocol architecture A protocol architecture having five layers and one or more protocols defined at each layer. Programs are written to implement the rules of a particular protocol. 259

Team surveys Forms of asynchronous communication in which one team member creates a list of questions and other team members respond. Microsoft SharePoint has built-in survey capability. 87

Technical feasibility Whether existing information technology will be able to meet the requirements of a new information system. 503

Technical safeguards Procedures designed to protect the hardware and software components of an information system. Examples include identification and authorization, encryption, firewalls, malware protection, and application design. 433

Telediagnosis A remote access system used by healthcare professionals to provide expertise in rural or remote areas. 256

Telelaw enforcement A remote access system that provides law enforcement capability. 268

Telesurgery A remote access system that links surgeons to robotic equipment and patients at a distance. 268

Terabyte (TB) 1,024 GB. 154

Test plan Groups of action and usage sequences for validating the capability of new software. 509

Text mining The application of statistical techniques on text streams for locating particular words and patterns of particular words and even correlating those word counts and patterns with personality profiles. 268

The Internet The public collection of networks used for transmitting data, worldwide. 246

The Singularity According to Ray Kurzweil, the point at which computer systems become sophisticated enough that they can create and adapt their own software and hence adapt their behavior without human assistance. 405

Thick-client application A software application that requires programs other than just the browser on a user's computer; that is, requires code on both client and server computers. See also *native application*. 161

Third-party cookie A cookie created by a site other than the one visited. 413

Threat A person or organization that seeks to obtain or alter data or other IS assets illegally, without the owner's permission and often without the owner's knowledge. 422

Three-tier architecture Architecture used by most e-commerce server applications. The tiers refer to three different classes of computers. The user tier consists of users' computers that have browsers that request and process Web pages. The server tier consists of computers that run Web servers and in the process generate Web pages and other data in response to requests from browsers. Web servers also process application programs. The third tier is the database tier, which runs the DBMS that processes the database. 252

Trade-off In project management, a balancing of three critical factors: requirements, cost, and time. 514

Train the trainer Training sessions in which vendors train the organization's employees, called Super Users, to become in-house trainers in order to improve training quality and reduce training expenses. 306

Transport Layer Security (TLS) The new name for a later version of Secure Sockets Layer (SSL). 437

Trojan horses Viruses that masquerade as useful programs or files. A typical Trojan horse appears to be a computer game, an MP3 music file, or some other useful, innocuous program. 438

Tunnel A virtual, private pathway over a public or shared network from the VPN client to the VPN server. 265

Unified Modeling Language (UML) A series of diagramming techniques that facilitates OOP development. UML has dozens of different diagrams for all phases of system development. UML does not require or promote any particular development process. Generally less popular that the E-R model. 213

Unix An operating system developed at Bell Labs in the 1970s. It has been the workhorse of the scientific and engineering communities since then. 163

Unstructured decisions A type of decision for which there is no agreed-on decision-making method. 79

Unsupervised data mining A form of data mining whereby the analysts do not create a model or hypothesis before running the analysis. Instead, they apply the data mining technique to the data and observe the results. With this method, analysts create hypotheses after the analysis to explain the patterns found. 390

URL (Uniform Resource Locator) An address on the Internet. Consists of a protocol followed by a domain name or public IP address. 252

Use increases value The concept that the more people use a site, the more value it has, and the more people will visit. Furthermore, the more value a site has, the more existing users will return. 342

User-generated content (UGC) Content on an organization's social media presence contributed by nonemployee users. 353

User tier In the three-tier architecture, the tier that consists of computers, phones, and other mobile devices that have browsers and request or process Web pages and other services. 252

Users Individuals and organizations that use social media sites to build social relationships. 329

Usurpation Occurs when unauthorized programs invade a computer system and replace legitimate programs. Such unauthorized programs typically shut down the legitimate system and substitute their own processing to spy, steal and manipulate data, or achieve other purposes. 426

Value As defined by Porter, the amount of money that a customer is willing to pay for a resource, product, or service. 124

Value chain A network of value-creating activities. 124

Value of social capital Value determined by the number of relationships in a social network, by the strength of those relationships, and by the resources controlled by those related. 336

Vanity metrics Measures that don't improve decision making. 348

Velocity In scrum, the total number of points of work that a team can accomplish in each scrum period. 523

Version control The process that occurs when the collaboration tool limits and sometimes even directs user activity. 94

Version management Tracking of changes to documents by means of features and functions that accommodate concurrent work. 89

Vertical-market application Software that serves the needs of a specific industry. Examples of such programs are those used by dental offices to schedule appointments and bill patients, those used by auto mechanics to keep track of customer data and customers' automobile repairs, and those used by parts warehouses to track inventory, purchases, and sales. 166

Videoconferencing Communication technology that enables online conferencing using video. 85

Viral hook An inducement that causes someone to share an ad, link, file, picture, movie, or other resource with friends and associates over the Internet. 330

Virtualization The process whereby multiple operating systems run as clients on a single host operating system. Gives the appearance of many computers running on a single computer. 164

Virtual machines (vm) Computer programs that present the appearance of an independent operating system within a second host operating system. The host can support multiple virtual machines, possibly running different operating system programs (Windows, Linux), each of which is assigned assets such as disk space, devices, and network connections over which it has control. 164

Virtual meetings Meetings in which participants do not meet in the same place and possibly not at the same time. 85

Virtual private cloud (VPC) A subset of a public cloud that has highly restricted, secure access. 263

Virtual private network (VPN) A WAN connection alternative that uses the Internet or a private internet to create the appearance of private point-to-point connections. In the IT world, the term virtual means something that appears to exist that does not exist in fact. Here a VPN uses the public Internet to create the appearance of a private connection. 263

Virtual reality A completely computer-generated virtual world. 155

Virus A computer program that replicates itself. 438

Volatile Data that will be lost when the computer or device is not powered. 155

Vulnerability An opportunity for threats to gain access to individual or organizational assets. Some vulnerabilities exist because there are no safeguards or because the existing safeguards are ineffective. 422

WAN wireless A communications system that provides wireless connectivity to a wide area network. 249

Wardriver People who use computers with wireless connections to search for unprotected wireless networks. 425

Waterfall method The assumption that one phase of the SDLC can be completed in its entirety and the project can progress, without any backtracking, to the next phase of the SDLC. Projects seldom are that simple; backtracking is normally required. 517

Web 2.0 A dynamic system that uses user-generated content. 350

Web application A software application that requires nothing more than a browser. Also called a thin-client application. 154

Webinar A virtual meeting in which attendees can view a common presentation on the computer screen of one of the attendees for formal and organized presentations. 85

Web page Document encoded in html that is created, transmitted, and consumed using the World Wide Web. 253

Web servers Programs that run on a server-tier computer and that manage http traffic by sending and receiving Web pages to and from clients and by processing client requests. 253

Wide area network (WAN) A network that connects computers at different geographic locations. 246

Windows 10 (mobile) A Windows operating system designed for mobile devices. 161

Windows Server A version of Windows specifically designed and configured for server use. It has much more stringent and restrictive security procedures than other versions of Windows and is popular on servers in organizations that have made a strong commitment to Microsoft. 164

Work breakdown structure (WBS) A hierarchy of the tasks required to complete a project; for a large project, it might involve hundreds or thousands of tasks. 511

Workflow control Collaboration tool feature in which software manages the flow of documents approvals, rejections, and other characteristics among a collaborating team. 95

Workgroup information system An information system that supports a particular department or workgroup. 287

Workgroup process A process that exists to enable workgroups to fulfill the charter, purpose, and goals of a particular group or department. 287

Worm A virus that propagates itself using the Internet or some other computer network. Worm code is written specifically to infect another computer as quickly as possible. 439

Zettabyte (ZB) 1,024 EB. 154

Index